School Library Management

School Library Management

SEVENTH EDITION

Judi Repman and
Gail K. Dickinson, Editors

 LINWORTH

AN IMPRINT OF ABC-CLIO, LLC
Santa Barbara, California • Denver, Colorado • Oxford, England

Library of Congress Cataloging-in-Publication Data

School library management / Judi Repman and Gail K. Dickinson, editors. — Seventh edition.
   pages cm
   Includes bibliographical references and index.
   ISBN 978-1-61069-140-6 (pbk.) — ISBN 978-1-4408-3456-1 (ebook)
 1. School libraries—United States—Administration.   I. Repman, Judi, editor.
II. Dickinson, Gail K., editor.   III. Library media connection.
   Z675.S3S354   2014
   025.1'978—dc23   2014037465

ISBN: 978-1-61069-140-6
EISBN: 978-1-4408-3456-1

19 18 17 16 15   1 2 3 4 5

This book is also available on the World Wide Web as an eBook.
Visit www.abc-clio.com for details.

Linworth
An Imprint of ABC-CLIO, LLC

ABC-CLIO, LLC
130 Cremona Drive, P.O. Box 1911
Santa Barbara, California 93116-1911

This book is printed on acid-free paper ∞
Manufactured in the United States of America

To Marlene Woo-Lun, our friend, mentor, leader, and visionary. She has created a community of learners that make up *Library Media Connection*; the magazine, the learning community, the circle of friends. We continue to be amazed by the energy and dedication that Marlene brings to helping school librarians "be the change!"

Contents

One Question Survey Results

CHAPTER 5: What Does the Future Hold?

Acknowledgment

To Sharon Coatney, for her unending patience, guidance, and support

Introduction

*L*ibrary Media Connection has always been at the forefront of a circle of friends. Our writers are our readers, and the conversation over the years has expanded to include an EdWeb community and webinars along with the print magazine. Our writers contribute articles and tips that reflect the breadth of the roles of the school librarian. This book, using reprints from *Library Media Connection* magazine, provides both a background and a context for sparking discussion about the job, tasks, roles, and functions of the school librarian.

Each chapter is divided into five important areas. Each issue of *LMC* contains an Editor's Note, and one of these will start off each chapter. Then, the hundreds of articles published in the last five years were combed through to find the perfect ones to complement the theme highlighted in the editor's note. We've included a handful of tips from the Tips and Other Bright Ideas section of *LMC*. Each issue of *LMC* also contains results from a One-Question Survey, and we've selected four of these for each chapter. Together the resources in each chapter highlight best practices and new ways of thinking about each of the five themes. One big change you will notice from the 6th edition is that technology is now woven throughout the content in each chapter.

Chapter 1—Putting Your Best Foot Forward

This chapter is designed for the librarian who is new to the profession or who may be moving to work at a different grade level school. The practitioner-focused articles in this section provide practical guidance about setting priorities, time management, basic management and administration practices, and establishing the school librarian's place in the culture of the school.

Chapter 2—The Big Ideas

The profession of school librarianship is predicated on the big ideas of intellectual freedom, equity and access. School librarians care about providing a rich diversity of resources to reflect the diversity of a global society. The articles in this section show how librarians are nurturing these big ideas in their schools. Many of the resources in this chapter encourage you to "think outside the box" and reflect new roles and responsibilities for school librarians in advocacy for these big ideas.

Chapter 3—The School Library and Student Learning

This chapter provides essential readings and resources to support the role of the school library as the learning laboratory/learning commons of a school. Topics covered include standards (Standards for the 21st Century Learner, ISTE's NETS, P21, and the Common Core), inquiry, and information literacy/21st century literacy. This chapter covers using data to both design and evaluate the instructional program of the school, along with suggestions for the use of 21st century technologies to achieve these learning outcomes. Articles that focus on the role of the school librarian in designing authentic assessments and new ways to approach collaboration will challenge you to take a central role in student learning at your school.

Chapter 4—Administration of a 21st Century School Library Program

The articles selected for this chapter highlight the strong voices of practitioners that are published in every issue of *LMC*. This chapter includes articles on a wide range of practical topics such as advocacy and public relations, facilities, collection development, personnel, technology administration, policies and procedures, program and personnel evaluation, action research, and staff development/professional learning. Many of these articles reflect how school libraries can survive and thrive in challenging economic times.

Chapter 5—What Does the Future Hold?

This final selection of articles addresses change and speculates about the future of school libraries and the school library profession. Look at these resources as a way to position your school library for whatever the future holds in teaching and learning. We all know that change is a constant and these articles will expand your thinking about the school library of the future.

How to Use This Book

Many school librarians and technology specialists have told us that each issue of LMC is like a conference that you can enjoy from the comfort of your home or office. So think of this volume as "the best of the best"—a superconference in one easy-to-use place. As we curated the articles and resources included here we considered how school librarians at different points in their careers might be able to use these resources.

School librarians enrolled in a pre-service school library education program are a natural audience for this book. The articles and other resources included in this volume make an ideal companion for a standard content area textbook, since they present voices from the field in real-world settings.

New school librarians (that is, those who have been on the job less than three years) or school librarians changing from one level of school to another will also find much practical guidance within these pages. These carefully selected articles address outstanding school library practice at all levels and creative school librarians will be able to adapt/modify/remix ideas to make them relevant to their own school library settings.

Practicing school librarians should find this compilation to be one-stop professional development. The wide range of topics ensures easy access to information exactly when you might need it. Whether you are in need of some ideas for new programming or new approaches, or whether you need some new administrative strategies, you are sure to find a relevant, useful article within this volume.

And school librarians from any setting will find this volume makes an excellent framework for a professional learning community. Select specific articles or focus on one of the thematic chapters and watch your PLC's discussion grow.

These resources will also be useful as resources to share with teachers, administrators and parents. They present a vision of high-service, cutting-edge school library programs in an accessible format so don't hesitate to share the ideas and strategies you find within these pages.

Join the *LMC* Family

Now that you've seen the best of what *LMC* has to offer, we'd like to extend an invitation to join our family. If you haven't joined our free community on EdWeb (http://www.edweb.net/lmc) now is the time to head to the computer and sign up. Take advantage of our free webinars delivered by leaders in our field. We hope you already subscribe to *LMC* but now we'd like to encourage you to give back to the profession by writing for us. Consider starting with a tip or maybe you're ready to dive in and write that first article! We are here to help and support you throughout that process because we know that our readers want to learn from your experience. You'll find all of the details you need to get started at our website: http://www.librarymediaconnection.com/.

CHAPTER 1

Putting Your Best Foot Forward

Editor's Note

And Still We Rise

So, here we are again on a September morning. You have been awakened by the alarm clock before dawn, your budget has been slashed, your load of library duties has been swelled by the non-library tasks now assigned to you, and you've lost your clerical assistant. When you think about the ever-decreasing amount of money allocated for public education along with the ever-increasing pressure for accountability, the burdens of the job seem overwhelming. Yet still you rise and slap the alarm clock with a high-five, caffeine up, and go off to another day of achieving the impossible dream of the school library.

Why? Why on earth are you not only getting up to go to work, but actually getting excited about the day ahead? The job, hard at best, has been made close to impossible through lack of resources, lack of time, and energy spent teaching to the test. The literature from the early 1900s is full of messages and tips to educate parents, classroom teachers, and school administrators on what a school librarian does all do. One hundred years later, and still we are pumping out the same message.

But every day, in spite of everything against us, there are still incredible successes. Sixth graders shout at the librarian in excitement over new books. High school seniors huddle over iPads to digitally curate resources for their debate chapters. Classroom teachers march to the principal, demanding reinstatement of the library staff. Middle schoolers use QR-coded posters to link to social studies projects. There is something about school librarianship that creates excellence.

The better we do at our jobs today, the better our students will be at their jobs tomorrow. We rise, because our students give us the respect and gratitude that keeps us going.

There used to be a myth that, according to the laws of aerodynamics, bumblebees should not be able to fly. Scientists have now found that bumblebees flap their wings incredibly fast to propel themselves clumsily through the air from flower to flower. They basically use sheer will power fueled by energy-rich nectar—same as school librarians do when flying against all odds using positive dispositions fueled by caffeine and chocolate. We power through without duty-free lunches, without planning time, and without a glance at the clock, because we have to. We rise, seizing every occasion for success.

Maya Angelou's classic poem *And Still I Rise* speaks to not only surviving but also succeeding, against all odds, against all prejudice, against all hope. Our pathetic whine of not being understood pales in comparison to the struggles of centuries she portrays, as it should. As a tale of courage, though, I see her poem every day in the celebrations school librarians share of their work with children and youth.

The future needs us. We are school librarians. We rise.

Angelou, M. *And Still I Rise. New York: Random House, 1978.*

Gail K. Dickinson
Editorial Director

Dickinson, Gail K. (2012). And still we rise. *LMC, 31*(1), 6.

Library LEGOs: Putting the Pieces Together

By Betsy Ruffin

LEGO is about building, creating, sharing, and connecting. School libraries can take a lesson from the popular and educational toy. A good library program can help build information literate students, create lifelong learners and share in student achievement by making connections with the school community through technology and more.

Making Connections with . . .

Students

Connecting with students is surely the foundation of our library LEGOs project. Studies confirm that good library programs help student achievement. Our best pieces need to be used in this part of the structure.

The first blocks support the curriculum, particularly reading since this is a foundational skill. Make sure you know where your state's or school's curriculum guides are located—most are online somewhere—and become familiar with the general objectives. Think about where the library program fits into this and the particular objectives the library can help students achieve. For example, in Texas, with its TEKS (Texas Essential Knowledge and Skills, www.tea.state.tx.us/index2 .aspx?id=6148), research is now included in the English Language Arts and Reading section, surely a place librarians can help!

A great and free website to help support the curriculum is Thinkfinity (www.thinkfinity.org). Supported by Verizon Foundation and subject partner sites, Thinkfinity has resources for almost every subject. Online databases such as Britannica School Edition, with elements for ESL, all school levels, and special features like read-alouds are a good paid option for curriculum support.

Learning can go beyond school days with blocks dedicated to helping build lifelong learners. Information skills instruction helps prepare

[handwritten margin note: make on your own]

students for college, vocational training, and other areas of life beyond school. A good research plan can help a student, not only in classes but also in finding information in real world situations. The Big 6, and its younger student corollary, the Super 3, is one such plan (www.big6.com). With links to information skills websites and lesson plan databases, the Resources for School Librarians Information Skills Instruction page (www.sldirectory.com/libsf/resf/ libplans.html) provides help for teaching these vital skills.

What about that important reading block? To get students reading those great library books, try capturing their interest with book trailers, such as those found at Book Trailers for All (http:// booktrailersforall.com), or make your own. You can find instructions at http://prezi.com/m68smuvk3bi9/ book-trailers-making-students-want- to-read-created-by-naomi-bates- northwest-high-school, courtesy of Texas school librarian Naomi Bates.

Teachers

Connecting with teachers builds on our project foundation as we collaborate with other educators to help students achieve.

Connect with teachers through online courses, including professional development courses (how to teach research) and student courses with librarians and classroom teachers working together. Moodle (moodle .org), an open source course management system, can be used for this. Courses can be built via modules with options including wikis, forums, quizzes, and much more. Find examples at http://moodle.cleburne .k12.tx.us.

Another online way to connect is Discovery Educator Network (http:// community.discoveryeducation.com). This Discovery Education companion (www.discoveryeducation.com) encourages collaboration among

educators with items such as shared educator resources, national and state blogs, and forums. Do not overlook the good options in Discovery Streaming (http://streaming .discoveryeducation.com). Items such as the My Builder Tools, My Content Sharing, My Classrooms, and Teacher Center take this wonderful tool beyond simply showing videos.

> *Learning can go beyond school days with blocks dedicated to helping build lifelong learners.*

Classroom 2.0 (www .classroom20.com), listservs such as LM_Net (http://lmnet .wordpress.com/subscribe), or your state library association group, and wikis such as http://librarygeekfeats .wikispaces.com and http:// wellesleyhighschoollibrary .wikispaces.com/Collaboration+Tools are good tools for collaboration ideas.

Parents

Connections with parents can be the missing blocks in a project, but those library LEGO elements are surely needed also. Parents can not only help your program connect with students but also provide advocacy with decision makers in the district.

Your library website is a good place to start with items such as an online catalog, library news, resource helps, and more (www.cleburne.k12 .tx.us/1019105616655243/site/default .asp). If your district has an automatic parent contact system, it can be used to send out library news such as book fair dates and end of year due dates.

More ideas for parent connections can be found at www .ala.org/ala/mgrps/divs/aasl/aboutaasl/ aaslcommunity/quicklinks/parents .cfm. It includes ideas for parental involvement and understanding the library's programs and its

[handwritten margin note: advocate!]

contribution to student learning. Resources for School Librarians & Parent Partnerships (www.txla.org/tasl/parent-resources) has links to presentations on school libraries, handouts for parents, and ideas for working with PTA (parent-teacher association). The School Library Link (www.theschoollibrarylink.com) is another helpful resource for promoting your program with parents.

Librarians

Sharing library LEGO pieces by connecting with other librarians helps both projects. There are many ways for school librarians to share ideas and best practices, including listservs and state/national associations. Join and participate in the discussions to build strong connections for strong projects.

Online resources for school librarians are plentiful. Resources for School Librarians (www.sldirectory.com/index.html) has categories such as program administration, teaching and learning, technology, and continuing education. School-libraries.net links to library webpages from around the globe, leading you to a world of ideas for your library LEGOs project. Librarian Links (http://home.gwi.net/brhs/lib.html) includes links to books and reviews sites, copyright and fair use help, lesson plans, research skills, and more.

The special collections at ipl2 (www.ipl.org/div/special) feature subjects such as e-readers, literary criticism, Native American authors, and web technologies. Check the pathfinders to see link collections

on subjects ranging from fairy tales, reading, and research to word and phrase origins, multicultural literature, and much more. Two particular pathfinders are resources for librarians and resources for the school librarian (www.ipl.org/div/pfarch/entry/83207). The latter is no longer maintained by ipl2 but still has good resources.

Web 2.0: Social Media

Technology has certainly added to our connection pieces, especially with the advent of Web 2.0. These tools, designed particularly to help people link and share, are rapidly becoming major elements in any library LEGO links project. They help link our libraries to students, teachers, parents, and other librarians.

Blogs and wikis are some of the best-known Web 2.0 tools.

Blogs can be used for book reviews (http://primetimebooks.edublogs.org) with permission sharing. Commenting allows others in the school community to share also. Blogs can also be used to share news of interest to the school community (www.computa-cat.blogspot.com), keep up with technology (http://community.discoveryeducation.com/blogs.cfm) or libraries (http://theunquietlibrarian.wordpress.com), or expand your own thinking about libraries and technology (http://doug-johnson.squarespace.com).

Wikis are good for online group sharing. They can be used by librarian groups for book reviews/selection (http://esc11librarians.wikispaces.com)

or program (http://makingarworkbetter.pbworks.com) help, by trainers as a professional development site (https://librarygeekfeats.wikispaces.com), or by classes for online assignments (http://onlineanimalpreserve.pbworks.com).

Web 2.0 goes beyond these, however, with more library-useful blocks.

Twitter gives news in a 140-character format. Twitter members to follow with (usually) relevant postings include (by Twitter name) mguhlin, joycevalenza, rmbyrne, blueskunkblog, mythbusters, or even bcruffin.

Ning allows you to create your own custom social networking community with tools such as blogs, forums, message broadcast to Ning members, Facebook and Twitter integration, and much more. Some Nings to note are www.classroom20.com, http://teacherlibrarian.ning.com, and http://web20schoollibraries.ning.com.

Looking for other ways to share books, whether professional or student? Try Shelfari (www.shelfari.com/groups/48361/about) or Library Thing groups (www.librarything.com/groups/schoollibrariansprof). Goodreads.com has mobile apps in addition to its website.

Good school library programs, like good LEGO projects, are built piece by linking piece. Building, sharing, creating, connecting—the program comes together to help those in our school community and beyond.

Betsy Ruffin *is the librarian/technologist at Irving Elementary in Cleburne, Texas. She can be reached at betsyx@fieldstreet.com.*

Ruffin, Betsy. (2012). Library LEGOs: Putting the pieces together. *LMC, 30*(6), 10–11.

Connect with teachers through online courses, including professional development courses (how to teach research) and student courses with librarians and classroom teachers working together.

connect! 2

Exactly How Big *Is* Your Head?

By Scott Hoskins

"Mr. Hoskins, can you come look at my computer?"
"Mr. Hoskins, my projector isn't projecting right."
"Mr. Hoskins, can you connect my printer to my computer?"
"Mr. Hoskins, why is this computer not letting me sign on?"
"Mr. Hoskins, can you show me how to . . . [place any computer skill here]?

I hear these questions on a daily basis in my role as a high school library media specialist. Notice that none of these questions are about books, locating them, using them for research, or sharing them with students for reader's advisory. Nor are they about information literacy, one of the hallmarks of being a media specialist. No, they are usually about investigating and repairing teachers' technology when it doesn't work, helping students do something with software with which they aren't familiar, or showing students how to do something that their teachers don't know how to do themselves.

If there is one thing I've learned in my short tenure as media specialist, it's that library media specialists have to have big heads in order to wear the many hats our positions require.

Hat #1: Technology Expert/ Coordinator/Repairer

One thing that distinguished me from the other candidates when I interviewed for my position was my experience with using and incorporating technology into lessons. As I have come to discover, however, this has been both a blessing and a curse. I knew that having a background in technology would be beneficial to being a media specialist, but little did I know that in today's educational environment, the media specialist is expected to be "the" expert on technology.

Two technology courses were required as part of my media specialist preparation program. The first dealt with learning parts of the computer; for example, identifying input and output devices, power components, memory modules, and types of disk drives. In addition, we had to design and create a webpage using HTML. HTML! I mean, who actually builds a website from scratch using HTML? The second course emphasized the more "creative" side of technology, using digital cameras, video cameras, and other digital media.

Sadly, both course prepared me for the expectations teachers and students have toward tech-savvy media specialists. There's a big difference between incorporating technology into a lesson and being asked to troubleshoot the actual equipment. From day one, I was expected to know how to connect devices to the wireless network, how to troubleshoot the network when the signal is lost, and how to connect computers to printers, projectors, and other peripherals.

> *Library media specialists have to have big heads in order to wear the many hats that our positions require.*

Even though our school system has a dedicated team of network and computer technicians, teachers have to put in work orders to get their issues resolved. While the technicians are incredibly competent and speedy, they are not speedy enough for teachers who need their technology working yesterday, if not sooner. I've learned so many technical points that I sometimes feel as if I should just be a network technician. A lot of it is honest-to-goodness trial and error. I probably couldn't replicate the fix if I had to. I feel like a shade tree mechanic tinkering under the hood of a Ferrari and occasionally saying "hmm" and "yes, that could be it" just to sound competent. In the end, either the problem is fixed and the teacher is happy, or the problem is not fixed and the teacher has to submit a work order.

> *I feel like a shade tree mechanic tinkering under the hood of a Ferrari and occasionally saying "hmm" and "yes, that could be it" just to sound competent. For anyone who claims that all creativity has been taken out of teaching, I say come to the media center to see the creative projects students are designing.*

Hat #2: Expert in Every Computer Program the School Uses and Probably Even More

Let's face it, there are a lot of software programs and even more web-based software. Students who use the media center will inevitably ask questions about how to use a particular function on the software. The main software culprits are Microsoft Office programs, which are ubiquitous in many school systems. Students bring in Word, PowerPoint, and Excel documents they created at home. The document was perfect there, but now, for some reason, it doesn't print correctly, it's laid out differently, or it has a number of other issues. Sometimes, they'll use an older version of Word that won't open on our computers. Some days, if the wind blows right, they'll even bring in a document that they created in WordPerfect.

I'm lucky that I've used Microsoft programs for a while and have a good grasp of the nuances of their functions; otherwise, I'd be as clueless as the students. Again, there was no "official" training in using software programs in library school. All I have to say is, thank goodness for Control-Z and Help menus.

Even though students are supposedly tech savvy, they fall short when it comes to understanding what they can and can't do on the Internet. For example, students typically want to spruce up their presentations with videos or music, but they don't understand that not all video and audio files can be downloaded and inserted into a file. I've turned away many disappointed students when they couldn't locate a "free" download of a popular song. (Most students don't understand copyright law. At least this area is definitely something I studied in library school.)

Hat #3: Demonstrator of Various Skills

For anyone who claims that all creativity has been taken out of teaching, I say come to the media center to see the creative projects students are designing. However, not all students have a clear picture of what their teacher expects—and not all teachers have a clear picture of what they expect.

Some teachers want their students to create something that they don't know how to do themselves. A good example is when a teacher wanted his students to create resumes for a chemical element (creative, yes?) but didn't show them an example of a resume and didn't show them how to create the resume. The students were lost. They were in the media center researching the element, and upon whom did it fall to at least show them what a resume looks like? You guessed it.

I've also had to show students how to create brochures using Word and Publisher, charts using Excel, and other projects using Web 2.0 tools. As a media specialist, I never know what skills I'll have to demonstrate from day to day. Once I learn these skills, I try to create how-to documents and post them on our media center website to guide other students.

I've had to teach myself Audacity, Google Earth tours, Xtimeline, TimeToast, and other web programs in order to become a more effective media specialist.

In addition, even though I taught English before becoming a media specialist, I have also had to become an expert on citing various types of sources in both MLA and APA styles. It's a 21st century librarian "thing."

Having a Big Head

These three areas alone could consume a lot of a media specialist's time. So when do I do "librarian" things like checking out books, shelving books, and finally, that old standby, telling kids to be quiet, you may ask? Honestly, these are no longer "librarian" things for a 21st century library media specialist. Any clerk with a normal-sized head can do those. Today's media specialist must truly have a big head, not only for the three hats mentioned above, but also for teaching information literacy to students and connecting students to resources.

After all, isn't it cool to have a big head?

Scott Hoskins *is a library media specialist at West Creek High School in Clarksville, Tennessee, and can be reached at empoweringthenatives@gmail.com.*

Hoskins, Scott. (2013). Exactly how big is your head? *LMC, 31*(2), 20–21.

Staying Focused During Tough Economic Times: Consolidating Our Research Base

By Melissa Allen

Introduction

Today school library media specialists operate in an environment of daily challenges and controversies. *No Child Left Behind* established mandates that all educators are scrambling to meet. No matter how people feel about the way the legislation is being carried out, it is difficult to argue against its purpose—that all educators must find ways to help all students to succeed regardless of race, ethnicity, dominant language, income status, or handicap. Education budgets are being slashed and media specialists across the country are losing their jobs and media budgets because they are not able to draw a direct connection between their programs and the school's achievement. Current research provides persuasive arguments for library investments and expanded responsibilities of the media specialist. This article presents an overview of factors that have been found to increase student achievement through multiple studies.

Media Programs' Relevance to Student Academic Achievement

To impact student learning we must emphasize research-based learning, not clerical duties such as cataloging and processing materials. A significant body of current research shows a positive relationship between media programs and student academic achievement. Like it or not, the bottom line in K-12 education today is student achievement and that achievement is being defined by standardized testing and *No Child Left Behind*. Todd (2003) summarized the importance of media centers:

The hallmark of a school library in the 21st century is not its collections, its systems, its technology, its staffing, its building, but its actions and evidences that show that it makes a real difference to student learning, that it contributes in tangible and significant ways to the development of human understanding, meaning making and constructing knowledge. (p. 13)

> *Current research provides persuasive arguments for library investments and expanded responsibilities of the media specialist.*

Research has shown that an effective media program must be in place to positively impact the learning that takes place in that school. Roscello and Webster (2002) conclude that effective media programs have the following common characteristics:

- Provide flexible scheduling and extended access to the collection beyond the school day.
- Address a broad range of reading levels and interests.
- Offer a broad range of materials including fiction, nonfiction, reference, print, non-print, audiovisual, and more.
- Are accessible to the entire learning community.
- Are cost effective by providing resources to be utilized by multiple patrons and by employing an automation system which minimizes lost resources and requires less staffing.
- Maintain an up-to-date collection through weeding and new collection development.
- Provide a sense of ownership that is shared by the entire learning community.

In 1992, Haycock found that students in schools with well-equipped media centers and trained media specialists performed better on achievement tests for reading comprehension and basic research skills. Media centers are equalizers for many students who may not have any resources at home. Haycock (2001) indicated that improvement to student self-esteem can be linked to a strong media center. Students in Haycock's pioneering study showed increased "confidence, independence and sense of responsibility in regards to their own learning" (2001, p. 34).

To a great extent, the quality of a school depends on the quality of that school's media program. A Colorado study entitled *The Impact of School Library Media Centers on Academic Achievement* (Lance, Wellborn, & Hamilton-Pennell, 1993) found that the size of the media center's staff and collection was the best school predictor of academic achievement. Students at schools with better funded media centers tended to achieve higher average reading scores, whether their schools and communities were rich or poor and whether adults in the community were well or poorly educated. Lance et. al. also found that in schools where the media specialist performed an instructional role the students tended to achieve higher average test scores. A study conducted by Topsy Smalley found that "students whose high schools include librarians and library instruction programs bring more understanding about information research to their college experiences" (2004, p. 197).

In 1999, Lance, Rodney, and Hamilton-Pennell conducted a study in 211 of Alaska's 461 public schools and included students in grades four, eight, and eleven. Not only did the level of media center staffing predict academic achievement, but so did the amount of time the media specialist spent delivering information literacy instruction to students, cooperatively planning with teachers, and providing inservice training to teachers. The more library/information literacy instruction the media specialist provided, the higher the students scored on the California Achievement Tests. In 2000, Lance, Rodney, and Hamilton-Pennell studied Pennsylvania public schools to determine the value of staffing school libraries with individuals with specific certification qualifications. Surveys were completed by 522 students in grades five, eight, and 11 from 435 public schools. For all three grade levels, the relationship between Pennsylvania System of School Assessment (PSSA) reading scores and the presence of adequate staffing of a full-time certified media specialist and a full-time support staff member is both positive and statistically significant.

Ester Smith (2001) collected data from a random sample of 600 Texas school libraries in *Texas School Libraries: Standards, Resources, Services, and Students' Performance*. The data was supplemented with state and federal records on school characteristics, community economic data, and Texas Assessment of Academic Skills (TAAS) test results. The study incorporated 200 variables to examine the relationship between libraries and academic performance. Staffing, collection sizes, technology availability, and the amount of interaction between the media specialist and the teachers and students had a positive impact on academic performance at all grade levels. Over 10 percent more students met minimum TAAS expectations in reading if they had a certified media specialist in their school.

In 2001, Lance, Rodney, and Hamilton-Pennell analyzed the relationship between media program development and reading/language test scores in Oregon. Oregon schools with the best reading scores tended to have strong media programs while taking into account other factors such as school differences, per pupil expenditures, teacher to pupil ratio, experience level of teachers, teacher salary scale, community differences, adult educational attainment, poverty level, and racial/ethnic demographics. The results showed that the relationship between media program development and test scores cannot be explained away by these other factors. Incremental improvements in the media program will yield incremental increases in test scores. Reading/language test scores rise with increases: in total staff hours, print volumes per student, periodical subscriptions, and school library media expenditures per student.

> To impact student learning we must emphasize research-based learning, not clerical duties such as cataloging and processing materials.
>
> *advocate*

In 2002, Lance and his colleagues again explored how the media program impacts student academic achievement. They analyzed data collected in Alaska, Pennsylvania, Colorado and Oregon. In addition, in each state a survey was given out at the school building level. The survey results provided information about the media programs in the school—staffing levels, staff activities, collection size, usage statistics and available technology. To overcome the previous studies' weaknesses, the researchers attempted to define the instructional role and the support given to the media specialists by the principal and teachers, and to analyze the relationship of information technology to the media program. The 2002 study showed that the results held up over time, were consistent from state to state, and were consistent whether state standards-based tests or norm-reference tests were used. The 2002 study acquired substantial amounts of information on the participating schools. The school information included test scores, teacher-pupil ratio, per pupil expenditures, percentage of students eligible for the National School Lunch Program (i.e. poverty), percentage of the community's adults who graduated from high

school, racial/ethnic distribution of students and teacher characteristics (percentage with advanced degrees, average years of experience, and average salary). Lance et. al. (2002) claimed that strong media specialists and integrated media programs can help ensure that America's schools "leave no child behind." The research suggested that academic achievement tends to be higher in schools where the media center is staffed with trained professionals (media specialists and support staff) and are better funded and better stocked. The media programs must have the support of teachers and principals, state-of-the-art technology must be a part of the media program, the library media specialist must teach information literacy skills (one-to-one for students and as large groups), and the library media specialist must provide inservice training to teachers (to keep them abreast of the latest information resources and technology) for there to be a documented increase in student achievement. The school media program predictors almost always outperformed other school characteristics, such as teacher-pupil ratio and per pupil expenditures.

In *Making the Grade: The Status of School Library Media Centers in the Sunshine State and How They Contribute to Student Achievement*, Donna Baumbach (2002) found that high performing schools are more likely to have a certified media specialist, an existing information-literacy curriculum, a significantly larger book collection, a school Web site, and more magazine subscriptions than low performing schools. This groundbreaking study also showed that media specialists in top performing schools spent more time collaborating with teachers and were more involved in reading activities. In 2002, Baughman used the 519 responses he received from the questionnaire he mailed to Massachusetts public schools to analyze the relationship between media centers and student achievement. At each grade level students scored higher on the Massachusetts Comprehensive Assessment System (MCAS) when there was a media program that provided instruction within the school. Higher scores on the MCAS occurred in schools with full-time media specialists.

Baxter and Smalley's (2003) report titled *Check It Out! The Results of the School Library Media Program Census* included 1,172 media specialists who responded to a survey to determine the correlation between the media center and achievement. The survey data showed that reading achievement was related to increases in media program spending—the larger the library expenditures for books and electronic materials, the higher students' reading achievement. The census data also showed that as a state Minnesota lags behind the averages for other states in expenditures for books for its media centers. Site visits confirmed the study's findings that the more hours a licensed media specialist worked in the media program, the more effective the program.

Burgin and Bracy's (2003) study of the relationship between media programs and student achievement in North Carolina was consistent with the earlier studies. The researchers found that media programs have a significant impact on student achievement. Scores on standardized reading and English tests in the North Carolina public schools tended to increase when school libraries had newer books, spent more on print and electronic resources, subscribed to more online and CD-ROM services, and were open and staffed more hours during the school week.

Todd and Kuhlthau (2004) surveyed 13,123 students in grades three through 12 and 879 staff members in 39 schools across Ohio with effective media programs to determine how students benefit from those effective programs. The 39 schools were selected based on the Ohio Guidelines for Effective Media programs and validated by an International Advisory Panel. 99.4% of the students surveyed believed that the media center and its services enhanced their learning. The study showed that an effective media center, led by a credentialed media specialist, served a critical role in facilitating student learning. "When effective school libraries are in place, students

[handwritten: students believe it helps]

do learn. 13,000 students can't be wrong" (Todd & Kuhlthau, 2004, p. 8).

In Lance, Rodney, and Hamilton-Pennell's study (2005) titled *Powerful Libraries Make Powerful Learners*, 657 Illinois schools from all grade levels and from all regions of the state participated in a voluntary survey. The survey gathered data on hours of operation, staffing, role of staff, media center collection and technology availability, expenditures, and patron usage of the media center. Test scores were higher in schools with flexible scheduling; with more staff; where media specialists spent more time collaborating with teachers; with larger collections; where students used the media center both individually and with their class; with better funding and higher expenditures; and where educational technology was more widely available. "In short, the findings of this study and its predecessors support the belief that powerful libraries—and librarians—do, indeed, make powerful learners" (Lance, Rodney, & Hamilton-Pennell, 2005, p. xiii).

The Impact of the Media Program on Reading Achievement

Stephen Krashen (1993) analyzed hundreds of voluntary reading studies in *The Power of Reading*. This report indicated that more voluntary reading resulted in better reading comprehension, a more fluent writing style, improved vocabulary, better spelling and grammatical development. Although everyone would acknowledge the numerous benefits of voluntary reading, Krashen specifically analyzed the media specialists' role in reading. He found that access to school media centers as well as to professional media specialists resulted in more voluntary reading by students. Krashen also concluded that larger media center collections and extended hours resulted in larger circulation rates and amounts read. Ramos and Krashen's (1998) later study concluded that one of the most powerful incentives for reading is to simply make interesting books

[handwritten: love for]

readily available to children, such as in a media center.

Conclusion

Information Power (1988) and *Empowering Learners* (2009) affirm that the mission of the library media program is to ensure that students and staff are effective users of ideas and information. The media specialist is an important partner in providing an integrated curriculum that prepares students to be lifelong learners. To summarize the previous research in this section:

- Students at schools with better funded media centers tended to achieve higher average test scores, whether their schools and communities were rich or poor and whether adults in the community were well or poorly educated. *[handwritten: donors choose]*

- In schools where the media specialist performed an instructional role the students tended to achieve higher average test scores. The more library/information literacy instruction the media specialist provided, the higher the students scored on achievement tests. Library/information literacy skills empower learners to construct meaningful questions, use multiple information sources to solve a problem, evaluate sources and draw original conclusions.

- Media specialists in top performing schools spent more time collaborating with teachers and were more involved in reading activities.

- Academic achievement on tests for reading comprehension and basic research skills tended to be higher in schools where the media center was staffed with trained professionals (media specialists and support staff), better funded and better stocked.

- The library media programs must have the support of teachers and principals, state-of-the-art technology must be a part of the media program, the library media specialist must teach information literacy skills (one-to-one for students and as large groups) and the library media specialist must provide inservice training to teachers (to keep them abreast of the latest information resources and technology) for there to be a significant documented increase in student achievement.

- Students believe that the media center and the services offered within the center enhanced their learning.
- Improvement to student self-esteem and sense of responsibility has been linked to a strong media center.
- Access to school media centers as well as to professional media specialists resulted in more voluntary reading by students.
- Larger collections and extended hours resulted in increases in voluntary reading.
- More voluntary reading resulted in better reading comprehension, a more fluent writing style, improved vocabulary, better spelling and grammatical development.

Media centers are powerful forces in the lives of children. Effective media centers have been shown to make a measurable difference on student achievement and learning, to positively impact students' self-esteem, and to increase students' desire to read voluntarily. Despite all of the research suggesting the positive effects of the media center on the learning community, several barriers exist that hinder media specialists from fully implementing their roles. The most commonly reported barriers were lack of time, lack of funding and resources, lack of support from administration and staff, lack of clerical staff, use of a fixed schedule, and too many schools or students to serve. Many of these factors might be overcome by presenting the research to school board members and administrators who control media funding, policies, schedules, and staffing.

Although one could argue that findings in one media center do not automatically apply to another, there are commonalities that are too strong to overlook and should become part of a media specialist's plan to improve the media program in order to increase student achievement. Analysis of the current research in the field about the true potential the media program has on learning outcomes should excite all educators. Media specialists need to conduct an informal assessment of their media program to determine how it matches up with the study findings to determine what changes need to be made. This research can be used to help set media program goals; write a media program mission statement; write a media specialist's job description; write a media clerk's job description; establish performance expectations for media staff; justify media staffing, schedules, and expenditures; set a standard for inservice training for media staff and much more.

References

American Association of School Librarians. *Empowering learners: Guidelines for school library media programs.* Chicago: AASL, 2009.

American Association of School Librarians and Association for Educational Communications and Technology. *Information power: Building partnerships for learning.* Chicago: American Library Association, 1998.

American Association of School Librarians and Association for Educational Communications and Technology. *Information power: Guidelines for school library media programs.* Chicago: American Library Association, 1988.

Baumbach, D. *Making the grade: The status of school library media centers in the sunshine state and how they contribute to student achievement.* Spring, TX: Hi Willow Research and Publishing, 2002.

Baxter, S., & A. Smalley. *Check it out! The results of the school library media program census.* St. Paul, MN: Metronet, 2003.

Burgin, R., & P. Bracy. *An essential connection: How quality school library media programs improve student achievement in North Carolina.* Spring, TX: Hi Willow Research and Publishing, 2003.

Haycock, K. *What works: Research about teaching and learning through the school's library resource center.* Vancouver, BC: Rockland Press, 1992.

Haycock, K. "School libraries and student achievement." *Teacher Librarian 31*(1) (2001): 34.

"Improving literacy through school libraries." (n.d.). The U.S. Department of Education. 10 May 2009 <http://www.ed.gov/programs/lsl/index.html>.

Krashen, S. *The power of reading.* Englewood, CO: Libraries Unlimited, 1993.

Lance, K., M. Rodney, & C. Hamilton-Pennell. *Measuring up to standards: The impact of school library programs and information literacy in Pennsylvania schools.* Greensburg, PA: Pennsylvania Citizens for Better Libraries, 2000.

Lance, K., M. Rodney, & C. Hamilton-Pennell. *Good schools have school librarians: Oregon school librarians collaborate to improve academic achievement.* Terrebonne, OR: Oregon Educational Media Association, 2001.

Lance, K., M. Rodney, & C. Hamilton-Pennell. *Make the connection: Quality school library media programs impact academic achievement.* Bettendorf, IA: Mississippi Bend Area Education Agency, 2002.

Lance, K., M. Rodney, & C. Hamilton-Pennell. *Powerful libraries make powerful learners: The Illinois study.* Canton, IL: Illinois School Library Media Association, 2005.

Lance, K., M. Rodney, C. Hamilton-Pennell, L. Petersen, & C. Sitter. *Information empowered: The school librarian as an agent of academic achievement in Alaska schools.* Anchorage, AK: Alaska State Library, 1999.

Lance, K., L. Wellborn, & C. Hamilton-Pennell. *The impact of school library media centers on academic achievement.* Spring, TX: Hi Willow Research and Publishing, 1993.

Ramos, F., & S. Krashen. "The impact of one trip to the public library: Making books available may be the best incentive for reading." *Reading Teacher 51*(7) (1998): 614–615.

Roscello, F., & P. Webster. *Characteristics of school library media programs and classroom collections: Talking points*. Albany, NY: Office of Elementary, Middle, Secondary, and Continuing Education, New York State Education Department, 2002.

Smalley, T. N. "College success: High school librarians make the difference." *The Journal of Academic Librarianship 30*(3) (2004): 193–198.

Smith, E. *Texas school libraries: Standards, resources, services, and students' performance*. Austin, TX: Texas State Library and Archives Commission, 2001.

Todd, R. J. "School libraries evidence: Seize the day, begin the future." *Library Media Connection, 22*(1) (2003, August/September): 12–18.

Todd, R., & C. Kuhlthau. *Student learning through Ohio school libraries: The Ohio research study*. Columbus, OH: Ohio Educational Library Media Association, 2004.

Dr. Melissa Allen *is a library media specialist at Glynn Academy in Brunswick, Georgia and teaches a class in the Instructional Technology department at Georgia Southern University.*

Allen, Melissa. (2010). Staying focused during tough economic times: Consolidating our research base. *LMC, 29*(1), 18–21.

First Year Firsts

By Gail Dickinson

[handwritten: virtual library tour ↓]

I remember my first day on my first job in the library. I was greeted with a hug from the school secretary. I was ushered down the hall and handed a key to the library. The door was opened for me, it was closed behind me, and I found myself utterly alone.

Almost every school library media specialist can recount a similar story about starting the job. Someone hands us a key, shows us where the door to the library is, and then leaves us to pick up the reins of the program. I suppose the assumption is that we know what to do. I suspect, however, that most of us would say that we managed to bumble through somehow until we figured it out.

As the years pass, the sense of fear, awe, excitement, and maybe sheer terror dims to an August of another year, another first day, and another group of students and teachers. Sometimes, however, it might be a good idea to pretend that it is the first year all over again. Here are some tips for the new or not-so-new library media specialist.

First Week

During the first week of school, the library media specialist's life will be filled with teacher work days, mandatory meetings, piles of stuff with no apparent purpose, and a line of teachers and other staff who want something from the library. There is little time to get to know the collection or the routine, and less time to figure out where everything goes. Try this list as a set of goals for the first week of school.

Introduce Yourself to Classroom Teachers and School Staff.

Start with your very first day, before school even starts. Each day, visit your prospective library, explore the halls. Many teachers spend a week or more at school before they have to be there. This is a good time for introductions. Obtain a list of faculty

and staff, and cross off the ones that you've met. When the first week of school arrives, set out with a purpose to find the ones you haven't met yet.

Find one Good Resource for One Teacher. *[handwritten: connect to curriculum]*

One of the reasons for meeting teachers in their classrooms is that you can easily find out what they will be studying during the first few weeks, simply by looking at their preparation materials and bulletin boards. Take notes so that you can be prepared for future needs, but then try to locate one really great resource. It will make you feel like you are already doing your job, and it will make one teacher see your value.

[handwritten: teachers talk]

Find one Good Book for One Student.

When school starts, have displays ready for student reading. Listen and engage in conversations about reading, books, magazines, and movies. Try to place yourself physically near students. Inexperienced teachers sometimes have a zone of fear around them, and approach students to answer a question and then quickly back off to safety. Place yourself in the thick of things. Be able to say after the first week that one student is reading a good book that you suggested. *[handwritten: connect]*

Put Up one Display.

Displays, bulletin boards, and library signage are important, but they are also time-consuming. Less is more. Remember that displays are part of the instructional process. A display should have a measurable educational objective. A display highlighting football fiction and biographies has a reading encouragement goal, measured by the number of books checked out from the display, and the number of students who found the resources interesting enough to talk about.

Do one Newsletter or Web Page.

Along with introducing yourself face-to-face with faculty and staff, you also have to introduce the library and its resources. Check with administration to find out whether e-mail newsletters or links to Web pages are preferred by faculty. Print newsletters tend to use a lot of paper. E-mail links may be preferred. Be careful with humor, although the tone can be light. School faculty can be touchy at times and unintended slights will last for years.

Be where the Students are.

It would be nice to say that you were so busy with students in the library that you did not have time to venture into the hall at all. Unfortunately, the reverse may be true, and you may find that the library is removed from the chaos of the rest of the school. Don't make yourself an island. Step into the halls when classes change. Visit the cafeteria during student lunch hours. Nod and say hello to students and teachers. You will find that for the most part they will be equally full of good cheer, and some may stop and talk. *[handwritten: (be in the thick of it all)]*

First Week Summary

Whew! Exhausted already. And this is just the beginning. At the end of the first week, you should have a sense of the faculty, staff, and student emotional climate. You should be able to talk specifically about your impressions of the school population. True, you still don't know much about the library or collections, but the first week needs to be a people-focused week. There is plenty of time for learning about the stuff.

First Month

Some brand-new school library media specialists make the mistake of first writing policy and procedures, goals and strategies, without ever meeting a single patron. Policy and procedures should be based on the people in the school, not inflicted on them. The end of the first month is plenty of time to think about the library program you could have in this school.

Set a Standard for Discipline Based on your Values and Beliefs and the Culture of the School.

If you believe that you are in the business of granting temporary privileges to use your library, you will work very hard to set up policies and procedures to keep as many students and staff out as possible. If, on the other hand, you believe that the resources paid for by parents and other taxpayers are owned by the students, and that you are the facilitator of their library, then you will take a very different approach. Spend some time thinking about what you believe. Read the mission, vision, and goals of *Information Power*, then set your standards accordingly. Remember that you will have the type and level of behavior that you either expect or that you come to accept over a period of time. Expect students to use the library. Refuse to accept disrespect from students or staff.

Offer to Collaborate with One Teacher.

Okay, you've casually mentioned working with a teacher to teach information skills. You put it in the newsletter Web page. And still no takers. Obviously, you will need to be a bit more direct. Choose one teacher who either owes you a favor, or who seems to be creative and innovative. Approach him or her directly and ask about doing a collaborative project together. If it works, fine. If not, plan on another teacher for next month. Sooner or later, you will find a yes.

Set Goals for The Year.

By the end of the first month, you should know what you want to achieve for the school and for the library program. Formulate at least three ideas into goals, each aligning to one of the *Information Power* roles.

Write a Scenario of your Vision for the Library Program in Terms of Instruction, Environment, and Collection.

One of the best things about being a school librarian is that we have the freedom and flexibility to concentrate on a variety of interests, since no one in the school truly knows what our job is. On the other hand, one of the worst aspects of the job is trying to explain what our job is to our peers who have no idea. A scenario is a picture of the future if everything worked out the way that it is supposed to. It time travels the reader into the future. A one-page scenario envisioning the library program five years in the future is a great way to explain and justify goals.

> *Policy and procedures should be based on the people in the school, not inflicted on them.*

First Month Summary

Wow. You have your feet under you now, although still at times you realize how much there is to know. Still, by now you have a good rapport with a few teachers, and are on speaking terms with most. You know some of the students by name, and are even able to identify a few regulars. You have your goals set, and have a fairly clear idea of what needs to be accomplished. You are ready to start achieving.

First Year

As busy as the first year is, at the end of five years you will look back and wonder what you did to keep yourself occupied. Program growth is exponential, and the more that you serve the needs of students and staff, the more needs there are to be fulfilled. At the end of each year, however, it's good to step back and reflect on the passage of the year. Here are some first year goals:

Survive!

Walking into your first year as a school library media specialist is like

jumping on a roller coaster going at top speed. Your only goal is not to fall off. Finesse moves such as waving your hands in the air will come later. Survival is the first real goal. Life cannot slow down while you catch up. You will have to hop on and hold tight. You need to feel good about doing that, instead of berating yourself for what you didn't do. You survived. For the first year, that was your job.

focus on the dids not the didn'ts

List Three Things that you are Proud of.

It's easy to see the disasters that happened, and there will always be some. For now, list three things that you are proud of doing. These may not be big program-changing events. In fact, what makes us proud to do what we do are sometimes the little things, like finding one book for one child, or having a really great research session with the ninth graders, or impressing a middle schooler with our knowledge of databases.

List Three Things that you want to Change.

Re-read your original goals and scenario that you wrote at the end of your first month. What are some of the barriers that are preventing that scenario from becoming a reality? Remember that your changes cannot address the behavior of others. People can change, but you can't change them. You can only change your response to their behavior. Keep your list to only three things. More will overwhelm you, less is not doing enough. You want to be able to assess how these changes will help your program, and you can't do this by changing everything at once.

Evaluate Your Program, Then Meet with your Principal to Discuss your Goals for Next Year.

There are several instruments available to evaluate your program and your performance. Search in the literature for one you are comfortable with, or develop your own. Contact your state school library office to see if there is a statewide instrument

Stars and wishes

Keep admin in the loop

available. Strive for an objective tone, neither too negative nor too positive. Write a one-page factual executive summary, and then make an appointment with your principal to discuss it. Try to schedule this after the students leave, when he or she has more relaxed time.

Take the Summer Off.

I know. You need to do inventory, catalog, reshelf, cover the shelves. Then you need to come in every few weeks to check on summer school, check for new boxes, see if the custodians have moved anything. Then midway through the summer, you need to come in to get the library ready for next year.

Relax. Go to the beach. Pick up some great reading. Clear your mind. You have a whole career ahead of you. Taking care of you is the most important job you have all summer. Put "Do Nothing" on your to do list as your only task. It may be harder than you think.

Plan for Next Year.

Summer is thinking time. Reflect on the past year, and plan to make small changes each month that will get you closer to your goals. Think also of the difference in your feelings between starting your first year and starting your second. Imagine what it will be like when you start your tenth year. Each year is different, but the elements of sameness will always make the library feel like home.

The more that you serve the needs of students and staff, the more needs that there are to be fulfilled.

Your First Principal

And while we are on the first year, here are some tips for the care and feeding of your first principal.

Work Toward School Goals.

It's not about you, or your little fiefdom of the library. The real question is how you contribute towards school goals. In each memo that you write, for each point that you achieve, connect the dots to show how your work in the library contributes toward school goals and student achievement.

Send a Monthly Report.

One of the most overlooked ways to keep your principal on your side is the monthly report of progress. List stats briefly and explain them, note significant accomplishments, then note challenges. Turn it in faithfully each month. This has several benefits. First, it will give you a chance to periodically reflect on the progress toward library goals. Second, it provides the principal with needed sound bites of what is happening in the library. Be sure to mention an instructional unit and a teacher by name. Also mention a few "coulda, woulda, shoulda" events. These are great things that didn't happen. Maybe you just didn't have time, maybe you didn't have the money, maybe the stars were not in alignment. Regardless, over a period of a few years, this will help you and your principal see recurring barriers to improved student learning.

Here are guidelines for the monthly report:

- One-page
- Circulation and other stats
- Accomplishments
- Notable instruction and assessments
- Almost home runs, and why you missed them
- Progress toward goals

Say "Thank You."

Principals sometimes take on the most amazing tasks. Every time you see your principal make an opening speech to the PTA, or face an angry parent, or defuse a simmering confrontation between students, be sure to let him or her know that you thought it was worth praise. Although at times we slip out the door to go home very happy that we are not sitting in the principal's chair, they rarely hear those thoughts spoken.

Remember that Kudos Come to Those Who:

- Show up. It's amazing how much of the time simply by always showing up and being on time people will think you are doing a great job.

- Support school goals. It also means enforcing school rules, even if you don't agree with them. School goals, however, need to be integrated into library goals for the year, and progress toward them evaluated.

- Care about student learning. We are not here to keep the books straight and in pristine condition. We need to care about assessments, help to figure out ways to increase student learning, and shoulder part of the responsibility when students do not achieve.

- Care about teaching. Good teachers are constantly searching for ways to improve their teaching. They scour journals, agonize over just-taught lessons, and ask for advice from others.

- Are professional. Professional teachers are members of their professional association, read widely in the education and subject-field journals, and are able to discuss trends and issues in education.

- Share turf. There is a difference between sharing turf and being a doormat. Value your space so highly that you want to share it with others so that students can benefit from the library.

- Make school work for everyone. The schooling process has worked for teachers and administrators. They are products of the system that they are engaged in promoting. There are others, however, for whom school did not and does not work. These include some parents, some students, and even some school staff. Find a way to make their involvement in the school a source of pride.

Just for You

A school library media specialist takes care of a wide range of needs for students, staff, and the school community. You can't do that unless you first take care of you. Starting with year one, put this to do list on top of the pile:

Join your State Professional Association.

Most state associations now have discussion lists, so it's a great way to get questions answered. It is also a great way to find out the names of the school library media specialists in neighboring schools and districts. It's usually fairly inexpensive to do this, and it helps to be able to talk with people who know the issues of your state and where to find resources.

Join AASL.

I don't want to hear that you don't have the money. You probably spend more on a month of diet soda than you would spend on a year's membership. You're a professional. It's just what you do. Enough said. And besides, AASL is your lifeline for the knowledge, continuing skills, and resources that you need to do your job. You get far more than you pay for with your membership.

Attend State and National Conferences.

You need to get away. At school library conferences, you will find people who understand you, your school, your trials and tribulations, and your enthusiasm for your job. The whiners tend to stay home, and that's a good thing. Even if you pay your own way, and most people do, use conference time as your own personal getaway time to relax, refresh, and rejuvenate.

Get in Touch.

Along with reading professional journals, you also should think seriously about joining a committee. It's nice to be involved in professional work outside of your school, and you will make some lasting friendships. Post a "hi, I'm new here" note to a school library discussion list. You will find others eager to extend a hand. Remember, school library media specialists are only as isolated as they allow themselves to be.

Make Long-term Goals.

Your program will do fine now that you're in charge, but remember you also have to be in charge of you. Make long-term goals for yourself as well in terms of professional growth, learning, and skills. Think seriously about applying for National Board of Professional Teaching Standards certification in a few years. It will be a tremendous challenge, but also a tremendous opportunity for you to join the community of school library media specialists as accomplished teachers.

Big Finish!

After it's all over, you've gotten through the year, and you can look back and be amazed at all you've accomplished. Go and out celebrate! You are well on your way.

Gail K. Dickinson, PhD, *is an assistant professor in the department of Educational Curriculum and Instruction, Darden College of Education, at Old Dominion University in Norfolk, Virginia. She is the author of several publications including* Empty Pockets and Full Plates: Effective Budget Administration for School Library Media Specialists *(Linworth Publishing Inc., 2003).*

Dickinson, Gail K. (2007). First year firsts. *LMC, 25*(7), 34–39.

yes

- join State Professional Associations
- join AASL
- attend conferences

Surviving Your First Year: Strategies and Tips That Will Get You through Your First Year as a Library Media Specialist

By Katie Cerasale-Messina

I was first hired as a library media specialist during late fall 2004. My library was only a year old and I was the first licensed LMS to work in the school in several years. I was 22 years old, fresh out of graduate school, and had energy to spare. On my first day, I vowed that I was going whip my program into shape by February vacation. Fast forward to February vacation—my library was nowhere near where I wanted it to be. I was behind on shelving, no one was signing up for flex time, and I was burned out. There was no way I could learn anything new, change a collection around, or research a grant opportunity. I could not wait until June so I could say "see ya later" and leave forever (preferably to non-library work). Needless to say I did not quit and I wised up. No matter your age, your experience, or energy level, there is only so much you can do at one time. I slowly began to collect strategies to get me through from the end of February to June.

Take your time and master one skill at a time. First-year library media specialists have a lot on their plates. Do not feel like you need to learn the ins and outs of the curriculum, Follett, Dreamweaver, and SMART Notebook all at once (that was my BIGGEST mistake). Take your time and focus one thing at a time. Try a quarter system—take a quarter to focus on something. For the first quarter, work on mastery of the curriculum and lesson planning; for the second, become an expert on your automation system; for the third, create a library blog, and so on. This strategy will prevent you from pulling out your hair and will slowly turn you into an expert on all things library related. This is one of the hardest things to do if you are a multi-tasker like me;

however, it pays off in the long run. When I first started out it took me two hours after school to plan for the next day. After spending three months organizing my plan book and studying the curriculum, I only devoted two prep times for planning my following week. Once I devoted three months to learning Dreamweaver it only took me five minutes a week to update my Web site.

Keep organized data. During the first three years of my career as a library media specialist, I was required to give evidence to support keeping the LMS position. So I started a data binder with sections for circulation statistics, flex time, media sign out, teachers' monthly topic and special unit alert forms, and student testing scores. Last year, I started an Excel spreadsheet for the data. Once a month, I input all of my data and at the end of the year I have an administrator friendly cover sheet for my data binder. Once you have your binder, your tabs, and the spreadsheet organized it only takes five minutes a month for data collection (saving you hours at the end of the year). Even if you are one of the lucky ones that never has to defend your position, it still is nice to have your all of your data in one spot.

Short staffed—no problem. In this economy school libraries are losing support staff. Daily tasks such as shelving and book repair are falling to the wayside. Parent volunteers can help but not all schools are blessed with parents that can be involved. Have students step up. At the beginning of library class have the students line up to check in their books. While they wait for their turn have them check their books for tears, marks, and loose spines. When it is their turn students can tell you if there

is anything wrong. This will save time for you and teach students basic book care. It will take a few weeks for students to get this routine down but once they get in the swing of things, students love helping out. Ask the local high school if they have a community service club. Some high school students may want to give back to their former elementary school, others may want brownie points for college applications. High school students are great for helping primary grades select books. They can show students how to use a shelf marker and make recommendations. Seek out MLIS students if your school is near a college or university with a MLIS program. Email a professor or admissions advisor to let them know you are willing to take on volunteers or pre-practicum students. MLIS students are great for special projects, such as collection development, weeding, and cataloging special collections. In return, you are giving a future professional experience in the library field.

Sing your library's praises. You are your library's biggest fan. There is no room for modesty; you need to brag about your accomplishments. Some teachers do not know the impact a licensed media specialist has on student learning. A lot of educators are under the impression that library class equals story hour. Displaying student work showcases your library's curriculum and teaching. When I created my library Web site I included a link for student projects. After a project is completed ask for volunteers to have their work uploaded. Once uploaded create a bookmark to pass out to everyone (students, administrators, and parents) so they can see what is happening in the media center.

Create a monthly newsletter. This may sound time consuming but once you create one, doing the next month's will take 10 minutes. Have your students help with the newsletter by writing a column about a library lesson taught or a book review. Do not want to waste paper? Have more tech savvy staff? Create a library blog using free blogger servers like Blogger <www.blogger.com>, Livejournal <www.livejournal .com>, or Wordpress <www .wordpress.com>. Blogs are easy to update and great for communicating library news to everyone in your community, including school staff, students, and parents. Try to update your blog once every other week. I even used my blog for writing exercises (double duty—updating the library community and showcasing student work).

Library media specialists are not like other teachers. In addition to teaching we have to manage a library and its collection. It can be overwhelming but manageable. My biggest mistake my first year was taking on everything at once. Once I started breaking up what needed to be done into manageable chunks I realized that I love my job. Everything will get done, when you have the time.

Katie Cerasale-Messina *is the Library Media Specialist at AC Whelan Elementary School in Revere, Massachusetts.*

Cerasale-Messina, Katie. (2010). Surviving your first year: Strategies and tips that will get you through your first year as a library media specialist. *LMC, 29*(1), 30.

My First Year

By Kristy Sartain

(handwritten left margin: ← take it all in 2)

(handwritten left margin: move things that do not belong)

(handwritten left margin: make a plan)

I imagine when most first-year librarians get to school that first day, they spend time wandering around the library, making mental notes of the locations of the fiction, nonfiction, and reference sections, and wonder if there is a way to take what previous librarians have done to the next level.

My first day of work as a first-year librarian at East Carteret High School in Beaufort, North Carolina, was spent taking inventory of a large number of boxes full of books, bookcases, and shelves strewn around the library, and wondering how in the world I was going to put the library back together. I was lucky to have a newly carpeted and painted library for my first day. Fresh paint, carpet chemicals—it smelled gloriously clean. My first order of business? Scented plug-ins. Everywhere.

Order from Disorder

Approximately 250 boxes were awaiting me with a total of about 12,000 books. Most of the bookcases were in some sort of loose approximation from the year before. Most. Thirty computers were set up in classroom formation in one section of the library. To create more space in the library, my principal, also in her first year, had the computers moved to an empty classroom across the hall, creating a true computer lab, and I got the remaining 20 percent of my library back to dedicate to tables and bookcases.

My second order of business was to figure out how I wanted the library set up. I wanted a lounge area where students could come in, relax, read a magazine, or just sit and chat with friends. I also wanted an intimate, comfortable fiction section, separated reference and nonfiction sections, and room for at least two classes to be in the library at the same time.

Book Cases and Books on the Move

Once I created a general floor plan I started moving bookcases. I recruited three students from our Alternative Learning Program (ALP) to help me move bookcases in the library. The students also helped me move bookcases to teacher lounges, classrooms, and book rooms for storage since I ended up with several extra bookcases. A lot of teachers were happy to help me make room in the library by taking the bookcases off my hands.

(handwritten vertical margin: still use any help you can get!)

Then we had to move the books. After long days of moving a few boxes here and there, and unpacking them to put on shelves, I convinced my husband—who teaches weight lifting—to bring in his class to help me. Since the boxes were marked with call numbers, the weight lifting students were able to line most of them up in order. It took them fifteen minutes to accomplish what would have taken me days to do! Then the three ALP students and I got down to business, shelving the books, moving the books when we missed a box, and making sure we had plenty of room. It took us six weeks to get the library exactly how I wanted it. I was lucky to have a principal who told me, "It's your library. Do it however you want it."

The Weeding Phase

My next order of business was to weed. By that time I was down to two ALP student helpers for an hour and a half every day. The average age of my fiction section was twenty-five years old. Yuck. We weeded 542 fiction books that were twenty-five years or older, hadn't been checked out in the last six years, and weren't classics. It took us a week to get that done. I sold about a hundred books for $1 each to faculty members and donated the rest to the Down East Regional Library, a library started by community members and run entirely by volunteers until it was acquired by the local library.

A Functional Facility, at Last!

Because my library now has enough room to accommodate two classes at a time, teachers have been bringing them in for group work. I have seventeen tables, more than enough for a class to spread out. In the past, with the computer lab in the library, another class couldn't use the library for research or group work because there was always someone teaching. My library is not large at all.

Another great thing that happened was that one of our teachers acquired new furniture and was trying to get rid of her old set. She tried selling it first. I told her to let me know if no one bought it, and I would happily accept it as a donation for a tax write-off. A week later she decided to donate it. I had my student lounge area! She donated a reclining sofa, reclining loveseat, and reclining easy chair. My students love it! They are able to come in, read a magazine, or hang out during lunch and before school, just like I envisioned.

> *It took us six weeks of work to get the library exactly how I wanted it. I was lucky to have a principal who told me, "It's your library. Do it however you want it."*

Literacy Outreach via a Book Fair

Would you believe our school had never had a book fair until I came along? I didn't hesitate. In my first week I called Scholastic and set one up for the week before the holiday break. I advertised the book fair for

(handwritten bottom: Out with the old! Someone's trash is another man's treasure)

weeks beforehand. I wanted our students to give gifts of literacy. Scholastic sent adult bestsellers, cookbooks, kid books, book gifts, and all the fun stuff that schools have at their book fairs. We literally had something for everyone. I stayed open late two nights, and parents actually came with their students (and sometimes by themselves) to buy books. When it was all said and done, the results were amazing. Our sales hit $1,000, which was phenomenal for a school of only 550 students that had never had a book fair. Teachers brought their classes in so the students would have time to browse and purchase. Honestly, I think our teachers were more excited about the book fair than the kids. Some teachers brought several classes in, so the teachers could have plenty of chances to browse. I'm already booked for the same week next year.

teachers love a good book sale

But It's Really about the Students

I'm most proud of the relationships I have built with some of my students. Norah and Gavyn in the Alternative Learning Program have put almost as much "sweat equity" into this library as I have. They have gone from being shy and introverted to outgoing, personable, well-respected students in the school, from teachers' and students' perspectives. Gavyn has turned into quite the reader since he is surrounded by books an hour and a half a day. He now assists me with book displays, book selections, and the library software by helping check students in and out. He has come so far in his school life that his supervising teacher and I submitted a conference proposal about how the library can help reach students who are on the edge. It was accepted, and we spread the message of the far-reaching potential of a library in helping students gain job skills, critical thinking skills, independence, and a sense of self.

give students accountability

I know I have had an impact on many of the students at our school. Several have asked me to be their mentor for their graduation projects. This is quite an accomplishment for a first-year teacher, but especially a librarian who doesn't have the same students every day. One student asked me if I could take her on a college visit because her mom couldn't take her. So we trekked all the way across the state to Asheville so she could see the college she had chosen.

career goal: every single year

> *When it was all said and done, we had amazing results from our book fair! Teachers brought their classes to browse and purchase. Honestly, I think our teachers were more excited about the book fair than the kids.*

I won a grant from the Margaret Alexander Edwards Trust to implement a program to encourage students to read for pleasure. To start that program I taught basic collection development and book research/review skills to a select group of students. After the class was completed, the students submitted lists of books they wanted to read that were appropriate based on our county's collection development policy. Once those lists were approved, we drove to Books-A-Million where the students purchased the books to add to the library's collection. These students will get to read and review the books they chose so they can encourage other students to read them as well. Already, the program has been a resounding success. I overheard one of the students telling two of her friends about the books she purchased and how good they were.

The Rewards of Teaching

One of my favorite things (that surprised me) was getting to teach classes. I have taught multiple classes on using Prezi, a web-based presentation tool. Students have absolutely loved it. One student told me she was mad I wasn't there before so she could have learned it for her senior project. Because Prezi is new to them, I have had no discipline issues while teaching it, and the students are creating some really great presentations and are generally very excited about using the tool. I have also taught classes about plagiarism and citations. While this isn't exactly an entertaining class, I try to make it that way so the students pay attention and maybe even remember some of my advice.

As a first year librarian, I have been absorbing so much information from the professional resources available. *LMC* has been instrumental in helping me. I have learned about building book displays and making my library seem more like a bookstore to encourage students to read. Implementing these tips as well as utilizing the help of my student library assistants and sharing the fact that I love these books and can recommend a book for anyone, circulation was up 36 percent this year. For a high school, this is a remarkable increase, and I have high hopes for next year as well.

Now that students know me, they feel more comfortable coming in and asking for a book recommendation or thoughts on a problem they're having. They know I'll give them straight-shooter advice, and I will ask questions that make them think about both sides of the issue they face.

one more reason to get to know kids!

Kristy Sartain *is the librarian at East Carteret High School in Beaufort, North Carolina. She can be contacted at kristy.sartain@carteretk12.org.*

Sartain, Kristy. (2013). My first year. *LMC, 31*(4), 20–21.

Everyday Best Practices

By Mary Alice Anderson

"Do what's best for kids!" My former principal said this often when we discussed media program needs. Media specialists can make media centers places where students and teachers want to be. This article looks at everyday, attainable, common sense best practices.

Putting Out the Welcome Mat

A welcoming environment makes the media center a place students want to be. Too often students are greeted with rules and "don'ts" instead of welcoming them. New Jersey media specialist Julie Greller's best practice is "always being available to teachers and students" (Greller). A newly hired media specialist plans to arrive at work early enough to have the computers on and be ready to welcome and assist teachers and students the minute they walk in the door. Keep your office door open, the window blinds up, and create a comfortable spot for teachers or students to sit when you are working together. If you have an office, create another workspace close to where the action is so you are visible and accessible. Increase your accessibility by walking around all spaces in the media center.

Following an unwelcoming predecessor is an opportunity to make lemonade from lemons. The response may be, "Really, we can do that?" One media specialist said "All of my teachers told the visitors that the library used to be a cold, unwelcoming place—but that it has really changed since I got there, because I tried so hard to get them what they asked for. Patience really does pay off, so hang in there. The word will spread." Do something out of the ordinary!

Loosen up on the rules, make yourself and resources more accessible, remove physical barriers to access. When I began a new job several years ago we got rid of fashioned pictures, signs, and dust bunnies. We brought in technology and allowed displays of student artwork, sending a strong message that a new environment with a kid friendly, lived-in look was in the

[handwritten: too real at Pembroke]

works. A media specialist starting a new career at an international school is "weeding ruthlessly, rearranging collections and furniture, hoping to create a more welcoming, current environment." Others are expanding accessibility with digital resources and giving students the freedom to use *their* digital information tools. Follow school guidelines and explain changes to staff and students who may be used to the way things were always done.

[handwritten: change can be scary but not bad]

Leadership in providing ongoing staff development helps teachers and will ultimately impact students. It's a career survival skills best practice.

Walking the Walk and Talking the Talk

A superintendent advised media specialists to make sure people see them doing professional tasks. Structure your work so people see you interacting with staff and students, modeling instruction and sharing your technology expertise. Give up jobs that don't matter or make a difference in student learning. Stop worrying about what doesn't matter. Are a few books lost? That might just be the cost of doing business.

It's all about relationships. Relationships with teachers will make or break a media program. A Wisconsin media specialist's best practice is "being very conscious of the fact that I am a specialist and do not have students 24/7 like classroom teachers." Share ideas for student success and connections

[handwritten: yes!]

to the classroom. I worked with an elementary grade teacher who was once a reluctant technology user but came to see me as his teammate. We developed authentic opportunities for his students to use technology resources and tools while supporting curricular goals and student success. "Eye Spy Math," for example, used primary source photos of buildings, such as the Pentagon, or people playing chess. As students viewed the photos, they observed and brainstormed geometric shapes. "Eye Spy Math" challenged the students to think as they reviewed geometric terms prior to a state math exam. Students used Excel to chart their reading fluency scores throughout the school year, developing pride in their reading and Excel skills.

Limited collaboration is a big frustration for media specialists, often leading to feelings of doing something wrong. Examine today's educational realities. Fewer media specialists, large class sizes, and mandates get in the way. Work with teachers in the areas in which *they* need help. Service is not a dirty word. One doable best practice is keeping the sign-up schedule close at hand to discuss possibilities from the start. If scheduling online, follow up with personal contact. A senior high media specialist switched to Google Docs for scheduling because it was more convenient for teachers; she said it has changed everything.

[handwritten: be willing]

Embrace technology. A senior high media specialist commented, "Too many media specialists believe computers are still a new technology and resist computers in the library for fear of noises." It's a best practice to fight for technology. Acquire and encourage the use of tools that support engaged learning. Model the use of Web 2.0 tools that make teaching and learning more relevant and efficient. A middle school media specialist introduced students to Prezi as an alternative to PowerPoint. She said Prezi's "busy" nature appeals to students. Consider allocating the budget differently to provide what today's students and teachers want. Supporting both the virtual collection and the tangible collection is a best practice.

Support technology initiatives throughout the school and empower others by being the "go to" person when teachers have questions about technology or need ideas for a new way to use technology. Understand district and school technology plans and policies. Participate in technology decisions made in the school and district.

(handwritten: the "go-to" person)

(handwritten: advocate!)

Leadership and Advocacy

Lead the way with real staff development. Debby Walters, a Wisconsin middle school media specialist, knows if media specialists don't lead the way, the technology training teachers want and need may not occur. Informal surveys by Dr. Mary Ann Bell (2010) and an NEA study (2008), show that instructional technology is underutilized. Training is more likely to be on instructional management rather than instruction and student use. After viewing the results of a survey Walters conducted through Survey Monkey, she planned a series of workshops. The first one was to "learn 360 and ECB VideoLink services. It was a good choice because it is something they can immediately use and will be helpful throughout the school year. Five people attended and I helped ten others with it at different times. We pay for it and it has been under utilized." "Train the trainer" models go far in helping teachers and ultimately students be successful.

(handwritten: need more hands on!)

Student instruction in technology can be a back door to developing staff skills. One media specialist described teaching students to use tools such as Zotero and Evernote as teaching staff through osmosis. Keep basic tech directions and tips readily accessible in print and electronic format so teachers and students can

be independent learners. Offer "Tech Tuesdays" or "Thirty [Minutes] on Thursday." Leadership in providing ongoing staff development is a career survival skills best practice.

> It's a best practice to fight for technology so that every student who enters a media center can use technology to access information and be a creative, productive learner.

Take time for advocacy so it is always in force, not just at budget cutting time. Develop ongoing relationships with people who will support your program. Even our most ardent, well-meaning supporters may not really know what we do. Basic and best advocacy practices include informational brochures and an online presence to inform about the media center and its resources, and show how students benefit from the media program. Work with district or school public relations personnel so the media program is represented in district press releases, newsletters, and the local news media, including locally broadcast television and radio programs.

(handwritten: Keep them informed)

(handwritten: Attention!)

(handwritten: yes!)

Web 2.0 tools kick advocacy up a notch and make a good impression in the digital age. Some media specialists are creating blogs with different topics for administrators, teachers, and families. Others are using e-marketing newsletters (one media specialist suggested MyMailout, an e-newsletter tool). Create a media center website that has photos or videos of students in the media center. A Flickr photostream or a short, lively video created with Animoto can send a strong message that "this is the place to be." Don't have a website? It's time to start. Let parents know what's *currently going on* in the media center as well as *what's available.* Invite students to share what the media center means to them. Include the media program mission statement and a familiar logo

(handwritten: make people aware!)

or slogan in all print and electronic communications to create recognition.

Tell stories with narrative, expository information to support your message. Instead of just informing people about available databases, tell a story about how the science students did research using a science database to find information for their successful papers and projects. One media specialist told her story through a multimedia presentation at a teacher sponsored open house to celebrate student projects.

Intentionally gather information. A weekly log of anecdotes yields an arsenal of stories to share. You never know when that might occur or who might stop by the media center to see or ask what you do. You may be pleasantly rewarded with unexpected public support from people who have paid attention. Can you tell your stories so they resonate with the school community?? If we don't tell our stories, who will?

(handwritten: board of ed meetings)

The Power of Families and Community

Reach out to families with special events. Family reading or technology nights are affordable options. A junior high media specialist worked with her principal to build a media center resources session into the parent back-to-school orientation session. Parents said it was the best part of the orientation. Keep the media center open on occasions that bring parents to school.

Extend program visibility in the community. If district facilities are available to community groups, make the media center available for use. It can be a lot of work, and it may mean wear and tear on the media center's equipment, but it's positive PR. A Minnesota media specialist had PR in mind when she made the school's video conferencing equipment available to a former professional football player who was speaking to students in another state. Taxpayers see what the media center has to offer and what it needs; they may become your best allies in the future.

Joint ventures with community cultural organizations are win-win

(local authors, Danbury museum)

partnerships. Arrange for museum displays to be brought to the school, work with a museum to develop a local history website or blog. Technology and telecommunications organizations and businesses are other groups to work with. Local government cable television stations may be looking for video clips to air. Small districts often have a close-knit community, and partnerships are obvious. Larger districts have various communities. No matter how small or large, there is potential.

Be the Change!

Ongoing connections with our profession help us understand the change that is constant and inevitable. The more you learn, the more you become energized and understand the big picture. Join professional organizations and networks, and attend conferences. Participate in committees, personal learning networks, and discussion groups. Explore and accept opportunities to participate in educational company advisory, editorial boards, or product beta tests.

Begin each day and each school year with a positive attitude. Each day is a new beginning and each year an even newer beginning for building community. A positive attitude and daily best practices make a difference.

These everyday best practices require your time, energy, new ways of thinking, and shifting priorities. But once you begin to implement them, you will see that they are attainable, rewarding, and essential for building a strong foundation for programs that successfully support today's standards and the needs of students and teachers, making every day one of your best days.

References

Bell, Mary Ann. "BELLTONES: What Teachers Know (and Don't Know) about Technology—And Does Anybody Know They Don't Know?" *Multimedia & Internet @ Schools* 7/8 (2010): 39–41.

Bell, Mary Ann. "BELLTONES: Who Knows What about Technology." *Multimedia & Internet @ Schools* 9/10 (2010): 27–30.

Greller, Julie. "Re: Best Practices." Message to Author. 22 Aug. 2010. E-mail.

Walters, Debby. "Re: Staff Development." Message to Author. 17 Sep. 2010. E-mail.

LM_NET Listserv Archives. Web. 20 Aug. 2010. www.eduref.org/lm_net/archive.

"Teachers: Downloads; Eye Spy Math in American Memory." Library of Congress. Web. 13 Oct. 2010. www.loc.gov/teachers/additionalresources/downloads.

"Access, Adequacy, and Equity in Education Technology." National Education Association. 10 June 2008. Web. www.nea.org/home/10908.htm.

Mary Alice Anderson *is a former Minnesota school media specialist now teaching in the online Professional Development Program at the University of Wisconsin-Stout (Menomonie). She can be reached at andersonmary@uwstout.edu.*

Anderson, Mary Alice. (2011). Everyday best practices. *LMC, 30*(3), 48–50.

If it doesn't challenge you, it won't change you

The School Media Specialist Organizational Survival Kit

By Julie Harris

Starting a new job or transferring to another school district can be an overwhelming experience for a school library media specialist. These basic survival tips, including networking and assessing your media center setup, will get you off to a great start!

Networking

Before you begin your position, consult with another experienced media specialist who is on your grade level. The person may be from your school district, a nearby school library, or someone you can e-mail. Pick someone whom you can easily reach throughout the school year.

Join library organizations, participate in listservs and other Internet groups, or subscribe to library periodicals. Sharing ideas, asking questions, and obtaining different viewpoints greatly enhance your chances to start your first year on the right path.

Assessing your Work Place

You usually begin several days before the staff and students. Take at least a day to get acquainted with your library setup. Check your office, the library seating and shelving arrangement, any storage areas, and space that may be used for a classroom.

Office

Arrange your office so you have ready reference access to material like circulation/cataloging manuals, budgets, inventory lists, scheduling, and forms for daily use. Be sure you know where all passwords are to computers, library software, and databases. Know the location of doors, cabinets, and keys, as well as owner's manuals. Keep a print or electronic list of the most frequently used numbers close-by, such as your technology supervisor, staff, maintenance, and businesses from which you want to order.

Work Room

Your work room should be arranged in a way that makes it easy for you to access equipment and materials. Set up a work table for the laminating machine, letter cutter, and cutting board. Some work rooms might have a sink and cupboards for storing supplies. Organize your work space so you have ample room to laminate, cut out letters, and repair books. Keep the following supplies on hand: laminating film, construction paper, rubber cement, glue, tape, markers, pens and pencils, rulers, scissors, stencils, and manila envelopes.

If library books or textbooks need repair, you can store supplies, such as book binding glue and tape, spine labels, paper towels, and protective book covers. If books are damaged in the spine, use book repair glue and let the books set overnight. Textbooks often need binding tape put on the spine as well as the front and back corners of the book cover. Plastic protective book jacket covers for books and paperbacks will help preserve the life of your book collection.

Media Room

The school library media specialist spends time taping, storing, cleaning, and checking out media equipment. You are responsible for an inventory list with models and serial numbers of all equipment. Update your list as you get new equipment, and delete discarded items. Be sure to notate the room number where equipment is housed. Give your principal and technology supervisor a revised copy at the end of the year.

Other networking tips:
Visit at least five other media centers before you start.
Have questions for each media specialist.
Gather information about cataloging, circulation, and management techniques.
Get copies of forms for statistics, reports, and patron usage.
Find out the Internet usage policy.

Additional supplies to store in the work room:
Printer paper, discs, file folders (letter and legal), clasp envelopes of various sizes
Masking, packaging, and adhesive tape, paper clips, notepads, glue, and liquid paper
Number two pencils (helpful for testing situations)
Pencil chains (helps prevent pencils or pens from being taken away from the counter)
Book binding and spine tape
Dusters, keyboard and household cleaners, paper towels, garbage bags, and furniture polish

In order for all teachers to have access to equipment, you can house TV and LCD projector carts in the library media center for checkout. If you have a larger TV monitor, be sure it is securely strapped to the cart. Set up a list at your counter so teachers can book equipment in advance. Make sure all electrical outlets are working properly on the cart.

Owner's manuals can be housed alphabetically in boxes by equipment type. On the top of the manual, write down in red ink the date purchased, model and serial numbers, and the warranty expiration date. Staple a copy of the warranty agreement and registration card inside the manual. When you need to troubleshoot your equipment, you can locate the owner's manual quickly.

Create an inviting, warm, and colorful environment in your media center so students will welcome the opportunity to return throughout the school year.

Media Center

One final area to consider is the arrangement of the media center. Begin by sketching a diagram. Keeping in mind the square footage of the library and the locations of doors, consider how to best arrange the furniture, such as the counter, tables and chairs, shelves, dictionary and atlas stand, computers and printer stations, and display counters. If possible, keep the circulation counter near the office so that you can go back and forth with ease to do various tasks. The checkout computer should be set up for circulation/cataloging along with Internet access and word processing. The printer should be located near your computer in order to run off such items as overdue or fine notices, daily reports, statistics of patron and material usage, and for student use while conducting research.

Sharing ideas, asking questions, and obtaining different viewpoints greatly enhance your chances to start your first year on the right path.

Students and staff should have plenty of room to study, read, browse, and work at a computer station. Space between furnishings should accommodate any type of activity, be it in a large or small group setting or for individual work. Place tables and chairs so you can see all students. A good way to maintain a quieter atmosphere with less disruptive behavior is when students know you can see them.

When setting up your computers, make sure that all computers with Internet access are facing you from the circulation counter. You can check at a glance what sites students are visiting.

Bright, colorful signs can be posted on top of shelves to indicate areas. Most media centers use the Dewey decimal system of classification. Other signs to post are fiction, reference, biography, story collection, paperback, easy, and professional.

Display centers can be set up to highlight holidays, new book arrivals, artwork of students, the top readers of special programs, reserved book sets for teachers of different grades, genealogy scrapbooks, and a book

Media supplies to have on hand:

Place cables, extension cords, and connectors in one drawer.

Store blank CDs, projector bulbs, etc. in a cabinet.

Label your remote controls and mark them so you know which TV or DVD player they go with.

Have a separate drawer for your batteries.

Keep a small tool kit on hand for equipment repair.

Store a silver or gold tipped permanent pen to mark equipment ownership.

Keep a small handheld vacuum cleaner and media cleaners on hand.

Store projector bulbs, headsets, and a tripod in the cabinet.

Extra items for the checkout counter:

Necessary items are stapler, tape dispenser, pencil sharpener, bookmarkers, pencils, scissors, highlighters, rulers, and metal chains for pencils connected to a self-adhesive base.

Additional items are notebook and printer paper, telephone directory, and calculator.

Have media center pamphlets and searching strategy guidelines available for research.

suggestion box for students. Create an inviting, warm, and colorful environment in your media center so students will welcome the opportunity to return throughout the school year.

Once you have set up your media center, you are off to a good start for the upcoming school year. By focusing on how you want the media center organized, you are in a unique position of meeting the challenges necessary to maintain a learning environment that will meet the needs of the entire school community.

Julie Harris *is a School Library Media Specialist at Raceland (Kentucky) High School. She may be reached at julieharris24@yahoo.com.*

Harris, Julie. (2012). The school media specialist organizational survival kit. *LMC, 31*(1), 14–15.

Shelving:

Use three to four shelves on the elementary level. At the junior high/high school level set up five shelves.
Keep fewer books on the bottom row.
Weed your collection regularly. Weeding is based on accuracy of information, last checkout date, year of publication, and condition.
Place reference books in a special section.
Have a professional collection in your office for autographed books, genealogy books, or your favorite read-aloud books.

Cross-Marketing Yourself: It ~~Doesn't Have to~~ Hurt to Work!

By Jennifer Coleman

No doubt you've encountered the art of cross-selling as a consumer. You needed shoes, and there also happen to be socks nearby. How about dessert to go along with that meal? You get the idea—it may not have occurred to you that you wanted or needed something, but having the idea planted in your head in a myriad of ways has a compelling effect. Cross-selling is the art of enticing customers with goods or services that are related to what they are already buying. Now think for a moment about replacing the word *customer* with *library patron*—they may not be buying anything per se, but they may be moving from being a non-user to a user. How can you apply cross-marketing to better offer the resources that you have on your campus?

Cross-selling is th[e art of] enticing customer[s with goods] or services that ar[e related to] what they are alre[ady buying.]

[handwritten note: Module 2: Flipgrid — Talk about the best way to market yourself to your school. Pg 26 &11]

...and positive way, one word at a time.

Simple Public Relations and Cross-Marketing Ideas

1. **Spend more time** with existing and long-using library patrons than you do appealing to new or non-users. Relationships require maintenance time. Do you have trouble getting new teachers to collaborate with you on library instruction, but you do have a few teachers who are the opposite? Spend time nurturing existing collaborative relationships. Word of your partnership efforts will spread through the voices of excited students who are the direct beneficiaries. Time will bring others into the fold if you strengthen those already strong relationships. The marketing idea at work here is: "We have a good thing going over here. Why don't you check out what we are up to?"

[handwritten note: teachers talk!]

2. **Ask questions** that are patron oriented. Get people talking about their needs and wants. Learn how to ask questions so that they are *user* focused, not *you* focused. Instead of asking "What do I need to do to help you?" ask "What keeps you from researching your paper with the online databases we have?"

3. **Join forces** and capitalize on your innate skills. Just like the socks near the shoes, be the value-added person in different areas of your building. For example, librarians are terrific organizers. Offer to come into any teacher's class and help students who might need a boost organizing their time or materials. Or offer an "After School Organizer Boot Camp" where you help kids get their school binders in order.

   Maybe you excel at being detail oriented. Can you partner with the secretaries, registrar, or other office personnel once a month or more to lend them a hand? Offer to proofread a newsletter or assist in a large project like schoolwide testing. Not only do you use your gifts and talents to enrich others, you help projects run more smoothly, people do their jobs better, and you are a demonstrated team player. Nothing but good comes from that.

[handwritten note: help organize]

4. **Offer up the space;** the library doesn't belong to you. The library is programs and people, not a warehouse of books. Allow people's energies to be part of the space. Offer to lend it out for meetings, book clubs, even baby showers and birthday parties for staff members. People who might come to those social gatherings will be looking around at your space while being engaged in an alternate activity. Take the opportunity to plant items in strategic places that might hook a non-user. If you know the staff party's refreshments are to be set up on a table near the biographies, display some new reads that you know might benefit certain classrooms. In cross-marketing lingo this might be called bundling.

   Think: You might just want cake and punch at the shower, but I'm going to make sure you leave with more, like a handful of books that you didn't even know would enhance your next science unit!

5. **Deliver more.** Use your big picture expertise! Use your knowledge of the curricular timeline to your advantage. Gather resources in advance and personally deliver items to teachers a week before they need them. If you make

[handwritten note: find them before they find you]

the point to create a personal connection with a teacher and what they are doing *before* their immediate point of need, it communicates a sense of caring community and enhances their performance. This simple act of being one step ahead will reduce your stress because it will cut down on those last minute panic requests. Keeping a careful eye on the big picture becomes a win-win for all involved.

6. **Write Notes.** In a world of e-mails and texts, written communication gets noticed. Few take the time to write and send cards anymore. Written notes really stand out and show that you care. Amass a stash of nice note cards and make it a goal to write one a week. Compliment a colleague on a lesson or thank them for stopping by the library to check out books for their literature circle. In four to five sentences a week, you can build your image in a strong and positive way, one word at a time. The marketing idea here is putting

yourself in a location that is unexpected.

Think: The teacher is hurriedly checking their mailbox in the lounge on a break, and in the midst of a stack of photocopied to-do lists and unsolicited catalogs, a personalized envelope emerges from the stack. It gets opened first! The librarian is in more than one place at a time? "Wow, I'm impressed. This reminds me, I need to go back to the library soon."

7. **Be short, concise, and relevant**. Everyone is busy. If you run into someone in the hallway, chances are they don't have much time. Respect your colleagues' time and they will appreciate you all the more. The cross-selling technique at play is: "Oh, they think they are just walking down the hall, but in 15 seconds I will let them know I was thinking of them and found three resources that can help with next week's language arts lesson—I'll drop them by this afternoon!"

"let's walk and talk"

Learn how to ask questions so that they are user focused, not you focused.

By applying one or two of these ideas to your already full plate does not have to be painful or laborious. It doesn't have to hurt to work. It just means being mindful of others, compassionate, and confident. Know what you have to offer and offer it. Reach out in a different way than you usually do. Not only will you grow professionally, you will grow personally. Bonus!

Jennifer Coleman *is a freelance writer and the librarian at St. Gabriel's Catholic School in Austin, Texas. She may be reached at jennandbrett@yahoo.com.*

Coleman, Jennifer. (2012). Cross-marketing yourself: It doesn't have to hurt to work! *LMC, 30*(5), 34–35.

confidence is key!

Practical Advocacy: Lead to Empower Learning

By Ann M. Martin

Second in a series of ongoing articles by guest authors.

The Education Revolution

Jell-O and quicksand are more stable than today's education environment. We are in the midst of an educational revolution demanding sweeping change. This creates instability. It is this volatile climate of educational reform that necessitates visible active leadership in the school. Communicating and then directing a meaningful vision restores stability. This is leadership.

An important addition to the national school library program guidelines, *Empowering Learners*, released by the American Association of School Librarians (AASL) is the guideline on leadership. It notes that the leadership role of the school librarian is critical to meeting local, state, and national goals. School library leadership takes advocacy to the next level. Leadership challenges librarians to extend their role of advocacy beyond influencing outcomes to directing educational initiatives in the school.

When revolutions occur leaders direct the path of change. In today's educational climate terms such as 21st Century Skills and Common Core State Standards are the new buzzwords. It is important to know and understand what these initiatives mean for the students and staff at the building level. More importantly it is critical to be able to communicate how the role of the library program is vital to meeting the demands generated by these initiatives. Accomplishing school program change is dependent on providing solutions and relevance to these new concepts. Leaders become experts on new ideas and implement the initiatives by gaining support and cooperation from decision makers. The school librarian who understands and adapts the latest educational trends provides relevance for the school community. This is how best practice is implemented and leadership is modeled.

> **Empowering Learning Through Leadership Guideline:** *The school library media program is built by professionals who model leadership and best practice for the school community.*

Seeing the Possibilities

If every school librarian will lead efforts to effectively infuse the vision of the 21st century library program into their building level educational agenda; then, the relevance of the school library program will be clear. Defining and clarifying the role of the school library program begins with understanding where the library program intersects with the school's annual goals. Schools develop objectives based on requirements to meet local, state, and national achievement standards. Successful library leaders embed the library program into the building level goals and objectives. When teachers and students are directed to the library as a source to achieve their benchmark goals then the school library program is actualized and viewed as critical to the school. School librarians who accomplish this are leaders because they empower learning for their students and teaching staff.

So there you have it. In this unstable quicksand-like educational climate library leaders must guide the instructional revolution by communicating and directing a meaningful vision to their school community. This is leadership. Consult *Empowering Learners* and put into action the leadership target indicators. Begin to lead your library today.

Ann M. Martin *is Educational Specialist, Library Information Services, at Henrico County Public Schools in Henrico, Virginia and is the Immediate Past President for the American Association of School Librarians.*

Martin, Ann M. (2009). Practical advocacy: Lead to empower learning. *LMC, 28*(2), 7.

Collaboration: Finding the Teacher, Finding the Topic, Finding the Time

By Angela Gess

Have you ever had a teacher say, "I'd love to bring my classes to the library more often, but we just don't have enough time because we have to prepare for our state standardized tests?" This response stems from a misconception about the role of library media centers and library media specialists. In some school environments, the library media center is viewed as a place for students to "waste" time reading fiction books, and the library media specialist as merely a babysitter who provides teachers with much needed planning time. This misconception by teachers and administrators must be changed. In light of the *Information Power* information literacy standards and the new 21st Century Learner standards, it is the role of the library media specialist to aide teachers and students in the preparation for standardized tests while teaching them crucial information literacy skills. This can be done through collaboration with the right teacher, on the right topic, at the right time.

The Foundation for Collaboration

Collaboration between the school library media specialist and classroom teachers is an excellent way to prepare students for a high level of achievement on state assessments. Collaboration, however, can be unsuccessful if proper planning does not occur. Successful collaboration occurs when planned with the *Information Power* and AASL standards in mind. The goal of any collaborative unit should be aligned with the *Information Power* mission statement in that students are effective users of ideas and information. Keith Curry Lance confirms this in the article, "Proof of the Power: Quality Library Media Programs Affect Academic Achievement." Lance states, ". . .the level of development of the library

media program was a predictor of student performance, and data on staffing levels correlated with test scores." He also states, "Levels of student performance were also related. . .to the extent to which library media staff engaged in particular activities related to the teaching of information literacy and to the exercise of leadership, collaboration, and technology."

The misconception that the library media specialist cannot help students prepare for standardized assessments must be eradicated. This can be done by examining data on the correlation between certified school library media specialists and higher test scores. According to the article, "School Libraries Do Make a Difference," published in *School Libraries Work* by the California School Library Association, schools in Colorado and Oregon where there were collaborative media teachers had ". . . the best statewide high school reading/language scores." Also, students had ". . . 21% higher elementary test scores." These statistics are just a few that have been published recently demonstrating the importance of utilizing the library media center and its certified media specialist. The key is having a media specialist who collaborates with teachers to further learning. Collaboration, when done conscientiously and often, is invaluable.

Off on the Right Foot

The first step in any good collaboration is finding the "right" teacher. The "right" teacher is eager to collaborate, values your role as the library media specialist, sees the need for integrating technology into the curriculum, and understands that both the library media specialist and the collection can aide in the preparation for standards of learning assessments.

Recently, I participated in a collaboration unit with the sixth grade science teacher at my school. She and I put a great deal of time and effort into preparing a unit that addressed the state assessment standards on the topic of weather. The unit was successful for several reasons; but mainly because we both believed in the collaboration, and we both knew our goal: to focus on how and what the students were learning that would prepare them for the state standards of learning test.

The second step in a successful collaboration is choosing the "right" topic. The right topic is one that lends itself to a connection with the "standards" in the library media field, and that allows for the integration of technology. The right topic is one that is fundamental for students to master in order to obtain a high level of achievement on state assessment tests. While our unit was on weather, we focused on several *Information Power* information literacy standards and AASL standards for the 21st century learner.

The following information literacy standards were addressed in the collaborative unit:

- Standard 1: The student who is information literate accesses information efficiently and effectively.
- Standard 2: The student who is information literate evaluates information critically and competently.
- Standard 3: The student who is information literate uses information accurately and creatively.

Likewise, the following AASL standards were a focus of this collaborative unit:

- 1.1.1–Follow an inquiry-based process in seeking knowledge in curricular subjects, and make the real-world connection for using this process in one's own life.

- 1.1.2–Use prior and background knowledge as a context for new learning.
- 1.1.4–Find, evaluate, and select appropriate sources to answer questions.
- 1.1.6–Read, view, and listen for information presented in any format (e.g., textual, visual, media, digital) in order to make inferences and gather meaning.
- 1.1.7–Make sense of information gathered from diverse sources by identifying misconceptions, main and supporting ideas, conflicting information, and point of view or bias.
- 1.1.8–Demonstrate mastery of technology tools for accessing information and pursuing inquiry.
- 1.1.9–Collaborate with others to broaden and deepen understanding.

Then the Right Time

The third step in any successful collaboration unit is finding the "right" time to integrate the unit. The right time is going to be different for each unit. Sometimes, it is best to do a collaborative unit as an introduction. Other times, it may be best to use the collaborative unit in the middle of inquiry. My collaborative partner and I found that it would be best to do the unit as a conclusion to her classes' study of the weather. We believed that this would afford the students the opportunity to demonstrate mastery of the *Information Power* and AASL standards.

The collaborative unit on weather began with a two-day review of weather terminology by the science teacher. There was also a focus on how to read and forecast the weather. During the next two days of the unit, the collaboration came into play. The science teacher and I worked together to create a webquest integrating information in several formats (AASL 1.1.6). The webquest allowed students to utilize our mobile laptop lab to research the topic of weather, thus integrating technology into the unit (AASL 1.1.1, 1.1.8). The students were guided through the research process with a webquest and graphic

organizer, but were required to access and evaluate information gathered from diverse sources in order to make sense of it and apply it to their science curriculum (AASL 1.1.4, 1.1.7, *Information Power* standards 1 and 2). This accessing and evaluating of information was essential in preparing the students for the state assessment test.

Without my collaboration with the science teacher, the students were less likely to be exposed to the information in so many formats. According to Debra Lau Whalen in the article "Study: Higher Test Scores Linked to Certified Media Specialists," in regard to the importance of library media specialists, ". . .preliminary results show that certified librarians are also more likely to provide students with materials that present more diverse points of view and that better support the curriculum than noncertified librarians." This was demonstrated in my collaboration unit with the science teacher.

Secondary Effects

This unit addressed several other *Information Power* information literacy and AASL standards. For example, *Information Power* standard 3: The student who is information literate uses information accurately and creatively, was addressed in the final two assignments of the collaborative unit. The first, when students were asked to apply their background knowledge (AASL 1.1.2) to imagine that they were realtors and to determine where a family would like to live based on their preferences about the weather. Also, in the final assignment where they were to "create" a forecast for their favorite city or town using the Microsoft PowerPoint program. The students could collaborate during these assignments, which led to a greater understanding of the topics (AASL 1.1.9).

The Importance of Inclusion

It is important when planning to remember that if you do not take into account students with special needs, you are unable to ensure the success

of all students. In this collaboration unit, we knew the demographics of our classes and planned accordingly. For instance, we had one class that included 13 students with special needs. We were fortunate to have a special education teacher in the room with us, who helped to facilitate learning by walking the students through the webquest inquiry on the Smart Board, reading the information aloud, and paraphrasing it for those students who may have had difficulty with the reading level of the information. When thinking about our state assessment scores, they encompass all students, including those with special needs, so we must not forget to plan for them as well.

At the end of each collaborative unit, an assessment tool determines the success of the unit. Include all who participated in the collaboration planning in the creation and implementation of this assessment. Did you meet all the standards laid out in the collaboration planning, and did students achieve success in the subject matter? The collaboration planners should be able to determine if the students were successful in obtaining knowledge and preparing for the state standardized test. For the collaboration unit on weather, we used a graphic organizer and a rubric to assess the students' success.

Collaboration between certified media specialists and classroom teachers can help prepare students for success on state assessment tests. Taking classes to the library should no longer be considered "free planning time" for teachers, but rather as an opportunity to improve information literacy skills while furthering an understanding of the state's standards of learning. The certified media specialist should be viewed as a partner in the planning and implementation of lessons dealing with classroom curriculums because of his/her ability to incorporate the *Information Power* literacy standards and the AASL standards for the 21st century learner. Collaboration benefits all members of the learning community when done correctly. Collaboration works when it is done with the right teacher, focuses on the right topic, and is implemented at the right time.

Works Cited

Lance, Keith Curry. "Proof of the Power: Quality Library Media Programs Affect Academic Achievement." *MultiMedia Schools* Sept. 2001 http://www.infotoda.com/MMSchools/sep01/lance.htm.

"School Libraries Do Make a Difference: Research Studies from 1993 to 2005 in Sixteen States." *School Libraries Work!* April 2005 California School Library Association.

Whelan, Debra Lau. "Study: Higher Test Scores Linked to Certified Media Specialists." *School Library Journal* 2 Feb. 2008 http://www.schoollibraryjournal.com/article/CA6531226.html.

Angela Gess *is a master's degree student of school librarianship, Darden College of Education, Old Dominion University, Norfolk, Virginia.*

Gess, Angela. (2009). Collaboration: Finding the teacher, finding the topic, finding the time. *LMC, 27*(4), 24–25.

Are You Listening?

By Trish Henry

In the spring of 2011, the Mead School District removed teacher-librarians from all its school libraries. The libraries are currently manned by para-educators under the direction of building committees. During the winter of 2012, the decision was made to hire one certificated teacher-librarian to act as an advisor to the committees and to the library para-educators. It is in this role as "teacher on special assignment to the libraries" that I have had the rare opportunity to see the inner workings of each of the district's libraries and gain insight into how we failed.

Where Did We Go Wrong?

We failed to listen to the needs of our patrons. We failed to recognize just who our patrons were. We failed to adapt to new technologies and recognize their importance. We were so locked into our own vision of what a library should be and in our perception of our role, that we lost sight of one critical factor: Libraries (and librarians) that fail to adapt to meet the needs of their patrons become irrelevant.

"Wait a minute! I was teaching critical information literacy skills that are not taught anywhere else in the curriculum. Teachers and students came to me for reading suggestions, research resources, and even tech support. How can you say that was irrelevant?" Unfortunately for our students, not every teacher-librarian could make that claim.

One principal told me, "We knew the librarians met regularly, but we never heard anything after the meetings. What do librarians teach at the various grade levels?" Another was excited at the prospect of getting e-books, something his librarian was not interested in obtaining. Teachers from across the district requested audiobooks, and yet, only one library had some. Resources vary from one building to the next, causing frustration for teachers and students. We were not meeting the needs of our patrons in part because we didn't recognize who all of our patrons were.

Supporting the Entire Learning Community

Naturally, as teacher-librarians, we focused on student learning, seeing the students as our primary patrons. We should have been looking at the entire learning community and how they use the library to support student learning. The learning community includes students, parents, staff, administrators, school board members, and the community at large. They are all our patrons.

Consider this: How many times has a student said to you, "I don't check books out from the library because . . ."? Do you ignore it or do you adapt to meet that student's needs? Now think about the times a fellow staff member or administrator has said those same words. Or even worse, they don't use your library at all! Are those "negative" comments ignorance or are they a warning call that your library is in danger?

Beginning with the End in Mind—Outside of the Box

A first step in creating a common vision is to eliminate the negatives from the discussion and set aside past practice. Instead, start with the end result as a goal and brainstorm ways to get there.

- "Our tech department won't let us." Include them in the conversation from the start.
- "I'm not good with technology." Take a class, work with a friend, or simply ask for help. Today's trained teacher-librarians are supposed to be information specialists. Information comes in a variety of formats, many of which include technology.
- "Not all kids have access to technology." Earlier this year, I had the privilege of teaching a fifth grade class. One boy in my class could verbally express himself, but he would not write—anything. Once we gave him a keyboard, however, he was happy to type his assignments. Should I have refused to provide the keyboard because I didn't have enough for everyone?
- "We've always done it like this." If the way it was always done worked, we wouldn't be having this conversation.

> We were so locked into our own vision of what a library should be and in our perception of our role, that we lost sight of one critical factor: Libraries (and librarians) that fail to adapt to meet the needs of their patrons become irrelevant.

If you look at the libraries that are winning national awards, you see libraries with extended hours, up to date technology, and collections that are constantly changing to meet the needs of their users. Their librarians are curriculum leaders who actively help teachers create engaging collaborative lessons. Administrative support is strong *not* because the administrator understands the librarian's vision, but because they *share* the vision. Award-winning libraries are learning commons where students are actively engaged and patrons share a common vision.

In Mead, we are in the beginning stages of creating a new vision of what our libraries will be. We are seeking to develop a vision that is consistent throughout the district, a vision that leads our libraries into the future, making them vibrant, relevant learning centers where everyone's voice is heard. We don't know yet what a 21st century library looks like, but we will.

Trish Henry is the district librarian for Mead School District 354 in Spokane, Washington. Trish has twenty-seven years of experience as a teacher-librarian. Her certifications include an endorsement in learning resources and a master's degree in educational technology.

Henry, Trish. (2013). Are you listening? *LMC, 31*(5), 26.

Rut Busters! How to Inject New Life into a Lifeless Library Media Center

By Jennifer Coleman

Are you mired in routine? Is your library media center dynamic and alive, or lifeless and humdrum? Just like an engaging teacher sets the pace for a conducive classroom learning environment, it is the library media specialist who "sells" the idea of what a library media center is and what a library media center can be to all patrons who walk through its doors. How can you break up and shake up the ruts that both library media specialists and patrons sometimes fall prey to when interacting with library media center materials so that true personal and educational growth can occur? The key is communication.

Step One: Communication with Yourself

By definition, *rut* means a "fixed course difficult to depart from." Doing things the same way just because that's the way you've always done them does provide some comfort but starves you from growth opportunities. Yet change can be difficult for some people to accept. One of the most vital factors in defining your career is *knowing yourself.* If you pause for honest self-reflection, you will have no choice but to grow personally and professionally. Make a vow to begin busting out of your ruts by answering some of the following questions. Type your answers on a word processor, or write them in longhand in a fancy journal—the manner in which you do the exercise isn't as important as communicating with yourself to discover (or rediscover) what you bring to the table.

Self-Reflection Questions:

- What activities do you enjoy and why?

- If you could study any subject(s) what would it/they be and why?

- When you enter a bookstore or library, what books attract you most and why?

- Would you rather work with people, things, ideas, information/data, or some combination of these?

- What types of people do you enjoy working or socializing with and why?

I get bored

Be honest. A few weeks before a new school year begins, what is your mood? Are you looking for new ways to present your "beginning of the year library media center rules presentation," or do you do the same thing year after year after year? Do your shoulders slump with dread at the thought of reading the same storytime selection for the 10,000th time, or do you present as freshly as you can, knowing that members of your young audience are hearing it with first-time anticipation?

Consider the half-time show during Super Bowl XL where the well-seasoned Rolling Stones performed "Satisfaction," probably for the 10,000th time. Aging rocker Mick Jagger's undeniable energy electrified the audience comprised of young and old alike. Don't you think he is sick of singing that song concert after concert, year after year? You couldn't tell by watching, and *that's* the point! True professionals do their best to give a fresh performance. Are you doing what you can to breathe life into your job performance? Communicate with yourself first by assessing how you do something as routine as a read-aloud.

Quick Storytime Rut-Busting Ideas

- Videotape yourself reading aloud to children. Watch the video objectively or with a peer who has offered to provide constructive criticism.

- Change your voice level, tone, and pitch as the story's mood dictates.

- Watch cartoons periodically and try to mimic a new voice, especially if you use the same voice for every character! Don't feel silly, children *love* voices.

- Before a read-aloud session, exercise your face muscles, do some deep breathing, and warm up your voice in an up-and-down trill (like in choir practice). These simple physical acts feel ridiculous but really will improve your stamina and reading performance. Have kids "help" you warm up—it gets their wiggles out and also provides anticipation for what you will do next!

Rut-Busting Reference Ideas

- Set a goal to find five new reliable Web sites a month.

- Go to someone else's library media center and pose a reference question of your own. How did the library media specialist's style differ from your own?

- Time yourself. How long did it take you to point someone in the right direction? Challenging yourself and making a "game" out of it keeps you on your toes.

More Rut-Busting Tips

- Do a little redecorating now and then. Move potted plants around. Display new posters each month.

- When visiting vendor booths at professional conferences, take the time to scope out three new vendors that you have never purchased from before, just to see what they offer. Take the opportunity to see what else is out there.
- Keep up with professional journals. Several are packed with refreshing new approaches that your colleagues around the country use.
- Don't just join your state's library association, get *involved*. Click on the Web site, volunteer for a committee, and write letters to your congressmen on the association's behalf. Meeting other proactive people will bolster you and stretch your current professional boundaries.

Step Two: Communicate with Your Peers

Experts advise that when beginning a new exercise regimen or weight loss program, the best way to stick with the changes is to share your goals and progress with others. In this context, maybe that means sharing your self-reflection responses with a colleague or direct supervisor. Maybe that means you extend yourself in different ways to the adult patrons that you serve and encourage *them* to move outside of their comfort zone as well. One way to do that is to volunteer to do a 10-minute library media center commercial at the beginning of a mandatory staff meeting. Through booktalking, share a few new reads that you have acquired! Hold up current professional journals and highlight some of their contents. Pass out a library media center patron inventory. Be the poster person for rut-busting!

For example, one year as an elementary library media specialist,

I set the specific goal of reading 10 new chapter books a month that I considered to be "out of my personal interest zone." One of those was Kate DiCamillo's *Tales of Despereaux*, which I would normally not be interested in because talking animal stories aren't my cup of tea. However, I found the novel to be charming and unique and thought it a good candidate for a certain teacher to read aloud to her class. The teacher I had in mind read E.B. White's *Stuart Little* without fail to her students year after year. Convincing her to *Jill* give DiCamillo's book a try was a bit of a challenge; however, she took me up on my suggestion and loved it as well. She ended up having her students draw comparisons between the mice characters in each novel through illustrations and compare/contrast paragraphs. I was thrilled! Because I had stretched myself, a teacher had stretched herself, thereby strengthening an already good lesson. The result? A richer literary experience for 21 students. Now *that* is rut-busting!

> Branching out and trying new approaches is not always the easy thing to do.

Step Three: Communicate with Student Patrons

Start early with young library media center users. Get on their level and find out how they are truly interacting with you and their library media center environment. Do they always sit in the same places during storytime? Mix up seating arrangements regularly. For instance, before students enter the library media center, have them line up according to their birthdays. For that day, they need to sit with their birthday month comrades. Do they

always!

always check out the same books from the same couple of shelves while dozens of other shelves go virtually ignored? Create scavenger hunts to send them to new sections and amaze the students with what has been right under their noses. Do chapter books with plain, solid-colored covers go untouched? Have a "Decorate an Ordinary Cover" day and assign each student to create a makeover cover on large construction paper that you will laminate and attach to the Plain Janes and watch your circulation soar! Yes it is true that students depend on routines to help guide them through the complicated school day. Yet routines need not be so strict to impede a child's natural desire to branch out and try something new once in a while.

Branching out and trying new approaches is not always the easy thing to do. New lessons require preparation and revision. There is a chance a lesson may fall short of your expectations. On the other hand, newness also acts as a spark to dry timber—it just might ignite a fire under someone! Thousands of freshly published books come out each year and beg to be explored and enjoyed. Take that next step. Branch out from your tried-and-true methods and stand-by book choices to incorporate the latest (or at least what is the latest to you!) books. The notion is similar to the familiar child's rhyme, "Make new friends but keep the old, one is silver and the other gold." Challenge yourself to break one or two of your own personal ruts and embrace both what you know well and what you don't. Happy rut-busting!

Jennifer Coleman *is a library media specialist and freelance writer from Carrollton, Texas.*

Coleman, Jennifer. (2007). Rut busters! How to inject life into a lifeless library. *LMC, 25*(5), 20–21.

blind date with a book

Yes!

Wait a Year before You Make Big Library Changes?

By Tammy Turner

I was beyond excited when I received the phone call saying a district high school wanted to hire me to be the new library media specialist. I had been a middle school librarian for the previous four years, and with the retirement of the high school librarian I was given the opportunity to move into the high school position. I distinctly remember getting this advice multiple times: "Don't change anything during the first year. Just see how things are before you make big changes." I've now been at the school for six months, and I'm glad I did not take that piece of advice. I haven't made changes arbitrarily, but rather came in with a plan of not only what to change to revitalize the library program, but how to go about making those changes, and advertising them.

What Changes to Make?

When deciding what changes to make in the library program, I felt it was important to understand my population and to get buy-in. To that end, my first task was to do both a student and a teacher survey. I sent the surveys out via e-mail and advertised the survey on the announcements. I had an over 50 percent response rate. Based on those results, I knew I needed to change the physical appearance of the library to make it more appealing to the clientele. I needed to expand the library programs offered. I needed to increase the hours of operation of the library. And I needed to increase collaboration between the library and the teachers. It wasn't a small task, and it would require huge changes. With almost no budget to make these changes, I knew it would not be easy.

Where to Start?

Now that I knew what areas needed to be changed, I started by getting the teachers and students involved. I solicited help from the teachers via e-mail and in-person requests. First, I asked the interior design teacher to have her students submit ideas to change the look of the library and my library office (as it's visible from the main library). I asked the graphic design teacher to have her students submit ideas for a new mural. I knew I could save money and increase student buy-in if I used a student design. I asked the photography teacher to have her students submit work to feature in the library. The result was enthusiastic buy-in.

It resulted in changing the appearance of the library in such a way that it was welcoming to the clientele.

> Students and teachers could see the changes in the library and knew that things really were changing. The library was a different place. More welcoming—a place where they wanted to be.

Using the suggestions the students made, I chose ideas that reflected a new, updated look in the library and were monetarily feasible. My office was painted red, I added a cushy seating area for student and teacher use, I put covers on the library chairs and loveseats, I made more vibrant curtains to hang in the library, and, for the biggest change, I took a student-submitted design and turned it into a mural. These changes took five months to complete, and I had to do my research to find the best, most cost-effective deals. I also had to learn how to use a sewing machine as I sewed the new curtains myself. The response was overwhelmingly positive from both teachers and students. They could see the changes in the library and knew that things really were changing. The library was a different place. More welcoming—a place where they wanted to be. The entire redo was accomplished for under $2,000, fully funded by my principal and student council.

What about Programming?

At the same time I was changing the look of the library, I was changing the library programming based on the survey results. I extended library hours by 45 minutes two days a week after school for those students needing to complete work and projects using library resources. I also added a staff book club, student book club, student technology corner (where students can learn about new apps and websites to help them with their studies and research), and a writing club. I advertised these new programs via e-mail, announcements, and posters. Since these programs were by request, I knew they would be well attended, and with the changing look of the library, the number of attendees grew as they felt more welcome in the library.

> New programs created a buzz about the library, and circulation statistics and use of library resources went up as a result, even though the programs themselves shouldn't have directly changed these things.

I also added a peer tutoring program. Students applied to be peer tutors and had to have teacher signatures indicating their capability of tutoring different subjects. I then created a schedule and online sign-up. I advertised the program via the student broadcasts, announcements, and e-mails to parents, teachers, and students. Soon, the slots were filled with students wanting peer tutoring.

The success of these programs was based on successful advertising and understanding of the needs of the population. The added benefit was additional traffic in the library and visibility of the library program. These programs created a buzz about the library, and circulation statistics and use of library resources went up as a result, even though the programs themselves shouldn't have directly changed these things.

And Collaborating?

Collaboration can be difficult to increase, but I was confident the staff was ready, based on the response I was getting with the other changes. I began by going to department meetings and team meetings. There were times the information presented did not apply to me or the library, but more often than not I was able to contribute to the conversation and offer assistance the teachers didn't know the library could offer.

Once I created research guides and WebQuests, word got out and I had regular customers. Word of mouth is by the far the best advertisement, and they were talking! I also built a rapport with my school's technology facilitator. This went a huge way toward creating a bridge between the teachers and me since the teachers already knew and trusted the technology facilitator. Having her advertise library services and include me in collaboration meetings was one of the items which increased library collaboration the most.

> *Word of mouth is by far the best advertisement.*

Success!

The success of this library revitalization effort rested on listening to both the student and the teacher populations. I'm excited to see the students attending the different clubs, the number of students utilizing the peer tutoring program, and my full

inbox of requests from teachers for help on different assignments. It's everything I wanted when I made the switch to high school. The number of check-ins each day (200–400 students daily) tells me I've created an environment that's welcoming to the students, and I couldn't be more satisfied with the changes I've made during my first year at the high school. Making big changes has to happen sometimes, and I don't think there is a time frame when you shouldn't make changes. I'm so glad I didn't wait a year, but that I dug in and made the changes now. Waiting could have resulted in it being too late to get buy-in. If I had it to do over, I'd jump in with both feet again.

Tammy Turner, MLS, MAT, *is a library media specialist, a UIL academic coordinator, and FISD research and curriculum library lead at Centennial High School in Frisco, Texas. She may be reached at turnerta@friscoisd.org.*

Turner, Tammy. (2013). Wait a year before you make big library changes? *LMC, 31*(1), 24–25.

From Professional Development to Personalized Learning

By Carolyn Foote

It's All about *Your* Learning Needs

Library advocacy. E-book content. Cell phones in the classroom. QR codes. What do these have in common? They are all things I have learned online through free webinars, online chats, global learning conferences, and many other formal and informal learning opportunities. How did I find out about them? Mostly through Twitter, email newsletters, and sites like the ALA, AASL, Library 2.0 Ning, Teacher Librarian Ning, and TL Virtual Cafe—all free sites to join. By reading the sites during the evenings, summer, or on weekends, I find learning opportunities galore, more than I can possibly follow up on. Online learning allows me to tailor my learning to *my* interests or needs. Personalized learning is what free online professional development is all about, and it's the real revolution in what we've traditionally called professional development.

"teacher gram." *Yes!*

Personalized learning means taking more control of your learning opportunities. It no longer needs to be something that your district "provides" for you—it's something that you do for the benefit of your own learning on your own time and at your own convenience, and it's tailored to what *you* need. That requires a change in thinking, but it is very empowering to be able to jump on opportunities and learn things and interact with other professionals from your living room. We cannot continue to draw the line between our work day and personal time, and stay ahead in our own learning. Personalized learning requires pro-activeness, not waiting on the district or conference to provide learning for you. And while online personalized learning doesn't replace the networking and learning you might get from a conference, for times when budgets are tight, it

don't feel like it's work

means that you can take advantage of professional development opportunities anyway. And there can still be networking involved. Lastly, much professional development in a district isn't tailored directly to librarians, but there is a plethora of library online learning available.

Plugging into the Twitterverse

Frankly, Twitter is my quickest gateway to online professional learning. It is an ongoing stream of sharing, from upcoming workshops to live tweets from professional conferences. I know some educators are intimidated by Twitter, either feeling like they don't have the time for it, or unsure how to get started and make it work for them. Twitter is just like any newsletter or email. Dip into it and read it when you have time, especially when first starting out.

> Personalized learning is what free online professional development is all about, and it's the real revolution in what we've traditionally called professional development.

There are many ways to use Twitter. To begin, you might just follow some library organizations and bloggers, and "lurk" to find learning opportunities. As time goes on, you might find yourself interacting with other librarians and educators on Twitter and building a larger network which leads to even more online professional development opportunities. Start by following a few key players; organizations like ALA, YALSA, AASL, and ISTE, and vendors like ABC-Clio and *School*

Library Journal, who frequently tweet out news and learning opportunities. Find and follow leaders like Joyce Valenza, Steve Hargadon, Gwyneth Jones, and Lisa Durff, who frequently share online learning opportunities. This becomes another key to making "lurking" work for you.

What Learning Opportunities Will You Find?

Webinars. Both formal webinars hosted by vendors or organizations, and informal webinars set up by volunteer contributors are regularly promoted. But don't think that you always have to pay for them—there are many free webinar opportunities, like those highlighted on the websites in the sidebar.

Livestreams. Live video from conference sessions can best be found via Twitter. These are usually spontaneous learning opportunities when someone tweets out a link to a livestream of a conference session they are attending. This is a "drop everything and learn" opportunity. You may not get much advance notice, but you get to attend a conference without leaving your chair. Also check conference websites where some livestreams are announced ahead of time.

> All of us have areas of expertise to share, and any of us can present online professional development in a podcast or start a webinar series using the free tools readily available.

23 Things. A great professional learning opportunity that is completely self-paced and could be helpful for librarians or paraprofessionals is 23 Things. Visit http://k12learning20.wikispaces .com/23Things.

Twitter chats. Another means of professional growth are Twitter chats. Various groups hold weekly chats. A good list of Twitter chats can be found on Cybraryman's website, http://cybraryman.com/ chats.html. This is also a good way to meet people on Twitter if you are building a network for the first time. To find the chat, just search for the hashtag in the search box on Twitter (e.g., #tlchat) and you will see all the thoughts being contributed. To add your ideas, type your 140 character message with the appropriate #hashtag at the end of your tweet. Some people enjoy participating in Twitter chats and some find them annoying. Even if they are not for you, just participating in your Twitter account by dialoguing with others is a way to contribute and learn.

Podcasts. Another means of learning on your own time are podcasts or videos like the TED Talks (www.ted.com/talks). Podcasts are often part of a series, either weekly or monthly, and are a great source of self-professional learning. Some great examples include Texas podcasts TechChef4U (www .techchef4u.com) and Tech Chicks (http://techchicktips.net).

Stick Your Neck Out!

Being a participant in these online learning opportunities is one way of learning. But when I am in the role of presenter, I find myself learning a great deal as well. Just like preparing for a conference presentation, preparing to present a webinar or podcast requires research, collaboration, creation of slides and materials for the listeners, and more. Presenting webinars or participating in Skype chats, etc. "forces" me to take the time to delve into something more deeply. All of us have areas of expertise to share, and any of us can present online professional development in a podcast or start a

webinar series using the free tools readily available. It pushes our presentation skills and it pushes us to be learners as well as presenters to take on this opportunity. It can even be done in-house for your own district. An in-district podcast or video of learning opportunities that is sent out regularly can help your staff be learners. Tools often used for webinars include Blackboard Collaborate, GoToMeeting, and WebEx.

> *Sometimes we have to stick our necks out there a little bit and offer to do something even when we have no idea how to do it, knowing that our fellow collaborators will help us along.*

Volunteering for various professional opportunities can help you learn many new tools. I took a deep gulp when I volunteered to help with the public relations for the K12 Online Conference several years ago (http://k12onlineconference .org). Through participating I learned how to collaborate with a group via Skype, wikis, and Google Docs when all of those tools were new. Sometimes we have to stick our necks out there a little bit and offer to do something even when we have no idea how to do it, knowing that our fellow collaborators will help us along. In fact, a lot of online learning involves sticking our necks out the first few times until we learn how to use the tools and how to navigate within them. The good news is that in almost every webinar or online chat, the moderator gets you started with instructions for using the tool, and everyone in the chat is happy to pipe in if you get lost or need help. The other good news is that most of the tools are extremely easy to use.

What you'll find once you embrace these personalized opportunities for learning is that they'll soon become a way of life for you; popping into webinars, workshops, or conferences will enhance your learning at your convenience.

Some resources for getting started in finding online learning opportunitees:

Library 2.0
www.library20.com

Teacher Librarian Ning
http://teacherlibrarian.ning.com

TL Virtual Cafe—Mondays,
8 p.m. EST
http://tlvirtualcafe.wikispaces.com

Chats on Twitter
#tlchat

Edutopia
www.edutopia.org

edWebnet
www.edweb.net

Global Education Conference
www.globaleducationconference
.com

K12 Online
http://k12onlineconference.org

ABC-Clio Webinars—LMC @
the Forefront
www.abc-clio.com

Many organizations sponsor free and fee-based virtual conferences and webinars, such as AASL, ISTE, and FETC.

Carolyn Foote *is a "technolibrarian" at Westlake High School in Austin, Texas. She is fascinated with the intersection between libraries, technology, and schools. Her blog, Not So Distant Future, can be found at www.futura.edublogs.org.*

Foote, Carolyn. (2013). From professional development to personalized learning. *LMC, 31*(4), 34–35.

Avoiding School Librarian Burnout: Simple Steps to Ensure Your Personal Best

By Margaux DelGuidice

It was 6:15 p.m. on a Wednesday night and things were not going well. I was already 15 minutes late for my part-time job at the public library because a professional development meeting in my school library began late. Sitting in traffic on my way to the public library, I tried to ignore my grumbling stomach, but my eyes lingered on a box of doughnut holes left over from my department meeting. Their final destination was supposed to be the office at the public library—a gift for the pages and a peace offering for the head librarian, who was growing tired of my late arrivals. After being on my feet since 7 a.m., and knowing that I would be working until 9 p.m., the donuts never made it to the public library. As I reached toward the cardboard box, the vehicle in front of me stopped abruptly. I slammed on my brakes, narrowly avoiding an accident. The box flew into the air. Doughnut holes, dried sugar, and colored sprinkles landed everywhere, including on a stack of student papers from the research class I teach at a local college. With shaking hands and a racing heart, I maneuvered safely to the side of the road. I realized that I had become a victim of librarian burnout.

Nearly a decade ago I remember sitting in my introductory reference course, Introduction to Information Sources & Services, listening to my professor speak about the dangers of librarian burnout. As she spoke, I had to stifle my laughter. At the time I thought that libraries were the quietest, calmest, most serene places in the world—it was one of the reasons I had enrolled in library school after working in the cut-throat world of corporate America. The thought that a librarian would be overwhelmed and frazzled by his or her job did not strike me as a reality. Of course, all that changed with my very first job as a library trainee and continued when I accepted a full-time position as a school librarian.

Like many school librarians across the country, I have always "moonlighted" in the realms of academia and public libraries at night. The intensity of this pace, sustained over many years, definitely plays a role in librarian burnout. However, all librarians, even those working one job, can become victims of burnout. It is simply the nature of our profession. As we strive to help the patrons around us, many times we neglect our own needs. It is an occupational hazard, especially as librarians are now working harder than ever to prove their worth in a fog of budget cuts and economic uncertainty.

> The thought that a librarian would be overwhelmed and frazzled by his or her job did not strike me as a reality.

Burnout can occur throughout the course of any career. It poses a serious threat. On a daily basis, librarians help patrons fight their way through a haze of misinformation and disinformation. A good librarian is always on the ready, shifting gears from MLA source citation to science to social studies to math and back to English, all within the course of a school day.

At the end of a long workweek, it is helpful to know that burnout can be avoided by following some simple steps. After having my car detailed and returning student papers that contained blue and green sugar specks, I made some basic lifestyle changes to avoid feeling so overwhelmed and frazzled. Here are some tips that I learned as I fought my way back into a healthier state of mind:

Attend Conferences and Workshops

If you have ever attended a professional conference and returned to your job with a renewed sense of vitality and enthusiasm, then you know how valuable this type of professional development can be for your state of mind. Attending a national, state or even local conference gets you out of your library and gives you the opportunity to mingle with other professionals. Conferences and other types of workshops are the perfect forums for everything from venting to networking as they provide an opportunity for self renewal and professional growth.

Sometimes all it takes is a day away from your job for you to step back and realize just how stressed out and overworked you have become. Attending a professional event at least once a year ensures that you will return to your library with a renewed, enthusiastic outlook and fresh ideas to keep that "conference high" going all year long!

If your employer lacks the funds to reimburse your expenses, apply for a scholarship or award provided by library organizations and vendors. In 2008 I was one of the recipients of the ALA/EBSCO Conference Scholarship, an award that is given annually to allow librarians to attend an ALA Annual Conference. I was given the opportunity to renew myself on a professional level while my school administration reaped the public relations rewards from showcasing my accomplishments in local newspapers and newsletters. Numerous awards, scholarships, and stipends are available. Begin your search at the ALA Web site on their "Awards & Grants" page.

Learn to Say No

If you have a choice when it comes to chaperoning school events and running extracurricular clubs and activities, always choose your assignments wisely. The job of a school librarian means that you wear many hats during the school day. It also means that there will be numerous interruptions throughout the day; especially when you are trying to sit at your desk and get some work done! On certain days, due to high traffic in the library, you may not get to take your regular "prep" period. According to the contract, your lunch period should be your own free time, but the reality is that many school librarians spend their lunch hour helping others. We are all guilty of assisting with research projects, helping students find books, and supervising groups of students when we should be taking a 40 minute break. At the end of the week those lost hours of peace and quiet take a toll on your body and state of mind.

If you spend your lunch hour and prep period squeezing in extra classes that need to finish a research project, or accommodating a teacher who is totally lost on the use of databases, make sure you compensate by keeping your afternoons or evenings free for you. Try not to chaperone too many extra activities or run numerous clubs after the school day has ended. Be sure to choose only those clubs and events that truly hold meaning and passion for you. Before you agree to cover any extra assignments, ask yourself this: *Will I really give the students in this club or on this team my all?* If you know that you will not be able to give your best after the school day has ended, pass up the opportunity.

Learn to Let Go

The library should be the hub of the school, but not at the expense of your health! Your contract allows for personal days and sick time for a reason. When you are ill, take a day off to help your body recover. If you need a personal "mental health day," take one. The books, databases, assignments, research projects, and lunchtime crowds will survive for a day without your presence in the library!

Many school librarians are the intermediary link between students, their teachers, and research projects. For this reason many school librarians are hesitant to take a day off when they know that a teacher will be bringing classes in for research assistance. The desire to help others is so innately ingrained in all librarians that it sets our profession down a path toward mental burnout and poor health. For example, a librarian who is reluctant to use sick time and miss a day of work for a minor cold may wind up contracting a more serious infection that lingers in the body. This scenario necessitates missing work for an even longer period of time and can be avoided by taking the time off when you know that your body needs the rest.

Ask for Help When You Need It

The library is the one place in the school where students are not expected to know all the answers. As information professionals it is our job to help them find the answers. Sometimes the librarian needs a little help as well. It is okay to put your trust in your co-workers when it comes to completing certain tasks. This includes your library aide or T.A. and well trained student workers or parent volunteers.

Many school librarians are reluctant to allow library aides or helpers to assist with shelving, downloading MARC records, processing books, disposing of weeded out titles or doing basic copy cataloging. As librarians, many of us insist on doing everything ourselves to ensure that our libraries are kept neat and orderly. Paying attention to details is always a good idea. However, we are not superheroes, and there is only so much time in the school day. After a week of teaching numerous research based classes, the last thing I want to do is stay late at work to check in and shelve carts of books.

Taking the time to provide in-depth training and orientation sessions for aides and other library workers will eventually free up more time for you to complete other tasks during the school day. Providing

ample training and holding regular monthly staff meetings to connect with your workers will provide the reassurance you need to know that the basic tasks in your library are being completed.

Beat the Budget Blues

School librarians often work within the constraints of a small budget that must be stretched to supply materials for an entire student body and school faculty. In this turbulent economy many school libraries have funds to purchase only a limited number of resources. If you find yourself struggling to make ends meet, or you are unable to provide proper materials for all your classes, consider reaching out to your librarian colleagues at the public library for assistance.

As the school year comes to a close, many teachers on the K-12 level look for different and fun activities to engage their students, especially as the weather turns warmer and standardized testing comes to an end. Teachers often turn to the school librarian at this point to plan collaborative lessons that utilize library resources. If you find that your collection lacks the tools needed to assist these teachers, consider contacting the public library. A good relationship with the public library allows you to reap the benefits of a symbiotic partnership and relieve you of certain pressures.

Working in tandem with your public librarian colleagues means that you may have the option of procuring certain titles and other resources for classroom use. This can all be accomplished through proper planning and coordination. It can be as simple as sending off a quick e-mail or making a phone call. The public library benefits because they now have access to new patrons that may not have visited the library, or utilized its services, without encouragement from their teachers.

Reach Out

Everyone feels stressed and anxious from time to time. If you are feeling overwhelmed for a prolonged period of time and getting up in the morning is a struggle, you may be past the point of professional burnout. There are many resources available to help you get past these feelings and into a healthier state of mind. Do not be afraid to ask a trusted colleague or friend for help. If you prefer to remain anonymous when seeking assistance, many employers provide the option of confidential counseling through an EAP, or Employee Assistance Program.

Consult your employee contract for further information, or search online for a directory of EAP providers. The information you share with an EAP counselor will be kept strictly confidential, and oftentimes you can receive a set number of counseling sessions for free. Most EAP plans also have provisions to provide assistance for immediate family members of the employee as well.

Avoiding an Occupational Hazard

Burnout is the unfortunate side effect of a career that puts the needs of others first. As librarians we give so much of ourselves to our patrons—the students, faculty, and colleagues in the schools we service. Do not forget to take the time to focus on helping yourself! Follow the steps above and do what is necessary to maintain proper physical and mental health. Keeping at your personal best ensures that your library will remain in top form as well.

Check Yourself—Signs That You May Be Experiencing Burnout:

Physical Symptoms
- Body aches
- Severe exhaustion
- Decreased immunity

Professional Behavior
- You are annoyed when students ask for your assistance during the school day.
- You view questions from students and teachers as an interruption to your work.
- You unnecessarily snap at your co-workers and lose patience when you are teaching lessons.

Social Indicators
- Your weekends are about recovering. You turn down invitations to social events because you know that you will be too tired to enjoy yourself.
- Your nights are spent on the computer, checking your e-mail and stressing about your workload for the next day.
- Your friends and colleagues no longer ask you what is wrong. Your behavior and attitude has become apathetic and indifferent.

Margaux DelGuidice *is a school librarian at Garden City High School in Garden City, New York. She also works part-time as a children's services librarian and adjunct professor of Academic Writing and Research. She can be reached at delguidicem@gcufsd.net.*

DelGuidice, Margaux. (2011). Avoiding school librarian burnout: Simple steps to ensure your personal best. *LMC, 29*(4), 22–23.

Are You the Next Leader in Our Profession?

By Carl A. Harvey II

I'll be the first to admit I'm not an athlete. The coordination and talent for anything related to sports was not in the gene pool. But, like most folks, when I was a child I played baseball for a few summers. Typically, I wanted to be as far away from the action as possible. The outfield was my home. Batting was even worse. I mean, who actually enjoys some kid throwing a hard round object at you very quickly and expecting you to hit it with a wooden stick, calling it fun? I don't think so! I would often duck or race right out of the batter's box. So my batting average was less than stellar. A few weeks ago I ran into the mom of one of my former teammates. I was telling her about my adventures the last few months. Most of it centered on my work at school, speaking at conferences, writing articles/books, and the leadership duties in our profession. She was kind of amazed and said, "All this from the kid who ducked when he was trying to bat!" We both got a good laugh out of it, but it got me thinking about how I got to this point in my career.

If someone with a crystal ball had told me I'd someday be president of our national organization (heck, any organization), or that someday I'd be speaking in front of groups of people (small and large), I would have been convinced they were nuts! I just never saw those as traits or talents I possessed. I was happy and content to work in the background. But sometimes a little push or shove can bring us out of the background. When I was student teaching, my supervising teacher decided we were going to present a session at our state conference. I wasn't too keen on the idea of talking in front of people (and was extremely nervous), but we got through it, and I learned so much during the process and presentation.

One Small Step

Another year at the conference, I was sitting in the session to learn about our state reading list nominees for the following year. While there, they passed around a sign-up sheet to be on the committee. I thought, "reading books"—I can handle that, and joined. After a year on the committee, they asked me to be the chair. They promised no major public speaking (which wasn't exactly true—being the emcee at the awards banquet was public speaking in my book!), but I loved the experience of working with all the committee members. It was a great place to get started in our association. The chair of our award committee also sits on the board of our state association. So this was my introduction to leadership in the organization.

Now more than ever our field needs the connections, the support, and the learning we get from our colleagues.

When Opportunity Knocks, Jump!

And the rest, as they say, is history. Someone suggested I write an article, so I did. The publisher liked it and suggested I write a book, so I did. Someone suggested I run for president of our state association, so I did. When AASL brought their conference to Indianapolis in 2001, I was asked to serve on the committee, so I did. Every time a new opportunity came along, I jumped. Not only was I building leadership skills in the profession, I was also taking those skills back to my school and putting them to use there. I became co-chair for our school improvement team. I represented librarians on districtwide committees. I became the chair of our department in the district. Each of these endeavors continued to build and further enhance my leadership skills.

As I look back now, I'm truly amazed at the journey I've had to this point. I've met so many wonderful friends and colleagues. I've learned so much from those I've worked with in my district, in my state, and all over the country. All of the people and experiences have enriched my life both personally and professionally.

Want to See a Leader? Look in the Mirror!

So, why am I telling you all this? Because the next leader in our field is sitting right there reading this article—you! Now don't laugh or roll your eyes! I'm serious. Every person who has ever led a committee, or been AASL president, or done a presentation at a conference, started out someplace. They are all normal, ordinary folks who got pushed out of the background. They saw the opportunities before them, and they seized them. No one in their first year on the job is running for president, but they should begin to take steps to get involved in the profession.

Each of us has 24 hours in a day and 7 days in a week. We get to choose how we allocate that time to our family, our work, our friends, and anything else. It is easy to say "I don't have time to be involved." But, if you ask anyone who has taken that leap, they'll say it was a very rewarding experience and worth the time they devoted.

Now more than ever our field needs the connections, the support, and the learning we get from our colleagues. Our professional organizations are one way to make those connections. Technology is making it more and more accessible for those who can't get to a conference to be active and involved in the work of the associations.

As we look to the future, I think one of the primary traits a school librarian has to have is leadership. We have to be one of the leaders in our building. We have to be one of the folks in the building to whom students and staff look for guidance, support, and encouragement. We want to be models; our patrons should see the librarian as someone who is a lifelong learner, always striving to make their programs better.

One way to build those skills is to get active and get involved. Opportunities exist at a variety of levels within our schools, districts, state organizations, and national organization. There are so many places within an association (committees, chairs, board members, etc.) that there is bound to be a perfect place or you. If you aren't someone who likes committee work, write an article or give a presentation at a conference. The possibilities are endless.

Perhaps one of the reasons I got involved is that I wanted to give back to our field. I have learned so much from so many people over the years. They have given me ideas, support, encouragement, etc. It is only fair I return that favor. We have to give back to the next group of school librarians, and being an active part of the field is a great way to do that.

So, I might still duck if someone throws a baseball at me, but I'm no longer content to be in the outfield. I want to be a part of the action! That's where we gain influence and find opportunities for leadership!

Carl A. Harvey II *is the school librarian at North Elementary School and president-elect of the American Association of School Librarians. He is also the author of three books from Linworth. He can be reached at carl@carl-harvey.com.*

Harvey, Carl A. (2011). Are you the next leader in our profession? *LMC, 29*(6), 14.

Be the Change, Live the Dream—From Day One!

By Kim Rodriguez

Where to Begin?

Librarians might remember that day, whether it was a month ago or over ten years ago. You may have asked yourself what you needed to know, how you should do it, how you could improve it, and, if change was needed, whether you could effect change with ease or would be met with opposition? Did we go in like lambs and became lions, or learned the lay of the land and find our place?

meet in the middle

We ask much of ourselves when we start something new, but what I've learned is the importance of focusing on the needs of library users and planning carefully. The library program of your making will not happen overnight, and it probably shouldn't, because a "flash in the pan" can be costly and disappointing. The time we take to thoroughly plan and timely implement our ideas will reveal its reward in the achievement of our users and the longevity of our programs. So the answer to my question is: Begin with a plan, starting with what you know, and then learn what you need and want to know. This is how I did it.

nothing ever does

New Beginning

I'm a career switcher. I was a professional computer geek and researcher for several years before my heart landed me in education, libraries to be specific.

My current employer graciously hired me at the same time I was leaving my previous employer and looking for placement as an intern, which was required to complete my education. I have since fallen in love with my job. The previous librarian, my good mentor, retired after twenty years and kept a solid collection for this small, private, Catholic school of approximately 310 students (grades 8–12). For the first month, I got to know faculty and students, all of whom I adore. The small assembly of people lends to familial warmth that I had not anticipated but fell into with ease.

The professional opportunities I have been given in my job play a major part of why my library program is working out so well, but being part of a non-secular environment does have its challenges. Challenges are expected and certainly not a bad thing. You can be transformed by challenges and succeed through them. I knew that it would be important for me to prepare accordingly. I reviewed my notes and pored over my texts and assignments from my university's school library preparatory program, as well as other publications from popular publishers in this field. I spoke with other librarians to make myself more aware of the differences between library programs in a private Diocesan school system versus a public school. Making copious notes of "things to do" from everyone and everything that gave me further insight has been and will be an ongoing task. After familiarizing myself with the collection and the community (about which I'm still learning), I have been able to do the following:

- Teach faculty and students about the databases available to them.
- Show students how to conduct responsible research and sharpen information literacy skills using authoritative sources of information.
- Provide training and assist students and teachers with hands-on hardware/software training (everything from how to scan USB drives for a virus to creating movies and wikis).
- Create a library web presence.
- Assist with policy, technology troubleshooting, and software/hardware recommendations as a member of the technology cadre.
- Draft a selection policy (using the ALA planner as a partial guide) and provide a lengthy addendum to the current challenged materials policy.
- Weed the entire collection and replace a good deal of outdated

fiction with popular, new titles. Circulation is going up!
- Provide readers' advisory services for students (when they talk about books, I love to listen).
- Purchase a new online database for cross curricular use, and budget for more next year. Note: Before purchasing one of the databases, I did an evaluation of the resource and submitted it to the vendor. As a result, I was invited by a marketing employee of the database company to submit my evaluation and testimonial for their website, which I thought was pretty cool.
- Serve as the moderator for the Student Council Association (SCA). Taking on a role outside of the library moves you from your area and into the school as a whole. Moderating the SCA is a great way to connect with the students.

> I feel like an artist—free to use everything in my arsenal to paint my profession with my own ideas, fueled by those of my peers in the field.

Professional Reading (and Surfing!)

I have kept all of my texts from my school library education program and regularly add to them when interesting titles become available. I also have my notes from school. I regularly weed them and add to them just as I would with any collection of data. I read my library periodicals, rip out the articles I want to keep, and put them in a folder for easy reference. I could build a database containing digital formats, but the truth is that sometimes I just like to read in bed without being wired. Besides, this type of information is dynamic and my database-building efforts could be put to better use elsewhere.

I regularly scan emerging apps and add the most promising links to my online bookmarks. I try everything web-related to see what's out there and what people are reviewing and using. I only add the most useful apps to my website. Most are free, so I don't hesitate to sign up. If I don't see how an app can serve my purposes, or if it seems redundant, I ditch it. There will be other like-minded applications out there to compete for my attention soon enough! Google's education applications have been mesmerizing me this year. It's like one-stop shopping for web tools. Through their Training Center, I'm studying to become a Google Apps Certified Trainer (www.google.com/a/help/intl/en/edu/certification_index.html). It's a bit of an undertaking, so plan carefully before embarking on this journey.

Simplify! (margin annotation)

> Taking on a role outside of the library moves you from your area and into the school as a whole. Moderating the student council is a great way to connect with the students.

Professional reading online and offline may seem to result in information overload at first, but you'll know you've done it well when you start to see similar ideas coalesce and patterns emerge. The connections I made started to make me think more like the bastion of knowledge I believe I need to be and less like a confused bystander. If I don't know something, I learn it. And I make sure I learn it fast because I don't want to be caught unaware of resources I should be responsible for explaining to others. It truly is my responsibility to seek knowledge every day because I will never know it all (for that, I'm thankful).

be alert & aware *up-to-date* (margin annotation)

Relationships

I got to know my fellow teachers, and I do not mean this in a collaborative

sort of way (that came later). I mean, I got to know them as colleagues. If your colleagues like working with you and trust your abilities, you'll go farther with collaborative efforts than if they do not. Some teachers have never collaborated with their librarian before. A lack of participation doesn't mean they don't want to; it just means you need to make the first move, armed with useful ideas.

I got to know the students and made sure they knew I cared by listening to them, speaking with them, and laughing with them. To show some personal attention (and to keep from being asked for a stapler every few minutes), I created a student supply table that holds a dry erase board with information, including the URL to the school library website. The table is stocked with bookmarks, scrap paper, notebook paper, password lists, pens, pencils, a glue stick, highlighters, scissors, a stapler, a three-hole puncher, and tape. Of course, what you stock at your supply center will vary by student needs and allowances. My biggest reward in this field is when students say things like, "Cool, thanks for doing that . . . makes it so much easier!" or "Wow, this is great. I never knew!"

Coming Soon

I have ideas to start a book club (the girls are excited about this), create a graphic novel section at the front of the library (the boys are excited about that), and teach a summer workshop on electronic portfolios for rising juniors and seniors. My plans also include:

- Create book trailers to be aired on school television.
- Create library binders for each teacher, showing services, collections, policies, and other information.
- Request curriculum guides.
- Participate in department chair meetings.
- Develop a two-year strategic plan.
- Offer software training as needed for students and faculty after school.
- Finish working on the online library schedule to replace the schedule

book (using a Google Docs spreadsheet widget embedded in my library webpage)

- Develop a library skills continuum plan, weed, and budget formula guidelines.
- Serve on a professional organization committee.
- Write grants.

> If I don't know something, I learn it. And I make sure I learn it fast because I don't want to be caught unaware of resources I should be responsible for explaining to others.

Conclusion

My first year as a librarian was all about learning. I learned about the culture of the school, the library program, the collection, the students, faculty and staff, the community, and the expectations. But it didn't end there. Once I had a fair grip on these areas, I broke out my notes, texts, and periodicals. Then I got online and "shopped" for ideas and examples. I began implementing some fresh ideas and improved on old ones, little by little.

I'm looking forward to watching my library program unfold and grow into a thriving entity. All of this requires thoughtful planning. Although the program of my dreams will not happen overnight, I'm getting closer to my goal. My goal is to create an environment that is conducive to the learner of the present and the future. I am fortunate to be among faculty who enjoy being part of this program.

There is so much to do and I'm in such a "whirlwind of wonderful" here that I'm afraid I'd start sounding like a fairy tale if I went on. I feel prepared to be a librarian for our times and technology. I feel like an artist—free to use everything in my arsenal to paint my profession with my own ideas, fueled by those of my peers in the field. I owe my

don't completely eliminate the old (margin annotation)

knowledge and preparedness to you, dear readers, writers, teachers, and peers, for equipping me with the right information to successfully navigate this field. Thank you.

Recommended Texts:

Bishop, Kay, and Phyllis Van Orden. *The Collection Program in Schools: Concepts, Practices, and Information Sources*. Westport: Libraries Unlimited, 2007. Print.

Bopp, Richard E., and Linda C. Smith. *Reference and Information Services: An Introduction.*

Englewood (Colorado): Libraries Unlimited, 2001. Print.

Doll, Carol Ann. *Collaboration and the School Library Media Specialist*. Lanham: Scarecrow, 2005. Print.

Hartzell, Gary N. *Building Influence for the School Librarian: Tenets, Targets & Tactics*. Worthington: Linworth Publishing, 2003. Print.

Repman, Judi, and Gail K. Dickinson. *School Library Management*. Columbus: Linworth Publishing, 2007. Print.

My Bookmarks:

www.google.com/bookmarks/l#!threadID=Go4KvP93b2Mw%2FBDSPKZQoQ-7vBy-wl

Kim Rodriguez *is a librarian from Newport News, Virginia. She may be reached at krodriguez@peninsulacatholic.com. You can also follow her on Twitter @kim1570 or visit her library website at http:// peninsulacatholiclibrary.wikispaces.com.*

Rodriguez, Kim. (2011). Be the change, live the dream—from day one! *LMC, 30*(1), 38–40.

ONE QUESTION SURVEY RESULTS

What Are You Doing During Standardized Testing Time in Your School?

By Gail K. Dickinson

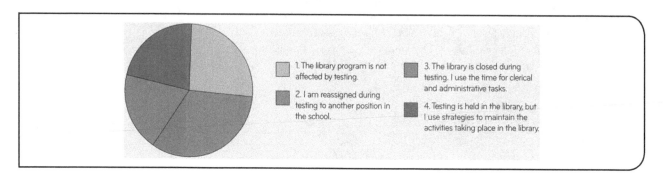

1. The library program is not affected by testing.
2. I am reassigned during testing to another position in the school.
3. The library is closed during testing. I use the time for clerical and administrative tasks.
4. Testing is held in the library, but I use strategies to maintain the activities taking place in the library.

One of the barriers to improving the library program in any school is the lack of comparison with peer schools. A classroom teacher can go up and down the hall to ask how to solve a classroom management situation or to glean new ideas for teaching. The school librarian does not have that option, which is one reason that social networking among librarians is so popular. The halls at conferences are filled with librarians starting conversations with "so what do you do when. . .?".

We asked our survey respondents what they did during standardized testing time. The response was smaller than our usual surveys at 119 respondents, and the resulting graph turned out to be very different from previous surveys. The answers were almost evenly split between the four questions.

Although most likely not high enough to be significant, the largest response came from those reassigned during testing time to other positions. Not surprisingly, the position most noted was that of proctor for the tests. A few respondents indicated that even though they were occupied with proctoring duties, students on an individual basis could still quietly use the library, but the reported use was severely limited. The smallest category, but not significantly lower than others, was reported by librarians attending to clerical and administrative tasks. Adding these two categories together means that when testing occurs, almost exactly half of the librarians report being unable to perform their primary function of teaching 21st century skills to students. Considering the amount of testing now happening in schools, the marginalization of the library program is in danger of becoming institutionalized.

It is not reassuring that only 26% of the respondents report that they are unaffected by testing, but it is encouraging that 21% of the respondents work to ensure that the library may be affected but that the library program is not. Librarians reported such strategies as taking resources to classrooms on carts and either using a laptop-based bar code scanner or plugging the scanner into a classroom computer. Some librarians altered their schedule to see more classes before and after teaching, or taking the library classes and resources to other areas, like the outdoor reading area, the computer labs, or the classrooms.

Standardized testing is not a learning activity. Students already know or don't know the material when they are taking the test, and testing uses time that could otherwise be spent on learning. A closed library closes the door on the serendipitous learning that can occur when students have full access to library programs and services.

LMC encourages the use of evidence-based practices to improve library programs. Lobby for positive change in your school and use these results to advocate to be one of the library programs where learning still occurs during testing weeks.

Question Surveys at www .librarymediaconnection.com. Have a good question? Be sure to let us know at lmc@ librarymediaconnection.com.

Dickinson, Gail K. (2012). What are you doing during standardized testing time in your school? *LMC, 31*(3), 53.

ONE QUESTION SURVEY RESULTS

How Do You Use Volunteers In Your Library?

By Gail K. Dickinson

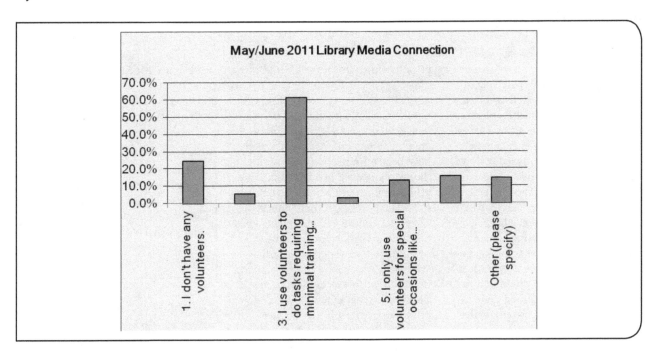

May/June 2011 Library Media Connection

(Bar chart showing percentages for categories:)
- 1. I don't have any volunteers.
- 3. I use volunteers to do tasks requiring minimal training...
- 5. I only use volunteers for special occasions like...
- Other (please specify)

If when looking at this question you are thinking "What volunteers?", you are in agreement with 24.5% of our respondents, who answered that they do not use any volunteers. Well over half of the 417 respondents use volunteers for tasks requiring minimal training, such as covering books, shelving, checking out, or inventory. Special events such as book fair were mentioned frequently. Very few respondents, 5% and 3% respectively, used volunteers for either advanced tasks requiring training or for instruction.

We did not specify either adult or student volunteers, and it is suspected that another more specific question may have had different results. Some librarians commented that they used students assigned to detention for tasks, including at least one respondent who included court-ordered community service hours for students as volunteer opportunities. One respondent commented that in a school of 360 students, the library could proudly boast the most popular volunteer program in the school, with about 120 volunteers.

Volunteers give freely of their time and energy to the school, but the school gets more than just free labor. They get advocates with a deeper understanding of the complex routines and processes that underlie today's libraries. Let's think of exciting and creative ways to draw students, parents, and local citizens into the school library that makes use of the talents that they have.

Did you know that all of the LMC One-Question Surveys are available for review? Check out this link: http://www.librarymediaconnection.com/lmc/?page=survey_results.

Dickinson, Gail K. (2011). How do you use volunteers in your library? *LMC, 30*(3), 57.

ONE QUESTION SURVEY RESULTS

Where Do You Mostly Find Reviews to Aid in the Selection Process?

By Gail K. Dickinson

All about Reviews

To those of us who prepare school librarians for their very first job, it is comforting to know that selection procedures still are in place. 55% of our participants (N-81) responded that they still use published reviews in print journals to select materials for school libraries. Another 31% reported that they use the database from their book vendor. The remainder reported using sources such as online sources or online book vendors such as Amazon or Barnes & Noble. We should be proud as a field that authoritative unbiased reviews by independent sources remain the bulwark of the selection process.

What is just a bit unnerving, though, is that the number of respondents to this month's 1QS is only 81. That's several hundred below normal, and it brings to mind several questions as to why. It could be technical, i.e., a broken link, blocked email, or some other factor. It could have been a function of time or that the survey opened at a busy time. It also though, could be that the question made some librarians uncomfortable. We all take shortcuts in our busy lives. Selecting materials for libraries is one of the most important jobs that school librarians have. It's important to do it right. If you are taking the time to read the reviews section of print journals to select materials, save this survey to validate the use of your time. 55% of librarians can't be wrong.

Library Media Connection encourages the use of evidence-based practices to assure your students have the libraries they deserve.

Next issue we will report on how you accommodate special needs students in the library program. Curious about our previous surveys? All are available online at www.librarymediaconnection.com.

Dickinson, Gail K. (2010). Where do you mostly find reviews to aid in the selection process? *LMC, 29*(1), 49.

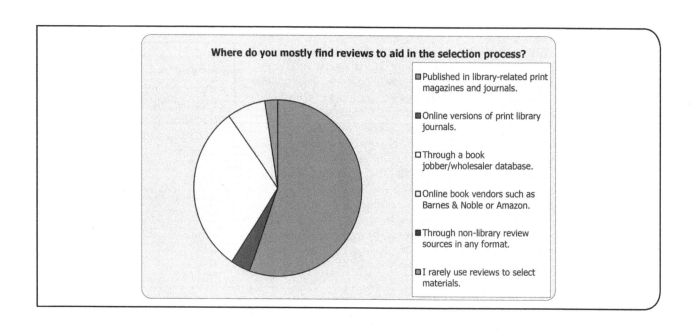

Where do you mostly find reviews to aid in the selection process?

- Published in library-related print magazines and journals.
- Online versions of print library journals.
- Through a book jobber/wholesaler database.
- Online book vendors such as Barnes & Noble or Amazon.
- Through non-library review sources in any format.
- I rarely use reviews to select materials.

ONE QUESTION SURVEY RESULTS

How Do You Accommodate Special Needs Students in the Library Program?

By Gail K. Dickinson

This month's One-Question Survey is a little bit different, since it allows our readers to choose many different options regarding how they accommodate students with special needs. For that reason, the percents do not add up to 100%.

It is not surprising to note that nearly all of the respondents (95%) provide a variety of materials so that all students can read and understand content material. Providing a range of materials on all levels has been part of our mission for over a century. With the push for differentiated instruction and a mandate to include all students in learning, modifying instruction so that all students can learn is also encouraging, although only 76.3% of respondents say that they did that.

Budget issues may prevent some librarians from accomplishing a deeper level of accommodation, namely providing non-book resources (55.4%) or assistive technology (28%). Of some concern are the low number (22%) of librarians who regularly borrow free materials from special source libraries for their students, although that number may change fairly dramatically if that question were limited to those librarians who had qualifying students. It would not be possible to borrow materials from the State Library for the Blind if the school did not have a student who met the requirements for those services.

Library Media Connection encourages the use of evidence-based practices to assure your students have the libraries they deserve. Use this chart to lobby for equitable funding to give all of your students strong support for success.

Next issue we will report on what reference tools are the most used in your library program. Curious about our previous surveys? All are available online at www.librarymediaconnection.com.

Dickinson, Gail K. (2010). How do you accommodate special needs students in the library program? *LMC, 29*(2), 43.

How do you accommodate special needs students in the library program? (Choose all that apply)		
Answer Options	**Response Percent**	**Response Count**
Non-book resources for those unable to read standard print.	55.4%	243
Special technology tools that can be checked out to specific students.	28.5%	125
Modification of instruction by differentiation to meet all students needs.	76.3%	335
Materials on a variety of intellectual or reading levels so that all students can find enough materials in the library.	95.2%	418
Use of resources from sources like the state library for the blind or other special source libraries.	22.8%	100
I don't make accommodations in the library for special needs students.	0.7%	3
Special needs students do not use the library.	1.4%	6
answered question		**439**

Tips

What's Going On?

Plan a Library Open House to demonstrate resources. Send Outlook invites based on planning periods so teachers will have a reminder on their computers. I had the following tables set up in the middle of our library:

1. Technology table: document cameras (one displaying onto our projector), flip cameras, set of clickers, DVD player, and Nooks and Kindles (already loaded with the literature titles we teach that are available on Gutenberg for free). One Kindle was checked out by a teacher!
2. Professional materials table (the best and newest; some were checked out!) with a basket for recommendations
3. Booktalk table with a selection of books about WWII
4. Database table: me at a computer to demonstrate databases to those interested
5. English learners/exceptional education table: hi-lo books, books in Spanish, and visual dictionaries
6. Refreshments and door prize table

Put brief descriptions on table tents to explain what is on the table, with possible uses in case you are busy talking to another teacher. What a success! Forty-nine certificated staff attended (out of 105).

Misti Jenkins
John Overton High School

Jenkins, Misti. (2012). What's going on? *LMC*, *30*(6), 8.

Hold That Display!

Librarians love it when children want to check out books on display, but that means that displays have to be refreshed constantly. Create a patron named "On Display" in your circulation system. Then put all the titles that you have on display on hold for that patron. When a student chooses one of the books, allow the system to override the hold and check the book out. When that student returns the book, the system will catch it as a hold and you know to put it right back on display. You can quickly restock your display without having to search for more titles!

Julie Hulbert
Ozark (Missouri) West Elementary

Hurlbert, Julie. (2011). Hold that display! *LMC*, *29*(6), 9.

Say Thank You!

With most library management software programs like Destiny or Alexandria, it is easy to track your biggest users each week or month! Simply run the Library Information report and search your Top Patrons. Check the past 5 days, 10 days, or month to see who your top patrons were during that time period. Then take a moment to send them a hand written note thanking them for using the Library/Media Center. Students love to get personal notes from their teachers and the Library Media Specialist teaches every student in the school. In your note, thank them for being one of the top users. You can also tell them to stop by for a free book mark or some other little reward. Just one more way to keep them coming back and to show them that their use of the Library/Media Center is appreciated!

Mimi Mayberry-White
Glynn Middle School Media Center
Brunswick, Georgia

Mayberry-White, Mimi. (2012). Say thank you! *LMC*, *31*(2), 8.

Google Me Organized

Google Forms is a great way to keep organized when asking staff to respond to a quick question (e.g., setup of checkout schedules, help with tech issues, or suggestions to add to the collection). The answers will be collected in a spreadsheet. This is much easier than combing through old e-mail messages to double check who answered in what manner! Google Forms could also be used with students as a way for them to suggest books, or as a simple assessment tool for a book club or reading promotion.

Angie Oliverson
Harmony Hills Elementary School
San Antonio, Texas

Oliverson, Angie. (2011). Google me organized. *LMC*, *29*(6), 9.

CHAPTER 2

The Big Ideas

Editor's Note

Putting the Big Rocks in First

Who can sleep the night before the school year starts? Everywhere, across the country, school librarians are sleepless with anticipation, thinking about the year ahead. The first day of school never gets old. We're wearing our shiny new clothes, taking out our cool new school supplies, and showing off our sleek new techie devices as we share the pictures from our summer vacations.

yes!

In thinking about the planning for what we in education call our New Year's Day, I remember a passage from Stephen Covey's book *First Things First* in which he describes a speaker placing a large jar on the podium. In the jar are several large rocks, filling the jar. "Is this jar full?" "Yes," the audience says. With a smile the speaker reaches under the table and pulls out handfuls of small rocks, pouring them into the jar, filling the spaces between the rocks. "Is it full now?" the speaker asks. Some in the audience still shout "yes," then watch as the speaker pours sand into the jar. The sand trickles through and around the spaces. "How about now?" asks the speaker. The audience, wiser now, says nothing as they watch water being poured into the jar.

The speaker goes on to explain that most people, overstressed, overextended, and overtired, take the meaning to be that the jar and our lives never get full; that if we work at it, be creative, and try harder, we can cram more into each day. That's a dangerous lesson for librarians to learn. Multitasking librarians running busy libraries can always find one more nook and cranny both in the schedule of the library and in their own day before and after school. Many librarians know the danger of starting a great new book at 10 p.m., or making just one more change on the library wiki as the evening news starts, only to glance at the clock in horror at 1 a.m., realizing that another busy morning is just hours away. No, we don't need to learn that we can shoulder the learning of the entire school if we just make a better plan. We know the limits of even our expert multitasking far too well.

The moral, though, of the science experiment is a far simpler but far more important lesson. The big rocks have to go in first. If they don't, there won't be room for anything else. We are librarians. We stand for something bigger than the resources on our shelves. We stand for something more important than just making sure all the books were returned in June to stand unused, waiting for us in September. We stand for inquiry, for equity, for access. We stand for the love of reading in all formats. We stand for curiosity and perseverance.

This year will bring us the usual challenges. We will struggle to teach students to wisely Google, to thoughtfully use Wikipedia, and to skillfully analyze the information found in tweets and blogs. We will encourage open checkout, wondering sometimes exactly how many will find their way back to us. We will reflect on opening access to e-devices without costly fees that are such barriers to the children who need them the most. We have to encourage, motivate, stimulate, and model information use in all formats, for all purposes, and by all users.

The challenges will be great. Our backpacks are stuffed with the water of the endless trivial details, the sand of the demands of our time and attention, and the pebbles of the pressure to do more than we can do. With such a year ahead of us, it's easy to forget the big rocks of our profession that take up so much room, but are so important to our students and teachers. For the start of this school year, let's put the big rocks in first.

Reference

Covey, Stephen, A. Roger Merrill, and Rebecca R. Merrill. *First Things First*. New York: Free Press, 1994.

Gail K. Dickinson
Editorial Director

Dickinson, Gail K. (2013). Putting the big rocks in first. *LMC, 32*(1), 6.

- dispositions
  - be the model of your expectations
- accepting of all students
- big rocks first
- learning looks like invention
- communication/resp

What Defines an Exemplary School Librarian? An Exploration of Professional Dispositions

By Jami Jones and Gail Bush

Student: *What should I do next?*
School Librarian: *If you were listening when I was demonstrating the database, you would know what to do. I really cannot spend the time right now to explain it to you again.*
St: *But this is my job in my research group.*
SL: *Well, you should have thought of that before you wasted the whole class period. Next time maybe you will pay more attention. You will have to excuse me; I need to help this group who is moving along nicely in their project.*
St: *Should I wait here?*

What Are Dispositions *Exactly*?

As former students ourselves, we know instinctively the qualities of exemplary educators even if we have difficulty naming these qualities. A natural responsive step of accomplished teachers is to simply ask students what their expectations are of us, which is exactly what Coalition of Essential Schools researcher Kathleen Cushman did in 2006. When Cushman asked 65 high school students to describe the qualities of the teacher they most wanted, these students responded that teachers must like their students, be trustworthy, and treat students as smart and capable of challenging work. In addition, students want engaging classes that are taught by teachers who like and care about the material they teach. Students want teachers who exhibit dispositions of care, trustworthiness, and respect for them. But what are dispositions *exactly*?

According to early childhood education scholar and leading expert on this topic, Lilian G. Katz, dispositions are a "pattern of behavior exhibited frequently . . . in the absence of coercion . . . constituting a habit of mind under some conscious and voluntary control . . . intentional and oriented to broad goals" that can be taught and caught through modeling (16). Dispositions are a "pattern of acts that were chosen by the teacher in particular contexts and at particular times" (Katz and Raths 7).

While this is the current buzzword in the evaluation of teacher performance, dispositions pose a problem for those seeking clean, lean assessment measures. One reason dispositions are so complex to understand is simply due to semantics. Terms such as skills, traits, attitudes, and habits are used interchangeably to describe a desirable characteristic or quality even if these words do not meet Katz's accepted definition of dispositions. Dispositions are not:

- **Skills**, which "carries with it a sense of mastery" (Katz and Raths, 1986, p. 5). One can be skilled without having a disposition for that skill. For example, even when students are skillful and comprehending readers, this does not ensure they will frequently and voluntarily engage with reading—in other words, exhibit the disposition of reading.

- **Traits**, which are consistent and enduring and independent of a situation. For instance, eye color, height, and extroversion/ introversion are inborn traits that cannot be changed. Traits and characteristics are often related to personality and temperament.

- **Attitudes,** which are judgments regarding likes and dislikes that can be changed, and are often measured using various scales that gauge one's positive or negative stances toward a situation or issue. Consider how your own adolescent attitudes might have developed as you have matured into an adult.

- **Habits** are learned behaviors displayed routinely without forethought or reflection. For instance, putting on a seat belt is a habit when we get into a car. (Katz and Raths 6–8)

The National Council for the Accreditation of Teacher Education (NCATE) describes dispositions as the "professional attitudes, values, and beliefs demonstrated through both verbal and nonverbal behaviors as educators interact with students, families, colleagues, and communities." NCATE "expects institutions to assess professional dispositions based on observable behaviors in educational settings." The two professional dispositions explicitly recognized by NCATE are fairness and the belief that all students can learn.

The National Board of Professional Teaching Standards does not define dispositions but expects that proficient teachers are able to employ the necessary "skills, capacities, and dispositions" (2002). The American Association of School Librarians refers to dispositions in its *Standards for Initial Programs for School Library Media Specialist Preparation* but does not define them.

A robust example of teacher dispositions is found in the Interstate New Teacher Assessment and Support Consortium (INTASC) Standards. The operating premise of INTASC is that an effective teacher must be able to integrate content knowledge with pedagogical understanding to ensure that all students learn and perform at high levels. INTASC Standards also state that teachers must hold certain dispositions that are congruent with effective teaching, which are included as part of the 10 INTASC principles. According to the INTASC Standards, the teacher is disposed toward:

- embracing reflection, being a lifelong learner and communicator, and reflective

- understanding the diversity of students and recognizing and promoting growth in others

- promoting positive social interaction and developing healthy and helping relationships with children and youth
- integrity and collaboration to advocate for children
- understanding and using a variety of instructional strategies, planning, organizing, and goal setting

How Do Our *Standards for 21st-Century Learners: Dispositions in Action* Fit into This Exploration?

The AASL *Standards for the 21st-Century Learners*, which comprise four learning strands each consisting of skills, dispositions in action, responsibilities, and self-assessment strategies, are the best example of dispositions for school librarians. While these dispositions are intended for students, they might also serve as specific dispositions of exemplary school librarians. Let us use the curriculum backward design strategy as we begin to consider what we want our students to learn. The dispositions in action of our learning standards become dispositions for school librarians because, in the words of NBPTS, accomplished teachers are "models of educated persons, exemplifying the virtues they inspire in students" (NBPTS). To successfully model these dispositions in action, school librarians must first have acquired and learned them.

be models↙

> Students want teachers who exhibit dispositions of care, trustworthiness, and respect for them.

Consider the full spectrum of 21st-century learner dispositions as crafted by AASL:

- Display initiative, engagement, emotional resilience, persistence, curiosity
- Demonstrate confidence, self-direction, creativity, adaptability, flexibility, personal productivity, leadership, teamwork, motivation

- Maintain (and employ) a critical stance, openness to new ideas
- Use both divergent and convergent thinking
- Have (and show) an appreciation for social responsibility

Further consideration of dispositions leads us to two questions for our preparatory higher education programs. First, how do we embed these dispositions in our programs and teach them to preservice school librarians and media program supervisors? And second, what is the best way to assess these dispositions?

How Do We Learn, Acquire, and Develop Dispositions?

By now you must have an inkling that this will not be a simple discussion. But there is a breakdown of dispositional behavior that might simplify our learning process. Shari Tishman and David Perkins of Project Zero at the Graduate School of Education, Harvard University, collaborate as principal investigators in the Patterns of Thinking Project sponsored by the John D. and Catherine T. MacArthur Foundation. They have identified three essential components of dispositional behavior; for illustrative purposes, let's assume that you have a caring professional disposition to illustrate each component:

- **Sensitivity**—to have your antennae up as you register or notice opportunities to carry out a specific behavior. *Do you recognize an appropriate occasion to act in a caring manner toward a student?*
- **Inclination**—to have the tendency and the impulse to act upon opportunities to carry out a specific behavior. *Do you feel inclined or motivated to invest in acting in a caring manner toward a student?*
- **Ability**—to have the follow-through knowledge that will allow you to successfully act upon this opportunity to carry out a specific behavior. *Do you have the capacity to act in a caring manner toward a student in this situation effectively?*

Tishman and Perkins's research on patterns of dispositional behaviors focuses on thinking dispositions

(their branding of habits of mind). Findings were surprising to these researchers as their gathered data uncovered a particular illumination of the sensitivity component. It seems to be the entry point for dispositional behavior. This gives us a specific direction for learning, acquiring, and developing. As you study the dispositions in action and reflect upon your own professional dispositions, consider your sensitivity to appropriate occasions to act; do you then feel inclined to engage the energy and effort required; and further, do you have the basic capacity to be effective? Consider what you can do to become more explicitly aware of your own dispositions. Perhaps focusing on your sensitivity to students might be a meaningful place to start.

How Do We Clarify Professional Dispositions for School Librarians?

Continuing our exploration of professional dispositions for exemplary school librarians impels us to be responsive to our students. Perhaps a caring disposition as revealed in Cushman's research should be our beginning point to identify the dispositions of an exemplary school librarian. It is difficult to imagine a situation where we could go too far afield by caring about our students' engagement to their own learning. Caring as a professional disposition might be a logical starting point because it brings us full circle back to the 21st-century learner dispositions in action. It is difficult to imagine modeling the dispositions without a foundation of caring equally about each student, believing that each student can learn, and understanding the equitable access to resources that translates to fairness for all students. And as this exploration continues, our skills as reflective practitioners will serve us well as we join together with dedicated scholars in our field to further define dispositions for 21st-century information professionals.

As you read the following scenario you might notice that it is handled by a school librarian whose dispositions are clearly different from our opening scenario. Consider a few select dispositions you personally believe are imperative to fulfilling your job as an exemplary school librarian and how these dispositions contribute to student learning. Just this reflection will strengthen the connection between our professional dispositions and our goals to model for students the AASL dispositions in action.

What do You Want to KNOW about School Libraries?

Watch for our one-question survey at www.linworth.com on the topic of Dispositions. LMC's One-Question Surveys are designed to provide building level school library media specialists with data they can use to advocate for their programs. Practitioners, whether they are building level, district level, or researchers at the university level are encouraged to suggest topics for future one-question surveys.

Student: *What should I do next?*
School Librarian*: Good question. Show me what you have completed. How do you think your research is going?*
St: *This is my job in my research group. This is what I have so far. What do you think?*
SL*: OK, this is what I call a good start. What do you think you should do next? . . . Well, that's one way to think about it. I have an idea. How about if you look here and I look there and we will compare notes? If I am working with another group, be patient with*

me and continue in your search until I am available for us to come back together.
St: *Should I wait here?*
SL*: Wait here? No sir, get to work but you take care to use your time wisely—you don't want me to beat you finding better information, do you? Ready, set, go!*

Standards Cited:

American Association of School Librarians. *Standards for the 21st-Century Learner* <http://www.ala.org/ala/mgrps/divs/aasl/aaslproftools/learningstandards/AASL_Learning_Standards_2007.pdf >.

American Library Association/ American Association of School Librarians. *ALA/AASL Standards for Initial Programs for School Library Media Specialist Preparation* <http://www.ncate.org/documents/ProgramStandards/ala%202001.pdf>.

Council of Chief State School Officers. *Interstate New Teacher Assessment and Support Consortium Core Standards* <http://resources.css.edu/academics/EDU/undergrad/forms/0405/INTASCStandards&EDUDispositionsAlignment.pdf>.

National Board for Professional Teaching Standards. *What Teachers Should Know and Be Able to Do* <http://www.nbpts.org/UserFiles/File/what_teachers.pdf>.

References:

Cushman, Kathleen. "Help Us Care Enough to Learn." *Educational Leadership* 63.5 (2006): 34–37.

Katz, Lilian G. *Dispositions as Educational Goals*. 1993. ERIC

Clearinghouse on Elementary and Early Childhood Education ED36354. 3 Dec 2008 <http://chiron.valdosta.edu/whuitt/files/edoutcomes.html>.

Katz, Lilian G., and James D. Raths. *Dispositional Goals for Teacher Education: Problems of Identification and Assessment*. 20–24 July 1986. World Assembly of the International Council on Education for Teaching, Kingston, Jamaica. 5 Dec 2008 <http://eric.ed.gov/ERICDocs/data/ericdocs2sql/content_storage_01/0000019b/80/32/26/62.pdf>.

Tishman, Shari, and Al Andrad. *Thinking Dispositions: A Review of Current Theories, Practices, and Issues*. 6 Dec 2008 <http://learnweb.harvard.edu/alps/thinking/docs/Dispositions.doc>.

Jami Jones, PhD *is an Assistant Professor and National Board Certified Media Specialist in the Department of Library Science, College of Education at East Carolina University in Greenville, North Carolina. Her latest Linworth title is The Power of the Media Specialist to Improve Academic Achievement and Strengthen At-Risk Students (2007).*

Gail Bush, PhD *is a Professor in the Reading and Language Department, National College of Education, and Director of the Center for Teaching through Children's Books at National-Louis University in Chicago, Illinois. Her 2009 upcoming AASL title is Best of Knowledge Quest: School Libraries in Action: Civic Engagement, Social Justice, and Equity.*

Jones, Jami, & Bush, Gail. (2009). What defines an exemplary school librarian? An exploration of professional dispositions. *LMC, 27*(6), 10–12.

effective and respected

Librarians as Incubators

By Connie Williams

Search YouTube for "Maker Faire," and you'll get a long list of interesting projects from Maker Faires worldwide. You will see the rich variety of the results of play, joy, and just plain messing around. At a Maker Faire people bring their already made products to share, learn new crafts, help design something new, or test drive someone else's prototype invention. At a Maker Faire kids teach other kids and families work together on a single project. The projects themselves may range from the smallest robots to life-size Rube Goldberg mousetrap contraptions. The best thing about a Maker Faire is that everyone can make something. Everyone.

Remaking School Libraries

In his TED talk, titled "We Are Makers," Maker Faire founder Dale Dougherty says, "All of us are Makers . . . We are born makers. We have this ability to make things . . . We don't just live, we create things" (www.youtube .com/watch?v=CX2Wo0_P_6o). Dougherty reminds us that we make things all the time. Even the most ordinary of tasks, like following a recipe (*making* dinner), demands activity that results in a product.

Imagine our school libraries as places where learning looks like invention. How can schools best support our kids so that they become confident learners, learning risk-takers, and explorers? How can we help them turn that learning into their own inventions and encourage them to make their own observations that allow them to turn *that* learning into making things or expanding on ideas?

> The necessary "between" space that exists between the classroom and "real life" needs a teacher, a resource facilitator, and an "incubator."

I wonder how many inventors identify with Mark Twain's quote "I've never let my school interfere with my education." What if we used David Loertscher's concept of the library as part of the larger school learning commons and applied Maker Faire philosophy to our libraries and ultimately our whole school? *That* could create real educational reform.

Libraries Are Everywhere!

How many times have you introduced yourself as a school librarian, only to have someone invariably chime in with an exclamation: "Libraries? Who goes to libraries anymore?" The pervasive perception among adults today is that kids are so wired in and know so much about computers that using a library seems anachronistic. This inaccurate perception allows administrators to chop their librarians first in a budget crisis and ignore them altogether in conversations about educational reform.

What is even crazier about this perception is that people create libraries wherever they live. Visit a lodge in the mountains, and there is a little dedicated space in the corner of the guest cabin to house books—useful for those snowy days when guests don't really want to leave the warmth of the fireplace. You'll find libraries in hotels, waiting rooms, and homes.

In many of the "Occupy" camps around the country, libraries became spaces where people could relax, read, and converse about their ideas. Nearly every institution where people congregate, a quiet space is designated—either by design or informally—where people begin donating books, magazines and/or equipment, and it becomes the "go-to" place for quiet conversation that may ultimately grow into something else: book clubs, crafts clubs, etc. It appears that we have an innate need for a "learning commons" wherever we are.

Libraries as Third Spaces

Dr. Susie Goodin (2011) discusses the concept of "third space" in a way that easily describes the school library today. She defines it as the "ideological space between traditional in-school instructional goals and out-of-school learning priorities" where the physical facility stands in the middle between assignments needing completion and personal learning needing to be accomplished. Think of a working professional who works in an office but may just as easily take work to the local café; using Wi-Fi to finish up that last report, meeting with clients, and hanging out with the local café population in between crunching numbers or sending e-mails.

The Communal Working Space

The school library absolutely plays a role in helping students learn how to work well. The time spent working on class assignments in a communal, and more relaxed environment can be productive when one knows how to balance the task with the demands of the environment. Third Space venues often require workers to learn how to work with distraction but also allow for that distraction to become a learning moment as needed. Students can assist one another, and with a librarian in close proximity, obtaining additional help is only a moment away.

> Getting faculty buy-in and helping them tweak their own perceptions about what makes a greater learning experience takes time, opportunity and persistence.

This idea particularly appeals to me because it seems to be the perfect description of what most of us are doing—creating that space where students can come from their classrooms to practice their skills and use the library as the place to meet and create via personal interest, classroom assignments, or school activities. A student named Sophie tells her story of getting failing grades until she began using the library as the go-to place for studying, because home was too distracting. Being in the library made sure that she had access to all the resources she needed (www.circulatethis.posterous.com, Our Story: Sophie).

At any given time the library might be hosting the writer's club while other students complete homework, make posters for a club activity, or use library resources to make podcasts, videos, and other media projects. Add in faculty members who drop by to join the conversation, and you have the makings of a true learning commons.

School Librarians as Incubators

But the library as "place" is only a part of the equation. It's the people—the librarian, the library team—that make this Third Space become a learning commons. That necessary "between" space that exists between the classroom and "real life" needs a teacher, a resource facilitator, and an "incubator."

Can we school librarians be the actual incubators for facilitating these kinds of learning? Is it simply a matter of hosting events in the library? Or, is there something deeper behind this kind of transformation? Does this include helping our classroom colleagues "incubate" some new learning ideas as we look at Common Core and other initiatives and mandates? Perhaps we can provide the professional development that nudges our classroom colleagues into tweaking some of their standard assignments into inquiry and/or project-based lessons that pull student creativity out of the doldrums and into the 21st century.

Imagine our school libraries as places where learning looks like invention. How can school best support our kids so that they become confident learners, learning risk-takers, and explorers?

From Finding to Making

iPad and other tablet/computer initiatives allow students and teachers to move beyond the classroom walls. Many articles show how the library can be a powerful influence on what and how these initiatives are played out in a school. When the librarian steps up to go beyond locating apps, configuring devices, creating policies, etc., and leads collaborations with teachers to develop project and inquiry-based lessons *and* re-creates the library space to accommodate this new way of working—maybe even creates the library as the Third Space for all kinds of learning—then librarians and the library space will truly become the center of students' working lives; *and* libraries will once again be seen as the important places they are, with the important people who run them.

We know that this is important for our students. We know that every time we offer programming (author visits, tech clubs, etc.) that lifts students out of the ordinary, they rise to the challenge and create fabulous things. We know that when we support an instructional change with a teacher, we see outcomes that often surpass our usual expectations. What if, after creating something for class or personal use, their work was displayed, if there were special days set aside for demonstrations, if there were "maker camps" held in the library? Might more students consider constructing things and maybe take a few more inventive risks to make something interesting and possibly useful? And might more teachers not consider changing some of their lessons into more activity/action-based lessons and assess learning

from these sorts of events rather than their usual essays or tests?

Making Space for Making

What do we need to do to make this happen? I've begun to make the transition toward becoming a Third Space for our students. Taking the lead from others, we've moved furniture, opened up a door to the hall that had been closed and alarmed, and brought in café style tables, a couch, and even moved my desk from a little back office to the middle of the library. Turning that little back office into a "creative room" is my next project.

Google workers work on Google projects for four out of their five working days. On day five they can work on their own projects alone or in groups. This creative work has generated amazing applications for Google, including Google Earth. This "20 percent time" could allow students to use some of their school time for something they want to pursue. (www.circulatethis.posterous.com, Our Story: Glen Warren). I've dubbed this room the "20 percent room" for now, but I'm going to have students come up with a better name for it. Then we'll advertise it as the place with tools, space, and an atmosphere for creativity.

When Dr. Doug Achterman was a high school librarian at San Benito High School, he offered up MAD Wednesdays where music, art, and drama were presented to students at lunch time—by students. In the period before lunch, chairs were moved to a corner of the library where student performances were staged. He obtained a theater style popcorn machine and served popcorn during each performance. MAD Wednesday performances included original music, dance, scenes from upcoming drama productions, poetry slams, open mic readings, and improvisational comedy. "MAD Wednesdays helped build a stronger sense of community, since students were coming to the library to share their own creative work. There was a kind of festival-like atmosphere that helped students feel even more comfortable in the library, and because it was about their performances, students came to

motivate and encourage imagination

lunch groups

communicate!

its the little things students will remember forever

view the library more as their own. At the same time, the library program helped build a reputation as a strong supporter of the arts and of student performance."

Making a Difference as an Incubator

The most crucial task is to provide solid professional development to our staff. "Maker camp" style of learning involves inquiry, passion, failure, and often frustration before success is achieved. We don't have such time in our classrooms given the constraints of standards, testing, and other mandates of the kind that discouraged Mark Twain. Determining the difference between curricular events and programming events might help to expand activities that could be assessed by teachers as a part of their lessons. For example, reading a book by an author who is coming to visit, and developing questions and asking them during the talk could become a part of a graded assignment for a particular student. Participating in a "MAD" presentation could be a graded event for a drama or music student. Using the "20 percent time" concept as a way for students to think out of the box, a teacher might ask students large questions toward the end of a unit and require them to come up with unique answers that count as 20 percent of their grade. Getting faculty buy-in and helping them tweak their own perceptions about what makes a greater learning experience takes time, opportunity, and persistence. Taking the baby step approach can help move things forward quickly enough without a huge investment of time.

One of the best things about being a school librarian is the opportunity to see the whole school curriculum, participate in creating the school climate, and help faculty and administration see where there are natural links between teachers and teaching ideas. Librarians are in the perfect spot to be incubators that allow for student and faculty ideas to blossom and flourish. It's a great time to be a school librarian.

- Move your desk to the middle of the library, or at least hang out there. It makes a huge difference in regard to accessibility and perception (both yours and theirs).
- Be prepared for surprises. Some activities flop big time, others are huge hits.
- While virtual projects are very cool, don't forget that the physical space we call library is equally important for events that bring people physically together.
- Maker events allow students and teachers to come to the library with stuff they've already made, so that others can see it and play with it. Other events invite people in to learn something new or to make something.
- Invite student clubs to the library for at least one meeting during the year where they can showcase their activities.
- Ecology clubs could use the library as an information station for their initiatives (gathering signatures, etc.).
- Health-related clubs could set up a card making event in the library where students make cards for children in hospitals.
- When thinking of a "big idea" project to do with classes, remember that they need their librarian!
- I'm not sure about this, but maker projects might best be accomplished toward the end of a unit. Knowing some basic information about a time period, a person, and a concept might enable students to spend more time creating with facts on hand versus spending time looking for those facts. But, here's where I waffle: What if we gave students the project and said "go forth." Maker activity isn't chaos, it's investigating, creating, testing, verifying, and collaborating. Depending on the students you have, and the project you're doing, starting with investigation might be the way to go.

- One of the joys of 20 percent time is that anyone can jump into a project they like. If one student likes to build things, she can offer her services to another student who has an idea but doesn't quite know how to pull it off. If two students like to read and talk about things, they could set up a debate and open it up to others who might like to join in.
- Susan Thompson, retired librarian from Casa Grande Library in Petaluma lived for many years in Hawaii. As an incubator activity, each May 1st (Lei Day) she brought flowers, greens, and all the supplies necessary to make *haku lei* (head leis). She had a library display about lei-making, and kids signed up ahead of time. "We made a mess, but it was so rewarding for me to pass on a lovely skill and tradition. As you can imagine, this was a hit with some of the Pacific Islander kids too. And at the end of lunch, I loved seeing the kids dash out the door with their head leis—they looked so adorable!"
- Anne Wick, at Sierra Junior/ Senior High School outside of Fresno, inherited a new room and is looking at the concept of how to open it to all as "the place where we can gather to think."

Work Cited

Goodin, M. S. *Room to Read: Tracking the Evolution of a New Secondary School Library*. Unpublished doctoral dissertation. Graduate School of Education, University of California-Berkeley, 2011.

Connie Williams *is the teacher-librarian at Petaluma (California) High School. She can be reached at chwms@mac.com.*

Williams, Connie. (2013). Librarians as incubators. *LMC 32*(1), 28–31.

Connecting Old and New Literacies in a Transliterate World

By Jamie Colwell

New digital technologies, along with different devices and platforms for reading, writing, and communication, are being developed at an astounding rate. Consider the average teenager. Recent Pew Research Center data suggests that 93 percent of adolescents ages 12–17, even in households with income levels below the poverty line, go online daily (Lenhart et al., 2010). They regularly engage in multiple types of new literacies—digital literacy practices such as texting and social networking—outside of school (Alvermann, 2002; 2008; Moje, 2000). They are continuously reading, writing, and communicating across digital mediums in an overlapping and harmonious manner. Navigating these literacies involves transliteracy. The skills students use to engage in transliteracy are different from traditional, or old, literacies used to read, write, and communicate.

Adolescents also need to develop their academic (or in-school) literacy skills by reading print-based texts, thinking critically about texts, and engaging in thoughtful discussion. How can we help students use and connect both sets of skills, supporting the development of well-rounded, multi-literate youth? How do we encourage both types of literacy in an already packed schedule? Consider the potential of discussion-based literacy practices that many students engage in every day, such as texting and social networking.

Keeping up with new technological advancements and how to effectively use them may be intimidating. Even the most tech-focused librarians and teachers are sometimes deterred by safety considerations and concerns that students will not engage as deeply in digital literacy practices because of the many distractions the Internet offers. Although these concerns are legitimate, think about how Internet "distractions" such as mobile technology and online social networks may be transformed into literacy enhancements to connect students' traditional and digital literacies. To do so, this article explores popular and common activities in education, specifically literature discussion and reflection, and how digital technology can connect old and new literacies.

Using Mobile and Online Social Technology in Literature Discussion and Reflection

Cell phones and online social networks can serve as powerful platforms to quickly and efficiently engage students in meaningful and thoughtful discussions about literature. Indeed, many schools are now re-evaluating cell phone and tablet bans in schools and allowing librarians and teachers to decide if students may use their personal phones and devices. These tools have the capability to connect academic learning to students' everyday lives. Four current, but not necessarily new, digital tools may enhance literature discussion and reflection and connect adolescents' traditional and digital literacies.

Cell Phones

Texting is a vital part of most adolescents' lives. Although the writing style differs from traditional writing, texting is still writing as students are putting into words, or symbols, reactions, thoughts, and ideas. Encouraging students to text in an academic setting for academic purposes creates an environment that promotes writing and expression of thought. For example, have students engage in group discussions about literature via texting to create a synchronous dialog about a book, story, or informational text, allowing them to participate in traditional (print-based reading) and digital (texting) literacy practices. This allows multiple interactive discussions in one classroom, particularly if the class is large and the room is small, without students talking over one another.

Worried that students will veer off topic? Have students verbally recap their main discussion points, integrating digital and oral discussion into the activity, or ask that students include you in their text discussions. Don't want to give students your cell phone number? Create free Google Voice accounts (www.google.com/voice). Your phone number(s) will be linked to your Google Voice account where you can access texts and voice messages. Students can leave a voice message on your Google Voice account number to summarize their texting discussions. Students can also create an account if they do not want to give other students their cell phone numbers.

Twitter

Tweeting may be fodder for celebrity and entertainment news, but the instantaneous and concise manner in which thoughts are projected to a group of people through Twitter (www.twitter.com) holds great potential. Have students react or respond to literature or text using a designated class Twitter hashtag. Because tweets are limited to 140 characters, students must find creative and succinct ways to express their opinions. Twitter allows students to post links to websites or videos that complement their responses. The links can be viewed by the rest of the class or the student book club. Students may respond to or retweet each other's tweets, encouraging an atmosphere of shared learning using mainstream social technology in conjunction with traditional literacy practices. Ask students to tweet from the perspective of a literary character to promote more critical thought and response.

> *The future of literacy is bright with the multitude of tools available for students to read and discuss texts and bridge school and life literacy practices.*

Connect librarians and teachers by having librarians engage in class Twitter feeds as a way to respond to students' ideas about literature or texts and to offer feedback and suggestions for future readings. Don't feel comfortable using Twitter or the terminology? Twitter's website offers tutorials and links to helpful videos. The site is user friendly, and students who are not already Twitter users should be able to navigate tweeting after a brief introduction and exploration of the site. Using Twitter for discussion may be an in-school activity if students are allowed to use their smartphones; or an out-of-school activity if Twitter is blocked by school Internet filters.

Ning Networks

A Ning (www.ning.com), an invite-only social network, can host a safe space for literature discussion and the sharing of ideas or web resources about literature. A Ning can host a large number of members and is available at no cost to educators through Pearson Education. Its structure is similar to that of Facebook, but the Ning content is developed and controlled by a librarian or teacher who serves as the site administrator, creating a safe, private space for students to discuss books. Librarians and teachers may even collaborate to create online book clubs for students to join and discuss literature pertaining to a certain genre, content topic, or student-selected books of interest. Forums and groups within the Ning can host the book clubs and allow

multiple discussions simultaneously. Like Twitter, students may upload or post videos, reviews, or other web resources related to the discussion topics, promoting multiple types of literacy as students read print-based texts and respond using multiple types of digital texts. A Ning can be formatted and personalized using different layouts and site themes to provide a customized space of learning.

Worried that students may be hesitant to write responses to literature or engage in online discussions open to all members of the Ning? Ning allows students to use screen names instead of their first and last names, so there is the option to discuss and respond to literature anonymously and share screen names only with the teacher or librarian. Thus, Ning networks hold great potential to expand students' thoughts and ideas about print-based literature through an online vehicle.

> *Encouraging students to text in an academic setting for academic purposes creates an environment that promotes writing and expression of thought.*

Edmodo

Edmodo (www.edmodo.com), another closed social network, was created specifically for education. While a Ning network offers more variety in layout and themes for personalization, Edmodo provides an easy to navigate, uniform layout with a low learning curve for students and educators. Edmodo also offers educators the option to set up different groups with separate home pages within their account, so a librarian could easily create a school library Edmodo account and host multiple discussions sorted by class or book club within one account. Discussion prompts and subsequent threads can be created and initiated on the main group page for whole

classes or large groups of students to discuss literature. Groups may also be divided into smaller groups using the Small Groups feature to engage students in discussion. Unlike group discussions in a Ning, small group discussions in Edmodo are private and only accessible by educators and students in their assigned group. This feature may provide an added level of comfort for students.

Additionally, Edmodo was designed for an educational context, so most school Internet filters do not block students from accessing the site. In fact, Edmodo is currently used in many educational settings, and educators can invite parents to the site to view students' discussions and work, connecting the discussion to home.

> *Even the most tech-focused librarians and teachers are sometimes deterred by safety considerations and concerns that students will not engage as deeply in digital literacy practices because of the many distractions the Internet offers.*

Anxious that the educational layout and traditional classroom-like features of Edmodo may not appeal to students or motivate them to actively engage in discussions in a school or out-of-school setting? The Edmodo site offers many youth-friendly features, such as unique emoticons and the capability for students to upload video and web links. Students may also upload photos along with their general profile information.

Edmodo offers students a voice. The site provides opportunities for them to react through direct messages or reaction emoticons that are sent to the librarian or teacher. Like a Ning network, Edmodo provides another possibility for connecting students' traditional and digital literacies as they discuss print-based texts using platforms applicable to the literacy practices they engage in during their out-of-school lives.

Final Thoughts on the Future of Literacy

As a literacy specialist, reflections about changing times often prompt me to think about where we have been and where we are going in terms of reading, writing, and communicating. I think back to my years as a high school English teacher. The rapid and exciting changes in classroom technology I, and my students, experienced were incredible, and sometimes a little overwhelming! At first, I admittedly struggled with making room for digital literacy practices in my curriculum that valued the traditional (and beloved to this English teacher) print-based text. But, I remember how engaging and relevant instruction became for my students after integrating technology to support and enhance literature or text discussion. I also saw students who had never enjoyed or felt comfortable speaking up in discussions shine with online discussion tools.

Now, as I work with librarians and classroom teachers across content areas, I further witness the power these tools hold to engage students in literacy and connect school and reading to their everyday,

technology-rich lives. Although transliteracy is usually referenced in terms of reading, writing, and communicating across digital platforms, I see a place for traditional reading and writing practices, such as reading print-based texts and writing reflectively and participating in discussion about those texts, as a part of that movement. Platforms of writing and methods to react or share opinions about texts may change, and language may shift to conform to the norms of the platform. Yet, reflection and critical thought will remain a constant objective. Internet tools and platforms provide a promising way to enhance and support these skills.

The future of literacy is bright with the multitude of tools available for students to read and discuss texts and bridge school and life literacy practices. Literacy is expanding to encompass online and digital skills, and those skills are rapidly growing in importance as we increasingly read, write, and communicate using digital technology. Traditional literacy skills are equally important to develop balanced adolescents and future adults. Technology holds promise to enhance students' traditional, print-based literacy skills, emphasizing the importance of both types of literacy and the power they hold when combined.

References

Alvermann, D.E. *Adolescents and literacies in a digital world.* New York: Peter Lang, 2002.

Alvermann, D.E. Why Bother Theorizing Adolescents' Online Literacies for Classroom Practice and Research? *Journal of Adolescent & Adult Literacy* 52.1 (2008): 8–19.

Lenhart, A., K. Purcell, A. Smith, A. and K. Zichuhr. *Social Media and Young Adults.* Pew Internet & American Life Project. 3 Feb. 2010. Web. http://pewinternet .org/Reports/2010/Social-Media-and-Young-Adults/Summary-of-Findings.aspx.

Moje, E.B. *"All the Stories That We Have": Adolescents' Insights about Literacy and Learning in Secondary Schools.* International Reading Association, 2000.

Jamie Colwell, Ph.D., *is an assistant professor of Literacy at Old Dominion University, Darden College of Education in Norfolk, Virginia. She may be reached at jcolwell@odu.edu.*

Colwell, Jamie. (2013). Connecting old and new literacies in a transliterate world. *LMC, 32*(1), 14–16.

Preparing Students for College: Whose Expectations Are We Meeting?

By Kathy Lehman

Are we underestimating our students? Do they have realistic expectations of the skills needed for college? Are we—teachers and school librarians—providing students with opportunities to master the skills that ensure success in higher education? The secondary curriculum covers content that school divisions and college admissions deem essential for success in college. Is mastery of course content enough?

Skill Building through an Internship

Emily McDaniel and I, librarians at Thomas Dale High School in Chesterfield County, Virginia, asked our students to name the top three skills they considered most important for success after high school. The skills most often mentioned were in the categories of research and study skills, time management, and responsibility. We were impressed. Attaining proficiency in these areas will take them far. Our challenge: incorporating strategies to require students to meet expectations in each of these areas while still meeting curriculum objectives.

Our library science class includes twenty-eight college-bound juniors and seniors, spread evenly over seven class periods. Students are able to combine the benefits of a school library internship with English elective credit. In each section, they divide their time between working the circulation desk, shelving materials, maintaining a section of the library, and completing units of study. The units are comprised of self-directed information literacy or literature modules designed to guide students through the research process and enhance their appreciation of literature. Some units are completed individually and some are completed in teams. One week students annotate resources on a topic, generating a

works cited list; another week they design a brochure on a specific genre for a Teen Read Week library display. A favorite group project is to research an aspect of Internet safety and create a multimedia online poster with original art or videos (Donovan and Lehman 28–29). Through these learning experiences, students build advanced research and study skills while developing excellent time management competencies and personal responsibility.

Student Voices

To determine which skills our library science students feel are important for college, we polled them using Edmodo, the Facebook style social learning platform our county promotes for posting assignments and student feedback. Edmodo allows instructors to pull students from across seven sections into a single online discussion.

Could a teacher or school librarian have said it better than Logan or Morgan?

Logan:

To ensure success in college, a high school student must master the following skills:

1. Students must be able to complete all of the components of a research paper correctly.
2. Students should also be able to do critical thinking on all types of reading materials. Critical thinking is very important for success in college because many times college students are asked to write essays using a lot of critical analysis.
3. Students should also know the dangers of plagiarism. Sometimes students do not understand the consequences of plagiarism, and students often do not know that they are doing it. Students should

practice reading things and turning them into their own words so that they don't get in trouble for plagiarism.

Morgan:

1. Students need to be able to read notes on the board and shorten them into something that they can understand but still gives the same information. There won't always be enough time to copy a whole slide.
2. Students need to be able to stay organized and keep track of all their own work and stay on top of assignments and when they're due. That's part of going to college and becoming independent.
3. Time management is a really important skill to have. Students need to be able to manage their time wisely in order to get everything done on time. There should be a lot of time put aside for homework and studying. College isn't just about your social life.

When the results were tallied, comments fell into five categories: Study Skills (88 %), Time Management (80 %), Responsibility (76 %), Social Skills (44 %), and Research Skills (40 %). Lumped together, Study Skills and Research Skills weighed in at 128 %. They were mentioned more than once as the top three skills students perceive to be necessary for college success. Clearly these students understand they need to be proficient in more than the content of their coursework. Now we need to ask ourselves, are we providing opportunities to practice research strategies, time management, and responsibility so they will master them at the level they need for college success?

Research and Study Skills

In a school of 2,200+ students, we know we are not reaching all students equally. Many teachers feel so pressed for time that librarians are fortunate to get one or two class periods with a section to introduce the resources available. Overview instruction is provided for locating and accessing materials, but with little time for guided practice. The finer points of analyzing websites for inaccuracies or bias are discussed with examples, but again time for students to practice evaluation strategies is limited.

In our library science class, however, these skills are emphasized and practiced in depth. As the year progresses, we witness our library science students with their other classes in the labs, helping their classmates during research assignments. We have had teachers come to us and request a lesson after one of the library science students told them about a library resource the whole class should use. Our library science students become expert ambassadors and skilled library resource users, spreading knowledge throughout the building.

Library students complete online modules covering web evaluation, bias, topic analysis, inquiry research, resource locating, note-taking, persuasive writing, plagiarism, and copyright. In every segment students cite their sources. These modules have been created in-house, researched online, found in journals, or discovered at conferences. Our students complete periodic TRAILS evaluations as well as our in-house assessments to evaluate their progress. The culminating spring project is to compile an online pathfinder on a research topic of their choice (see http://tdale.wikispaces.com/Student+Pathfinder+Contents).

The lessons developed for library science students can be used or adapted with classroom teachers. The class doubles as a laboratory to test new ideas and strategies to recommend for collaboration between classroom teacher and librarian. Each year we revise and update units for the library science class as we embrace new Web 2.0 applications or discover new online modules.

Before the end of the course we will have students exclaim, "Everyone should take this class!" or "I wish I had known this before I wrote my history paper last year." Our goal is to raise students' comfort levels with online resources so they can analyze a website with confidence and search an online subscription database with the same ease with which they use Google. Their first research goal on their college campus should be to learn the subscription databases available through the college library, and how to use the library on-site and from their dorm rooms.

In library science we are "learning how to learn," in the spirit of Thomas Friedman's famous phrase from in his book *The World Is Flat* (2006). As we model our love of learning, Emily and I hope our commitment to "learning for learning sake" will be contagious. Curiosity stimulates learning. Determining what you want to know, setting up the reference questions, and refining the keywords to construct meaningful result lists become the ultimate quest.

We do not write papers in library science, but we set them up and generate brief blogs describing what we found. Learning how to approach a research project is key to college success. Alison Head and Michael Eisenberg (2010) explain this major research finding when they state, "Even though many students may consider themselves adept at evaluating information and applying techniques for tackling one course-related research assignment to the next, the sheer act of just getting started on research assignments and defining a research inquiry was overwhelming for students—more so than any of the subsequent steps in the research process." Our library science students practice on multiple projects to master the opening steps of the research process that are so difficult for many students entering college, including setting up essential questions, using critical thinking to assimilate information from multiple sources, and composing original sentences. Proficiency and mastery take hours of time on task. In *Outliers* (2008), Malcolm Gladwell refers to it as the 10,000 hour rule. We may not approach 10,000 hours of searching,

questioning, reading, thinking, and writing in one school year, but we log hours and hours of practice.

Students clearly understand they need to be proficient in more than the content of their coursework.

Time Management and Responsibility

Library science students must manage their time and complete their assignments and work schedules on their own with minimal supervision. They are responsible for completing their circulation and shelving responsibilities and supporting their team. The four students each period determine the desk schedule and cover if anyone is absent. They are given a calendar of due dates for assignments as well as a section of the library to keep straight, which rotates each month. They have part of every class period to work on assignments. If they work diligently, their assignments can be completed during library class. Assignments and due dates are posted online. They complete periodic self-assessments to determine how well they are meeting their responsibilities.

Students are graded not only on their class assignments but on work ethic, interaction with patrons, teamwork, and willingness to take on additional library tasks, such as processing materials for the shelves or setting up displays. They are library interns getting English elective credit. They can move about freely, and they have more choices than in other classes in regard to how they spend their class time. However, they do not have time to squander. They are members of the library staff who have an opportunity to exhibit qualities future employers and admissions officers are looking for, such as punctuality, strong work ethic, proper dress, good manners, teamwork ability, academic excellence, and the ability to complete tasks with minimal supervision. We remind them that librarians write excellent letters of recommendation for students who exhibit these high expectations. This class is one of the few opportunities college-bound students have to obtain class credit and work experience during the school day.

Social Skills

When 44 % of our students emphasized the need for social skills in college, they were not talking about their social lives. They meant interacting positively with others and gaining self-confidence. Library science class provides many opportunities to work with the public, team with each other on projects, and interact politely with other students and staff. Desk duty means being proactive to address patrons, inquire how we can help them, and enforce library pass and borrowing regulations. At the circulation desk they take responsibility for daily functions, calling on the adult staff only when a patron needs assistance they cannot provide.

Library Science Is Not Just about Research

Library science students have literature-based projects that allow them to use creative software products to produce presentations and movie trailers of books and authors. While research units exercise the more analytical side of the brain, literature-based projects engage students creatively. Daniel Pink, in *A Whole New Mind* (2006), emphasizes the need for education to balance out the right and left brain functions. Alternating creative literature projects with analytical research quests helps our students keep their thinking active in multiple venues. Research and creativity may overlap on some projects. Collecting material for a book trailer may include gathering information on an author, time period, or historical event. Assembling Internet safety information for an online poster incorporates creative use of color, formatting, and images,

as well as an opportunity to design an original video.

> *As long as we keep listening and meet students' expectations, they will meet ours.*

Two years ago, Lori Donovan and I compiled this curriculum into a book, *Power Researchers: Transforming Your Library Aides into Action Learners* (2011). We developed the class together after determining that study hall style library aides were not working for us. Students in ungraded periods have no incentive to excel. More importantly, we were missing an opportunity to teach in depth the very skills researchers such as Alison Head and Michael Eisenberg are telling us freshmen lack. Our book has done exactly what the title states. We now have more college-bound students wanting to take the class than we can accommodate. Their success in college has validated our curriculum. We have designed a course that meets their expectations. We are teaching research skills, providing opportunities for students to manage their time, and requiring students to take responsibility for their work. If you ask them, most will say library science is their favorite class. As long as we keep listening and meet their expectations, they will meet ours.

> *Our library science students become expert ambassadors and skilled library resource users, spreading knowledge throughout the building.*

Works Cited

Donovan, Lori, and Kathy Lehman. "Internet Safety and High School Students: What Do They Know and What Do They Need to Know?" *LMC* 29.6 (2011): 28–29. Print.

Friedman, Thomas L. *The World Is Flat: The Globalized World in the Twenty-first Century*. London: Penguin, 2006. Print.

Gladwell, Malcolm. *Outliers: The Story of Success*. New York: Little, Brown and, 2008. Print.

Head, Alison J., and Michael B. Eisenberg. *Truth Be Told: How College Students Evaluate and Use Information in the Digital Age. Project Information Literacy Progress Report: Truth Be Told.* Rep. University of Washington, 1 Nov. 2010. Web. 15 Oct. 2012. http://projectinfolit .org/pdfs/PIL_Fall2010_Survey_ FullReport1.pdf.

Lehman, Katharine B., and Lori E. Donovan. *Power Researchers: Transforming Student Library Aides into Action Learners*. Santa Barbara, CA: Libraries Unlimited, 2011. Print.

Pink, Daniel H. *A Whole New Mind: Why Right-brainers Will Rule the Future*. New York: Riverhead, 2006. Print.

Student Pathfinder Contents: TDale— Student Pathfinder. May 2012. Web. 15 Oct. 2012. http://tdale.wikispaces. com/student pathfinder contents.

TRAILS: Tool for Real-time Assessment of Information Literacy Skills. N.d. Web. 15 Oct. 2012. www.trails-9.org.

Kathy Lehman, NBCT, *is the librarian at Thomas Dale High School in Chester, Virginia. She may be reached at kathy_ lehman@ccpsnet.net.*

Lehman, Kathy. (2013). Preparing students for college: Whose expectations are we meeting? *LMC, 31*(5), 10-12.

Culturally Responsive Leadership in School Libraries

By Laura L. Summers

Students need culturally responsive teacher-librarians who focus on 21st century skills for all students. Basic principles for culturally responsive leadership in school libraries are articulated by multicultural educators who know that social equity is more important than ever, as the number of diverse and underserved students increase each year. In Denver Public Schools (DPS), a district in which I am familiar, there are now over 73,018 students and 80% of the students represent minorities. By 2010, it is predicted that over 30 percent of all school-age children will be English Language Learners. Ethnicity, race, disability, gender, language, and socioeconomic status define diverse students who enter school libraries every day. Since teacher-librarians interact with *all* students within a school, it is a natural fit to look toward our school library personnel to model culturally responsive leadership for educators within their schools and communities. School librarians can be a primary voice in promoting the importance of social equity for all students. School librarians must focus on enhancing their professional competencies and promote positive intercultural interactions between students (Jackson) in order to create the best learning environment in the 21st century.

James Banks' has designed four levels of multicultural curriculum reform that teacher-librarians can use to measure their effectiveness in helping all students be more successful in a culturally diverse society. Teacher-librarians can use his four levels to evaluate if their research curriculum and information literacy skills are culturally responsive.

Level 1: The Contribution Stage

At this first stage of curriculum reform a teacher-librarian focuses only on the superficial aspects of culture. This is where most teacher-librarians stop because it is the easiest level to incorporate. One example is when the school library puts up posters for Cinco de Mayo, Martin Luther King's birthday or African-American History Week. At this level no conversations occur among faculty and students about current issues like racism, poverty, and oppression. Students miss out on the opportunity to see the value their cultures bring to a multicultural society. At this level, stereotypes of ethnic groups remain central to one's ethnic identity which can contribute to students limiting their ambitions based on the heroes they see. One black student explained in my class that he thought he could only succeed in sports based on the media coverage of other black men. It took a teacher who cared about his academic success to show him educational alternatives. I rarely hear about such conversations with teacher-librarians even though teacher-librarians have the ability to have many one-on-one conversations with students while they are lounging in the magazine section or working on class research.

Level 2: The Additive Stage

At this second stage a teacher-librarian makes more of an effort to integrate cultural content into curriculum, but when collaborating with other teachers, a teacher-librarian who is unaware of alternative resources may only introduce resources that are written from the viewpoints of mainstream writers and historians. A culturally responsive teacher-librarian will need to spend time investigating alternative resources and books. To advance to the next stage, a teacher-librarian must evaluate resources based on language, pictures, topics, and stereotypes. Through collaborative conversations, and teacher-librarian modeling, children and adults can be taught to notice cultural biases they may not have otherwise noticed. Teacher-librarians who want to be culturally responsive need to think about the following questions:

- Who wrote the book: male, female, dominant culture, non-dominant culture?
- What is the copyright?
- Is it a book about non-dominant culture written by a person from the dominant culture? (If so, the book may have a Eurocentric perspective.)
- How are women treated in the book?
  - Are they strong or submissive, lead or supporting characters, do they need the men to approve the decisions or help them carry them out?
  - What is the language style? (e.g. Does the book use "he" to talk about both genders?)
  - Who are the main characters?
    - Look for stereotypes in pictures and character descriptions.
    - Does the book describe non-dominant culture characters as evil, crafty, lazy, shady, and so on . . .?
    - How are the characters illustrated?
    - Do the non-dominant culture characters have subservient roles; or do they get to make decisions, take part in or lead the action, and move the story forward?
    - Do the non-dominant culture characters get to solve problems or are they shown as causing problems?
    - Do they have to gain acceptance or acquiesce to dominant culture characters?
    - Are lifestyle and cultures represented accurately and

respectfully; is there negativity or judgment about lifestyle, language, socioeconomic status, gender, religion, sexual preference, ability or color (black is bad, white is good)?

o Who are the heroes (men, women, dominant, or non-dominant)? If the hero is non-dominant who are they serving, the dominant culture group or their own?

> *Since teacher-librarians interact with all students within a school, it is a natural fit to look toward our school library personnel to model culturally responsive leadership for educators within their schools and communities.*

Level Three: The Transformational Stage

Finally at Level 3, a transformation of curriculum begins to occur as the teacher-librarian introduces colleagues and students to resources that offer multiple cultural perspectives and viewpoint, and teaches students to know and praise their own and each other's cultural heritages. For example, a language arts unit on poetry should not just focus on the works of Robert Frost or Donald Hall, but include African-American poets such as Maya Angelou, Langston Hughes, or Paul Laurence Dunbar to gain a different perspective of society and culture. In history, students studying the significant events should be introduced to the perspectives of African Americans, Native Americans, Japanese Americans as well as other ethnic groups affected by the same historical events that have been reported on by mainstream, white men in the past. As Banks explains, "One irony of conquest is that those who are conquered often deeply influence the cultures of the conquerors" (63).

Level 4: The Social Action Stage

The decision-making and social action approach is the highest and most complex level. Banks explains that in this approach students study a social problem based on their own community or school's issues. The purpose at Level 4 is to teach students critical-thinking skills; empower them as cultural individuals; and create more self-efficacy (63). At this stage, teacher-librarians team with colleagues and administrators to encourage parental and community participation in discussing issues that are critical to the community to build meaningfulness between home and school experiences. Culturally responsive teaching is comprehensive and teaches the whole child. Being a culturally responsive instructional leader as a teacher-librarian means caring about students; having high expectations of all students; communicating with students; and being sensitive to diverse learning styles.

> *One simple strategy for building trust is to learn students' names when students visit the library. Acknowledge the students with a smile and let them know that you are glad they came into your classroom—the school library.*

so important!

As a role model for other colleagues, students, parents, and community members, a culturally responsive teacher-librarian can foster student achievement through the following proactive actions:

1. Build trust

All students bring their culture into school. Trust is built when students feel valued and cared about just as they are. If students feel valued, student achievement will increase. Geneva Gay writes about this notion of the power of caring and encourages all educators to send the message to students that "I have faith in

your ability to learn. I care about the quality of your learning, and I commit myself to making sure you will learn" (45). One simple strategy for building trust is to learn students' names when students visit the library. Acknowledge the students with a smile and let them know that you are glad they came into your *classroom—*the school library. Promote a higher level of cultural awareness within your school community by having students conduct research and share stories about their own family's ethnic background. All students have a culture and should be aware of their own ethnic roots (Jackson).

2. Value cultural awareness

First as instructional leaders, school librarians need to be aware that "culture determines how we think, believe, and behave, and these, in turn affect how we teach and learn" (Gay 9). To be a leader in cultural responsiveness and model appropriate attitudes and behaviors with other colleagues, one much first be aware of one's own culture. Take time to think about cultural norms of home, school, district, and community to better assess one's own influence on the level of cultural acceptance within a community. A teacher-librarian needs to be aware of how she treats others who are different. Be aware of misjudgment based on stereotypes. Research shows that white, middle-class people see themselves as cultureless which can unintentionally become a measure of white racial superiority (Perry). School librarians are often left out of the professional development that other educators in their district receive so a culturally responsive school librarian will seek out opportunities to learn more about the students within their learning community. Often referred to as "color-blind" or "cultural blindness," white educators believe they are being non-discriminating when in reality, more subtle forms of negative experiences exist due to lower expectations of students of color (Gay; Irvine). A school librarian may have good intentions but is not aware of how current instructional practices reflect European American cultural values. Also, there may be a subconscious intent to assimilate students of color into mainstream society. Instead, celebrate differences and know that it is okay to notice differences among each other while assuming positive intent. Accept that each culture finds different values and behaviors as important (Lindsey, Robins, & Terrell).

"Culture is a system of shared beliefs, values, customs, behaviors, and artifacts that the members of society use to interact with their world and one another" (Zion & Kozleski). Culture does not have to be defined in terms of race, ethnicity, or national boundary. Diverse and underserved populations in K-12 schools include the following characteristics: ethnicity, race, neurological (e.g. autism, Asperger's Syndrome), religion, physical differences (e.g. visual or hearing-impaired), sexual orientation, gender, and age. Even working-class, single-parent, and low-socially economic families represent cultures which are more than likely different from the mainstream (Dean). A school librarian can be a stakeholder in dispelling any myths and prejudices that may exist in a school by learning more about the students' language, learning styles, and values. In addition, "ethnically different students will deliberately sabotage or camouflage their intellectual abilities to avoid being alienated from their ethnic friends who are not as adept at school" (Gay 19). For example, African-American females and Chinese Americans operate in "intentional silence." They may purposefully not speak up in class, or answer questions tersely or without elaboration in order to avoid bringing attention to themselves. They are more comfortable with their anonymity. In addition to some ethnic groups who avoid eye contact, students with autism may also avoid eye contact. If a teacher-librarian is not aware of this difference, she may expect a different behavior from the student then what is possible.

To get to know students better, Jackson, a multicultural educator, recommends that educators should observe students in nonschool settings, visit community churches, talk to community leaders, and make home visits with other teachers to show that they care and to encourage parents to become more involved in the school community, which leads to a higher investment in education. One of Jackson's principles for culturally responsive educators is to establish positive relationships between home and school. The library is a perfect place to hold evening meetings to discuss important issues in the community. Welcome families into the library to learn more about college opportunities as well as to discuss issues like Internet safety to further build upon the relationship between school and home.

3. Foster motivation.

"Engagement is the visible outcome of motivation" (Wlodkowski & Ginsberg). Teacher librarians can foster motivation by engaging students in what they are learning and making it relevant to their real-world experiences (Wlodkowski & Ginsberg). This is more possible when the teacher-librarian has taken time to get to know her students and to develop trust among the learners. A culturally responsive teacher-librarian develops a library connection that appeals to different cultures as personal relevance creates a more positive attitude towards school; a place that has not always been welcoming to the underserved populations because of their differences. She also finds ways to create performance assessments that are based on students' strengths and ask students to offer feedback on how they would like to be evaluated. A culturally responsive leader is not afraid to empower learners with learning choices, knowing there are often multiple ways to teach to state standards. As Wlodkowski and Ginsberg explain, "Rather than trying to know what to do to students, we must work with students to interpret and deepen their existing knowledge and enthusiasm for learning."

4. Establish inclusion.

Through the process of inclusion, a culturally responsive teacher-librarian creates a learning community in which learners and educators feel respected by and connected to one another. A culturally responsive teacher-librarian emphasizes the purpose for what is being learned and its relationship to students through collaboration and cooperation. For example, when learning how to conduct research, the culturally responsive teacher-librarian assigns students to small groups where they discuss previous experiences about conducting research. Then, the teacher-librarian has each group share their perspectives in order to understand their concerns and connect with them. The teacher-librarian is also aware that some cultures are more comfortable than others revealing their personal feelings and must feel safe to do so; she then explains that most people are researchers and shares examples. The last step is when she asks students what they would like to research. After a lively discussion, the class decides to investigate a common interest. This example portrays a learning opportunity that connects students with each other and promotes a personal connection between the learners and what they are being asked to learn.

Works Cited

Banks, James. *Cultural Diversity and Education: Foundations, Curriculum, and Teaching*. 4th ed. Needham Heights, MA: Allyn and Bacon, 2001. Print.

Dean, Patricia K. "Working Toward Cultural Responsiveness in the New Millennium." National Association for the Education of Young Children's Annual National Institute for Early Childhood Professional Development. Albuquerque, NM. 2002. Print.

Gay, Geneva. *Culturally Responsive Teaching: Theory, Research & Practice*. In J.A. Banks' (Ed) *Multicultural Education Series*. Columbia University, New York: Teachers College Press, 2000. Print.

Irvine, Jacqueline J. *Educating Teachers for Diversity: Seeing with a Cultural Eye*. New York: Teachers College Press, 2003. Print.

be aware!

Jackson, Francesina. "Seven Strategies to Support a Culturally Responsive Pedagogy." *Journal of Reading,* Volume 37. Issue 4 (1993): 298–303. Print.

Lindsey, Randall B., Robins, Kikanza N., and Raymond Terrell. *Cultural Proficiency: A Manual for School Leaders*. Thousand Oaks, CA: Corwin Press, 1999. Print.

Perry, Pamela. "White Means Never Having to Say You're Ethnic: White Youth and the Construction of "Culturelessness" Identities." *Journal of Contemporary Ethnography,* Volume 30. Issue 1 (2001): 56–91. Print.

Wlodkowski, Raymond and Margery B. Ginsberg. *A Framework for Culturally Responsive Teaching*. San Francisco: Jossey-Bass, 1995.Print.

Zion, Shelley and Elizabeth Kozleski. *Understanding Culture*. Tempe, AZ: Arizona State University, National Institute for Urban School Improvement, 2005. Print.

Laura L. Summers, PhD *is an assistant professor and coordinates the online school library graduate program in the Information and Learning Technologies program at the University of Colorado Denver. She can be reached at laura.summers@ucdenver.edu.*

Summers, Laura L. (2010). Culturally responsive leadership in school libraries. *LMC, 28*(5), 10–13.

Students as Global Citizens: Educating a New Generation

By Patricia Montiel-Overall

Today's young learners are members of a global community and will face enormous challenges in making decisions about issues affecting planet Earth. Students need to understand the connectedness of local and world economies, ecologies, and technologies. They will have to make informed decisions about how choices made in one part of the globe affect other parts, how disasters on one continent require concern and aid from other continents, and how environmental changes affect all living creatures.

Global citizens of the future will need educators and mentors who have the ability to examine international issues through a critical lens. They need to see issues and solutions from a new paradigm in which borders matter less than global well-being. Educators and librarians will be needed to prepare students to participate in this global community which is closely connected through the media, the Internet, and financial institutions. Educators and their librarian partners will help students develop new ways of thinking about complex issues and to be able to balance global and nationalistic interests.

This article introduces key issues for new global citizens and highlights the roles of teachers and librarians in providing students with toolkits for becoming leaders and future policy makers. Included is the ability to think critically, solve difficult problems, and demonstrate a high degree of cultural competence. For teachers and librarians these tools are the cornerstone of their profession.

Background

The idea of global citizens evolves continuously. With the advent of each new technology (writing, ships, trains, telephone), communities have become more closely connected and are in closer communication. Today global issues affect us in ways not previously conceived of. Before discussing the critical role teachers and librarians have in developing global citizenship, let's examine some of the issues likely to be at the forefront of the agenda for the next generation of global citizens.

Global Issues

Globalization

In 1983 Theodore Leavitt, an economist and professor at Harvard Business School, popularized the term "globalization" in his book *The Marketing Imagination*. Since then, the term has become a buzzword synonymous with increased international cooperation in commerce, economic growth, and development. The economic value of globalization has been central to discussions by economists and their vision of the United States as a major player in promoting relationships across borders. The American Library Association's definition of globalization as "the process of integrating regions via communications and economics" exemplifies the extent to which economists' definition of globalization is understood across disciplines. To the general American public, globalization is also associated with world trade, free trade, call centers, wages, employment, immigrants, imports, and foreign investments.

While many members of society, including LIS professionals, have accepted globalization as the product of the information age in an increasingly connected world, a small but growing number of voices have raised questions about underlying assumptions of globalization and its real (not proposed) benefit to local and global communities. For example, in the United States, some have attributed the loss of jobs to other countries as an important factor in unemployment. In India, the rise in mental health issues associated with long call center hours and work schedules are a growing concern (e.g., rising early and sleeping when families are active isolates workers from families).

> Global citizens must be culturally competent in order to recognize different ways of perceiving, promoting, debating, disputing, and approaching global issues.

Ecology

Ecology refers to the study of organisms and ways in which they interact with each other within their environment. Global ecosystems include land, water, and atmosphere. For decades, we have studied the planet as one interdependent ecosystem. A new generation of global citizens will have to make decisions that reflect this understanding. Recent global disasters have demonstrated the interconnectedness of ecosystems and raised the level of awareness about the effects of human intervention on ecosystems. For example, the volcanic eruption of Mount St. Helens in 1980 resulted in research on the effects of the eruption on ecosystems. Findings indicate that human intervention to protect property influenced the rate of natural reparation and calls into question prioritizing short-term financial losses over long-term ecological benefits.

← bring in relative examples

Technology

Technology refers to the specialized application of knowledge and includes a broad range of topics, including writing, teaching, and digitization. Technological tools include pencils, stoves, respirators, computers, the Internet, and resources such as ERIC. The next generation of global citizens will face enormous challenges regarding the use and distribution of technologies, particularly new technologies. The ethical use of new and old technologies will have to be re-examined to determine their effect on the planet. For example, coal-burning electrical plants are currently considered a major contributor to global warming by scientists. However, for a variety of reasons, including the cost of re-equipping current coal-fired facilities with electrical plants fueled by natural gas generators, solutions to this challenge have not been implemented. The next generation of global citizens will need to examine new technologies such as solar and wind power, hydroelectric dams, and nuclear reactors. They will also have to consider technologies that haven't yet been invented (e.g., "capturing the carbon dioxide produced by fossil-fueled power plants and storing it permanently underground;" http://dge.stanford.edu). Policies and regulation of pollutants and hazardous waste are some of the challenges to be addressed. Global citizens will also have to examine the extent to which global communities have access to technologies. In 2010, only 22 percent of the global population had access to computers. "North America, with 5 percent of world population, is home to 50 percent of Internet users and has more computers than the rest of the world combined. South Asia, by contrast, has 20 percent of world population but only 1 percent of the world's Internet users" (Conachy, 1999).

Policy

Policies are decisions or actions that guide practices related to the delivery of services, behavior, use of resources, and other endeavors. Future global citizens will be involved in policy making about economics, the environment, finances, and business practices. Policies that affect global communities and will become

increasingly problematic include disposal of toxic and hazardous wastes and international cooperation to avoid physical, ecological, and economic harm. Current policies often depend on voluntary mechanisms for enforcement. For example, the labeling of packages is generally not regulated unless a product is perceived as high risk. Creating mandatory policies may be required in the future as new, higher risk products emerge. Cross-national policy making will require extreme diplomacy and knowledge of culture.

Culture

Culture has been defined in multiple ways, including belief systems, habits, customs, and activities. In general, culture involves the daily activities that occur in the lives of groups and organizations. Global citizens have unique cultures which reflect differences in activities despite similarities brought about by international product distribution (i.e., videos, music, and food). Global citizens also have distinct languages although English has become a global language. The new generation of global citizens may determine that Americans should become more linguistically diverse and initiate more second language instruction as the population of the United States becomes more diverse and the number of Latinos/Hispanics and Spanish-speaking citizens increases. Spanish for English speakers may be included in schools and libraries with English as a second language classes.

Global citizens of the future may realize that language policies have been inadequately examined and are a critical issue for participation in global societies. In the United States, culture and language issues are highly political and have little relationship to scientific evidence about the benefit of bilingualism (which has been compared to having more RAM in your hard drive). Bilingual education may be revisited, and research regarding its value as a successful strategy for second language acquisition may need to be reconsidered. The next generation of U.S. global citizens must examine language policies related to

immigrants and consider alternatives to eliminating Spanish, which is the third most commonly spoken language in the world.

These themes are interrelated, despite regional and national alliances. For example, when thinking of globalization, which has dominated the thinking in economics for decades, cultural issues become a major consideration. Economists such as Leavitt (20–49) believe that products do not need not be customized inasmuch as globalization has done away with individual preferences. At the same time, resentment by locals toward Americanization reflects the concern by some about a loss of local cultural practices, values, and beliefs. Global citizens will need to determine the extent to which concerns must be considered and whether it would even be possible to override the perspective of economists.

The opportunity for teachers and librarians is being able to provide an education which truly demonstrates the democratic principles of our country.

Cultural Competence

Global citizens will have to be culturally competent. Cultural competence means understanding and respecting diverse perspectives. Using a framework of cultural competence for library professionals (Montiel-Overall 175–204), the following definition is used:

Cultural competence is the ability to recognize the significance of culture in one's own life and in the lives of others; and to come to know and respect diverse cultural backgrounds and characteristics through interaction with individuals from diverse linguistic, cultural, and socioeconomic groups; and to fully integrate the culture of diverse groups into services, work, and institutions in order to enhance the lives of both those being served by the library profession and those engaged in service.

Global citizens must be able to understand the nuances of global issues from diverse perspectives. Those whose lives are affected by decisions will need to be brought into discussions to ensure global peace and stability. Global citizens must be culturally competent in order to recognize different ways of perceiving, promoting, debating, disputing, and approaching global issues.

> *Teachers and librarians can be instrumental in bringing students to a higher level of understanding about global issues through strategies identified in the Common Core State Standards, and through rigorous and honest evaluation of issues critical to the planet.*

Figure 1 illustrates the interconnectedness of these issues.

The Role of Educators and Librarians

Educators and librarians are uniquely situated to ensure that all students develop into global citizens who

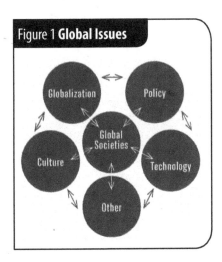

Figure 1 **Global Issues**

are capable of managing complex systems and processes discussed above. Through collaboration, teachers and librarians work together to design lessons based on inquiry-based instruction and problem solving. The current shift toward Common Core State Standards (CCSS) opens the door for this type of instruction which librarians have promoted for decades. It involves critical thinking, doing research to answer questions and solve problems, evaluating information, and analyzing situations. Drawing on these abilities, now specified in national standards, teachers and librarians are able to go beyond previous prescriptive standards based on direct instruction and designed to teach discrete information. The new standards enable teachers and students to ask tough questions and find solutions that fit a wide range of complex problems. Teachers and librarians will be able to focus students on the validity of underlying assumptions and re-evaluate the merit of those assumptions so that discrepancies can be revealed and reconciled rather than ignored.

According to the CCSS Initiative Standards-Setting Criteria, the standards were designed to provide rigorous content that is "internationally benchmarked, so that all students are prepared for succeeding in our global economy and society . . ." and "will set the stage for U.S. education not just beyond next year, but for the next decade [to] ensure *all* American students are prepared for the global economic workplace."

To meet these criteria, students will need to be knowledgeable about international benchmarks and actively participate in how these benchmarks are established and which criteria are used to evaluate them. Teachers and librarians must help students become knowledgeable about workforce practices to ensure that standards established for American citizens apply to global citizens as well as workers in the United States. Educators and librarians must facilitate difficult discussions and act as "academic guides" who "transfer responsibility into the hands of the

students" (Jaeger 11). Questions such as "Who benefits economically when jobs are outsourced?" and "Is pollution a global issue? If so, how do local communities collaborate with outside communities to address the issue?" will inevitably be raised by students engaged in inquiry-based instruction. Students must be encouraged to think about these questions and come up with innovative answers to them if we are truly interested in fostering "higher level thinking" and producing "graduates who are problem solvers" (Jaeger 11).

Conclusion

Preparing students for global citizenship is a challenge and an opportunity for educators and librarians. The challenge will be to transition into new ways of teaching and help students transition into new ways of learning, which includes more independent critical thinking and objectivity. The opportunity for teachers and librarians is being able to provide an education which truly demonstrates the democratic principles of the country. Global citizens will have to be rigorous in their decision-making to ensure that equality across borders occurs even when decisions are in conflict with those of special interest groups. If the United States truly believes in democratic ideals of equality and justice for all, it must be willing to apply these principles internationally to retain a position of global leadership.

Teachers and librarians can be instrumental in bringing students to a higher level of understanding about global issues through strategies identified in the core standards, and through rigorous and honest evaluation of issues critical to the planet. The next generation of global citizens must be able to appreciate the urgency of acting responsibly to address the global issues outlined above. New educational standards are a starting point for forward-thinking and vigorous action. However, it will take teachers and librarians who are willing to support students as they come up with creative and innovative solutions that change the status quo. It will take educators and librarians who accept the challenges and opportunities of educating a new generation of global citizens.

Works Cited

ACRL. "Diversity Standards: Cultural Competency for Academic Libraries (2012)." *American Library Association.* Web. 20 May 2012. www.ala.org/acrl/standards/diversity.

Carnegie Institution for Science/ Department of Global Ecology. "Only the Lowest CO2 Emitting Technologies Can Avoid a Hot End-of-Century." 16 February 2012. Web. 25 June 2012. http://dge.stanford .edu.

Conachy, Michael. "Social Inequality and the World Wide Web." World Socialist Web Site. 17 August 1999. Web. 25 June 2012. www.wsws.org/ articles/1999/aug1999/www-a17 .shtml.

Common Core State Standards Initiative. www.corestandards .org.

Jaeger, Paige. We Don't Live in a Multiple-choice World: Inquiry and the Common Core. *Library Media Connection* 30.4 (2012): 10–14.

Leavitt, Theodore. *The Marketing Imagination.* The Free Press, 1983. pp. 20–49.

Montiel-Overall, Patricia. "A Cultural Competence Framework for Library and Information Science Professionals." *Library Quarterly* 79.2 (2009): 175–204.

Dr. Patricia Montiel-Overall *is an associate professor of the School of Information Resources and Library Science at the University of Arizona. She may be reached at overall@email.arizona.edu.*

Montiel-Overall, Patricia. (2013). Students as global citizens: Educating a new generation. *LMC, 31*(3), 8–10.

Character in the Library

By Heather Moorefield-Lang

Building Better Citizens

Character education has been called many things over the years, such as values education, character development, pro-social education, efficacy training, civic development, moral instruction, and peace education (Hall xxiii; Helterbran, 2009). The definition for character education can be as changeable as the name itself. Overall, character education can be defined as teaching, training, or practices that promote positive behavior traits within students. Those who teach this type of education instill good values and teach how to best act on those values. Moral rights and wrongs also come into play (Lockwood 12). Character education can sometimes be embodied by virtues such as respect, tolerance, self-discipline, effort, perseverance, and fairness, to name a few (Benninga, Berkowitz, Kuehn, & Smith, 2006). No matter how it is defined, character education teaches our students how to be better citizens, more respectful human beings, and kinder peers—traits that should be taught in every classroom, the library included.

> *Allow students to build their own characters and write stories around them. Having students share their stories with peers and families is a wonderful way to connect their work to character education.*

Those teaching in schools have to compete for students' attention when it comes to character education. Young people are rarely told on television, in video games, and on the Internet to be kind and respectful to their peers, parents, elders, or anyone in authority. Character education can lead to a calmer, more peaceful and respectful educational atmosphere that can aid in student learning. Students can create closer relationships with their peers and teachers because they are thinking outside of themselves; they are thinking of others (Brannon, 2008). Complete character education cannot be done by one or two educators in a school building. It must be a schoolwide commitment from the principal to the cafeteria staff. Everyone has to be involved in creating a safe, caring environment where the staff and faculty come together to model the behavior that they expect from the students (Benninga et al., 2006). When educators, administrators, and support staff exhibit positive behaviors, students will begin to emulate them. While modeling is incredibly important, many student activities can aid in further implementing character education. This is where the library and the school librarian can be fully integrated into this schoolwide initiative. The following examples show how literacy, activities, and technology character education can be implemented in the school's media center.

Literacy

Books are one of the best ways to discuss and show examples of good characteristics for character education. Many books, such as Susan Hall's *Using Picture Books to Teach Character Education*, focus on this very topic. If the literature is rich, it will be easier to include it in a lesson involving character education (O'Sullivan, 2004). Pick literature with characters from different backgrounds, races, and genders. Choose a character who is close in age to the students you are teaching. Look for stories where decisions have to be made or where there are dilemmas to be solved (Helterbran, 2009). Have the students talk through the character's choices. Let them compare and think on their own about options and preferences, and whether they would have made the same judgments.

> **The Hunger Games Trilogy.** Written by Suzanne Collins, *Hunger Games, Catching Fire,* and *Mockingjay* are perfect for discussing character traits, decisions, and right and wrong. The lead character, Katniss Everdeen, faces decisions that she has to make each moment of every day that she is in and out of the Hunger Games. Students in middle and high school will be engaged by these fast paced books. Character traits such as courage, hope, justice, loyalty, resourcefulness, and forgiveness are all a part of the story. The opportunities for writing exercises, playwriting, game design, art projects, and more are endless with this series. The character education opportunities are plentiful, and it is a very powerful read.
>
> ***The Invention of Hugo Cabret.*** Written in pictures, this story by Brian Selznick is a wonderful book for elementary and lower middle school. Courage, diligence, hope, kindness, and resourcefulness are only a few of the many traits that are portrayed. Video and podcasts on character education in black and white movie style could be a fun way to teach with this novel. Creating sculptures with peers as representations of the automaton in the book would be a wonderful way to encourage collaboration and positive peer interaction.
>
> **Olivia.** This picture book series by Ian Falconer features a young, precocious pig by the name of Olivia. No matter how active or nerve-wracking she may be, her mom and dad always love and accept her. The Olivia books show

positive character traits such as patience, courage, tolerance, and loyalty. School librarians can act out scenes from the books in the library and discuss with students whether or not Olivia made positive or negative decisions. Olivia likes to paint and draw. Students can be assigned a positive behavior trait and draw out what they think that attribute looks like. Then the library can have a character education art wall.

Activities

Physical and artistic activities get students thinking and moving. Not every student likes to write, and some struggle with reading, but incorporating other types of activities will bring out the artists, actors, poets, singers, and more amongst students. Young people enjoy being creative. Here are some examples of how to be innovative with character education.

Acting/role playing. Have students act out scenarios where positive and negative behavior traits are displayed. The performances can be scripted and planned out or improvised. Have students discuss what they are seeing and come up with alternatives to negative behaviors or traits. Another way this can be done is to have students act out scenes without an ending and then have the students discuss how each scenario should end or what decisions the characters should make (Lockwood, 2009).

Character education collage/wall. Have a wall in the library that is completely for character education. It can be used to feature artwork. Each month a different grade, team, or class can take over the wall and display their work. Poetry, writing, art, music, and more can be shared on the wall. If there isn't a wall to spare, unroll long sheets of bulletin board paper and have students create their own character education wall that can be posted in the library or school halls. (This can also be done with classroom door decoration contests.)

Game design. Have students create their own character education game. It could be a board game, video game, or app. Students can create a story, characters, conflict, decisions, and a conclusion to the game. Then they can design and storyboard the game. The project can be finished with presentations to their peers or families. Storyboards can be shown in the library. If there are any programmers in the school, these games could go on to be designed and created in computer classes.

Technology

Many Web 2.0 tools and apps for handheld and tablet devices can be used in conjunction with character education. Use these sites to complement the books and activities that you have been reading. Below are examples of free sites and how they might be used with your students.

Get artistic. Use sites such as Flockdraw (http://flockdraw .com), Odosketch (http://sketch .odopod.com), or Draw Island (http:// drawisland.com) to create images, drawings, and sketches online in order to accompany character education projects. Read a story based on a character education trait and have students draw about it. Have them create the school's new character education campaign design or slogan. The possibilities are endless.

Word clouds. Try Wordle (www.wordle.net), Tagxedo (www .tagxedo.com), or ABCya (www .abcya.com/word_clouds.htm) to create character education word clouds. Do this as a class or have students design their own. Create a character education wall in the library. Some students don't feel comfortable writing long passages, but creating these gorgeous graphic word designs will be a great way to express what they want to say.

Write a story. Let students write their own stories and create characters with sites like My Storymaker (www.clpgh.org/kids/ storymaker/embed.cfm), Comic Master (www.comicmaster.org.uk), Zooburst (www.zooburst.com), and Storybird (http://storybird.com). All of these sites allow students to build their own characters and write stories around them. Having students share their stories with peers and families is a wonderful way to connect their work to character education.

Conclusion

Lessons and activities in values, positive behaviors, and civility are important. Though we as educators may feel that these traits should be taught at home, we cannot guarantee that this is the case. We can make sure positive behaviors are modeled, taught, and witnessed in the school halls and classrooms. Character education is essential throughout the school, and it shouldn't stop in any one classroom. The school library as a central element in student learning should also be the hub for character education. Incorporating traits and values into books, activities, technology, and other lessons can only help fellow educators enhance the work they are doing in their classrooms. Character education makes for a safer, kinder school, for work and learning.

References

Benninga, J.S., M.W. Berkowitz, P. Kuehn and K. Smith. "Character and Academics: What Good Schools Do." *Phi Delta Kappan* 87.6 (2006): 448–452.

Brannon, D. "Character Education: A Joint Responsibility." *Kappa Delta Pi Record* 73.8 (2008): 56–60.

Hall, Susan. *Using Picture Storybooks to Teach Character Education.* Oryx Press, 2000.

Helterbran, V.R. "Linking Character Education and Global Understanding through Children's Picture Books." *Kappa Delta Pi Record* 45.2 (2009): 69–73.

Lockwood, Alan. *The Case for Character Education: A Developmental Approach.* Teacher College Press, 2009.

O'Sullivan, S. "Books to Live By: Using Children's Literature for Character Education." The Reading Teacher 57.7 (2004): 640–645.

Heather Moorefield-Lang *is the education and applied social sciences librarian at Virginia Tech. She can be reached at hmlang@vt.edu. Follow her on Twitter @actinginthelib and find out more about her research and work at www .actinginthelibrary.com.*

Moorefield-Lang, Heather. (2012). Character in the library. *LMC, 31*(1), 10–12.

School Library Media Collaborations: Benefits and Barriers

By Dawn Frazier

Introduction

The British writer Aleister Crowley once noted, "The joy of life consists in the exercise of one's energies, continual growth, constant change, [and] the enjoyment of every new experience." If this is true, today's school librarians experience an abundance of joy in their lives! A school librarian's curricular role has expanded from resource provider to educational partner with the goal of creating 21st century learners. The American Association of School Librarians encourages school librarians to generate opportunities for students' becoming "independent lifelong users and producers of ideas and information" (*Empowering Learners* 20).

In addition to promoting lifelong learning, *Empowering Learners: Guidelines for School Library Media Programs* defines multiple literacies and emphasizes the learning process. It challenges the school library media center to evolve from "a confined place to one with fluid boundaries that is layered by diverse needs and influenced by an interactive global community"(5). Amid this evolution, school librarians expect their primary responsibilities to shift from teacher and information specialist to that of instructional partner (16). Thus, this article focuses on a school librarian's collaborative role, exploring its beneficial outcomes for teachers and students, as well as implementation barriers and possible solutions.

Collaborative Benefits for Educators

Meaningful collaborations between school library media specialists and classroom teachers occur when both parties unite to create lesson plans, facilitate engaging student activities, and develop authentic assessments for evaluating student progress. AASL recognizes that undertaking a collaborative partnership requires

"creativity, an openness to trying new approaches, and a willingness to take risks"(*Empowering Learners* 20). These risks offer many rewards. Successful collaborative partnerships may:

- Create a mutual awareness of learning standards across multiple disciplines as instructors explore the alignment of academic content standards and National Educational Technology Standards (NETS) with information literacy standards.
- Expose teachers to new technology as school librarians suggest a wide range of new learning tools and materials formats.
- Allow teachers to realize the school librarian's full potential as a knowledgeable ally, supporting inquiry-based learning with current, high quality materials and resources.
- Strengthen the library media center's collection development plan. A school librarian gains insight into the collection's gaps when collaborating teachers and students pursuing answers to Essential Questions express the need for additional resources on specific topics.
- Inspire other faculty members to participate in future partnerships as reluctant teachers witness colleagues and students demonstrate enthusiasm for the collaborative process.
- Underscore the school library media program's relevancy and instructional impact in the eyes of administrators, parents, and the community.

Today's students demonstrate enthusiasm and renewed interest for learning because school librarians intentionally embed a myriad of digital tools into their collaborative activities.

Collaborative Benefits for Students

Students reap many rewards when the school librarian engages in collaborative partnerships. A school librarian provides students with comprehensive guidance in the research process as a key component of collaboration. Using incremental research models with students, such as the *Big 6* or the *Super 3*, the school librarian promotes learning on both affective and cognitive levels.

For students engaged in research, emotional pitfalls such as uncertainty, confusion, frustration, and doubt traditionally correlate with the initiation and exploration stages of information seeking, causing some pupils to abandon the process altogether (Kuhlthau 367). A school librarian helps students avoid research anxiety by equipping them with tools such as resource pathfinders to effectively locate relevant information. In addition, the school librarian builds student confidence and understanding by incorporating appropriate research models that guide pupils step by step. This practice directs students' focus away from worry to genuine cognitive interest and provides a framework for successful lifelong knowledge seeking—the foundation of information literacy.

Students further benefit from collaboration in the area of achievement. When the school librarian is part of the planning and teaching team, focusing on information literacy skills, research indicates students perform better academically (Lance 16). In addition, studies endorsed by the Colorado Department of Education note, "After the wealth of a district, the second largest influence on test scores is the school library and its teacher librarians" (*Your School's Team*).

Finally, today's students demonstrate enthusiasm and renewed interest for learning because school librarians intentionally embed a myriad of digital tools into their collaborative activities. Guided by standards set forth by the International Society for Technology in Education and AASL's *Standards for the 21st Century Learner*, school librarians elevate students' critical thinking skills with lessons on Web site evaluation and use of digital applications. Tech savvy students plan, design, and create digital products to showcase their learning. For example, high school instructor Brian Beard reflects on his students' reaction to online Web publishing with "It motivates them to work to the best of their ability, because there is a huge difference between writing a paper for the teacher and writing one for your peers . . . [Students] enjoy looking at their published work and reading their friends' work as well" (qtd. in Driscoll par. 19).

> *A true information professional worries less about managing the collection's attrition, caring more for marketing every resource available to foster students' lifelong learning.*

Overcoming Collaboration Barriers

Though educators and students benefit from collaborative partnerships, several barriers may inhibit the process.

Barrier #1: Time—Teachers often have little planning time embedded in their day. Some may perceive a collaborative effort with the school librarian as an intrusion on the few precious minutes they do have. Conversely, school librarians with no support staff independently manage administrative duties, circulation, and patron requests with time for little else.

Solutions: A school librarian can utilize support staff and volunteers to visit teachers during planning periods or attend grade level meetings to learn about upcoming units of study. At its best, this practice allows a school librarian to open the door for possible collaborations as teachers gain awareness of a school librarian's knowledge, skills, and services. At a minimum, it affords the school librarian an opportunity to recommend resources and activities that enhance existing classroom lessons.

An alternative approach, likely to become popular with the faculty, is the implementation of a weekly free beverage day. One local elementary school librarian sends school-wide email reminders to market "W.O.W.—Wired on Wednesdays." On a portable cart in one corner of the media center, she provides large pots of coffee and hot water alongside small baskets with packets of creamer, hot chocolate, and tea. On Wednesday, staff traffic in the media center is heavy. With informal chats, the school librarian builds rapport with her colleagues, suggesting resources and collaborative services when the conversations turn to future curricular plans.

Barrier #2: Technology Troubleshooting Demands—Conducted by Library Media Connection, a February 2008 survey of 992 school media specialists revealed 65% consider themselves "the secondary technology support person" in the building and 15% "the primary technology person" (58). The latter figure may be on the rise as many school districts, faced with deep budget cuts, have downsized IT personnel. The result is an increased demand for school librarians to troubleshoot staff technology concerns. Such demands sap time from collaborative efforts.

Solutions: School librarians must create and maintain a balanced schedule. Collaboration requires advance preparation and commitment. School librarians should keep appointments with teachers and students for collaborative planning and lesson implementation while setting aside specific blocks of time to address technology issues. To maximize efficiency, the school librarian may keep a technology log of submitted troubleshooting requests, noting the date and time, the teacher's name, and the nature of the concern. A log allows problems to be addressed in order of receipt and documents frequently recurring issues. A school librarian may respond to common problems by offering a school-wide inservice training or publishing a step-by-step troubleshooting guide. When one-on-one assistance visits to a classroom do occur, the school librarian can use the opportunity to expand the teacher's technology skills while marketing the librarian's expertise as an instructional partner, eager for collaborative efforts to expand student knowledge.

Barrier #3: Narrow Focus—Though well-suited and eager to implement information literacy standards, a school librarian may lack knowledge of content specific academic curricular objectives. Such a gap impedes a school librarian's ability to align information literacy standards with academic standards. Thus, no framework exists to provide classroom teachers with a meaningful connection between the two sets of learning objectives.

Solutions: A school librarian must become well acquainted with state academic standards, especially those assigned to the represented grade levels at her school. To garner a faculty member's collaborative support, a school librarian must "illustrate the obvious connection between information literacy and content-related objectives [and] indicate the mutual benefit of integrating the two sets of objectives where the accomplishment of one set promotes the fulfillment of the other" (Wolcott par.19). One need not memorize the academic standards but become familiar with what classroom instructors are teaching. For example, at the start of each school year, teacher-librarian Debbie Belue requests copies of faculty members' long range plans. From this broad list of units, she creates an easy to follow matrix including teachers' names, months of the year, and planned topics of study. Using this matrix as a blueprint for proposing collaborative projects, she proactively gathers unit-related materials and reflects upon ways to combine information literacy activities with the classroom teachers' existing plans. While a unit matrix may be impractical for a school librarian serving a vast population, such as a large high school, the librarian could target specific academic departments each quarter, i.e. planning collaborative lessons with selected science classes the first nine weeks, social studies classes the second nine weeks, and so forth as required by subject areas and teachers.

Barrier #4: Faculty Perceptions—English teacher Angela Gess notes, "In some school environments, the library media center is viewed as a place for students to 'waste' time reading fiction books, and the library media specialist is merely a babysitter who provides teachers with much needed planning time"(24).

Solutions: To promote an information specialist's expertise, a school librarian can approach constructivist teachers to initiate collaboration efforts. Such teachers appreciate the school librarian's influence on student achievement. The successful outcomes of these collaborations, underscored by genuine student interest in a topic, may be too tempting for others to resist climbing on board in the future. With those educators less open to partnerships, a school librarian recognizes opportunities, no matter how small, to market her services to faculty and students. For example, instead of displaying annoyance that a colleague waited until the last minute to seek resources for an imminent lesson, capitalize on the opportunity to exercise the "information specialist role to the hilt" by demonstrating eagerness and enthusiasm for the challenge (Wolcott par.18). The librarian's positive attitude may be just the key for approaching this colleague in the future with collaborative intentions. Finally, a school librarian can change staff perceptions by increasing her visibility, actively participating in staff development, attending grade level meetings, and volunteering on the school's improvement committee (Colorado Department of Education, *Your School's Team*).

Barrier #5: Restrictive Control—In some schools, teachers may feel detached and uninformed of the media program's resources and the librarian's good intentions if the school librarian exhibits tight control of materials through restrictive circulation policies or if she independently executes collection purchases.

Solutions: In this scenario a school librarian needs to revisit and reflect upon the media program's mission. Resources sitting on a library shelf accomplish nothing but dust accumulation! A true information professional worries less about managing the collection's attrition, caring more for marketing every resource available to foster students' lifelong learning. In addition, an effective school librarian actively solicits "assistance in evaluating and selecting appropriate resources in the collection," especially those areas with noted deficiencies (Wolcott par.19). Collaboration is an ideal format as a school librarian may obtain formal or informal feedback from the partnering teacher and students regarding the collection's strengths and weaknesses. Furthermore, a school librarian may enlist vendors to display materials for purchase consideration on tables in the media center and invite faculty members to stop by, browse the options, and record preferences with sticky notes affixed to specific items. Not only will teachers feel more invested in the school media program, they will appreciate the librarian for assigning value and worth to their opinions.

Barrier #6: Lack of Administrative Support—Principals and school officials may simply lack awareness of collaboration benefits. Perhaps students have always been served in the media center on a fixed schedule and the principal has never doubted this practice as sound pedagogy.

Solutions: For uninformed administrators, a school librarian should supply copies of sound research underscoring the positive effect meaningful collaborations have on student achievement. Few principals can dispute hard evidence in the form of increased test scores, as noted in this paper's section on collaborative benefits for students. To maintain effective collaborative practices, a school librarian must advocate for partial or full flexible scheduling over fixed scheduling, presenting administrators with additional research findings to indicate "group library media center visits [do] not demonstrate . . . a correlation" with increased test scores (Lance 18). To this end, a school librarian needs to be realistic, recognizing that manipulating school-wide schedules is often difficult. An agreeable compromise may be a combination of fixed and flexible schedules on alternating weeks.

Conclusion

Effective school librarians embrace their evolving role as an instructional partner for student success. Director of the Colorado State Library, Eugene Hainer, uses this metaphor, "Think of school as a tapestry, where all the threads woven together create a picture of what students need to be. If you take out any of those threads, pretty soon you lose that tapestry, you lose that picture . . . we want that picture to be complete and a teacher librarian is part of that complete picture" (Colorado Department of Education, *Your School's Team*). Today's school librarians are not just part of the tapestry, they represent the vital golden thread that pulls it all together, connecting teachers and students to the information and modern day tools necessary for 21st century success and lifelong achievement.

Works Cited

American Association of School Librarians. *Empowering Learners: Guidelines for School Library Media Programs*. Chicago: American Library Association, 2009.

American Association of School Librarians. *Standards for the 21st Century Learner*. Chicago: American Library Association, 2007. 14 Jan. 2009 <http://www.ala.org/ala/mgrps/divs/aasl/guidelinesandstandards/learningstandards/standards.cfm>.

Belue, D. Lecture on School Library Media Collaboration. University of South Carolina. Columbia. 2006. 15 Jan. 2009 <http://www.sc.edu/mediaservices/courses/lib_sci.html#SLIS_J742>

Driscoll, K. "Collaboration in Today's Classrooms: New Web Tools Change the Game." *Multimedia and Internet @ Schools* (May 2007). 8 Feb. 2009 <http://www.mmischools.com/Articles/ReadArticle.aspx?ArticleID=12691>.

Gess, A. "Collaboration: Finding the Teacher, Finding the Topic, Finding the Time." *Library Media Connection* 27.4 (2009): 24–5.

Kuhlthau, C. "Inside the Search Process: Information Seeking from the User's Perspective." *Journal of the American Society for Information Science* 42.5 (1991): 361–71.

Lance, K. "Proof of the Power: Quality Library Media Programs Affect Academic Achievement." *Multimedia Schools* 8.4 (2001): 14–20.

"One Question Survey." *Library Media Connection* 27.1 (2008): 58.

Your School's Team Deserves a Star Player. Prod. Colorado Department of Education. 2006. Denver Film and Digital. 26 Apr. 2009 <http://www.cde.state.co.us/media/cdelib/video/StarPlayer/StarPlayer.html>.

Wolcott, L. Planning with teachers: Practical approaches to collaboration. *Emergency Librarian*, 23.3 (1996).

Dawn Frazier *is a recent graduate from the University of South Carolina's School of Library and Information Science and an early childhood educator for the Berkeley County School District in South Carolina.*

Frazier, Dawn. (2010). School library media collaborations: Benefits and barriers. *LMC, 29*(3), 34–36.

School Librarians & English Language Learners

By Larry Ferlazzo

It was a day when 40 intermediate English Language Learners (ELLs) from two classes could choose among several options when they entered the library media center. Some chose to read the bilingual books in Hmong, Spanish, and Russian the librarian had set out for them, while others went to a graphic novel cart that had been rolled out. Several went to work creating a public display highlighting the arrival of the Hmong New Year. Others picked up their headphones/microphones and went to the computers to easily create and post online animated movies they had written, or they practiced their reading, listening, and speaking skills at some of the other 9,000 free and accessible Web sites linked to the school's Web page.

Well over 10 percent of all students in K-12 schools in the United States are English Language Learners today, and, according to the Educational Testing Service, that number is expected to grow to 25 percent by 2025. Much of that growth is happening in communities (and in schools) that do not have a history of large immigrant populations. Given these demographics, let's consider different strategies school librarians can use to effectively assist ELLs and their teachers.

Building Your Library of ELL Resources

Having age-appropriate bilingual and graphic novel books available for students is important in this goal to assist ELLs. As more and more immigrant families come to the United States from different countries (Somalia and Bhutan are two of the more recent countries of origin for many ELLs), librarians might also find that another way to have bilingual books available is by working with students to create their own. Also, displaying books and materials—including those created by students—that share information about students' native countries can help develop a welcoming atmosphere to ease student anxiety, which can be a major barrier to language acquisition. Those resources can also help introduce new cultures to the broader school population.

> Computers can also be used to help students feel more comfortable about making mistakes and learning from them. Thousands of free online activities allow students to practice listening, speaking, writing, and reading with instant feedback—without anyone else seeing their mistakes.

The Internet is not a "magic bullet" but, if used strategically, English Language Learners can use it as another tool to assist language development. Becoming familiar with the most suitable sites and introducing them to teachers and their students can be a key role for librarians. The Internet resources I use with my ELL students have to meet very strict criteria. First, they must be available at no charge, Second, they must provide some kind of value-added benefit to students. In other words, some additional learning opportunity must be provided to students by using the computer over a lesson that doesn't use technology. I have to admit, however, on occasion doing something on the computer that could just as easily and effectively be done in the classroom can be a nice change of pace and result in increased student engagement. One value-added benefit can be creating online content for an "authentic audience"—someone other than the teacher. Computers can also be used to help students feel more comfortable about making mistakes and learning from them. Thousands of free online activities allow students to practice listening, speaking, writing, and reading with instant feedback—without anyone else seeing their mistakes. This obviously won't eliminate making errors around others—and, in an effective classroom, mistakes are celebrated for the risks they entail—but it can build greater student self-confidence. Third, I must be able to learn how to use the application within one minute. Fourth, it has to be possible for a non-tech-savvy student or English Language Learner to understand how to use it within a minute, too—with a little guidance. And, finally, it has to be allowed through most school content filters.

Here are some of my (and my students') favorite resources that meet those criteria.

Speaking

At English Central <http://www.englishcentral.com/en/videos> students can watch scenes from popular movies, see what is being spoken, then repeat what they hear. They are then graded instantaneously by the site on how well they pronounce the words, which also takes into consideration the students' particular accent. It's likely that every teacher of English Language Learners in the world who uses the Internet in their teaching would identify it as the best Web site that came online in 2009. To use the site you must have earphones and microphones for each student. You can purchase them at a local store or buy them from Schoolphones <http://www.schoolphones.com/products-frame.htm>, which offers quality headphones to schools at a low cost. An additional piece of good news about English Central is that Google is one of its primary investors, so it's likely to be around for a long time to come.

Vocaroo <http://vocaroo.com/> is a simple site where students can easily and quickly record their own voice and post it on a class blog or just email it to a teacher. No registration is required, and there are no ads on the site.

Writing

BBC Bitesize KS 2 for Writing <http://www.bbc.co.uk/schools/ks2bitesize/english/writing/> and BBC Bitesize KS 3 for Writing <http://www.bbc.co.uk/schools/ks3bitesize/english/writing/> are excellent sites that provide numerous interactive games and activities for students to practice multiple writing skills.

Edublogs <http://edublogs.org/> is a great place to create a class blog where teachers can easily post assignments and students can share their completed work. In addition, students can comment on the work of their peers. You can see our class blog here <http://sacschoolblogs.org/burbankeld/>. It's free, but if you want a blog free of advertisements, and the ability for students to leave audio comments (plus many other additional features), the cost is $40 per year.

Listening

Henny Jellama's TPR site <http://www.digischool.nl/oefenen/hennyjellema/engels/tpr/voorbladtpr.htm> is a brilliant online creation of a teaching strategy often used in the ELL classroom—Total Physical Response. On the site, many images of actions are shown, and the user has to choose the correct written and audio description of the activity.

English Listening Online <http://www.elllo.org/> has thousands of engaging listening activities and games.

Reading

Into The Book <http://reading.ecb.org/student/index.html> is designed to help students learn reading strategies such as visualize, predict, and summarize. Users are led through the process of learning each reading strategy with interactive exercises.

Reading Skills Stories 1 <http://www.marshalladulteducation.org/reading-skills-for-todays-adult/group-1> and Reading Skills Stories 2 <http://www.marshalladulteducation.org/reading-skills-for-todays-adult/group-2> provides a large selection of engaging and accessible stories for older English Language Learners.

Literactive <http://www.literactive.com/Home/index.asp> and Starfall <http://www.starfall.com/> are unparalleled sites for younger ELLs.

The best language learning occurs when students use the knowledge gained in the computer lab to help develop and deepen face-to-face interaction with their peers and teachers in and out of the classroom.

All in One

Mingoville <http://www.mingoville.com/en.html> is an exceptional site from Denmark designed to teach younger beginning English Language Learners. There are many interactive exercises and games, it's very colorful, and there are both listening and speaking activities, including a voice recording feature. You can experiment with it as a guest for a few minutes, but then you have to register. It's completely free, and registration takes about 20 seconds.

USA Learns <http://usalearns.org/index/> is an incredible Web site to help users learn English. Even though it's primarily designed for older learners, it's very accessible to all but the very youngest ELLs. It's free to use.

My own Web site <http://larryferlazzo.com/english.html> is designed for student self-access, and has 9,000 categorized links that are accessible to English

Language Learners in every content area.

Teaching Ideas

English Raven <http://www.englishraven.com/main.html> is designed by an experienced teacher of English Language Learners, and has thousands of teaching ideas and downloadable activities. Much of it is available for free. If you access certain resources on the site, you are asked to pay whatever you can—there is no set fee.

EFL Classroom 2.0 <http://eflclassroom.ning.com/> is an online community of thousands of English teachers from around the world. Thousands of resources are available, as well as free advice.

For more ideas on how librarians can assist English Language Learners, visit Colorin Colorado's "10 Ways To Support ELLs In The Library' <http://www.colorincolorado.org/article/33008>.

Redwoods and Language Learning

Computer resources, when used appropriately, can be a great asset to English Language Learners and their teachers. One caution, however, is to not get seduced by its ease of use and its apparent effectiveness. Here in Northern California, you can find many redwood trees. The ones that grow on their own can get very tall. It's the trees found in groves, though, which are the ones that can reach extraordinary heights. Their underground trunks interlock and provide needed support. Students relating to the computer screen can take advantage of exceptional language learning opportunities. However, the best language learning occurs when students use the knowledge gained in the computer lab to help develop and deepen face-to-face interaction with their peers and teachers in and out of the classroom.

Librarians and teachers together can make a dynamic combination to respond to the needs of this rapidly growing high-risk student population. By focusing on the assets of the vast majority of ELL students (their appetite to learn, their rich cultural histories) instead of their perceived deficits, everybody can win.

_____

Larry Ferlazzo *teaches English Language Learners at Luther Burbank High School in Sacramento, California. He is the co-author (with Lorie Hammond) of "Building Parent Engagement in Schools" and the forthcoming "English Language Learners: Teaching Strategies That Work" (April, 2010). Both are published by Linworth Publishing. He writes a popular resource-sharing blog at <http://larryferlazzo.edublogs.org/>.*

Ferlazzo, Larry. (2010). School librarians & English language learners. *LMC, 29*(3), 24–25.

The Role of the Media Specialist to Improve Academic Achievement and Strengthen At-Risk Youth

By Jami L. Jones and Alana M. Zambone

American education is failing many students, but especially students of color, from low-income families with disabilities or those who have limited English proficiency. These students are the focus of *No Child Left Behind* (NCLB), the 2001 revision of the Elementary and Secondary Education Act of 1965, which was signed into law on January 8, 2002. As much as educators complain about NCLB, it is difficult to argue against its purpose that all students will succeed regardless of race, ethnicity, family income, dominant language, or disability.

For media specialists, the tipping point for at-risk students is not graffiti, but rather the 3 Cs: connection, competence, and contribution.

NCLB as a Positive Force

From the passage of ESEA in 1965 to its latest version—NCLB, the goal is to ensure that students who have previously been left out, pushed to the side, and received inadequate schooling will no longer be ignored (Thernstrom and Thernstrom). The message to educators is that they must find ways to reach all students. There are numerous examples of other education legislation aimed at improving educational opportunities for all students, most notably, the *Individuals with Disabilities Education*

Act (IDEA) which established educational opportunities for students with disabilities. Despite over 40 years of legislative efforts to resolve the conditions that place students at-risk for low achievement and school failure, America continues to face a growing crisis in education. Oftentimes, we blame educational laws such as NCLB and IDEA for the increasing decline of education for at-risk students; however, these laws are not the problem, although regulations and procedures for implementing them may obscure their intent to provide all children with a high quality, appropriate education.

The Tenth Amendment of the U.S. Constitution gives

each state the power and the responsibility to provide benefits such as education, while the federal government provides funds for specific services, such as those required by NCLB and IDEA (Yell and Drasgow). Historically, education was the responsibility of each state and they set their own standards and designed their own educational systems. The Federal government has increased its role in response to changes in student populations and growing numbers of at-risk students and has attempted to reform education through legislation and funds to more effectively meet the needs of at-risk students.

States cannot pass education laws that require fewer services

Resources to learn more about education laws:

- American Library Association. *Your School Library Media Program and No Child Left Behind.* Chicago, IL. 2004 26 Jan 2007 <www.ala.org/ala/aaslbucket/AASLNCLBBrochureweb.pdf>.
- "Close Up: NCLB—Improving Literacy through School Libraries." *NCLB: The Achiever.* 15 Sep 2004 <www.ed.gov/news/newsletters/achiever/2004/091504.html>.
- NCLB is highly controversial. Visit <http://www.civilrightsproject.ucla.edu/> to read several research studies and policy analyses outlining strengths and concerns about

the law. Education of students with disabilities is one of the controversies surrounding NCLB.
- The federal government's role in education is described at <www.ed.gov/about/overview/fed/role.html>.
- To learn more about how to support students with special needs visit <http://www.ed.gov/parents/needs/speced/resources.html> or <http://www.cec.sped.org/>.
- To learn more about the accessibility requirements for school libraries and other facilities visit <www.access-board.gov/ada-aba>.

than those provided in federal laws, although they can pass laws that require more services than are identified in the federal laws. All school personnel are responsible for implementing educational services that satisfy the intent and the letter of the federal and state laws that govern education. Although media specialists might not be specifically named, they are nevertheless in a powerful position to truly implement the intention of these laws to improve academic achievement. Media specialists are in a strong position to strengthen at-risk students through mentoring, making connections with them and helping them connect to others in the school, and supporting their learning in creative and motivating ways.

What Is the "Turnaround" Media Specialist?

In the book, *The Power of the Media Specialist to Improve Academic Achievement and Strengthen At-Risk Youth*, Jones and Zambone identify affective and instructional strategies for working with low achieving students. They introduce the concept of systems change to transform the school library into a "turnaround place" for students and schools, and the media specialist into a "turnaround teacher."

What is a "turnaround teacher?" In their renowned longitudinal research to identify the protective factors that contribute to resiliency, Werner and Smith determined that the participants often named a teacher who had "become a role model, friend, and confidant for them" (57). The connection with this teacher gave them the strength to become resilient adults despite childhood traumas and trials. Bonnie Benard coined the term "turnaround" to describe a teacher who could promote resiliency by providing the at-risk student with three crucial environmental protective factors: connection, competence, and contribution (Benard).

The "turnaround" media specialist cares about students and connects with them. She is proactive, creative, and able to think divergently to create a school library program that benefits each of the diverse students in her school. The "turnaround" media specialist analyzes, synthesizes, and applies research findings to build a library program that meets the unique needs of students in the school and community.

The First C: Connection

The first of these "turnaround" qualities identified by Benard is connection. One example of a "turnaround" media specialist is Nelle Martin of West Palm Beach, Florida. When Martin noticed that the same students came alone to the school library every day during lunch instead of spending time with friends in the cafeteria, she sat down and talked to each of them. Martin learned that most were new to the school and had not yet made friends. To help them with this transition, Martin encouraged these students eat lunch together in an out-of-the-way spot in the school library. She purchased games for them to play during lunch. Sometimes "The Lunch Bunch" students helped Martin by performing minor chores around the media center. Martin was truly astounded to see how these students flourished as they developed friendships within the group and connected to the school through the library. Media specialists who recognize the importance of helping youth develop social skills, make friends, and establish connections can easily replicate the supportive program that Martin developed in other schools. This program won Martin the Florida Association for Media in Education's (FAME) first Amanda Award in 2002. The Amanda Award recognizes media specialists who develop programs that strengthen and develop the self-esteem of students. If Martin had not intuitively understood the value of spending time with students, she would not have learned about their sense of isolation, thus starting a program to strengthen their connection within the school. Often, students at-risk for academic failure are those who do not connect with school.

The Second C: Competence

The second "turnaround" quality identified by Benard is competence. "Turnaround" media specialists use research-based instructional strategies that make a difference. Research identifies a core of effective instructional and behavioral practices and strategies that help students achieve. Marzano, in reviewing his own and others' research, found that "if we follow the guidance offered from 35 years of research, we can enter an era of unprecedented effectiveness for the public practice of education—one in which the vast majority of schools can be highly effective in promoting students learning" (1). In *What Works in Schools: Translating Research into Action,* Marzano organizes research findings into three categories: school-level factors, teacher-level factors, and student-level factors. He writes, "We know what works in education. The research is prolific. The question today is not what works or what does not work. Rather it is why is it that we know what constitutes good teaching and effective learning and yet we fail to implement what we know?" (16).

Let us consider one way that media specialists can combine the "turnaround" qualities of connection and competence to influence what is perhaps the biggest academic shortcoming faced by students— reading. For children to become literate they must have the vocabulary to understand ideas, concepts, and experiences, but many of the students who are the focus of NCLB come to school without the background knowledge to support vocabulary development and literacy. Even the most carefully chosen collection is not going to improve this situation, but a proactive media specialist who connects with students, identifying their interests and strengths as well as their needs, will be able to use her competence to build the students' background knowledge. Interestingly, Marzano found that one way to develop background knowledge is through mentoring. In their resiliency research, Werner and Smith found that mentoring was the most significant way to strengthen struggling youth.

The Third C: Contribution

A third quality of the "turnaround" media specialist is contribution. The impact studies by Keith Curry Lance and his colleagues clearly show how media specialists contribute to the school's academic climate. Although socioeconomic status (SES) is perhaps the most significant predictor for high school dropout and low student achievement, Lance and his colleagues found that after accounting for socioeconomic status, "library media predictors almost always outperformed other school characteristics, such as teacher-pupil ration and per pupil expenditure" in improving student achievement" (6). The message for media specialists is than an effective school library benefits students. He and his colleagues identify those predictors in the summary of their research, noting that "reading scores increase with increases in the following characteristics of library media (LM) programs: LM program development, information technology, teacher/library media specialist (LMS) collaboration, and individual visits to the library media center (LMC). In addition, as participation increases in leadership roles, so does collaboration between teachers and LMSs. The relationship between these factors and test scores is not explained away by other school or community conditions" (3).

To learn more about these studies go to <www.lrs.org>. There is also an excellent review of impact study findings by state in the North Carolina report titled *An Essential Connection: How Quality School Library Media Programs Improve Student Achievement in North Carolina* by Robert Burgin and Pauletta Brown Bracy. This report is available at <www.rburgin.cm/NCschools2003/NCSchoolStudy.pdf>.

The message for media specialists is that an effective school library benefits students achievement and increases the resiliency of at-risk students. According to Lance, the school library contributes to student achievement when the media specialist collaborates with classroom teachers to deliver instruction; develops and manages quality collections to support the curriculum; integrates state-of-the-art technology into learning and teaching processes; and cooperates with other types of libraries, especially public libraries.

The Media Program as a Tipping Point

If the media specialist doubts her power to serve as the "turnaround teacher" for at-risk students, they need only to look at Gladwell's notion of a "tipping point"—a small focused effort that leads to big changes. In *The Tipping Point: How Little Things Can Make a Big Difference,* Gladwell describes how the theory of "Fixing Broken Windows" can turn around negative situations. Epidemics, which he defines as negative situations affecting a large number of persons [authors' note: low test scores and significant gaps in achievement fit this description], "can be reversed, can be tipped, by tinkering with the smallest details of the immediate environment" (146). One example he offers is his description of how, in the 1980s, one small change turned around the impending collapse of the New York City subway, which was overwhelmed by crime, filth, and trains that did not run on schedule. At the urging of a consultant, the New York Transit Authority focused on eliminating graffiti. Singling out this problem may seem inconsequential compared to other challenges facing the subway system, but the graffiti was viewed as the "symbolic collapse of the system" (142). Eradicating graffiti was the tipping point—the small change—that transformed a beleaguered subway system into one of the world's best. "Turnaround" media specialists recognize the

importance of implementing the small changes—the tipping points—that can transform low-achieving students into high-achieving ones. For media specialists, the tipping point for at-risk students is not graffiti, but rather the 3 Cs: connection, competence, and contribution.

Works Cited

Benard, Bonnie. "How to Be a Turnaround Teacher." *Reaching Today's Youth: The Community Circle of Caring Journal* 2.3 (1998): 31–35.

Gladwell, Malcolm. *The Tipping Point: How Little Things Can Make a Big Difference.* New York: Little, Brown and Company, 2000.

Jones, Jami L., and Alana Zambone. *The Power of the Media Specialist to Improve Academic Achievement and Strengthen At-Risk Youth.* Worthington, OH: Linworth. 2007.

Lance, Keith Curry. "How School Librarians Leave No Child Behind: The Impact of School Library Media Programs on Academic Achievement of U.S. Public School Students." *School Libraries in Canada* 22.2 (2002): 3–6.

Lance, Keith Curry, Marcia J. Rodney, and Christine Hamilton Pennell. *How School Librarians Help Kids Achieve Standards: The Second Colorado Study.* Denver, CO: Colorado Department of Education, 2000.

Marzano, Robert J. *What Works in Schools: Translating Research into Action.* Alexandria, VA: ASCD, 2003.

Thernstrom, Abigail, and Stephan Thernstrom. *No Excuses: Closing the Racial Gap in Learning.* New York: Simon & Schuster, 2003.

Werner, Emmy, and Ruth S. Smith. *Overcoming the Odds: High Risk Children from Birth to Adulthood.* Ithaca, NY: Cornell University Press, 1992.

Yell, Michael, and Erik Drasgow. *No Child Left Behind: A Guide for Professionals.* Upper Saddle River, NJ: Pearson Prentice Hall, 2005.

Dr. Jami L. Jones *is an assistant professor at East Carolina University, Department of Library Science and Instruction Technology in Greenville, North Carolina. Dr. Alana M. Zambone is an assistant professor at East Carolina University, Department of Curriculum and Instruction in Greenville, North Carolina. Jami and Alana are co-authors of the new title from Linworth, The Power of the Media Specialist to Improve Academic Achievement and Strengthen At-Risk Students (2008).*

Jones, Jami L., & Zambone, Alana M. (2008). The role of the media specialist to improve academic achievement and strengthen at-risk youth. *LMC, 26*(7), 30–32.

Together We Can: Collaborating to Meet the Needs of At-Risk Students

By Karen Gavigan and Stephanie Kurtts

With an annual dropout rate of roughly 1.2 million students, far too many children and youth are being left behind in our nation's schools. As a consequence of the large dropout rate, it is estimated that the United States loses almost $320 billion in potential earnings each year (CNN.com, 2010). It is apparent that educational reform is needed in order to identify at-risk students, and to develop programs to prevent them from leaving our schools. With the increasingly diverse educational needs of all students, it takes a team of professionals to ensure student success. School librarians can be integral members of these professional teams. Through collaborative activities, librarians can meet the needs of at-risk students by working to implement strategies designed to help them experience academic success and prevent them from dropping out of school. As stated in the common beliefs of the American Association of School Librarians (AASL) *Standards for the 21st-Century Learner* (AASL, 2009), "school libraries are essential to the development of learning skills" and "School librarians collaborate with others to provide instruction, learning strategies, and practice in using the essential learning skills needed in the 21st century" (p. 11).

Defining At-Risk Students

Data collected as a result of federal and state legislation are a good indicator of which students are meeting standards and which students are most at risk. For example, the White House recently reported that almost half of our nation's dropouts are Latino or African-American students (CNN.com, 2010). In addition to race and ethnicity, other characteristics of at-risk students include:

- Low socioeconomic status
- English Language Learners

- Disabilities and identified as special ed
- Moves frequently
- Poor reading skills
- Grade retention one or more years
- Multiple suspensions and expulsions
- Single parent households
- Home alone more than three hours a day
- Pregnancy
- Drug use
- Bored with school (Jones, 2006, p. 11)

Once at-risk students have been identified, the challenge is to implement comprehensive school-wide initiatives for keeping them in schools and to close the existing achievement gap. School librarians offer information literacy and technology instruction that is crucial for 21st century learners, particularly marginalized at-risk learners who may not have access to resources and computers in their homes. Furthermore, school libraries can provide students equal access to print and digital resources to help close the gap between privileged and at-risk students.

Keith Curry Lance and library researchers nationwide have consistently demonstrated that quality school library programs have a positive impact on academic achievement (Lance, 1994; Lance, 2002a, 2002b; Lance, Wellburn & Hamilton-Pennell, 1993; Lance, Rodney & Hamilton-Pennell, 2003a, 2003b). Unfortunately, however, administrators and stakeholders are often slow to recognize the role that school librarians can play when it comes to the needs of at-risk learners. Furthermore, in spite of the fact that most at-risk students have poor reading skills, school libraries are often ignored when it comes to dropout prevention efforts.

Therefore, it is imperative for school librarians to be a part of collaborative student support teams. Furthermore, principals need to understand the potential of the library program on student learning. As stated by Shannon (2009), ". . . the school librarian must be proactive in showing him or her how the library program supports the school's goals and impacts student achievement" (p. 19).

Using their knowledge of the overall curriculum, technological expertise, and the ability to locate resources, school librarians are in a unique position to collaborate with the educational team to teach and evaluate at-risk students. Librarians can support at-risk students in their academic, social, behavioral, and emotional success by offering them engaging and relevant instruction, increased personal attention, and improved relationships with adults (Jones & Zambone, 2007, 2009). Furthermore, caring and compassionate librarians can make school libraries places where at-risk students' differences are acknowledged and respected.

Working side by side with others on the team, the school librarian can help to implement school-based interventions such as mentoring programs. For example, the LISTEN (Linking Individual Students to Educational Needs) program proved to be successful for at-risk students in Tennessee (Lampley & Johnson, 2010). School librarians, administrators, counselors, teaching assistants, cafeteria workers, and retired teachers met with the students twice a week during the school year to establish relationships with at-risk students. These mentors were trained to work with the students on study skills, interpersonal relationships, problem solving, and communication skills. The results were positive, with 49 of the 54 LISTEN participants experiencing improvement in the areas of GPAs, discipline referrals, and attendance records.

Librarian's Role as a Member of a Collaborative Educational Team—Response to Intervention

All educational professionals, including librarians, should have knowledge of the services available to identify students at risk for academic failure. Increasingly, schools are turning to Response to Intervention (RtI), a student-focused approach using evidence-based tiered instructional practices that promotes early identification for students who struggle academically or behaviorally (Hawkins et al., 2008; Mellard & McKnight, 2008). Addressed specifically in the reauthorized Individuals with Disabilities Improvement Education Act of 2004, RtI is based on individual student educational needs (U.S. Department of Education, 2005). RtI is founded on the premise that with data-based decision making and evidence-based practices many children, who otherwise may have been identified with a disability, will have the opportunity to have their educational needs met in general education settings. Overall, RtI has the potential for keeping a class together by promoting instruction in inclusive learning environments and may lead to better achievement and behavior outcomes for all students (Fletcher et al., 2004).

Caring and compassionate librarians can make school libraries places where at-risk students' differences are acknowledged and respected.

Evidence-Based Practices and Strategies for Intervention

Evidence and research-based practices are critical components of intervention to be used by teams of educational professionals as they

address the needs of their students. Listed are several key practices that librarians should understand as they develop collaborative partnerships with teachers. These interventions are not exclusive; however, they may be used to implement a student-focused approach such as RtI to address the needs of struggling students.

Differentiated instruction. In a differentiated classroom, all students are included in the learning experience based on their individual learning styles. Teachers who incorporate differentiated instruction ensure that each student is equally important to the learning process. For example, through activities such as peer teaching and cooperative learning, students have the opportunity to become active learners, decision makers, and problem solvers. Differentiated classrooms challenge children of all ability levels (Jenkins, 2005).

Universal Design for Learning (UDL). The use of UDL offers students with diverse strengths and abilities, along with their teachers, multiple and flexible opportunities to make curricular goals accessible (Hitchcock, 2001). The function of UDL is not to modify or add on to a pre-existing lesson but rather to transform instruction from the outset in order to broaden the definition of the learners who are expected to succeed in the general education environment (Pisha & Coyne, 2001). UDL can support teachers as they anticipate a wide range of learning styles and abilities in the classroom.

Culturally Responsive Instruction (CRI). Teachers who practice CRI foster a climate of caring, value, and respect to promote student performance. As such, educators are able to use a student's cultural and societal context as a vehicle for learning (Klump & McNeir, 2005). Culturally responsive classrooms make real-life connections based on children's experiences. Activities can include developing literacy skills across curricula, as well as learning from and about culture, language, and learning styles (Lipka, 2002).

In addition to academic support, many at-risk students will be in need of behavioral interventions that can

be enhanced by the involvement of the librarian. Two examples of these interventions include a positive behavioral support system and positive classroom management.

A positive behavioral support system is a school-wide approach that focuses on proactive and preventive, rather than aversive and punitive, behavioral techniques (Sugai & Horner, 2001). Interventions are designed to decrease problem behaviors and to improve the quality of life for students exhibiting those behaviors. This is accomplished through increasingly intensive supports and data-based decision making. School faculties, of which librarians are an integral part, develop school-wide management plans while incorporating these plans into the daily routines of the school thus providing a framework for reinforcing compliance. Students are taught what behaviors are expected and held accountable and rewarded for meeting expectations (Kern & Manz, 2004).

Positive classroom management includes behavior management processes and interventions to enhance the development of student behaviors that are personally fulfilling, productive, and socially acceptable (Salend, 2008). Interventions may include creating a reward system, setting clear social and instructional goals instruction or a combination of the two (Cheney, 2008). As interventions are implemented, progress monitoring activities are conducted to make informed, data-based decisions about the students' progress in developing appropriate behaviors.

While working in collaborative partnerships with teachers, librarians may also take time to get to know their at-risk students by applying specific strategies that meet individual student needs. These strategies include:

■ Developing library collections that include universally designed resources on a variety of levels and in a variety of formats to meet the unique needs and learning styles of at-risk learners (examples include bilingual titles, graphic novels, and interactive books)

- Developing library collections that include culturally relevant curriculum materials based on students' backgrounds, languages, experiences, and interests
- Providing opportunities for students to become engaged and feel successful in their reading (examples include book clubs, reader's theater, poetry slams, and Teen Read Week)
- Educating themselves about at-risk students and providing information literacy instruction and library services that can be customized to their learning needs
- Making the library a welcoming and supportive place for students to come before, during, and after school by including comfortable reading areas, posters, and creative signage
- Involving the community by encouraging active participation from parents and community leaders through programming and/ or tutoring services

Closing

In today's global economy, a high school degree is a stepping stone to success whether a student is pursuing a career or higher education. It will take a school-wide effort to help at-risk students become engaged in learning, and choosing to remain in school until they graduate. As an active member of a school team supporting at-risk students, school librarians should work with other educational professionals toward the common goal of helping at-risk students experience academic success in a non-threatening school environment.

References

American Association of School Librarians. *Standards for the 21st-Century Learner in Action.* Chicago: American Association of School Librarians, 2009.

Cheney, D. *RTI and the Behavior-Response to What Intervention? Part II. CEC Blog.* 2008. 3 June 2010 <http://cecblog.typepad.com/ RTI/2008/10/RTI-and-the-b-2 .html#more>.

CNN.com. *Obama Highlights Federal Funds to Lower High School Dropout Rate.* 2010. 10 June 2010. <http://www.cnn.com/2010/ POLITICS/03/01/obama .education/index.html>.

Fletcher, J. M., M.W. Coulter, D.J. Reschly & S. Vaughn. "Alternative Approaches to the Definition and Identification of Learning Disabilities: Some Questions and Answers." *Annals of Dyslexia* 54(2) (2004): 304–31.

Hawkins, R., S. Kroger, S. Musti-Roa, D. Barnett & J. Ward. "Preservice Training in Response to Intervention: Learning by Doing an Interdisciplinary Field Experience." *Psychology in the Schools* 45(8) (2008): 745–762.

Hitchcock, C. "Balanced Instructional Support and Challenge in Universally Designed Learning Environments." *Journal of Special Education Technology* 16 (2001): 23–30.

Jenkins, R.A. "Interdisciplinary Instruction in the Inclusion Classroom." *Teaching Exceptional Children* 37(5) (2005): 42–48.

Jones, J.L. "Dropout Prevention through the School Library: Dispositions, Relationships, and Instructional Practices." *School Libraries Worldwide* 15(2) (2009): 77–90.

Jones, J.L. "The Numbers Are Astounding? The Role of the Media Specialist in Dropout Prevention." *Library Media Connection* 25 (2) (2006)10–13.

Jones, J.L. & A.M. Zambone. *The Power of the Media Specialist to Improve Academic Achievement and Strengthen At-Risk Students.* Santa Barbara, CA: Linworth Publishing, 2008.

Jones, J.L. & A.M. Zambone. "The Role of the Media Specialist to Improve Academic Achievement and Strengthen At-Risk Youth." *Library Media Connection* 26 (7) (2008): 30–32.

Kern, L., & P. Manz. "A Look at Current Validity Issues of School-Wide Behavior Support." *Behavioral Disorders* 30 (2004): 47–59.

Klump, J. & G. McNeir. *Culturally Responsive Practices for Student Success: A Regional Sampler.* Northwest Regional Educational Laboratory. 2005. 7 June 2010. <http://www.nwrel.org/ request/2005june/what.html>.

Lampley, J.J. & J.C. Johnson. "Mentoring At-Risk Youth: Improving Academic Achievement in Middle School Students." *Nonpartisan Education Review* 6 (1) (2010): 1–12.

Lance, K.C. "The Impact of School Library Media Centers on Academic Achievement (in Colorado)." *School Library Media Quarterly* 22(1994): 167–170.

Lance, K.C. "The Impact of School Library Media Centers on Academic Achievement." *Teacher Librarian: The Journal for School Library Professionals* 29 (3) (2002): 29–34.

Lance, K.C. "What Research Tells Us About the Importance of School Libraries." *Teacher Librarian: The Journal for School Library Professionals* 30 (1)(2002): 76–78

Lance, K.C., L. Wellburn & C. Hamilton-Pennell. *The Impact of School Library Media Centers on Academic Achievement.* Castle Rock, CO: Hi Willow Research & Publishing, 1993.

Lance, K.C., M. Rodney & C. Hamilton-Pennell. *How School Libraries Improve Outcomes for Children: The New Mexico Study.* San Jose, CA: Hi Willow Press, 2003.

Lance, K.C., M. Rodney & C. Hamilton-Pennell. *The Impact of Michigan School Librarians on Academic Achievement: Kids Who Have Libraries Succeed.* Lansing, MI: Library of Michigan, 2003.

Lipka, J. *Schooling for Self-Determination: Research on the Effects of Including Native Language and Culture in the Schools* [ERIC digest]. Charleston, WV: ERIC Clearinghouse on Rural Education and Small Schools. 2002. 6 June 2010 <www.indianeduresearch.net/ edorc01–12.htm>.

Mellard, D., & M. McKnight. *RTI Implementation Tool: Best Practices for Grades K-5. (2008).* National Center on Response to Intervention. 2008. 6 June 2010 <www.RTI4success.org>.

Pisha, B. & P. Coyne. "Smart from the Start: The Promise of Universal Design for Learning." *Remedial and Special Education* 22(2001): 197–203.

Salend, S. *Creating Inclusive Classrooms: Effective and Reflective Practices* (6th ed.). Upper Saddle River, New Jersey: Prentice Hall, 2008.

Sugai, G. & R. Horner. "Features of an Effective Behavior Support System at the School District Level." *Beyond Behavior* 11(1) (2001): 16–19.

U.S. Department of Education, Office of Special Education and Rehabilitative Services, Office of Special Education Programs. *26th Annual (2004) Report to Congress on the Implementation of the Individuals with Disabilities Education Act* 1 (2005): 20–47.

Web Resources

Center on Instruction—Information on Research-Based Instruction
http://serge.ccsso.org
A collection of scientifically based research and information on K-12 instruction.

Differentiated Instruction—Education World
http://www.educationworld.com/a_curr/virtualwkshp/virtualwkshp006.shtml
A virtual workshop on differentiated instruction with lists of additional resources.

Intervention Central—Response to Intervention (RtI)
http://www.interventioncentral.org

A comprehensive site for RtI resources; includes academic and behavior interventions.

SERGE—Special Education Resources for General Educators
http://serge.ccsso.org
Contains some of the most widely implemented strategies to help all students succeed.

Understanding Problem Behavior—An Interactive Tutorial
http://serc.gws.uky.edu/pbis
Part of a series of training materials to support the efforts of the Center on Positive Behavioral Interventions and Supports.

Karen Gavigan *is an assistant professor at the School of Library and Information Science at the University of South Carolina in Columbia, South Carolina.*

Stephanie Kurtts *is an assistant professor in the School of Specialized Education Services at the University of North Carolina at Greensboro (North Carolina). She can be reached at sakurtts@uncg.edu.*

Gavigan, Karen, & Kurtts, Stephanie. (2010). Together we can: Collaborating to meet the needs of at-risk students. *LMC, 29*(3), 10–12.

Using Assistive Technology to Meet Diverse Learner Needs

By Stephanie Kurtts, Nicole Dobbins, and Natsuko Takemae

Implementing new and advanced technology for instruction and access to the curriculum for the increasingly diverse student populations in our schools can be a daunting task for even the most tech-savvy school personnel. This task can be even more challenging when devices, tools, and systems associated with assistive, or adaptive, technology are part of an individualized education program (IEP) for students with disabilities. School librarians should be knowledgeable about how assistive technology (AT) becomes part of a student's learning. Being a member of the team of classroom teachers, administrators, specialists, and parents who are striving to meet the needs of children who learn differently and require instructional accommodations or modifications to the curriculum using AT can be an essential role for school librarians.

Legislation and Assistive Technology Defined

While all students can benefit from the implementation of technology into the delivery of effective instruction, students with identified educational disabilities may have individualized education plans which require devices, tools, or systems as part of their instruction. The Individuals with Disabilities in Education Act (IDEA) in 1990 (P.L. 105–476) defined assistive technology, mandated schools to provide AT devices and services for students with disabilities, and addressed what those would be for an individual student's individualized education plan (Assistive Technology Training Online Project, 2005). Further legislation, IDEA 1997 (P.L. 105–17), reinforced students' rights to receive AT devices and services addressed on IEPs, and allowed students to use these AT devices and services outside school settings (Office of Special Education and Rehabilitative Services, 2003).

One thing that has been consistent across the legislation is the definition of assistive technology. The Individuals with Disabilities in Education Act 2004 defines an assistive technology device as "any item, piece of equipment, or product system, whether acquired commercially off the shelf, modified, or customized that is used to increase, maintain, or improve functional capabilities of a child with a disability" (U.S. Department of Education, 2011). In addition, the IDEA 2004 supports the uses of AT devices and/or services in order to encourage students' maximized access to learning. This also includes training and technical assistance for service providers and educators so that AT can be selected, acquired, and utilized in a way that a student's needs are met (U.S. Department of Education, 2011). As such, the technology associated with serving students with disabilities has evolved. A variety of devices have been invented, reinvented, and advanced.

With over 5,400,000 children receiving special education services across the country, increasingly in general education classrooms and in inclusive educational settings, the need for effective and innovative technology-based programs that respond to individual student needs is critical (U.S. Department of Education, 2005). The school librarian can provide a valuable service for teachers, related service providers, and families in integrating media resources to assist in the delivery of instruction and providing access to the curriculum while using instructional AT tools and devices. School librarians are in a unique position to do this based on their comprehensive understanding of the curriculum, expertise in the areas of instructional technology, and the ability to locate a variety of resources (Gavigan and Kurtts, 2010).

Universal Design for Learning and the Tools of Assistive Technology

The evolution of AT includes the creation of more sophisticated educational software as well as more responsive and unobtrusive assistive devices. Technology can enhance the academic and social success of the students as well as provide a link between the information taught by the teacher and the expected academic and social behaviors the student is expected to perform (Reisberg, 1990).

> With over 5,400,000 children receiving special education services across the country, the need for effective and innovative technology-based programs that respond to individual student needs is critical.

Curriculum that considers the specific needs of students with disabilities and makes use of technology should include appropriate content as well as the method of instruction. Universal Design for Learning (UDL) can enhance the use of technology integration and assistive technology for all students, including those with disabilities. UDL transforms instruction from the outset in order to broaden the definition of the learners who are expected to succeed in the general education environment without "adding-on" accommodations or modifications (Pisha and Coyne, 2001).

By implementing the principles of UDL along with the use of assistive technology teachers can rethink how they plan instruction for their students and their needs in the classroom. Teachers who understand the principles of UDL in lesson planning consider diverse students' needs to be the result of normal variance within a heterogeneous population rather than isolated instances of difference or disability (McGuire, Scott, and Shaw, 2006). Lessons planned using innovative strategies supported by UDL indicate that teachers anticipate a wide range of learning styles and abilities in the classroom, and are prepared to adapt instruction that will most effectively meet all students' needs (Kurtts, Matthews, and Smallwood, 2009). By definition, the UDL lesson is flexible and deliberately multifaceted in order to engage all students as they work to meet curricular goals through multiple and varied interactions with instructional materials and activities (Gavigan and Kurtts, 2009; Orkwis, 2003).

Assistive technology tools and devices are an integral part of the implementation of UDL principles across instruction. AT tools and devices can be low-technology, mid-technology, and high technology. Low tech tools, which could be used by all students in the classroom, thus enhancing access to the curriculum, might include specialized writing tools, pencil grips, planners, raised-line paper, or highlighting pens and tapes. Mid-tech tools, also used by all students, might include timers, spell checkers, tape recorders, digital recorders, calculators, and alternative keyboards. Low, mid, and high-tech tools can serve as assistive technology when indicated in an IEP as a tool to provide access to instruction or can also serve to enhance engagement with the curriculum (Gavigan and Kurtts, 2009).

Universal Design for Learning (UDL) can enhance the use of technology integration and assistive technology for all students, including those with disabilities.

Focus on High-Tech Tools

High-tech AT tools are becoming more common as advanced and specialized technology becomes increasingly available to classrooms and all students. School librarians may be frequently called upon to provide assistance in implementing the use of the tools and should have the opportunity for training in the use of the technology tools.

While high-tech tools and devices are too numerous to list here, school librarians and teachers may be familiar with touch screens, adapted computers, software programs, portable keyboards, audiobooks, word processing software, word prediction software, instruction websites, and communication (Hitchcock and Stahl, 2003). The chart provides examples of high-tech tools along with a description of each tool, what the tools are used for, and what type of learning difference may be supported. Through these tools, school librarians can lead collaborative activities with teachers as they work to improve learning outcomes for students with disabilities or diverse learning needs.

Preparation for school personnel in the use of high-tech tools is a must for the most effective implementation of instruction supported and enhanced by the technology. School librarians may be the key to this training and assistance, encouraging collaboration between educators while enhancing the implementation of UDL principles and the use of AT tools with innovative technology-based strategies to improve outcomes for all students.

Bibliography

Assistive Technology Training Online Project (ATTO), (2005). *Assistive Technology Legislation.* Web. 22 Aug. 2011. http://atto .buffalo.edu/registered/ATBasics /Foundation/Laws/atlegislation .php.

Gavigan, K., and S.A. Kurtts. "AT, UD, and Thee: Using Assistive Technology and Universal Design for Learning in 21st Century Media Centers." *Library Media Connection* 27.4 (2009): 54–56.

Gavigan, K., and S.A. Kurtts. "Together We Can: Collaborating to Meet the Need of At-Risk Students." *Library Media Connection* 29.3 (2010): 10–13.

Hitchcock, C., and S. Stahl. "Assistive Technology, Universal Design, Universal Design for Learning: Improved Learning Opportunities." *Journal of Special Education Technology* 18.4 (2003): 45–52.

Kurtts, S.A., C. Matthews, and T. Smallwood. "(Dis)Solving the Differences: A Physical Science Lesson Using Universal Design." *Intervention in School & Clinic* 44.3 (2009): 151–159.

McGuire, J.M., S.S. Scott, and S.F. Shaw. "Universal Design and Its Application in Educational Environments." *Remedial and Special Education* 27 (2006): 166–175.

Office of Special Education and Rehabilitative Services. *IDEA '97: The Law.* 2003. Web. 14 Aug. 2011. www2.ed.gov/offices/ OSERS/Policy/IDEA/the_law. html.

Orkwis, R. *Universally Designed Instruction* (ERIC digest No. E641). ERIC Clearninghouse on Disabilities and Gifted Education. 2003. Web. 2 Jul. 2008. www .ericec.org/digests/e641.html.

Pisha, B., and P. Coyne. "Smart from the Start: The Promise of Universal Design for Learning." *Remedial and Special Education* 22 (2001): 197–203.

Reisberg, L. "Curriculum Evaluation and Modification: An Effective Teaching Perspective." *Intervention in School and Clinic* 26 (1990): 99–105.

U.S. Department of Education, Office of Special Education and Rehabilitative Services, Office of Special Education Programs. *26th Annual (2004) Report to Congress on the Implementation of the Individuals with Disabilities Education Act, 1.* Washington, D.C., 2005: 20–47.

U.S. Department of Education. *Building the Legacy: IDEA 2004.*

2011. Web. 14 Aug 2011.
http://idea.ed.gov/explore
/search?search_option=all&
query=assistive+technology&
GO.x=0&GO.y=0.

Stephanie Kurtts *is an associate professor in the Department of Specialized Education Services at the University of North Carolina Greensboro.*

Nicole Dobbins *is an assistant professor in the Department of Specialized Education Services at the University of North Carolina Greensboro.*

Natsuko Takemae *is a doctoral student in the Department of Specialized Education Services at the University of North Carolina Greensboro.*

Kurtts, Stephanie, Dobbins, Nicole, & Takemae, Natsuko. (2012). Using assistive technology to meet diverse learner needs. *LMC, 30*(4), 22–23.

Taking a Page from the Art Museum: Curation as Mediation

By Sue C. Kimmel

Imagine walking into an art museum for the first time. Move past the lobby into the exhibit rooms. The museum is divided into rooms. Each room has several works of art facing out on the walls. Your eyes take in the entire room and notice the content and arrangement of works. You may notice how works were chosen and displayed to represent the work of a single artist, a theme, or a time period. Then you focus on a particular work, and walking closer you begin to take in other details. You stop to read the title, the medium used, and the artist's name. Moving around the room, you may find that the arrangement causes you to notice relationships among the works that are chronological or that cause you to notice the way an artist uses a particular color, medium, shape, or theme in the chosen works. A bench may be placed in front of a particular piece, inviting you to linger and study it more.

How Is a Library Like an Art Museum?

Now let's think about the museum visit as a mediated information-seeking activity and compare it with a visit to a library. When you enter a library, you have access to the entire collection, while in the museum a curator has selected particular pieces for you. In the library, the collection has been carefully selected to meet the needs and interests of the community of which an individual visitor is one member. A visitor may find what he or she needs, but will often require further mediation or help from the library catalog or library staff. In the museum, an art expert has pulled particular pieces from a collection and displayed them in such a way that their arrangement also provides information about unifying themes or distinct differences. Labels are unobtrusively placed next to the artwork, providing information about the title, artist, medium, and date. The room itself may have a plaque with a statement from the artist or curator. Scanning the room, a newcomer could go immediately to a work of interest, linger there, and then attend to adjacent pieces for contrast or comparison. Much of the work of mediation has already been completed in the selection, display, and annotation of the museum exhibit.

The Need for Digital Curation

The best libraries borrow from the museum concept with book displays, themed sections, and annotated suggestions. Libraries also provide access to virtual collections through the Internet. While the library has collected and cataloged materials for a well-defined community, the Internet is an amassed collection of links that have not been cataloged and represent the universe of needs and interests. The visitor who wanders into this space will soon experience information overload and little, if any, mediation or assistance in his or her information search. Some have compared it to a huge library with all the materials in one big pile. Others have said it's like trying to drink from the forceful flow of a fire hydrant. As information professionals, how can we begin to offer some form of mediation for our patrons in their use of this space? Led by the work of Joyce Valenza, the field of school librarianship has turned to the concept of "digital curation." Valenza describes the work of curators: "Curators make sense of the vast amounts of content that are continually produced. They are talented at scouting, identifying relevance, evaluating, classifying, organizing, and presenting aggregated content for a targeted audience" (Valenza, 2012).

Digital curation borrows heavily from the museum format. Curation provides a very selective collection, designed and arranged to meet the needs of a particular audience. A curated collection differs from a collection because it is tailored to a particular audience or need *and* it is presented in a manner that adds value to the selection. A digital curation is a curated collection of digital objects available online or through the Internet. In schools the particular audience and need are most often curricular. School librarians might digitally curate objects related to a fourth grade unit on electricity, the study of an author, or a high school unit on cell biology.

Digital Curation vs. Pathfinders

Digital curation builds on the kinds of services school librarians have traditionally provided, such as curricular pathfinders or collected links. Curation differs from pathfinders in the intended purpose. A good pathfinder is a navigation tool that leads the user to choose their own path, making decisions based on their information need and topic. A pathfinder scaffolds the user in creating their own targeted search strategies in order to conduct their own research. Curation brings together the results of the curator's research and reflects decisions made by the curator about what to include and how to present the resources. The selector adds value through curation in terms of the very focused selection, the arrangement of the material, and the addition of tags or annotations.

Digging Deep

Let's return to the museum model to think about these distinctions. Like a museum curator, a school librarian is a professional who understands the big picture of what's available and can select particular objects that represent unique perspectives, avoid duplication, or might be lost in a crowded collection. In a curated collection, the school librarian is not going to leave a student on the front steps of a large museum or on the front page of a large site such as the Smithsonian website (www .si.edu). Instead, the curator will dig deeper into a site to find the page that provides an aspect of the topic that is not available elsewhere.

A curated collection does not provide multiple links that repeat the same information. Think about a famous person, such as Rosa Parks. It's possible to find numerous sites that provide her written biography. Beyond the first one or two sites, a student may struggle to really find anything new about this subject. The curator of this topic might find one very good textual biography of Rosa Parks to include in the curation. A great digital curation takes advantage of the multimedia available on the Internet and looks to extend this textual resource with images, video, audio, and simulations that engage students in new understandings of the topic. While a collection of links about Rosa Parks might include the Henry Ford Museum Rosa Parks Bus site (http://www.thehenryford .org/exhibits/rosaparks/home.asp), the curator would dig deeper into this site to find the famous bus and a three dimensional scan where the

visitor can virtually board the bus and see where Rosa Parks sat (www .thehenryford.org/exhibits/rosaparks/ images/restored/ROSA_PARKS_ BUS.mov).

Value Added

A curator in a museum carefully arranges objects so that they tell a chronological, topical, or thematic story. A digital curation should also be carefully arranged. In a digital curation, the platform determines the way the content will be displayed and the kinds of relationships the structure demonstrates. Platforms such as Pearltrees, Pinterest, and Livebinders each offer different kinds of arrangements and should be selected to best present the particular topic to an audience.

Pearltrees offers a branching or hierarchical arrangement that is suitable for more complex kinds of information. Value is added to Pearltrees in the arrangement of the pearls; the curator offers information about how the topics relate to each other by the placement of pearls on various branches.

Pinterest provides very visual access to a page of images that each lead back to a website. Tags, or brief descriptions, or instructions can be provided for the user for each of the websites. Like the room in the museum, it's possible to scan the

room to find an image of particular interest but also move through the page in a linear order.

Livebinders look like tabs in a notebook or file drawer. Content curated in a Livebinder is subdivided by tabs that could be arranged by date or subtopic.

A curator decides how to display and group content. Like a museum, the curator may add labels to each object and include a "curator's statement" about how the items were chosen and arranged. In a curated collection, the expertise of the curator is apparent through the choices made regarding what to include (and exclude) from the exhibit, how the selections are displayed, including their arrangement, and through the labels or other brief but relevant information. Librarians are particularly skilled at this because we understand selection, description, and organization of information.

The Librarian as Concierge

Clearly the work of digital curation is time consuming and requires a level of knowledge and critical thinking about content. Digital curation is a concierge level of library service. How can busy librarians possibly do this? First, school library professionals *are* doing this. The busy school librarian should look for digital curations that have already been created and begin to "curate" those. For example, combine your search for the Harlem Renaissance with Livebinder, or a search for fractals with Pinterest.

When Valenza says that curation is the "new search" she means that we begin looking for what others have curated as a search strategy (Valenza, 2011). Digital curation is the type of knowledge work that we are especially trained for; it's an area where we can display our skill and knowledge in terms of available content, curriculum, and the needs of our users. In an era of information overload it's a service our users need. And finally, we can begin to teach our students to create digital curations. School librarians should curate because we have the particular expertise. We can share with others and look for what others have shared. And we can teach our students

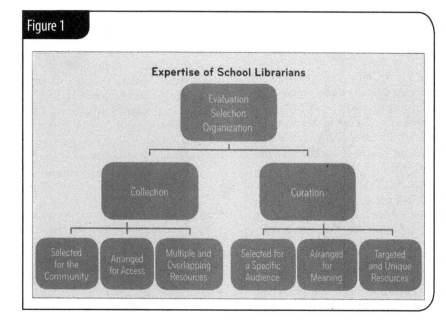

Figure 1

Expertise of School Librarians

Evaluation Selection Organization

Collection

Curation

Selected for the Community

Arranged for Access

Multiple and Overlapping Resources

Selected for a Specific Audience

Arranged for Meaning

Targeted and Unique Resources

to curate and to collect and share their creations.

Works Cited

Valenza, J. "Curation Is the New Search Tool." Neverending Search Blog. 30 Sept. 2011. Web. http://blog.schoollibraryjournal.com/neverendingsearch/2011/09/30/curation-tools-are-also-search-tools.

Valenza, J. K. "Curation." *School Library Monthly* 29.1 (2012). Web. www.schoollibrarymonthly.com/articles/Valenza2012-v29n1p20.html.

Sue C. Kimmel, *Ph.D., is an assistant professor, School Libraries/Dept. of Teaching and Learning, Darden College of Education at Old Dominion University in Norfolk, Virginia. She may be reached at skimmel@odu.edu.*

Kimmel, Sue C. (2013). Taking a page from the art museum: Curation as mediation. *LMC, 31*(5), 16–17.

Stemming the Tide of Plagiarism: One Educator's View

By Kathy Lehman

Is cheating widespread among high school students today? The unfortunate answer is YES. Do they see themselves as cheaters? No. What steps can teachers and school librarians take to stem the tide of cheating? Absolutely.

Last fall a class of Teacher Cadets at my high school participated in a round table discussion on ethics in the classroom. Teacher Cadets make up an elective dual enrollment class with the community college for future teachers. The round table was part of an effort to provide student input for a webinar produced by Linworth and iParadigms (Turnitin). These students were assigned a background e-text reading "Cheating in Academic Contexts" as preparation for the classroom and online group discussion which preceded the round table. We asked: "How well do you measure up? Are academic pressures along with time management challenges tempting students to cross the line? Are students who fail to learn the process of writing papers and to study course content preparing themselves for the rigors of college and the workplace?" Students' frank and open comments opened our eyes to a startling point of view. Behaviors teachers and school librarians label as an ethical or moral are interpreted differently by students who regularly cheat. To them it is simply a time management issue solved by technology.

Student Voices

Students today feel the same time crunch as parents who fill their calendars with extracurricular activities. One student wrote, "Students cheat because they feel it is the easy way out. They feel like they are full to the brim with academic and outside of school activities, and they simply 'don't have the time' for homework and the like. They know that they have a safety net available. So, they think, 'So what!'" Another wrote, "Not only are there now more ways to cheat via technology, but more students are spending a lot of time using the technology. They will sit around texting, watching TV or on MySpace, Facebook or Aim. Maybe just listen to their iPod and put off the work they have to do. Given there are also so many kids involved with sports or clubs who don't have time to sit around and procrastinate. So if they cheat, it is because of poor time management. But why do we have poor time management? We're used to getting what we want when we want it." These young people know exactly what they are doing and why. Other student comments include:

"They just want the grade for completion and turning it in on time."

"I think the main reason students cheat is that most students are lazy. They wait to the last second to do their work and the only way to get it done is to get it from another source."

"Cheating is seen as the easy way out in many aspects and students love to make things easier for themselves."

"Students are more inclined to cheat when they have other academically challenging classes such as honors classes or AP classes. Other obligations such as sports or part time jobs can also create more pressure for students to cheat when they lack time to study and prepare themselves for an upcoming test or exam."

"Using the things around us to get something done is NOT 'cheating.'"

"Technology and other sources have provided so much information that it takes less effort to cheat than it does to actually do the assignment and learn from it."

"Cheating doesn't have the consequences it should."

> *When teachers break research steps down into sections with separate assessments, students will not be able to put a major project off to the last minute.*

Are all students in this camp? Many are frustrated and angered by their peers' behavior. One wrote, "To me cheating is like stealing, it should make you feel bad that you stole someone's idea or paper that they worked hard on . . . I work really hard to write my papers and do my school assignments." These students understand they need to study in school and learn the information in their school's curriculum. Their comments include: "Cheating won't help cheaters obtain the knowledge they need for the real world."

"Cheating is dumb and pointless. If a person cheats on a constant basis then they aren't retaining any information . . . so they have to cheat again and again."

"Cheating can become an extremely aggravating situation for students who honestly put forth effort needed to do well in their classes. When I see students cheating and receiving grades similar to mine, it really gets to me. While I'm spending hours studying terms and theories for psychology, they're off having fun and getting the same grades as me."

Nothing much has changed. For decades we have had morally upright students and students who have cheated on assignments. The difference is that today's technology makes it so easy that more are sliding down the slippery slope. Cutting and pasting off the Internet is so accepted, many simply do not understand that what they find and paste together is not their work. They need to learn beginning in their elementary years that research, writing papers and creating presentations involves not simply locating information but reading, paraphrasing, summarizing, and synthesizing from multiple sources to formulate their own ideas into a new product.

Some Possible Solutions

What can educators do to reduce cheating and support the students making the effort to study hard and earn honest grades?

- **Structure the environment to discourage cheating.** There need to be clear expectations for what constitutes cheating with enforced consequences for infringements. For each assignment from overnight homework to long-term projects, teachers must explain what can be done together and what must be completed individually.

- **Major assignments should engage learners.** Studies show students cheat less when they like their topic (Murdoch and Beauchamp). Teach good research skills in all grades and content areas following AASL's new *Standards for the 21st Century Learner.* When gathering and synthesizing information is well practiced it will not be such a formidable task put off until the last minute and impossible to complete properly. When teachers break research steps down into sections with separate assessments, students will not be able to put a major project off to the last minute.

- **Detailed rubrics are needed throughout the research and writing process so students can self assess as they move through each stage of the project.** Examples of rubrics for research, note cards, source cards, essays, peer editing, presentations and citations can be generated using rubric generating applications such as Rubistar <http://rubistar.4teachers.org< or Teach-nology <http://www.teach-nology.com/>.

- **Subscribe to a plagiarism checking subscription service such as Turnitin.com to allow students to check their work for originality before turning it in.**

This is an excellent self checking strategy to learn proper paraphrasing and summarizing as well as a deterrent to plagiarism. In our school, Turnitin is our number one defense against cheating. Turnitin's reports match a student's paper with others in the database. There will usually be some exact word matching due to direct quotes from literature texts and identical sources being used in frequently assigned topics.

To establish a proper classroom test environment to discourage cheating, the students agreed with the advice given in the studies listed in the article they read by Murdock and Beauchamp.

- **Constant monitoring by the teacher is the most important factor.** Students know if the

teacher is paying attention and resent teachers who are unaware of students pulling out cell phones against school rules to search the Internet, text back and forth or photograph questions and answers. One scenario was brought up of a teacher who said the first student to answer a bonus question at the end of a test would get extra points. Student A finishes the test, asks to be excused, pulls out a cell phone in the restroom and Googles the answer before the rest of the class finishes the test.

- **Students want teachers to require cover sheets during tests.** In another scenario a student describes her best friend asking if she can copy off her paper during a test. The night before the friend had a game and could not study. In this case loyalty to a friend trumps

Figure 1

THOMAS DALE HIGH SCHOOL RESEARCH RUBRIC

Name: _____ Teacher: _____

	Criteria				Points
	4	**3**	**2**	**1**	
Introduction/ Topic	Student(s) properly generate questions and or problems **around a topic.**	Student(s) **generate questions** and or problems.	Student(s) **require prompts** to generate questions and or problems.	Questions or problems are **teacher generated.**	
Conclusions Reached	**Numerous** detailed conclusions are reached from the evidence offered.	**Several** detailed conclusions are reached from the evidence offered.	**Some** detailed conclusions are reached from the evidence offered.	**A** conclusion is made from the evidence offered.	
Information Gathering	Information is gathered from multiple electronic and non-electronic sources and **cited properly.**	Information is gathered from **multiple** electronic and non-electronic sources.	Information is gathered from **limited** electronic and non-electronic sources.	Information is gathered from non-electronic or electronic sources **only.**	
Summary Paragraph	Well organized, demonstrates **logical** sequencing and sentence structure.	Well organized, but demonstrates illogical sequencing or sentence structure.	Well organized, but demonstrates illogical sequencing **and** sentence structure.	**Weakly** organized.	
Punctuation, Capitalization, & Spelling	Punctuation and capitalization are **correct.**	There is **one error** in punctuation and/ or capitalization.	There are **two or three errors** in punctuation and/ or capitalization.	There are **four or more** errors in punctuation and/or capitalization.	
				Total —>	

Teacher Comments:

ethics in her choice. She said wistfully, if the teacher required a cover sheet, I could have said, "Sorry, I have to use a cover sheet."

- **Students resent having studied and worked hard to make A's in a class and having another cheat to receive the same grade.** One student smiled and said, "Sometimes I just give them the wrong answers." In these last two scenarios, both students succumbed to peer pressure and shared answers. One even thinks she was not cheating because she gave wrong answers—she rationalizes that only the one receiving, not giving, the answers was cheating. Surely the one receiving the answers thinks she cheated.

Talk about It!

Ask your colleagues and share ideas in your building. Make multiple copies of the test with multiple answer keys. Change the order of essay questions. Change some details in essays so they are not exactly the same.

Organize discussions in your buildings so students have an opportunity to think about these issues and the implications of their choices on their future academic success as well as their current grades. They need to reconcile the ethical choices they are making between school, home, and friends. Have upperclassmen mentor lowerclassmen and lead the sessions. Models are available through organizations such as Integrity Works, <http://www.ethicsed.org/programs/integrity-works/index.htm>. Many of our students think differently about their choices as a result of our open dialogues.

At first I was shocked by the comments and attitudes of the students. I decided to have a heart to heart talk with one of our top library science students. I told him about David Conley's *Habits of Mind*—those qualities of higher order thinking and reasoning which include evaluating resources, and persisting with difficult tasks that every college freshman needs to acquire during their high school years before going on to college or university level work. I asked him, "Don't students realize they need to learn how to do research? If they take short cuts and cheat, they will not be prepared for college level work?" My student grinned and shook his head, NO. "They don't think about that, they are just thinking about getting through the week. Finishing this paper and going out with their friends."

We are dealing with many immature adolescents who will learn hard lessons after graduation when they struggle in college and the workplace because they did not learn their school's core curriculum or the basics of research in middle and high school. Banning cell phones and limiting access to the Internet is not the answer. They will find a way around these rules. **As educators, our task is to guide them to use this technology to become master researchers and to instill in them a determination not to be satisfied until they find the best sources.** Praise and reward is always the best motivator. Yes, subscribe to plagiarism software such as Turnitin but reward students who have 25% or less originality reports with extra points. We have to catch the cheaters and enforce penalties with significant consequences to deter them. We also have to set classroom parameters to protect those students who do not want to cheat and are forced by peer pressure to choose between their friends and their conscience. Their friends will win 90 % of the time.

Best practices have not changed. The technology has. Students have always procrastinated and looked to their peers to get help with their school work. Teachers have always worked to stay one step ahead of their students. As educators we need to be vigilant in the classroom and subscribe to online software that can track past submissions and monitor online sources. If we do not, our students will not be motivated to research, write original papers, and gain the critical thinking skills they will need to be successful in the 21st century.

Works Cited

American Association of School Librarians. *Standards for the 21st Century Learner*. Chicago: ALA, 2007.

Conley, David T. "Toward a More Comprehensive Concept of College Readiness." *EPIC: Educational Policy Improvement Center*. Bill and Melinda Gates Foundation, Mar. 2007. 27 Jan. 2010 <http://cepr.uoregon.edu/upload/Gates-College%20Readiness.pdf>.

Murdock, Tamera B. and Anne S. Beauchamp. "Cheating in Academic Contexts." *21st Century Education: A Reference Handbook*. Ed. Thomas L. Good. Thousand Oaks, CA: Sage Publications Inc., 2008. 426–433. *Gale Virtual Reference Library*. Gale. Thomas Dale High School. 22 Oct. 2009.

Plagiarism in the Digital Age: Voices from the Front Lines: What's Happening in High Schools Today? Moderator: David Wangaard, Executive Director, School for Ethical Education. 18 Nov. 2009. 27 Jan 2010 <http://www.plagiarism.org/plag_webinar_high_schools.html>.

Kathy Lehman *is an NBCT librarian at Thomas Dale High School in Chester, Virginia.*

Lehman, Kathy. (2010). Stemming the tide of plagiarism: One educator's view. *LMC, 29*(2), 44–46.

Deep Reading: Using Technology to Engage, Connect, and Share

By Sue C. Kimmel

[handwritten: I use book length as motivation ✓]

Our reading lives are increasingly digital and saturated with technology. Readers today are likely to be reading from a screen such as a webpage, a PDF, a Facebook or Twitter feed, or a text on a cell phone. With a sense of irony, I recently finished reading *The Shallows: What the Internet is Doing to Our Brains* on a Kindle and posted it on Goodreads, a social networking site for readers. In *The Shallows*, Carr suggests that new technologies are changing the reading brain and leading us away from the deep reading promoted by printed books toward the more surface and multitasking kinds of reading promoted by hypertext, Twitter and Facebook feeds, and multimedia. Carr makes a persuasive argument that new media detract from the deep thinking and sustained reading promoted by traditional printed texts. *[handwritten: yay!]*

The Changing Reading Landscape

Carr's caution about how changes in reading habits may be related to changes in our brains, our thinking, and our culture should give us pause as we think about using technology to promote reading. What kinds of technology should we be using to promote what kinds of reading? Today's new readers are as likely to encounter texts on screens as they are on printed pages. They need to be nimble and critical readers of all kinds of messages in a variety of media. How can we ensure that they also acquire the skills and stamina for deep reading and the deep thinking that accompanies it? Media use by youth ages eight to eighteen has increased over the past ten years, according to a study by the Kaiser Family Foundation, in all areas except the reading of print text (Rideout, Foehr, and Roberts, 2010). The study found that youth report reading fewer magazines *[handwritten: so sad]*

and newspapers, but book reading (for pleasure) has remained fairly constant. The drop in reading periodicals was offset somewhat by reading online. Youth did report an increase in multitasking, except when it came to reading books. The proportion of youth who reported multitasking most of the time while reading has remained fairly constant since 2004. The study was conducted in 2009 and did not report on e-readers, but it did report a dramatic increase in cell phone usage and texting. We can all attest to the experience of information overload and the easy distraction of email, messaging, and hyperlinks, yet this study suggests that young people still read in sustained and relatively quiet spaces. How could technology and the burgeoning use of social media in particular support deep reading and perhaps increase membership in a community that values deep reading and thinking?

Technology and Reading

Reading has always been supported by technology. Books were printed and bound, and required a source of light. A highlighter or pencil allowed one to mark or annotate passages. Today e-reading devices come either with a screen that is backlit or attachable lights so that reading may take place in a dimly lit or dark space. Often these devices weigh less than a book, automatically bookmark for you, and allow you to search for keywords or passages. Passages can be highlighted and annotated. Yes, at some point you are tethered to a source of electricity to recharge batteries, but in fact these generally last a long time—much longer than our cell phones. Books that filled shelves and weighed down suitcases can now fit on one device that we carry with us. The electronic book offers the ease of the printed book and accessories in *[handwritten: something about a good 'ole book]*

one handheld device. An e-reader may be less intimidating than a thick book because of the limited amount of text on the page and the ability to change font size. The kinds of devices available are rapidly expanding with numerous devices dedicated to reading and others, such as cell phones and iPads, have apps for reading e-books. These portable devices have wide appeal and application. E-book sales have skyrocketed and libraries are scrambling to determine how to offer access to all patrons. The Kaiser Foundation study found that youth are increasingly owners of cell phones; in 2009, eighty-five percent of youth aged fifteen to eighteen reported owning a cell phone. It shouldn't be a huge step for us to ensure that they have books on those devices. Many of the classics are available for free download. Let's teach our students how to add a book app and load free books to their smartphones so that they always have something to read. *[handwritten: yes! ✓]*

> Books that filled shelves and weighed down suitcases can now fit on one device that we carry with us.

Enhancing the Reading Experience

Reading is about making connections. E-readers often have a small library loaded on them for readers to browse and discover books they might not otherwise read. The ability of these devices to contain several titles and different formats allows an ease of connecting from text to text. Put a dictionary on the device and definitions are a click away. The addition of audio enables words, or even an entire book, to be read aloud. *[handwritten: podcasts too]*

A beginning reader can follow along, building a sight vocabulary needed for eventual reading fluency. And as long as we can put a dictionary on the device, let's add an atlas. While you're reading about the Galapagos Islands you can locate them on a globe. Curious about Route 66? There's a road map for that. There are book apps that allow young readers to play with or manipulate the pages. The new *Pop-Out Peter Rabbit* preserves the text and illustrations from Beatrix Potter but allows a child to touch the screen and watch leaves fall or Peter hide. It's not much of a stretch to imagine pages of books that become doors to alternate endings or offer enhanced content, including images, audio, and video that connect with the text. Suppose the main character is listening to the big band sounds of Glenn Miller on the radio, and the reader could click to hear the actual music. Think of all the enhancements authors have added to books through sidebars or back matter. In addition to maps and charts, what about recipes, lists of further reading, or even discographies or videographies. What might these become as hyper-links in a book? Yes, many have made the point that these are no longer e-books, they are book apps, but I suspect this distinction will become increasingly blurred as technology and the market drive innovations.

The Social Side of Reading

Reading has always included a social element. Perhaps one of the most powerful features of reading is the permeable boundary between the experience of the individual reader and the larger social world of that reader. Reading allows an individual in a certain place and a certain time to be both in that place and in another place: the one created on the written page. Our lives as social beings in families and communities allow us to fashion meaning from books, but the books also have power to influence those social lives. We recommend books to friends and follow their suggestions in our own choices. Social networking sites were reported in the Kaiser Foundation study as the most popular computer activity.

Forty percent of young people, ages eight to eighteen (fifty-three percent of those ages fifteen to eighteen) visited a social network site daily, and those who did, spent about an hour a day on those sites. Goodreads offers readers similar social opportunities to "friend" or follow other readers, message others, and post comments. One cool feature allows you to post your progress reading a book and follow it on a graph. In libraries we can allow patrons to "tag" catalog entries or rank books with stars. Library catalogs now allow readers to see what's currently popular. We should be adding links to our library catalogs that allow readers to find "read-alike" titles with similar genres or appeal elements. We could be using technology to create tailored lists of books for reader tastes and abilities, and to provide e-mail or text message alerts about new books or similar books. Readers on the Kindle can now upload highlights or annotations to sites for others to see. What's the part of *Hunger Games* most often highlighted by readers? What about *A Wrinkle in Time* or Hawthorne's *The Scarlet Letter*? Imagine the possibilities for homework assignments that included sharing passages and annotations.

Sharing Meaning

Reading requires the reader to be actively engaged in making meaning from the text. Technology with social media allows entirely new possibilities for creating and sharing these meanings. Readers have numerous ways to share what they are reading in addition to sites such as Goodreads, Twitter, and Facebook. Word clouds created with Wordle or Tagxedo offer a new way to explore word choice and meaning. Fans can create flashy multimedia book trailers with Animoto or other video tools to entice others to read the book. QR codes could be created that connect print titles or book lists with book trailers, author websites, and other extensions to the book (think again about links to maps, music, recipes, or informational videos). Numerous youth bloggers (e.g., Book Nerd, Laura's Life, and Reading in Color) are writing about what

they are reading and are networking with other bloggers. What's even more interesting is the growth of "fan fiction" on the web where peers post reactions, extensions, or alternatives to favorite books for others to read and comment on. Fan fiction (www.fanfiction.net) exhibits the manipulation of content that evidences higher level thinking, and the addition of peer reviews ramps this up to be a powerful learning engine. In her blog Edtech Vision, Colette Cassinelli regularly posts examples for using VoiceThreads, Prezi, and other web tools to celebrate and extend books for young adult readers.

> We can look at new technologies as competition for the time and attention of young people, or we can look for ways to harness these technologies to put more "books" in the hands of more readers.

Making Reading an Active Experience

Technologies allow readers to "write" into the experience of reading: to annotate an e-book, blog about the reading experience, author fan fiction, or transfer the experience and the meaning into other media. Technology allows the solitary reader to become a social reader and join a community of readers. Perhaps the book as we know it—the portable bound pages—may change, but that miraculous ability of authors to take the printed word and shape a vision, an understanding, and a story through the formation of letters is the true gift of writing and reading. The communion of writers and readers that has endured through centuries, across distances, and through translations, crossing boundaries of culture, economics, gender, age, and ethnicity, is the organic, living, and breathing

Handwritten margin notes:
epic + raz kids
animated always catches attention
competition
"more like this" netflix
live in books
a new way of looking at reading

creation we need to celebrate, name, and nurture. Whether the words are handwritten, composed on a typewriter, or keyed into an iPad, it is the written word and its ability to reach and touch the minds and experiences of others that is truly miraculous. Our essential work of turning kids on to reading has not changed. We can look at new technologies as competition for the time and attention of young people, or we can look for ways to harness these technologies to put more "books" in the hands of more readers. Handheld technologies and social media offer us the portability, connectivity, and sociability to accomplish that.

[handwritten in left margin: way of thinking]

References

Book Nerd Blog. www.booknerdblog.com.

Carr, Nicholas. *The Shallows: What the Internet Is Doing to Our Brains.* W.W. Norton, 2010.

Ed Tech Vision (blog). http://edtechvision.org/?p=861.

Fanfiction.net. www.fanfiction.net.

Laura's Life (blog). http://lauramitolife.blogspot.com.

Pop Out: The Tale of Peter Rabbit (app). Loud Crow Interactive Inc. http://itunes.apple.com/us/app/popout!-the-tale-peter-rabbit/id397864713?mt=8.

Reading in Color (blog). http://blackteensread2.blogspot.com.

Rideout, V, J., U. G. Foehr, and D. F. Roberts. *Generation M(2): Media in the Lives of 8- to 18-Year-Olds: A Kaiser Family Foundation Study.* Henry J. Kaiser Family Foundation, 2010. www.kff.org/entmedia/8010.cfm.

Web Tools

Amazon Kindle: http://kindle.amazon.com

Animoto: http://animoto.com

Facebook: www.facebook.com

Goodreads: www.goodreads.com

I-Nigma (QR codes): www.i-nigma.com/i-nigmahp.html

Prezi: http://prezi.com

Tagxedo: www.tagxedo.com

Twitter: http://twitter.com

Voicethread: http:/voicethread.com

Wordle: www.wordle.net

Sue C. Kimmel *is assistant professor at Old Dominion University in Norfolk, Virginia, and can be reached at skimmel@odu.edu.*

Kimmel, Sue C. (2012). Deep reading: Using technology to engage, connect and share. *LMC, 30*(5), 10–12.

[handwritten note across lower half of page:]

post: one way to use technology to connect your students

↳ challenges on Goodreads

↳ book trailers on Animoto with QR codes
print titles → trailers

↳ networking

Rules or Reading?

By Anne E. Ruefle

An Unexpected Question

During a bookstore presentation about literary programming, a woman raised her hand and asked if I would give my opinion about library procedures. Always eager to give my opinion, I leaned forward to hear her question. Her question, though, was not what I was expecting. She explained that her three daughters dreaded library day at their school, because they lived in fear that they might forget their library book. According to the mother, if a student forgot just one book, the child lost the right to select any other library book until the forgotten book was returned. Worse than that was the harsh scolding they received from the librarian about their "lack of responsibility." The librarian seemed more interested in rules than reading.

The mother said she had questioned the librarian about a missing book. She was certain the book had been returned; the librarian said it was not. While the two adults were wrangling for more than a month via e-mail about the missing book, the kindergartner was not allowed to select another book, which broke her heart. Parents had complained to each other about the harsh atmosphere in the school library, but nobody wanted the hassle of fighting with the librarian. The new rule for the woman's children became: Never take your library books out of your book bag. What did I think, the woman asked. Was this a typical school library policy?

Oh My, Stereotype Alert!

Her comments made me wince, in part because it was not the first time I had heard of such a situation. It called up every awful stereotype about school librarians: grouchy, humorless, more concerned with neat shelves than engaged students. Author Pat Conroy, in his new memoir *My Reading Life*, recalls a dreadful librarian he knew as a student: "For [this librarian], I think that the state

of Nirvana would be a library clear of all readers and the books all shelved and accounted for. As a librarian, she was legendary in all the wrong ways, and for all the wrong reasons."

Our Basic Values

With all the innovative, interesting, important things school librarians are doing, it is dismaying that a perception of school librarians still lingers as obsessed guardians of the books, rather than as a force in the literacy development of students. But the real problem here is not the perception people have of librarians; rather, it is limiting student access to books, which directly impacts students' literacy development.

> *The freedom to select multiple books resonated with students. No longer did they have to decide between five great books; now, they could check out all five of them. No longer was a child reduced to tears because library books were inadvertently left at home.*

Research shows that an important step in the development of readers is having access to books. Steven Krashen, in *The Power of Reading*, cites multiple studies that demonstrate access to books is crucial in developing strong readers: "the richer the print environment, the better the literacy development." Limiting access runs counter to research and to the American Association of School Librarians' *Standards for the 21st-Century Learner*: "All children deserve equitable access to books and reading, to information . . . in an environment that is safe and conducive to learning." Librarians

need to oversee book circulation, but are we really promoting reading and literacy development if our library environment values neat shelves and prompt book returns as more important than regular access to books?

"That's the Way We've Always Done It" Is Not Good Enough

> *The real problem is limiting student access to books, which directly impacts students' literacy development.*

I was not always a proponent of open access to books. Once upon a time I followed the ubiquitous two-book checkout policy at my K-8 school: Students checked out two books at a time on library day, and those who forgot to return one book the next library day, could check out only one book. Students who forgot both books, well, they didn't get to check out another book, even though no one was ever very happy when they had to leave empty-handed. I used that policy for years, mostly because that was the policy I inherited when I started at my school, and I never thought to question it. But years ago, at an AASL conference, I attended a session where the speaker said in a most offhand way, "How many of you follow the two-book limit with your students?" The speaker said it sweetly, and nearly all of us in the room raised our hands. The woman almost barked at us, "Why?! Why just two books? Why do you need to keep those books on the shelf? What would happen if they could take out more books? Wouldn't there STILL be books on your shelves? Get the books out to the kids!"

It was an eye-opening moment. I had never thought about my policy before, but as soon as I returned to my library, I changed the policy and removed most of the restrictions on checkout. I said that students could check out up to ten books. If students forgot one book, or three books, or five books, they could still select other books. They could renew a book as long as they wanted, unless there was a waiting list for the book.

> *Regular access to books, with open checkout policies, unhampered by the pursuit of overdue fines, has been instrumental in creating a culture of literacy at our school.*

Amazed and Delighted Readers

The response from students was immediate—they were delighted. The freedom to select multiple books resonated with them. No longer did students have to make a decision between five great books; now, they could check out all five of them. No longer was a child reduced to tears because library books were inadvertently left at home.

Part of becoming a reader is seeing oneself as a reader; having many books is central to that role. I want all of my students to value reading, to consider themselves readers, and to participate in our reading community. Regular access to books, with open checkout policies, unhampered by the pursuit of overdue fines, has been instrumental in creating a culture of literacy at our school.

Our checkout policy has been in place for many years now, but every time we get a new student, I am reminded how significant the policy is for students. New students usually ask, "How many books can I check out?"

"How many books do you want?" I answer. The typical response is a timid, "Uh, I don't know. Two?" I respond, "Sure. But what about five books? Six? Can you fit seven books in your desk?" I love seeing the look of surprise spread across their faces and the new eagerness with which they attack the shelves to find multiple books.

The Rewards of Building Trust

None of my worries about excessive overdues or lost books came to fruition. We still have overdue books and lost books, certainly, but those numbers have *never* increased from when we had the two-books-at-a-time policy, though our circulation has gone through the roof. Students are more attentive to their books because they feel more connected to the library. It's not just about letting students have more books; it's about saying you trust them as readers and you trust them with the materials.

I am often asked about extending this policy to younger students: "Do kindergartners really need more than one book at a time?" "Isn't it wise to wait several months into the year before kindergartners check out books?" "Are kindergartners capable of selecting books without making a mess?" The answer is yes—even the kindergartners need to be engaged as readers. To ensure that students develop into lifelong readers, making strong connections between kindergartners and the library might be among our most important tasks.

It's Never Too Early to Start

I begin kindergarten checkout the first day they come to the library. They can check out two books every week. Kindergartners are happy to select two books, and they also quickly learn that once they get to first grade, they will be able to check out even more books. Kindergartners are instructed to take their books home. I tell them the books will cry in their book bags if the books are not taken out and read at home.

If they forget their books the next visit, I still let them take out another two books. And the week after that, I will do the same. Knowing that many kindergartners regularly use computers, iPods, game systems, and other sophisticated technology tools, it seems counterproductive to think that these same students can't handle selecting and returning library books.

Of course, some kids struggle to remember to bring back their books, but almost every student gets into the habit of returning books on a timely basis. If a student has 10 books (and

that rarely happens), I tell them they need to bring me back a few before selecting a new one.

We do have to work at instructing students of the importance of returning books in a timely fashion. I send home a letter to parents explaining library policies and asking them to participate in the reading development by reading with their children *and* returning books each week. One of the benchmarks for Kindergarten Information Literacy in Ohio is that students need to "know that books may be taken home but must be returned." That's part of our job: instructing the students (even the youngest ones) that they are part of a larger system that allows them to borrow and return books.

No Fear!

Yes, my library is often messy, and yes, the bookshelves can be a disaster. However, I often think of the horror stories from parents at other schools who tell me they NEVER even take their child's library books out of the book bags because they are terrified of having a late library book. And that is the real disaster, I think: instilling a sense of worry about the school library rather than instilling the joy, excitement, and wonder that should come with books and reading and libraries.

Works Cited

American Association of School Librarians. *Standards for the 21st-Century Learner.* Chicago: AASL, 2007.

Conroy, Pat. *My Reading Life.* Doubleday, 2010.

Krashen, Steven D. *The Power of Reading: Insights from the Research.* Libraries Unlimited, 2004.

Anne E. Ruefle *is the teacher-librarian at Saint Mary School in Columbus, Ohio. She is the author of Creating a Culture of Literacy (Libraries Unlimited, 2009) and was a 2008 National Catholic Education Association distinguished teacher of the year. She can be reached at aruefle@cdeducation.org and www .cultureofliteracy.com.*

Ruefle, Anne E. (2011). Rules or reading? *LMC, 29*(6), 34–35.

Unrestricted Checkout: The Time Has Come

By Kathryn K. Brown

What's the Issue?

In our politically charged culture, people have strong opinions on everything from the environment to health care. I have recently found myself in the middle of a debate about the benefits of unrestricted checkout in my elementary school library.

I believe that the time has come to let children check out the number of books they want. My only requirements are that they must be able to carry them ("No, you may not ask your teacher to carry some for you, and no fair bringing a wagon!"), and if the student has an overdue book, he or she is restricted to one book until the overdue is resolved. In an ideal world, I would not impose that last restriction either, but one does have a budget, and children are learning organization and responsibility skills.

Other members of our faculty are concerned that unrestricted checkout is depleting our library of resources, that students aren't reading the books they check out, that they are irresponsible and don't return them, and that the books don't fit in their desks or backpacks.

AASL's Position and Some Research

In its *Position Statement on the School Librarian's Role in Reading*, the American Association of School Librarians (AASL) states, "library media centers are to provide students, staff, and families with open, non-restricted access to a varied high quality collection of reading materials in multiple formats that reflect academic needs and personal interests." In *The Power of Reading: Insights from the Research,* 2nd edition (2004), Stephen D. Krashen writes that reading and having access to good books are critical to achievement in reading, writing, and spelling. Research has shown that students who are given the opportunity for free voluntary reading (FVR), show dramatic improvement in test scores over time. FVR improves vocabulary development, grammar test performance, writing, and oral/aural language ability (Krashen 3). Students who are speakers of English as a second language dramatically improve fluency and comprehension when they have access to quality books (Krashen 149).

Assigned reading has its place in reading instruction, too. It challenges students intellectually and exposes them to books they might not choose on their own, thereby expanding their free reading horizons. These are powerful arguments for surrounding children with books.

Krashen's research also shows that students in poverty have access to fewer books than students who are more affluent. Not only are there fewer book stores and libraries in poor neighborhoods, there are fewer books in classroom libraries and school libraries. In a California study by LeMoine, Brandlin, O'Brian and McQuillan (1997), researchers found that

> . . . students in high-achieving schools in affluent areas are able to visit the school library more frequently, both independently and as a class, and are more likely to be allowed to take books home. Seven out of the fifteen low-achieving schools they studied did not allow children to take books home (Krashen 72).

Affluent children have more books at home and more ways to get the books they want. Low-income students are more dependent on the school for their books (Krashen 68–73).

Our challenge is to provide books that are rich in content and variety, reflecting the curriculum and the diverse needs of our students (AASL 2010), and to make sure that children have the opportunity to read. We need to take every advantage of every tool in our arsenal to get them to read.

> *The best collection, the tidiest shelves, and the most inviting library will do no one any good if books sit on the shelves. Library books are to be used.*

The Power of Choice

Children have strong opinions about what they like to read. When I was a brand new librarian, I assumed (incorrectly) that children would prefer picture books, as I always took my own children to the picture book section when we visited the public library. I was surprised to discover that many students prefer nonfiction books, which was reinforced when I began really paying attention to what my kids were bringing home from their visits to the school library (army books, cat books, dinosaur books). If no books are of interest to students, or if they are not allowed to check out the books they want to borrow, reading becomes an exercise in frustration, and the library is a place to waste time.

Just like adults, children like books that are attractive and in good condition. If shelves are overcrowded, children become overwhelmed and can't find the "good" books they want. This is why weeding is a critical activity for the librarian. Allowing unrestricted checkout reduces overcrowding on shelves, too. The more books students check out, the easier it is to find the books they want!

Celebrating Empty Shelves

The best collection, the tidiest shelves, and the most inviting library will do no one any good if books sit on the shelves. Library books are to be used. In the process some books will be damaged and some will be lost. If the loss rate is too low, it indicates that the collection is not being used. Anne E. Ruefle, in the article "Rules or Reading" (*Library Media Connection*, May/June 2011) shared a story about a woman whose three daughters dreaded library day because they might forget their library books, in which case the children would not be allowed to check out another book and would be reprimanded by the librarian. In other libraries, children check out books but are afraid to take them out of their backpacks for fear of forgetting them. Every September, during our library orientation, I ask students, "What is the *most* important thing to do with your library book?" The answers include taking care of them, returning them, not tearing the pages, not letting little brothers or sisters read them, not writing in them, and not letting the dog chew them. Rarely does a child get the right answer: "The most important thing to do with your library book is to *read* it!" Have we become so rule driven that reading is an afterthought? If the time ever came that the shelves were empty, that would be cause for celebration! Can you imagine a library that is so intriguing and inviting that children can't wait to check out whatever book is available?

> *If the time ever came that the shelves were empty, that would be cause for celebration! Can you imagine a library that is so intriguing and inviting that children can't wait to check out whatever book is available?*

When students are first given the opportunity to have unlimited checkout, they check out more books than they can possibly read (and in some cases, carry). If they have unrestricted access, however, they quickly learn that when they finish the books they have, they can return and get more. They learn to self-limit their selections. When a student is told that she can get three books, she feels that she a) *must* get three books and b) must select absolutely perfect books because she can only get three. Thus, limiting checkout creates anxiety and tension in the library as students are rushed because it is time to go and they haven't yet found the exact number of exactly the right books.

Addressing Concerns

A teacher shared with me that assessing independent reading is very difficult if a child abandons books without finishing them. What an opportunity to collaborate with her to come up with solutions to this problem! I suggest that if students are allowed to check out as many books as they like, they will take more risk in their reading. If I can only get two books, I'd probably make sure they are books I already know I will like. If I can take more, I might be more willing to try a science fiction title (not my personal favorite), knowing that if I hate it, I still have something else to read. As the librarian I can work with the teacher to ensure that each student has one book for her to evaluate the student's reading and several other books to explore.

> *Our students deserve unrestricted access to a collection of high quality, high interest books. Our goal is to get them to read.*

Children check out books for reasons that have nothing to do with reading them. Is there really anything wrong with just looking at the pictures? That is how I read magazines. Some children just want to look cool or grown up. I still remember the first "grown up" book I read. I was in fourth grade, and I read Laura Ingalls Wilder's *Little House in the Big Woods*. To my young mind it was a grown up book because it was thick. Many children have someone at home happy to read aloud to them, if there is something to be read. My children allowed me to read all seven Harry Potter books to them, even though my son was a senior in high school the summer we read the last one.

What Students Deserve

Our students deserve unrestricted access to a collection of high quality, high interest books. As teachers, our goal is to get students to read. As students, their goal is to find something interesting that will entertain them and please us. Overall their goals are the same as anyone else's: to find happiness, to be treated with respect, and to be valued as individuals. If we restrict checkout, we are violating at least one of those goals. We are telling them we don't trust them to return their books. We are telling them we don't care what *they* like—that we as educators know what is best for them; and so we are not valuing them as individuals. We are teaching them that reading is a chore that is controlled by us. That is in no one's best interest.

While a collection of print resources is the most obvious measure of a library, the library of the 21st century is not hampered by walls. There is a wealth of useful databases for students and professionals. Electronic books and programs such as TumbleBooks and myON books provide books to be read online. No collection of print resources can meet everyone's needs, and that is the beauty of electronic resources.

Our students need to read, and they need to be able to get the books they want when they want or need them. A flexible schedule is another way to provide unrestricted access to the library. If a student finishes a book on Tuesday, it does him no good to have to wait until Wednesday to check out another. On the other hand, if he checked out a book on Tuesday, why does he need to come to the library on Wednesday? Students need the books when they need them, not necessarily on their assigned library day. I have seen classes come to the library where half of the students leave without books because they already have something to read. What a waste of instructional time!

AASL's *Standards for the 21st-Century Learner* lists four standards: learners use skills, resources, and tools to inquire, think critically, and gain knowledge; to draw conclusions, make informed decisions, apply knowledge to new situations, and create new knowledge; to share knowledge and participate ethically and productively as members of our democratic society; and to pursue personal and aesthetic growth. Unrestricted checkout for students assists them to use their skills of locating information to answer the questions they are curious about. They gather new knowledge by taking risks with their reading. They learn to share their knowledge as they discuss the books they are reading, and learn to participate by being responsible book users. Most of all, unrestricted checkout allows students to grow as individuals, as they read about topics of interest to them.

Limiting access to books might have been important fifty years ago, but that time has passed. It is time to allow our students free use of our school libraries. After all, aren't the libraries for them?

Bibliography

Hoyt, Linda. *Spotlight on Comprehension: Building a Literacy of Thoughtfulness*. Heinemann, 2005. Print.

Johnson, Peggy. *Fundamentals of Collection Development and Management, 2nd edition*. American Library Association, 2009. Print.

Krashen, Stephen D. *The Power of Reading: Insights from the Research, 2nd edition*. Heinemann, 2004. Print.

Routman, Regie. *Invitations: Changing as Teachers and Learners K-12*. Heinemann, 1991. Print.

Ruefle, Anne E. "Rules or Reading?" *Library Media Connection* 29:6 (May/June 2011): pp. 34–35. Print.

"School Librarian's Role in Reading Toolkit." American Association of School Librarians. 1 September 2010. Web. 14 February 2012. www.ala.org/aasl/aaslissues/ toolkits/slroleinreading.

"Standards for the 21st-Century Learner." American Association of School Librarians, 2007. Web. 12 February 2012. www.ala.org/ aasl/guidelinesandstandards/ learningstandards/standards.

Woolls, Blanche. *The School Library Media Manager, 3rd edition*. Libraries Unlimited, 2004. Print.

Kathryn K. Brown *is the library media specialist at Woodlawn Elementary School in Alexandria, Virginia.*

Brown, Kathryn.K. (2012). Unrestricted checkout: The time has come. *LMC, 31*(2), 32–34.

The Need to Shift and Widen School Library Advocacy Efforts: An Opinion Piece

By Gary Hartzell

Editor's Note: *Library Media Connection* is pleased to share this important work on advocacy. Read the executive summary below. To access the full paper (including references) visit: bit.ly/lmc.hartzell.

For more than twenty years, school librarians have focused advocacy efforts on principals, superintendents, and board members in the field, arguing that libraries should be institutionalized elements of K-12 education. It hasn't worked. Libraries remain vulnerable to cuts and elimination. This individualized field-based advocacy may have forestalled greater disaster, but it has not and *cannot* by itself make libraries and librarians secure in our schools.

To do that, librarians need to widen their advocacy efforts and give priority to two new targets: (1) the educational administration (Ed Ad) professors who shape beginning administrators' perceptions and values and (2) the professional associations that have a powerful influence on how administrators approach their work challenges once they are in the field. In effect, this widening represents a shift from battling for current school leaders' support to preemptively conditioning the next generation of administrators to support libraries as they take up their new responsibilities.

Right now the most successful school and district advocacy campaigns aimed at current school administrators cannot produce lasting results. Even when today's educational leaders appreciate what libraries can contribute, they move in and out of schools and districts too quickly to create lasting library support systems. In the 2007–2008 school year, for example, more than half of America's principals changed schools. Nationally, superintendents average little more than five years in office and only about three and a half

years in large urban areas. Because their individual time on the scene is too short, their support can only be transitory, and there is little hope of institutionalization. When school and district leaders move on, all the work librarians have done in those buildings and offices to secure administrative support can be wiped out. Too often, succeeding leaders don't understand what libraries and librarians can contribute, and advocacy efforts must begin all over again. This Sisyphean situation will endure until something is done to produce new leaders who arrive believing in libraries.

The keys to producing library-valuing new administrators are found in the university training they receive before they enter the field and in the guidance they receive from their professional associations once they're in them.

Let's look at university educational administrator preparation programs first. Most regular faculty Ed Ad professors are former practitioners; virtually all adjunct professors are still practitioners. They didn't learn the value of libraries in their own university training, nor did they learn it on the job. Carrying that ignorance back into the university when they become academics, they don't integrate any sense of library value into the administrative preparation courses they teach—and another generation of library-blind administrators graduates into our schools.

It will take a long time to get a critical mass of Ed Ad professors to think of libraries differently, but changing their perspective is imperative: The tipping point for school libraries won't come until the current body of educational leaders has been replaced by people who think libraries are indispensible. That won't occur until Ed Ad professors who don't value school libraries have been replaced by professors who do.

This effort will involve not only widening advocacy to the university level, but also enlisting a wider set of advocates. The first challenge will be capturing the professors' attention. Unlike the administrators with whom school-level librarians interact every day, professors don't work in the K-12 setting and are not anywhere near as physically accessible to our current library advocates. This means that library media faculty will have to become school library advocates and undertake concerted efforts to build relationships with administration faculty. They must bridge the gulf between departments and open communication lines through which pro-library evidence and argument can flow. They must reach out to administrative professors to participate in joint research and teaching projects that will make them witness to what libraries can contribute to student achievement. Collaborative cooperative endeavors, particularly those resulting in joint publications, will help build the connective tissue vital to these relationships and help tie the partnered administration professor to library support.

At the same time, library media faculty need to publish more of their individual work in journals that Ed Ad professors read, particularly refereed research journals. Administration professors, especially those associated with advanced degree programs, deal in research. Research and publishing are required if they are to keep their tenure-track jobs and earn promotion, and they must guide their students in thesis and dissertation research projects. This is an important group for school library advocates to connect with because a doctorate is increasingly required for a superintendency, and increasing numbers of principals are pursuing post-master's degrees.

Ed Ad professors must be brought to respect the research demonstrating library value. Since they don't read librarian publications, there is virtually no hope that any significant number of them will ever become aware of the growing mass of library impact research unless it begins to appear in journals they read and trust. Trust is the important element here. An article touting libraries in a library journal will be perceived as inherently self-serving. This is why there isn't much to be gained by giving an administration professor a copy of a librarian publication. To come to administration professors' attention, library research must be published in refereed and popular *administration* journals.

Studies show that administrators seek evidence for decision-making that fits into frameworks of what they already know. This strongly suggests that if aspiring administrators read library-positive research reports in their preparation programs, and their professors simultaneously speak to library importance, the odds probably go up that they will later seek and pay greater attention to library-supportive research and opinion.

Now, what about professional associations? School administrators listen to their professional organizations. They consistently cite professional association conferences and publications when they are asked to identify specific sources they turn to for research evidence. Perceived as unbiased providers that can help administrators find and prioritize research, associations serve as intermediaries between raw research

results and meaningful application. Administrators trust their associations to deal in credible material and to help them apply it to specific local issues. Getting into association publications and on to conference presentation schedules could open a pipeline into schools and district offices across the country.

Infiltrating administrators' professional organizations will require an effort similar to influencing university Ed Ad professors, taking time and partnership development. Just as it may take co-authored articles for library research to break into administrative research journals, it may take co-authoring to break into association publications and to get on conference and annual meeting presentation schedules. But it will be worth the effort.

Professional groups are important targets, and the work needed to partner with them will be intensive. But there's a likelihood that capturing their attention and support may consume fewer advocacy resources as time goes by if Ed Ad professors are brought around. Library-positive university prepared administrators will take their places in the field, join professional organizations, and, over time, come to lead those organizations, and, because *they* believe in library efficacy, become advocates themselves. For right now, and for at least the next decade, building relationships and partnerships with associations that administrators listen to will be an important component of any plan to turn the field around.

A Final Word

I realize that the arguments above are unattractive, that the notion that current school library advocacy approaches are insufficient is frustrating and disappointing, and that the advocacy shift I propose is daunting. Nonetheless, it seems clear to me that present advocacy approaches alone are not going to change things. The only hope for lasting change is to capture the hearts and minds of those who shape practicing administrators' perceptions at the outset of their careers.

Gary Hartzell *is emeritus professor of educational administration at the University of Nebraska at Omaha. The author of Building Influence for the School Librarian, lead author of a book on assistant principals' work lives, and numerous articles, he was invited to speak at the White House Conference on School Libraries in 2002 and has spoken about school libraries and workplace relationships at many professional association conferences and school district programs, both nationally and internationally. He is a member of the Laura Bush Foundation for America's Libraries advisory board, on the advisory board for Linworth's Library Media Connection, and on the editorial board for the International Association of School Librarians' School Libraries Worldwide journal. He has been listed on the American Association of School Librarians honor roll and is a winner of its Crystal Apple Award.*

Hartzell, Gary. (2012). The need to shift and widen school library advocacy efforts: An opinion piece. *LMC*, *30*(6), 12–13.

meet them at their level

not easy but achievable

ONE QUESTION SURVEY RESULTS

What Do You Do During Back-to-School Night?

By Gail K. Dickinson

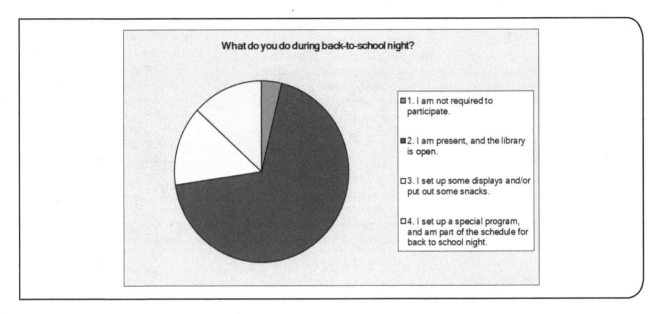

What do you do during back-to-school night?

■1. I am not required to participate.

■2. I am present, and the library is open.

□3. I set up some displays and/or put out some snacks.

□4. I set up a special program, and am part of the schedule for back to school night.

Ah, back to school night. For classroom teachers, it's a stress-filled anticipation waiting to see which parents will show up along with rigorous preparation and scripting of exactly what to say to help struggling parents help struggling students. Classroom teachers decorate their classrooms with student artwork, work to ensure their gradebook is up to date, and review individual student progress in order to develop a clear understanding of what to say to each child's parents, even though most schools stress that back-to-school night is not parent-teacher conference night.

School librarians, on the other hand, look forward to back to school night as a great time when they can work in the library without distraction. As nearly 75% of our respondents indicate, they are in the library during back to school night, the lights are on, and the library is open. But whether the library is home for any activities during back-to-school night is a different story. We didn't ask, and we don't know, if any of our respondents

attend back-to-school nights because the library is packed with parents waiting to talk to their librarian about information skills or the best reading resources for their child.

The answers to questions three and four, though, suggest a different scenario. Some of the activities noted for question four suggest that school librarians work hard to try to see a variety of parents. Several noted that they planned a book fair for back-to-school night. One high school librarian planned college information resources, as well as showing freshmen how to login to their accounts, with the added advantage of having parents signing the required acceptable use policy. And, of course, the tried and true method of getting anyone to show up anywhere is to feed them, and putting the snacks or activities in the library is a method used by about 15% of our respondents.

Only a handful of respondents, less than five percent, are not required to attend back-to-school night. It is heartening that the percentage is so small, but still alarming that any

school librarian is not required to fulfill this important duty.

The challenge of back-to-school night, as with any instructional activity, is to make it meaningful to today's parents and within the context of the instructional environment of the school. It's our chance to be seen on an equal footing with the other teachers in the school, so although the lure of the back room is tempting, get out there. Stand outside the door, act as tour guide and information expert, and make sure that every parent knows that your school has a librarian.

Find data for past One-Question Surveys at www.librarymedia connection.com. Have a good question? Be sure to let us know at lmc@librarymediaconnection.com.

Dickinson, Gail K. (2013). What do you do during back to school night? *LMC*, *31*(4), 41.

ONE QUESTION SURVEY RESULTS

The Librarian's Role in Teaching Internet Safety

By Gail K. Dickinson

Internet safety has become a required part of most school curricula. In many states, some form of instruction in staying safe on the Internet, on responsible use of information, and on cyberbullying is mandated by state or district regulation. Surprisingly, despite these mandates, slightly more than 23% of our nearly 300 respondents noted that Internet Safety is not taught in their schools. Also of note is that for 36% of our respondents, Internet Safety is taught in their schools by someone other than the school librarian. Those that do teach it tend to develop their own curriculum, as opposed to purchasing a canned curriculum. Some comments submitted with the survey responses indicate that librarians teaching Internet Safety want some help with materials and resources. They want to know how to adapt curricula to the middle school level for Internet Safety, and how to integrate Internet Safety into regular library lesson planning, and also how to make Internet Safety a whole-school responsibility.

LMC is always looking for Tips or articles on teaching Internet Safety. Send your ideas to LMC@librarymediaconnection. com. Curious about our previous surveys? All are available online at www. librarymediaconnection.com.

Dickinson, Gail K. (2011). The librarian's role in teaching Internet safety. *LMC*, *29*(6), 51.

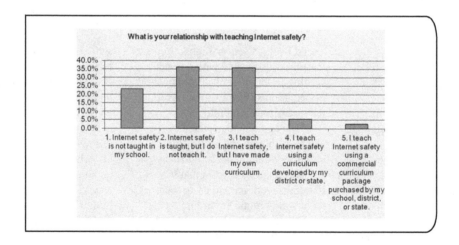

ONE QUESTION SURVEY RESULTS

What Is Your Requirement for Lesson Plans?

By Gail K. Dickinson

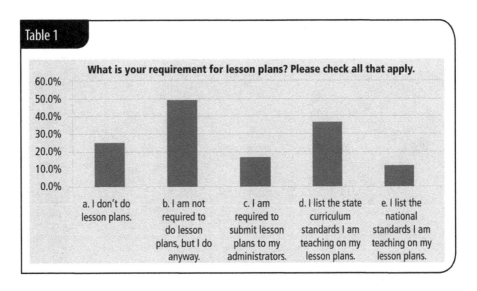

Table 1

What is your requirement for lesson plans? Please check all that apply.

This month's survey asked participants to tell us about one of the most common instructional routines, lesson planning. The results are a bit of a shock. 162 of our respondents, exactly one fourth, reported that they don't do lesson plans. Another 37% reported that they are not required to but that they do them anyway. It's hard to believe that after around a century of complaining that school librarians are not respected as teachers, we are still fighting the same battles. We need to be modeling the behavior of the latter group above who write lesson plans, therefore reinforcing that yes, they, too, are teachers. For the 25% who do not do lesson plans, it is a bit depressing that such a significant portion of the respondents are not doing teacher tasks, whether they are required to or not.

It's encouraging to see, though, that some school librarians are listing the state curriculum standards on their lesson plans, and that a smaller number are listing national curriculum standards. Aligning instruction with curriculum is not just good teaching practice, it's great advocacy for school library programs. What better way to show the school-wide impact of a strong school library instructional program than by linking what we teach to what is taught elsewhere in the schools. If all politics is local, surely all advocacy is as well.

It's as simple as this: Teachers write lesson plans. Teachers put state and national curriculum standards on their lesson plans. If school librarians want to be considered teachers, then we have to walk the walk, not just talk the talk.

Curious about our previous surveys? All are available online at www.librarymediaconnection.com.

Dickinson, Gail K. (2010). What is your requirement for lesson plans? *LMC*, *28*(4), 53.

ONE QUESTION SURVEY RESULTS

What Are You Doing Differently Because of the Common Core?

By Gail K. Dickinson

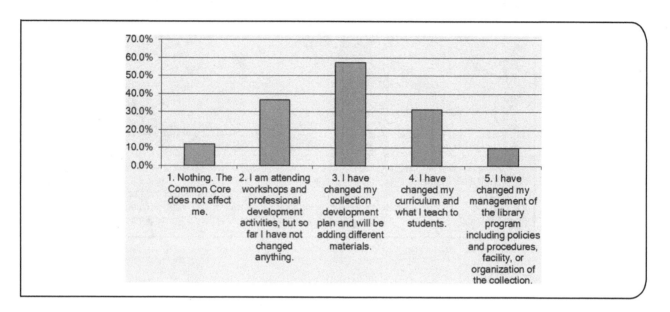

What is that looming on the horizon? It's Common Core State Standards! Whether you believe that the Common Core State Standards are a portentous black cloud or a hint of blue skies to come, implementation of the Common Core is a hot topic for school librarians. We wanted to know exactly how Common Core implementation was affecting what school librarians did on a daily basis in libraries, so we gave choices that included both instructional and administrative elements of the school library program.

We found that nearly 40% of our respondents (N=150) are attending trainings and learning about the Common Core, but at the time of the survey had not yet changed any part of their program. An additional 10% have not changed anything, and it may be assumed are unaffected

by the Common Core. Indeed, some respondents noted that their states had not adopted Common Core, and some shared frustration that they did not see a coordinated response to Common Core implementation coming from the state level.

For the respondents who have made changes, well over half of our respondents indicated that collection development was the area most affected by the Common Core. That in some ways is the most visible change to patrons, and in some ways it's also the easiest change for school librarians to make. Comments submitted with the surveys indicate that most of the changes in collection focus on nonfiction. One librarian was engaged in examining picture books to see if some could be reclassified as information texts. Others noted that they were

purchasing more nonfiction, and several were reorganizing the collection to highlight nonfiction, even to the extent of moving from Dewey to Library of Congress classification.

There were other changes beyond collection development. Approximately 30% of our respondents have changed their instructional program, and another 10% have changed the way that they administer the library. School librarians reported more collaboration, and a stronger focus on inquiry and the use of nonfiction materials, as well as some policy and procedural change.

For most of the country, implementation of the Common Core is an ongoing process. School librarians, along with other teachers, are reading articles, attending trainings, rewriting curriculum, and making plans. We suspect that a repeat of this survey next year may show that change processes because of the Common Core are more evenly spread across library activities. For now, though, this One-Question Survey is a snapshot of implementation.

LMC encourages the use of evidence-based practices to improve library programs. Lobby for positive change in your school and use these results to advocate to be one of the library programs where the school library is at the heart of change.

To review previous LMC One-Question Surveys, visit www .librarymediaconnection.com.

Have a good question? Submit it to lmc@librarymediaconnection. com. We will be waiting to hear from you.

Dickinson, Gail K. (2013). What are you doing differently because of the Common Core? *LMC, 31*(6), 23.

Tips

Picture Me in High School

For freshman orientation, most librarians have a PowerPoint template listing such information as library hours, location of various collections, fines, and rules of conduct. Each year, during the first few days of school, invite freshmen students to have their pictures taken in poses to illustrate the PowerPoint slides. When the presentation is played, the students listen very attentively as they watch to see if they or their friends are featured on one of the slides.

Judi Wollenziehn
Bishop Miege High School
Shawnee Mission, Kansas

Wollenziehn, Judi. (2011). Picture me in high school. *LMC, 29*(6), 9.

Dewey Do Decimals

Collaborate with a math activity that benefits everyone! One instructional topic that all students learn is decimal places. A fun activity for a small class is to have them come to the library on a weekly basis and be "shelf wizards," shelving nonfiction books and straightening the shelves. In addition, take their pictures and laminate the photos at the top of book ends. Students can move their photos each week to the section they straightened and shelved.

Mitzy Cromwell
Plaza Middle School
Virginia Beach (Virginia) City
Public Schools

Cromwell, Mitzy. (2011). Dewey do decimals. *LMC, 29*(6), 8.

Summer Book Bags

Don't leave all your middle and high school books locked away over the summer. Start a program called Summer Book Bags, which allows students who have permission from home to take care of twelve books over the summer. There are no fines or overdues to worry about. Students return the book bags during their first week back to school. It makes for a lot of shelving at the beginning of the school year, but the students really look forward to having a great supply of summer reading books.

Suzanne Dix
Caravel Academy
Bear, Delaware

Dix, Suzanne. (2011). Summer book bags. *LMC, 29*(6), 8.

Book Fair Fare

Make sure that all students can join in the book fair fun. Have a collection jar for loose change to buy books for the library. In exchange for donating coins to the jar, students can also nominate a book for purchase from the book fair. If a book garners enough "votes," the students who nominated the book move to the top of the waiting list to check out the new book. This way, even if students cannot afford to buy a popular book at the book fair, they have a chance being among the first to check it out from the school library.

Janice Gumerman
Bingham Middle School
Independence, Missouri

Gumerman, Janice. (2012). Book fair fare. *LMC, 31*(1), 9.

The School Library and Student Learning

Editor's Note

Strengthen and Support

For decades the school library field has agonized over how to describe the relationship between the school library and the teaching and learning processes in the school. It's hard to find just the right word that places the school library at the center of the interaction between curriculum, teaching, and learning.

To say that the library program enriches the teaching of the curriculum is certainly true, but to enrich means that the library program is somehow extra. In other words, it hints that teaching and learning work perfectly fine without the library program, but somehow the process becomes extra special when the librarian is involved, that is, the cherry on top of the ice-cream sundae. Although the fact that we do enrich learning is nice, in difficult times sometimes the extra pieces are the first to go.

To say that the library program *reflects* the curriculum was my favorite. In the days of print-only collections, I thought that it was possible to walk the stacks and see the spectrum of the curriculum reflected on the shelves. This included, of course, the stated curriculum from state frameworks along with the hidden and unwritten curriculum of traditional school and seasonal topics, student hobbies and interests, and local historical and cultural influences. But *reflect* also means to stand apart from, to not be one with, the mirror, but opposite it. The word does not accurately describe the integrated relationship of the school library program in the school.

Support is the term most commonly used, but that also can have a negative connection. Support, although certainly descriptive of the very hard work that school librarians do to assist teaching and learning processes, can also mean "less than." To be a support person would indicate that someone else is the main event, and that the role of the school librarian is to be under or beneath that effort. We support the classroom teacher, we support administrators' efforts to make a positive change in schools, we support the curriculum, and we support student learning of digital literacy. We support. By common use and by definition, it is a passive word that does not cover the active nature of the true relationship between the school library program and teaching and learning.

Thanks to Terry Young, a librarian in the Jefferson Parish Public School System in Louisiana and a member of the LMC Advisory Board, I found a new word that is more accurate to portray the relationship. "Not support, *strengthen*," he chastised me. Of course. To strengthen. To turn creativity into innovation, motivation into persistence, and curiosity into knowledge. School libraries strengthen school improvement efforts by focusing on specific areas with specific teachers and groups of students. The school librarian has a unique vantage point to work with teachers and students who need assistance with translating state curricula.

Strengthen. School librarians work with all teachers and all students to strengthen the teaching and learning processes, to make the link between the curricula and student achievement so much more than just scores on tests. School libraries strengthen learning in ways that create lifelong readers, develop informed and critical users of information resources, and require students to act as ethical digital citizens.

It's true that this whole discussion may be just a matter of semantics. It's true that the work of school librarians does not change by using a different term to describe that work. What is also true, though, is that the school library profession has to articulate our place in the educational process so that we can be seen as the critical element in learning. Support won't get us there, but strength just might.

Gail K. Dickinson
Editorial Director

Dickinson, Gail K. (2012). Strengthen and support. *LMC, 31*(3), 6.

The Journey Begins Here: Aligning Information Literacy with Common Core, State Standards, and Assessments

By Colet Bartow

A Puzzle with Many Pieces

In 1994, when I started my teaching career as a high school English teacher and librarian in rural Montana, I wished for a curriculum that clearly charted a path for developing information and literacy skills for my students. I wished for assessment strategies, defined by clear descriptions of learning expectations, I could use to really know how well my students were progressing. At the time, there were no state standards to rely upon, much less a fully developed information literacy curriculum aligned with the English curriculum. I did have a good understanding of the Big6™ information problem solving process and the interest of my fellow English teachers in improving research and writing assignments. Out of that common goal we eventually developed a Big6-based research guide still used in the district (Manhattan High School). The piece of the puzzle that remained missing was a well-crafted approach to assessing and reporting information literacy achievement. This has become a primary focus of my work at the Montana Office of Public Instruction as the state's library-information literacy curriculum specialist. The current standards-based education landscape provides interesting opportunities to bring information literacy and critical thinking skills more clearly into the center of instructional and assessment practice.

Challenges for Teachers

For teachers, assessing information literacy and critical thinking skills can be far from the top of the priority list. Our national focus on summative assessments for accountability has left untested subjects out in the cold. At the same time, 21st century skills have grown in recognition and importance as the critical skills students must

master for college and career readiness. Teachers of all grade levels struggle to create a balance between providing opportunities for students to develop skills for communication, critical thinking, creativity, and deep content knowledge while also ensuring that students perform well on summative accountability tests.

With the arrival of the Common Core State Standards (CCSS) for English Language Arts and Mathematics, in combination with the development of the Smarter Balanced and PARCC assessments, schools have an increased focus on what is being taught at each grade level (standards) and how well students are meeting the expectations set in the standards as they progress toward graduation. While some believe that the Common Core Standards and tests are just a continuation of business as usual, the standards and new assessment systems are opportunities for a change in focus to information literacy and how those skills are assessed. Fortunately, teacher-librarians (TLs) are well suited to lead the effort to implement the CCSS with their expertise in teaching and assessing information skills.

Leaders Need Resources and Plans

The opportunity for teacher-librarians to lead and inform the infusion of information skills into the CCSS points out the need for resources and strategies for putting the spotlight on information skills where they exist in the CCSS. With this in mind, I analyzed the CCSS through the lens of our Montana K-12 Information Literacy/Library Media Content Standards as our state went through the process of adopting the CCSS. With the help of Montana TLs and further assistance from my fellow curriculum specialists at the Montana

Office of Public Instruction, I drafted an alignment chart. The excerpt from that chart can be used by TLs as they partner with classroom teachers to create learning opportunities for students with clearly identified learning expectations that include information skills. When classroom teachers develop units or lessons that focus on specific writing, speaking, listening, and mathematical practices, the TL can include the aligned information skill in the learning expectations and create performance tasks that allow students to demonstrate their proficiency levels in meeting the standards.

> *While some believe that the Common Core Standards and tests are just business as usual, the standards and new assessment systems are opportunities for a change in focus to information literacy and how those skills are assessed.*

The following example presents a suggested alignment of the Common Core State Standards for English Language Arts College and Career Readiness Anchor Standards for Reading, Writing, Speaking and Listening, and the CCSS Mathematical Practices with the Montana Information Literacy/Library Media Content Standards. This alignment is used with content area curriculum guides and maps to develop units and lessons that provide students with rich opportunities to practice information literacy skills in the context of standards for writing, speaking, listening, and mathematical practices.

Table 1 Information Literacy and Common Core Standards Alignment

Montana Information Literacy Standard 3 The student will evaluate the product and learning process.	College and Career Readiness Anchor Standards for Writing Production and Distribution of Writing 5. Develop and strengthen writing as needed by planning, revising, editing, rewriting, or trying a new approach. Range of Writing 10. Write routinely over extended time frames (time for research, reflection, and revision) and shorter time frames (a single sitting or a day or two) for a range of tasks, purposes, and audiences. College and Career Readiness Anchor Standards for Speaking and Listening Comprehension and Collaboration 3. Evaluate a speaker's point of view, reasoning, and use of evidence and rhetoric.	Common Core Standards for Mathematical Practices 1. Make sense of problems and persevere in solving them. 8. Look for and express regularity in repeated reasoning.

Source: (Bartow)

Table 2 Grade-by-Month Information Literacy/Library Media Curriculum Guide

Grade: 7	Standard	Essential Learning Expectations	Vocabulary	Assessment	Reporting
December	Standard 3: The student will evaluate the product and learning process.	The student will 1.A. evaluate the product's strengths and weaknesses according to task criteria. 1.B. critique the final product (e.g., self, teacher, peers). 1.C. identify areas for improvement of the product. 2.A. examine task completion process (e.g., self-regulation, time management, etc.). 2.B. identify areas for improvement in the process.	Benchmark 1: evaluation Benchmark 2: self-regulation, time management, peer evaluation, evaluation	Formative strategies	Assignment grades Feedback forms Check-logs

"Unpacking" to Move Forward

With the assistance of Montana TLs, I have outlined at each grade level the essential learning expectations that "unpack" the information literacy standards. We identified vocabulary, assessment focus, and suggested general ways to report student progress. The model is based in our standards but also reflects the Big6 by the Month approach (Eisenberg). For each grade level and in each month, the TL can focus instruction and assessment on specific information literacy skills in the context of classroom or content assignments.

Assessment and Outcomes Inform Planning

From the standards and essential learning expectations for information literacy, performance rubrics have been developed that describe how well students perform according to the criteria specified at each grade level. Further, the performance is defined for four levels: novice, nearing proficiency, proficient, and advanced. The example in Table 3 is a "meta-rubric," an analytic but generic rubric. To use the rubric in a specific task or assignment, the teacher-librarian or classroom teacher must select only the most appropriate descriptors. If the rubric is to be used by students for self-evaluation, the language should also be translated into student friendly language.

Tasks and products that closely match the learning expectations and provide students authentic and engaging learning opportunities will most certainly help the practice of critical thinking and problem solving skills.

Information Literacy Performance Rubric: a set of criteria describing student performance along a continuum from novice to advanced. The criteria define how well students apply the knowledge and skills set forth in the standards ("Standards-based Curriculum").

With clearly defined levels of performance, our next step is to develop units and lessons with targeted information skills identified and included in the performance tasks and assessments.

The sample unit plan in Table 4 uses an Understanding by Design template (Wiggins). A thoughtful, strategic, and complete planning process ensures that information skills are seamlessly integrated into lessons. As teachers, we need to carefully select and focus on what students are expected to know and be able to do. We have to employ our best skills in creating learning opportunities that go beyond isolated activities. Most importantly, assessment of content and skills must be identified before performance tasks and work products are developed. Tasks and products that closely match the learning expectations and give students authentic and engaging learning opportunities will most certainly help the practice of critical thinking and problem solving skills. For great ideas and examples of tools, rubrics, and strategies for assessing information literacy, I highly recommend Violet Harada and Joan Yoshina's book *Assessing for Learning: Librarians and Teachers as Partners*.

Table 3 **Performance Rubric for Standard 3, Grade 7**				
Performance Criteria	**Novice**	**Nearing Proficiency**	**Proficient**	**Advanced**
The student will assess the quality and effectiveness of the product.	The student will A. evaluate product strengths and weaknesses without regard to task criteria. B. trust the authority of teacher or peer evaluation of the product. C. have a general sense that the product could be improved.	The student will A. evaluate the product's strengths and weaknesses with limited consideration of task criteria. B. critique the final product independent of teacher or peer evaluation of the product. C. recognize differences in quality between products.	The student will A. evaluate the product's strengths and weaknesses according to task criteria. B. critique the final product with consideration of teacher or peer evaluation of the product. C. identify areas for improvement of the product.	The student will A. evaluate the product's strengths and weaknesses according to task criteria throughout the process. B. critique the final product and compare differences in self-evaluation and teacher or peer evaluations. C. reflect on ways to improve the product in novel ways.
The student will evaluate how the process met the need for information.	The student will A. identify elements of the task completion process with no future projections for improvement. B. identify steps in the process with limited understanding of strengths or weaknesses in a given step.	The student will A. present confusing statements or facts about the task completion process. B. recognize need for improvement in the process.	The student will A. examine the task completion process. B. identify areas for improvement in the process.	The student will A. self-critique and reflect on the task completion process. B. identify areas for improvement in future applications of the process.

Table 4 **Sample Unit Plan**

Grade 7 Sample Unit Plan

Title of Lesson: Montana Citizens of Note

Stage 1: Desired Results

Montana Standards
Social Studies: Analyze the significance of important people, events, and ideas (e.g., political and intellectual leadership, inventions, discoveries, the arts) in the major eras/civilizations in the history of Montana.
Writing: Production and Distribution of Writing
5. Develop and strengthen writing as needed by planning, revising, editing, rewriting, or trying a new approach.
Information Literacy 3: Students will evaluate the product and learning process.
Technology: 2.3 Communicate the results of research and learning with others using digital tools.

Students will	Essential Questions
1. be able to evaluate work products according to established criteria. 2. be able to identify steps in the learning process and reflect on how well they worked through the process. 3. be able to apply knowledge of digital tools to share learning results. 4. analyze the significance of people, events and ideas.	■ What makes a person, event, or idea significant? ■ How do I decide the best way to share information with a particular audience? ■ How do I know when information is reliable?

Stage 2: Assessment Evidence

Performance Tasks
Each student will select a current or historical figure in Montana and create a wiki page that includes biographical information, geographic context, the significance of the figure's contributions to Montana history, at least one picture, and a map. The student will include an annotated works cited list that includes a brief statement about why the source was chosen and what made it a reliable source.

Evidence
Wiki page with annotated works cited list, MLA style

Performance Description Rubric

Novice	Nearing Proficient	Proficient	Advanced
Cites each source with many errors	Cites each source with few errors in MLA format	Cites each source in MLA format	Cites each source in MLA format
Evaluates the product's strengths and weaknesses without regard to task criteria	Evaluates the product's strengths and weaknesses with limited consideration of task criteria	Evaluates the product's strengths and weaknesses according to task criteria	Evaluates the product's strengths and weaknesses according to task criteria throughout the process
Has a general sense that the product could be improved	Recognizes differences in quality between products	Identifies areas for improvement of own product	Reflects on ways to improve the product in novel ways
Identifies steps in the process with limited understanding of strengths or weaknesses in a given step	Recognizes need for improvement in the process	Identifies areas for improvement in the process	Identifies areas for improvement in future applications of the process

Stage 3: Learning Plan

Learning Opportunities
Students will work in pairs to research a figure from Montana history and create a wiki page according to completion criteria. The wiki page will include biographical information, geographic context, the significance of the figure's contributions to Montana history, at least one picture, and a map. The student will include an annotated works cited list that addresses the relevance, appropriateness, authority, and currency of each source. Students will present the project wiki to members of the local historical society.

Lesson Progression
Introduction of unit objectives and overview of project; activation of knowledge of Montana history; organization of teams; instruction in evaluating sources and citing sources; instruction in wiki construction; group and individual assistance for research and wiki construction; evaluation of product and process.

Materials/Resources Needed

Wiki completion checklist

✓ Website evaluation rubric
✓ Works cited checklist
✓ Process evaluation checklist

Websites/Reference Sources

Montana, Stories of the Land: http://mhs.mt.gov/education/textbook/textbookmainpage.asp
Montana Place Names: http://mtplacenames.org
Montana Memory Project: http://cdm15018.contentdm.oclc.org

Are We There Yet?

The development of information literacy standards, essential learning expectations, performance rubrics, Common Core Standards alignment, and a curriculum framework has felt like an epic journey—a journey that is by no means complete. We have provided essential resources to help teachers and teacher-librarians effectively implement assessment of information and critical thinking skills. The essential learning expectations and their corresponding performance rubrics clearly define what students must be able to do and describe how well they are progressing toward meeting the learning expectations.

It is my hope that the work we have done will benefit fledgling teacher-librarians and those who have been flying solo for a few years. As these resources were developed, we benefitted from the advice and guidance of Mike Eisenberg, Bob Berkowitz, Janet Murray, and Doug Johnson. Thankfully, the journey toward creating these resources has also been shared by the best and brightest librarians in my state.

Works Cited

Bartow, Colet. "Montana Teacher Librarian Wiki." Montana Office of Public Instruction. Web. 03 June 2012. http://opi.mt.gov/groups/mtl.

Eisenberg, Michael B., Janet Murray, and Colet Bartow. "Big6 by the Month." Big6. Web. 03 June 2012. https://sites.google.com/site/big6xthemonth.

Harada, Violet H., and Joan M. Yoshina. *Assessing for Learning: Librarians and Teachers as Partners*. Santa Barbara, CA: Libraries Unlimited, 2010. Print.

Manhattan High School. "Manhattan High School Research Handbook." Manhattan Public Schools. Web. 3 June 2012. http://manhattan.schoolwires.com/1525101210115112210/lib/1525101210115112210/revised_11_research_handbook.pdf.

"Standards-based Curriculum." Montana Office of Public Instruction. Web. 3 June 2012. www.opi.mt.gov/Curriculum/Curriculum-Development-Guide/index.php#gpm1_4.

Wiggins, Grant P., and Jay McTighe. *The Understanding by Design Guide to Creating High-quality Units*. Alexandria, VA: ASCD, 2011. Print.

Colet Bartow *lives in Helena, Montana, where she works for the Montana Office of Public Instruction (OPI) as library-information literacy curriculum specialist. She can be reached at cbartow@mt.gov.*

Bartow, Colet. (2012). The journey begins here: Aligning information literacy with Common Core, state standards and assessments. *LMC, 31*(2), 10–13.

We Don't Live in a Multiple Choice World

Inquiry and the Common Core

By Paige Jaeger

Common Core and the Why Questions

As she spoke to attendees at a Common Core gathering, Lily Ekelsen, vice president of the National Education Association (NEA), painted a picture of her civil rights instruction. She described a deep, authentic learning model experienced by her elementary students as they dug into civil rights, desegregation, equal rights, and America. Then came the test. The assessment asked who won the Nobel Peace Prize in 1964. None of her students answered that question correctly even though it was probably more important to know *why* Martin Luther King received the Nobel Peace Prize, rather than *who* received the prize. Despite her students' scores on the multiple-choice assessment, they understood civil rights. That is why she and the NEA were thrilled with the Common Core State Standards (www.corestandards.org). They foster higher-level thinking.

From Kalamazoo to Kansas

Despite many wonderful aspects, the Common Core Standards remain unfamiliar to most educators. Many stressed-out educators view the new standards as another mandate that might fade. I beg to differ. Across America, the states have adopted these new learning standards, and we are all going to be on the same page. When a family moves from Kalamazoo to Kansas, they will not have to worry that their children will be out of sync with instruction in the new state and waste a year to align their knowledge. The Common Core raises the bar for states struggling to decide what should be taught or tested. As low-performing schools strive to improve instruction, the blueprint has been defined. The

Common Core defines the curriculum in enough detail and specifies ways to teach that content creatively and innovatively, to produce graduates who are problem solvers and globally competitive.

As America strived to do well on assessments, authentic learning went the way of the dinosaur. Assessment became the curriculum. Educational administrators and communities feared the annual newspaper issue that reported assessment and ranked schools in their areas. The pressure was on to score well, which often surpassed the need to teach well.

What's in the Common Core for School Librarians?

As the Common Core curriculum is adopted and unpacked, librarians should celebrate that finally, from the beginning, directions for inquiry and inquiry-based learning are embedded throughout. The Partnership for 21st Century Skills states that America needs graduates who can think creatively, solve problems, are information and technologically literate, and are able to collaborate. That is the language of inquiry. We have been waiting for this moment.

Repackaging Research

In our area we encourage teachers to "repackage research" for the Common Core. When we use the phrase "repackage," teachers are more apt to consider collaborating when they realize they do not have to recreate but can merely redesign. Often an old research unit can be redesigned by:

- Initiating the project with a critical, compelling question for students to answer rather than a "deadly packet" asking students to dig for information

- Allowing students to create the questions for research collaboratively
- Embedding technology as a working platform
- Changing the final knowledge product into a 21st century communication product

Explaining Inquiry in the Common Core Framework

As the date approaches when the new learning standards take effect, we find teachers slowly trying to digest these new standards. This is our chance to shape teachers' understandings and bring them into our information haven. To recognize inquiry in the Common Core, you must have an understanding of the process. Here is a simplified explanation:

> *The Common Core defines the curriculum in enough detail and specifies ways to teach that content creatively and innovatively to produce graduates who are problem solvers and globally competitive.*

Inquiry starts with a question. This question will inspire students to create questions and research to find answers. Evaluation and synthesis of this information is imperative to foster long-term retention and deep learning. Students draw conclusions from information and create a knowledge product to share with others.

Inquiry is not a clean fill-in-the-blank search for predetermined facts a teacher has predefined. Inquiry transfers responsibility into the hands of the students. Inquiry fosters student ownership of the process and student pride in the product. It works! In a well-defined unit, the teacher serves as a learning concierge and academic guide, ensuring that learning goals are met, content vocabulary is understood, and assessment is authentic.

The Anchor Standards

If you examine the Common Core Standards, you will see that College and Career Readiness standards are highlighted as the anchor standards. Inquiry language is embedded in all of the anchor standards. Even in subjects such as math and science you will find this language (see images). The Common Core Standards can be a labyrinth of material to digest. Start with the following link: www.corestandards.org/the-standards/english-language-arts-standards/anchor-standards-hssts/college-and-career-readiness-anchor-standards-for-writing.

Consider printing out the anchor standards, such as the pages that hold these statements:

Writing

- The ability to write logical arguments based on substantive claims, sound reasoning, and relevant evidence is a cornerstone of the writing standards, with opinion writing—a basic form of argument—extending down into the earliest grades.
- Research—both short, focused projects (such as those commonly required in the workplace) and longer term in-depth research— is emphasized throughout the standards but most prominently in the writing strand since a written analysis and presentation of findings is so often critical.
- Annotated samples of student writing accompany the standards and help establish adequate performance levels in writing arguments, informational/explanatory texts, and narratives in the various grades.

Speaking and Listening

- The standards require that students gain, evaluate, and present increasingly complex information, ideas, and evidence through listening and speaking as well as through media.
- An important focus of the speaking and listening standards is academic discussion in one-on-one, small-group, and whole-class settings. Formal presentations are one important way such talk occurs, but so is the more informal discussion that takes place as students collaborate to answer questions, build understanding, and solve problems.

From: "Key Points in Language Arts," Common Core State Standards Initiative, www.corestandards.org/about-the-standards/key-points-in-english-language-arts

Research to Build and Present Knowledge

7. Conduct short as well as more sustained research projects based on focused questions, demonstrating understanding of the subject under investigation.
8. Gather relevant information from multiple print and digital sources, assess the credibility and accuracy of each source, and integrate the information while avoiding plagiarism.
9. Draw evidence from literary or informational texts to support analysis, reflection, and research

From: "College and Career Readiness Anchor Standards for Writing," Common Core State Standards Initiative, www.corestandards.org/the-standards/english-language-arts-standards/anchor-standards-hssts/college-and-career-readiness-anchor-standards-for-writing

> *The Common Core English language arts anchor standards state that students should "read and comprehend complex literary and informational texts independently and proficiently." The keyword is rigor, and rigor is not Google.*

Literacy and Rigor

For years librarians have supported and enhanced literacy instruction, but now alarm bells are ringing. With Race to the Top (RTTT), the old-fashioned meaning of literacy is stressed. Embracing literacy is a Common Core objective, presenting literacy not just in English class. We should encourage teachers to include various forms of literacy within their lessons. In an inquiry-based model, the student often searches for the reading material. Print, electronic, media, and other electronic formats are recognized in the Common Core.

The Common Core Standards acknowledge that students arrive at college unprepared to read and comprehend difficult text. Our goal as educators is to graduate college and career ready seniors, and we are failing this task. The Common Core English language arts anchor standards state that students should "read and comprehend complex literary and informational texts independently and proficiently." The keyword is rigor, and rigor is not Google.

Offer your services to teachers as they search for appropriate material to meet Common Core requirements of literacy rigor. Encourage students to move from Google to databases that are challenging, credible, and more efficient. That is vastly different from the online habits we observe, such as "super-squirreling" and "website kangarooing." We must model how to slow down, read, comprehend, and analyze for credibility and accuracy on an electronic platform. We need to teach students to be skeptical of all information heard and read on the Internet so that they innately take the time to evaluate the source appropriately. Common Core Standards ask us to focus on complex textual writing in order to graduate college and career ready students.

Navigate the pages on the Common Core State Standards Initiative website. I found some of the best language for librarians by following these clicks:

Corestandards.org > The Standards > English Language Arts Standards > Anchor Standards >

College and Career Readiness Anchor Standards for Reading (or Writing, Speaking and Listening, Language)

Promoting the Common Core

As you find a page with "library lingo," print it. Highlight the research language. Highlight the references with statements such as "comparing primary and secondary sources." Highlight statements such as, "Use technology, including the Internet, to produce and publish writing and to interact and collaborate with others." Share these findings at team meetings; share them with your building principal and at faculty meetings. Suggest developing professional learning activities that focus on inquiry-based learning. Offer to help teachers create units aligned with the Common Core Standards. Hold lunchtime picnics in your library and introduce teachers to inquiry.

If you are looking for a good inquiry document to help teachers understand this process, visit http://wswheboces.org/files/419/wise%20curriculum%20–1stedition1.pdf. Additional inquiry resources can be found at http://wswheboces.org/SSS.cfm?subpage=419. This material is copyrighted, so please ask for permission to print.

Paige Jaeger *is the coordinator for school library services at the Washington-Saratoga-Warren-Hamilton-Essex (WSWHE) Board of Cooperative Educational Services, Saratoga Springs, New York.*

Jaeger, Paige. (2012). We don't live in a multiple choice world: Inquiry and the Common Core. *LMC, 30*(4), 10–12.

Tools of the Trade

How Do the Common Core Standards Impact School Library Programs?

By Peggy Milam Creighton

Reading standards require:

- Wide and deep reading of increasingly complex, high-quality text that expands students' views of the world
- Greater emphasis on independent reading of informational text
- Vocabulary development driven through a wide range of relevant text
- Literacy-rich classroom environments

Writing standards require students to:

- Construct a solid opinion, narrative, or informational writing by citing specific text evidence and evaluating the relevance and range of that evidence
- Conduct short- and long-term research, gathering information from multiple credible formats without plagiarizing
- Utilize multiple sources, both print and digital, as tools to strengthen evaluation and reflection on the research process
- Expand or reduce the research as needed, and integrate the findings
- Use technology tools to create, collaborate with other students, and publish work

Content area literacy standards require students to:

- Evaluate primary and secondary sources

- Connect ideas, evaluate various points of view, and integrate concepts for logical reasoning
- Establish relationships among primary ideas and supporting details
- Comprehend key phrases and vocabulary pertaining to specific domains
- Evaluate theories and facts by verifying or challenging conclusions with their own arguments

To prepare for the road ahead, school librarians should:

- Increase the number and range of high quality, informational resources, including reference resources in various formats
- Obtain copies or excerpts of text exemplars from the standards
- Clear library schedules of unnecessary activities to devote adequate time for all grade levels to engage in research and library media instruction
- Work with teachers and administrators to make technology resources available to students in support of reading, research, and writing projects
- Identify a wide range of high quality print and digital resources with an appropriate level of text complexity to strengthen curricular themes

- Become familiar with the Common Core Standards and the anchor standards for all levels
- Focus information literacy skills instruction on evaluating sources (especially primary), citing evidence, building a strong argument, and drawing conclusions from text evidence
- Show documents such as this one to administrators, teachers, parents, and other stakeholders to build support for staffing, scheduling, and budgeting for the school library media program

Reference

Common Core State Standards Initiative 2012. Web. 28 July 2012. www.corestandards.org/the-standards.

Peggy Milam Creighton, Ph.D., NBCT, *is a school library media specialist. She is author of The Secret Reasons Teachers Are Not Using Web 2.0 and What School Librarians Can Do about It, Perceptions of Web 2.0 Tools as Catalysts for Teacher and Librarian Collaboration: A Case Study, National Board Certification in Library Media: A Candidate's Journal, and InfoQuest: A New Twist on Information Literacy.*

Creighton, Peggy Milam. (2013). Tools of the trade: How do the Common Core Standards impact school library programs? *LMC, 31*(4), 45.

Outfitting Yourself as a Core-brarian

By Peggy Milam Creighton

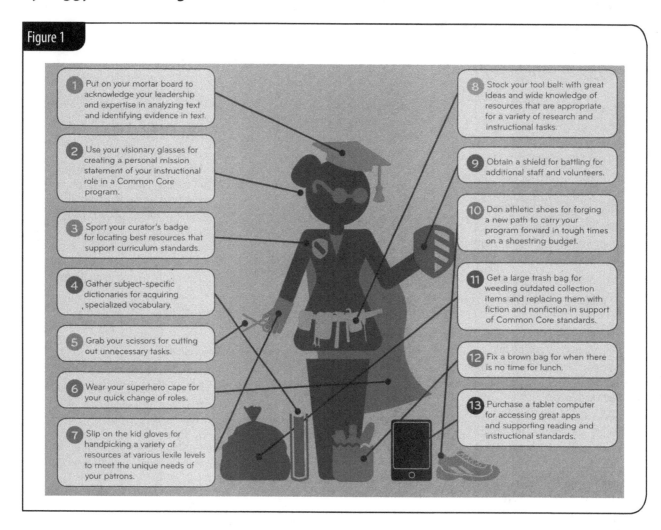

Figure 1

1. Put on your mortar board to acknowledge your leadership and expertise in analyzing text and identifying evidence in text.

2. Use your visionary glasses for creating a personal mission statement of your instructional role in a Common Core program.

3. Sport your curator's badge for locating best resources that support curriculum standards.

4. Gather subject-specific dictionaries for acquiring specialized vocabulary.

5. Grab your scissors for cutting out unnecessary tasks.

6. Wear your superhero cape for your quick change of roles.

7. Slip on the kid gloves for handpicking a variety of resources at various lexile levels to meet the unique needs of your patrons.

8. Stock your tool belt: with great ideas and wide knowledge of resources that are appropriate for a variety of research and instructional tasks.

9. Obtain a shield for battling for additional staff and volunteers.

10. Don athletic shoes for forging a new path to carry your program forward in tough times on a shoestring budget.

11. Get a large trash bag for weeding outdated collection items and replacing them with fiction and nonfiction in support of Common Core standards.

12. Fix a brown bag for when there is no time for lunch.

13. Purchase a tablet computer for accessing great apps and supporting reading and instructional standards.

	Item Above	Designates	The Following
❑	1. Mortar board	Knowledge leadership	School librarians promote their Common Core leadership and expertise by analyzing text and citing evidence within text, modeling this skill for all stakeholders.
❑	2. Visionary glasses	Visionary goal-setting	School librarians advocate for their programs by creating a vision statement for their programs' roles and their personal roles in supporting Common Core instructional standards.
❑	3. Curator's badge	Curating resources	Common Core teacher-librarians skillfully curate best resources for their collections and publicize them through pathfinders, newsletters, email, blog posts, and face-to-face instruction.
❑	4. Special subject dictionaries	Acquiring special vocabulary	School librarians strategically support all subject areas in the Common Core with specialized dictionaries and reference media to meet the diverse needs of their patrons.

☐	5. Scissors	Cutting out unnecessary tasks	School librarians are time management experts and professional multitaskers who eliminate all unnecessary activities and focus on most critical functions in Common Core schools in this era of extreme budget cuts.
✳	6. Superhero cape	Quick role changes	Common Core teacher-librarians are quick-change artists who can jump from reader's advisory to teacher collaboration to administrator support to homework help with a minute's notice.
☐	7. Kid gloves	Handpicking resources	School librarians are experts at identifying and meeting the unique needs of their populations with a variety of Common Core media on a wide range of lexile levels.
✳	8. Tool belt	Tools of the trade	Teacher-librarians organize their Common Core tool belts with great ideas and a wide knowledge of resources appropriate for a variety of instructional tasks.
☐	9. Shield	Battling for necessary staff	School librarians passionately battle for necessary staffing and funding to continue critical Common Core library programs.
✳	10. Athletic shoes	Forging new paths	Teacher-librarians identify personnel, programs, and policies to carry their programs down new Common Core pathways on shoestring budgets.
☐	11. Trash bag	Strategic collection weeding	Common Core requires school librarians to evaluate the rigor of their collections, weed strategically, and then obtain a wide range of exemplary nonfiction and fiction supporting new curriculum standards.
✳	12. Brown bag	Lunch on the run	Busy Common Core librarians often hold a working lunch on their tight schedules when short-staffed.
☐	13. Tablet computer	Reading and instructional apps	Teacher librarians are technology leaders and trailblazers who model the latest and best in reading and instructional apps for mobile computing devices for Common Core.

Peggy Milam Creighton , Ph.D., NBCT, *is a school library media specialist. She is author of The Secret Reasons Teachers Are Not Using Web 2.0 and What School Librarians Can Do about It, Perceptions of Web 2.0 Tools as Catalysts for Teacher and Librarian Collaboration: A Case Study, National Board Certification in Library Media: A CandidateÊs Journal, and InfoQuest: A New Twist on Information Literacy .*

Creighton, Peggy Milam. (2013). Outfitting yourself as a core-brarian. *LMC, 32*(1), 50-51.

The Data-Driven Library Program

By Judith Dzikowski, Mary Tiedemann, and Justin Ashworth

Collaboration empowers each of us in different ways: in the school setting it brings partnerships with colleagues and relevance to the cycle of ongoing instructional improvement; in a regional setting it provides an understanding of the various facets that make up an exemplary library media program along with the challenges of the classroom. School librarians need to embrace a collaborative mindset because it is the world we live in; it is the world our students live in, and it is the world they will be working in. This article is written in the spirit of collaboration.

Onondaga-Cortland-Madison Board of Cooperative Educational Services (OCM BOCES) School Library System (SLS) is a state and district funded consortium of 24 districts, 117 schools, and 64,000+ students. The SLS's mission is to empower school librarians to be instructional experts and leaders in their school community.

A question our member school librarians have been asking over the past few years is, *"How can the library program be instrumental at leading efforts to school-wide improvement in student learning?"* Our response to this question was the creation of the PALS initiative. Throughout the last five years, 42 School Librarians, 61 Teacher Partners, and 3 Instructional Specialists from 17 school districts within our region have participated in the Partners in Achievement: Library and Students (PALS), Improving Student Achievement through Data Use for Library Media Specialists service. This article is written by Judi Dzikowski, the Director of the OCM SLS who initiated the process with vision, leadership, and membership feedback; Mary Tiedemann, the OCM SLS librarian and a BOCES Curriculum Staff Development Specialist, who guided the design and implementation of the program and

Justin Ashworth, a school librarian who participated in the program for three years.

Justin's Story Begins . . .

If you had asked me five years ago to define my role as a school librarian, taking a leadership role working with student assessment data wouldn't have been part of the conversation. Such work is usually reserved for curriculum coordinators or administrators. In 2006, my second year as a K-5 school librarian, my school district registered me with a cohort of my fellow school librarians in PALS.

The focus of PALS was to glean student achievement data from state assessments to inform and enhance library collections and collaborations with classroom teachers and to plan units of instruction to address identified student learning needs. At first I was skeptical, even a little annoyed, at the idea that the school librarian needed assessment data to justify collaboration. After all, annual standardized assessments prepared by the state are just a snapshot of where students are at a single point in time. The essential question posed by PALS became, *"How could my library program in partnership with classroom teachers leverage data from standardized state assessments to respond to students' academic strengths and challenges?"* Starting out, the learning curve was steep. PALS provided a model for the program but there was no step-by-step instruction manual for the school librarian to take the lead as a data facilitator.

The first step in PALS (we met for five full days throughout the school year) was to identify a teacher partner to participate in the program with you. I worked closely with a 3rd grade teacher partner who had mastery of grade level curriculum and a willingness to participate in the collaborative inquiry process.

During the PALS training sessions we began to learn how to use the Web application DataMentor. This is a reporting tool that warehouses results from standardized assessment data over time and allows for various levels of aggregation. The reporting features allowed us to access Web-based reports which helped us answer questions like:

- How do New York State (NYS) assessment questions relate to NYS and AASL Standards for various grade levels?
- How is a grade level performing on a specific standard/performance indicator?
- What are grade level student strengths and challenges (gaps)?
- What are our steps for planning targeted instruction?

My classroom teacher and I focused on reviewing test questions and identifying performance and trend gaps from the NYS English Language Arts assessment results. In addition, my teacher partner contributed summative and formative assessment data for us to consider.

In answering these questions, we developed a two-year action plan which detailed the specific ELA standards and performance indicators where grade level students were outperformed by the state. The data showed that the 3rd grade cohort were struggling on the performance indicator—making predictions, drawing conclusions, and making inferences. The next step was to develop a collaborative instructional unit designed to address the identified gap(s). Once we pinpointed this, my teacher partner and I designed learning experiences for our students. This involved creating, producing, and differentiating lessons using research-based strategies for a unit that targeted the skills that make students more proficient at predicting and making inferences. Our library was the perfect place to work on these gaps with its abundance of resources and a curriculum that has a focus on the AASL standards for the 21st century learner.

A valuable component of the program was the two sessions of on-site coaching. Experts from the SLS, in collaboration with the BOCES staff development department, facilitated one to one or team coaching as needed, and provided another set of eyes to analyze our data and give us feedback. We focused on student performance data, unit/lessons being developed, collection development, and the library curriculum/information literacy skills.

A parallel activity was the use of various circulation reports to analyze the library collection and devise a two-year action plan to address areas that needed alignment to the curriculum. At this point my teacher partner and I implemented the Prediction/Inference Unit and I began to work on collection development, alignment, and weeding. By year two, the word about our work began to gradually spread through the school. Other teachers inquired as to my willingness to work with them and their students in a similar fashion. Each collaboration afforded me the opportunity to develop my instructional expertise and data analysis skills. In year three I became recognized as a person who shared in the responsibility of analyzing standardized student assessment data results, and I facilitated sessions with teachers as they focused instruction on identified achievement gaps of their students.

I now co-chair the building planning team with my principal. Principals play a critical role in structuring time for the school librarian to collaborate and setting the expectation that the data team works to regularly examine student work. Becoming a school-wide leader and increasing my own data literacy has paid dividends for the students. Data-driven dialogue between the school librarian and grade level teachers has resulted in collaborative, informed instruction that is targeted at the identified achievement gaps. Leading

an effective data dialogue requires focus, guiding questions, and an understanding of the collaborative inquiry process. The increase in the use of data in our school has become a strategy for me to evaluate my instructional program and make changes aimed at improving student achievement. This year, I have had an opportunity to present to 35 members of the Parent Teacher Association (PTA) on the data cycle. I was able to show the relevance of the data analysis process and the impact that assessment data has on their child's learning. The feedback was positive; they were impressed that instruction is well-informed, dynamic, and responsive to student learning needs.

What Was the Effect on the Library Program?

How Did the PALS Service Develop?

New York State's 41 SLSs are a state-funded consortia designed to support the school library media programs for students, school librarians, faculty, and administrators in public school districts and nonpublic schools. SLSs provide services and programs that support the learning process by: promoting 21st Century skills emphasizing 21st Century Learning Standards, supporting preK-12 curriculum and NYS Learning Standards, providing professional development on the latest advancement in technologies, and providing access to print and digital resources locally, regionally, statewide and nationally.

Starting in 2004 OCM SLS began to ask the question *"How do librarians use various types of data to inform their instruction and to build a library collection aligned to curriculum and recreational reading?"* As we investigated throughout the region and beyond, the answer we heard most often was that their use of data was linked to the creation of annual reports on library usage, circulation and programming, and nothing further.

SLS envisioned that student assessment data could be a powerful

tool for librarians to use to leverage their program in addressing student learning needs. Our goal was to develop a pilot program that came to be known as (PALS). From its inception the program was a collaborative effort as SLS partnered with the curriculum and data departments within our BOCES organization to help design and implement this pilot program.

The intent of PALS is to address the challenge of improving library instruction in information literacy skills and strategies, and library collections, by linking to identified student learning needs based on standardized assessment data results. In the first year of the program (2005), 15 librarians participated. Their teacher partners joined in for the second year as the design of collaborative units began. In subsequent years librarians and teacher partners participated for one, two or three years depending on their team goal.

Using data analysis tools we focused on reviewing test questions, establishing the connection between NYS standards and the AASL Standards, analyzing assessment results, and identifying performance and trend gaps. The resulting identification of student learning need was applied to collection development, library instruction, and lesson design done in collaboration with classroom teachers. Two-year action plans were created that focused on collection alignment and development, curriculum development, and collaborative unit design.

The general purpose of the coaching visits was to support the collaboration between the school librarian and their teacher partners and to improve instruction based on student performance data.

During the next four years SLS continued to grow the program. The work was modified yearly as needed with a clear focus on data analysis. The school librarians used the data to improve the quality and relevance of their instruction, and to guide the alignment of the collection to better support the curriculum and student learning needs.

beneficial! (handwritten margin note, left)

relevance (handwritten margin note, right)

"How do I begin to identify student learning needs in my building and how do I connect this to the library program to improve student achievement?"

In the area of instruction:
- Accept the reality that you have the authority to ask for and use student achievement data.
- Consider how you utilize the AASL Standards for the 21st Century Learner to guide instruction as you align it to content areas (Language Arts, Social Studies, etc.).
- Become informed about data-driven collaboration.
- Investigate your local curriculum documents, strengthening your understanding of the content areas.
- Connect with your principal and ask, "How do I become a part of the standardized assessment data analysis process in this building?" Yes, it is a mouthful!

- Embrace that opportunity and assist with the interpretation of test results with teachers.
- Begin to develop curriculum connections and offer to collaborate with teachers on focused instructional units which address identified gaps.

In the area of collection development:
- Generate circulation/age/holdings reports to gain an understanding of collection use by grade level, gender, age, balance, and alignment to curriculum.
- Collaborate with teachers involving them in the analysis of targeted sections of the collection, developing a sense of shared ownership of the collection.
- After developing an understanding of the collection needs, develop a statement or pictogram of collection strengths and needs.

Teachers— "By collaborating with the librarians I can provide more varied and interesting lessons for the students."

"Librarians are essential to literacy development."

We hope this article has inspired you to consider the tools described, tailored to your district/school strategic plan, and the role school librarians have in 21st Century student learning as you rethink, retool, and reinvent your library program.

Suggested Reading

American Association of School Librarians. *Empowering Learners: Guidelines for School Library Media Programs.* Chicago: American Library Assoc., 2009.

Buzzeo, Toni. *The Collaboration Handbook.* Worthington, OH: Linworth, 2008.

Harada, Violet H., and Joan M. Yoshina. *Assessing Learning: Librarians and Teachers as Partners.* Westport: Libraries Unlimited, 2005.

Koechlin, Carol, and Sandi Zwaan. *Q Tasks. How to Empower Students to Ask Questions and Care about Answers.* Markham, Ontario, Canada: Pembroke Publishers Limited, 2006.

Loertscher, David V., Carol Koechlin, and Sandi Zwaan. *Beyond Bird Units: 18 Models for Teaching and Learning in Information-rich and Technology-rich Environments.* Salt Lake City, UT: Hi Willow, 2007.

Standards for the 21st Century Learner in Action. Chicago: American Library Assoc., 2007.

Using the data gathers, the next step is to create an action plan comprised of two sections— one for instruction and one for collection development—detailing the steps to implementation of your targeted collaborative curriculum units including gaps identified, standards addressed, teachers involved, resources needed, and time frame for implementation. Create an action plan for collection management clearly stating the weakness identified, steps you have identified to rectify those weakness, and time frame for completion of this work.

The following is a sample of an Action Plan Template you may wish to use. For additional examples of data analysis results, action plans, collection development, and instructional units, please see the SLS Web site (http://sls.ocmboces.org).

So, now that you have heard Justin's story and the PALS story, we would like to encourage you to write your own story.

Recognizing the impact the library media program has on student achievement, we suggest you take what we have shared and apply it to your district's goals and strategic plans.

Comments from some of our participants:

Librarians—"PALS has changed how my library program is carried out. It has allowed for growth in how I teach, what I teach, and how I develop lessons."

"PALS has empowered me, I have the data to back up what I want to do with classroom teachers."

How	Why	Who	When
Action Steps	Supporting Assessment Data	Persons Responsible/ Involved	Timeline
How Much	Support		Resources
Costs/Time	Professional Development (If Needed)		Web, Print

Zmuda, Allison, and Violet Harada. *Librarians as Learning Specialists: Meeting the Learning Imperative for the 21st Century.* Westport, CT: Libraries Unlimited, 2008.

Judith Dzikowski *is the director, School Library System at OCM BOCES in Syracuse New York. Mary Tiedemann is the school librarian at OCM BOCES School Library System in Syracuse New York. Justin Ashworth is the school librarian at McNamara Elementary School in Baldwinsville (New York) CSD.*

Dzikowski, Judith, Tiedemann, Mary, & Ashworth, Justin. (2010). The data-driven library program. *LMC, 29*(1), 10–12.

Making the Case for Evidence-Based Practice

By Joanne Bates, Janelle McClure, and Andy Spinks

Opening Arguments

Ladies and gentlemen of the jury, you are about to be presented with facts that will prove, beyond any reasonable doubt, that data can be used to enhance the effectiveness of your library media programs and gain support for them, even in the toughest budget climates. Evidence-based practice is the collection, interpretation, and use of data, such as collection statistics or assessment results, that measure the effectiveness of a library media program. We, the prosecutors, will present various forms of evidence and show that any library media specialist can use data to make informed decisions that improve the impact of the library media program, and he or she can also use data to demonstrate the quality of the program and garner support for it.

Establishing a Motive

Why would a busy library media specialist want to bother with collecting, tabulating, analyzing, and publicizing data about his or her program? Evidence-based practice sounds like a lot of work, and it clearly requires some premeditation. However, a library media program can reap substantial benefits from evidence-based practice, and in the long run, it can even eliminate some of the work required of that busy media specialist.

Most importantly, a library media specialist can use data about his or her own library media program to guide decision-making and spur immediate improvements. For example, if a library media specialist learns that students visit the library media center twice as often before school as they do after school, she might choose to open earlier in the morning and shorten afternoon hours. Similarly, if a library media specialist uses a formative assessment tool to discover that a particular lesson was not effective, he can re-teach the concepts

using a different instructional strategy. Dedicating time and resources to the most powerful practices (and eliminating those activities that are not effective), makes programs operate more efficiently and eliminates unnecessary work.

Data that reflect the effectiveness of an individual program can also be an incredibly powerful tool for public relations and advocacy. For example, data showing that after completing a research project, 87% of students in an eighth-grade science class were able to successfully organize scientific information in an appropriate chart or graph, could be used to persuade other science teachers to collaborate on similar projects. The same data could support a request for funding to update the book collection—or to support a plea to hold "picture day" somewhere other than in the library media center!

> A library media program can reap substantial benefits from evidence-based practice, and in the long run, it can even eliminate some of the work required of that busy media specialist.

Make no mistake, administrators and policymakers give priority to programs that they believe work, and this kind of specific data is a powerful tool for conveying the effectiveness of a library media program. If those leaders understand the impact of their library media programs, they will do their best to provide them with adequate funding and staffing. Also, they will try to avoid saddling their library media specialists with those dreaded "other duties as assigned." Library media specialists can use data to avoid unnecessary and unrelated

work, garner support for their programs, and enjoy the satisfaction of knowing they make a difference, so they have strong motives for using evidence-based practice!

Exhibit A: Indirect Evidence

Indirect evidence is a sort of "circumstantial" evidence; it shows that the library media program in question has done the kinds of things that have proven to be effective in other programs around the nation. To establish "guilt" we must compare existing research findings with data about the library media program in question. Here are several examples:

Collection Statistics: Research has shown that achievement is higher when students have access to larger, more up-to-date library media collections. If the collection statistics for a library media center show a significant improvement in the quantity and quality of information resources available, a case can be made that the program is making a greater contribution to student achievement at that school.

Accessibility Data: Research has shown that achievement is higher in schools where library media center resources are more accessible. If evidence shows hours have been extended, its collection has been supplemented with online research databases that extend accessibility into the classroom and the home, or its loan periods and circulation policies have been adjusted to maximize the accessibility of its resources, a case can be made that the program is making a greater contribution to student achievement at that school.

Usage Statistics: Research has shown that achievement is higher in schools where students use their library media center and its resources more frequently. If measures of book circulation, database usage, or foot traffic show that students are using a library media center more, a case can be made that the program is making a greater contribution to student achievement at that school.

Collaborative Instruction Data: Research has shown that achievement is higher in schools where library media specialists collaborate with classroom teachers to offer information literacy instruction that is integrated with subject area content. If collaborative planning documentation and the library schedule or calendar show that the library media specialist has provided more and better information literacy instruction, the case can be made that the program is making a greater contribution to the overall level of student achievement at that school.

For more information, jurors are encouraged to examine the briefing filed by Lance and Loertscher that outlines the research findings on the impact of library media programs on student achievement. As in the examples above, research findings can be paired with data collected at a local school to establish "guilt by association."

> *Make no mistake, administrators and policymakers give priority to programs that they believe work, and this kind of specific data is a powerful tool for conveying the effectiveness of a library media program.*

Exhibit B: Direct Evidence

Direct evidence can be used to prove that one's library media program is guilty of improving student achievement. These kinds of evidence are incontrovertible; they show that the actions of the library media specialist *directly led to student learning*. Fortunately, this type of data can be collected easily as part of the assessment process.

Some examples are very simple, such as using a "ticket out the door" to check students' grasp of a concept at the end of a lesson.

In this activity, students respond to a brief prompt such as, "Give one reason that it is important to cite the sources of your information in a research paper," or "List three ways to determine the quality of a Web site." The students turn in their responses (their "tickets out the door") as they leave. Afterward, the teacher or library media specialist tallies correct responses to measure the impact of the lesson.

Other types of direct evidence require more advance planning and greater collaboration with the classroom teacher, such as comparing the results of pre-tests and post-tests results, or using project assessment rubrics to measure students' ability to apply a skill. Several examples of direct evidence will be discussed in the eyewitness testimony to follow, and many more are included in the briefing on collaborative assessment of library media instruction filed by Harada and Yoshina.

Eyewitness Testimony

Now, the prosecution would like to call our first witness, Joanne Bates, to the stand. Ms. Bates, would you describe for the jury how you became involved with evidence-based practice?

My data use began a few years ago as I was trying to get more teachers to collaborate on instruction. At that time, most of my library media lessons were planned and delivered without any true teacher collaboration, and I never did any formal assessment of what students learned. In hopes of motivating teachers to collaborate more, I decided to create an assessment to see just what the students already knew.

Instead of beginning the year with the usual orientation, I gave our fifth-graders a simple pre-assessment consisting of 10 general questions about information literacy. I administered the pre-assessment using a student response system, which made it more fun for students and made it easier for me to collect and tabulate the data. I used Promethean's ActiVote system, which allowed me to export

the responses for each class as a color-coded Excel spreadsheet, with all the correct responses highlighted in green and the incorrect answers highlighted in red.

I asked the fifth grade teachers if I could talk to them during their team planning session, and I came armed with a printed copy of each class's spreadsheet, exported from the ActiVote system. As I handed out the spreadsheets, they were visibly shocked. After seeing the amount of red on the spreadsheets, the teachers could not deny that their students needed more instruction in information literacy. They agreed that we needed to meet on a more regular basis to collaboratively plan their students' library media instruction.

Throughout the year, I worked with the fifth grade teachers to plan a series of lessons and projects to develop these information literacy skills. I conducted formative assessments and made adjustments as necessary. Finally, I gave a post-assessment that paralleled the pre-assessment from the beginning of the year. The results revealed that *every class* made improvements in their understanding of information literacy skills. Overall, the mastery level increased by 43 percent. Since I used the ActiVote system to conduct the post-assessment, I was able to generate a color-coded spreadsheet for each class. Seeing the shift from mostly red to mostly green convinced the teachers of the effectiveness of our collaboration.

That was three years ago. Each year since, I have expanded my use of assessment and improved the tools I use. I use pre- and post-assessments with third and fourth grades, and I have aligned them more closely to the curriculum standards for each grade level. I use formative assessments to measure student progress during individual units, either with the student response system, project-based activities, "tickets out the door," or other strategies. The formative assessments allow me to see if the students grasped the key concepts, or if I need to go back and re-teach using a different approach.

Figure 1 The shift from mostly blue to mostly green is a strong visual representation of the progress students made.

Class 5A - Individual Student Responses

	Pre-Assessment (9/4/2007)											Post-Assessment (5/8/2008)										
Student	%	Q1	Q2	Q3	Q4	Q5	Q6	Q7	Q8	Q9	Q10	%	Q1	Q2	Q3	Q4	Q5	Q6	Q7	Q8	Q9	Q10
A 1	50	D	C	A	A	A	D	C	B	D	D	80	C	C	A	D	A	B	C	B	A	D
A 2	50	B	C	D	D	A	D	B	B	B	D	100	B	C	A	D	A	B	C	D	A	D
A 3	80	C	C	A	C	A	B	C	D	A	D	90	B	C	A	D	A	B	C	D	A	B
A 4	70	C	C	A	D	A	D	C	B	A	D	60	D	C	A	D	A	A	C	B	A	B
A 5	70	B	C	D	D	A	D	C	B	A	D	90	B	C	A	D	A	B	C	B	A	D
A 6	70	B	C	D	C	A	B	C	B	A	D	80	B	C	A	D	A	B	C	D	C	C
A 7	80	B	C	A	D	A	D	C	B	A	D	90	B	C	A	D	A	B	C	B	A	D
A 8	80	B	C	A	C	A	B	C	C	A	D	80	B	C	A	C	A	B	C	B	A	D
A 9	70	B	C	A	D	A	D	A	B	A	D	90	C	C	A	D	A	B	C	D	A	D
A 10	70	C	C	A	C	A	B	C	B	A	D	90	B	C	A	D	A	B	C	B	A	D
A 11	50	D	B	A	B	A	B	C	B	A	C	80	B	C	A	D	A	B	C	B	D	D
A 12	40	D	C	A	A	B	C	B	B	A	D	90	B	C	A	D	A	B	C	B	A	D
A 13	80	C	C	A	D	A	A	C	D	A	D	90	B	C	A	C	A	B	C	D	A	D
A 14	80	B	C	A	C	A	B	C	B	A	D	90	B	C	A	D	A	B	C	D	A	B
A 15	60	A	C	A	C	A	D	C	B	A	D	90	B	C	A	D	A	B	C	D	A	B
A 16	30	B	C	B	A	C	A	A	A	D	D	80	B	C	A	C	A	B	C	D	A	C
A 17	70	B	C	A	B	D	B	C	C	A	D	80	B	C	A	D	A	B	C	B	A	B
A 18	60	B	C	A	C	D	A	C	B	A	D	70	B	C	A	D	A	D	C	C	A	B
A 19	60	B	A	A	C	C	B	C	B	A	D	90	B	C	A	D	A	B	C	B	A	D
A 20	30	D	C	C	D	D	C	A	A	A	F	100	B	C	A	D	A	B	C	D	A	D
A 21	10	D	B	A	A	D	C	A	A	D	B	90	B	C	A	D	A	B	C	D	B	D
A 22	60	C	C	A	C	A	B	C	B	A	F	80	B	C	A	C	A	B	C	D	A	B
A 23	70	B	C	A	D	B	B	B	B	A	D	100	B	C	A	D	A	B	C	D	A	D
A 24	30	A	A	C	A	A	D	C	B	A	B	70	C	C	A	D	A	B	C	B	A	C

Green highlighting indicates correct responses. Blue highlighting indicates incorrect responses.

Because of the initiative I took to begin using assessment and collecting data, the majority of my teachers now actively collaborate with me on information literacy instruction. Now that I have been collecting assessment data for a few years, I use it to prove to teachers, administrators, and the school community that my library media program has a direct impact on student learning at our school. (I can even say that my efforts have had an effect beyond the school level. Our assistant superintendent came in once while I was giving a post-assessment using the student response system. She was so amazed to see a library media specialist using assessment this way that she asked me to give a presentation to all of the principals in our area! I don't know what took me so long to start, but I'm proud that I did. Now I couldn't imagine doing my job *without* using data.

Thank you, Ms. Bates. Now the prosecution would like to call Janell McClure to the stand. Ms. McLure, could you describe for the jury some of the ways you have used data in your library media program?

I admit, I have personally engaged in a number of data-gathering activities, including pre/post tests, student performance observations, and student reflections. I used the results of these formal and informal assessments to improve instruction and deepen collaboration with my professional accomplices.

Two years ago, elementary, middle, and high school educators in our area met in "vertical teams" to examine ways to improve our students' transition from elementary to middle school and from middle to high school. High school library media specialists reported that students were entering ninth grade without several crucial information literacy skills, including searching databases, citing sources, and even saving documents. Based on these discussions, I collaborated with the eighth grade language arts teachers at my school to create a series of six lessons that would give students the information literacy skills they would need to be successful in ninth grade. The lessons focused on the concerns expressed by our high school colleagues, but they also aligned with approximately 25 state curriculum standards and AASL information literacy standards. We called the project "Eighth Grade Academy," because all six lessons were taught in the final four weeks of the school year, after the administration of Georgia's high-stakes Criterion-Referenced Competency Test (CRCT).

At the beginning of the program, the teachers and I gave a brief pre-test to determine the students' current proficiency in our focus areas. After each lesson, students were also asked to write a one-sentence "ticket out the door" describing what they learned during that day's activities. After three lessons, we gave a quiz to assess the students' comprehension of the concepts and their ability to apply these new skills. After the final lesson of the "Academy," the students completed a post-test that mirrored the pre-test given before the first lesson. I charted the results, and the teachers were pleased to find that their students' overall mastery of the concepts had improved in a majority of the classes.

We further examined the data to determine how it might help

improve our own performance as educators. We realized that our pre- and post- test questions were not as well aligned with our lessons as we would have liked. Also, we discovered a consistent lack of growth in student performance in some specific areas, indicating that our instruction had not addressed those topics as successfully as we had hoped. Finally, we noticed that in the students' reflections, their perception of their own information literacy skills were slightly different than what had been observed by our high school colleagues; the students felt they had mastered skills, such as saving documents and understanding effective search terms, but the high school library media specialists reported otherwise. Based on the insights from this data, we modified the pre-test questions and the lessons for the following year to better address the concerns of the high school library media specialists and the needs of the students.

After the second year, our collaborative team made more improvements to the instructional goals, lessons, and the test questions. We also began using an online survey tool called SurveyMonkey <http://www.surveymonkey.com> to administer the pretest. The reporting feature of SurveyMonkey automatically generated charts that visually represented the overall responses for each question. At a glance, we were able to determine which skills students had already mastered and which ones needed the most instructional attention.

Now that I have several years' worth of data to show that this instructional program is effective, it has been much easier to convince teachers to start the lessons before the CRCT is administered. We have also continued to improve the quality of the pre- and post-test items, and we are using better formative assessments to ensure that students are retaining the

skills they learn and can apply them in context.

After seeing the power of data in improving my instruction and promoting my library media program, I have started to use it more and more. CRCT test results reveal areas where our students struggle, and within those areas, I have identified specific topics that library media instruction can support and collaborated with teachers to develop instructional units that address these target areas. I'm so addicted to data, that when it is not readily available, I do whatever is necessary to get it. I have even used SurveyMonkey to poll students regarding their reading habits and preferences, then used this data for reading promotion and collection development. I can't get enough!

Thank you, Ms. McClure. I believe that the jury is now beginning to see how powerful evidence-based practice can be.

Figure 2 **Students showed no progress on some questions, indicating that our instruction had not effectively addressed those topics or that our questions were not valid measures of their knowledge in those areas. In response to these findings, we modified our assessment questions to ensure their alignment with the standards and adjusted our instructional methods to improve their effectiveness.**

Number of Incorrect Student Responses, Pre-test vs. Post-Test

Question #	Class 8A Pre	Post	Class 8B Pre	Post	Class 8C Pre	Post	Class 8D Pre	Post	Class 8E Pre	Post
Q1	3	0	1	1	1	0	0	0	6	2
Q2	11	8	10	4	4	1	13	3	9	3
Q3	5	5	8	4	7	8	11	3	9	6
Q4	5	4	4	5	4	2	5	0	1	4
Q5	8	4	10	3	11	3	14	4	16	7
Q6	11	8	5	5	10	8	12	10	8	10
Q7	11	12	12	9	8	7	12	10	12	10
Q8	12	12	10	10	9	15	10	13	15	10
Q9	12	14	12	11	13	2	15	15	19	10
Q10	6	6	3	4	6	6	2	2	9	8

Green highlighting indicates questions on which the class showed had the same or a greater number of incorrect responses.

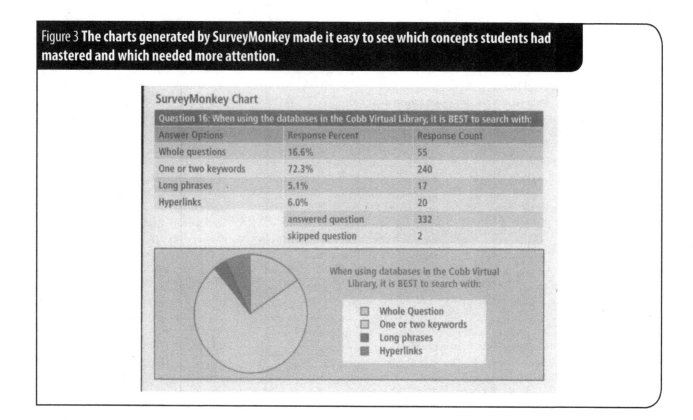

Figure 3 The charts generated by SurveyMonkey made it easy to see which concepts students had mastered and which needed more attention.

SurveyMonkey Chart

Question 16: When using the databases in the Cobb Virtual Library, it is BEST to search with:		
Answer Options	Response Percent	Response Count
Whole questions	16.6%	55
One or two keywords	72.3%	240
Long phrases	5.1%	17
Hyperlinks	6.0%	20
	answered question	332
	skipped question	2

When using databases in the Cobb Virtual Library, it is BEST to search with:

- ☐ Whole Question
- ☐ One or two keywords
- ■ Long phrases
- ■ Hyperlinks

Closing Arguments

Ladies and gentlemen of the jury, you can clearly see that these various types of evidence are sufficient to prove the effectiveness of a school's library media program. Indirect evidence, such as circulation or usage data, establishes that the library media program and its staff have engaged in practices known to impact student achievement. Furthermore, direct evidence collected from instructional assessments proves that a library media specialist is guilty of teaching in the first degree! (Such an effect on student learning could not have occurred unless the act was intentional and premeditated.) Library media specialists have a clear motive for engaging in such practices, because they provide a mechanism for improving the effectiveness of their programs, eliminating unnecessary work, and gaining support from teachers and education leaders during a time when it is needed more than ever.

Court Documents

Harada, Violet H., and Joan M. Yoshina. *Assessing Learning: Librarians and Teachers as Partners*. Westport, CN: Libraries Unlimited, 2005.

Lance, Keith C., and David V. Loertscher. *Powering Achievement: School Library Media Programs Make a Difference: The Evidence Mounts* (3rd ed.). Salt Lake City, UT: Hi Willow Research, 2003.

Loertscher, David V., with Ross J. Todd. *We Boost Achievement! Evidence-Based Practice for School Library Media Specialists*. Salt Lake City, UT: Hi Willow Research & Publishing, 2003.

Joanne Bates *is a library media specialist at Tritt Elementary School in Marietta, Georgia.*

Janelle McClure *is a library media specialist at Palmer Middle School in Kennesaw, Georgia.*

Andy Spinks *is the supervisor of library media education for the Cobb County (Georgia) School District.*

Bates, Joanne, McClure, Janelle, & Spinks, Andy. (2010). Making the case for evidence-based practice. *LMC, 29*(1), 24-27.

Five Years Later: A Look at Building and Triangulating Evidence in a School Library

By Susan D. Yutzey

In 2005, I attended an evidence-based practice workshop sponsored by the Ohio Educational Library Media Association (OELMA) featuring Professor Ross Todd. Professor Todd, who had recently completed his groundbreaking research study entitled "Student Learning through Ohio School Libraries: Background, Methodology and Report of Findings," presented two scenarios to his audience:

> If your local newspaper asked you "We want to do a story on your school library and how it really helps students learn."
>
> OR
>
> If your school board was trying to make a budget decision and asked "how your school library impacts students."

"What would you answer?" was the challenge for those of us sitting in the room. Participation in the workshop was a transforming experience. The traditional statistics that I had painstakingly gathered and recorded for our annual report did not provide evidence of actual learning. Evidence acquired through assessment, both formative and summative, provides the evidence that "school libraries are more than repositories of information or alternatives to study halls—school libraries are places of essential learning for every student in the school" (Logan 7).

So five years later what kind of evidence about the school library program's effect on learner achievement can I give to the school board or to the local newspaper? Rather than statistics on the number of books circulated, number of classes in the library, number of teacher collaborations, number of students from study halls, I provide data on a variety of measures related to information literacy and research skills. These "process skills" are typically not measured with the high stakes content-oriented tests but are recognized by the Partnership of the 21st Century Skills as the "skills, knowledge and expertise students should master to succeed in work and life in the 21st century" ("Overview," pars. 4).

Beyond gathering evidence through assessments, we attempt to triangulate the evidence, that is to say, we collect data from various points of view or vantage points (Champlin, Loertscher, and Miller ix, Todd, pars. 5). We use the strategies described below to gather evidence from multiple vantage points about our students' achievement in information literacy.

Simple Class Reflection after a Teaching/Learning Session in the Library

At some point during our teaching sessions in the library or in a classroom, we take five minutes to ask some important questions.

These could be part of a class discussion, a quick survey, or a quick write. Here are some of the questions we ask:

- How many were successful in finding information last night? Why or why not?
- What three important things did you learn today about (fill in the blank)?
- How did your experience today improve how you conduct research?
- Is research a process? Explain your answer and use evidence from your past experience.
- What part of the research are you finding the most difficult?
- How can we as teacher and librarian help you succeed better?
- If you were doing this project again, how would you do it differently?

Champlin, Loertscher, and Miller in *Sharing the Evidence: Library Media Center Assessment Tools and Resources* provide some other simple reflection questions such as:

- What tricks helped you to find the information you needed quickly?
- How did you know when you found high quality information?
- When you get stuck in the research process what should you do next?
- Why isn't Google always the answer?
- What did we do today that helped you summarize the information you found?
- Did working in teams help you get more done?
- What database gave you the best results?
- What would help us get more done in the time we have in the library?
- What tools do we have at school that you need at home?
- What tools do you have at home that we should have at school?

Our favorite question is "What part of the research are you finding the most difficult?" The students write down their thoughts on a 3 x 5 library catalog card and we quickly thumb through looking for patterns. We respond to their concerns throughout the period. If you're looking for triangulation of evidence, compare the patterns that emerge with those found in Kulthau's *Model of the Stages of the Information Process in her Seeking Meaning: A Process Approach to Library and Information Services.* Kulthau describes the thoughts and feelings students experience at every stage of the research process, what kinds of strategies teachers can employ to help students and what kinds of actions students can take to help themselves. Building those "self-reliance" and problem-solving skills are essential to prepare our students to compete in a global economy.

These formative assessments provide powerful information to students and teacher librarians. First, the immediate and careful analysis of this assessment data reveals patterns of student understanding and confusion. Second, it informs teaching practices that can then be adjusted as students are working.

Information Literacy Lessons: Multiple Types of Evidence

Students can be evaluated at any stage of the information literacy model being used. For example, they may be evaluated in their skill at finding relevant information using a search engine or a fee-based subscription database. When an entire model such as the

Big 6 or the Savvy 7 is used, rubrics can be created for each one of the components to assess student success at that level. At the "Sorting and Sifting" stage of Jamie McKenzie's Research Cycle we want students to begin analyzing their sources and developing rationales for why these sources are critical to their research. We created an annotation rubric that assesses their ability to analyze their sources. The rubric helps us assess their ability to recognize the type of source (e.g., book, journal, magazine); establish the credibility of the source (author's expertise in the field); determine the rationale for choosing the source; summarize the significant arguments; discuss its significance to the research; and identify its limitations.

> *Our favorite question is "What part of the research are you finding the most difficult?" The students write down their thoughts on a 3 x 5 library catalog card and we quickly thumb through looking for patterns.*

At the beginning of the Gathering stage of the Research Cycle, my colleague gives students a sample annotation and a brief lesson on the components of an annotation. Students submit a works cited with two sources and their accompanying annotations and are assessed by my colleague using the rubric shown in Table 1. Year after year, student scores reveal that they have difficulty in several areas: purpose and summary of the source; rationale for using the source; and limitations of the source.

My colleague returns to the classroom and shares the group scores for the class. As with the formative assessment described in the previous section, this formative assessment reveals patterns of student understanding and confusion. My colleague re-teaches the lesson using a variety of high-interest books (cookbooks, automobiles, true crime) to demonstrate how sources have different purposes. Our favorite example involved a student who in evaluating a cookbook realized that the book was created for diabetics but specifically diabetics who had recently been diagnosed with the disease. By taking the time to read the preface and introduction of a book, the students realized how they could use that information to further determine the book's purpose. The students re-submit the works cited with revised annotations. Using the same rubric, my colleague assesses the revised annotations, and the scores in the areas of purpose and summary of the source, rationale for using the source, and limitations of the source improve by at least one level. This exercise builds students' confidence as well as self-reliance.

To triangulate the data, teacher librarians and collaborating teachers can examine the student's revised annotation scores and compare them with the student's score on the TRAILS assessment, particularly the scores from "Evaluate Resources" and "Identify Sources." TRAILS or Tools for Real-Time Assessment of Information Literacy Skills is a project of Kent State University Libraries. "TRAILS is a free, self-guided, self-administered assessment tool used to determine the information literacy competencies of their students" ("Ideas for Using," pars. 1). Each assessment is composed of multiple-choice questions targeting a variety of information literacy skills based on sixth and ninth grade *Ohio Academic Content Standards* and AASL's *Information Power*. A ninth grade version of TRAILS was released in 2006 and the sixth grade version was released in 2008. Third grade and twelfth grade versions are being developed and tested this year. Since its inception through fall 2009, over 7,600 librarians throughout the U.S. and 30 plus countries have administered TRAILS to more than 211,000 students. For more information on this assessment tool go to <http://www.trails-9.org/index.php?page=home>.

Ninth graders' proficiency with databases was the focus of this information literacy lesson. Coiro (2003) states that: "The Internet, in particular, provides new text formats, new purposes for reading, and new ways to interact with information that can confuse and overwhelm people taught to extract meaning from only conventional print." The idea of a fee-based subscription database as "new literacy" for students—one that could confuse and overwhelm students—evolved into an intriguing collaborative lesson for ninth graders enrolled in Honors English and an opportunity to assess their proficiency with databases. Students were divided into database groups: Bloom's Literacy Reference Online; Biography Reference Bank; Oxford Reference Online; ProQuest Learning Literature; and a search engine (Google, Clusty). Within their groups students were first asked to find specific information on John Knowles's *A Separate Peace* and use the various tools found within the database or search engine (email, print, listen to text, cite). Within their groups students used a database rubric to analyze the characteristics of their respective database and then compose a review of the database. The reviews appeared on our course management system, Moodle, for students within the class to read. Each student was then to compare and contrast at least two features of one database with his or her assigned database. The final step was for each group to develop a slogan to advertise the database. Students across all six ninth grade Honors English classes voted for their favorite slogan.

Table 1 Annotated Citations Scoring Rubric

Category	Proficient (2 points)	Novice (1 point)	Beginner (0 points)
Source Type	The resource type is accurately determined	A source is mentioned, but not accurately determined	The type of source is not addressed
Primary or Secondary	Identification of source as primary or secondary is accurate	Source is identified as primary or secondary, but identification is inaccurate	Identification of source as primary or secondary is not noted
Credibility	Annotation provides significant background information about author's/creator's authority in the research field	Annotation somewhat addresses the author's/creator's authority ("Professor," "PhD," etc.)	Annotation does not address the author's/creator's authority in the research field
Purpose/ Summary	Annotation clearly summarizes the main idea and purpose of the work and accurately identifies the scope of the source	Annotation contains a general/ vague statement instead of identifying the central idea/ purpose of the entire source	Annotation does not include a summary of the purpose of the source
Rationale	Annotation contains a clear rationale for both choosing and using the source	Annotation contains rationale for choosing, but not how the source is being used	Annotation contains no rationale for choosing and using the source
Limitations	Annotation contains a clear description of the information still needed for research	Annotations contain a statement of how the resource is limited, but not which information is still needed	Annotation does not address the issue of limitations at all

Voted the Best Slogans

To celebrate and honor the students' creativity we converted the slogans into banners that now hang from the ceiling in the Learning Center. To assess proficiency with these specific databases, I developed a reflection tool centering on the pre-determined learning targets that asked students about their confidence with the database and their group experience (Table 2).

Since this assignment was done at the beginning of the school year, I could use the results of this summative assessment to work with students on their database proficiency throughout the school year. In addition, the scores could be triangulated with TRAILS scores, specifically "Identify Potential Sources;" and "Develop, Use, and Revise Search Strategies."

In the five years since my EBP training, there is no doubt that our sophistication in creating different types of evidence from multiple perspectives has grown. This research-derived evidence helps us shape and direct what we do as we work with students one-on-one

Figure 1

ProQuest Learning Literature: Quick and Easy Like Oatmeal

7 billion people on the planet. Search one. Biography Reference Bank

The search goes zoom when you use Bloom!

and in groups and how we design and implement our collaborative lessons with teachers. It helps us make decisions about how the school library can best meet the instructional goals of the school and become the lifelong learning center. The lifelong learning center, as we envision it, is one in which we know that through the systematic collection and analysis of evidence our instructional practices impact student achievement. More importantly, that the student achievement goes beyond good scores on high stakes, multiple-choice tests—it means developing deep knowledge and understanding and the

competence and skills for thinking, living, and working in a competitive global society.

Works Cited

Champlin, Connie, David V. Loertscher, and Nancy A.S. Miller. *Sharing the Evidence: Library Media Center Assessment Tools and Resources*. Salt Lake City: Hi Willow, 2003.

Coiro, Julie. "Reading Comprehension on the Internet: Expanding Our Understanding of Reading Comprehension to Encompass New Literacies."

Table 2 Self-Reflection

Say to yourself, I can	I can do this	I cannot do this	I am okay but need more work
Locate and summarize information found on a database or search engine			
Identify the features of a database or search engine			
Apply some of the features of a database or search engine to answer my information needs			
Compare and contrast my understanding of a database feature to another database			
Explain the features of a database and how it would help my information needs to my peers			
Write a database review based upon criteria identified by my teacher			
Synthesize my learning by creating an original slogan for a database			
Work collaboratively with peers in my product review group to achieve the above-mentioned learning targets			

Feb. 2003. *Reading Online* 8 Apr. 2010 <http://www.readingonline.org//_index.asp?HREF=///2–03_Column/.html>.

"Ideas for Using TRAILS." *Tools for Real-time Assessment of Information Literacy Skills (TRAILS)*. 2010. Kent State U Libraries. 8 Apr. 2010 <http://www.trails-9.org>.

Logan, Debra Kay. "Practical Advocacy: A Measure for Success." *Library Media Connection* (Mar.-Apr. 2010): 7.

"Overview." *Partnership of the 21st Century Skills*. 2004. 6 Apr. 2010. <http://www.p21.org/.php?option=com_content&task=view&id=254&Itemid=119>.

Todd, Ross. "The Evidence-Based Manifesto for School Librarians." *School Library Journal*. 8 Apr. 2010 <http://www.schoollibraryjournal.com>.

Susan D. Yutzey *holds a doctorate from The Ohio State University and an MLS degree from Kent State University. She is currently the Director of the Learning Center at Upper Arlington High School, Columbus, Ohio, a position she has held since 2002.*

Yutzey, Susan D. (2010). Five years later: A look at building and triangulating evidence in a school library. *LMC, 29*(1), 14–16.

Teaching in the Zone

Formative Assessments for Critical Thinking

By Leslie K. Maniotes

An Impressionist Vignette of Guided Inquiry in the Library Media Center

Enter the Library Media Center in a public high school in Denver. The students are sitting in small groups engaged in conversation, with notes and laptop computers at their tables, as well as primary source images, letters and objects. They are in the exploration phase of an inquiry project looking at the topic of the post-emancipation African-American experience 1865–1917. One group is talking about freedom and the challenges that newly freed people faced. Another group is delving into identity creation, how African Americans, during that time period, came to define themselves. Another is looking at the institutions that shaped the African-American experience. A fourth group is talking about the politics and leadership that arose within the African-American community.

As students immerse themselves into the inquiry, the instructional team encourages them to bridge the connections from the information they are finding into their own interests and lives. Students fill out "connection journals" to help them purposefully and explicitly relate what they are reading to their own experience and thinking.

A closer look at the groups uncovers the emerging individuality. Under the group topic of freedom, Destiny and Brianna are interested in finding out about the women, looking at images of women's dress, as well as songs and mottos. Marcus, in the leadership group, is interested in Frederick Douglas' writings. Derek, in the identity group, has uncovered a paper on "Pigmentocracy" and is interested in how skin tone of African Americans creates an unspoken hierarchy

(Harris). He wants to look closer at the historical underpinnings of this value system. Talking to Derek about his topic has made Alicia curious about the biology of race and she is examining the human genome project and relating it to the beliefs of the post emancipation time period.

> As students immerse themselves into the inquiry, the instructional team encourages them to bridge the connections from the information they are finding into their own interests and lives.

Figure 1

Topics and resources for this impressionist vignette came from the National Humanities Center toolbox. Find much more about this topic and others at: http://nationalhumanitiescenter.org/pds/index.httTi

Derek and Alicia are not the only two conversing. The students are grouped in ways that enable conversation around topics and provide a supportive environment for questioning and puzzling through ideas together. The instructional team recognizes the power of social learning and provides the structure for that learning to happen. The teachers also recognize the power of intrinsic motivation and encourage the students to connect the information that they

find to their own lives. It takes a bit more time for students to find their own path through the information, but the end result is much more powerful learning. The teachers have decided that the time invested is worth the learning rewards.

The history teacher and the school librarian are sitting with different student groups. When you look carefully, they are mostly listening and taking notes. Each has an observational focus for the session. The school librarian's goal is to gather information about how students are engaging their critical-thinking skills. The history teacher is examining how students are synthesizing connections between their current understandings with what they are discovering about the time period and its people. This instructional team is facilitating learning by guiding the inquiry.

Learning Is Complex within an Inquiry Framework

The previous impressionist vignette (Van Maanen) demonstrates of the complexity of constructivist learning that occurs within an inquiry frame. It describes the social learning context of inquiry while highlighting, at the same time, the customized and individual nature. These complexities of inquiry pose a problem for assessing the learning that occurs. The conclusion of this vignette highlights how the instructional team takes on the task of assessment (Harada and Yoshina). The librarian hones in on the assessment of students' critical thinking. Her teaching will be guided by the formative assessments of observation and focused note taking during group work. What should these notes include? How can she help students improve their critical thinking and strengthen their higher order thinking skills through the inquiry process? The goal of this article is to help answer these questions.

First, we'll look at the big picture, using a Guided Inquiry approach to examine how we teach higher order thinking skills within an inquiry paradigm. Next, we'll consider how formative assessments can be used to match the teaching to the student's learning needs during inquiry. Finally, we'll look at a critical-thinking checklist, a formative assessment tool to help teachers focus on specific learning targets of critical thinking during observations. A post-observation worksheet follows to help analyze the observational notes to create meaningful next steps for instruction.

As we implement the AASL standards, students must continually be locating, evaluating and using information in meaningful contexts to construct new understandings. AASL states that inquiry "provides the framework" for students to learn how to "thrive in a complex information environment." Through inquiry, students are using thinking skills and the habits of mind of information seekers while expanding their information literacy skills within a community of practice (Wegner; Yuckawa & Harada).

In Guided Inquiry, Kuhlthau, Maniotes & Caspari unpack the complexity of learning in inquiry by defining the five kinds of learning in practice. The simultaneous nature of learning in inquiry creates a complex design problem for the instructional team. How do we teach in this complex learning environment? How can we assess all this learning going on at once? Each kind of learning requires guidance or targeted instruction.

Assessment of Learning within Inquiry

Shepard explains that within a learning culture, such as with inquiry, the assessment changes. Educators are comfortable with assessing the end product, as grading is common practice. We are familiar with using rubrics and looking at products to assess student learning. Using a rubric as a summative assessment has value, but it is not enough (Harada and Yoshina; Zmuda and Harada; Kuhlthau, Maniotes and Caspari). To facilitate learning in the inquiry context, we have to guide the learning. This requires formative assessments (P21 ereport). Through formative assessments we can recognize gaps in learning, and find ways to coach students to improve.

Consider the school librarian in the opening vignette. She wants to assess critical thinking. If she waits until the end there is no opportunity for improvement and instruction. How does she assess during the learning process to intervene? Shepard recommends some tools that can be used to inform our teaching within the learning cycle.

Tools for Formative Assessment

Shepard suggests that when we are teaching within a constructivist framework, the assessments must be "dynamic and ongoing." They must be placed "in the middle of the teaching and learning process instead of being postponed as only the end-point of instruction" (10). She agrees that assessments within the learning cycle help teachers to create "perfectly targeted occasions to teach and provides the means to scaffold next steps" (10). With these tools in use Shepard reminds us that educators "must engage in a systematic analysis of the available evidence" (8) in order to create the targeted customized instruction we seek to accomplish. The analysis must include evidence for specific learning traits resulting in an action plan for assisting or coaching the student toward improving skills, behaviors, and dispositions in action. The research on the Information Search Process helps us to envision this type of teaching as occurring within a "zone of intervention" (Kuhlthau).

What is a zone of intervention for critical thinking?

Unfortunately, most schoolwork is limited to shallow processing in response to simple or superficial questions with prescribed answers. Deep processing requires engagement and motivation that stimulate inquiry within a constructivist approach to learning.

Figure 2	
Interventions for Learning in the Inquiry Process	
Five Kinds of Learning	**Types of Intervention**
Curriculum Content	for fact finding, interpreting, and synthesizing
Learning How to Learn	for initiating, selecting, exploring, focusing, collecting and presenting
Information Literacy	for locating, evaluating and using information
Literacy Competence	for improving reading, writing, speaking and listening
Social Skills	for interacting, cooperating and collaborating
Kuhlthau, Maniotes, & Caspari 2007, 141	

Figure 3
Tools for Data Gathering
Observations
Interviews
Reflective journals
Projects
Demonstrations
Collections of student work
Student's self-evaluations *(Adapted from Shepard, 2000)*

Deep processing fosters higher order thinking that requires intervention at critical points in the learning process…

The zone of intervention is that area in which a student can do with advice and assistance what he or she cannot do alone or can do only with great difficulty. Intervention within this zone enables students to progress in the accomplishment of their task. Intervention outside this zone is inefficient and unnecessary, and may be experienced by students as intrusive on the one hand and as overwhelming on the other. (Kuhlthau, Maniotes & Caspari, 27)

The zone of intervention, an extension of Vygotsky's zone of proximal development concept, is an area for targeted instruction. Teachers can use the wide scope of research around the ISP (Kuhlthau et al.) to inform teaching decisions.

Within these phases there are rich opportunities for learning and developing thinking skills. "The studies of the ISP indicate that the exploration and formulation stages are when higher order thinking is developed by carefully planned advice and assistance of the instructional team" (23).

What Does Teaching in the Zone Look Like?

True inquiry learning requires a customized approach. For example, teaching in the zone requires that students aren't all handed the same graphic organizer at once and taught how to use it. This may happen at the elementary level when students are just learning what graphic organizers are. But having all students do the same thing is standardized teaching (Christensen). Many times teaching is facilitating, more like a conversation

with a student, asking questions, pushing their thinking, wondering with them, and then making a small useful suggestion at just the right time to move them ahead. The assessments we use must help us to make good teaching decisions during the learning process.

Using Observation to Assess Critical Thinking

Are there zones of intervention for critical thinking? What do they look like? Kuhlthau's research suggests that there are. When do you intervene? So how do we know who needs what lesson? Teachers who adopt a constructivist approach are constantly observing students and keeping records of what students are doing, saying and demonstrating. At times these observations are informal. However, when students are working on a specific skill set an in-depth observation is necessary.

Observations can include a variety of record keeping devices from note taking, audio recording, video recording, to scripting conversations. Different forms of recording may be employed, depending upon the learning goals. For example, if the goal is student collaboration, then an audio recording of their conversation during inquiry circles would provide the needed data (Kuhlthau et al., 43). But if the goal is to facilitate the development of higher order thinking skills, then observations of students engaging in higher order thinking would be necessary.

Observing critical thinking during inquiry is a complex problem and checklists are useful when you have a complex problem (Gawande). Checklists break down the core features or elements of a more complex whole to help see its component parts. This checklist was created considering what habits of mind and observable behaviors critical thinkers would employ through the inquiry process (Wiggins and McTighe). It is designed to help focus teachers' observations on critical-thinking behaviors in action.

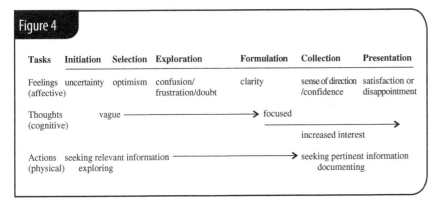

Figure 4

Tasks	Initiation	Selection	Exploration	Formulation	Collection	Presentation
Feelings (affective)	uncertainty	optimism	confusion/ frustration/doubt	clarity	sense of direction /confidence	satisfaction or disappointment
Thoughts (cognitive)		vague ———————→ focused				
				increased interest ——————→		
Actions (physical)	seeking relevant information ——————→ exploring				seeking pertinent information documenting	

Figure 5

In the creation of the checklist I used these online resources on critical thinking:

http://www.criticalthinking.org/

https://my.wsu.edu/portal/page?_pageid=177,276578&_dad=portal&_schema=PORTAL

http://litre.ncsu.edu/sltoolkit/Critical_Thinking_Rubrics.htm

http://educate.intel.com/en/AssessingProjects/OverviewAndBenefits/

Once these behaviors were identified, the list was arranged in the order that these skills would be put to use in the inquiry. For example, we want students to ask questions throughout the inquiry, but students' questions in the beginning of inquiry steer the thinking across the entire process. Then as students find sources relevant to their interest, they must evaluate those sources and make choices whether to include them or not. As they read, critical thinkers use connections to help bridge information from a variety of sources as well as from their life experiences. During the inquiry the students would share their perspective with others, listen to other people's ideas and respond to them. Reflecting and reasoning occurs when students synthesize information, interpret ideas and create their own arguments. Students use organizing tools across the inquiry to manage and interpret information. Finally students will draw conclusions and adapt a critical stance to create a logical argument to share with others.

This critical-thinking checklist is meant as a template. All of the higher order thinking skills as well as habits of mind/dispositions in action that occur in a well-designed inquiry can be broken out in this way.

How Do I Use This Checklist?

The blank checklist is an observational note-taking template. As you observe students, only write observations of what the student did, said, and wrote. For example, when you hear a student ask a question, write the question down in the question block. It is important not to add any value judgment to the data. Your analysis can come afterwards. This takes some practice. Before you start, familiarize yourself with the checklist and the elements of critical thinking listed there. Make an audio recording of the conversation you observe as a backup to your note taking.

The first time you observe, focus on one student at a time. As you get better at writing observations, you may be able to take notes on a whole group at a time. This takes practice and some organization in note taking. As with anything new, try a little at a time.

Share these observations with the instructional team to help communicate about students' needs and collaborate on making teaching decisions. Google applications and other Web 2.0 tools can facilitate that sharing and collaborating.

Analysis of the Observation

As you take observational notes in the blocks you are beginning to analyze the information into meaningful units from which you can consider instructional interventions. The categories help guide your interactions with students to assist the development of critical thinking skills and behaviors. The questions on the analysis form help you to reflect further on the data.

Consider what the student is doing well and what gaps in knowledge or use of skills are evident. Both the strengths and weaknesses of the student's skills can inform teaching decisions and help to take appropriate action. A skilled inquiry coach or facilitator is a keen observer of student learning. As you practice, you'll become better at knowing how to use the data you gather to teach in the zone for the greatest impact on learning.

Conclusion

The librarian in the vignette provides an example of using careful observations as assessments that inform instruction. As the librarian completes her observation she notices a few key patterns from the data. She has difficulty separating out process from the thinking but the careful observation, note taking, and subsequent analysis has helped her to be thoughtful about how she moves forward. She has discovered that some students need assistance developing critical thinking and has created a list of teaching points for when she sees the students again. The first item on the list is to sit down one-on-one with Marcus. At this point, Marcus is only collecting facts about Frederick Douglas. The librarian knows that fact finding will lead to shallow learning and she wants to help him begin to dig deeper into the ideas and connect the pieces. Her plan is to model her own connection making and help him understand that these types of connections are what he can include in his "connection journal." This approach will provide him with a strategy that he can continue independently and help her to monitor his progress. Her goal for Marcus is to foster deep processing of the ideas and he may need more than one intervention to get him there. Without these assessments Marcus might have been disappointed in the outcome of his inquiry, but now the instructional team can work together to help him reach a higher level of learning and understanding as he proceeds through the inquiry.

Figure 6 **Observations—A note taking form**		
Name:		**Date:**
✓	**Elements of Critical Thinking**	**Notes: observations, quotes, evidence**
	Questioning	
	Evaluating & Choosing	
	Making Connections	
	Listening & Responding	
	Reasoning & Reflecting	
	Organizing	
	Drawing Conclusions	

Figure 7 Reflection & Analysis—Post-observation for instructional decision making

Name:		Date:	
✓	**Elements of Critical Thinking**	**Strengths**	**Indication of ZONE & Intervention strategy**

	Questioning:
	What kind of questions?
	Levels of questioning:
	   1. Who? What? When? Where? How Much?
	   2. OR Why? How? What if?
	Range of questions		

	Evaluating & Choosing
	How was information evaluated?
	  ■ Expertise
	  ■ Accuracy
	  ■ Currency
	  ■ Perspective
	  ■ Quality
	Determining importance, relevance
	Decision making –
	  ■ what to add?
	  ■ what is enough?		

	Making Connections To their life experiences To the world To other texts or materials Explicit connections or inferred		
	Listening & Responding Understanding others Incorporating multiple viewpoints Developing own perspective		
	Reasoning & Reflecting Interpreting facts Synthesizing information Citing supporting evidence Reasoning is logical		

	Organizing
	Using organizing tools
	  ■ charts/timelines/flowcharts
	  ■ graphic organizers
	  ■ outlines/notes/journals		

	Drawing Conclusions What conclusions were drawn? Test against evidence On what basis? Divergent/convergent thinking Adopting a critical stance		

References

Christensen, C.M., M.B. Horn, and C.W. Johnson. *Disrupting Class: How Disruptive Innovation Will Change the Way the World Learns*. New York: NY: McGraw Hill, 2008.

Gawande, A. *The Checklist Manifesto: How to get things right*. New York, NY: Metropolitan Books, 2009.

Kuhlthau, C.C. *Seeking Meaning: A Process Approach to Library and Information Services*. 2nd ed. Westport, CT: Libraries Unlimited, 2004.

Kuhlthau, C.C., L.K. Maniotes and A.K. Caspari. *Guided Inquiry: Learning in the 21st Century*. Westport, CT: Libraries Unlimited, 2007.

Harada, V.H., and J.M. Yoshina. *Assessing learning: Librarians and teachers as partners*. Westport, CT: Libraries Unlimited, 2005.

Harris, Trudier. "Pigmentocracy." Freedom's Story, TeacherServe©.

National Humanities Center. 8 March, 2010 <http://nationalhumanitiescenter.org/pds/index.htm>

Partnership for 21st Century Skills. 2007. "21st Century Skills Assessment." 1 March 2010 <http://www.21stcenturyskills.org/index.php?option=com_content&task=view&id=82&Itemid=185>

Shepard, L. "The Role of Assessment in a Learning Culture." *Educational Researcher* 29:7 (2000): 4–14.

Standards for the 21st Century Learner. 2007. American Association of School Librarians. 2 March 2010 <http://www.ala.org/ala/mgrps/divs/aasl/guidelinesandstandards/learningstandards/standards.cfm>

Van Maanen, J. *Tales of the Field: On Writing an Ethnography.* Chicago, IL: University of Chicago Press, 1988.

Vygotsky, L. *Mind in society: The development of higher psychological processes.* M. Cole, V. John-Steiner, S. Scribner, & E. Soubermen, Eds. and Trans. Cambridge, MA: Harvard University Press, (Original work published 1934) 1978.

Wenger, Etienne. *Communities of Practice: Learning, Meaning, and Identity.* New York, NY: Cambridge University Press, 1998.

Wiggins G. and J. McTighe. *Understanding by Design.* Expanded 2nd ed. Alexandria, VA: Association for Supervision and Curriculum Development, 2005.

Yuckawa, J. and V. H. Harada. "Librarian-Teacher Partnerships for Inquiry Learning: Measures of Effectiveness for a Practice-Based Model of Professional Development." *Evidence Based Library and Information Practice* 4.2 (2009): 97–119.

Zmuda, A. & V.H. Harada. *Librarians as Learning Specialists: Meeting the Learning Imperative of the 21st Century.* Westport, CT: Libraries Unlimited, 2007.

Leslie K. Maniotes, Ph.D. *is an independent consultant with Denver (Colorado) Public Schools and can be reached at lesliekm@mac.com. Leslie is also a co-author of Guided Inquiry: Learning in the 21st Century, Libraries Unlimited.*

Maniotes, Leslie K. (2010). Teaching in the zone: Formative assessments for critical thinking. *LMC, 29*(1), 36–39.

Using TRAILS to Assess Student Learning: A Step-by-Step Guide

By Patricia L. Owen

Introduction

Teacher-librarians nationwide seek to produce evidence of the library's impact on student learning and achievement. While classroom teachers demonstrate their impact through the use of standardized test scores including end-of-grade tests and SAT/ACT tests, teacher-librarians have long used informal or in-class assessments to gauge student learning. While effective, these assessments can be augmented by the use of standards-driven information literacy tests, such as TRAILS-9 (www.trails-9.org).

What Is TRAILS?

TRAILS-9 (Tools for Real-Time Assessment of Information Literacy Skills) is a knowledge test made up of multiple choice questions. Funded by ILILE (Institute for Library and Information Literacy Education) and based on Ohio K-12 Library Academic Content Standards as well as *Information Power* (Kent State University Libraries and Media Services), TRAILS-9 offers two 30-question tests and ten 10-question tests focused on five information literacy areas: 1) Develop Topic; 2) Identify Potential Sources; 3) Develop, Use, and Revise Search Strategies; 4) Evaluate Sources and Information; and 5) Recognize How to Use Information Responsibly, Ethically, and Legally. Because TRAILS-9 is available free online, it's easy for both teacher-librarians and students to access. Teacher-librarians can set up as many test sessions as they need and all student scores are password protected.

Why Do TRAILS?

The primary reason to use TRAILS-9 is to assess student learning of information literacy skills. Additionally, because TRAILS-9 is

formatted as a standardized test, it offers some unique benefits. First, tests like TRAILS-9 capture a large amount of information about student learning quickly (Oakleaf 236). By including questions in five areas of information literacy skills, teacher-librarians can get a thorough picture of student skill weaknesses and strengths. Second, TRAILS-9 can be used for pre- and post-testing of students such as measuring differences in student learning from freshman year to graduation. Third, the report module in TRAILS-9 provides easy access to student scores, both individually and as a group. This minimizes the time

teacher-librarians spend analyzing assessment data. Finally, tests like TRAILS-9 are widely accepted by stakeholders including students, teachers, parents, administrators, and library colleagues as acceptable measures of student learning. TRAILS-9 is a great program advocacy tool.

Teacher-librarians also understand that the assessment of student learning is a professional responsibility. Both the Ohio K-12 Library Academic Content Standards and the National Board for Professional Teaching Standards underscore the importance of learning assessment (see Figure 1).

Figure 1 **Professional Responsibility for Assessment**	
Ohio K-12 Library Media Academic Content Standards	■ 1 .C.3. Collaborate with teachers to assess student learning. ■ 1 .C.4. Assess the progress of and collect data on all library instructional activities.
NBPTS Library Media-ECYA Standards	■ Standard IV. Accomplished library media specialists integrate information literacy through collaboration, planning, implementation, and assessment of learning.
AASL Empowering Learners Guidelines	■ Guideline: The school library media program is guided by regular assessment of student learning to ensure the program is meeting its goals—implements critical analysis and evaluation strategies ■ Guideline: The school library media program is built by professionals who model leadership and best practice for the school community—uses research to inform practice and makes evidence-based decisions

Step-by-Step TRAILS-9 Process

The process for using TRAILS-9 can be divided into five steps and further subdivided into multiple tasks (see Figure 2).

At my high school, I used this step-by-step TRAILS-9 process as a guide to collaborate with classroom teachers and gain an initial assessment of student learning that I am using to revise future information literacy instruction.

1. Devise an Action Plan

All freshmen are required to take social studies in my school district, so I began my action plan by getting on the agenda of the first social studies department meeting of the year. I shared the TRAILS-9 Web site and provided refreshments and handouts to give teachers background information about TRAILS-9 and how it can be integrated into their social studies curriculum. At the conclusion, all of the social studies department teachers had a better understanding of how this pilot would eventually impact the information literacy instruction of all students. The freshman teachers agreed to allow their students to take the TRAILS-9 test, choosing a test date in October for the pre-test and one in May for the post-test. As an incentive, the teachers decided to give students points for taking the test regardless of their scores.

Then I launched the TRAILS-9 pilot project. The third week in September, I created a bulletin board to attract student and teacher interest in TRAILS-9 and put a flier in the social studies teachers' mailboxes and the teachers' lounge. I mentioned details of my

Figure 2 Step-by-Step Process for using TRAILS

Devise an Action Plan	Administer Test	Analyze Results	Share Results with Teachers & Students	Revise Instruction
■ Initiate conversation to set up meeting with teacher(s) ■ Arrange specific time, location, place, and resources ■ Place meeting date on building calendar to avoid schedule conflicts ■ Invite teachers in other departments ■ Inform and invite principal ■ Prepare short presentation demonstrating TRAILS ■ Create a bulletin board and a flyer to ignite interest ■ Hold meeting and discuss selection of target classes with teacher(s) ■ Decide whether to collect class results vs. individual student results ■ Discuss workarounds to any barriers to the administration of TRAILS	■ Finalize specific testing dates and periods with teachers ■ Continue sharing information with teacher(s) about the uses of TRAILS results ■ Offer to share TRAILS results with students and teacher(s) ■ Open a TRAILS session for all students and assign codes with or without names ■ Assemble students in library at computers. Provide directions and explain goals ■ Distribute codes to students ■ Administer 30-question test ■ Close session (when all students are finished)	■ Generate and print reports ■ Begin analysis of TRAILS results by skill area ■ Map incorrect answers to matching information literacy skill areas ■ Create an informal report analyzing the significance of the TRAILS results	■ Secure a spot on department team meeting schedules ■ Prepare informal presentation of aggregated results ■ Share results with teacher(s) ■ Specify date to share results with students ■ Share results with students	■ Identify areas of information literacy skill weakness ■ Align skill weaknesses with instruction content ■ Collaborate with teacher(s) to discuss skill weaknesses ■ Replace/revise current instruction targets with ones designed to address weaknesses ■ Prepare new instruction

plans in casual conversation with colleagues. Next, I generated a list of TRAILS-9 student codes and familiarized myself with the Web site by examining the sample tests, reports, and the related resources. Since the October test date coincided with Teen Read Week, I decided to motivate students by placing the names of all students taking TRAILS-9 in a random drawing for prizes. Advertising the drawing generated a lot of interest; students asked repeatedly how they could win.

2. Administer Test

Just before the pre-test, participating social studies teachers reminded me about sharing the class and individual test results with both teachers and students, so a date for sharing was set in early December. Students could come to the library and view their individual results at their leisure.

I launched TRAILS-9 by explaining the directions and handing students strips of paper that contained their names, pre-assigned codes, and the TRAILS-9 session Web address. During each class period, the teacher and I assured students that they would receive points for taking the test and noted that points would not be deducted if some of their answers were wrong. I told them we were trying to find out how "information literate" the freshmen were, and that the TRAILS-9 results would help their teachers and I learn what skills to teach this year and what changes to make to future information literacy lessons.

Students displayed various behaviors during the test ranging from confusion to excitement. One or two students in each class typed in the wrong address and could not access the test until I helped them re-type the correct URL. A few students simply clicked answers randomly and hit "finished." Others labored for up to 40 minutes, working diligently to respond to all of the questions. I overheard the term "Boolean?" muttered frequently.

Teacher-librarians nationwide can use the TRAILS-9 process to collaborate with classroom teachers, assess student learning, revise their information literacy instruction, and produce evidence of their library's impact on student achievement to share with stakeholders.

As each student finished TRAILS-9, they placed their student code strips into the random drawing and received a candy treat. Students who had been absent came in during the next week to "make up" the test. No technology glitches occurred during any TRAILS-9 sessions.

3. Analyze Results

During the first week of November, I generated reports and began the analysis by skill area. I mapped incorrect answers to each skill area and created an informal report of the results. Some of the initial information was significant. Most of my freshmen students understood the concept of primary resources, which pleased social studies teachers because it is an Ohio Graduation Test (OGT) requirement. 91% of my students placed importance on asking a librarian for help and 95% knew that the public library is the best source for new books.

4. Share Results with Teachers and Students

I created a results chart and began an ongoing discussion about the information literacy skill strengths and weaknesses revealed by TRAILS-9. Next, I shared the TRAILS-9 results with each class of freshmen students and told them about the post-test schedule for May. Some freshmen came to the library and viewed their individual results online.

The primary reason to use TRAILS-9 is to assess student learning of information literacy skills.

In addition to the quantitative results, interviews and personal observation revealed some notable affective and behavioral results. My freshmen thought some of the questions had "too many parts" causing them to lose focus so they moved on to the next question. One freshman said he liked to do anything that involves a computer. A few students were worried about running out of time but then just settled in, relaxed, and advanced through the test pretty quickly. Another student was surprised by the charts and screen shots on the test. He mentioned the OPAC and book title pages. Another student liked that she could go back at the end and check her answers. One student said the prizes weren't that great. A sample of student comments are below:

- "What's Boolean?"
- "Did anyone get all the answers right?"
- "It took too long; I skipped to the end."
- "Doing the test online made me nervous."
- "How come we had to put numbers [codes] in?"
- "Are we going to take more tests and draw prizes?"
- "The OPAC question was easy; we did it in middle school!"

Some students concentrated the entire period and reviewed earlier questions. Maybe they were challenged by the fact that I mentioned students all over the country took the test and someday they might be able to compare their "performance with the national average" (Schloman and Gideon 47). One person muttered about the chart that covered nearly half a page and indicated it was complicated. Several freshmen needed reassurance that points would not be deducted from their guaranteed points when they realized the test was challenging.

The comments of teachers and administrators were also revealing:

- "The codes were interesting."
- "I didn't realize the test questions would be in a different order for each student."
- "My students heard about it; can they take it too?"
- "Will you share the results with my students?"
- "Can you tell me how each student did?"
- "Teachers seem okay with it so it's okay with me."

5. Revise Instruction

Throughout the balance of the school year, the social studies teachers and I worked collaboratively to determine the information literacy skills on which freshmen needed to concentrate as revealed by TRAILS-9. Once we identified their strengths and weaknesses, we addressed future freshmen orientation lesson content, and I revised my current and future lesson objectives in collaboration with several subject area teachers. I began adding new content across grade levels in order to bridge all of my students' information literacy skill gaps. For example, TRAILS-9 revealed that 85% of the freshmen understood a table of contents; 81% recognized a book publisher, 87% knew how to search by title in a library OPAC, and 85% have internalized MLA citation

format elements. I will limit coverage of these terms to a brief review and insert more complex skills into future lessons.

In May a TRAILS-9 post-test was administered to freshmen to determine skill acquisition. These results also contributed to the revision of future freshmen library lessons. In a separate development, senior teachers agreed to permit graduating seniors to take the TRAILS-9 test to establish a graduate benchmark for the purposes of comparison with future classes.

Conclusion

By using this step-by-step approach, any teacher-librarian can devise a TRAILS-9 action plan, administer tests, analyze the results, share reports with teachers and students, and revise instruction. Teacher-librarians nationwide can use the TRAILS-9 process to collaborate with classroom teachers, assess student learning, revise their information literacy instruction, and produce evidence of their library's impact on student achievement to share with stakeholders. TRAILS-9 is an effective assessment tool to use to measure your information literacy instruction program.

Works Cited

Institute for Library and Information Literacy Education. *ILILE*. 28 July 2009 <http://www.ilile.org/>.

Kent State University Libraries and Media Services. *TRAILS: Tool for Real-time Assessment of Information Literacy Skills*. 2009. 28 July 2009 <http://www.trails-9.org>.

National Board for Professional Teaching Standards. *NBPTS Library Media Standards*. 2001. 28 July 2009 <http://nbpts.org/userfiles/File/ecya_lm_standards.pdf>.

Oakleaf, Megan. "Dangers and Opportunities: A Conceptual Map of Information Literacy Assessment Approaches." *Portal: Libraries and the Academy* 8.3 (2008): 233–253.

Ohio Department of Education. *Academic Content Standards: K-12 Library Guidelines*. 2004. 28 July 2009 <http://education.ohio.gov/GD/DocumentManagement/DocumentDownload.aspx?DocumentID=13969>.

Schloman, Barbara F., and Julie A. Gedeon. "Creating TRAILS: Tool for Real-Time Assessment of Information Literacy Skills." *Knowledge Quest* 35.5 (2007): 44–47.

Patricia L. Owen *(NBCT) is a teacher-librarian at Eastwood High School in Pemberville, Ohio, and can be reached at powen@bex.net.*

Owen, Patricia L. (2010). Using TRAILS to assess student learning: A step-by-step guide. *LMC, 28*(6), 36–38.

Inquiry Unpacked: An Introduction to Inquiry-Based Learning

By Barbara A. Jansen

"Inquire, think critically, and gain knowledge." "Plan strategies to guide inquiry."

As our national educational organizations' standards evolve from students mastering discrete skills to demonstrating broad learning behaviors, often referred to as 21st century learning skills, pedagogy is slowly shifting from teacher- and textbook-centered dissemination of facts and information to student-centered construction of learning and knowledge. In this environment, students use a wide range of resources to collaborate with others to solve authentic problems by thinking critically, actively create content, and communicate with a wide audience. The Partnership for 21st Century Skills succinctly categorizes these participatory skills into the four Cs: "critical thinking and problem solving, collaboration, communication, and creativity and innovation" (P21 mission statement). Both the American Association of School Librarians (AASL) and the International Society for Technology in Education's (ISTE) National Educational Technology Standards for Students 2007 call for students to use an inquiry approach when engaged in the research process. The AASL standards refer to inquiry seven times, including having students "inquire, think critically, gain knowledge," and to "follow an inquiry-based process in seeking knowledge in curricular subjects, . . ." and "continue an inquiry-based research process by applying critical-thinking skills . . ." in addition to "conclud[ing] an inquiry-based research process . . ." (AASL). ISTE standards call for students to "plan strategies to guide inquiry" ("NETS for Students").

The inquiry process is not linear but occurs as a cyclical series of actions or events.

But what does it look like for a student to be engaged in inquiry? What is inquiry-based research, commonly referred to as inquiry-based learning or "guided inquiry" (Kuhlthau, Maniotes, and Caspari)? A recent post on the AASL email forum underscores the confusion that school librarians and educators in general have about inquiry. A librarian questioned the use of the term "inquiry-based project" in the standards in lieu of "research project" and considered whether she should teach her students the meaning of inquiry. A search for "inquiry-based research" on Google results in 102,000 links. "Inquiry-based learning" returns over 151,000 links. A search for "inquiry-based learning" offers 101 titles on Amazon.com, over 8,400 results on Google Books, over 9,760 results on Google Scholar, and over 52,000,000 results on Bing.

Not to Be Missed Reading and Viewing for School Librarians

Kuhlthau, Carol C., Leslie K. Maniotes, and Ann K. Caspari. *Guided Inquiry: Learning in the 21st Century*. Libraries Unlimited, 2007.

Rheingold, Howard. "Librarian 2.0: Buffy J. Hamilton." *Digital LM Central*. MacArthur Foundation, 3 May 2010. Web. 10 Oct. 2010. http://dmlcentral.net/blog/howard-rheingold/librarian-20-buffy-j-hamilton.

Stripling, Barbara. "Teaching Students to Think in the Digital Environment: Digital Literacy and Digital Inquiry." *School Library Monthly* 26.8 (2010): 16–18. EBSCOhost Professional Development Collection. Web. 16 Sept. 2010.

Inquiry Defined

What is inquiry? What does it look like? What are its components?

The *Oxford English Dictionary* defines inquiry as "the action of seeking, . . . for truth, knowledge, or information concerning something; search, research, investigation, examination; a course of inquiry, an investigation; and the action of asking or questioning."

Educational organizations explain inquiry as it relates to learning. In *Standards for the English Language Arts*, the National Council of Teachers of English (NCTE) describes inquiry as "the learner's desire to look deeply into a question or idea that interests him or her" (27). AASL's explanation in *Standards for the 21st-Century Learner* offers inquiry as a "stance toward learning in which the learners themselves are engaged in asking questions and finding answers, not simply accumulating facts (presented by someone else) that have no relation to previous learning or new understanding" (17). Inquiry-based research—or learning—consists of a "process of learning that is driven by questioning, investigating, making sense of information, and developing new understandings, it is a process of active learning, [and] it is cyclical, not linear" ("Chapter 3: Inquiry in Action") and is determined "by one's own curiosity, wonder, interest or passion to understand an observation or solve a problem" ("A Description of Inquiry").

Traditionally, the teacher tells students what to "look up" during the research phase of a given project, which may typically occur after the teaching of the content as enrichment or a follow-up activity. Inquiry-based research allows the student to ask questions in which he or she is interested and use all available resources to investigate the problem. Key components of inquiry-based research include "framing school study around questions developed and shaped by kids," "handing the brainwork of learning back to the kids," and focusing on the "development of kids' thinking first, foremost, and always" (Harvey and Daniels 56–57). And, inquiry occurs not at the end but at the beginning of the study, allowing students to construct the content knowledge necessary to understand concepts and make connections.

Inquiry does not necessarily follow a logical or neat process. Models of inquiry-based learning show a variety of approaches (see additional resources below) that librarians and teachers can use to guide students. All emphasize that the process is not linear but occurs as a cyclical series of actions or events. The six-phase Stripling Inquiry Model makes good sense for school librarians who seek a structure for collaborating with teachers (Stripling) to bring inquiry into the learning process. The model's phases—connect, wonder, investigate, construct, express, and reflect—allow for nonlinear thinking as illustrated below:

Ideally, the process begins "when the learner identifies a problem or notices something that intrigues, surprises, or stimulates a question—something that is new, or something that may not make sense in relationship to the learner's previous experience or current understanding" ("A Description of Inquiry").

> *Inquiry-based research allows the student to ask questions in which he or she is interested and use all available resources to investigate the problem.*

Inquiry Practiced

In reality, other than the occasional self-selected research paper or science fair topic, state- or school-mandated curriculum standards leave little time for students to explore their own interests. By turning the curriculum into engaging problems for students to solve, students can participate in inquiry while practicing many curriculum-mandated skills (i.e., reading, writing, listening, research) as they investigate subject-area content (social studies, science, health, math, etc.). Instead of teachers dictating the information students need to locate, allow them to determine what they know, want to know, and need to know to solve the information problem. Encourage students to use a variety of online and offline resources, and allow them to show their results by creating products that go beyond the traditional report and PowerPoint presentation. Targeting specific audiences for students' efforts raises their level of concern and provides a focus for their writing and knowledge sharing. For example, turn the traditional report into an article synthesizing important concepts for the general consumption of *Time* magazine readers or an editorial for the opinion page of a newspaper. Multimedia texts combine the important skill of writing along with those involved in visual and audio production. Students can display these texts on blogs or wikis for public consumption.

Inquiry is not easily nurtured through standalone library instruction that occurs once a week. Successful inquiry-based learning involves students engaging in topics originating in their subject-area courses for extended periods of time on consecutive days, preferably in collaboration with the school librarian. Kuhthau, Maniotes, and Caspari suggest that "inquiry instructional teams" help students develop competencies in research and subject knowledge while helping to support essential 21st century skills, and require "careful planning, close supervision, ongoing assessment, and targeted intervention . . . " (2–3).

Buffy Hamilton, librarian at Creekview High School in Canton, Georgia, offers useful insights to the inquiry process through a collaboration with a tenth grade teacher of literature composition. According to Hamilton,

> collaboration with the classroom teacher benefits students in several ways: scaffolding information literacy skills, introducing new online tools to students or showing them how to use familiar ones in effective ways, teaching evaluation of multimedia texts, and establishing a climate that promotes participation, inquiry, and risk taking in a safe environment. Students see

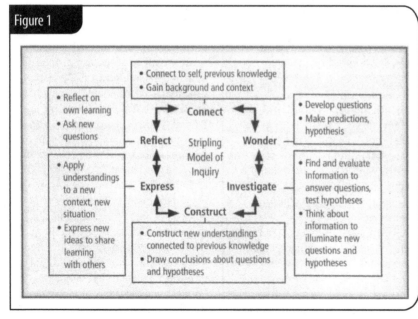

Figure 1

- Connect to self, previous knowledge
- Gain background and context

Connect

- Reflect on own learning
- Ask new questions

Reflect

Stripling Model of Inquiry

Wonder

- Develop questions
- Make predictions, hypothesis

- Apply understandings to a new context, new situation
- Express new ideas to share learning with others

Express

Investigate

- Find and evaluate information to answer questions, test hypotheses
- Think about information to illuminate new questions and hypotheses

Construct

- Construct new understandings connected to previous knowledge
- Draw conclusions about questions and hypotheses

Used with permission. For more about the Stripling Model, see the additional resources below.

[handwritten margin notes:] letting kids be in charge of learning

Not forced but engaged and motivated

multimedia texts on display

collaborate

two or more professionals working together and learning with them (qtd. in Rheingold).

Through self-selected topics within the greater problem of veteran's issues, students in Hamilton's school engaged in the inquiry process with the support of these professionals. Students "effectively learn to become their own information filters, which is the ultimate act of information fluency. [Using a variety of online resources and presentation tools such as NetVibes] allows us to privilege multiple forms of literacy and for our students to engage in transliteracy— the ability to read and write and share information across a variety of platforms" (Rheingold).

By collaborating with teachers to connect students to subject knowledge, developing their information fluency, and supporting the vital skills of collaboration, creation, and communication through inquiry, school librarians will solidify their place as an essential teaching professional at their schools.

yes.

Works Cited

American Association of School Librarians. *Standards for the 21st-Century Learner*. American Library Association, 2007. Web. 30 Aug. 2010. http://www.ala.org/ala/mgrps/divs/aasl/guidelinesandstandards/learningstandards/AASL_LearningStandards.pdf.

"Chapter 3: Inquiry in Action." Supporting Inquiry with Primary Sources. Library of Congress, n.d. Web. 16 Sept. 2010. http://www.loc.gov/teachers/professionaldevelopment/selfdirected/inquiry/index.html.

"A Description of Inquiry." Institute for Inquiry: Examining the Art of Science Education. Exploratorium, 1998. Web. 16 Sept. 2010. http://www.exploratorium.edu/ifi/about/inquiry.html.

Harvey, Stephanie and Harvey Daniels. *Comprehension and Collaboration: Inquiry Circles in Action*. Heinemann, 2009. Print.

International Reading Association and National Council of Teachers of English. *Standards for the English Language Arts*. International Reading Association and the National Council of Teachers of English, 1996. Web. 3 Sept. 2010. http://www.ncte.org/library/NCTEFiles/Resources/Books/Sample/StandardsDoc.pdf.

Kuhlthau, Carol C., Leslie K. Maniotes, and Ann K. Caspari. *Guided Inquiry: Learning in the 21st Century*. Libraries Unlimited, 2007. Print.

"NETS for Students 2007." International Society for Technology in Education, 2007. Web. 17 Sept. 2010. http://www.iste.org//for-students/student-standards-2007.aspx.

"Our Mission." Partnership for 21st Century Skills, 2004. Web. 1 Oct. 2010. http://www.p21.org/index.php?option=com_content&task=view&id=188&Itemid=110.

Rheingold, Howard. "Librarian 2.0: Buffy J. Hamilton." Digital LM Central. MacArthur Foundation, 3 May 2010. Web. 10 Oct. 2010. http://dmlcentral.net/blog/howard-rheingold/librarian-20-buffy-j-hamilton.

Standards for the 21st-Century Learner in Action. Chicago: American Association of School Librarians, 2009. Print.

Stripling, Barbara. "Teaching Students to Think in the Digital Environment: Digital Literacy and Digital Inquiry." *School Library Monthly* 26.8 (2010): 16–18. EBSCOhost Professional Development Collection. Web. 16 Sept. 2010.

Additional Resources for the Stripling Inquiry Model

Supporting inquiry with primary sources (multimedia from the Library of Congress; with Barbara Stripling, primary sources, and 5th graders): http://www.loc.gov/teachers/professionaldevelopment/selfdirected/inquiry/index.html

Supporting inquiry learning from the Library of Congress's *Teaching with Primary Sources Quarterly* publication: http://www.loc.gov/teachers/tps/quarterly/0907/pdf/TPSQuarterlySummer09.pdf

"Student Inquiry and Web 2.0" by Pam Berger (includes using Stripling Inquiry Model with Web 2.0 tools): http://www.schoollibrarymonthly.com/articles/Berger2010-v26n5p14.html

Other Models

Historical Inquiry (ABC-CLIO):

Tasks of Inquiry (Anna J. Warner and Brian E. Myers, Department of Agricultural Education and Communication, Florida Cooperative Extension Service, Institute of Food and Agricultural Sciences, University of Florida): http://edis.ifas.ufl.edu/wc075

8Ws of Information Inquiry (Annette Lamb): http://virtualinquiry.com/inquiry/ws.htm

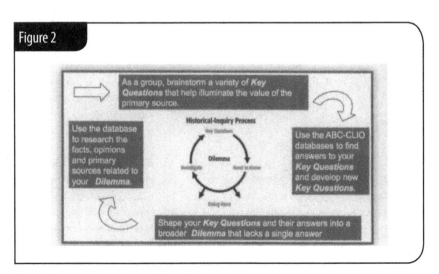

Used with permission from ABC-CLIO.

Inquiry-based Learning (Paula
Sincero): http://www.inquirylearn.
com/Inquirydef.htm

Inquiry Process (The Inquiry Page,
University of Illinois, Urbana-
Champaign): http://inquiry.illinois.
edu/inquiry/process.php3

Assessment

"Enhancing Inquiry through
Formative Assessment" by

Wynne Harlen (Exploratorium
Institute for Inquiry): http://www.
exploratorium.edu/IFI/docs/harlen_
monograph.pdf

"How can we assess student
learning in an inquiry
classroom?" (The Inquiry
Page, University of Illinois,
Urbana-Champaign): http://
inquiry.illinois.edu/php/
assessment2.php

Barbara A. Jansen *is the librarian/
technology coordinator at Saint
Andrew's Episcopal High School in
Austin, Texas. She is the author of
several titles from Linworth
Publishing.*

Jansen, Barbara A. (2011). Inquiry
unpacked: An introduction to inquiry-based
learning. *LMC, 29*(5), 10–12.

Project-Based Learning: Rigor and Relevance in High Schools

By Violet H. Harada, Carolyn Kirio, and Sandy Yamamoto

Note: This article is based on excerpts and summaries from the authors' new Linworth publication, *Collaborating on Project-Based Learning in Grades 9–12*.

High schools are under tremendous pressure to increase graduation rates and lower dropout numbers. A survey conducted for the Bill and Melinda Gates Foundation indicated that over a third of students entering high school never graduate on time (Bridgeland, Dillulio and Morison 2006). Students who drop out claim that the curriculum is disconnected from real life and that their schools are impersonal systems where no one really cares about them (Wagner 2002). Over half of these students are disadvantaged minorities of color, e.g., Hispanic, African, and Native Americans. High schools are responding to this challenge by creating smaller learning communities and academies that focus on interdisciplinary learning environments and team teaching (National Association of Secondary School Principals 2004). This type of reform is fertile ground for Project-Based Learning (PBL).

> *Project-Based Learning frames an approach to learning that actively engages students in deeper levels of comprehension and interpretation about what and how they study.*

Project-Based Learning (PBL) is a potentially powerful means to produce relevant and rigorous learning. Although developing projects is not new in education, PBL is a more holistic instructional strategy (Railsbeck 2002). With our increasingly diverse student population, PBL takes on greater importance because it builds on students' individual strengths and allows them to explore their interests in the structure of a defined curriculum.

Major Features of PBL

The major attributes of PBL include the following:

First, issues, themes, or problems form the core of PBL and require in-depth exploration. There are no quick and easy answers or definite solutions. Issues or themes are directly related to content standards in the various disciplines. These standards provide an anchor to foundational concepts and processes in the curriculum.

Second, students develop ownership in two important ways. They first select topics that are personally relevant to them. Students then develop a new sense of responsibility as they start to take charge of their own learning. They do this by determining goals, identifying critical tasks and appropriate resources, and devising feasible timelines for accomplishing the work.

Third, instructors take on the roles of facilitators and coaches. They do not relinquish control of the learning situation but share it with their students. The facilitative role affords them rich opportunities to differentiate and tailor instruction to specific student needs. They administer this assistance at the point of need. Instructors also assume the responsibility for ensuring that the projects satisfy a prescribed framework determined by the parameters of the established curriculum.

Fourth, students use essential tools and skills that include application of technology for accessing, retrieving, and producing information. These skills range from searching online databases to using various methods for gathering data and creating presentations.

Fifth, students collaborate with peers and adults. They establish project teams where they share responsibilities and exchange ideas and points of view. They confer with instructors to assess their progress and determine next steps. They establish contact with peers in other schools and with experts in the community. As a result of this process, they strengthen their skills in active listening and intelligent, coherent communication.

Sixth, students reflect continuously as they work through their projects. Key questions they must ask themselves include: What is my goal? How well am I achieving this goal? What is working well? What problems am I having? How might I deal with these problems? What are possible solutions? This type of self-analysis builds students' abilities to focus on their strengths and consider areas for improvement.

> *Project-Based Learning is a potentially powerful means to produce relevant and rigorous learning.*

Finally, PBL culminates in a product that presents possible solutions to a problem, analyzes a dilemma from multiple points of view, or develops an idea in original and thoughtful ways. This final product is evaluated for quality. As the culminating event, it should be celebratory and shared with a wider audience. According to the Buck Institute for Education (2002), PBL has the following benefits:

- It merges thinking and knowledge by helping students master both the content and the process.
- It emphasizes real-world skills including problem solving, communication, and self-management.
- It integrates disciplines by focusing on themes, issues, and deeper investigations of topics.
- It capitalizes on concerns and skills valued in the community.
- It acknowledges and meets the needs of learners with a range of learning styles and needs.

Planning for PBL

There is no one "best way" to implement PBL. However, starting early and developing a plan are crucial requirements. Effective instructional planning starts with an idea of what the students must be able to do *at the end of the learning experience*. Wiggins and McTighe (1998) popularized the term "backward design" to describe this concept in curriculum planning. A possible sequence in planning is outlined in Figure 1.

Librarian's Role in PBL

Why should school library media specialists promote PBL? For one, it contributes significantly to teacher collaboration because project-focused teaching encourages multidisciplinary approaches to learning. As partners in PBL, enterprising library media specialists can seize this opportunity to infuse information literacy skills into the school-wide curriculum. Library media specialists become active co-facilitators as they work alongside classroom teachers to help students refine their abilities in solving information-related problems. They help students develop strategies to be critical consumers of information and discriminating producers of newly acquired knowledge.

Importantly, library media specialists are key partners in identifying the relationships existing between thinking skills and core knowledge embedded in various disciplines. They introduce the notion of information literacy as the foundation for deeper understanding. Library media specialists play several important roles in PBL:

- As a connector: Library media specialists, working with entire school populations, have a "big picture view" of school needs and priorities (McGregor 2003, 210). Having this holistic view of the school enables library media specialists to facilitate discussions

with faculty about integrating and merging priorities across content areas.

- As an integrator: They promote the connections across the disciplines and negotiate the links with the necessary information resources. As part of the integrative process, library media specialists also suggest ways to incorporate the information literacy skills at various phases of the projects.
- As an instructional partner: They possess special skills and tools to help both teachers and students in the accomplishment of their instructional and learning goals. Figure 2 is a checklist to gauge one's leadership readiness.

PBL in Practice

What types of projects motivate students in a high school? The following brief snapshots originated from Kapolei High School in Hawaii. These projects range in duration from two weeks to a semester. Fuller descriptions of the projects along with instructional aids appear in *Collaborating for Project Based Learning in Grades 9–12* (Harada, Kirio and Yamamoto 2008).

Are You My Clone? The Controversy Over Genetics

Students in grades 11 and 12 engage in this interdisciplinary unit that integrates human physiology and American problems. They participate in a statewide Bioethical Genetic Summit to present summaries of various genetic discoveries and their positive and negative impacts on society. At the summit, students prepare a debate to share various points of view on each topic. They also collaboratively develop guidelines to regulate policies and practices related to genetics and present their recommendations to a panel of legislators and other public policy makers.

Figure 1 Steps in Planning a Project

1. Identify key student outcomes and content standards to be addressed.
2. Brainstorm project ideas that deal with issues and topics that will motivate thinking and student interest.
3. Decide on a project that targets the outcomes and standards identified.
4. Identify prior skills and knowledge students must have for this project.
5. Develop the essential or overarching question for the project.
6. Determine criteria to assess the final project or performance.
7. Develop tools to perform the assessment.
8. Identify key benchmarks in the project where you plan to conduct periodic checks on progress.
9. Outline the project–include a timeline and the activities planned.
10. Identify and agree upon the instructional team's roles and responsibilities in the project.

Figure 2 **Checklist to Gauge Your Leadership Readiness**

Leadership Characteristics	Self-Rating		
	Strong	**Adequate**	**Weak**
Character			
I maintain people's trust and confidentiality.			
I am resilient and flexible.			
I am willing to take risks.			
I am approachable.			
Organization and Management			
I have a vision and goals for the library media center.			
I have a strategic plan of action to achieve my goals.			
I maintain clear and continuous avenues for communication with the rest of the school community.			
I get things done in a timely manner.			
I anticipate and plan for what may be coming next.			
I follow through on promises made.			
I can juggle a multitude of jobs and responsibilities.			
Interpersonal			
I listen carefully to what is being said.			
I suspend judgment.			
I encourage others to express their ideas and feelings.			
I strive to confirm and clarify information received.			
I am sensitive to facial expressions and other nonverbal cues.			
I acknowledge the accomplishments of others and give them credit.			
Conceptual and Technical			
I see the bigger picture and facilitate problem solving in this larger context.			
I seek connections between the school's mission and goals and those of the library media center.			
I keep abreast of current issues and research in school reform as well as my profession.			
I am knowledgeable about learning theories and research that inform my teaching.			
I keep abreast of the latest trends and research in the applications of technology for teaching and learning.			
I regularly reflect on what I am doing to improve my professional practices.			

PBL culminates in a product that presents possible solutions to a problem, analyzes a dilemma from multiple points of view, or develops an idea in original and thoughtful ways.

A Taste of Culture

Students in grades nine through 12 investigate the preparation, ingredients, and significance of parts of the globe. They ultimately stage a cultural fair where they share their research through multimedia presentations or displays. The students combine their studies of social studies (geography) and foreign languages in this unit.

A Forensic Approach to Scientific Inquiry

Students in grades nine and ten combine physical science and U.S. history in this introduction to various forensic techniques as they conduct an investigation of their own.

First, students study a criminal case from the past and consider how the results might have been different if current forensic techniques had been available. They then get involved in a mock crime scene staged at the school. As investigators, they evaluate the crime scene and gather evidence. Through scientific inquiry and research, students collect and analyze clues, uncover motives, and apprehend the suspect. They also participate in a mock trial where justice is administered. Based on the presentation of evidence and persuasive arguments, a student jury determines the verdict.

Helping Our Environment, Helping Ourselves

In this unit of study that integrates biology, economics, and language arts, students in grades 11 and 12 gather information on an environmental issue relating to sustainability in their own communities. The students develop possible alternatives to address the issue and actually design and implement their strategies. The projects range from beach clean-ups and recycling to saving endangered native species and water conservation.

Voices Alive: Oral Histories Tell Us About Communities

Students in grades 9 through 12 combine social studies and language arts to preserve the personal experiences and historic perspectives of the community. They conduct oral history research and create multimedia presentations based on their investigations. The students also have the opportunity to share their products with community members. Ultimately, their presentations are added to a repository of local history accessible through the school library media center.

Raising the Bar: New Sports for a Challenging Tomorrow

Students in grades 9 through 12 focus on extreme sports that have become the center of current pop culture. This project, which integrates social studies and physical education, challenges students to conduct in-depth investigations of existing sports. Selecting one game, their objective is to create a new "extreme" version. Students produce manuals with clearly written instructions, detailed directions, and descriptive guidelines.

Conclusion

Project-based learning frames an approach to learning that actively engages students in deeper levels of comprehension and interpretation about what and how they study. While the classroom teacher has the disciplinary knowledge, the library media specialist can assist the teacher with the process or thinking skills necessary for students to create meaning for themselves. The synergy of working together provides a learning frame that can be a seamless blend. PBL is an approach to teaching and learning that brings curriculum in line with the way the world really works.

References

Bridgeland, John M., John J. Dillulio, Jr., and Karen B. Morison. *The Silent Epidemic: Perspectives of High School Dropouts.* A Report by Civic Enterprises in Association with Peter D. Hart Research Associates for the Bill & Melinda Gates, Foundation, 2006. 30 July 2007 <http://www.gatesfoundation.org/UnitedStates/Education/TransformingHighSchools/Announcements/Announce-060302.htm>.

Buck Institute for Education. *Project Based Learning Handbook.* Novato: Author, 2002. 30 July 2007 <http://www.bie.org/pbl/pblhandbook/intro.php>.

Harada, Violet H., Carolyn Kirio, and Sandy Yamamoto. *Collaborating for Project-Based Learning in Grades 9–12.* Worthington, OH: Linworth Publishing, Inc., 2008.

McGregor, Joy. "Collaboration and Leadership." *Curriculum Connections Through the Library: Principles and Practice.* Ed. Barbara K. Stripling and Sandra Hughes-Hassell. Westport: Libraries Unlimited, 2003. 199–219.

National Association of Secondary School Principals. *Breaking Ranks II™: Strategies for Leading High School Reform.* Reston: Author, 2004.

Railsback, Jennifer. *Project-Based Instruction: Creating Excitement for Learning.* Portland: Northwest Regional Educational Laboratory, August 2002. 30 July 2007 <http://www.nwrel.org/request/2002aug/>.

Wagner, Tony. *Making the Grade: Reinventing America's Schools.* New York: Routledge/Falmer, 2002.

Wiggins, Grant, and Jay McTighe. *Understanding by Design.* Alexandria: Association for Supervision and Curriculum Development, 1998.

Violet H. Harada *is a professor in the Library and Information Science Program at the University of Hawaii. Her email: vharada@hawaii.edu*

Carolyn Kirio and Sandy Yamamoto *are cybrarians at Kapolei High School in Hawaii. Their email addresses: carolyn_kirio@notes.k12.hi.us, sandy_yamamoto@notes.k12.hi.us*

Harada, Violet, H., Kirio, Carolyn, & Yamamoto, Sandy. (2008). Project-based learning: Rigor and relevance in high schools. *LMC, 26*(6), 14–20.

STEM, eSTEM, and the Cybrarian: What Every Librarian Should Know

By Paige Jaeger

Math, the Basis of Most STEM

While technology is widely praised for its social role in communicating and collaborating, we should thank technology's role in mathematical advancements. Math is at the core of technology, math is at the core of engineering. Math is at the core of math. So, while we speak of eSTEM, it's almost all math in a technology and digitally focused STEM curriculum.

Nearly thirty years ago, I stepped into the computer world as a programmer for Electronic Data Systems (EDS) where I was quickly swallowed up in the inner core of computer logic. When the banking system's program would crash, we would get a green-striped 11 x 17 inch paper printout almost a hundred pages long. The printout was mathematical binary code mumbo jumbo called a "dump." The dump code is called *Hexadecimal*. It is the equivalent of base 16 logic. The world works in a base 10 number system. In base 16, you run out of usable digits, so they insert a few alphabet letters. The alphabet letters and digits work together to represent every number and every letter in the alphabet. That is the core of your computer logic—mumbo jumbo. These dumps could be dreadful, or they could be viewed as a puzzle to be solved. They were paying us to solve puzzles.

http://en.wikipedia.org/wiki/Hex_dump

That experience taught me that math was the essence of all STEM and all computers. Technology, engineering, and math boil down to numbers and digits. Science, on the other hand, uses math, elements, biology, laws of physics, and centuries old discoveries to organize and study the laws of our physical world. Sometimes, science includes math. Sometimes it does not. Even electrical engineering, for instance, uses calculus and cosines to plan alternating currents which feed our coffee machines. That is one reason the Common Core has concentrated on math as much as it has focused on literacy. We need to communicate. We need to calculate. We need to drink coffee.

Students today have a great aversion to math. In fact, I don't know which aversion is greater: the aversion to reading or the aversion to math. Librarians find it easy to support literacy, but we can also support science, technology, engineering, and math (STEM). We have to be creatively conscious to support math. It is mathematics, after all, that has given us Dunkin' Donuts and Starbucks.

Books and Programs to Creatively Support Math and STEM

To support the Common Core math focus, a librarian can dig into math ratios. Purchase books like the new Infographics-filled baseball book *Flip Flop Fly Ball: An Infographic Baseball Adventure*. Hold competitions for kids to find mathematical applications in real life and fill a bulletin board. Keep a ratio board in the library where students can post ratios they find in advertisements or discover on their own. Run a mathematical running total and competition, posting ratios of the winners and losers. Keep your circulation statistics by ratios and post the grade to grade ratios on your board. Graph your genre checkouts on your bulletin board. Have the students update it weekly for you. Identify students who need help understanding ratios and let them do this task, checking their calculations.

Figure 1


```
0000000 0000 0001 0001 1010 0010 0001 0004 0128
0000010 0000 0016 0000 0028 0000 0010 0000 0020
0000020 0000 0001 0004 0000 0000 0000 0000 0000
0000030 0000 0000 0000 0010 0000 0000 0000 0204
0000040 0004 8384 0084 c7c8 00c8 4748 0048 e8e9
0000050 00e9 6a69 0069 a8a9 00a9 2828 0028 fdfc
0000060 00fc 1819 0019 9898 0098 d9d8 00d8 5857
0000070 0057 7b7a 007a bab9 00b9 3a3c 003c 8888
0000080 8888 8888 8888 8888 288e be88 8888 8888
0000090 3b83 5788 8888 8888 7667 778e 8828 8888
00000a0 d61f 7abd 8818 8888 467c 585f 8814 8188
00000b0 8b06 e8f7 88aa 8388 8b3b 88f3 88bd e988
00000c0 8a18 880c e841 c988 b328 6871 688e 958b
00000d0 a948 5862 5884 7e81 3788 1ab4 5a84 3eec
00000e0 3d86 dcb8 5cbb 8888 8888 8888 8888 8888
00000f0 8888 8888 8888 8888 8888 8888 8888 0000
0000100 0000 0000 0000 0000 0000 0000 0000 0000
*
0000130 0000 0000 0000 0000 0000 0000 0000
000013e
```


Librarians find it easy to support literacy, but we can also support science, technology, engineering, and math.

It is easy to find apps to support science, technology, engineering, and math on an iPad or portable device. You could post award-winning apps that the students have discovered. It is important to have the students manipulate the variables and understand the principles before we launch them into an entertaining BrainPop video. Apps will dance and help them dream, but at the core, students need to comprehend. As librarians we tend to operate in a linguistic world, but we should be thankful for math, too, which brings us the technology to collaborate, communicate, create knowledge products, and write books to our heart's content.

I love math because I love to write, read, and drink a good cup of coffee. Thank you, Einstein, thank you, Pythagoras, and thank you, Rear Admiral Grace Hopper!

eSTEM = STEM-Energized Educational Focus

Across the United States, charter schools are multiplying quickly. One booming charter school movement is eSTEM. Librarians automatically equate "e" with online, connected, and technology-dependent. When you see eSTEM, you are viewing a deliberate, integrated educational paradigm shift where digital, technology-focused STEM is the "driver" of the curriculum. Even physical education teachers integrate STEM into their curriculum and shifting the focus from STEM to eSTEM makes it even more relevant to 21st century learners.

> When you see eSTEM, you are viewing a deliberate integrated educational paradigm shift where digital STEM is the focus throughout the curriculum.

One such movement in the Northeast began in 2001 with a think tank seeking to integrate engineering at the elementary level. Their initiative, now known as "Engineering is Elementary" (EiE), successfully developed a curriculum that tied into the existing curriculum. Concurrently, Massachusetts adopted STEM as a main point and framework in their curriculum standards. Christine M. Cunningham, founder and director of EiE explained it this way:

"Children are born engineers—they like to design their own creations, figure out how things work, and take things apart. Could this natural curiosity be tapped to teach engineering principles in elementary schools, alongside math and science content skills? Could we create a curriculum that interests and engages *all* students, including girls and boys, children of all races and ethnicities, children from a variety of socioeconomic backgrounds, and children who are most likely to be "at risk"? And, could we do so in a way that is readily accepted and implemented by elementary school teachers who are often uncomfortable with science and engineering topics?"

Check out some of their curriculum at http://legacy.mos.org/eie. Research investigating the implementation of this curriculum has found significant improvements in student understanding of various STEM concepts (http://legacy.mos.org/eie/pdf/research/EiE_Executive_Summary_May2012.pdf). You can find additional information about public eSTEM charter schools that are now operating in Arkansas at this link: https://www.estemlr.net/.

A New Call Number Is Born

One example of how EiE schools have tied engineering into the curriculum is insects. Curriculum designers tapped into the agricultural engineering characteristics of some insects. Each of the twenty curriculum areas begins with a picture book where a child encounters a problem. These picture books were chosen from international titles. The settings are linked to global locations and problems. If I were an elementary librarian, I would immediately note my catalog with problem solving (PS) books. A new call number is born for STEM!

> As academic coaches, we need to encourage, enhance understanding, apply the principles, and provide mentoring that cannot be replicated by a handheld device.

Apps for eSTEM: Academic Coaches Wanted

For those schools fortunate to have iPads, iPods, or other portable devices, you may wish to look at the long list of apps for STEM. In 2012, OnlineUniversity.com published their list of the best fifty apps for STEM, including: Mythbusters HD, Science Illustrated, Khan Academy, Seismograph, Science Glossary, PLoS Reader, Science 360 , The Ultimate Dinopedia, 3D Sun, Muscle System Pro II, Molecules, Simple Physics, The Elements, Planets, NASA, 3D Brain, D. Bones, and Paperbridge (www.onlineuniversities.com/blog/2012/05/50-best-ipad-apps-for-stem-education).

When I download and examine these apps, I cannot help but wonder how teachers can compete with this engagement. Our value added has to be one of *relationship*. As academic coaches, we need to encourage, enhance understanding, apply the principles, and provide mentoring that cannot be replicated by a handheld device.

Librarians need to be thoroughly acquainted with the online STEM world, apps included, and seek to understand how we can enhance the exploration of science. Often these apps offer explanations and experiments, online glossaries, and more. They do not offer high quality problem-based, inquiry-driven units. This is where librarians can shine. Apps do not hold answers to unique questions. Educators need to become academic coaches, ready to rescue those who don't understand, support those who have additional questions stemming from what they have learned, and lending a hand in discovering connections to other content areas. STEM, after all, is more than technology integration and gaming on a device. Our Common Core curriculum models must move science beyond the engagement or connectedness of a device into real life applications which will connect the importance of science to a person's well-being, advancement, and success.

STEM Is More than Technology Integration

I spoke with a high school librarian from Long Island who was seeking to repackage a science unit for a science teacher. The teacher had previously done a project that was all over science without many parameters. Here is a glimpse into this low level, poorly-planned project, which had very little direction:

Our ninth graders do a science fair project every year. They can choose any topic that has to do with the living environment. Most students choose a disease such as breast cancer or diabetes. Other topics include endangered species, global warming, and cloning. This is basically a research and recall project. Students are asked to research their topic and write a three page paper. In March they put their information along with illustrations on a poster board to

be displayed. They are required to use a variety of sources (books and databases) and cite their work. They don't have to answer an essential question. Is there one essential question you can have for so many different topics? I can think of individual questions for each topic but am wondering if there is one major essential question for the project that the group can think of?

This project is just one example where the teacher has not identified the project (and curriculum topic) with an enduring understanding and life application. "What do you really want the students to remember at the end of the road?" I asked and suggested an essential question (EQ) to at least focus the project and give it a STEM application. The project was repackaged in this direction: "Why is your future brighter because of the scientific research and advances that have been done/made on your topic? Why should [topic] be funded under the new U.S. administration? You could have the students plead for funding and compete for grants."

This essential question gives the teacher a unit that embraces Common Core verbs such as:

- Solve problems.
- Research an issue.
- Support a position.
- Argue persuasively.
- Support conclusions with evidence drawn from the text.

It also gives the librarian the opportunity to take the content away from a handheld device into a deep

research-based learning experience. This is our value added. As librarians we need to embrace inquiry-based learning and get intimately acquainted with crafting "problem solving" units. STEM is not about learning the facts; it is about applying science and math to real-world issues, problems, and more.

Resources:

Common Core State Standards www.corestandards.org

Engineering is Elementary: EiE Unit Overviews http://legacy.mos.org/eie/20_unit.php

Franco, M., N.H., and Lindsey, J. "Are STEM High School Students Entering the STEM Pipeline?" *NCSSSMST Journal* 17.1 (2012): 14–23. www.ncsssmst.org/publications/journal.

Online University: 50 Best iPad Apps for STEM Education www.onlineuniversities.com/blog/2012/05/50-best-ipad-apps-for-stem-education

Partnership for 21st Century Skills www.p21.org

PBS STEM Resource Center www.pbs.org/teachers/stem

Paige Jaeger *is the coordinator for school library services at the Washington-Saratoga-Warren-Hamilton-Essex (WSWHE) Board of Cooperative Educational Services, Saratoga Springs, New York.*

Jaeger, Paige. (2013). STEM, eSTEM, and the cybrarian: What every librarian should know. *LMC, 31*(6), 10–12.

24/7 STEMulation: Reinventing Discovery

By Terrence E. Young, Jr.

A Literate Nation Not Only Reads. It Computes, Investigates, and Innovates.

—From Change the Equation,
changetheequation.org

Can you imagine a world without science? Science permeates our lives. Our lives are spoiled by science. The television series *Revolution* portrays a world without electric power. In June 2012 the world quietly moved to Internet Protocol version 6 with 340 undecillion web addresses available. Whether it's the discovery of a new element or species, the Mars rover, wireless technology innovations, or the cloning of extinct creatures, we have become accustomed to imaginative and brilliant minds bringing us new wonders. As educators we are responsible for producing the imaginative and brilliant STEM minds of the future.

From Why? to Aha!

The Merriam-Webster dictionary (m-w.com) defines the "aha moment" as "a moment of sudden realization, inspiration, insight, recognition, or comprehension." To a student it is usually a moment of clarity, the moment where they gain real wisdom that they can use to change their life. To a scientist it is the moment of amazement and euphoria, the moment when the "why" question is answered.

Elementary school students are natural scientists who ask anything about everything: "Why is the sky blue? Why do I need to eat? Why do cats bury their droppings?" This is the way it should be. Posing questions is the first step to learning. Middle school students begin to lose interest in science because of the way science is presented to them. If a middle school student loses interest in science, they will not take the necessary courses to major in science at a later time.

College, Careers, and STEM

The acronym STEM stands for science, technology, engineering, and mathematics. STEM education is critical to preparing students for college and careers. Successful STEM education transforms the typical teacher-centered learning space by encouraging a learning that is driven by problem-solving, discovery, and exploratory learning, and requires students to actively engage in a situation in order to find its solution. Millennial students gravitate toward group work, find it cool to be smart, and consider technology fascinating, so finding a solution can be both challenging and rewarding. Problem-solving, discovery, and exploratory learning require resources that are associated with print and virtual library resources. They also require learning and innovation skills; information, media, and technology skills; life and career skills; adaptability; complex communication/ social skills; non-routine problem solving; self-management/self-development; and systems thinking. These are skills that school librarians teach every day. School librarians must become participatory partners in STEM education. Our libraries and schools need inspiring STEM education programs so our students will develop the basic analytical, problem-solving, and critical thinking skills that are central to academic achievement and workforce readiness for today's world. The following learning challenges provide strategies for "STEMulating" your school library program!

Putting STEM education into practice involves all of the resources of the school library—engaging literature, hands-on activities, interactive displays, reference sources, and projects for specific scientific concepts.

Learning Challenge: Perform a collection analysis through one of the major book jobbers and weed your STEM resources. Update your collection with e-books, online resources, etc. Add STEM apps to your iPads, tablets, and other smart devices. Remember that a collection analysis does not factor in electronic resources as there are no physical copies associated with them.

In 2010 President Obama commissioned a study about the country's STEM education program. He then launched Change the Equation (http://changetheequation. org), a CEO-led effort to dramatically improve STEM education. The website is a must for all educators to explore.

The major findings of the 2011 National Assessment of Educational Progress (NAEP) in science (www. nationsreportcard.gov/science_2011/ summary.asp) and mathematics (http://nationsreportcard.gov/ math_2011) provide a state by state status of science and math achievement.

The National Research Council defines the four STEM subjects as follows:

1. Science is the study of the natural world, including the laws of nature associated with physics, chemistry, and biology, and the treatment or application of facts, principles, concepts, or conventions associated with these disciplines.
2. Technology comprises the entire system of people and organizations, knowledge, processes, and devices that go into creating and operating technological artifacts, as well as the artifacts themselves.
3. Engineering is a body of knowledge about the design and creation of products and a process for solving problems. Engineering utilizes concepts in science and mathematics and technological tools.

4. Mathematics is the study of patterns and relationships among quantities, numbers, and shapes. Mathematics includes theoretical mathematics and applied mathematics.

Learning Challenge: Become familiar and disseminate the current STEM status and standards adopted for your state. What can you do to share the findings and strengthen your library STEM education program?

STEM literacy is the ability to apply understanding of how the world works within and across the areas of science, technology, engineering, and math, and the ability to problem-solve, analyze, communicate, and understand technology. The Next Generation Science Standards (NGSS) were completed in March 2013 and are located at www.nextgenscience.org. Over 90 percent of the standards were revised using feedback provided after the May 2012 draft release. In addition, the NGSS team finalizing the definition for college and career readiness in science to ensure the standards supported this definition.

The National Educational Technology Standards (NETS) are the standards for learning, teaching, and leading in the digital age, available at www.iste.org/standards. The NETS set a standard of excellence and best practices in learning, teaching, and leading with technology in education.

The Common Core State Standards for mathematics are available at www.corestandards.org/assets/CCSSI_Math%20Standards.pdf.

The 2011 State STEM ED Report Cards provide information on your state rankings and are available for download at www.stemedcoalition.org/reports. Additionally, ASCD (formerly the Association for Supervision and Curriculum Development) has links to each state's Common Core Standards at www.ascd.org/common-core-state-standards/common-core-state-standards-adoption-map.aspx.

Learning Challenge: Plan and implement professional development on STEM literacy and resources for your stakeholders.

Think science has to be boring? Not when your students experience it through informal science education. Informal science education provides stimulating experiences as learning happens outside of formal classroom environments through media, exhibits, and community-based programming. The Center for Advancement of Informal Science Education (CAISE), http://caise.insci.org/uploads/docs/MakingScienceMatter.pdf, works to strengthen and connect the informal science education community by catalyzing conversation and collaboration across the entire field—including film and broadcast media, science centers, museums, zoos, aquariums, botanical gardens, nature centers, digital media and gaming, science journalism, and youth, community, and after-school programs. CAISE focuses on improving practice, documenting evidence of impact, and communicating the contributions of informal science education.

> *All STEM programs and activities should be fun, engaging, hands-on, break preconceptions, and stick in the mind forever.*

All STEM programs and activities should be fun, engaging, hands-on, break preconceptions, and stick in the mind forever. In our fast-changing world, people of all ages continue to seek knowledge and enrich their lives beyond the formal education environment of the classroom. The informal science education community offers a plethora of programs, field trips, speakers, and information. U.S. Government departments and agencies with science connections also offer activities and programs. NASA's Science Education Program, http://science.nasa.gov/educators, creates products using NASA's results in earth science, heliophysics, planetary science, and astrophysics research. The program sponsors educational activities at all levels

of formal and informal education to provide opportunities for learners to investigate their world and their universe using unique NASA resources.

The Informal Science Education Network (ISEN) listserv offers an environment for the exchange of ideas and knowledge regarding informal science education. Museum staff and educators participate in the discussions. Subscribe to the listserv at www.astc.org/profdev/listserv.htm

An excellent resource that is a free PDF download is the book *Learning Science in Informal Environments: People, Places, and Pursuits*, available at www.nap.edu/catalog.php?record_id=12190.

Learning Challenge: Collaborate with school librarians in your community to investigate, compile, and disseminate a digital directory of informal science education resources in your community. Invite scientists into your school to discuss with students what got them excited about science.

> *We need to pay extra attention to supporting females and minorities because they are greatly underrepresented in STEM college programs and careers.*

Professional associations, organizations, and companies are genuinely interested in improving STEM education. Search their websites for grants, speakers, and resources. The American Association of School Librarians (AASL) has partnered with the Carnegie Science Center: Girls, Math & Science Partnership to inspire girls through gaming and online activities to see themselves in STEM careers. Visit www.canteengirl.org/library for more information on the Can*TEEN Career Exploration initiative. We need to pay extra attention to supporting females and minorities because they are greatly underrepresented in STEM college programs and careers.

How will we meet the needs of society in the future? Where will the scientists, mathematicians, technologists, engineers, and innovators of the next generation come from? How can we increase student interest in STEM programs and careers? By strengthening our collaborative planning we can develop and implement lessons that introduce creativity and innovation, and as a result assist students with career exploration and development.

Traditionally, school libraries have supported the humanities and social studies classes more than STEM classes. Thus, it is critical that school libraries support STEM education proactively. Now is the time to correct this imbalance of resources. Putting STEM education into practice involves all of the resources of the school library—engaging literature, hands-on activities, interactive displays, reference sources, and projects for specific scientific concepts. The literature component alone includes trade books, biographies, government documents, atlases, periodicals, online databases, and websites. Keeping pace with our technology savvy students requires us to purchase as many STEM resources in electronic and/or digital formats.

No Time to Waste

Technology and media play a large role in the ways that young people connect to STEM learning. Functioning successfully in today's world requires scientific literacy, and the current pace of scientific and technological change requires our students to learn quickly and think critically. The increased dependence on technology will require all students to have a solid foundation in the STEM disciplines. As the 21st century progresses, STEM graduates will be as essential as electricity. Our students will need a solid understanding of STEM—and the problem-solving and creative thinking skills it involves—to have success in science and in business. Business and industry will demand that students have the skills that make

them creative thinkers, excellent problem solvers, and capable of good decision-making. Successful STEM education creates critical thinkers, increases science literacy, and enables the next generation of innovators. Innovation leads to new products and processes that sustain our economy.

We don't have a second to waste. The very future of our children and our economy is at stake. It is essential to our society that educators and learners at all levels are actively engaged in, motivated by, and able to work effectively on the complex issues involving STEM disciplines. By improving access to resources for students and teachers, and raising the community's understanding of the value of science literacy, school librarians will be doing their part to develop the scientists of tomorrow. Let's strive to provide our students with important "aha moments."

Outstanding STEM resources

AAAS Science Netlinks: http://sciencenetlinks.com
AAAS Science Update: www.scienceupdate.com
Common Core State Standards: www.corestandards.org
National Science Digital Library: http://nsdl.org
PBS STEM Education Resource Center: www.pbs.org/teachers/stem
Project Lead the Way: www.pltw.org
STEM Education Coalition: www.stemedcoalition.org/reports
STEMResources: www.stemresources.com

References

Bayer Corporation. *STEM Education, Science Literacy and the Innovative Workforce in America: 2012 Analysis and Insights from the Bayer Facts of Science Education Surveys, 1995–2011*. Pittsburg: Bayer Corporation, April 2012. Web. http://bayerus.online-pressroom.com/bayerus/assets/File/Final%20 Bayer%20Compilation%20Report.pdf.

Bell, Philip, et al., eds. *Learning Science in Informal Environments: People, Places, and Pursuits*. Committee on Learning Science in Informal Environments, Board on Science Education, Center for Education, Division of Behavioral and Social Sciences and Education. Washington, D.C.: National Academies Press, 2009.

Change the Equation. changetheequation.org.

Falk, J.H., and L.D. Dierking. "The 95 Percent Solution." *American Scientist* 98.6 (November/December 2010): 486–493.

Slavin, R.E., et al. *Effective Programs for Elementary Science: A Best-Evidence Synthesis*. Baltimore: Johns Hopkins University, Center for Research and Reform in Education. May 2010. Web. www.bestevidence.org/science/elem/elem_science.htm.

Subramaniam, Mega M., et al. "Reimagining the Role of School Libraries in STEM Education: Creating Hybrid Spaces for Exploration." *Library Quarterly* 82.2 (April 2012): 161–182.

U.S. Department of Commerce: STEM: Good Jobs Now and for the Future. 2011. Web. www.esa.doc.gov/sites/default/files/reports/documents/stemfinalyjuly14_1.pdf.

Young, Terrence E., Jr. "No Pain, No Gain . . . The Science Teacher and You Working Together." *Library Media Connection* 21.4 (January 2003): 14–16, 18–21.

Young, Terrence E., Jr. "STEM: Sparking Innovation and Imagination in School Libraries." *Library Media Connection* 30.5 (March/April 2012): 14–16.

Terrence E. Young, Jr. *is the library media specialist at West Jefferson High School in Harvey, Louisiana. He may be reached at bestman@att.net.*

Young, Terrence E., Jr. (2013). 24/7 STEMulation: Reinventing discovery. *LMC, 31*(6), 20–22.

Using Inquiry Groups to Meet the Next Generation Science Standards

By Laurie Dole

Students will
- Ask questions that can be investigated based on patterns such as cause and effect relationships. (3-PS2–3)
- Gather, read, and synthesize information from multiple appropriate sources and assess the credibility, accuracy, and possible bias of each publication and methods used, and describe how they are supported or not supported by evidence. (MS-LS1–8)
- Communicate technical information or ideas (e.g., about phenomena and/or the process of development and the design and performance of a proposed process or system) in multiple formats (including orally, graphically, textually, and mathematically). (HS-PS4–5)

Sound familiar? When I first read through the *Next Generation Science Standards*, I found myself checking the bibliography to see if AASL's *Standards for the 21st-Century Learner* were listed as a reference. The ideas and wording are so similar; I was surprised not to see AASL mentioned. Regardless, throughout the new science standards, you will recognize skills, dispositions, responsibilities, and self-assessment strategies very similar to our own.

The Next Generation Science Standards

The Next Generation Science Standards (NGSS) are a state-led initiative that present specific science standards all K-12 students should meet. Representatives from States across the country describe a vision of what it means to be proficient in science. The Next Generation Science Standards were developed on eight essential practices: asking questions and defining problems; developing and using models; planning and carrying out investigations; analyzing and interpreting data; using mathematics and computational thinking; constructing explanations and designing solutions; engaging in argument from evidence; and obtaining, evaluating, and communicating information.

All inquiry learning models are similar in their goal of active wonder and questioning. Students connect, question, and pursue knowledge in order to create new understanding.

"The goal of the new K-12 Science Education Standards is to ensure that by the end of 12th grade, all students have some appreciation of the beauty and wonder of science; possess sufficient knowledge of science and engineering to engage in public discussions on related issues; are careful consumers of scientific and technological information related to their everyday lives; are able to continue to learn about science outside of school; and have the skills to enter careers of their choice, including (but not limited to) careers in science, engineering, and technology" (www.nap.edu/openbook.php?record_id=13165&page=1#). This goal was developed as part of the Framework for K-12 Science Education by the National Academies of Science in partnership with the National Research Council (NRC), the National Science Teachers Association (NSTA), the American Association for the Advancement of Science (AAAS), and Achieve.

The AASL Connection

The Next Generation Science Standards present the perfect opportunity to integrate 21st Century Standards into our curriculum. Even those states will be affected that chose not to implement the standards directly. The Next Generation Science Standards were developed on eight essential practices that can be directly connected to the standards set forth by AASL (see Table 1). One of the common beliefs stated in the AASL *Standards for the 21st-Century Learner* is that "inquiry provides a framework for learning." There are many models of inquiry learning, but they are all similar in their goal of active wonder and questioning. Students connect, question, and pursue knowledge in order to create new understanding. For teacher-librarians, classroom content and district curricula provide the framework while inquiry is the foundation.

AASL's standards reflect the shift from a narrow focus on informational literacy to the broader thinking needed by the 21st century learner. Visual, digital, textual, and technological literacies work together to prepare our students for a global world of information. Visual literacy requires students to know how to "read" and evaluate visual media as well as be able to express their understandings through visual representations. Digital literacy asks students to use websites and resources to collect, organize, and create information. Textual literacy applies to the skills needed to find and use information, such as reading, writing, analyzing, and evaluating. Technology literacy asks students to master the various technologies to read, write, and communicate. Teacher-librarians have the expertise needed to support the classroom curriculum and can help the classroom teacher address these literacies as they connect to the Next Generation Science Standards. Students are expected to demonstrate grade appropriate proficiency in the eight essential practices in order to demonstrate understanding of the core ideas. For example, in Practice 2: "Developing and Using Models," modeling includes diagrams, analogies, and computer simulation. This is addressed in AASL's visual and digital literacies. Practice 8: "Obtaining, Evaluating, and Communicating Information" addresses textual and technology literacies.

Savvy teacher-librarians can teach students to connect visual images and ideas, make inferences, and justify interpretations in science as well as other content. Students should be taught to use Web 2.0 tools to create and present their learning. They can self-assess their products and communication. "The digital environment presents both opportunities and challenges which affect students' ability to process the evolving information available" (Stripling, 2010). Teacher-librarians must provide access to a variety of texts, regardless of learner ability, in order to support growth. By integrating new literacies into the curriculum, the teacher-librarian can have a positive impact on student learning.

Instructional Implications

In its *Standards for the 21st-Century Learner*, AASL shares the common belief that learning has a social context. Learners use skills, resources, and tools to "share knowledge and participate ethically and productively as members of our democratic society" (AASL, 2009). The Next Generation Science Standards address this need in essential Practice 7 and 8. Practice 7: "Engaging in Argument from Evidence" tasks the students from the earliest grades with comparing their ideas to others. They must listen actively and determine between facts, opinions, and bias. Practice 8: "Obtaining, Evaluating, and Communicating Information" expects that students share information, evidence, and ideas in a variety of ways. Complexity increases throughout the grade level bands, but ideas are shared orally, graphically, and textually. This simply cannot be achieved without students working together.

"Only true education comes through the stimulation of the child's powers by the demands of the social situations in which he finds himself"(Dewey, 1897). Over the years, research has continually extolled the benefits of group work. Greater motivation, satisfaction, and retention of knowledge are reported. But many teachers resist group work or find it ineffective. One of the easiest mistakes teachers can make is to assume content will take precedence over the social learning in the group. Before a group can be successful, it must figure out how to work together. Building the community of learners will take time, but collaboration allows students to "raise questions, hear other perspectives, try out ideas, and share their own views at various stages in the inquiry process" (Kuhlthau, 2012). Once students have experience sharing their questions and ideas, they are ready to learn from each other.

Kuhlthau, among others, has outlined a process for student inquiry that teaches students to construct subject as well as social knowledge. Clear procedures for sharing and giving feedback need to be established. Kuhlthau sets out intervention strategies, "The Six Cs," in her most recent publication on guided inquiry design to help groups transition smoothly through the stages of inquiry. The strategies—collaborate, converse, compose, choose, chart, and continue—support a constructivist approach to knowledge building. But whether you use Kuhlthau's process or one of the many others available, the intervention strategies she suggests will make your groups run more smoothly. Through time, inquiry communities and circles learn to value input from their peers and become better able to achieve the Standards for the 21st Century Learner and the Next Generation Science Standards.

The Next Generation Science Standards present the perfect opportunity to integrate 21st Century Standards into our school library curriculum.

Excerpted from *Standards for the 21st-Century Learner* by the American Association of School Librarians, © 2007 American Library Association. Available for download at www.ala.org/aasl/standards. Used with permission.
A Framework for K-12 Science Education: Practices, Crosscutting Concepts, and Core Ideas. The National Academies Press, 2012

Need more suggestions for lesson plans linked to the Common Core? Try the AASL Lesson Plan Database, available at www.ala.org/aasl/standards-guidelines/lesson-plan.

Table 1 **Connecting Next Generation Science to 21st Century Learning**

Science and Engineering Curriculum Essentials	21st Century Learning Standards
Practice 1: Asking Questions and Defining Problems Students at any grade level should be able to ask questions of each other about the texts they read, the features of the phenomena they observe, and the conclusions they draw from their models or scientific investigations. For engineering, they should ask questions to define the problem to be solved and to elicit ideas that lead to the constraints and specifications for its solution (NRC Framework, 2012, p. 56).	1.1.3 Develop and refine a range of questions to frame the search for new understanding. 1.2.1 Display initiative and engagement by posing questions and investigating the answers beyond the collection of superficial facts.
Practice 2: Developing and Using Models Modeling can begin in the earliest grades, with students' models progressing from concrete "pictures" and/or physical scale models (e.g., a toy car) to more abstract representations of relevant relationships in later grades, such as a diagram representing forces on a particular object in a system (NRC Framework, 2012, p. 58).	3.1.4 Use technology and other information tools to organize and display knowledge and understanding in ways that others can view, use, and assess. 3.3.4 Create products that apply to authentic, real-world contexts.
Practice 3: Planning and Carrying Out Investigations Students should have opportunities to plan and carry out several different kinds of investigations during their K-12 years. At all levels, they should engage in investigations that range from those structured by the teacher—in order to expose an issue or question that they would be unlikely to explore on their own (e.g., measuring specific properties of materials)—to those that emerge from students' own questions (NRC Framework, 2012, p. 61).	1.1.1 Follow an inquiry-based process in seeking knowledge in curricular subjects, and make the real-world connection for using this process in own life. 1.4.1 Monitor own information-seeking processes for effectiveness and progress, and adapt as necessary.
Practice 4: Analyzing and Interpreting Data Once collected, data must be presented in a form that can reveal any patterns and relationships and that allows results to be communicated to others. Because raw data as such have little meaning, a major practice of scientists is to organize and interpret data through tabulating, graphing, or statistical analysis. Such analysis can bring out the meaning of data—and their relevance—so that they may be used as evidence. Engineers, too, make decisions based on evidence that a given design will work; they rarely rely on trial and error. Engineers often analyze a design by creating a model or prototype and collecting extensive data on how it performs, including under extreme conditions. Analysis of this kind of data not only informs design decisions and enables the prediction or assessment of performance but also helps define or clarify problems, determine economic feasibility, evaluate alternatives, and investigate failures (NRC Framework, 2012, p. 61-62).	1.1.6 Read, view, and listen for information presented in any format (e.g., textual, visual, media, digital) in order to make inferences and gather meaning. 2.2.3 Employ a critical stance in drawing conclusions by demonstrating that the pattern of evidence leads to a decision or conclusion.
Practice 5: Using Mathematics and Computational Thinking Although there are differences in how mathematics and computational thinking are applied in science and in engineering, mathematics often brings these two fields together by enabling engineers to apply the mathematical form of scientific theories and by enabling scientists to use powerful information technologies designed by engineers. Both kinds of professionals can thereby accomplish investigations and analyses and build complex models, which might otherwise be out of the question(NRC Framework, 2012, p. 65).	1.1.2 Use prior and background knowledge as context for new learning. 3.1.6 Use information and technology ethically and responsibly.

(*Continued*)

Practice 6: Constructing Explanations and Designing Solutions Asking students to demonstrate their own understanding of the implications of a scientific idea by developing their own explanations of phenomena, whether based on observations they have made or models they have developed, engages them in an essential part of the process by which conceptual change can occur. In engineering the goal is a design rather than an explanation. The process of developing a design is iterative and systematic, as is the process of developing an explanation or a theory in science. Engineers' activities, however, have elements that are distinct from those of scientists. These elements include specifying constraints and criteria for desired qualities of the solution, developing a design plan, producing and testing models or prototypes, selecting among alternative design features to optimize the achievement of design criteria, and refining design ideas based on the performance of a prototype or simulation(NRC Framework, 2012, p. 68-69).	2.1.6 Use the writing process, media and visual literacy, and technology skills to create products that express new understandings. 2.2.4 Demonstrate personal productivity by completing products to express learning.
Practice 7: Engaging in Argument from Evidence The study of science and engineering should produce a sense of the process of argument necessary for advancing and defending a new idea or an explanation of a phenomenon and the norms for conducting such arguments. In that spirit, students should argue for the explanations they construct, defend their interpretations of the associated data, and advocate for the designs they propose. (NRC Framework, 2012, p. 73)	2.3.2 Consider diverse and global perspectives in drawing conclusions. 3.3.3 Use knowledge and information skills and dispositions to engage in public conversation and debate around issues of common concern.
Practice 8: Obtaining, Evaluating, and Communicating Information Any education in science and engineering needs to develop students' ability to read and produce domain-specific text. As such, every science or engineering lesson is in part a language lesson, particularly reading and producing the genres of texts that are intrinsic to science and engineering (NRC Framework, 2012, p. 76).	1.1.4 Find, evaluate, and select appropriate sources to answer questions. 1.1.5 Evaluate information found in selected sources on the basis of accuracy, validity, and appropriateness for needs, importance, and social and cultural context. 1.1.7 Make sense of information gathered from diverse sources by identifying misconceptions, main and supporting ideas, conflicting information, and point of view or bias.

References

American Association of School Librarians. *Standards for the 21st-Century Learner.* AASL, 2007. Web.

American Association of School Librarians. *Standards for the 21st-Century Learner in Action.* AASL, 2009.

Dewey, John. *John Dewey: My Pedagogic Creed.* N.p., n.d. Web. 23 April 2013.

A Framework for K-12 Science Education: Practices, Crosscutting Concepts, and Core Ideas. The National Academies Press, 2012.

Kuhlthau, Carol Collier, Leslie K. Maniotes, and Ann K. Caspari. *Guided Inquiry Design: A Framework for Inquiry in Your School.* Libraries Unlimited, 2012. Print.

Next Generation Science Standards: For States, By States. The National Academies Press, Draft, 2012.

Smith, M. K. Bruce W. "Tuckman—Forming, Storming, Norming and Performing in Groups, the Encyclopedia of Informal Education." Infed.org, 2005. Web. www.infed.org/thinkers/tuckman.htm.

Laurie Dole *is a third grade teacher in at Hermitage Elementary in Virginia Beach, Virginia. She can be reached at laurie.dole@vbschools.com.*

Dole, Laurie. (2013). Using inquiry groups to meet the next generation science standards. *LMC, 32*(2), 34–36.

I-LEARN: A Tool for Using Information for Learning

By Delia Neuman

Ideas and Information in the 21st Century

Library media specialists understand better than anyone that students must learn to engage with a wide variety of information types and formats to be efficient and effective learners in the 21st century. Whether presented through print, audio, visual, multisensory, or digital media, it is the information itself—not the "carriers" that deliver it—that learners must use to make meaning. To become lifelong learners in a world where information flows freely and sometimes overwhelmingly, students must develop strategies for engaging with a near infinite variety of ideas that come in all information formats.

A Model for Learning from Information

The I-LEARN Model—Identify, Locate, Evaluate, Apply, Reflect, kNow—both describes the process of learning with information and provides a teaching tool linked directly to information-age learning. A learning model that builds on but expands traditional information-seeking models, I-LEARN assumes that learning itself is the goal of information-seeking in schools. The model builds on the well-known information literacy paradigm—accessing, evaluating, and using information—to "operationalize" an inquiry approach to learning.

I-LEARN assumes that learning itself is the goal of information-seeking in schools.

The I-LEARN model includes six major stages, which describe the overall process of learning with information, and eighteen elements, three related to each stage, that flesh out the major stages with suggested ways to implement them. Table 1 shows the stages and elements and defines each. In practice, these elements might change—and the number might even increase or decrease—according to the needs of students and the demands of particular learning tasks. The elements listed under "Evaluate," for example, might include only two of the three or focus on comprehensiveness rather than timeliness in the use of information to learn about a hot-button political or social issue. In other words, while the stages are stable, the elements are possibilities rather than formulas.

Table 1 The I-LEARN Model

Identify	**Choose a problem or question that can be addressed through information.**
Activate	A sense of curiosity about the world
Scan	The environment for a suitable topic within that world to investigate
Formulate	A problem or question about the topic that can be addressed with information

Locate	**Access information, either recorded or in the environment, related to the question/problem.**
Focus	On what is to be learned
Find	The information needed for that learning
Extract	The most relevant and salient information for that learning

Evaluate	**Judge the quality and relevance of the information found.**
Authority	Credibility of source and/or author; internal logic; accuracy
Relevance	Topic at hand; level of learning/ depth required; appropriateness
Timeliness	Currency; accessibility

Apply	**Use the information for a learning task.**
Generate	Construct new understanding, personal meaning.
Organize	Determine appropriate cognitive structure (e.g., chronological, hierarchical, etc.).
Communicate	Create appropriate product to convey that structure.

Reflect	Examine product and process.
Analyze	Adequacy of both form and content
Revise	Improve as necessary
Refine	Polish as appropriate

kNow	Instantiate knowledge gained so that it can be used in the future.
Internalize	Integrate with previous knowledge.
Personalize	Recognize meaning as personal construct.
Activate	Draw upon as necessary and/or appropriate.

I-LEARN in Theory and Practice

As explained in detail in Neuman (2011), I-LEARN is grounded in the research and theory of both information studies and instructional systems design. The research and theory yield a highly practical outcome as well: a strategy that can be taught to help students master the process of learning with information. By operationalizing learning with information in only six stages and a few elements within each, the model is a tool that library media specialists and teachers can use to break the task of learning with information into manageable chunks that fit into a logical overall structure.

Now that I-LEARN's theoretical background is in place, validating the model in practice is the next step in its development. Template 1 is the vehicle by which that will happen. Individual school library media specialists as well as teams of school library media specialists and teachers are invited to use it as the basis for (1) identifying information-based questions related to various curricular areas and (2) developing scenarios for applying I-LEARN to solve them. The scenarios would then be used to guide students' research as they seek answers to these questions. The students' experiences, which will enrich and expand the ideas on each template, will form the basis for revising and refining the scenarios. Ultimately, a collection of tested and revised scenarios will be made widely available in digital and other formats—much like the familiar collection of WebQuests that library media specialists have used for years.

Figure 1 provides a template that shows the format such a scenario would take. Like any template, this one provides only a structure and some suggestions for ways in which its central topic might be addressed. How the scenario would play out

Figure 1 An I-LEARN Scenario

The Magic of Oz

Identify:

Activate: What's unusual about Australia?
Scan: Australia is in the Pacific Ocean, but it is linked to Great Britain.
Formulate: Why is Australia associated with Great Britain?

Locate:

Focus: What are the historical ties between Australia and Great Britain?
Find: Books, databases, documentaries, newspaper archives, etc., dealing with Australian history; information from conversations with Australians who live in my town or city
Extract: Specific information about the British settlement of Australia, developments over the years, military history, current status, etc.

Evaluate:

Authority: Credentials of the creators of the information; reasons for different views (e.g., stories of British descendants vs. those of Aboriginal peoples); informed opinion vs. propaganda; etc.
Relevance: Records of specific incidents, genealogical information, descriptions of cultural considerations, etc.
Timeliness: Contemporaneous accounts vs. later examinations of developments, current viewpoints, etc.

Apply:

Generate: Create a personal theory about the reasons for Australia's ties to Great Britain.
Organize: Make a topical outline of reasons related to each topic, along with supporting evidence.
Communicate: Design and create a multimedia presentation about Australia's ties to Great Britain based on the outline.

Reflect:

Review: Is the presentation logical, complete, balanced, etc.? Does it include all the appropriate information and avoid irrelevant information? Is it attractive and well designed?

Revise: Find more information, crop and re-position pictures, etc.

Refine: Polish narrative, add soundtrack, etc.

kNow:

Internalize: Integrate with existing knowledge about Great Britain, other parts of the British Empire, etc.

Personalize: Acknowledge ownership of ideas, explanations, etc.

Activate: Use new understanding as the basis for exploring other aspects of the British Empire or Australia.

---

is dependent on the interests and research paths taken by particular students, and these are virtually unlimited. The template is only a template, a guide to the overall structure of I-LEARN scenarios whose content can (and should) be tweaked to meet students' needs.

If you are interested in working with I-LEARN in your school, please get in touch with me (delia.neuman@ischool.drexel.edu) and we can discuss what you might do and how I can help you. I look forward to seeing how library media specialists can make the

model work as an effective tool for students!

> *Library media specialists understand better than anyone that students must learn to engage with a wide variety of information types and formats to be efficient and effective learners in the 21st century.*

Reference

Neuman, D. *Learning in Information-Rich Environments: I-LEARN and the Construction of Knowledge in the 21st Century*. Springer, 2011.

Delia Neuman *is an associate professor and director of the School Library Media Program at Drexel University, College of Information Science and Technology in Philadelphia, Pennsylvania. She may be reached at delia.neuman@drexel.edu.*

Neuman, Delia. (2012). I-LEARN A tool for using information for learning. *LMC, 30*(4), 18–19.

The Librarian's Role in Reading Instruction

By Beth Andersen and Megan Frazer Blakemore

The AASL *Standards for the 21st-Century Learner* state that "reading is a foundational skill for learning, personal growth, and enjoyment." In fact, this is the first statement of the standards. Though reading is a core skill, few librarians have time to teach it. We are called upon to do so much—technology, information literacy, professional learning communities—that reading, the very thing that likely drew many of us to the profession, often falls through the cracks.

It is important, though, for librarians to be a part of the reading team at the school. First you need to understand how reading is taught in your school. All teachers may use the same program, or the approach may vary from room to room. What follows are some common approaches.

Building Blocks of Reading Instruction

At the youngest grades, students work on the building blocks of reading. Print awareness is the first skill; it is the understanding that those squiggly lines on the page are actually representations of the words that we say. From there, students learn phonemic awareness, or the idea that sounds go together to make words. Phonemic awareness is different than phonics. As students grasp phonics, they understand the ways that letters and letter patterns make words, as well as the relationship between the letters and the sounds they make.

As students get older, they begin to work on fluency. The ability to correctly read text with expression is a constantly moving target; a child's fluency must grow as the texts he encounters become more complex. Likewise, students begin to master text comprehension, or the ability to understand what words mean beyond merely decoding them. This skill, too, grows more difficult as the child grows older. Once students have the

basic skills under their belts, the way the reader is grown and nurtured can vary widely.

Skills may be taught using the phonics approach where children learn rules for correctly decoding and pronouncing the words. Typically this approach uses repetition to drill students in the rule. For example, teachers might be focusing on the short vowel sound of the letter "a" (*The cat sat on the mat with the bat.*). Students read a short story or picture book which emphasizes words using that sound. In this approach, decoding is the fundamental skill of reading; once students can decode, meaning will follow.

> Both the Common Core Standards and the Next Generation Science Standards ask all teachers to focus on literacy. Science and math teachers may be anxious about taking on a literacy role. This provides a perfect opportunity for collaboration.

In contrast, the whole language approach argues that reading skills come from reading comprehension and appreciation. Students are given authentic, enjoyable texts with the goal of fostering a lifelong love of reading. When students bring appreciation and background knowledge to a text, comprehension becomes easier.

Like most dichotomies this one has its limit, and teachers employ a mix or balance of the two strategies. For example, teachers can teach phonics using authentic texts. It's not a big jump from the cat example to Dr. Seuss's *The Cat in the Hat*. Balance also comes into

the reading classroom in the form of the Balanced Literacy approach. Balanced Literacy sees literacy not only as reading, but also speaking, writing, listening, and viewing—an idea of literacy that should sound familiar to librarians.

Dystopias across the Curriculum

In her school visits, author Kate Messner uses a lesson on dystopian novels to help with world building and creative problem solving. This activity can be adapted to bring literature across disciplines.

Step 1: Read and Reflect on the Literature

Messner begins by asking students to think about dystopias they have read, such as *The Hunger Games* by Suzanne Collins, and how society might have gotten to that point. As the librarian, collect a number of dystopias at varying reading levels that students can choose to read. Titles would vary based on student age, but could include *The Giver* by Lois Lowry, *Brave New World* by Aldous Huxley, *The Handmaid's Tale* by Margaret Atwood, or Kate Messner's *Eye of the Storm*.

Step 2: Read and Imagine from the News

Next, in social studies and science classes, students can read newspapers, magazines, and online articles to learn about troubles facing the world's nations today. Once again, be sure to find current events material in a variety of formats and lexiles. Next comes the world building, which Messner explains as "imagining a world years, decades, or even centuries away by looking at current events and projecting possibilities for the future." Ask students to imagine the worst possible outcome of the scenarios. Messner suggests students do a five to ten-minute quick-write about their ideas. Repeat this activity, but this time ask students to come up with the best possible outcome.

Step 3: Reflect and Reverse-Engineer

We are asking our students to be creative thinkers and problem solvers. Here is where we put those skills into action. Students use their visions of the worst and best case scenarios to reverse-engineer the better outcome. What choices can we make today that will lead to that best outcome as opposed to the worst?

A dystopia activity is easy to connect to the curriculum: current events, totalitarianism (either in general or a specific dictatorship), climate change, or the environment. As the librarian, you can select dystopias at multiple reading levels; connect the history, English, and science teachers for collaboration; and construct a powerful interdisciplinary unit. Along the way, you can help the teachers instruct students on reading skills appropriate for each discipline.

Reading and Writing Workshop

Within and across these philosophies, there are a number of classroom models that teachers may use. One approach is the Reading and Writing Workshop. Pioneered by Lucy Calkins, this model focuses on frequency. Every day, students participate in read-alouds, individual reading assignments, and reading groups. The literature provides the content and context for student reading skills acquisition. Students are asked to engage with the text. They mark passages, generate vocabulary lists, and ask questions, practicing the skills of a strategic reader. The other half of the workshop model is writing about reading. Journals allow students time to write authentically about texts

and record their individual ideas and questions. In conjunction with reading assessment, evaluation of students' writing may shed light on why a student is having difficulties. Looking at each student's writing can reveal difficulty with print awareness versus phonics.

Colby Sharp, a fourth grade teacher from Michigan, uses this approach in his classroom. He begins the reading class with a mini lesson, typically around a skill and often modeled with a picture book. Kids spend thirty to forty-five minutes a day reading independently from books they have chosen themselves. While the class is reading, Sharp holds one-on-one reading conferences, explaining, "This gives me a chance to focus on reading strategies, reading habits, and other skills that my students need help with." Sharp is quick to point out that the workshop model does not mean leaving kids alone to teach themselves reading skills, but rather tailoring instruction to the individual student on an as-needed basis and giving them specific strategies for success. Reading skills are taught, but in the context of authentic reading experiences. This approach is of course similar to a school librarian teaching information literacy skills in the context of an authentic research process rather than in isolation.

> *Taking the lead on lesson development is a way to shape literacy instruction in your school.*

Building Reading Routines

A more formal approach is the use of programs such as Accelerated Reader from Renaissance Learning. These programs recognize the importance of routine when it comes to reading: "AR serves as the practice component of a comprehensive reading program by promoting personalized practice combined with data to monitor and manage that practice" (www.renlearn .com/ar).

The data monitoring and management takes two forms. First, before beginning the program, students are assessed for reading level. Their reading choices are determined by this assessment, with the idea that they will not be bored or frustrated by reading material that is too easy or too difficult. Students work with their teacher to set goals. They are given ample time during the day to practice reading authentic texts, after which they take a test. The frequent testing allows teachers to carefully track reading comprehension. Often there are rewards associated with earning points in the system. Although these programs are controversial, proponents argue that it motivates students to read and demonstrably raises comprehension.

While all of these programs may continue into high school, grades nine through twelve reading instruction is traditionally dominated by all-class reading assignments. In the context of the class book, students are taught to read critically, mining the text for theme, symbolism, and other layers. It is also in these years that focus is placed on discipline-specific reading, such as reading primary sources in social studies or a lab report in science.

Support Comes in Many Forms

Once you understand what methods your teachers use, you can better support them. If your teacher is using a program like Accelerated Reader, you may be asked to organize your library by lexile so that students can easily find books within their range.

A teacher using the workshop is going to need texts, and lots of them. As the librarian, you can alert your teachers to the latest books and recommend titles that go along with the specific skills. For emerging and struggling readers, Calkins proposes a literacy team for more individual work. Although she does not mention the librarian specifically, it is easy to see teachers needing support to find the differentiated titles needed for read-alouds and individual reading.

I am lucky to have a combination schedule at my high school. My primary schedule is a flexible schedule, but I meet with certain populations of students (ELL and Special Education) on a fixed schedule. This allows me to create a continuous strategic approach to teaching literacy with these classes. This year one class chose the 2012 Newbery Award Winner *Dead End in Norvelt* by Jack Gantos for our read-aloud.

Empowering Learners defines skills for strategic reading: Build upon prior knowledge, ask questions before, during, after reading, summarize, predict, make connections, draw inferences, and create new knowledge (AASL 22). Class activities line up with these skills.

Build upon prior knowledge:
- We pulled everyday vocabulary from the book and had dictionary races. Everyday vocabulary is an extension of daily class activity.
- Eleanor Roosevelt is an important historical figure in the novel. Many students knew she was the wife of President Roosevelt, but to learn more about her, students used a database.

Ask questions before, during, after reading:
- Stop reading in the story to ask questions to model this behavior of question asking.

Summarize:
- Students spent the final ten minutes of each class creating a collage of pictures for visual clues to the plot which we review at the beginning of each class.

Predict:
- Students who were able, wrote down predictions at major plot points in the book. Their thoughts provided material for authentic student-lead, class discussions.

Make connections:
- Student volunteers read books from the *Rotten Ralph* series to the class and connected themes to *Dead End in Norvelt*. During these readings, students had to sound out words. Both the classroom teacher and I commented on the readers' technique and skills: "I like the way Sophie sounded out the words she didn't know."
- A Google search led students to find current photos of Norvelt.
- Students became readers of the "This Day in History" column in our local paper, making connections to historical events outside of the novel.
- Students then examined other Newbery Award winning books. They were encouraged to check these out for summer reading.

Draw inferences:
- The main character's face is covered on the front of the book. When we were halfway through, students drew pictures of Jack based on descriptions of Jack in the book and author pictures.

Create new knowledge:
- Students became interested in learning the history of their own city. They planned to work with the historical society to review primary sources and create a presentation for the school.
- This has made the library the hub of literacy for the Special Education department. Students come in independently to check out books.

Coordinate Curricular Efforts

If your school uses curriculum mapping, you should read and know those maps so you can make sure your work with students goes along with that of the classroom teachers. Use your library time to enhance and promote the curriculum. If you are teaching research skills, have the subject be an extension of the classroom unit.

With the adoption of the Common Core Standards (CCS), teachers are feeling overwhelmed and looking for guidance. "As we adopt the Common Core Standards, I've done a lot of consulting on which texts are appropriate for various grades," says Cathy Potter, an elementary school librarian in Falmouth, Maine. She is already planning specific CCS lessons: "We're planning a Tale of Peter Rabbit unit with Kindergarten. We're going to have students retell the story using finger puppets, because retelling important events is part of the CCS." In other words, if you don't already know them, it's time to learn the Common Core Standards.

Similarly, the librarian can coordinate to fill gaps that the classroom teachers cannot meet. Potter is meeting the CCS of multiple literacies with a graphic novel reading/writing unit: "We're bringing in a comic artist to art classes in May, and students are going to write their own comic strips. I'm going to teach students and teachers some lessons on how to read graphic novels." Finding and filling these holes with your areas of expertise is one way to work with teachers to enhance reading instruction.

Coordination can be based around skills or content. For example, in the younger grades at Potter's school, "phonemic awareness in the library is in the context of rhyming stories, poetry, and nursery rhymes we read to Kindergarten and first grade classes." The activities in the library model and reinforce the lessons of the classroom. Carl A. Harvey II, past-president of AASL, puts it this way: "Any time I'm working with a class and a teacher and those skills can be practices, enhanced, taught, etc. I think we have to use all those opportunities."

Collaboration at the Core

John Schumacher, a school librarian perhaps better known as Mr. Schu, works with teachers to teach reading within the research environment. "I incorporate reading strategies when teaching students how to be effective and productive researchers. I consult with the homeroom teacher to see if he or she wants me to emphasize a specific strategy." Some reading strategies you might tap include accessing previous knowledge, summarizing, and asking questions.

Both the CCS and the Next Generation Science Standards (NGSS) ask all teachers to focus on literacy. Many teachers, especially in science and math, may be anxious about being asked to take on a literacy role. This provides a perfect opportunity for collaboration. Looking at the science standards officially published in April, each standard includes three dimensions: content, practices, and cross-cutting concepts. The cross-cutting concepts are the ELA and math standards connected to each science standard. Students may be asked to pull information from multiple sources to create an argument to support a scientific claim. Working in collaboration with the science teacher, the librarian can provide these resources and teach these skills. The librarian can also analyze the products with the teacher. If a student submits a poorly written piece, it is important to go back and analyze the work. Together the science teacher and the librarian can begin to isolate whether a student is experiencing difficulty with content versus literacy skills.

Leading the Way

One of the biggest challenges of the Common Core Standards will be to raise text complexity levels. Do so not merely by raising the lexile levels, but also by deepening the reading assignments so that students of all levels can interact with complex texts. The librarian can and should take the time to build the scaffolding, look at lexiles, and build standards-based lessons to bring to teachers.

Taking the lead on lesson development is a way to shape literacy instruction in your school. It is also important to be involved in reading and literacy work outside of the classroom. "You need to be a part of the school improvement team," states Harvey. "You need to be at data meetings where you are analyzing test scores. You need to have conversations with teachers and administrators about what areas our students need to improve on and how the library can be a part of that."

Don't Sit on the Sidelines!

Like so much of education, literacy is a team effort. The days of closed doors and isolated lessons at all levels are over. Just as the new standards are asking our students to be active participants in the creating and sharing of knowledge, it is our professional responsibility as well. Many librarians may not have a degree in literacy, but literacy skills have always been integral to our job. We share our passion for reading by helping students learn to be more effective readers and learners.

References

American Association of School Librarians. *Standards for the 21st-Century Learner.* Chicago: ALA, 2007. Web.

Calkins, Lucy. *The Art of Teaching Reading.* New York: Longman, 2001. Print.

Common Core State Standards Initiative. Web. 8 May 2013. www.corestandards.org/ELA-Literacy.

Empowering Learners: Guidelines for School Library Programs. Chicago: AASL, 2009. Print.

"Overview." Renaissance Learning. Web. 9 May 2013. www.renlearn.com/se/overview.aspx.

Elizabeth Andersen *is the librarian at Westbrook (Maine) High School.*

Megan Frazer Blakemore *is an author and librarian. Find her at www.megan frazerblakemore.com.*

Dynamic Partnerships to Improve Reading Scores

By Connie Ulmer, Carol Truett, and Nita Matzen

Today's media specialist can and should become an integral part of the school's efforts to improve student reading and test scores. "But how," asks the busy media specialist, "can I have a direct impact on reading scores? I only see some students once or twice a week and then only to help them check out books and possibly collaborate with their teachers on a research project." Contrary to this belief, there are many ways that a media specialist can have an influence on student reading. One should always remember that our ultimate goal is to develop in our students a love of reading as a pleasurable activity and a lifelong habit. "Adults who model reading behaviors and remain approachable help students learn about reading for pleasure, which is the key to lifelong learning" (Fenn, 2005, p. 51), and a major reason many adults go to the library. Minkel, (2002) quoting Mike Eisenberg, reminds media specialists that they have three major roles to perform: information literacy teacher for students and staff, reading advocate, and information manager in charge of print and electronic resources.

A recent national survey reported that "less than half of the adult population now reads literature, and . . . trends reflect a larger decline in other sorts of reading, [and] the rate of decline for the youngest adults— those 18 to 24—was 55 percent greater than that of the total adult population" (Whelan, 2004, p. 1). Whelan also states the concern that in 10 years this same group [at the age] of 28 to 34 years old may well pass on their apathy toward reading to their own kids.

Sharon Coatney says many media specialists seem to have forgotten that the first information literacy is the ability to read. Not only does Glick (2005) maintain that media specialists play a role in teaching students to read, but they need to perform that role if they want school administrators and politicians to see them as key players in that role.

A Reading Teacher and a School Media Specialist Partnership

Carolyn Icard, a reading teacher hired as an Instructional Coach at Heritage Middle School in Valdese, North Carolina, has a dual role in the school as reading instructor and consultant. Her office is located in the library media center which is supervised by media specialist Travis Childers. Childers helps his teachers with the Accelerated Reader (AR) Program; however, he is much more involved than that with reading promotion. He noticed when he first took the position that when AR books were shelved in a separate section no one would read the non AR books. He now mixes AR books with regular fiction and nonfiction on his bookshelves. To encourage students to choose other books to read, he regularly pulls books off the shelves and displays them. Since these books are singled out, students check them out thinking they must be special like the AR books even when they are not.

> Our ultimate goal is to develop in our students a love of reading as a pleasurable activity and a lifelong habit.

How do Icard and Childers actively work together to improve student reading? For one thing their office proximity fosters a continuing dialog that allows both parties to keep up with the other's job and to brainstorm ways they can collaborate. Icard coaches students for both math and reading improvement, and maintains that reading is fundamental to both areas. Students who can't read frequently don't even understand a math problem, let alone know how to solve it on a test. A sixth grader who is reading at a second grade level cannot read a social studies book written at his grade level. Some teachers, Icard explained, don't use a textbook partly for this reason, but assign other projects or reading including research-related activities illustrating the same concepts as the text. One example is using a social studies story written on the second grade level describing the Civil War, the topic of the week.

The media specialist can also recommend publishers, such as Steck-Vaughn, as well as books written on lower reading levels that would interest sixth graders. Jean Fritz, a well-known children's author, writes high interest, low reading level children's books in genres such as history and geography, for example *Traitor: the Case of Benedict Arnold*. Since her books are written like graphic novels, younger and older students appreciate reading them. The reading teacher could use these graphic novels as models for student writing in the class, which ultimately improves their reading abilities. This relationship between the media specialist and the teacher is paramount to the objective of enhancing the literacy skills of not just slow, but average and advanced readers.

Together Icard and Childers peruse book catalogs so he may order books for the library which she feels will help the poor and reluctant readers. And Childers does order graphic novels which appeal particularly to reluctant male readers and other high interest, low reading level books (often call high-lows) such as sports biographies. He maintains that he cannot keep his lower level mysteries such as the Boxcar Children Series, written at the elementary level, on the shelves of his middle school. Easy books, also known as E or picture books, of interest to middle schoolers are also purchased and inter-shelved among the other fiction and nonfiction books. In summary, Icard and Childers tackle the problem of low reading scores, not to mention school-wide literacy, as a team effort.

Public and School Library Cooperation

The public library children's summer reading program, part of virtually every public library's mission, is another area where the media specialist can help promote reading. All too often students' reading abilities decline over the long summer vacation. Promoting and publicizing the public library's summer reading program is an excellent way for school media specialists to help combat this situation. Minkel (2003) offers seven methods that librarians can use to collaborate with schools in order to promote summer reading programs, and savvy media specialists can take advantage of these tips. The school media specialist can invite public librarians to visit their schools and sign children up for the programs, help arrange to send literature publicizing summer reading home to parents, get permission to send summer reading program stickers home on student report cards, and schedule follow-up for the programs in September in the school library.

An example of public and school library cooperation is the Seattle Public Library's joint program with Seattle media specialists who worked together on their "What if Everyone Read the Same Book" campaign (Minkel, 2002). This program encouraged every fourth and eighth grader to read and discuss Louis Sachar's novel *Holes*. This concept has caught on in many communities throughout the country such as Boone, North Carolina, where the Watauga Public Library and Appalachian State University encourage and promote the program for students and adult readers.

Good Writers Are Good Readers: The Reading and Writing Partnership

Many of the programs discussed thus far relate to silent and oral reading, motivation, and quality books to help improve reading scores. However improving reading goes beyond how or what one reads. Research shows that enhancing all of the literacy modalities (reading, writing, speaking, listening, and visualizing) helps improve reading abilities. Rosenblatt (1978) suggests that the transaction between the reader, text, and context of the reading event also determines a student's comprehension. In the context of reading, students often write to describe, synthesize, analyze, and critique their understandings, especially in a testing context. And Applebee (1978), according to Stephen Krashen (1993), a nationally recognized expert on reading research, "found that outstanding high school writers (i.e., winners of the National Council of Teachers of English achievement awards in writing) were pleasure readers. They reported reading an average of 14 books for pleasure over the summer vacation and an average of four books during the first two months of their senior year" (p. 9).

The idea that the media specialist's role may not end just with reading instruction is a concept also proposed by Janet Boltjes (2005), media specialist at Gilbert High School in South Carolina. When Boltjes heard keynote speaker Brod Bagert speak at a state conference, she was so taken with his idea of a poetry writing club that she started one at her own school. She was both shocked and pleasantly surprised when 12 students actually showed up to participate, not just the anticipated two. This number gradually grew to 20. The poetry seminars resulted in a weekly interchange of poetry tips, writing, and readings. No formal poetry lessons were included in these sessions. Response and participation from the students involved was intensive, the diversity of students notable, and interactions dealt with personal and sensitive teen issues.

Brod Bagert himself visited the school, responded to many of the seminar students' poems, and performed before whole classes, composing a poem "on the spot" about science topics much to the amazement of a live student audience. One of these poems, a humorous piece titled "The Decay of Radiant Bodies," may be found in the article, and similar poetry is included on Bagert's Web site.

> *The relationship between the media specialist and the teacher is paramount to the objective of enhancing the literacy skills of not just slow, but average and advanced readers.*

In Conclusion: We Are What We Do (and Read)

Modeling and sharing a love of reading and literature is probably one of the best ways to instill this in students. Ala Sue Moretz, media specialist at Mountain City Elementary in Tennessee, maintains that the best way to motivate student reading is to read yourself, especially the books in your own collection. "If you don't know the books, you can't get kids to read them," says Moretz (2007). "If **you** have no excitement, they can sense that. I also believe in reading to them—at **all** ages." And didn't most of us get into this profession because we love books and reading?

References

Fenn, Jane. "8 Ways Your Librarian Can Help Promote Literacy." *Principal Leadership (High School Ed.)* 5 Feb. 2005: 49–51.

Glick, Andrea. "Reading Teacher, Meet the Librarian." *School Library Journal* 51 (June 2005): Eric Doc. No. EJ714269

Icard, Carolyn and Childers, Travis. Interview conducted at Heritage Middle School, Valdese, North Carolina, Burke County Public Schools, on Sept. 17, 2007.

Krashen, Stephen. *The Power of Reading: Insights from the Research*. Englewood, CO: Libraries Unlimited, 1993.

Minkel, Walter. "Making a Splash with Summer Reading." *School Library Journal* 49 (January 2003): 54–56.

Minkel, Walter. "Making Every Librarian a Leader. The Future of the Profession. Part 2." *School Library Journal* 48 (Oct. 1, 2002): 46–49.

Moretz, Ala Sue. Interview conducted at Boone, North Carolina on Sept. 18, 2007.

Rosenblatt, Louise. *The Reader, the Text, the Poem: The Transactional Theory of the Literary Work.* Carbondale, IL: Southern Illinois Press, 1978.

Summerford, Steve. "Creating a Community of Readers to Fight Functional Illiteracy [Program with Heart in North Carolina]." *American Libraries* 28 (May 1997): 44–48.

Whelan, Debra Lau. "Librarians Respond to Decline in Reading." *School Library Journal* 50 (September 2004): Online 1–2.

Woolls, Blanche. "Changes, Changes: Count on Reading." *School Library Media Quarterly* 21 (Summer 1993): 237–39.

Dr. Connie Ulmer *is associate professor of reading in the Department of Language, Reading and Exceptionalities at Appalachian State University in Boone, North Carolina.*

Dr. Carol Truett *is professor of library science in the Department of Leadership and Educational Studies at Appalachian State University in Boone, North Carolina.*

Dr. Nita Matzen *is assistant professor of library science in the Department of Leadership and Educational Studies at Appalachian State University in Boone, North Carolina.*

Ulmer, Connie, Truett, Carol, & Matzen, Nita. (2010). Dynamic partnerships to improve reading scores. *LMC, 28*(5), 18–19.

Can Web 2.0 Strengthen Reading Skills?

By Tammy Story

"I don't like to read." "This book is boring." "It's too hard to read!" These statements are all too familiar and common from students who are struggling with reading. As a media specialist, I have observed how challenging it is to strengthen the reading skills of struggling readers. Many will give up trying to read or will not read at all. As 21st century teachers, we must continually seek engaging interactive literacy tools to use with struggling readers in order to strengthen their reading skills.

Reading the Web 2.0 Way

With everything online or converted to an app, how do we strengthen the reading skills of the struggling reader in the 21st century? Teaching them to read the traditional way is not as effective. It is important to use tools that will engage students.

Many young learners who struggle in reading enjoy electronic devices, such as smartphones, tablets, smart TVs, and wireless game systems. It's amazing to see how a student who struggles in reading plays a video game for hours but cannot focus on reading a book. Can Web 2.0 strengthen reading skills? Many struggling readers prefer to do an activity that is interactive and engaging versus reading a hardcopy book.

David Ligon (2009) defines a 21st century learner as "someone engaged in educational gaming and multi-user virtual environments (MUVEs), collaborating through social media (blogs, wikis), listening to podcast lectures on iPods and smartphones, watching YouTube videos, connected to and communicating with the global village through wireless laptops and PDAs. Always plugged in, always on, 21st century learners are mass-consumers of information on demand at the speed of thought."

> *Web 2.0 tools can help the struggling reader and make learning to read fun, interactive, and engaging.*

Based on these traits, how do we help the 21st century learner who struggles in reading? Web 2.0 tools can help the struggling reader and make learning to read fun, interactive, and engaging. As a leader of literacy, my interest lies in researching Web 2.0 tools that can strengthen reading skills.

I began my research by defining Web 2.0: "Web 2.0 is defined as a new way of creating, collaborating, editing, and sharing user-generated content online. The tools are user friendly; furthermore, there is no need to download, teachers and students can master many of these tools in minutes; in addition, Web 2.0 tools are accessible 24 hours a day and 7 days a week" (http://web2012.discoveryeducation.com). Then I identified Web 2.0 tools that would help struggling readers improve their reading skills. Let's explore some of these tools.

Presentation Tools

Presentation tools such as Prezi and Glogster allow one to create interactive presentations and promote visual literacy. These tools give teachers and students the ability to upload, create, edit, and share interactive and engaging presentations at any time from any place. Prezi and Glogster may be utilized to create an engaging and interactive word wall. "Word walls are a literacy tool used mostly in classrooms as part of a reading instruction program. Word walls should be interactive and dynamic" (About.com, 2012). Presentation tools will enable you to create word walls that students find interactive and engaging. They are used as an interactive resource that students can refer to during literacy exercises at any time of the day. "The large visual nature of Word walls helps students to naturally gain familiarity with these high frequency words as well as to gain reinforcement of vocabulary" (About.com, 2012).

Another Web 2.0 tool for creating word walls is Wordle. "Wordle is a visual tool used for generating "word clouds" from text that you provide" (Feinburg, 2011). For example, you could take a list of vocabulary words from any book and create a Wordle word wall to which students can refer during literacy exercises.

Figure 1

Wordle Word Wall created with words from Dr. Seuss' *Hop on Pop*.

Video and Audio Tools

Video Podcast and Photostory 3 allow teachers to create videos or photo stories that are used as a read-aloud to help strengthen the reading skills of struggling readers. Video tools allow a teacher to take a book and create a digital copy with voiceovers that will enable the student to read a book independently by listening to the words that are read aloud in the video.

Web 2.0 Tools to Help Strengthen Reading Skills

Audacity: http://audacity.sourceforge.net
Edmodo: www.edmodo.com
Glogster: www.glogster.com
GlogsterEDU: http://edu.glogster.com/l
PhotoStory 3: www.microsoft.com/download/en/details.aspx?id=11132
Prezi: www.prezi.com
Wordle: www.wordle.net

Apps:
Android: https://play.google.com
Apple: www.apple.com/macosx/whats-new/app-store.html

Another option is to take the video and upload it to a video hosting site. This way students will have access to the video at any time. Be sure to review your school's copyright policy before uploading videos to public sites. As students watch and listen to the video, they will become familiar with the vocabulary, and they will be less reluctant to read the book.

Audio tools such as Audacity allow a teacher to create mp3 files for a student to download and listen to while following along in the book. Again, be sure to review your school or district's copyright policy to determine fair use. Audacity gives a student the opportunity to practice reading passages aloud and self-access their oral reading skills. Sharon Thornton shares the following insight: "Audacity creates a starting place for students as they see and hear their reading first hand; in addition, students now have a way which serves as a starting point in order to start improvements. As students progress, they become engaged in creating recordings in Audacity, which allows them to become active participants in their learning" (Thornton, 2011). The more often students actively participate in oral reading exercises, the more they strengthen their reading skills.

Community Tools

Social networks and wikis provide a range of tools that help teachers and students to communicate, collaborate, and share work. Edmodo is a safe social network where teachers can post reading resources, videos, and literacy exercises for students, all in one location. It's a safe place for students to communicate and collaborate with teachers and peers while having access to literacy exercises at any time. Students can help each other out with assigned literacy exercises and take part in engaging and interactive book discussions.

From Web 2.0 to Mobile Tools

Mobile tools are engaging interactive resources that can help strengthen the reading skills of the struggling reader. They are great for reading, podcasting, blogging, social networking, and media sharing. Mobile tools allow students to practice literacy exercises, communicate with teachers, and read books while on the go—and they can be accessed 24/7 from various mobile devices, including smartphones, tablets, and wireless gaming devices.

Mobile tools allow students to practice literacy exercises, communicate with teachers, and read books while on the go.

References

About.com: Special Education. "Teach Reading with Word Cards and Word Walls." 2012. Web. http://specialed.about.com/od/wordwalls/a/wordwall2.htm.

About.com. "Word Walls: Definition of the Education Glossary Term Word Walls." 2012. Web. http://k6educators.about.com/od/educationglossary/g/gwordwalls.htm.

Discovery Education. "Web 2.0 Tools." 2012. Web. http://web2012.discoveryeducation.com/web20tools.cfm.

Feinburg, J. "Wordle: Beautiful Word Clouds." Wordle, 2011. Web. www.wordle.net.

Ligon, D. "21st Century Teaching & Learning." Classroom 2.0, 9 August 2009. Web. www.classroom20.com/profiles/blogs/21st-century-teaching-amp.

Seuss, T. *Hop on Pop.* New York: Beginner Books, 1963.

Story, T. "*Hop on Pop* Wordle." Wordle, 21 April 2012. Web. www.wordle.net/show/wrdl/5176208/Hop_on_Pop_Wordle.

Thornton, S. "Improving Literacy with Audacity Recording Software." Audacity, 2011. Web. http://audacity.pbworks.com.

Web2teachingtools.com. "Glogster, a Web 2.0 Teaching Tool Supporting 21st Century Learning Skills. Web 2.0 Teaching Tools, 2009. Web. www.web2teachingtools.com/glogster.html.

Tammy Story *is a library media specialist at Norris Elementary School in Thomson, Georgia, and can be reached at trstory@mail.com.*

Story, Tammy. (2012). Can Web 2.0 strengthen reading skills? *LMC, 31*(3), 38–39.

You Can't Fool Me: Website Evaluation

By Jennifer Bromann-Bender

The pregnant man. Exploding Pop-Tarts. The Tree Octopus. Baby cages. The jackalope. And the Online Pregnancy Test (my favorite). We often teach website evaluation using fake websites. These extreme examples show students that we need to evaluate online information because even though it looks real and valuable, it is completely fabricated. Students love these fun examples and realize that not all information out there is accurate. As an example of how easily we can be fooled, my sister bought me a stuffed jackalope for my baby shower, and I said, "Now, the jackalope is not real, right?" But many people at the shower swore that it was, even a librarian. Can students transfer this understanding about what is obviously false to an article on stem cell research, published on a website with a specific viewpoint behind it?

Motivated by the desire to collaborate, promote database use, and be a larger part of the classroom, I developed my own website evaluation tool. I knew what I wanted students to consider so they could make decisions about the validity of the sources they hoped to use. As I showed teachers what I was working on and began working with students, the evaluation form evolved and will likely continue to change.

Available Resources

I love Joyce Valenza's *Power Tools Recharged*, a handbook that consists of handouts. I use the resources as a starting point and adapt them to my own needs. Included are the Web Page Evaluation Checklist from Joe Barker (2002) and the CARRDSS method Valenza developed in collaboration with Carol H. Rohrbach. This method includes the categories of credibility, accuracy, reliability, relevance, date, sources behind the text, and scope. In addition, she includes questions like "Why Should I Take This Author Seriously?" as a way to examine the

authority of an author. I also looked at the Five W's of Website Evaluation (who, what, when, where, and why).

After I had developed the form, I attended a workshop that mentioned an online source called the Website Evaluation Wizard from the Illinois Math & Science Academy (http://21cif.com/tools/evaluate). It does not tell you if your source is good or not, but you can enter the answers to various questions and print out a report to hand in to a teacher or for self evaluation. I like this resource since it allows students to complete the evaluation process online as they pull up a website. Wouldn't it be great if there really were a source where you could submit a URL and a flashing green or red light would indicate if the site is approved?

Getting Started

It began with the curriculum our district librarians were creating based on the I-SAIL standards from ISLMA (Illinois School Library Media Association.) We planned to use this curriculum as a starting point for working with teachers based on the skills that the Illinois State Board of Education, AASL (American Association of School Librarians), and ISLMA believed were necessary for our students to master by the end of high school. With the draft of this document in hand, I met with our Reading Department chair Bridget Scheer and our English Department chair Renee Goldie to discuss what knowledge from our curriculum could be combined with the goals for their curriculum. I had mentioned that some teachers had been using our website evaluation form. The English chair was interested in having more classes use this method. She presented the form to her teachers and brought comments back for me so I could make revisions. The original form was a one-page document with little space for notes. The teachers felt that students needed more room to write

down their notes. I revised the form, and after working with students and receiving additional suggestions from English teachers, I revised the form again and again. With the support of the English Department, I worked with most classes using this form. We decided that students would complete the form on their own and return it to me, the librarian, for approval (or teachers might choose to "grade" the forms themselves). This can be time consuming, but it is exciting to have a larger part in the research process.

How It Works

I present a 15-minute lesson, showing the students a good and a bad example of a website on a topic related to their assignment while going through the concepts on the evaluation form. Occasionally I have to make adjustments to the time needed, but for most classes the students answer the questions on their own and submit the form to me to review. That is why I wanted the form to be detailed; students should be able to answer most of the questions on their own.

Ideally, I go through the answers and approve the forms. However, most of the students approve their own bad website choices, using the form as a self evaluation tool. So when I get the forms, I often have to look up the websites or review the copies they provide and do further evaluation myself. Also, many of the students do not complete all the steps. Does this defeat the purpose? I do not believe so. I give students feedback on their evaluation of the websites. If they agreed that a website did not include bias, I often point out how the website does include bias. I try to offer students something to consider before they use these sources in their papers.

The goal is also to secretly promote database use. One teacher had me describe all the steps to her students and pointed out how much work it is to thoroughly evaluate a website. The students then realized that it is easier to use the more reliable subscription databases.

Instruction or modeling should guide students through the process of website evaluation. Why not take the opportunity to show them how to conduct a search for more reliable information? I decided to include some pre-searching tips at the beginning of the process.

- **Try adding .edu, .org or .gov to your search to locate more reliable sources.**

Government, organizational, and educational websites are more likely to contain reliable information. Students should be aware that they can do a search for just these websites by adding the domain abbreviations to their searches (e.g., cloning .edu).

For more scholarly articles, try www.scholar.google.com. Google Scholar may not always provide the best or most full-text hits. However, it is a starting point that could narrow a search and lead students to scholarly or professional resources.

- **Use the advanced search in a search engine to search by date and eliminate unwanted information.**

Most students do not realize that even search engines like Google have an advanced search. Here they can narrow or expand their searches to receive results with a more relevant focus.

- **Try a Boolean search (and, or, not) to eliminate unneeded information.**

Discuss Boolean searching even if it may be the default in the search engine students choose. Other searching techniques, such as phrase searching and truncation, could also be discussed if there is time.

- **Use an index such as www.ipl.org. This source features preselected websites that were verified for accuracy by others.**

Show students an index like Internet Public Library where websites have been pre-selected. You can also share databases with selected websites. Most have already been determined as reliable sources.

- **Try a reliable news source, such as a well-known newspaper or news organization (*New York Times*, *Chicago Tribune*, CNN).**

Students may locate news articles in a general search, but starting off in these sources may avoid wasted search time. Articles from these sources will likely be accepted.

If time is not devoted to pre-searching, students will revert back to their old ways of typing their topics word for word into a search engine and selecting the first results.

Website Evaluation Instruction

After making suggestions about finding a reliable website, instruction on website evaluation can take place. Website evaluation is best explained by showing two examples of articles, one good and one bad, on the same topic. Then model your approach to evaluation.

Whereas the "pregnant man" is obviously not real by the title alone, a website such as Borderland Beat (www.borderlandbeat.com) is more likely to fool students. This was an actual website submitted by a student. The article she had selected looked accurate and may have been true. But the About section of the site listed the founder as Buggs. Buggs, who has roots in Mexico where he has traveled extensively, and J, a collaborator for the site, may be highly qualified individuals, but Buggs and J just aren't names that are usually used on a reliable website. There is also the statement "Most of the information and content is derived from open source media, unconfirmed individual sources, and personal viewpoint of author. Most content is for information purposes only and is not from direct official sources and in most cases not confirmed. Some content is graphic and discretion is advised." Would you want to base your research on facts from a site that claims most of their sources are unconfirmed? The site looks valid, but when you investigate further, you find that it's not as good as it seems.

As part of the instruction, I share an article from Borderland Beat and go through all the questions on the website evaluation form, explaining what to look for and where to find it on a website. If time permits, students can also select random articles to review or go through the steps as a class, using an article of their choice related to their topics.

Student Evaluation

The next step is for the students to evaluate their own website selections. They may ask if they have to fill out a form for a specific website. That is generally up to the teacher. Usually they have to fill one out for each website unless it is from a subscription database. Teachers may not require a form for authoritative sites such as BBC, *Chicago Tribune*, or CNN since they are likely to be approved. I review the forms and return them to the students or teachers, depending on how the teachers want it handled.

Background Information

What do I need to know to approve students' selections? For me to approve their website evaluations, I need to know some basic facts, especially the nature of the assignment given to the students. Otherwise I may find myself writing to the teacher to verify if an article with bias would be appropriate for a pro/con paper, if bias was allowed.

Students also need to state their topic. Evaluating a website for relevance can only be accurate if the topic has been specified.

Asking students to include the website title is useful as well. If a student does not provide a copy of the article or write the URL legibly, you need the website title to help locate the article. Students should be instructed on where to find the title. Finally, they should add the URL or provide a copy of the article.

Final Approval

The students may approve themselves, but ideally the librarian should have final approval. I originally only included the categories "A good source" and "Not a good source" to check off. I soon realized that some articles might have a great quote or a good fact, but they were not from the most reliable sources. Or they weren't the best choice. Due to this, I decided to add an option to check off "Acceptable for a quote or fact, but should not be used as a main source. Better information can be found." After finding myself constantly writing about bias, I decided to add the evaluation "Acceptable for a research assignment that allows for bias, such as a debate or pro/con paper. This article is from a website with a specific agenda. Be sure to indicate the organization behind the information in your paper. Be careful if using the site for factual information."

Of course, students will not continue to fill out such a form for every website they use, and they won't take a stack of them to college. The idea is that, after filling the form out a few times, they will begin to internalize the criteria and think about what makes a good website each time they are searching, even when the librarian is not there. Or they will prefer to use the databases instead.

In the notes section of the website evaluation form I have provided comments on what students should be looking for and what you should be looking for when reviewing the evaluations.

Name _____   Teacher _____

Website Evaluation—Lincoln-Way West High School

Searching for Reliable Sites—Tips

1. Type in your topic and add .edu, .org, or .gov to locate more reliable sources.
2. Try www.scholar.google.com for more scholarly articles.
3. Use the search engine's advanced search function to search by date and eliminate unwanted information.
4. Try a Boolean search (and, or, not) to eliminate unneeded information.
5. Use an index such as www.ipl.org. This source has preselected websites that were verified for accuracy by others.
6. Try a reliable news source, such as a well-known newspaper or news organization (*New York Times, Chicago Tribune*, CNN).

Topic:

Assignment:

Website Title:

URL/Address:
(Please write clearly or attach the article, including URL.)

Questions to Consider:	Notes (answer as many of the following questions as possible with proof):	Is this a reliable site based on these questions? Yes/No
Domain and URL: 1. What is the domain? (.edu, .org, and .gov are more reliable, although .com is often reliable too. Just because it is a .org site does not make it automatically reliable) 2. Search link:yourURL. This will identify if your selected website was linked from any other site. Are the sites reliable? 3. Check the URL in online databases to see if it has been cited in articles.	Although .edu, .org, and .gov are generally more reliable, they may also exhibit bias or inaccuracy. If on the fence, these would generally be approved, but should still be checked. Search for the URL in a search engine by typing in the address, using link:yourURL or in databases. Was this website linked to other reliable (or unreliable) sites? Demonstrate this approach to students. Most teachers will automatically approve sites from reliable news sources. Inform students that some websites will fake an article and put a newspaper logo above it. Students should make sure the article was originally published in the news source.	Yes No

4. Is the article from a reliable news source such as *New York Times, Chicago Tribune,* or CNN, etc.? These are automatically acceptable, but make sure you find the article on the actual news website to be sure it is not a fake.

Credibility:

1. Who is the author? A professor/expert/scholar/researcher?
2. Any credentials listed?
3. What do you find when you search for the author's name in a search engine or subscription database?
4. Who is the sponsor of this site? Is the organization credible? Check Wikipedia or use a search engine for more information.

One of the main things to look for is whether or not an author is listed and credentials can be found. If they are a staff reporter or have an educational background in the field for which they are writing about, they are generally approved. This may need to be sought out beyond the original website. What is even more important is the organization behind it. Often, if you search deep enough, you find a religious or political organization behind the facts. This may indicate bias. The student should check another online source to find out more about the legitimacy of that organization.

Yes
No

Date:

1. When was this website created and updated?
2. Does your information need to be more current or can it be historical?

Look for a current date or one that is relevant to the time you are researching.

Yes
No

Sources:

1. Were credible sources used?
2. Are references from other articles or websites cited?
3. Copy and paste some of the references into a search engine. Are these sources cited elsewhere? Do they really exist?

It takes a lot of work to conduct a precise search. However, it is a good idea to look for references. If none are provided, it is a red flag. Where is all this information coming from? The references should be within the article or listed somewhere on the page. They should be checked to make sure they are real sources.

Yes
No

Bias:

1. Does the author or organization argue only one side of an issue?
2. Is the purpose to promote a specific agenda? If it is one-sided and your purpose is to argue this point of view in a debate or pro/con paper, the website may be acceptable if you identify the organization behind the opinions. If you are writing a factual paper, you may want to look for a different site. For example, is the information from a political website?

Students need to consider whether or not they can include articles with bias for a particular assignment. Often this would be appropriate if arguing an issue. Students should still identify the organization behind the article or ideas, or explain an opposing view from another organization. Sometimes the purpose of a website will identify this. The organization itself is a big clue into whether or not the article and information is biased.

Yes
No

Accuracy:

1. Can you verify the facts in other sources? Double-check the facts by searching for them on other sites or in a book. 2. Based on your own knowledge, does the information seem accurate?	Students often respond that they know the facts are correct. They should also try to provide evidence. Even if they cannot verify facts for obscure information, the website may still be reliable. Ask students to consult a book or search for a fact on another website. Bob Marley's birthday has been listed incorrectly in different sources. If the article has information a student really wants to use, but the website is questionable, they may find the information from a more credible source by searching the content of the article.	Yes No
Relevance: 1. Does this source answer your questions and support your topic/thesis/hypothesis?	The student would best be able to answer this question. Look at their topic provided and compare. Tell students to skim the article or use the "find" option to search for key terms to help confirm relevance.	Yes No
Appearance: 1. Does the website have a professional appearance? (This can also be misleading.) 2. Does the information appear to be as good or better than a journal article?	Show some examples of professional-looking websites which are fakes. Show examples of websites that are littered with ads.	Yes No

This website is

____ A good source ____ Not a good source

____ Acceptable for a quote or fact, but should not be used as a main source. Better information can be found.

____ Acceptable for a research assignment that allows for bias, such as a debate or pro/con paper. This article is from a website with a specific agenda. Be sure to indicate the organization behind the information in your paper. Be careful if using the site for factual information.

Comments:

__ Credible author provided __ References included __ Reliable organization/news organization

Created by J. Bromann-Bender, 2010/2011

Works Cited

Heine, Carl, and Dennis O'Connor. "Citation Wizard." *Information Fluency Home*. The 21 St Century Information Fluency Project, 15 Dec. 2011. Web. 24 Jan. 2012. http://21cif.com/tools/evaluate.

Schrock, Kathy. "The Five W's of Web Site Evaluation." Kathy Schrock's Home Page. Web. 24 Jan. 2012. http://kathyschrock.net/abceval/5ws.htm.

Valenza, Joyce Kasman. *Power Tools Recharged: 125+ Essential Forms and Presentations for Your School Library Information Program*. Chicago: American Library Association, 2004. Print.

Jennifer Bromann-Bender *is a librarian at Lincoln-Way West (Illinois) High School and can be reached at bromannj@hotmail.com.*

Bromann-Bender, Jennifer. (2013). You can't fool me: Website evaluation. *LMC, 31*(5), 42–45.

Create, Curate, Celebrate: Storytelling in the Library

By Diane Cordell

Long before there was a written language, stories served to entertain, enlighten, and connect groups of people through the sharing of universal themes, common history, and accumulated wisdom. Stories are a rich source of language experience for children, stretching their understanding, and giving them the vocabulary to begin crafting a sense of self.

During traditional library story hours, children sit and listen to works of imaginative literature read by adults. While this remains a valuable practice, libraries can also build on the power of storytelling in another way, by taking it from a passive activity to an active process, inviting students to begin telling their *own* stories, the fascinating, ongoing, and very personal history that they will be generating throughout their entire lives.

Create

Stories begin with raw material, from small anecdotes to adding clarifying points for variety, interest, and color. Print and electronic resources are standard library starting points, but there are other rich veins to mine when developing a good storyline.

Displaying photographs found in archival collections might spark a young person's interest in viewing, scanning, and researching the contents of family albums. Other types of objects—mementos, ephemera, even well loved toys—can also be primary source artifacts, adding a sense of time and place.

Perhaps the most valuable resource for crafting a story is people. Relatives, friends, and community members all hold pieces of the shared story that is human life. Encourage students to seek out those who have personal knowledge of historical events and days gone by. It might be helpful to create an interview form that will facilitate conversations and could trigger half-forgotten memories. Remind student interviewers to ask questions about old photos and to record names, dates, and places, when possible. Supporting details give a story depth and texture.

Build a reflection component into the creation process. This might entail casual dialog about stories in progress, formal conferencing sessions, or storytelling opportunities. Students would also benefit from access to a mentor who could help guide their efforts to construct meaning.

Suggestions (each of these ideas has a virtual equivalent, e.g., images can be located via Flickr or creative commons searches):

- Look at yearbooks and consider student clubs, productions, and even local business ads in the back.
- Study objects—eggbeaters, rotary phones, washboards—to talk about how technology has evolved.
- Examine the clothing and accessories of another era—dresses, pants/knickers, shoes, hats, white gloves, aprons, handkerchiefs—for clues about life and society.
- Read old cookbooks, postcards, letters, diaries, and autograph albums.
- Visit local cemeteries in search of familiar names and interesting historical data.
- Research local trades and industries.

My Father's Story

Among the old photos I found in my parents' house was a picture of my father's second grade class, from about 1925. For a man known for his warm smile, my dad looks very solemn. He also seems younger than most of the other students. When I asked him about this, he gave a fascinating explanation: My paternal grandparents emigrated from Italy, settling in upstate New York. Because they wanted to become American citizens, each of them had to learn how to read and write in English. My father was four when his mother began this process, and he studied right along side her. School regulations were quite different in the 1920s, so when he proved his literacy, he was admitted to first grade. A year later, he began second grade, at the ripe old age of five.

Imagine the conversations such a story could spark about immigration, schooling, social and emotional development, and other issues!

Curate

Curating is defined as locating, grouping, organizing, and sharing the best of relevant content. It's much more complex than simply collecting resources. In order for a learning activity to be authentic, it should be real, meaningful, and valuable. Throwaway projects do not inspire passion or fuel the desire for knowledge. By consciously and publicly curating student stories, we affirm their value, acknowledging their significance to their creators and to members of the larger community. Digital tools make this process more comprehensive, providing the means to preserve text, images, and sound. Tagging material (adding keywords) makes search and retrieval easier.

A storytelling festival would be a wonderful opportunity to publicly demonstrate how students value family and community, making the entire process real and authentic.

Suggestions:

- Create a Facebook memory page for your school or community.
- Teach students how to tag and search photos that are stored in online albums or collections.
- Maintain a local history section in your library.
- Purchase and archive copies of school yearbooks (families may be willing to donate older editions).
- Collaborate with local or county historians and public libraries.

The King's Story

My mother enlisted in the WAC (Women's Army Corps) during WWII, serving in England and France. Among her keepsakes from that time is a photograph of the British royal family setting out in a car from Windsor Castle. King George VI is at the wheel, Queen Mary rides beside him, and the princesses Elizabeth and Margaret sit with an older woman in the back seat. There is no visible security personnel, and the photo was taken from fairly close range. Fortunately, my mom noted on the back, "King and queen of England with the princesses leaving Windsor Castle, 1944," so I can be sure of when and where the photo was taken. It is fascinating to view this artifact and put it into historical context, particularly since the movie *The King's Speech* spurred public interest in this quiet, courageous monarch. The photo tells the story of a man who happens to be king, setting out for a drive with his family. It puts a human face on a historic personage. I was careful to tag this picture and share it on Flickr and on several social networking sites. To date it has been viewed more than 2,000 times, as compared to being buried or lost in a hodgepodge of personal mementos.

Celebrate

When it's time to share, make sure that the experience is interactive, allowing participants to not only create their own stories but also hear and respond to the stories of others. A storytelling festival would be a wonderful opportunity to publicly demonstrate how students value

family and community, making the entire process real and authentic. Such events help foster an emotional connection to the library as a facilitating institution, creating new generations of library advocates and demonstrating the value of libraries to other stakeholders.

Suggestions:

- Provide gallery space for student creations, including both audio and video capabilities.
- Share students' stories online, in district newsletters, or in a self-published book.
- Host storytelling exhibits that coincide with special events like concerts or parents' night.
- Use display cases to showcase a rotating collection of items that tell an individual student's story.
- Encourage students to contribute to a school yearbook or class memory book.
- Work with teachers to embed storytelling techniques in cross-curricular projects.
- Help students write and film a documentary about their town.
- Plan a storytelling festival and invite those whose stories you are sharing (family, friends, community members).
- Invite parents, veterans, and senior citizens to share their stories with students as part of the celebration.

My Fifth Graders' Stories

During one school year, my schedule included covering a fifth grade class on alternate days. With no set curriculum, I tried a variety of instructional activities, ranging from genre exploration to note-taking to critical thinking games. One afternoon, I commented that maybe the students should take over some of the teaching—to my surprise, the suggestion was a hit. Students signed up for half hour slots to present a topic that interested them. A sports enthusiast brought in the gear he wore for motocross races and suited up for us. Another classmate did a similar demonstration with hockey equipment. A talented dancer showed us stretching exercises and went

en pointe, earning the amazement and admiration of her classmates. Students who were 4-H members shared photos of farm animals they were raising and displayed ribbons earned at the county fair. These presentations told us stories about individuals and their passions. Those

who were not academically gifted had the chance to gain respect in the eyes of their peers. This was not about school, it was about life.

Perhaps the most valuable resource for crafting a story

is people. Relatives, friends, and community members all hold pieces of the shared story that is human life.

Storytelling

There are many types of stories. There are stories to inspire, stories to explain, stories to define, stories to connect, and stories to create meaning. By incorporating storytelling into the library experience, we not only tap into creativity but also foster a lifelong skill.

Author Ursula LeGuin remarked, "There have been great societies that did not use the wheel, but there have been no societies that did not tell stories." In this age of technology, in a time of turmoil and change, storytelling remains a common thread that links people to each other and to their shared history. Where better to nurture the storytellers of the future than in the library?

Diane Cordell *is a retired NYS-certified school library media specialist and an online facilitator and research consultant for CyberSmart Education Company. You can read her blog at http://dmcordell. blogspot.com.*

Cordell, Diane. (2012). Create, curate, celebrate: Storytelling in the library. *LMC, 30*(6), 40–41.

"Hey, Did You See This?"

Teaching and Learning through Digital Storytelling

By Cathy Jo Nelson

Wander around any venue with an abundance of middle or high school students, and you are likely to hear, "Hey, did you see this?" and see clusters of students gathered around a smartphone. Students of the generation we teach are more than ever aware of digital sharing and networking. Even our youngest elementary students tuck a mobile phone or iPod Touch into their backpacks as they head off to school. The small device has become the preferred mode for sharing, whether it's a one-line text massage or a cute video. Many use their mobile devices for capturing photos or video, adeptly understanding and taking advantage of the one-touch upload feature to any number of sites for sharing. More often than not, friends go well beyond the simple sharing of content and produce a creative remix or mash-up of their digital content to relay a message. A digital story is born.

BYOD (Bring Your Own Device)?

Most schools prohibit electronic devices that can transform the "real" story. How many have seen YouTube videos of school fights or teachers who lost their patience? For these and other reasons, many schools work to keep the devices out of the school environment. But is powering down, blocking, or banning beneficial to our students? We are missing an opportunity.

Libraries have standards, and they are up to date with the ever popular "21st century" jargon that librarians and teachers use every day in their lesson plans, job descriptions, blog posts, and grant applications. Truly a buzzword in the educational arena, it may be finally losing ground. It is overused to a degree where no one is sure what it really means anymore.

Grounding Digital Storytelling in Standards

The LMS and library media program standards were written to reflect the 21st century learner. Our most current documents, *Standards for the 21st-Century Learner* (AASL, 2007) and *Standards for the 21st-Century Learner in Action* (AASL, 2009), have embraced the 21st century learner jargon, despite how vaguely the terms are defined. The library standards, although written as action statements, are useless as a stand-alone document. Our standards are written with collaboration in mind. These standards make sense when a collaborative effort is made to implement them along with content standards from classroom teachers.

How does digital storytelling fit into the library standards? Based on the *Standards for the 21st-Century Learner*, media sharing and digital storytelling align well with the following:

- 2.1.4—Use technology and other information tools to organize and display knowledge and understanding in ways that others can view, use, and assess.
- 3.3.4—Create products that apply to authentic, real-world context.
- 4.1.8—Use creative and artistic formats to express personal learning.

It is easy to see how digital storytelling can be a conduit to getting even the most resistant teacher to collaborate. By being an instructional partner in activities that include digital storytelling, the librarian has the opportunity to also introduce a wide variety of topics and standards. Additionally, the ethical use of resources can be discussed, particularly images, music selections, and videos. Copyright and fair use can be complicated topics

that students may not understand, or worse, decide they are not relevant to them. But teaching about the resources selected for a digital storytelling project in the context of copyright and fair use allows for appropriate modeling of ethical and legal principles. Students will have a more personal experience, which means the otherwise dry topics will suddenly be relevant and meaningful to them.

> By being an instructional partner in activities that include digital storytelling, the librarian has the opportunity to introduce a wide variety of topics and standards.

Below are some user friendly digital storytelling resources that anyone can use. Some of them are online applications while others are standalone computer applications.

Windows Live Movie Maker or iMovie

Windows Live Movie Maker or iMovie (for Mac) are just two of many video creating/editing software applications. These programs contain features such as effects, transitions, titles/credits, audio tracks, and timeline narration, and allow users to edit a series of frames (photos or video) to create a video. The user can view it in storyboard format or timeline format, and can apply basic effects to audio tracks, such as fade in or fade out. The final product can be saved as a movie that can be shared in a digital format but can also be exported to DVD. Both are relatively simple to use.

OurStory: www.ourstory.com

OurStory permits users to develop and save collaborative timelines that can be personalized with annotations, photos, and videos. Stories (timelines) can be printed in book format, archived on DVD, or even sent as postcards. You can teach your students to develop content-specific timelines that are linked to the teaching of research and information literacy skills.

TeacherTube: www.teachertube.com

Much like YouTube, TeacherTube is a video hosting site. It is perfect for teachers and students as it offers videos solely for the field of education. Videos are created by teachers and students to be shared with other teachers and students. TeacherTube is a great way to have students share their work with parents. It is also a way for teachers to share with other teachers, peers, and administrators, both on-campus and off. The site is generally not blocked by filters, like YouTube and other video hosting sites may be.

VoiceThread: http://voicethread.com

PowerPoint has fallen out of fashion in many classrooms due to the notion that one person "presents" or "teaches" a topic. Many elements of digital storytelling are used in PowerPoint, such as images, sounds, videos, music, etc., but the audience is typically expected to "sit and get" from the presentation. Consider VoiceThread the end of the boring slideshow. It allows users to share images, documents, and videos with added narration, but there is a twist in that a viewer can add to the narration, thus enhancing the final product. A classroom can bring oral history to life as students narrate a series of images that relate to the skills and ideas they have learned in a particular lesson.

> *Teaching about the resources selected for a digital storytelling project in the context of copyright and fair use allows for appropriate modeling of ethical and legal principles.*

Prezi: www.prezi.com

Prezi is primarily a presentation tool and an alternative to PowerPoint. But it offers the ability to embed links, images, and even videos or audio files. Prezi uses a zoom feature to focus in on the added elements. The zooming in, out, and around connected circles can literally cause a viewer to feel dizzy. Perhaps check with your classes regarding sensitivity to motion sickness before committing to the tool. The creator is not limited by linear design typically associated with a storyboard plan. Instead, the creator can utilize the space as she sees fit, using the capability to fly over the space and zoom on finer points.

Jing: www.techsmith.com/jing

Jing is a screencasting program that is downloaded to the computer. It allows for whatever is viewed on the screen to be captured for video and video editing purposes. It is great for creating computer program tutorials or sharing what is viewed on the screen. Jing is free but offers a paid service as well that gives a user more bells and whistles to add to their screencast.

Take a Stand for Learning

These are just a few tools that educators and librarians can use in the classroom. As you consider digital storytelling, think about how you can address your own information literacy standards while collaborating with colleagues to teach their standards, too. In fact, you don't even have to tell the collaborating teachers that your standards are being addressed. Just keep it focused on the students and their final products. You will know that your students (and likely their teacher, too) are actively involved in a standards-based lesson.

You will probably come across various online digital storytelling tools that may be blocked because of the settings used on the network for filtering. Write up the lesson, including goals, objectives, and all standards (and by all I mean yours as well as classroom standards of the collaborating teacher), and present the project to the powers that be who control the filter. If this audience will not include anyone who is trained in pedagogy, ask for your principal and/or curriculum coordinator (or similar administrative leader in your school or district) to be part of your pitch. Ask for reconsideration of the site or tool for your project. Negotiate based on pedagogical principles. Negotiate by asking for the tool or site to be allowed for the duration of the project. Remind everyone that the students will be supervised and taught how to make good choices, and that the planned activities will be engaging enough that students won't have time to get off task. Finally, invite everyone who will make this decision to observe first hand the activities, excitement, and engagement. Do not settle for a change in lesson plans without trying first. It's for the sake of learning.

Cathy Jo Nelson *is the library media specialist at Dorman High School in Roebuck, South Carolina. She may be reached at cathyjonelson@gmail.com.*

Nelson, Cathy Jo. (2011). "Hey, did you see this?" *LMC, 30*(1), 10–12.

ONE QUESTION SURVEY RESULTS
What Student Organizations Do You Supervise?

By Gail K. Dickinson

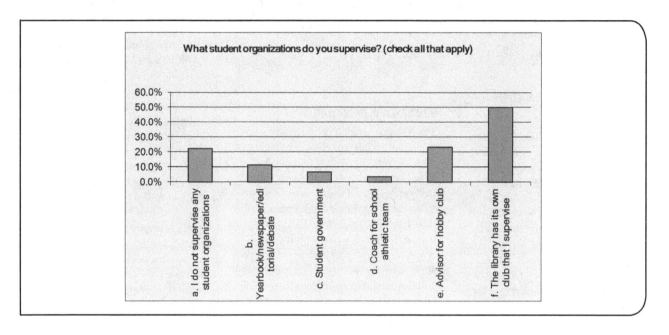

Our One-Question Survey this month touched a chord with our readers, with 519 respondents. We wanted to know about the interactions with students that are considered extracurricular, but that good teachers know are crucial to student success. So we asked school librarians to tell us about the type of activities they supervised. To be sure we were inclusive, we asked them to check all of the categories that applied to their situation, so the total percentage will add up to be more than 100 percent.

Almost 1/4 of our respondents reported that they do not supervise any student organizations. Very few (3.5% and 6.6% respectively) note that they are advisors to student government or coach an athletic team. Surprisingly, just a bit more than 10% supervise what could be considered a literary activity, namely the yearbook/newspaper/debate or other type of editorial team.

The organizations that librarians seem to sponsor or supervise are based on student interests. Half of our respondents have their own library clubs. A sampling of these are book clubs, morning announcement teams, or library volunteers. More interesting, though, are the clubs and groups that strike at the heart of today's digital learners who are active and engaged in learning. Librarians sponsor Anime/Manga clubs, poetry and writing groups, gaming, photography, and a range of other student interests. At the heart of the tenets of the library field is attention to access and equity, and librarians share that responsibility with students, sponsoring groups such as the Gay/Straight Alliance and affinity groups for students of color. At least one librarian reported managing an art club, because due to budget cuts they no longer have an art teacher.

The school librarian has the ability to build multi-year relationships with students, watching them grow and mature from year to year. That relationship is both cross-curricular and extra-curricular. As a profession, we are able to understand that a student may approach science differently than she approaches social studies; that he may hate reading biographies of mathematicians but loves writing poetry. It's that special understanding than enables school librarians to be the glue to hold student interests through clubs and other activities, and that may ultimately keep students in school.

All of the LMC One-Question Surveys are freely available online. Use this link http://www.librarymediaconnection.com/lmc/?page=survey_results to find a survey that will help you advocate for a strong school library program. Have a good question? Submit it to lmc@librarymediaconnection.com. We will be waiting to hear from you.

Dickinson, Gail K. (2013). What student organizations do you supervise? *LMC, 32*(1), 17.

ONE QUESTION SURVEY RESULTS
Have You Considered Getting Administrator Certification?

By Gail K. Dickinson

There are two jobs in the school that are similar to being a school librarian. The first of these is the sports coach. Like a coach, the school librarian celebrates the achievement of skills without the arbitrary walls of age or grade level. We work at the one-on-one level to motivate students to constantly improve those skills, and we delegate responsibility based on the student's capability to work responsibly. We focus on the whole child, not just the piece of the brain that shows up in the 6th period grade book.

The school librarian also functions much like the building principal. There are few other jobs in the building that work with the entire curriculum and the entire range of grade levels. School librarians collaborate with every teacher and integrate activities with all support staff, from the lunch ladies to the custodians. The relationships that we build with adults in the school learning community determine, in a large part, the success of our programs.

It is small wonder, then, nearly 10 percent of the respondents to our One Question Survey have either achieved or are working on administrator certification, and over 20 percent have considered it. School librarianship is the perfect training ground for administrators. Good school librarians know how to stay a teaching peer, even though at times they find themselves in a position to observe both good teaching and bad, to hear raging rants and over-the-top praise from parents regarding specific teachers, and to see the

effect of teachers on student learning and behavior. They know when to offer a silent shoulder and when to proffer experienced advice. They know, or soon learn, not to engage in gossip that can turn a school into a maelstrom of malcontents. School librarians are, in fact, already administrators managing complex programs that change with every minute of the day.

Maybe it's no surprise then that nearly 1/3 of the field has considered or is working on administrative certification. We don't have the statistics that will tell us how many school librarians already are principals or superintendents. We don't know how many slide into the job down the hall for which they have actually spent many years preparing. We also don't know the answer to the

opposite and more complex question, which is how many administrators decide to become school librarians. As a school library educator, I have several students each year who want to keep their school-wide and curriculum-wide perspectives, but who decide to train for a job that is more fun and has fewer hassles from parents and central administration.

One of the reasons that district level library supervisors may state for why they accept positions out of the building level is that they want to effect change on a broader level. It may well be why classroom teachers study to become principals, and why principals decide to seek superintendencies. Perhaps this is a reason that we need to begin using to recruit to the field. Classroom teachers who are looking for a

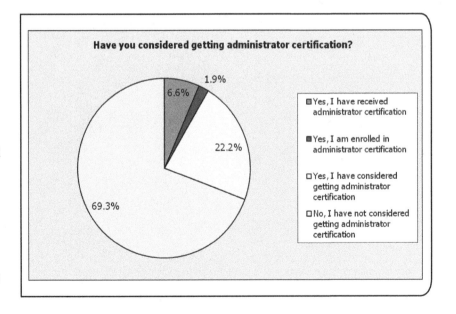

Have you considered getting administrator certification?

1.9%
6.6%
22.2%
69.3%

- Yes, I have received administrator certification
- Yes, I am enrolled in administrator certification
- Yes, I have considered getting administrator certification
- No, I have not considered getting administrator certification

change may welcome the opportunity to still be a teacher, but also have the broader influence to change entire schools.

Linworth encourages the use of evidence-based practices to help you ensure that your students have the libraries they deserve. Use this graph to illustrate the importance of your job in the school.

Next month we will report on how your funding has been affected this school year. Curious about our previous surveys? All are available online at www.linworth.com.

Dickinson, Gail K. (2009). Have you considered getting administrator certification? *LMC, 28*(3), 44.

ONE QUESTION SURVEY RESULTS
How Are You Acting in a Leadership Role in Your School?

By Gail K. Dickinson

It is a positive indicator of professional leadership that most respondents to our latest LMC One-Question Survey found the questions difficult to answer. We asked respondents to choose a leadership role, and many found that they either could not or simply did not want to answer the survey the way it was written. They fulfilled several leadership roles and choosing just one was difficult. The difficult choice, though, was intentional. It is easy to say that busy school librarians active in leadership roles do everything. They are on administrative councils, they mentor new teachers, they are a prime source of professional development, and they work with students. A harder task is to check just one box as the activity that you perceive that you do, leaving the other boxes unchecked. If this graph is reviewed with that task in mind, an interesting picture emerges.

In the 1980s and early 1990s, site-based management swept into schools. School librarians, afraid to be left on the decision-making sidelines, insisted that their position be a permanent fixture on those councils. The urgency of the field to not be left behind made an impact, since nearly one third of respondents claimed that role. The other roles represented in this chart may represent the choices offered by the district as well as the personal choice of the librarian. If there is no official mentoring program for new teachers in the school,

obviously the librarian cannot act in that role, even with a strong desire.

Of great concern is the percent of librarians who reported rarely pursuing a leadership role in the school. Over one out of every ten librarians admitted that they not only do not currently have a leadership position, but that they rarely take one. This is unacceptable. No superintendent or school board would be proud of the fact that 10% of the teachers chose not to do part of their jobs, and certainly no superintendent or school board would allow them to continue to make that choice. Choosing to become a school librarian means choosing to become a leader in the school, district, and

community. Our profession cannot afford any other choice.

Library Media Connection encourages the use of evidence-based practices to assure your students have the libraries they deserve.

Next issue we will report on where you mostly find reviews to aid in the selection process. Curious about our previous surveys? All are available online at www. librarymediaconnection.com.

Dickinson, Gail K. (2010). How are you acting in a leadership role in your school? *LMC, 28*(6), 53.

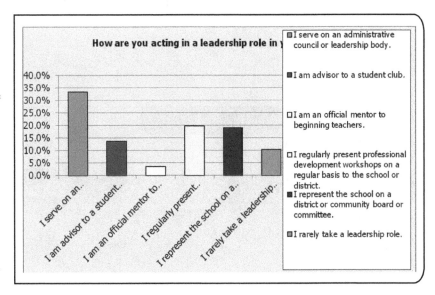

ONE QUESTION SURVEY RESULTS
How Much of Your Resource Budget Is Spent on Materials in Languages Other Than English?

Years ago a debate raged over the proper word to describe the relationship between the library collection and the school curriculum. *Support* was thought of being, well, too supportive, meaning less than. *Enrich* was tossed out because to enrich would mean that the library collection was not central to the curriculum, it was in fact extra. The word that most people agreed with was *Reflect*, in that the library collection should reflect the curriculum.

What was not debated, but probably should have been, is the word to describe the relationship between our library collections and our students. Perhaps Reflect is still the right word. We want our collections to reflect the faces of our students and the faces of our world. We want to present information and ideas to our students in packages that describe their world and the world beyond

them. The last bastion of acceptance may be examining the collection to see if it fits the most basic definition, i.e. are the materials in the languages that our students speak?

According to our latest one-question survey, the answer is clearly no. Nearly 40 percent of our 261 respondents only buy materials in English. Another 36 percent buy fewer than 10 materials a year in Spanish. Of course, some librarians, mainly in the OTHER category above, noted that they do not have funds to buy any materials, either English or Spanish. One librarian reported buying one foreign language book a year, to support the foreign language department.

This is a non-scientific survey to be sure, since it does not reflect the demographics of the school. It could very well be that our respondents are librarians in schools where there

are no speakers of other languages. That's doubtful, though. Discussions of equity and access have to include whether or not the materials are in the languages of the students. Libraries have always been the one place where students can read on their level, to their interests, and find materials with characters just like them. Let's expand that definition to include languages.

> Curious about our previous surveys? All are available online at www.librarymediaconnection.com.

Dickinson, Gail K. (2011). How much of your resource budget is spent on materials in languages other than English? *LMC*, *30*(1), 47.

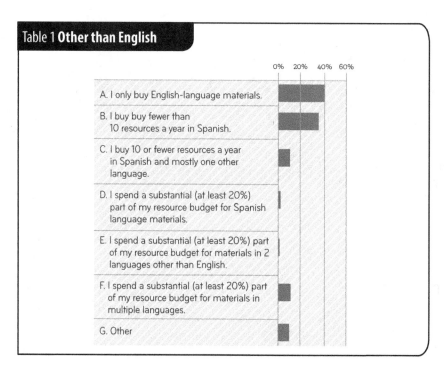

Table 1 **Other than English**

A. I only buy English-language materials.

B. I buy buy fewer than 10 resources a year in Spanish.

C. I buy 10 or fewer resources a year in Spanish and mostly one other language.

D. I spend a substantial (at least 20%) part of my resource budget for Spanish language materials.

E. I spend a substantial (at least 20%) part of my resource budget for materials in 2 languages other than English.

F. I spend a substantial (at least 20%) part of my resource budget for materials in multiple languages.

G. Other

Tips

Get Carded at the Library (Editor's Choice)

With so many Web 2.0 applications and students doing projects from home with their own devices, students often need the help of a school librarian outside of the regular school day. Try making up a batch of business cards with your name, picture, email address, and Twitter account. Give these to students on an as-needed basis and let them know they may contact you whenever they need it. It has really worked at my school! I've even had students tell me that they've kept my business card and want to know if it is OK if to contact me on other projects too. I found this to be an easy way to promote the fact that you are there to help the students, and it lets the student feel very grown up, because you are giving them a business card.

Robyn Young
Avon (Indiana) High School and Advanced Learning Center

Young, Robyn. (2012). Get carded at the library. *LMC, 31*(2), 8.

Review Me!

Need a quick and easy way to build library enthusiasm and have more opportunities to meet new students? If your catalog allows students to submit book reviews, create a contest. I received 374 book reviews, with over 100 of our 240 students participating in the contest. What is even more thrilling is that the book reviews continue to pour in. The kids love to see their names "published" in our catalog! I was so impressed by all the efforts from my students that I rewarded the top three reviewers with special gifts, and all participants received a piece of candy. Smiles all around!

Suzanne Dix
The Seven Hills School
Cincinnati, Ohio

Dix, Suzanne. (2013). Review me! *LMC, 31*(6), 8.

Book Safari

Teach your upper elementary students to quickly find books they love. Collect books in a range of levels that fit the groups coming in for a library lesson, so that each child gets a stack of five books. Set a timer for 2 minutes, and tell them that they have to spend the entire 2 minutes with one book. In this time they can look at the cover, read the back or inside flap, look at pictures if there are any, and read a little of the book. Make sure that they remember the five finger rule to help them understand when a book is a good match for them. After 2 minutes, the students write down the title and give it a ranking, using either numbers or symbols (star: really like this book and I want to check it out; happy face: sounds good, may want to check it out another time; sad face: not interested or not a good fit). Once they get through their stack of five books, if time allows, they swap their stack with the person next to them. By the end of class they have a list of books they can bring with them to the library for future visits. They can also check out books they discovered during the activity, or they can find something on the library shelf. Most of the time, children leave with a book from their stack and are really excited about it.

Rebecca Flowers
Walker Upper Elementary School
Charlottesville, Virginia

Flowers, Rebecca. (2013). Book safari. *LMC, 32*(1), 8.

Take a Hike for Source Citations

Sometimes upper elementary students have trouble remembering to capture all of the parts of the citations for their research projects. We created "source walks." We wrote out each part of a citation on a strip of duct tape and placed them in key areas of the library. Now, when students are doing their research, they can take a source walk to cite their resources and double-check their finished projects.

Kathy Bargeloh
Franklin Elementary Center Library
Parkersburg, West Virginia

Bargeloh, Kathy. (2012). Take a hike for source citations. *LMC, 30*(6), 8. All of

CHAPTER 4

Administration of a 21st Century School Library Program

Editor's Note

Pilot Study for School Librarianship

"If you're having trouble getting permission, just call it a pilot." I heard that advice last week in a completely different context and a completely different set of circumstances, but the beauty and usefulness of that advice, applied to the school library setting, appealed to me. Sometimes in school libraries we have difficulty getting permission to implement new procedures, try new instructions, or lift restrictions on student access. Busy principals sigh at the thought of any perceived risk-taking behavior at the beginning of the year while they are dealing with new students, new district initiatives, and new staff to supervise. The school library programs on the table, however wonderful and promising, become just one new flavor on the decision plate of busy principals.

But spring is different. In spring, the end of the year is so close you can smell it in the clean, just-washed air and the first few flowers. Teachers, parents, students, and administrators are starting to relax. The promise of hours of daylight after the school day puts everyone in a great mood as spring sports, great weather, and after-school nonschool activities beckon. It's a great time to start testing out new ideas in preparation for the next school year, even though it seems so far away, especially when summer seems tantalizingly close.

Perhaps you want to try removing limits to book checkout, or blowing the dust off those hardly used DVDs and shelving them in the regular collection where they will actually intrigue students to learn. Maybe you want to try different ways of organizing just one section of the collection, or create a genre display to match just one student interest. It works with teachers as well, giving you a chance to beg a teacher to bring the students into the library and hold back the worksheets to try some different strategies for mastering classroom content. You could even ask the IT director to unblock some favorite websites.

It's a pilot. It's not like you are starting out the year with requests for projects that might cause later problems as unanticipated consequences arise. You aren't standing at the principal's door with the next latest and greatest decision as a hundred other decisions both large and small crowd around you vying for the principal's attention. The year is about to end. This group of students will leave, teachers will close their grade books, and principals will wave goodbye at the door and face a too short summer preparing for the next year.

It's a pilot. It's a chance to play at changing the world just a little bit. Next year, if disaster strikes, you can put it all back and pretend it never happened. At a time when energy is fading all around you, you can spark life into a school through the school library. Pilot studies steer the school library from winter into spring. It's truly playtime for the program as the batting around of ideas inside mirrors the sounds from the playground outside.

The definition of a pilot is a small-scale project designed to test premises and procedures before full-scale implementation. It can also be called a feasibility study, which makes it sound more important, but the idea is the same. Pilots are meant to be temporary and set in a definite time frame, for instance, the last two months of school. They are conducted with just a handful of teachers or students, sometimes but hardly ever the entire school. After the pilot is over, the analysis begins in order to determine whether or not a full-scale project is warranted. The first question, especially if the change is drastic, is always "Did the sky fall?" If the answer is no, then on to implementation.

Spring pilot projects smooth the way for change. Sometimes the greatest obstacles turn out to be no problem at all. Sometimes the biggest objections just melt away when the positive outcomes thaw the resistance. The best part is that no one is nearly as tense about change as they would be at the beginning of the year. After all, it's just a pilot. Just until the end of school. When the year ends, uncross your fingers, analyze your results, plan to incorporate the changes for fall, and plan the next year's pilot.

Gail K. Dickinson
Editorial Director

Dickinson, Gail K. (2013). Pilot study for school librarianship. *LMC, 31*(5), 6.

Going Back into the Trenches

By Kelly M. Hoppe

To gain a fresh perspective as a librarian, go back into the classroom for a year. In reality, this is not possible or even desirable for librarians. Library jobs are hard to come by, and no school would hold someone's position while they ventured off into the classroom. However, a year ago, I found myself in exactly this situation. Due to circumstances beyond my control, after seven years as a librarian, I found myself back in the classroom. I tried to view this as an opportunity instead of a roadblock to my library career. It excited and frightened me at the same time because I had finally gotten a foothold in the library profession and was afraid I would lose all the connections and progress I had made. Could I be a teacher again? Could I rise to the challenge?

Apprehensive at first, I found myself growing more excited as my time to re-enter the classroom drew near. I found myself looking forward to sharing entire novels with a class, teaching various writing skills and grammar, and doing all the things one does as a 7th grade English Language Arts (ELA) teacher.

Unfortunately, my enthusiasm did not last. I quickly became bogged down in the day-to-day reality that is teaching in the 21st century. Being a veteran teacher, I never expected to experience the range of emotions and frustrations that I did upon reentering the classroom. I could not believe how much things had changed in the seven years I had been out of the classroom. Teachers now have absolutely no down time. In addition to recreating activities and lessons I had gotten rid of when I left the classroom, every moment of my day was consumed with things that didn't involve actual classroom instruction, like daily department meetings, daily grade level meetings, getting individual assignments to the In School Suspension (ISS) teacher, after school workshops, testing stress, evaluating testing data, filling out special education paperwork, obtaining Texas English Language Proficiency Assessment System (TELPAS) writing samples and evaluating them, after school tutoring programs, becoming English as a Second Language (ESL) certified so I would fall into the "highly qualified" category, hall duty, before and after school duty, etc. Even getting to the bathroom was a challenge! Honestly, there was little time to enjoy actual teaching. I got to work an hour early and stayed late to complete tasks, and I never could get caught up. Through this experience, I developed a new respect for this generation of teachers.

> I had happily lived in my library bubble for the past seven years, and while the faculty was pleased with my services, I now realize I wasn't doing all I could.

New Students, New Attitudes, New Challenges

For me personally, a huge struggle was the disposition of many of the students I was teaching. Most were at the lower end of the socio-economic scale, what some might think of as "inner city" students, and quite honestly, they weren't responding to the teaching style I had used in the past. Several students had a shocking sense of behavior entitlement. It was as if they felt they had a right to be rude or misbehave, and they were incredibly defensive. I could just calmly say, "Sit down John," and they would puff up and become extremely aggressive. At the beginning of the year, it wasn't unusual for outbursts of "Shut Up!" to fly across the room. I was working with the toughest bunch of students I'd ever experienced in my eighteen years of education. I had to re-assess my discipline style to make it more effective.

I had happily lived in my library bubble for the past seven years, and while the faculty was pleased with my services, I now realize I wasn't doing all I could. Back in the classroom, the Texas Assessment of Knowledge and Skills (TAKS) test consumed my day. Additionally, being a 7th grade ELA teacher meant I was responsible for two TAKS tests, a writing test in March, and a reading test in April. I just did not have time to get to the library. Plus, my classroom was miles away from the library. Just getting there and back would have taken up valuable class time. Finally, any change in routine really seemed to agitate my students, and the few trips we made to the library for book checkout resulted in chaos.

I was teaching in a Title I school. The student demographic included many ESL students, including from Mexico, Somalia, Egypt, and Thailand. The range of reading levels was vast. The majority of my students did not value reading for pleasure, so going to the library was seen as a time to chase each other around and socialize. All of this frustrated me, but I didn't know what to do. As a librarian, I knew the "power" of the library, yet I felt paralyzed and unable to reap the rewards of the library due to the overwhelming frustration I felt with my endless teaching duties and responsibilities.

When I was a librarian, there were teachers, mostly English teachers, who were always in the library, and there were others who never used the library's services. I just assumed it was because they didn't NEED to do research or something, but what if they were experiencing the same difficulties, pressures, and time constraints as I? I had never thought about it from that perspective.

Most of my students were not recreational readers. For the majority of the year, I would have to stand at the front of the classroom and literally watch them while they read silently. Any attempt on my part to sit down or grade papers would result in some sort of mischief. Noticing this lack of interest early on, I wanted to do everything I could to encourage their interest in reading. I tried to expose them to as much literature as possible. In addition to reading novels as a class, I frequently incorporated picture books into my lesson plans. I've always loved using picture books with students and have witnessed their power to draw in even the oldest reader, but that wasn't enough. I did not have a good classroom library, so I decided to have shorter books available for students to at least look at if they finished an assignment before others and had some free time. But I was always hard pressed to get to the library to pick something out. My librarian jumped to the task. She was happy to pick out and deliver thirty books for me to keep in the classroom for an extended period of time. In addition to high interest/low level books, there were graphic novels and titles that had high appeal for middle school students. Being a librarian is all about service. Besides meeting students' needs, I've always felt that my first priority was to meet the needs of the teachers. My librarian's willingness to step outside the library services box by consistently providing books in this way was a great help and a valuable benefit to the students. By the end of the year, I did not have to constantly monitor my students while they read silently for an extended period. My students were starting to show more of an interest in reading, and some would even talk to me about books they had read. I felt I had achieved a small victory.

Since there is usually only one librarian per campus, librarians never get the chance to observe other librarians in action like a new teacher might observe a veteran teacher.

By the end of the year, we were struggling to complete the new Texas Essential Knowledge and Skills (TEKS) research strand. When the school year started, my librarian had made it clear that she was willing to help us with this and even made research folders with ideas in them. The other 7th grade ELA teachers and I had good intentions and started the year off by attending a plagiarism presentation in the library with our students. However, we rapidly became snowed under with TAKS responsibilities. Research was put on the back burner. Throughout the year, my librarian would revisit the topic of research, but she was never pushy. She knew how busy we were with two TAKS tests hanging over our heads and the amount of material we had to cover. Once the TAKS tests were over though, we met with our librarian as a 7th grade team and mapped out a plan. Because we were running out of time and computer labs, she agreed to come to each of our classrooms to do a presentation on citations. Additionally, we met one more time, as combined classes, in the auditorium for a presentation on citations for images and how to put that in a PowerPoint presentation. She developed and presented both lessons, which was a huge relief to all of the grade level teachers. While I was a veteran librarian with experience teaching research skills, the other ELA teachers had never really done this and were not sure how to proceed. Finally, because the library was totally booked throughout the end of the year, the librarian gave us two carts with two sets of encyclopedias and books on the topics that our students were researching. Since we couldn't get to the library or computer labs, we could still do research in our rooms with the mini mobile library.

This was the year for ELA textbook adoption. With each adoption, you could choose an "x" number of novels. Many of the novels on the list were what one might think of as classics, but there were others the department was unfamiliar with. While textbook adoption, by no means, falls under the category of library services, our librarian volunteered to locate a synopsis and reading level for each

novel on the list, which was no small task. Again, it is all about service. This saved us hours of valuable time trying to figure out which books would be suitable for selection.

Lessons Learned

Early on, I decided to see how I could use my classroom experience to make myself a better librarian.

One thing I decided is that I would find ways to politely force myself on classroom teachers. As a librarian I had faithfully attended department meetings and was always happy to go to the classroom if asked, but I had never considered inviting myself into a classroom. Were there other teachers out there who felt the way I did as a teacher? That it was basically impossible to get out of the classroom and go to the library? Librarians need to consider attending grade level meetings because each grade level deals with things that are specific to that grade level.

Another thing that was clear to me was that I needed to help teachers more in the area of discipline. I was always an effective disciplinarian as a librarian and disciplined students when necessary in the library, but if a teacher was with her class, I usually let her make the first move and followed her lead. If she was more laid back, I would be more laid back. If she was a strict disciplinarian then I was too. However, even as a veteran teacher, I struggled this past year to find an appropriate discipline style that would work. I now know that, as a librarian, I need to make sure I am a visible presence and support for those teachers who are obviously grappling with discipline issues and who are not just laid back.

One service that I will offer is to go to classrooms once every two weeks so students can return books. If there is a scanner for remote checkout, I'll take that and, if possible, arrive with books, sort of like a mini mobile library or book mobile. In the classroom, there is very little free time to allow students to run to the library to return books. Add to this the fact that on some campuses students have to have a pass to go to the library before school. While I understand the necessity of a rule like this, it can be just another obstacle, making it almost impossible for some students to get to the library. So a classroom visit from the librarian could be a perfect solution and help reduce overdue books.

A Final Thought

This past year was the perfect opportunity to observe a fellow librarian, to be able to see how someone else did the job. Since there is usually only one librarian per campus, librarians never get the chance to observe other librarians in action like a new teacher might observe a veteran teacher. This was a unique opportunity for me. And what I learned!

What really stood out to me was my librarian's willingness to serve. She constantly went above and beyond with her library services. She went out of her way to make the library's resources as well as herself available to us. She topped it all when she volunteered to be on the rotation for the after school tutoring program. This was huge to me. Even though we teachers received a stipend for this program and were told our participation wasn't mandatory, everyone knew the program needed to be available for our struggling students, so when our librarian wanted to be included, I was impressed. It was another way for the students to get to know the librarian. Plus, the librarian demonstrated that she was a fellow educator and team player. If the teachers had to stay after school until 5 p.m., then so did she.

I am now back in the library world where I belong. While I would never choose to go back into the classroom, this experience made me stronger and I will be a better librarian for it—one with a clearer understanding of the reality teachers face every day.

Kelly M. Hoppe *is a library media specialist at Palo Duro High School in Amarillo, Texas, and can be reached at khop12@gmail.com.*

Hoppe, Kelly M. (2011). Going back into the trenches. *LMC, 29*(4), 20–21.

The Principal Factor

By Audrey P. Church

Once upon a time the principal ruled the school from the office ivory tower, emerging only in late spring wearing soft-soled shoes to conduct end-of-the-year teacher evaluations. This is no longer the case. Today's principals must have knowledge of content area standards and be involved in curriculum planning and pacing. They assign strong master teachers as mentors to new teachers. They are involved in what's happening in their classrooms and practice ongoing assessment of the classroom teaching, focusing on improving student learning. Today's principal is the instructional leader of the school and sets the tone and expectations for teaching and learning. In this role, the principal can make or break the library program.

Numerous studies completed in various states show that strong library programs contribute to student achievement (School Libraries Work!). Student learning is higher in schools in which the library is adequately funded and appropriately staffed and the library media specialist takes an active role in instruction. As Gary Hartzell noted in his presentation at the 2002 White House Conference on School Libraries, "The principal is a key player, perhaps the key player, in library media programs that make a difference." This key factor is the basis for three important questions:

1. How does the principal support your ability to contribute to teaching and learning?
2. Where does the principal's perception of your job originate?
3. What exactly does the principal expect from you instructionally?

1. How Does the Principal Support Your Ability to Contribute to Teaching and Learning?

Financial Support for the Library Program

In most schools the principal controls budgets and funding. Adequate funding is necessary to purchase print and electronic materials which support the reading interests and the instructional program of the school. Principals have to know that money invested in the library collection and the library program serves every student and teacher in the school, not merely Mrs. Taylor's classroom or the 3rd grade or the social studies department. When your principal supports the library financially, you are able to purchase up-to-date resources and provide teachers and students with a collection that serves their needs and interests.

Staffing Support for the Library Program

To be most effective instructionally, you need time to collaboratively plan, teach, and evaluate with fellow educators. It is difficult to do this if you are the lone ranger of the library. Principal support is key to providing additional staff in your library— clerical assistance or additional professional library media specialists. When your principal supports the library program with adequate support staff, you are more fully able to implement your teacher and instructional partner roles.

> It is the responsibility of the school library media specialist to realize the critical role that principals play in full implementation of the library media program.

Scheduling Support for the Library Program

The principal impacts the library program with scheduling decisions. At the secondary school level, this plays out when the library is used for testing or occupied for meetings and closed for all other uses. At the elementary level, it is noticeable in the fixed vs. flex debate, as the principal chooses either regularly scheduled library visits (fixed), most often to provide classroom teacher planning time; or access at the point of need (flex), with library use based on instructional needs. When your principal facilitates open library access (flex), you are better able to build a library program that meets the needs of students and teachers.

Verbal Support for the Library Program

Principals serve as the instructional leaders of the school. They make a powerful statement if they emphasize to teachers that the library media specialist is a teacher and an instructional partner, that collaborative instruction is expected and supported, that the information literacy skills taught in the library are key to helping students become critical thinkers and lifelong learners, and that the library program is an integral part of the teaching and learning taking place. In some instances, principals would like to provide more funding for the library, or hire a full-time clerk, or implement a fully flexible schedule, but are not able to do so. They can emphasize, however, in both words and actions, that the library plays a critical role in student learning.

Today's school library media specialist's role has expanded from that of keeper of the books to facilitator of lifelong learning. Library media specialists understand that their roles have evolved and they must take an active role in instruction, yet many principals still hold the narrow, stereotypical, limiting view of our jobs.

2. Where Does the Principal's Perception of Your Job Originate?

How Do Principals Learn What We Do?

Hartzell notes that principals are extremely busy individuals and that, ideally, the time to inform them of our instructional role is prior to their move to the principal position. Research demonstrates, however, that topics of school libraries and school librarians are not addressed in coursework in principal preparation programs. Information about school libraries and librarians does not typically appear in administrators' professional journals nor are there sessions which address this at their professional conferences. Principals learn what library media specialists do from library media specialists with whom they work, either as a principal or as a teacher prior to becoming a principal. In a recent survey of elementary school principals in Virginia, 65.5 percent of the respondents noted that their knowledge of the instructional role of the library media specialist came from interactions with library media specialists during their administrative careers. Over 26 percent (26.4 percent) stated that their knowledge of the instructional role of the library media specialist came from interactions with library media specialists during their teaching careers (Church). Principals learn what you do . . . from you!

3. What Exactly Does the Principal Expect from You Instructionally?

So, what makes your principal happy? What types of activities and initiatives will help your principal better understand the contributions that you make to help students become successful, independent 21st century learners? In a recent survey of elementary school principals in Virginia, principals who displayed a solid understanding of the instructional role of the library media specialist identified relational/attitude items and informational/content items that helped them to form their positive views of the library media specialist as teacher and instructional partner.

Relational/Attitude

Principals want library media specialists who create warm, welcoming environments in their library media centers. They want library media specialists who offer

inviting spaces for learning; spaces where instructional activities related to the classroom take place. They want library media specialists who are proactive and collaborative, who exhibit leadership skills, and who interact well with fellow educators. They want team players who are enthusiastic and excited about what they do every day and who are invested in the school culture. They want library media specialists who demonstrate good interpersonal relationships with students and teachers alike and who display and share with others a positive attitude toward the library program and toward the school.

> In a recent survey of elementary school principals in Virginia, 65.5 percent of the respondents noted that their knowledge of the instructional role of the library media specialist came from interactions with library media specialists during their administrative careers.

Informational/Content

Principals identified numerous areas in which library media specialists contribute to the instructional program of the school. First, they noted that strong library media specialists connect to state curriculum standards. Library media specialists are knowledgeable regarding state standards, integrate library information skills instruction with classroom content, and proactively provide quality resources to classroom teachers to support teaching and learning. Secondly, taking this connection a step further, library media specialists who rated high on the principals' instructional scale were knowledgeable about what was going on in each classroom at any particular time of the academic year, and they used this knowledge to make relevant connections between classroom and library instruction. Planning and teaching collaboratively, they made the

library an extension of learning in the classroom.

Third, principals recognized and rated highly library media specialists who showed an interest in test data and who were cognizant of student standardized test scores. With the current educational emphasis on student scores and accountability, this action demonstrated to the principal and to teacher colleagues the library media specialist's commitment to the overall instructional program of the school and concern for student achievement. It also facilitated targeting of library information skills instruction to reinforce areas in which students' scores were the lowest. Fourth, principals praised library media specialists who actively taught research skills that students needed to be successful 21st century learners. Principals acknowledged that the information-seeking processes learned in the library provided critical-thinking and problem-solving skills applicable across content areas and transferable to real-life situations.

Next, principals applauded library media specialists who provided staff development for faculty and parents in the area of information technology and resources. When library media specialists provided workshops and training on topics such as the use of subscription databases and effective searching on the Web, principals took note. Finally, principals expressed their expectation that the library media specialist be the primary initiator of collaboration with classroom teachers at both the individual teacher level and the school level. They wanted library media specialists who were proactive, who stepped out to promote their instructional role, who took the initiative and approached classroom teachers to inform them of the instructional potential that exists.

The Principal Factor

It is the responsibility of the school library media specialist to realize the critical role that principals play in full implementation of the library media program. Principals expect positive attitudes and relationships, and they appreciate your active participation in curriculum and instruction. According to Hartzell, "The principal is an absolutely essential element in maximizing the return on library investment." Daily, you invest quite a bit of time, energy, and effort in your library program. It is up to you to take a proactive stance and address the principal factor in your school.

Works Cited

Church, Audrey P. *The Instructional Role of the Library Media Specialist as Perceived by Elementary School Principals.* 27 August 2008. American Library Association, *School Library Media Research.* 14 December 2008 <http://www .ala.org/ala/mgrps/divs/aasl/aasl pubsandjournals/slmrb/slmrcontents/ volume11/church.cfm>.

Hartzell, Gary. *What's It Take?* 4 June 2002. White House Conference on School Libraries. 13 December 2008 <http://www.imls.gov/news/ events/whitehouse_2.shtm#gh>.

School Libraries Work! 2008. Scholastic Library Publishing. 13 December 2008 <http://www2 .scholastic.com/content/collateral_ resources/pdf/s/slw3_2008.pdf>.

Dr. Audrey Church *is Assistant Professor and Coordinator of the School Library Media Program at Longwood University in Farmville, Virginia. Her latest title from Linworth is Your Library Goes Virtual (2006).*

Church, Audrey P. (2008). The principal factor. *LMC, 27*(6), 40–41.

Reinventing Ourselves in the Digital Age

By Joanne K. Hammond and Chris Barnabei

As our profession embraces the charge to incorporate digital technology, school librarians are aware that we must change how we teach. We are redefining ourselves in myriad ways to remain vital in our schools. This article reveals how a librarian at a STEM high school in Pennsylvania has dramatically reinvented himself and how he is adapting to his new role.

From Library to Knowledge Commons

The new Chambersburg Area Career Magnet School adjoins a vocational technical school to provide easy movement from the academic pursuits of science, technology, engineering, and math to the hands-on classrooms for technical and trade pursuits. Admission is competitive and includes an interview to gauge potential for success in a different learning environment.

> The "knowledge commons" would forego bookshelves to create space for collaborative groupings and comfortable chairs with built-in outlets that would accommodate recharging electronic devices.

Planning for this launch began with a search for teachers willing to use flipped classrooms, digital resources, and no textbooks. Central to the plan would be a new media center designed to be a place for knowledge to be created and shared rather than be the standard repository for books. The "knowledge commons" would forego bookshelves to create space for collaborative groupings, and comfortable chairs with built-in outlets would accommodate recharging electronic devices. With a 1:1 iPad

initiative, flat-screen televisions and palm-sized Apple TVs would replace interactive whiteboards. AirPlay would allow sharing of iPad views. The librarian would provide 20 percent of the teaching while the students would accomplish 80 percent of their own instruction via project-based-learning. It was a goal that called for an innovative librarian to make it happen.

Recognizing the impact our librarians have on education, administrators requested that a member of our department take on a new role: technology integrator/librarian. Chris Barnabei, with five years' librarian experience at an urban elementary school, accepted the challenge, which involved a total revamping of the prevailing philosophy and methods of teaching. He would also be responsible for bringing the rest of the staff on board.

Chris's Story: One Friday Afternoon in the Life

It was Friday, 3 p.m., and like every other teacher, I was packing my things so I could leave and start my weekend. Since moving from an elementary library to my new position as a technology integrator at a grade 9–12 STEM magnet school, I hadn't had too many opportunities to take advantage of the hour-earlier dismissal time that secondary teachers enjoy, but today was going to be different. Yes, today I was going to be able to enjoy some daylight at home and accomplish some yard work. As I started to turn off the lights, a teacher came in with an emergency. Change of plans. During my five previous years as a librarian, end of the day emergencies were nothing unusual, and I welcomed the opportunity to help a colleague no matter how late I stayed. Usually these emergencies entailed supplying a teacher with a book, giving a recommendation, or scheduling a last minute class during my flex time, but in my new position this emergency was different than any other.

The teacher with the emergency was teaching Algebra I and Geometry. She needed help with a project on the topic of slope and rate of change. Specifically, she needed to know how students could place a coordinate plane over top of a manmade or natural structure, like a mountain or bridge, so they could determine the slope of that structure. Now, instead of recommending a book or planning a lesson on information literacy, I had to play the role of a graphic designer to create a transparent picture of a coordinate plane that could be layered over another image in a photo editing app.

> To make matters more difficult, one might find an app, create a sample project in that app, and have it work fine, but then malfunctions arise when 100+ students begin to use it.

Problems like these are common in my school where we are seeking to do things differently through project-based learning, real-world applications, a focus on STEM, flipped classrooms, a more collegial environment, and a 1:1 student to iPad ratio. Our model is not unique and is gaining ground in this country, especially in the use of iPads and going 1:1. I'm hoping the story of my experience as a librarian turned technology integrator will provide valuable advice for librarians who would like to integrate iPads in their libraries, who are at a school that is going 1:1, or who are looking to reinvent themselves.

Collaboration and Communication with Technology Personnel

Before I talk about my work with students, teachers, and curriculum, I need to address the technical

goal

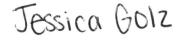

challenges of going 1:1 with iPads. My job description is based solely on instruction and coaching, but, not surprisingly, I found myself doing a lot of troubleshooting during the first weeks of school. I gained a new appreciation for how complicated it is to maintain a network that supports over 550 devices. These devices will not support learning unless they are working properly. A good working relationship and open communication with one's technology department is essential. Even though I am still a member of the library department, I attend our tech department's monthly meetings. I also maintain contact with our network administrator, as iPads require Internet access in order to be effective. Too often the tech department receives undeserved criticism. Maintaining close contact will help you better understand complicated issues that this department faces as well as allow you to communicate your needs to them.

> The challenge is to design projects that are relevant and meaningful.

Enhancing and Supporting Professional Learning

We librarians have always served as technology coaches for our teaching staff, but in my new position this role has taken on new dimensions. In addition to group instruction for staff, I work with individual teachers on a daily basis, planning projects with technology and helping them use apps and resources in their daily instruction. In addition to teaching research and literacy while working with classes, I have often made myself available to teach technology skills or be on hand in the classroom to offer tech support. Our school uses only Apple products, so our teachers who previously used PCs had to learn how to use MacBooks and OS in addition to the iPad. This, when combined with a new school and a new model of teaching, caused great anxiety among our staff. To help ease tensions, and in the spirit of flipped

classrooms, I created many video tutorials for teachers on MacBook topics, using a screencasting app. At the request of my teachers, I also hold short, informal workshops on technology-related topics before and after school.

The App Gatekeeper

The world of apps can be difficult to navigate. For instance, of all photo editing apps, which is the best one for a particular project? To make matters more difficult, one might find an app, create a sample project in that app, and have it work fine, but then malfunctions arise when 100+ students begin to use it. After using a video editing app for a ninth grade history project, students found that the audio narration they recorded would not save when they exited the app. This had not been an issue for me when I tested this app.

Our school favors app consistency from class to class, so students don't have to relearn apps when going from project to project. I have taken on the role of "app gatekeeper" and created a guide of recommended apps (http://chambersburg.libguides.com/cmsapps). I am selective about the apps I recommend and post only those that I have tested and that have worked for students. Though consistency is nice, I also found success with giving students the freedom to discover, choose, and evaluate apps themselves. When introducing a project, I might show students an app that I recommend but tell them they are welcome to discover their own. Giving students this freedom has greatly helped me, and I have learned a lot from them.

Focusing on Quality in Project-Based Learning

It is not technology that will distinguish our school from traditional options, but rather the way in which we deliver instruction. We are committed to project-based learning. I see myself not so much as a media specialist but rather as a project specialist. I am often approached by teachers and asked for input on projects. With emphasis on project-based learning,

teachers can easily focus on churning out a large quantity of projects rather than focusing on their quality. The challenge is to design projects that are relevant and meaningful. We, as a career- and STEM-focused school, need learning experiences that have real-world applications.

To help us to this end, we have formed a business advisory board comprised of members from local companies who meet and advise on curriculum decisions for our school. The primary goal of this group is to provide real projects that our students can complete for their companies. For instance, our students are currently researching geriatric fitness and designing exercise stations for a local retirement home. In the very near future, our students will also be searching for job openings, applying for that job, and conducting mock interviews with some of our business partners who will provide them with feedback. Our business partners are eager to be involved in this project because they have expressed that people in the workforce need better soft skills (dress, communication, punctuality, etc.). As a technology integrator I foster this partnership by maintaining a blog where business partners and teachers can post and respond to ideas as well as provide assistance to teachers when planning these projects. The business community is very eager to work with us, and our board contains members from all rungs of the corporate ladder, including presidents and CEOs. Your school may not have such an organization; however, if you reach out, I am confident that you will find receptive people in the business community who are excited to work with you and your students.

Establishing Expectations

While we have had many successes so far, we have also encountered several challenges. As you might imagine with teenagers, time management along with appropriate use of the iPads have been issues. Our students required an education on digital citizenship and Internet safety, which librarians are in a prime position to provide. Furthermore, we see a need that students receive this education before iPads are distributed. Our program calls for one day of instruction during all English classes, since all students have an English class. All teachers during this time teach the same lesson that includes student-created videos. On the following day, students must pass a written exam in order to receive their iPads. Students need refreshers on these lessons throughout the year; however, that initial lesson and exam establishes expectations.

If going 1:1, take little for granted. Do not assume that students will know how to properly conduct themselves online. Also do not assume that students will come to you ready to learn in an online environment. Our science and math teachers are working toward flipping their classrooms. A flipped classroom is when the majority of homework entails watching instructional videos on concepts, and the majority of class time is spent practicing these concepts and completing real-world projects. Students often want to watch these videos like they watch television. It is common to multitask by accessing social networking sites, gaming, socializing, etc. while the TV is on, but this does not work when watching a video on how to solve a complex algebra equation. We had to model and teach our students how to take notes and be fully engaged when viewing an instructional video.

Taking Risks to Move Forward

This year has been quite a learning experience for us all at the Chambersburg Area Career Magnet School. Though a lot of work, I have found this opportunity to be very rewarding. If you are undertaking a similar endeavor, my biggest piece of advice would be to have a willingness to take risks and learn from your failures.

Joanne K. Hammond *is the head librarian at Chambersburg (Pennsylvania) Area School District and a librarian at Chambersburg Area Senior High School. She can be reached at joanne.hammond@ casdonline.org.*

Chris Barnabei *is the technology integrator/librarian at Chambersburg (Pennsylvania) Area Career Magnet School. He will be presenting "An iPad for Every Student: Lessons from a Librarian Turned Technology Coordinator" at the Pennsylvania School Librarians Association annual conference.*

Hammond, Joanne K., & Barnabei, Chris. (2013). Reinventing ourselves in the digital age. *LMC, 31*(6), 14–16.

Survive and Thrive: Managing Multiple Libraries

By Heidi Hammond

Year after year, school librarians find their hours reduced or find themselves assigned to more than one library. The Google map "A Nation without School Librarians," created by Shonda Brisco, confirms this. As the coordinator of the school library track within a library school, I felt I would be remiss if I didn't prepare my students for this possibility. A search of the literature for articles about managing multiple libraries found few. When you think about it, it's easy to understand why. School librarians managing more than one library don't have the time or the energy to write articles about their experiences! So I contacted school librarians and also posted a query on LM_NET asking how they cope when their hours are reduced or they are assigned to more than one building. *School Library Journal*'s annual spending survey stated, "As the economy limps along and federal dollars dwindle, school librarians are turning into resourceful survivors" (*SLJ*, March 2011). I share with you advice and strategies from some of those survivors.

Advice from the Surviving and Thriving

If you manage more than one library, you may not be able to do all the professional duties you were trained to do, know you should do, and would like to do. One thing you always can do is *be* professional. Rather than focusing on what you can't accomplish, concentrate on what you can do. It's frustrating to be placed in these situations. You may want to cry; many librarians have. But, as Mr. Quimby said in *Ramona the Brave*, "Buck up, Ramona. . . . Show us your spunk."

Attitude is everything. Remember, you are managing the libraries; don't let the work manage you. "Your attitude is your choice," was the advice I heard from many librarians. Their most frequent advice was to smile, focus on the positives, and try to make the library a place where students and staff feel welcome, even if you

feel overburdened. If your goal is to change your situation, you will find people more supportive if they can see you are trying to make the best of things. Other advice included:

- Treat all of your schools equally, as much as time allows. Make the teachers and students feel like they are your priority while you are there.

- Try to attend functions at all the schools, though not all the functions. Students appreciate seeing you. Teachers and administration will think of you as part of their "family."

- Post your hours at each building so students and teachers know when you will be there. Provide each classroom and the office with a schedule of your hours. If your teachers use Google Calendar, that would also be a good place to post your schedule. Signs are more effective for students.

- Be visible as much as possible, especially to administration. Pop in to say hello as you enter or leave the building. Keep them informed.

- If you have aides, give work such as cataloging and preliminary weeding to them. Welcome their initiative, but ask that you be consulted before they implement their ideas. Do make sure aides understand that you are the librarian and you are the one who makes final decisions. Communicate daily to keep connected.

- Remember to treat your aides well, and bring them treats.

- Keep treats and coffee in the library for teachers and staff. You may not have time to go visit them, so draw them to you. While they are in the library, use that time to find out what they are teaching and suggest resources to them. Offer to collaborate.

- Use a rolling cart to transport materials to save your back.

- Go home at the end of the day listing the things you've accomplished, not the things that didn't get done.

- Find a way to re-energize daily. One librarian bought a puppy. That took her mind off work!

- Get enough rest.
- Recognize that you will not be able to everything. You will have to let some things go and do just the essentials. Working with students is our most important work.

> *If you manage more than one library, you may not be able to do all the professional duties you were trained to do, know you should do, and would like to do. But one thing you always can do is be professional.*

Our Most Important Work

A school library media specialist has many roles, but we would all agree that our instructional role is most important. Though we are information and technology specialists and provide professional development to our faculty and staff, our primary role is working with students. Collaborating with teachers affords us the best opportunity to reach the most students.

You may not be able to meet with all the teachers individually face-to-face to collaborate on lesson plans, so make use of cloud computing and Web 2.0 tools such as Google Docs or wikis. These tools allow you to work on anything, anywhere. Documents are accessible to you and the teachers you work with so all of you can make contributions.

You can share lessons between buildings by saving them on a district network drive. Or you can save them in a cloud-based storage application such as Dropbox rather than in a file on a particular computer in a particular building. Duplicate lessons between buildings, if possible, but to avoid boredom, don't teach the same lessons at each of your buildings at the same time. Staggering lessons between buildings will allow you to share materials, too.

Attitude is everything. Remember, you are managing the libraries; don't let the work manage you.

Create some online lessons for when you can't be at a site. You can make instructional videos and podcasts of skills that aren't site specific. Post them on the library webpages under tabs for a particular grade level or course, and coordinate with teachers for students to do the lessons. You might create an orientation video for new students that you can't meet with individually. It could serve as a review for returning students at the beginning of the school year.

Promote your virtual library. Your library's webpage is a valuable tool for communicating with students and staff. Be sure to teach them what's included on your site and how to use the resources you provide.

Nuts and Bolts Work: Prioritize, Organize, and Duplicate

Administrative work is our behind the scenes work. Others are unaware that we do these tasks because they don't always see them. Prioritize long-term and short-term tasks (annually, monthly, weekly, daily) to assure they get accomplished.

Organize, both physically and digitally, so you can locate materials efficiently. Take the time to clean cabinets and throw out what is no longer needed. Label cabinets and drawers to help you find things quickly.

Organize digitally, too. Have email folders for each building, and within the folders, create subfolders for grade levels or subject areas. Create email groups so you can send messages to all teachers at a grade level or within a content area. Make use of Google Docs for storage. Establish an iGoogle page for your home page and keep sticky notes and "to do" lists on it.

Order books processed with MARC records. It costs a bit more, but if you don't have enough clerical help, it's worth it. It is easier to tweak a MARC record than to generate one from scratch or search for one to copy.

Duplicate as much as possible. This has enormous potential for saving time.

- Besides duplicating lessons, duplicate bulletin boards. Don't create seasonal bulletin boards, but rather bulletin boards and displays that can be used year round. Then, move them from building to building.

- Duplicate website material and newsletters, customizing items to fit buildings.

- Duplicate book orders as much as possible so that when you create holiday or subject-based booklists for students or teachers, you can use the same lists for each school. Buying multiple copies sometimes expands your purchasing power for books and equipment.

- Create templates for forms and notices so they can be used at each building by just personalizing them for the particular library.

Realize and accept that you will need help. You cannot do it all. Time spent recruiting and training volunteers can pay off in the long run. Students can assist with numerous tasks, from checking in books to shelving and maintaining their own specially assigned shelves.

Your Leadership Role

It may seem that you have no time to assume a leadership role in any of your buildings. However, fulfilling this role may have the most impact on your situation.

A school librarian is trained to be a leader. You have valuable skills and knowledge to share. Your participation on building and district committees attests to your professionalism and provides you an opportunity to influence what happens in your buildings and in your library. It gives you a platform to promote your contributions to the learning community.

Display your expertise by providing professional development training for staff and faculty. Sometimes that professional development happens discretely when you are working with classes of students and the teachers learn while they observe. And, don't forget

to continue your own professional development by attending conferences and workshops.

Advocacy

Much has been written about school library advocacy. The AASL School Library Program Health and Wellness Toolkit contains valuable information and resources. Advocacy is defined as "a long-term, deliberate plan that is designed to build stakeholder support." It's not a one-time activity.

People are advocating for you at the state and national levels. Even so, there is much you can do. Remember that when you advocate for the school library, it is not about you. Focus on the students. When you advocate for increased funding and staffing, you are advocating for increased student learning. Build stakeholder support and they will advocate for the library, too. Show your stakeholders what they have to gain, and they won't want to compromise their advantages.

This may seem daunting when you feel overwhelmed with a multitude of responsibilities. Make a plan, one day at a time. Recognize and appreciate what you gain from your situation: relationships with students and teachers for whom you can make a difference. Your limited time in each of your buildings is valuable to everyone, including you.

Works Cited

AASL. "School Library Program Health and Wellness Toolkit." ALA. Web. www.ala.org/ala/mgrps/divs/aasl/aaslissues/toolkits/slmhealthandwellness.cfm.

Brisco, Shonda. "A Nation without School Librarians." Google Maps. 2012. Web. http://maps.google.com/maps/ms?ie=UTF8&oe=UTF8&msa=0&msid=117551670433142326244.000482bb91ce51be5802b.

Heidi Hammond, *Ph.D., is an assistant professor in the MLIS program at St. Catherine University, St. Paul, Minnesota, and can be reached at hkhammond@ stkate.edu.*

Hammond, Heidi. (2012). Survive and thrive: Managing multiple libraries. *LMC, 31*(3), 28–29.

Sweet vs. Snap! Effective Dispositions in the Media Center

By April Standard

"Sugar!"

Place a "reserved" sign on the conference room door, pull books for Mr. Mack's research project, add new book requests to book order . . .

"Oh, Shoooo-gar!"

. . . meet with language arts teachers during 3rd period, prep materials for literary circle, finish plagiarism pathfinder . . .

"Whooo-hoo!"

. . . put pen down, look up, and smile. Uggghhh!

A teacher was poking her head into my office, bright curls bobbing.

"Yes, Mrs. Smith?" I asked patiently.

"I just wanted to thank you, sweetie, for fixin' my computer yesterday. Let me tell you, I thought I would never get that thing to do anything but mock me! And here you come and it just whizzes right along like a little bee." She giggled. "And let me tell you, it was really nice that you did it with a smile. With some people around here, you never know if you're gonna' get sweet or snap!"

Wow . . .

It's impossible for me to adequately describe how small I felt as she sashayed out of the media center, her Southern drawl echoing in my office. She took time out of her busy day to walk several wings over and thank me for doing my job, and I had to hold myself back from brushing her off in exasperation because I was busy. How many times do we snap at colleagues and students simply because we are overwhelmed or preoccupied?

In "What Defines an Exemplary School Librarian," Jami Jones and Gail Bush make a strong argument that our professional disposition is the key to a successful library media program. The authors emphasize the relevance of INTASC standards which specify that teachers must promote "positive social interaction and [develop] healthy *and* helping relationships with children and youth." Now, the services of a school library media program should target not only our students but our teachers as well. Therefore, an entry point into reforming our social interactions and relationships is to provide a positive appeal in the media center for students and teachers.

Who knew that a coffee station could tempt teachers from different content areas to congregate in the media center and discuss how they can build bridges across disciplines?

I know exactly what you are thinking. You can't imagine placing your hand on the shoulder of a disgruntled co-worker who is snarling at you with contempt. Forget apologizing! Why should we have to apologize for technological glitches caused by the Internet?! Or compose our features into an expression of sympathy for a teacher who adamantly proclaims the LCD projector is broken when the problem is merely that lens cap is still on?

Here's the thing. We have a choice. We can either be a "Rocky" or a "Tyson." Rocky goes the distance but remains humble and respectful in all fifteen rounds. Tyson, well, he bites your ear. Since it is vital that we promote positive social interaction with students and teachers, we must develop strategies that let us become a Rocky.

First, we should ask ourselves what students and teachers need the most to feel they are valued and welcome in the media center. The answer seems universal. Everyone wants to have their presence acknowledged, their needs met, and be appreciated for their hard work and patronage. We must find ways to promote a positive atmosphere and provide unique services which reward our patrons and promote our programs.

After putting research into action in a high school media center, I found the following strategies effective in providing immediate, positive results for the school library media program.

Master Plan #1: Just a Little Bribe . . .

Do you remember the scene in *A Christmas Story* where Ralphie brings the teacher a huge fruit basket in hopes of improving his grade? We can pull a "Ralphie" without being ashamed. For the most part it will work! The following student and teacher strategies will create a cordial and productive atmosphere in your media center.

Students: Provide one reward for each visit during which a student checks out a book. One option is to start with a bag of Jolly Ranchers. (Who knew the blue one has the highest demand but the lowest number count in any given bag?) You may eventually want to expand your reward repertoire to include non-sugary treats, such as bookmarks, pens, and frequent verbal messages of thanks for being a valued patron.

Not only will students be pleasantly surprised about their "recognition" but they will eventually begin making comments such as, "I'm bringing a couple of friends tomorrow. They want to check something out . . ." and "You know, I didn't know you had books like this in here . . ." Student traffic will increase tremendously in a short amount of time and you may even witness students dropping off trinkets for your reward stash. What starts out as a materialistic endeavor will transform into a sincere appreciation for your media center program. You are guaranteed to reap the rewards you are giving to others—tenfold!

Teachers: Provide coffee that is convenient, quick, and suited to their tastes. Strategically place a donation jar nearby. The rationale behind this: caffeine = energy= motivated teachers who frequently visit the media center, which in turn provides us with opportunities to promote co-teaching sessions, collaboration, and services.

You may find that coffee, espresso, or cappuccino will bring teachers to the media center on a daily basis. It will inspire even the most technologically insecure teachers to ask you to co-create a wiki unit. Who knew that a coffee station could tempt teachers from different content areas to congregate in the media center and discuss how they can build bridges across disciplines? And like the students, teachers are generous. You will soon have enough consistent donations to make the coffee station pay for itself!

> Offer "concierge services," such as taking coffee to busy secretaries who can't leave their desks, placing requested books in teachers' mailboxes for quick pickup, and registering students with online testing services for teachers by class period to save class time.

Master Plan #2: Let's Get Ready to Rumble or . . . EMBRACE?!

How many times have we been deeply engaged in a task only to have one or more interruptions sidetrack us and steal valuable time? While I was immersed in registering three classes for online test preparation services, I was repeatedly interrupted by teachers and students needing immediate assistance. By the time I was able to return to my task, I found my session had timed out and my Internet connection had been severed. Immediately, my pulse began to pound, my

teeth began to clench, and a surge of burning rage began to swell inside my chest.

Then, a student timidly approached the circulation desk and said, "Can you help me, please?! Like, I've totally lost my source cards for my research paper and I can't finish the "Works Cited" page without them. I'll never find them on my own!" At that moment I realized that everyone's tasks are vital and of utmost importance to each individual. How can we consider one person's needs to be more important than another person's needs when our school's success depends on the success of everyone on our team? Jones and Bush remind us of the importance of everyone's success. Unfortunately, this means we must sacrifice some of our time to go above and beyond for the success of others. The rewards of this action will be overwhelming in the end. By implementing the following teacher and student strategies, you will find that others will come to your much needed rescue during your most stressful moments.

Teachers: Respond to all requests within a 24-hour period by providing either a resolution or a discussion to solve the problem. Many times this will mean visiting a teacher's classroom to verbally assure her that you are working on the issue. Provide "comfort resources" for faculty and staff. New mouse pads, smooth writing pens, and wrist rests for keyboards do the trick. Offering smooth pens to teachers who are frustrated with grading piles of essays will help brighten their spirits. Just having something tangible to remind them that others do know how hard they work gives them a second wind. Offer "concierge services," such as taking coffee to busy secretaries who can't leave their desks, placing requested books in teachers' mailboxes for quick pickup, and registering students with online testing services for teachers by class period to save class time. It will be much appreciated and rewarded.

Teachers will visibly pause in surprise and thank you when you visit their classes to offer reassurance that you are working on their problems. You may notice very quickly that they

will begin troubleshooting many of their problems before sending you new requests. This, in turn, will save you a tremendous amount of time. Teachers who would never attempt to fiddle with plugs or restart devices will adopt these procedures as a first step before contacting you to do it for them. They will become more comfortable with taking a proactive approach to technical problems, and their pride will be obvious in the emails you will receive from them proclaiming success.

Students: Offer book concierge services in the form of individualized book recommendations and deliver requested books to a student's homeroom. Provide headphone checkout to football players during away games for use on the bus. If you manage to draw in one athletic team, chances are you will snag new patrons from other teams as well.

The concierge services will prove to be very effective in building relationships. Students will refer their friends who have never visited the media center before to request a book. Knowing they can drop by and write down in private an author or genre they would like to read allows them to enjoy extracurricular activities without sacrificing after school time searching for a book. The headphone checkout for student athletes will serve as a starting point. At first, they will probably only listen to music at a computer station but eventually a couple of them may begin asking for help finding a book. Also, you may want to consider designating a "good luck" display in the media center. Every morning of a game, a student athlete can place a team helmet, baseball, or basketball on top of a book shelf for good luck. This will be an opportunity for your library media program to branch out into all areas of the school.

A final consideration is to send out MVP (most valuable patron) cards to the top ten patrons of your media center every three months. Include a short note of thanks for their patronage and a pass to a dessert table at lunch. This shows students and teachers that you are appreciative of their hard work and dedication to academics. You will also have the opportunity to achieve more diversity on your library committee by identifying students and teachers who are less vocal with their opinions.

Implementing these strategies will take time out of a busy day to go the extra mile, but it will end up saving you time in the long run. Teachers, students, and staff will soon develop a new appreciation for the work you do in the media center and you will find your program will expand exponentially. So the next time you are overworked, overtired, and overwhelmed, consider choosing to be "sweet" rather than "snap." Take Jami Jones and Gail Bush's advice and put research into practice. Implement a positive, welcoming disposition into your school library program and see immediate results!

Work Cited

Jones, Jami and Gail Bush. "What Defines an Exemplary School Librarian? An Exploration of Professional Dispositions." *Library Media Connection* 27.6 (2009): 10–12.

April Standard *is the media specialist for Jefferson County High School in Louisville, Georgia. Her goal is to create and implement an effective school library media program. April can be reached at standarda@jefferson.k12.ga.us.*

Standard, April. (2011). Sweet vs. snap! Effective dispositions in the media center. *LMC, 29*(6), 36–37.

Dream Big: Empowering Middle School Students

By Mary Virginia Meeks and Maria Cahill

In February 2012, crews from Nickelodeon descended upon the T.C. Marsh Middle School library to feature students in a *Nick News with Linda Ellerbee* segment (2012) attempting to answer the question "If a school is broken, can kids fix it?" The cameras filmed students from the 1,200 student Title One campus who had been empowered to take ownership of their library and turn it from a tired and abused book warehouse into a vibrant learning commons Tech Café.

T.C. Marsh Middle School Library Makeover

How does a new librarian enter an unfamiliar school setting and successfully jumpstart a struggling library program? I, Mary Virginia Meeks, did so by dreaming big, but realistically aligning my dreams with the "mission, goals, and objectives of the school" (AASL, 2009: 30). I formulated my dreams into a tangible plan and began to take action. I started by first conducting formal and informal surveys of teachers, students, parents, and administrators to identify stakeholder perceptions and priorities. To document campus needs, I gathered demographic and achievement data about students and reviewed campus and district goals. I then established a few core library goals aligned directly with campus goals.

With tentative goals in place, I created an informal library advisory board. Coffee and muffins helped generate inquisitive attendees who I'd like to think were "hungry" for change. I shared my ideas with the group, but remained open to alternate suggestions and directions. I worked with the library advisory board and sketched out a plan for meeting immediate and long-range goals and objectives. Our group instituted initiatives directly connected to the campus improvement plan and inspired students to build the library program. Through collaboration with students, teachers, parents, and administrators,

we were able to revitalize the library program.

Get the Students Back!

One of the first initiatives was to entice students to come back to the library. Outstanding fines for lost books had kept students from using library resources. The uninviting, unattractive environment had discouraged staff and students from utilizing the library program. I broke down these two barriers by offering students amnesty for book fines in exchange for student help with a "library make-over." During Thanksgiving break, over forty students signed up for two-hour shifts and cleaned, scraped, painted, and added life to their library with elbow grease and a few cans of paint. In the weeks following, the colorful change brought in curious students and teachers. This led to a dramatic increase in circulation, collaboration, and a gradual evolution of the library program. The makeover also instituted a sense of student ownership of the library which resulted in a thriving library club that boasted more than seventy members this past year.

> *Review your campus improvement plan. Think outside the box in considering how the school library might be involved in addressing key issues within the plan.*

As students, staff, and administrators began to recognize how the library program contributed to the campus goals for student success, grass-roots fundraising efforts such as read-a-thons, pizza sales, and community book fair nights helped secure needed funds to grow the program despite severe budget cutbacks. Soon

corporate and individual donors also took notice and pitched in their support to help build the students' dream of a Tech Café where students could sip cocoa and use laptops for research. When the Dallas Advocate magazine got wind of the changes afoot, they tracked the progress of the program with small news pieces, and in March 2012 they featured a print and video story about the library program.

Steps for Reinventing a School Library Program

If you are wondering how to replicate some of the successes of T.C. Marsh Middle School library at your own campus, here are the steps that we suggest.

> *Beyond simply communicating your goals, sharing the plan with stakeholders also increases the likelihood that you will actually carry out your plan.*

If school libraries are to be seen as essential and more importantly contribute to student learning, base library goals on the goals of the school and perhaps even the district. In August 2009, then president of AASL Ann M. Martin posted a message on the AASL forum discussion list addressing the importance of aligning school library goals with those of the school. She wrote, "To be thought of as essential we must contribute to solving the needs of the school board. The politics of scarce resources is fickle. All departments and members of the educational community are fighting for the same resources of time, money, and visibility. What needs to be done is to figure out what is the most important goal, agenda item, objective of your local school board. Once you find that out then show how the library helps to meet that goal."

Step 1: Align your program with school goals.

First, determine your school's goals. Most likely school goals will be written, but sometimes administrators have unwritten goals and priorities as well. Review your campus improvement plan. Think outside the box in considering how the school library might be involved in addressing key issues within the plan. Schedule conversations with your administration. Doing so will not only help you gather the information you need, it will also convey to them that your interests and programs support their goals—and that you are a team player. Talk to teachers to find out their needs within their classrooms as well as their perceptions of the library program and its role in student learning. These conversations just might be the first steps in developing a collaborative relationship. Formally and informally survey students and parents. By soliciting input, you will have opportunities to reiterate that this is *their* program. Review school board minutes to determine key issues and priorities across the school district.

Step 2: Formulate a preliminary plan and take it to your stakeholders.

Once you have an idea of the school goals, review the professional literature and talk with other librarians to understand how others have successfully addressed similar goals. Formulate library goals based on school goals and create a tentative plan.

Meet with a library advisory board to flesh out and finalize the goals and the plan. This is a critical step because you want these to be more than just your goals—you want to have stakeholder buy-in so that your plan has teeth. Because it tends to be easier for groups to revise than create, come to the advisory board with the draft of your goals and plan; do so with the mindset that the goals are preliminary and likely to change. If you don't have a library advisory board, create one. Invite one or more members from each stakeholder group (admin, teachers, students, parents,

community) to help you steer the direction of the library—and use their input! As part of this planning process, consider how you will measure the effectiveness of activities, instruction, and programming, and include the collection of evidence and data analysis in the plan.

Step 3: Share your plan with stakeholders and ask for further input.

Sharing your plan with all stakeholder groups is essential. Doing so will convey that the library program is focused on accomplishing school goals (i.e., the library is important and the librarian does more than simply manage resources). This type of communication also imparts the notion that the library program has a plan based on researched best practices, and the librarian is proactive rather than reactive. Finally, it reassures your stakeholders that you value them and want to partner with them. Beyond simply communicating your goals, sharing the plan with stakeholders also increases the likelihood that you will actually carry out your plan.

> *Visibility is key if the goals are to be met—not for job security's sake alone, but for the continued growth of a library program that truly is the hub of the school and clearly contributes to student success.*

Step 4: Partner with stakeholders to accomplish your plan.

More than likely you will not be able to accomplish your plan solo—nor do you want to. You want this to be your stakeholders' plan that you help carry out. Undoubtedly, your plan involves instruction (you might be in trouble if it doesn't). Establish partnerships with teachers as early as possible

to plan collaborative units. Talk to students, parents, and community members to begin forming partnerships and discussing strategies to realize goals.

Step 5: Implement your plan.

Begin to carry out your strategies and initiatives related to accomplishing each goal, and collect evidence to evaluate each strategy. While it is easy to get caught up in the day-to-day management tasks of the library, remember to follow through on carrying out your plan. Create a schedule for routine procedures that address plan goals and adhere to your self-imposed schedule. Do whatever it takes to make sure that you accomplish what you set out to do. For example, if one of the tasks to accomplish a goal is to booktalk a set of books with a different group of readers each week, schedule that task on your calendar for each week. Also, be sure to create a schedule for collecting and analyzing data. Though some data will only be collected once, other data will need to be collected and analyzed on a somewhat regular basis. Be sure to put it on your schedule.

Step 6: Communicate.

Building a library program based on the school's goals is the starting point, but you must share the evidence. Get evaluative information from your stakeholders and share with them what you collect. Communicate the activities and evaluative data with all stakeholders regularly. Visibility is key if the goals are to be met—not for job security's sake alone, but for the continued growth of a library program that truly is the hub of the school and clearly contributes to student success.

Communicating highlights and "bragging rights" every six weeks in a concise but stakeholder-friendly way gives principals a snapshot view into what goes on in the library program. We must assume that if we don't tell them, they won't know. You must be consistently proactive in sharing how the library program is critical to the school's goals for student achievement.

To increase cohesiveness among staff:	To increase cohesiveness among students:	To increase cohesiveness among the extended Marsh community:	To increase academic behavior and extra-curricular activity involvement:	To increase technology use:	To increase college awareness and AVID use:
Review curriculum/TEKS for collaborative needs.	Maintain an open library schedule.	Survey parents, staff, and students on measures to improve the library	Improve the print collection for ELL students.	Conduct tech surveys with teachers, parents, and students to measure abilities.	Teach students and staff how to use the "Career Cruiser" database.
Study TAKS data.	Provide service options for students to reduce library fines.	Host a coffee for FOL adult volunteers in the fall, and market volunteer opportunities year long.	Provide student-to-student academic support in the library before school through the Library Club.	Provide staff training in databases, Web 2.0, and other electronic resources.	Promote College Awareness Week with displays.
Host workshops for Tech Tools.	Seek student input on improving the library environment.	Organize a Tech Café dedication, and include press, community, and sponsors.	Promote Bluebonnet and RAL programs; host year-end celebrations.	Offer extra training for students implementing Microsoft Office and Web 2.0 projects.	Promote college awareness by being a speaker to AVID classes.
Attend curriculum meetings.	Visit elementary feeder schools in May to introduce the library and promote summer reading.	Attend and present at PTA meetings.	Create a Novel Book Room with an inventory list, self check-out, and planning calendar for the ELAR dept.	Train students and staff in database research skills.	Promote Cornell note-taking skills and AVID techniques in the library.
Maintain a calendar and communicate the availability of the library to staff.	Entrust Library Club to host Cocoa Mornings at the Tech Café.	Invite corporate sponsors, parents, and teachers to participate in a virtual book club with students.	Develop year-long book club: Teach students how to blog about books with students, staff, and community sponsors.	Serve as webmaster for the campus and assist with webpage development.	Host evening AVID events in the library for parents.
Create a library newsletter every six weeks.	Expand student ownership of the library through Library Club.	Host a book fair, book swaps, and special guest events.	Improve campus literacy awareness through year-long library events.	Promote e-reader use.	
Host a monthly staff coffee.	Display student photos, book reviews, and events.	Promote the library program by speaking at library conferences.	Acquire academic games.	Maintain forty-five Netbooks.	
Help build classroom libraries.	Host library social events for students.	Create/maintain a library webpage.			

Possible areas to include in a "Six Weeks Library Update" for stakeholders: Statistics (circulation, class visits, before/after school visitors, database use); how the activities addressed school goals; a couple of cool snapshots and highlights of events; a sidebar with quotes from students, teachers, or parents about something that went on in the library. It doesn't have to be complicated or award winning. Just start simple and do it. Get ideas by looking at how other libraries share their news with stakeholders in print and online formats.

A newsletter is a traditional way to communicate, but consider using different ways to send your message. Videos and photographs are engaging and informative communication tools. Be sure to place information and data analyses on your library website. Blog about how your program is addressing school goals. Invite the local media to cover exciting events and accomplishments. Turn your students and teachers into walking billboards with stickers and t-shirts.

Step 7: Analyze for Self-Improvement.

What a wonderful year it would be if everything worked out as planned. However, since life does not always unfold according to plan, be ready to adapt your plan to circumstances that arise. Regularly revisit your plan and identify shortcomings. Consider ways to alter the plan in order to rectify any problems now or in the future. Critically analyze your data and identify opportunities for improvement. Again, solicit the input of stakeholders along the way and at the end of the year to gather their assessments and ideas. This puts you right back at the beginning and positions you to repeat the evidence-based process!

References

American Association of School Librarians. *Empowering Learners: Guidelines for School Librarians.* Chicago: American Library Association, 2009.

Martin, A.M. "Does Any of This Go to Libraries?" [electronic mailing list message]. 7 August 2009. Web. http://lists.ala.org/sympa/arc/aaslforum/2009–08/msg00013.html.

Nickelodeon. "*Nick News*: If a School Is Broken, Can Kids Fix It?" [video]. 18 March 2012. Web. www.nick.com/videos/clip/nick-news-126-full-episode.html.

Toman, E., and D. Fulgencio. "Marsh Students Take Back Their Library." *Advocate Magazine* (March 2012). Web. http://prestonhollow .advocatemag.com/2012/02/24/ marsh-middle-students-take-back-their-library.

Mary Virginia Meeks *is a librarian at Cobb Middle School in Frisco, Texas. She may be reached at maryvmeeks@gmail .com.*

Dr. Maria Cahill *is an assistant professor at the School of Library and Information Studies at Texas Woman's University in Denton, Texas. She may be reached at mcahill1@twu.edu.*

Meeks, Mary Virginia, & Cahill, Maria. (2013). Dream big: Empowering middle school students. *LMC, 31*(4), 30–33.

Something New . . . Planning for Your New School Library

By Leigh Ann Jones

Opening a new school library is a bit like planning a wedding. It is an expensive process, with months of planning required. Every decision impacts how smoothly the big event will go. A bride has colors and fabric swatches to examine, selections to make, and countless vendors to consider. Librarians may peruse paint chips, choose shelving and furniture, select thousands of books and other materials, and weigh the merits of myriad jobbers.

In the same way that a wedding coordinator can lend experience and offer advice to a bride, a full-time library coordinator can facilitate the process of opening a new school library. If a coordinator isn't in the picture for your district, careful advance planning and attention to detail will allow you to prepare for a library that will serve your students and staff well.

Glossy bridal magazines have a planning calendar with monthly benchmarks. The bride is advised to book the wedding venue one year in advance while the groom should be fitted for his tux three months prior to the wedding. Applying this type of calendar to the opening of a school library may help librarians in planning as well.

The Planning Calendar

Planning for new school libraries is a yearly process in Frisco (Texas) Independent School District (ISD). Ranked as one of the fastest growing school districts in the nation, Frisco opens three to six new campuses each year. In the fall of 1990, the district enrolled 1,310 students in one elementary, one middle school, and one high school. Nineteen years later, 30,908 students currently attend 40 campuses. By August 2010, nine more campuses will open.

Because we are fortunate to have the strong support of our Board of Trustees and administration, each of our libraries has a certified librarian. Our district library services department consists of a full-time coordinator and half-time cataloger. Each person plays an active role in planning for new libraries. While the process in Frisco ISD may differ from your own situation, a monthly benchmark calendar may be useful in shaping your own new school library.

One Year in Advance (August)

- Look at the big picture first.
  - Revisit state standards in regard to facilities and the collection.
  - Review local selection policy and guidelines.
  - Re-read state and local curriculum applicable to the campus.
  - Form a strategy for developing the opening collection (ODC).
- Meet with architects.
  - Offer input on the location of the library within the campus, the size and storage space available, if possible.
  - Offer input on the layout of the library, electrical outlets, data drops, and built-in storage components.
- Meet with your district technology department.
  - Discuss the number of computers needed, data projector and screen, circulation scanners, and other equipment.
  - Review placement of electrical outlets and data drops.
  - Form a timeline for installation of hardware and software.
- Meet with your district purchasing and finance departments.
  - Discuss budget allocations and deadlines.
    - Campaign for funds which will allow your new library to open at the recognized level according to state standards.
      - In Texas, this would provide a collection of 10,800 items or 18 items per elementary student, 16 per middle school student, or 14 per high school student, whichever is greater.
- Promote funding which will provide at least an acceptable level of materials according to state standards if recognized level is not possible.
  - In Texas, an acceptable collection provides a minimum of 9,000 items or 16 per elementary student, 14 per middle school student, or 12 per high school student, whichever is greater.
- Find out purchasing requirements such as bids and vendor specifications.
- Confer about ordering procedures and timelines.

> "Opening a new school library is a bit like planning a wedding. It is an expensive process, with months of planning required."

Eleven Months in Advance (September)

- Devise a formula for a balanced collection.
  - Assign each a percentage of the total opening day collection funds for each Dewey designation.
    - Use H.W. Wilson's core collections as a starting point for this formula.
    - Tweak Wilson's suggested percentages for each Dewey designation to reflect state and local curriculum, projected circulation patterns, and the age of students at the campus.
  - Apply the final formula to obtain a dollar amount to be ordered for each Dewey designation.

- Remember to include periodicals, professional materials, and other formats including audiobooks, DVDs, and online resources.

Ten Months in Advance (October)

- Organize a new school committee comprised of librarians, if help is available.
  - Enlist committee help for all phases of the process including designating a timeline with intermediate and final deadlines, ordering supplies, and reviewing the opening day selections.

Nine Months in Advance (November)

- Submit lists to the district purchasing for office and library supplies to be ordered.
- Touch base with district technology staff and meet as needed throughout the process.
- Divide the Dewey designations of the ODC among the number of professional librarians available to help select the collection.
  - Review the collection development plan and selection policy and guidelines with each librarian responsible for ordering one or more sections.
  - Stress the importance of selection based on professional reviews, the curriculum, quality, and currency. Each book in the ODC should be selected individually using the criteria above.
  - Set a deadline for completion in mid-April.
- Proceed carefully if no professional selection help is available and you must outsource the list.
  - Consider each title on a vendor-provided list carefully with attention to reviews, the curriculum, currency, and bindings even if the vendor makes assurances that their ODCs are selected by librarians.
  - Develop important target sections such as fiction and easy, personally using reviews rather than vendor suggestions.

Eight Months in Advance (December)

- Choose vendors for books and periodicals, reference, nonprint, and professional materials.
- Consider price, customer service, experience, fill rate, and the quality of processing and cataloging.
- Remember that small things make a huge difference. Does the vendor offer a service to shelve the books upon arrival? Will the books arrive packed in Dewey order? Are property labels available?
- Ask around—what has been the experience of other libraries using these vendors for an ODC?
- Request processed and cataloged samples of a variety of media to check quality.
- Simplify the process by selecting as few vendors as possible.

Seven Months in Advance (January)

- Select library shelving and furniture in conjunction with district purchasing.
- Obtain quotes for capital request items and submit to district purchasing.

Six Months in Advance (February)

- Touch base with librarians who are selecting sections of the new collection.
- Offer assistance as needed so that final deadlines are met.

Five Months in Advance (March)

- Order dumb barcodes printed with the new library's name.
- Set up barcode tracking service, if applicable.
- Work with your automation vendor to put the new location in your circulation system.
  - Ensure that circulation parameters are consistent with other libraries in the district.

"Glitches may happen, but it's likely that your organization and forethought will ensure that all will go smoothly."

Four Months in Advance (April)

- Place periodical orders, specifying the new library's correct mailing address.
- Contact all vendors to review detailed cataloging and processing specifications.
- Convene a meeting between librarians who are selecting the ODC and librarians and teachers who are well versed in curriculum.
  - Provide one copy of the printed list of proposed titles for each Dewey designation in the ODC.
  - Ask librarians and teachers to rotate and read the list for each section carefully, attending to curriculum needs, student needs, publication dates, grade level(s) for which materials are reviewed, and bindings.
  - Ask the group to add or delete titles as appropriate.
  - Check for newly-published materials to add.
- Compile and review the revised lists.

Three Months in Advance (May)

- Complete requisitions and place all orders for books, audiobooks, DVDs, professional materials, and online resources.
- Contact the district facilities office to determine when a certificate of occupancy will be given for the new campus.
- Consult campus administration before setting delivery dates.
- Work with the district purchasing office to coordinate the dates for delivery and assembly of shelving and furniture.
- Coordinate dates for all deliveries accordingly.

- Communicate dates to construction, purchasing, maintenance, administration, and vendors.

Two Months in Advance (June)

- Follow up with vendors. Is everything on track for timely delivery? Are cataloging and processing specs being followed correctly?
- Check in with construction. Has the date for occupancy changed?

One Month before School Starts (July)

- Ensure that shelving and furniture are in new condition and assembled and arranged correctly.
- Estimate the number of books for each Dewey designation and plan a shelving arrangement accordingly. Remember to leave shelf room for growth.
- Place a sticky note showing where each Dewey designation will begin.
- Have the vendor from which you ordered the largest number of items shelve first.
- Schedule one vendor at a time to intershelve other materials.
- Post attractive call number signage that is easily moved as your collection grows.
- Decorate the library in an attractive, uncluttered way that is appropriate to the age of your students.
- Consider procedures for the library that will enhance efficiency without overly restricting patrons.
- Rest, relax, and celebrate!

After a busy year of planning, August has arrived and the start of school is imminent. As in planning a wedding, there is a great deal of excitement and anticipation as the awaited day nears. Will the big event go off without a hitch? Glitches may happen, but it's likely that your organization and forethought will ensure that all will go smoothly. Now all that's left is to open the doors on the first day of school and warmly welcome students and staff to their beautiful new library.

Leigh Ann Jones, PhD *is coordinator of library services at Frisco (Texas) Independent School District and can be reached at jonesl@friscoisd.org.*

Jones, Leigh Ann. (2009). Something new . . . planning for your new school library. *LMC, 28*(1), 34–36.

Tactics for Tough Budget Times

By Ann M. Martin

Library supplies—cut 35%. Library subscriptions—cut 25%. Library books—cut 20%. How do you maintain high goals for instruction with dwindling funds? On a district level, the ability to do more with less is just not possible. It is the capability to reposition available resources that achieves critical goals. One way to visualize this concept is to think of a stretched elastic band. When that band is extended, it changes its shape to achieve different functions. So, to deliver more value for district dollars, it is necessary to stretch available funds by changing purchasing decisions. To maximize your budget allocation you need to prioritize, shop the best buy, and find funding support from additional sources. In a sense you are recreating purchasing power by using alternative solutions and innovative techniques to meet user demands.

A District-Level Decision Making Process

Prioritizing at the district level requires analyzing where the dollars are currently being spent and which resources serve curriculum needs best. If my database or book budget is cut, then obviously the same number of databases and books cannot be purchased. Holding the pricing at the same level as last year does help; yet a drop in budget means less money to spend. Since my budget has fewer dollars than in the year before, maintaining last year's pricing still means adjusting what is purchased. At the district level, prioritizing requires input from the field. Districtwide committees charged with the task to review resources provide critical decision making information. Their input assists in determining which purchases are essential to fulfill curriculum requirements and meet different skill levels. The committees advise me on what the librarian at the building level considers vital in order to deliver instruction.

Working with the database committee helped me to make smart decisions when decreases in the variety of databases offered by the state created additional financial burdens on the district. Many of the eliminated databases in my state are relevant to schools. This is a blow to school libraries who are dealing with diminishing local funds. So the combination of fewer state-provided databases and reduced local funds negatively impacts the number of available resources. To prioritize budgeting for this year, my district library database committee reviewed each of the database subscriptions as well as researched databases from other providers. As part of the vetting process, this committee surveyed all the librarians at each level elementary, middle, and high school to set priorities on the databases currently in use. The results provided a definite preference in content and vendor product. Wherever possible, they review two databases that contain similar subject matter but are offered by different providers. The idea is to provide choices in pricing. Based on the committee's recommendation and data, a $24,000 database was eliminated. Ironically, the database was a resource that everyone loved, but when examined we found that it was minimally used. Cutting this resource enabled the purchase of a database with a higher priority and need. This same process is possible for the variety of resources used in the school library.

> To maximize your budget allocation you need to prioritize, shop the best buy, and find funding support from additional sources.

Shopping for Alternatives

Shopping the best buy means finding alternatives, whether it is for databases or for print resources. Start by asking questions as they relate to your resources. Often the answers will frame choices for spending funds. For example, are there Web sites that offer information to replace resources? We replaced a poetry database with a Web site that provided similar information. Will teaching students how to use and evaluate RSS feeds, apps, and other digital means bring information to them? Instructing students on how to set up and evaluate information portals such as Google Alerts, RSS feeds, and expert opinions can reduce cost by providing a resource stream to users. Should e-books be considered? Often the e-books are priced lower than the print version. In our district, where there is a one-to-one laptop initiative for all secondary students, e-books makes sense. They are about half the price of hardbacks. Reading devices like the Kindle and Nook reduce expenses because a purchased title can be downloaded to six of these devices. If you are planning a community read, book club, or have a required reading program like Virginia Reader's Choice then perhaps purchasing those titles for an electronic reading device is an economical way to provide multiple copies of those titles.

Exploring answers to vendor related questions will also frame better decisions. Will a vendor offer better pricing if other districts purchase the resource together? Sometimes consortium buying is helpful. Collaborate with colleagues in other districts to write a Request for Proposal (RFP) for specific resources. It is time consuming to write an RFP, but if you team up the process is not so overwhelming. I need to mention that you must comply with your specific district and state purchasing guidelines when creating a joint RFP.

Can a vendor deliver deeper savings when you purchase several resources at once? Bundling resources may provide a broader range of products and expand your purchasing power.

Check Your Contracts and Your Contacts

In addition, determine how changes in contracts and billing can stretch budget dollars. Will an extended contract continue services and stabilize increasing prices? This past year I completed a service contract with the intention of alleviating the rising cost for our software maintenance. Working with the purchasing department, the school lawyer, and the vendor resulted in a contract for service that is renewable each year for five years. As a word of caution, be sure to have the contract reviewed by your legal department. In our district, funds for future years cannot be encumbered since the budget is dependent on variable revenues. This often means that coming to a decision on extended or multiple year contracts may be a complex, difficult legal process. The monetary benefit resulting from developing an extended contract is well worth the time invested working through the details. For example, I currently have a software service contract that spells out specifically the amount that my district will pay each year for five years out. Not only did I save $12,000 dollars the first year, but the cost for this maintenance is locked in for five years out. Continue to ask questions such as what am I actually paying for? Review your invoices. I found that one vendor was billing us without a line item explanation. When I asked for the line item breakout, I found that we were being charged for items that were no longer in place. It seems so obvious that a company would send detailed statements, but it doesn't always happen. By removing several items that were no longer used, approximately $2,000 was saved.

Work with others outside your district to obtain funding for your libraries. Target is a company that provides makeovers for school libraries. Visit your nearby Target to see if any of your schools qualify for

this grant. It helps to visit personally because the managers are able to put a face with a need. Our local newspaper has an online subscription to the newspaper that is cheaper than the print. By working with the management of the newspaper I was able to obtain pricing that maintains delivery of a print newspaper as well as a digital copy for each school. Some newspaper companies provide a digital subscription free with the print. Be sure to explore online newspaper parameters. Sometimes the connections to the digital paper are limited. You might decide that a print copy that can be read by multiple users is a better option. Options and considerations like these assist in saving money while stretching the budget.

Special Funding Initiatives

Also, look within your district to see where the money is flowing. Funds often follow federal programs, state mandates, and district initiatives. To become a viable recipient of these funds, formalize how the library program supports district objectives. Create a one page handout that relates the library mission and vision to instructional goals. Include an implementation timeline for the library support. It is effective to include additional data detailing the cost for the library program to support the initiative. When the preK program became a district priority, I surveyed the library collections and determined that preK materials in the school libraries were lacking and in some cases not evident. A committee of librarians, preK teachers, and public librarians developed a core list of titles needed to support the curriculum. Working with our book vendor, the suggested titles were reviewed for availability and binding preference. Then, armed with the resource list and pricing, I was able to seek financial assistance to purchase a preK core collection for each school library. What I thought was exciting about the addition of these books was that we gave the librarians essential tools to support a segment of the student population with unique needs. Funding for these materials

came from outside the district library budget to assist with instructional goals for the district.

Rather than initiate arbitrary budget decisions, plan to reposition your budget.

Communication Is Critical

Maintaining high expectations and curriculum goals can be achieved in spite of budget cuts, but it takes careful budgeting to position the available funds in a way that meets user needs. It also requires honesty when dealing with change. So be honest with the librarians and also with the vendors. Today, there is a level of understanding that was not present in times when money was more abundant. Yet consider giving your librarians as well as your vendors an opportunity to work with you. Let's face it. There is an extensive change occurring at the district level, which ripples down to the librarians and the vendors. Just because change is prolific, it does not make it any easier. Even though every school district is rethinking how to spend their dollars, I feel it is my responsibility as a district supervisor to constantly anticipate how each decision impacts instructional delivery. Change creates a domino effect, and the librarians in the buildings are impacted. For example, when resources are replaced, then instruction must be modified. So, it is important to talk with the librarians and let them know how the budget allocation creates a need to think differently. Inclusion means that the librarians are provided with the opportunity to understand the how and why of smarter spending. In the same way, it is important to be clear and explicit with vendors. Communicate your budget parameters to your vendors. This gives them an opportunity to work with you. Vendors know their pricing structure and options. In the end they may find a product pricing solution that enables you to make smart decisions.

There are Web sites devoted to elastic band tricks. What I have shared with you are not tricks but effective ways to take the budget you have and stretch it in a different direction. You can make impressive changes in order to impact instruction in a positive way. So rather than initiate arbitrary budget decisions, plan to reposition your budget. Visualize how the funds; though less, can be optimized to effectively meet your libraries' operational and instructional goals.

Ann M. Martin is currently the educational specialist for library information services at Henrico County Public Schools in Richmond, Virginia. She is president of the American Association of School Librarians (AASL), a Virginia Educational Media Association past president, an AASL board member, and a recipient of the 2002 AASL National School Library Media Program of the Year Award. Ann is author of Seven Steps to an Award-Winning School Library Program by Libraries Unlimited.

Martin, Ann M. (2011). Tactics for tough budget times. *LMC, 29*(4), 24–25.

Grant Writing without Blowing a Gasket

By Alicia Vandenbroek

Why Should I Fundraise?

No one woke up this morning asking for a budget cut, but the harsh reality is that in today's economic downturn it is becoming more and more common. Even libraries seen as a vital part of the educational process are subject to reductions because districts are suffering financially. Just as you've been tightening your personal finances, schools face the conundrum of funding exceptional programs with inadequate funding. The answer? Grants. They aren't a perfect solution, but there is a lot of financial support available for those who ask.

Besides the monetary gain, one commonly overlooked reward of grant funding is campus revitalization. This renewal comes in several forms. Other teachers are encouraged by your success and willing to take risks. Sometimes those risks involve using the materials you've acquired through your grant, and sometimes the risks involve funding for their own creative projects. Grants typically allow students access to a unique experience. This experience makes them broader educationally and usually involves a cross curricular project that develops lifelong learning.

Begin with the End in Mind

Beginning a grant can seem overwhelming if you don't break it into manageable pieces. Always start with the end in mind. In other words, what do you want? This can be money, supplies, experiences, and so on. Find the best deal by pricing these items in advance. Be honest with vendors so they know you might not actually place an order, but work out a deal that gets you the most value.

After you know exactly what you want, be creative and find a way to use those items or experiences in a student-friendly manner that directly supports curriculum. For the most part grants are geared toward directly impacting education; therefore, your proposal must be educationally

sound. Be careful not to over commit yourself; this is the voice of grants gone badly talking. You don't have to build the space shuttle, just engage and educate your students. Sometimes less really is more. Focus on your strengths or areas you would like to become your strengths. For example, I'm kind of a tech nerd, so a lot of times my grants focus on Web 2.0 tools and projects. If technology scares you (yes, I know you are out there) then focus on a different form of grant until you have had time to increase your technology prowess and feel comfortable taking on more challenging projects.

Check your progress:

- What supplies, projects, or experiences do you hope to gain?
- What classroom/library goals do those supplies, projects, or experiences support?
- Does the grant provide opportunities to be successful or highlight my skills?

The Perfect Pair

I wish I could tell you that there is a magical grant out there with your name on it already . . . but you know that doesn't even happen in fairy tales. That said the perfect paring of grant writer to grant funder is actually easier than you might expect. Once you know what outcomes you hope to achieve then you are ready to look for a perfect partnership.

Focus on grant funders whose goals and programs support your desired outcomes. For example, the first grant I ever applied for was a science grant. I submitted an innovative hands-on activity to a company who prides themselves on being cutting edge in their field. I got the grant with no problems. Of course no one is perfect, because recently, I applied for a grant to a very conservative library supporter for a somewhat out-of-the-box after school program. I didn't receive that grant because the proposal did not support the private

organization's opinions of what constitutes a strong library program.

After you find a source learn a little more about the company behind the funding. Are they a company with which you would feel proud to have your name/your school's name linked? If not, perhaps you should consider another funding source. All funders evaluate your program and ideas, so you should take time to ensure this is a mutually beneficial partnership.

Check your progress:

- Is the grant proposal a good match for the place that I'm applying?
- Is the company one of integrity and financial responsibility?

A Name Says a Lot about You

Think about your own name. Few people are ambivalent about their own name; it's usually either love or hate. It's not quite the same with grants, but it is pretty close. A grant proposal is only really as good as it can be remembered; this is where a catchy title comes into play. A simple catchy title will make your grant memorable and can speak volumes about the content of your grant before the reader even begins consideration.

Some easy pitfalls include using titles that say nothing (e.g. Grant Proposal), using titles that say too much (e.g. Grant Proposal to Use Digital Cameras to Teach Habitats on Wikis with Student Involvement and Corresponding Library Resources), or worse, using titles that say something only to people in your field (e.g. Region 11 NKLB Wiki Title I Grant Proposal). The latter is especially important because frequently people in other states or outside of your educational venue view these grants, so bogging them down in jargon distracts from the grant content.

Check your progress:

- Is your title creative (will it stand alone)?
- Is your title clear of buzz words or trite expressions?

Establishing a Budget

As you research the items for the grant, make sure you are following district policy. Some items, like technology, must be on an approved bid list, while others need only be from an approved vendor. Keep copies of quotes or catalogues so that when you receive the funding you will know exactly where the money goes. Work with vendors for discounts like free processing or shipping. Buying in bulk often means deeper discounts, so allow time to contact vendors directly. Include an itemized budget in the written proposal. If the grant is only one portion of the funding, be sure to reflect where additional funding sources are provided.

Check your progress:

- Have you followed district guidelines for purchasing?
- Do you have clear records or quotes for reference after you earn your grant?

Creating a Timeline

If you've ever been part of writing a campus plan you understand the importance of an accurate timeline. The timeline must be detailed but loose enough to allow flexibility. Always pad the time, allowing for Mr. Murphy to make his presence known. Build in time for processing, completion, reflection, evaluation, and reporting.

Your timeline should follow the S.M.A.R.T. principles:

Specific—detailed step by step
Measurable—results need to be quantifiable
Achievable—should be accomplished in the designated time
Realistic—clear expectations that are developmentally and academically appropriate
Time bound—succinct time structure, can be days or weeks but be consistent

Check your progress:

- Does your timeline cover every important part of the grant?
- Is the timeline flexible enough to allow for changes or difficulty?
- Does your timeline meet the S.M.A.R.T. principles?

Write, Write, Write

If you spent time in the first stages, this should prove to be a fairly easy part of the process. Be sure to refer to the helpful sites listed below for suggestions about where to locate frequently needed information. If a template is provided you are ready to start compiling the necessary information. If no template is provided, start with subject headings.

To ensure you meet all the guidelines of the grant, look at the directions and write the requirements of each section under the subject heading. Include information relating to word limits, required detail, information of importance, and so on. Once you have this shell you are ready to write. These bullet points will help keep you from getting off track and ensure you address all required items.

There are two schools of thought on writing a grant. Some grant writers suggest you write one section at a time, perfecting it before you go on, and some suggest a more holistic approach to writing the entire grant and then going back to fine tune the details. My suggestion is to do what makes the most sense to you.

Check your progress:

- Have you located a copy of the template or created your own document with subheadings?
- Have you used the directions and rubrics to make notes under each subheading?
- Have you written the necessary narratives adequately answering each item?

To Rubric or Not to Rubric—That is an Easy Question!

Grants always come with a written set of directions and protocols for grant submission. Consider this your primary rubric. In addition to those directions, grants frequently come with a rubric for scoring. If the company provides this type of rubric PLEASE use this valuable tool. Failure to use a rubric is no different than a student not utilizing a rubric you provide for a research paper and then failing because they didn't meet your expectations. Rubrics are the keys that set your grant apart from others

and take your proposal from average to exemplary.

If a template is not provided, use the directions of the grant to structure the proposal. After you write the grant, proofread it several times. The first proofread is for grammar and spelling. Second, screen for conceptual problems, and lastly review your rubric and directions, ensuring that you've adequately met the requirements. If time permits, allow a day in between each reading. Mistakes are caught easier with a fresh eye. Ask a colleague to review your work and compare it against the rubric. Frequently, they will catch contextual issues potentially overlooked.

Check your progress:

- Have you located a copy of the complete directions?
- Does your grant provide a rubric? If not, have you created your own rubric?
- Have you checked your rough draft for spelling?
- Have you checked your rough draft for conceptual problems?
- Have you compared your rough draft to the rubric and directions and made the necessary changes?
- Are the word counts at or below the required number?

Administrative Musts

Make sure your principal supports your project. Without administrative support your funding will not be approved. If your project involves collaboration, be sure all parties involved are committed. This can be a double-edged sword. There is strength in numbers and often working with partners provides flexibility; however, there is nothing more frustrating than having participants back out at the very last minute or not carry their portion of the workload.

Every school district has slightly different policies so it is important to adhere to the rules for your district. Typically, you will write a grant and submit it to the grants office for approval. After reviewing their suggestions, you submit the revised grant for the final necessary board approvals.

Check your progress:

- Does your principal support your program?
- Have you determined if you will work alone or with a partner?
- Have you followed the school district grant process?

After the Celebration

Take a moment to celebrate . . . you got grant funding! Remember this feeling, because this satisfaction fuels the desire for future success. But your work has only just begun. This next stage is critical for compliance with grant guidelines. If you apply for more than one grant in a calendar year, consider tracking your commitments using a spreadsheet.

Write down the dates on the timeline on your personal calendar with reminders of due dates a few weeks before required. Also jot down notes about what sort of documentation you will need. Throughout the project take photos for school publicity and photos for funders. Be sure any photos that leave the school do not have faces of students or faculty unless you have written permission from all parties involved. It is also helpful to keep copies of handouts or promotional items. If possible highlight the project using Web 2.0 technology on your school Web site. Not only will this increase parent support of the library, but potential donors usually take time to preview a school Web site before donating, and it is an easy commercial for effective collaboration.

Check your progress:

- Did you actually celebrate?
- Does your calendar reflect important upcoming events?

Submitting a Written Report

When you submit your report track the items you said you would. With that in mind, think about confidentiality of students. Make sure the information collected is aggregated rather than using individual student names. When sending the final report, a thank you goes a long way. This can be from

students or just from you but take a few minutes to thank the people who made your success possible. Before final submission, review the guidelines to ensure complete compliance.

Submit a duplicate copy of the written report to your principal and set up a meeting to review the success of the grant. Not only will this confirm you've completed the grant requirements, but it also shows administration your commitment to the school's success. Favorable outcomes mean more principal support not only for future grants but good money/supply management encourages the endowment of more funds when they become available.

The last copy goes in your personal portfolio. If you don't have a portfolio, start a simple three ring binder with copies of reports. This is a great tool when showcasing your classroom or library or when trying to procure additional funding.

Check your progress:

- Have you confirmed your written report met all the requirements of the grant?
- Are photos of students clear of student faces or do you have appropriate permissions?
- Did you review the written report with the principal or other supervisors?
- Does your portfolio contain a copy of the final report?
- Have you included Web 2.0 representations of the project on the school Web site?

Helpful Sites (Just a few to get you Started)

Grant Writing Sites

http://www.npguides.org/
http://712educators.about.com/od/grantwriting/Grant_Writing.htm
http://www.libraryspot.com/features/grantsfeature.htm
http://foundationcenter.org/getstarted/tutorials/shortcourse/index.html
http://librarysupportstaff.com/find$.html

Grant Sites

http://www.ed.gov/fund/landing.jhtml
http://school.discoveryeducation.com/schrockguide/business/grants.html
http://www.schoolgrants2009.com/
http://www.grantwrangler.com/
http://www.homeroomteacher.com/teacher_grants.html
http://www.donorschoose.org/homepage/main.html?zone=321
http://www.realschoolgardens.org/en/
http://librarygrants.blogspot.com/
http://www.technologygrantnews.com/grant-index-by-type/library-grants-funding.html
http://www.scholastic.com/librarians/programs/grants.htm

General Information

Community Demographics http://factfinder.census.gov/home/saff/main.html?_lang=en
Accountability Reports http://ritter.tea.state.tx.us/perfreport/aeis/index.html
TEKS http://ritter.tea.state.tx.us/teks/
School District ID http://nces.ed.gov/globallocator/

Bibliography

AISD. "Grant Application Procedures." [Online] 26 May 2009. <http://www.aisd.net>.

AISD. "Grant Process." [Online] 26 May 2009. <http://www.aisd.net>.

Browning, Bev. *Grant Writing for Dummies.* 2nd. Hoboken, NJ: Wiley Publishing, 2005.

Karsh, Ellen, and Arlen Sue Fox. *The Only Grant Writing Book You'll Ever Need.* New York: Carroll & Graff, 2003.

Susan M. Heathfield. "Beyond Traditional S.M.A.R.T. Goals." [Online] 26 May 2009. <http://http://humanresources.about.com/cs/performancemanage/a/goalsetting.htm>.

Alicia Vandenbroek *is a library media specialist at Shackelford Junior High in Arlington, Texas.*

Vandenbroek, Alicia. (2010). Grant writing without blowing a gasket. *LMC, 28*(6), 28–30.

Your School Needs a Frugal Librarian!

By Sara Kelly Johns

As budgets tighten and the use of library resources increases, your ingenuity, skill, and planning can ensure that your students and staff have the best you can select, buy, borrow or solicit. Strategizing for lean times includes a vigorous, deliberate promotion and marketing campaign. Administrators, teachers, parents, and the community will support a program they know about; you will develop a core of advocates as your program is perceived as vibrant and crucial.

At one of the earliest library conferences I attended, school librarian Joanne Stickler of Canton, New York, described her curriculum-based budgeting technique. Every requisition was submitted with a tie to a course (a new one or a data-supported lack of resources for an existing one) or a curriculum initiative. Our budgets support the entire curriculum; our resources are essential to learning. Every time a requisition is processed, it's obvious to administrators why it's crucial for the school, building support for your program.

Working with Vendors

Speaking of conferences, connecting with the vendors' representatives face-to-face in the exhibits reaps discounts, advice, tips on grant sources, the best swag—all available to you. If you walk in with a targeted list of needs, you will get to compare prices and specs, often concluding a great deal with a conference discount. On Facebook, John Sandstrom, El Paso Public Library, advised, "Never be afraid to ask questions of vendors. Ask if they are giving you the best discount, the most service, the greatest help available. The worst that can happen is they say no."

Taking sales reps' phone calls with e-mail follow-ups, signing up for companies' e-mail alerts, and "friending" companies on Facebook are all worthwhile. Debra L. Maier, Ontario Primary School, Ontario Center, New York, is always ready for the Bound to Stay Bound $6.00 sale at the beginning of October. Other vendors might offer deals such as, "Buy 4 books and get one free" or "Spend $350 and get $150 worth of free material."

> *"When you have credibility and logic on your side, you can make some interesting offers that can't be refused."*

Careful Selection

When funds are limited, it's time to sharpen your selection process, choosing those materials that are most effective at enticing students to read and provide high quality information. Amy Ipp, Millburn Middle School, New Jersey, checks circulation records for series books. If circulation is low, she does not purchase sequels beyond the second title.

In presentations I attended this year, Joyce Valenza, Springfield Township High School Library, Pennsylvania, said that we no longer can or need to have a physical collection of "just in case" materials available. The perfectly balanced collection that we learned to assemble in library school is not possible and may not even be needed. It IS necessary for us to provide access to high quality materials and information. Through interlibrary loan, immediately streamable downloads, accessible audio/ebook collections, and such services as PaperbookSwap.com, we can provide "long-tail" books for our students, whose interests are wider than ever. Local bookstores offer discounts for "just in time" books—and there are no shipping costs.

Our physical collection needs to reflect the students we have coming through our doors now. Our virtual collection needs to take advantage of state-provided databases while studying usage statistics to subscribe to others that are actually used—at the best price you can negotiate or obtain through consortia. Albany, New York, school library system director Linda Fox suggested on Facebook, "Take advantage of consortia. If you don't have a school library system or regional consortium—start one! There is strength in numbers."

To stretch your dollars, virtual resources need to include wide accessibility with remote passwords. Churchville-Chili (New York) Middle School librarian Marie Barron suggests, "When buying e-books, look for companies offering unlimited simultaneous users. Patrons might have to enter a password to access it remotely but it's worth the inconvenience to have multiple copies available."

About five years ago, I scrutinized my magazine order to remove titles that were readily available in databases, replacing many with the titles that would encourage students to read more—titles like *Dirt Bike*, *Transworld Snowboarding* (remember, it's Lake Placid), *Games*, and *Junior Miss*. Pauline Herr, LaGrange (New York) Middle School librarian concurs: "I can't buy a lot of periodicals anymore. I buy some that I hope will entice readers. I encourage students and teachers to use our databases for those periodicals that may [offer] more research and current events (such as *Newsweek*)." EBSCO's recent purchase of exclusive rights to several magazines makes it difficult if you don't have access to their databases. One solution is adding links on your Web site to free online versions of the magazines that are no longer full-text in your databases.

Bartering

When you have credibility and logic on your side, you can make some interesting offers that can't be refused. Mindy Holland from Pinewood Elementary School in Rotterdam, New York, convinced her principal to give the library half of the money that used to go into classroom libraries, a considerable amount. She used the money to set up an organized, catalogued book room that is available to all.

Sharing resources with another department is possible, too. After years of searching for instances of suspected plagiarism with mixed results, the English department chair and I shifted funds (with the help of the business manager) to purchase a subscription to Turnitin.com, keeping the connection to ethical use of information part of the school library program (we ordered and administered it).

> "Donations are great—if they fit in your library's collection. Always ask yourself whether the resource is worth more than the barcode and book pocket."

depends

Community Help

The investment in press releases, informative Web sites, board presentations, presentations to community groups, participation at PTO meetings, and other visibility and promotion activities pays dividends when your own budget needs to be supplemented. Amy Ipp wrote a proposal for her PTO when they lost the state funding for a database (EBSCO), and they agreed to fund it for the coming year.

Marie Barron's PTO purchases paperback book giveaways during *Teen Read Week* and *Black History Month* while Lisa Von Drasek, Bank Street College of Education School for Children Librarian, New York City, tries not to buy paperback series books like *Magic Tree House* or *Goosebumps*. Instead, she puts out a fall request to parents whose kids have outgrown them to donate them to the library. She also asks for donations for duplicate copies of high-interest series books like *Lemony Snicket* and *Lightning Thief*.

Lisa Hunt, librarian at Apple Creek Elementary School in Moore, Oklahoma, expected low or no funding this year, so she planned

strategically by talking to her PTA, "Although we do book fairs each year (and use the money for the library), I know the PTA always targets their fundraising project for something the school needs. They were prepared that I would ask for this in August 2010. I did and they voted to support the library with 85 percent of their fundraising efforts this year."

Henrico County's very resourceful Theresa Harris from Glen Allen Elementary School, Virginia, gets support from parents for supplies during open house/back to school night: "I put book-shaped stickies on my door with a catchy phrase about supplies. On each sticky is a supply that I could use if parents want to donate items to the library. I usually put items such as a ream of colored paper, markers, stickers, hand sanitizer, tissues, empty coffee cans (for crayons, markers, etc), old wallets (we use those for *Bunny Money* by Rosemary Wells), etc. While I don't get all the items, it is an easy, less invasive way to "beg" for supplies."

Hermosa's (California) fifth annual Taste at the Beach event will offer fine food from their best restaurants and a silent auction hosted by the Kiwanis Club. Proceeds from the social will benefit the libraries at Hermosa Valley School and Hermosa View School since the libraries' hours of operation were cut back. The community is aware of the need and is supporting their students' learning.

Debra Maier creates a "Celebrate with a Book" shelf display for a special event or birthday celebration, with inexpensive Junior Library Guild books from their backlist to offer gifts at a low cost. The PTA helps her by floating the original funds, and the checks or cash go back to them.

Consortia Leveraging

Make full use of any cooperative services that might be available. In New York state, the regional Boards of Cooperative Services (BOCES) and school library systems provide services that can cut costs. In addition to negotiating the best database prices and loaning displays and professional books, Marie Barron's BOCES media library loans iPod Shuffles to students. She shares that, "They are

also willing to take suggestions for new purchases and have the ability to purchase the titles immediately, download the audiobook, upload it to the iPod, and ship it to the school. It's an amazing service." As Linda Fox said above, if you aren't part of a consortium, start one.

Grants

This is certainly the time to write small and large grants. Lisa Hunt applied for the Dollar General Youth Literacy Grant and a Wal-Mart Grant. She says, "I've discovered the beauty of the small numbers grants. I used to skip over the things that were $100 or $200 maximum. However, I've learned that small amount is just enough to get the ten personal CD players I need, or two Flip cameras. Over the last five years, I've changed my planning strategy because we always have less money instead of more."

Central New York school library system director Judy Marsh was recently awarded an Improving Literacy through School Libraries grant for $339,335 for two elementary school libraries, Geneva West and North Street. The funds have to be expended in a year! That grant was originally authorized at $250 million but has never been funded at more than $19.4 million. ALA successfully lobbied for it to be separated from other federal grants this year. ALA Council passed a unanimous resolution urging funding for at least $100 million to greatly benefit school libraries. Watch for advocacy opportunities to support this initiative.

Free!

You sure can't beat the price when resources are free. Donations are great—if they fit in your library's collection. Always ask yourself whether the resource is worth more than the barcode and book pocket. Seriously, a donation policy or clause in your selection policy is helpful. My standard phrase is, "If we can't find a place in our collection, I will offer them to teachers." And I do. If they don't need them, ALA has a donation fact sheet listing worthy causes: http://www.ala.org/ala/professional

resources/libfactsheets/alalibrary factsheet12.cfm.

Setting up wish lists is a strategic way to be ready if requests to help or monetary donations come your way. Colette D. Eason, librarian at the Marsalis Elementary School ISD, Dallas, Texas, suggests one way: "Mackin has a great program where parents, community, or others may donate to an account that you set up for the purpose of this program." Other companies do so, too, as well as book fairs, both actual and virtual. Along with Scholastic's fairs, Christine Schein, District Tech Strand Coordinator/Information Literacy Specialist at Academy District 20, Colorado Springs, Colorado, suggests book fairs through Barnes and Noble or Borders because they set up and you can purchase through them with educator discount cards.

Marie Barron increases her collection by tying print and online resources together: "I can't afford to purchase multiple copies of the popular graphic novels. So when the titles or volume numbers are out, I suggest the student try reading the missing volumes online. I have links to a few of the more popular Web sites for reading online on the library's Web site."

Karen Kliegman, Searingtown School in Albertson, New York, suggests stretching your library dollars virtually: "Take advantage of free Web 2.0 tools to take the place of expensive word processing, presentation, and mindmapping software." Christine Schein suggests using open source software to replace or extend

expensive software licenses. She listed Google Docs, Wordle, Wallwisher, Photostory, Audacity, Epearl, Moodle, and Moviemaker.

Christine Schein also suggested showing students how to use the online catalog at the public library. Students can use the holds feature and then pick up their materials. Lisa Weinstein, librarian at Century Junior High in Orland Park, Illinois, suggested borrowing displays from other librarians. One of her colleagues borrowed all the pieces needed for a bulletin board about books made into movies, saving money AND time. Not free, but cheap and helpful to the public library, is shopping library book sales, such as the Friends of the Library book sale where Stefanie Halliday of Bellville High School Library, Michigan, finds two to three books every week.

"Strategizing for lean times includes a vigorous, deliberate promotion and marketing campaign."

Debra Maier enters contests and free drawings, once winning a classroom set of paperback Curious George books. She also subscribes to free magazines, such as the LEGO magazine.

School libraries are crucial to learning but need resources to close

the digital and print divide that widens as school budgets shrink. Your time and ingenuity can make a difference for your students. Your efforts will be appreciated by your staff, administration, and the public as you provide virtual resources and get those grants, donations, and loans from other libraries. And, of course, publicize your efforts. You will build that core of advocates to keep your program strong.

As preparation for this article, I surveyed school librarians by using my state school library association discussion list, AASLForum, LM_NET, and Facebook. To extend the "hit" beyond this article, I created a wiki. Check out http://frugalschool-librarian.wikispaces.com to adapt an idea for your library—and add YOUR best tip. In these lean times, let's keep this going!

Reference

Howard, Jacqueline. "Taste at the Beach Benefits School Libraries." *Hermosa Beach Patch*, 23 Aug. 2010. http://hermosabeach.patch.com/articles/taste-at-the-beach-benefits-school-libraries.

Sara Kelly Johns *is an instructor for the Mansfield University School Library & Information Technology Program, ALA councilor at large, AASL Legislative Committee in Saranac Lake, New York, and AASL past president.*

Johns, Sara Kelly. (2011). Your school needs a frugal librarian! *LMC, 29*(4), 26–29.

No Budget? Build a Community of Library Supporters!

By Lelia Rogers

Last year I left my position as a ninth grade English teacher to become school librarian of Prospect Elementary School in rural Seymour, Tennessee. Our Title 1 school serves about 400 students in grades K-5. I was thrilled to take my first library position in a brand new school with computers and Smart Boards in every classroom and with the most supportive, encouraging, and capable principal I could have hoped for.

Real Life, Not a Fairy Tale

Only one part of this fairy tale fell short of wonderful—an annual library budget of zero! I was given $10,000 to start my collection, which purchased about 700 books from Follett. You can compare that to the $70,000 in startup money given to a grades 4–8 school that opened in a neighboring school district. After receiving the money to start up the collection, I was told that I had no hope of receiving funding in future budget years and should also not expect supply money to purchase the basics, like barcode labels or even a shelving cart.

> All this time spent fundraising means less time working face to face with kids and developing the top-notch programming I want to offer.

Looking for Support

Despite these obstacles I was still thrilled to be part of this new school and optimistic about the future. I had great visions for this place and shared my excitement. I got busy immediately looking for help.

Within a week of landing the job, I created a handout titled "Ways to Help the Prospect Elementary School Library." I started asking everyone I knew for donations of books that could either be used in the library or traded for other books. My mother painted signs for the different sections. With my own money I purchased a rocking chair and a decorative tree from Cracker Barrel. The library was starting to take shape.

That first month I also got busy applying for grants, particularly through Donors Choose. I have found that most people recognize the importance of giving kids access to books and are eager to support such a worthy cause. I begged for help everywhere, from Facebook to craigslist. I fundraised every way I could. In December I decorated a holiday tree in the library with small paper trees, each listing a book title that was needed for the library. Students donated over $1,000 for the titles we needed, and in return I placed a sticker bookplate inside the new books to recognize the donation. Steadily over the course of a year the donations kept coming.

A Supportive Community

Supporters of the library included a local Sunday school class, the Kiwanis Club, a grant from Samsung for a document camera, matching funds from the Modern Woodmen and Denso, a grant from Lowes, our school PTO, the Coordinated School Health Committee, Scholastic Book Fair, Prestige Cleaners, Adopt-a-Classroom, a Titlewave fundraiser, and, of course, money and book donations from our parents. In two years, over $20,000 has been raised. Our book collection has jumped from 700 to 8,500 titles. Now our kids can actually find books that interest them (most of the time)!

> Most people recognize the importance of giving kids access to books and are eager to support such a worthy cause.

Tradeoffs and Rewards

When I think of how far we have come and how full our shelves are, it sometimes takes my breath away. I cannot take full credit for it—this amazing community rallied behind the many needs of our library and helped transform this place. Do we have all the books, periodicals, and technology we need now? Absolutely not. Does running my library like a nonprofit agency sometimes come at a high price? Yes. All this time spent fundraising means less time working face to face with kids and developing the top-notch programming I want to offer. I currently have $500 in my library account for next year. I have no idea how, or even if, I will be able to raise the money to purchase more books and supplies. Still, I do everything I can to fight for the resources these kids crave and need to grow. I hope one day our library will be properly funded and I can focus on doing what I love and am trained to do.

Lelia Rogers *is the librarian at Prospect Elementary School in Seymour, Tennessee. She may be reached at lelia.rogers@ blountk12.org.*

Rogers, Lelia. (2013). No budget? Build a community of library supporters! *LMC, 32*(2), 22.

If Kids Designed School Libraries: The Top-10 List + Wild Things

By Sue Stidham

What would kids say if asked to design a school library? Ninety-two students from twenty-three schools were interviewed to find out. Four students from each school were interviewed: an avid reader, a nonreader, a nonconformist, and an artistic student. Money was not to be an issue. This study, not meant to be scientific, provided an insight into what kids want in a school library.

Technology: Super laptops for every student in the school library were the number one request. Databases, color printers, and tech support for when the computers didn't work were viewed as a must. Students expressed a concern about filtering systems that blocked valuable sites. Time before and after school to use the computers was requested, as was 24/7 access. Having the ability to log in from home and reserve books for the next school day was also important. Finally, students wanted the rows of computers to go away. Instead, they wanted laptops on tables and they preferred round tables over rectangular ones.

Design: A futuristic café-style design with a skylight was envisioned. Wood was to be avoided because it "makes the library look old." Instead of one all-purpose room, three areas were preferred: one for reading, one for lounging, and one for projects. The project room would include stations for school-related projects, while the lounge area would include i-Pods with earphones, a large plasma television, and video games. The preference was for different sizes of tables in small and large groupings. Carpet was preferred to tile. A common request was for background music similar to mall stores.

Seating: Students wanted modern, ergonomic furniture that was designed specifically for their size. Descriptive words included comfy, squishy, and soft. Older students wanted leather couches with accompanying end tables, and these couches were to be spread throughout the library along with comfy chairs. Bean bags were repeatedly requested and futons and recliners were mentioned. Younger students wanted chairs that represented different books like a rocking chair for reading Goldilocks. All furniture needed to be in bright colors.

> *"We need librarians because they know what they are doing and know how things work. They specially know more about books than maybe anyone in there."*

Color: Students didn't want boring "adult" colors. Instead, they wanted bright, vibrant and eye catching colors like yellow with bright green, pink with silver, turquoise, orange, yellow, blue, hot pink with black, dark blue with light green, purple, red, white, and bright neon. More than one group mentioned using school logo colors. Also suggested were random colors in a blend of different, fun patterns. Students echoed that the current look was "really boring and dull" and "wanted colors that made them feel happy."

Walls: Walls were also considered boring. The majority wanted interesting, promotional posters that carried a powerful message. Another suggestion was to decorate the walls with murals of characters in children's literature. One group suggested a theme painted on the walls, but they wanted the students to vote on the theme. Finally, students reported emphatically, "No posters about drinking milk!"

Noise level: Students reported that noise level should be lower for those reading and higher for those working on projects. They believed that noise should be regulated but that soft talking should be allowed. One summed up the thought of others: "I think there should be a specific room or area for kids who are actually bothered by the noise and another for kids making noise. There are times when students just can't be quiet and it's not their fault."

Books and Reading Materials: Students wanted enough books for everyone, and they wanted new hardback books in larger quantities. They also wanted magazines, comic books, and book related videos. I-students wanted downloadable books and CD-formatted books. Students requested two computers dedicated to inventory search and checkout, and they preferred touch screen book finders like commercial book stores.

Games: Boys were especially focused on games—brain games, board games, and puzzles. Boys also wanted video games located in a room away from the "reading" room in the library so students wouldn't be disturbed. They wanted access to games before and after school and believed that video games should be used for reward during school. The system of choice was Nintendo DS Wii with all of the educational games available.

Social Networking: Social networking was requested with both Facebook and MySpace at the forefront. The i-students wanted to send text messages to each other in the library. And no concern was expressed for Internet safety.

Librarian: A consensus was reached—librarians were wanted and needed. "Of course a librarian would be in charge of the library. Librarians have gone to college and learned how to run the software, how to keep records of books, and how to handle certain books. They are the ones that check us out and dedicate their lives to books." And another said, "We need librarians because they know what they are doing and know how things work. They specially know more about books than maybe anyone in there." For schools that didn't currently have a librarian, students wanted a "real" librarian.

Wild Things: The "out of the box" thinkers suggested a tree house, a loft, and a crow's nest located above the main level so students could have a private area to read. They wanted a real alligator and sharks in the project area. Other ideas included a haunted house, Starbucks, water fountain, snack bar, dessert bar, exercise equipment, vending machine, and gift shop to purchase books, t-shirts and movies. And the final two "wild thing" requests—turning books upside down for a creative effect and a holographic librarian.

So what could be learned from this survey? Kids had ideas about what they wanted and needed in a school library, and they even had a sense of humor. And some of their ideas were realistic and could be implemented without much expense or time, while other suggestions were just the opposite. When kids were asked to design a school library, they were sensitive to their own wants and needs and to those of others. More important, they were still optimistic enough to see their school library as an opportunity for change.

_____

Sue Stidham *is an associate professor in the Library Media Program at Pittsburg State University in Pittsburg, Kansas.*

Stidham, Sue. (2010). If kids designed school libraries: The top-10 list + wild things. *LMC, 29*(1), 22.

Creating a Lean, Green, Library Machine

Easy Eco-Friendly Habits for Your Library

By Amy S. Blaine

It's T.G.I.F. at the Wasteful Elementary School Library. Teachers and students alike are ready for the weekend. Before the library media specialist turns out the lights (if she remembers) she takes a final look at the library media center, making a mental note of all the things she should do upon her return. Leaving the computers and monitors on will save time come Monday morning, that's for sure. The trash can, filled with extra handouts from a recent lesson on note taking, needs to emptied into the school dumpster. Colorful, albeit expensive, sticky notes next to each computer terminal help students jot down a call number as needed. Earth Day and Television Turnoff week are coming up fast, but who has time to single-handedly plan for yet another "Day" let alone an entire "Week"? The door closes and the LMS heads out into the early June heat, leaving the well air-conditioned comfort of her media center behind.

If this scenario sounds familiar, you are probably not alone. For some library media specialists, implementing the three Rs of recycling, reducing, and reusing comes easily; they've been environmentally conscious well before the concept of going green made its way into the vernacular. Yet for some of us, the thought of greening our library, let alone the entire school, can seem rather daunting. Whether you want to begin eco-friendly practices in your library in response to school-based initiatives or to take the lead in developing a school-wide program, it can be helpful, and encouraging, to learn some eco-friendly ways to become a lean, green, library machine.

> The library is often the technology hub of the school yet, as a result, can become the school's energy hog as well.

Get Energized

Let's face it; the library is often the technology hub of the school yet, as a result, can become the school's energy hog as well. If you have pods or banks of computer terminals, know that even equipment that is shut down still draws small amounts of power; to prevent this, switch power strips to the off position when the equipment is not in use for extended periods of time. The United States Department of Energy recommends that you turn off computer monitors when they will remain unused for more than 20 minutes and shut off both the computer and monitor if unused for more than two hours. While this may not be practical or even needed in a high traffic library, shutting down equipment for the weekend and during longer breaks makes your library a bit more energy efficient and cooler. If you are fortunate enough to have an individual thermostat for your library, consider turning the heat down just a couple of degrees in winter and putting on that sweater or shrug instead. For those of us in hazy, hot, and humid climates, take a hard look at your use of air-conditioning or make sure that your thermostat is keeping you comfortably cool but not frozen. Ceiling fans, window blinds, and cross-ventilation help keep costs and energy use down.

> For more information, and inspiration, on going green at your library, visit the following resources:
> **Treehugger** (<www.treehugger.com/>)
> For information and related links on everything from no VOC paints to thinking green in the classroom, this Web site is one-stop shopping for all things green.
> **U.S. Environmental Protection Agency Earth Day**. <www.epa.gov/earthday/>

> **Earth Day 2010**. (ww2.earthday.net/)
> Earth Day 2010 will mark the 40th anniversary of this annual celebration. These are just two Web sites of many that have suggestions for promoting this April event at your school and in your community.
> **U.S. Department of Energy Energy Savers**. <www.energysavers.gov>
> This government site provides energy saving strategies for both the home and workplace.
> **How Can I Recycle This?**
> This Web site is a librarian's dream. Originating from the United Kingdom, this clever site relies on its readers to come up with novel ideas for reusing common (and sometimes not so common) goods from expired instant coffee to old compact discs.

Where Have You Bin? Using That Strange Blue Bucket

Is your waste bin truly that: a *waste* bin? Or is it filled with items that really belong in the recycling bin: that oft forgotten, usually blue bucket that somehow manages to become another catch-all for trash? If your library is anything like mine, it plays host to everything from teacher appreciation luncheons to coffee hours for the parents of rising fifth graders. Make it easier for your guests to recycle by having designated bins (a cardboard box lined with a garbage bag will do) in obvious places. Simply marking them "Recycle your cans and bottles here!" will let your library users know that the library considers recycling important. Recycling is all well and good, but it still takes energy to give your used goods a second life. One of the smartest ideas I ever saw was at a bake sale at a local church. People de-cluttered their kitchens by donating their unwanted ceramic coffee mugs. Later, at the bake sale, those who bought a cup of coffee had it served to them in a real (not Styrofoam or paper) cup that you could then take home with you. A mug with coffee included all for 50 cents! To introduce this idea at your school or library, ask staff, teachers or parents to clean out their cupboards. No doubt you'll have a stash of reusable mugs for your next library coffee or tea.

> *Picture books that teach stewardship of the earth such as Barbara Cooney's* Miss Rumphius *can inspire entire lessons that focus on the positive.*

From Cartridges to Cleaners

Office supplies are not unique to school libraries, of course, but we do have some rather specialized functions that can lend themselves to recycling or reusing. How do you handle interoffice mail such as interlibrary loans? Do you use a brand new envelope each time or can you use a transmittal envelope with room for more than one address? Don't forget to recycle any and all ink cartridges and toners from printers and photocopiers. Suppliers have programs that allow you to mail back used cartridges or toners at no cost. Your local office supply store may have a similar program, sometimes with incentives. Also, how many extra library supply catalogs are you receiving each year? Call library supply companies to have the number of catalogs mailed to

you reduced, or better yet, ask to be removed from their mailing list and shop via their Web sites instead. And while you're cleaning house by recycling all those catalogs, think about how you clean your physical space as well. You may not be able to convince the custodial staff to go green with their cleaning products, but for your own daily use you can make some simple changes. Spray bottles filled with water and white vinegar solution (the smell dissipates as it dries) is often all you need for cleaning tabletops and countertops. Or you may want to stick with a name brand green cleaner that is a more natural alternative. Of course, if a flu outbreak or stomach virus is making the rounds, you'll want to follow the direction of your school's administration when it comes to cleaning and disinfecting. Finally, if you're fortunate enough to have some extra funding for your library space, consider purchasing items made from recycled or eco-friendly materials. This can mean anything from carpet squares made from recycled plastic bottles to no or low VOC (volatile organic compounds) paints. While no or low VOC paints can be budget-busters, consider them if you are re-painting or painting a smaller section of your library such as a reading nook.

Earth Friendly Program Planning

Earth Day and Television Turnoff Week occur during the same week each year, providing us with a great way to link stewardship of the earth with a reduction in screen time. When I came on board at my elementary school, our school's green team was already in full force, with a fifth grade teacher as the team's advisor. While the green team handled a week's worth of events from recycling juice pouches to sponsoring an endangered animal poster contest, I assisted by creating Earth Day activity reminder fliers for teachers to place over their classroom television sets each day. For schools that rely on their closed circuit television system for morning announcements, it can be a bit of a challenge to get the word out about Television Turnoff Week without turning on the televisions! Use fliers

(but consider one per classroom to conserve paper), ask if students can use the overhead intercom for Earth Day announcements, or have a brief school assembly. If your budget allows, BPA-free plastic or stainless steel water bottles are nice prizes for students who are "thirsty for books." Does your school distribute an annual "school spirit" item? Suggest a reusable library book bag with your library media center logo on it!

If your school does not already have a green team, think about what it would take to establish one. Library media specialists are in a unique position because they are often the only teachers that interact with every student and every teacher. If hosting a plethora of activities sounds like biting off a bit more than you can chew, focus on just one green activity for the year. For example, library media specialist Elena Rodriguez of Gunston Middle School in Arlington, Virginia, readily admits she used her position as a "bully pulpit" to establish and coordinate a recycling program for her entire school. How did she do it? She piggybacked recycling education onto her school-wide "Reading is Fundamental" (RIF) programming, held three times a year. "I also used my role as Web master," she says, "to create a fairly comprehensive Web site with recycling information." To see what Ms. Rodriguez and her school's green team are up to, visit their Web site at <http://bit.ly/2HgP0r>.

In Print and Online

And finally there are the library resources themselves. Consider when electronic resources can substitute for paper resources. Do you need to purchase a hard copy of an encyclopedia every other year or, with an online database as your backup, would every five years suffice? In addition, a student (or staff) book swap is a great way to reuse books that students have purchased on their own. Make it easy on yourself by instituting a simple one-for-one rule (students can pick as many books as they donate) and nothing more. Remember, the goal is to get used books into the hands of new owners and not be a stickler for complicated rules and procedures.

Collection development is another important opportunity to spread the gospel of green. Think out of the box when it comes to fiction and nonfiction that address environmental topics. Nonfiction titles about recycling and global warming are the most obvious examples, but what about fiction choices such as Hoot by Carl Hiaasen or Seed Folk, by Paul Fleischman? Both make excellent choices for student books clubs (over waste-free lunches) that focus on the environment. Picture books that teach stewardship of the earth such as Barbara Cooney's Miss Rumphius

can inspire entire lessons that focus on the positive. Consider fun nonfiction additions to your collection such as arts and crafts books that provide instruction on making crafts from recycled materials. Encourage students by offering to display their works of recycled art in the library.

It's T.G.I.F. at Wastenot Elementary School Library. Teachers and students alike are ready for the weekend. Before the library media specialist turns out the lights (an adorable light bulb die cut affixed to the switchplate reminds anyone who passes by), she takes a final look at the library, making mental note of all the things she should do first thing on Monday morning. Her student assistants will start the day by turning on all the lights and the power strips before they boot up the computers. Next, two third-graders will swing by to take the bin of used paper to the recycling bin on the school's loading dock. Cans and bottles left over from the previous

week's staff meeting will be carted off as well. Before opening the doors to the students, she'd better be sure that the holders next to the computer terminals are re-stocked with scrap paper cut into squares for note-taking (sure saved her money on those expensive sticky notes that were used once and then tossed). And finally she makes a mental note to have her latest ideas ready for her meeting with the green team's advisor. There's not much time to coordinate activities for Earth Day and Television Turnoff Week! The door closes and the LMS heads out into the early June heat. Ahhhh… it's good to be green!

Amy S. Blaine *is a library media specialist at Jamestown Elementary School in Arlington, Virginia. She can be reached at amysblaine@gmail.com.*

Blaine, Amy S. (2010). Creating a lean, green library machine: Easy eco-friendly habits for your library. *LMC, 28*(4), 24–26.

Making Your School Library More Functional to Individuals with Autism

By Andrea Bress

Imagine going to a school library in search of a certain book, but when you look on the shelves you perceive that the books are arranged by color or by size as opposed to the Dewey Decimal system. As we go about our daily routines at home or in school, it is easy to take for granted that our world is conducive to the way most of us think and process information. We tend to overlook the notion that not every brain works the same way. Autism spectrum disorder (ASD) is a neuro-developmental disability that affects an individual's social interaction and communication development and may result in restrictive interests, repetitive or problem behaviors. Individuals with ASD struggle to live in a nonsensically structured world.

Libraries as Comfortable, Low Stress Places

The number of individuals with ASD visiting school libraries continues to increase as the diagnosis of the disorder increases. The Centers for Disease Control and Prevention (CDC, 2012) reported one in every eighty-eight children is identified with ASD. Rather than being another confusing environment, school libraries have the potential to contribute to the students' educational plan. Autism Speaks, the world's largest autism science and advocacy organization, has identified leisure participation in libraries as excellent environments for individuals with ASD (Autism Speaks, 2011). Libraries are comfortable, interesting, and low stress places for people with ASD. Libraries have predictable rules, logical layouts, systematically arranged materials, and some quiet areas—all characteristics of environments that support this

population. Technology—another common interest of students with ASD—that enables them to function independently is often available (Ennis-Cole & Smith, 2011). Libraries are important avenues for accessing community resources and have the potential to serve as a safe and acceptable location to explore interests, connect with others, and participate in self-directed learning.

Modifications, Big and Small

How does your school library support this very diverse group? Let us consider how adjustments can be made in the school library environment to support the needs of individuals. A problem that persists in settings such as a classroom or library is the number of distractions. For an individual with ASD, these aspects of the environment can make or break their concentration and comfort level. It is easy to overlook certain things, like posters on the wall, the pattern on the floor, and even the amount of light in a room that may result in the student fixating or focusing all attention on the pattern rather than engaging with the learning materials. Lighting is also a common problem when there are bright lights or large windows distracting.

Students with ASD generally benefit from routine, another reason why the library can be a good learning environment for them. Students with ASD are likely to be more comfortable knowing that every time they visit a place they will have a similar experience. This can be supported by keeping the furniture and books in the same place, having a specific place for technology, and paying close attention to the structure of walkways. Using a self-checkout system is also helpful because this

process is consistent, and once the student learns to use the system successfully, it can be continued on each visit.

A Simple Space Solution

A simple corner can be utilized to create an environment with minimal distractions. Furniture can be turned to face the corner, away from any windows or other disturbances. The reason a corner is more effective than just a desk barrier is that "even when some learners have a visual barrier, they are so distracted by the noise of other activities that they constantly get up and look over or around the barrier" (Janzen, 2003). Sometimes the barrier itself can be somewhat distracting. Remove any clutter or decorations from the walls. If possible, replace bright overhead lights with lamps or low light. This quiet space may enhance the student's ability to focus comfortably and help him or her feel in control of the environment.

Visual supports and cues can play a critical role in understanding the layout and structure of the library, the process for finding and checking out books, and the library rules. Visual cues can be anything from item labels to describing the procedures of checking out a book. Visual supports provide an alternate format to enhance understanding of the library's structure, organization, and processes.

Benefits for All

Making slight adjustments in the school library will reap benefits for individuals with ASD. These adjustments might have the added benefit of helping all students who need structure and routine.

Suggestions from the point of view of an individual with ASD:

A simple, clutter-free environment will help me focus.

- I am more comfortable in a space with limited visual or auditory stimulation. Piles of books on carts or papers on the walls divert my attention and may increase my stress.

I like things to be the same.

- Consistency is important. I like it when the furniture and other materials stay in the same place. A simple floor map can help me get started and will help again if furniture or displays have been rearranged. Once I find my way around, I can rely on that knowledge when I return.

I am most comfortable when I can access a quiet space.

- A desk or a soft, comfortable chair placed in the corner of a room is ideal. Having secluded workstations throughout the library can make me feel like I can work and read without being disturbed. It can also serve as a spot I can go to when being involved with the other students gets to be too much for me. I can take a few minutes to refocus and de-stress.

For me, picture signs and simple written text are more helpful than oral directions.

- I am a visual learner. A list or picture board of the library rules is important. Pictorial labels on bookshelves at the end of aisles make more sense to me and may provide the support I need to learn the Dewey Decimal System. Directions on how to check out books or use the computer are also very helpful.

It may be hard for me to communicate my wants and needs or ask for help.

- I may not be able to speak to you easily. Looking at people's faces and initiating conversations can be difficult, especially if I do not know you. I can use visual cues, such as pointing or nodding, or a communication device such as picture symbols. A self-checkout desk would be beneficial to me because I could be independent. I feel comfortable not needing to interact with someone else.

I have special interests.

- This is a good thing because when I come to the library, there are topics or activities I am going to enjoy. However, it can also be difficult for me when I do not get to spend time on what I want. I prefer doing what I want to do, and making changes to different topics or activities can be very hard.

I may get stressed or upset and not be able to tell you what is happening.

- The behaviors I exhibit when I am upset or stressed are my way of communicating. I may have different hand or arm movements, may squeal or make odd noises, walk or appear agitated. I want you to be aware that there is something wrong. Help me by remaining calm and prompting me to communicate using pictures, or showing you if I am having trouble using words to communicate.

I may respond to noise, lights, crowds, or distractions differently than other students.

- Windows or the hum of fluorescent lights can be especially distracting when I am trying to focus. Too much sensory input, e.g. lights, noise, textures, or smells can affect my ability to participate and learn. You may not even notice this, but I do. I am not being "difficult" on purpose. It is just the way my system works.

Signs and labels will help me understand my environment.

- There is much to be aware of in a library environment. Labeling will help me learn to interact effectively. Screen shots are terrific (my neurotypical friends like them too!) for directions in specific areas, like computers.

I aim for independence.

- I want to be able to use a library like everyone else. Once I know the correct procedures and have the supports I need, I can enjoy the benefits of the library on my own.

Resources about Autism and Libraries:

Libraries and Autism:
We're Connected: www .librariesandautism.org
This website provides guidance for librarians and library staff to help them better serve individuals with autism and their families.
Project ENABLE: http://projectenable .syr.edu
Housed at Syracuse University's School of Information Studies

Center for Digital Literacy, this project provides a high quality, comprehensive, train-the-trainer continuing education program for New York's school librarians to help them create and deliver effective library and information services to students with disabilities, but it is open to anyone.

References

Autism Speaks. http://autismspeaks. org.

Centers for Disease Control and Prevention. "Prevalence of Autism Spectrum Disorders." *Morbidity and Mortality Weekly Report* 58. SS10 (2011): 1–20.

Ennis-Cole, D., and D. Smith. "Assistive Technology and Autism: Expanding the Technology Leadership Role of the School Librarian. *School Libraries Worldwide* 17.2 (2011): 86–98.

Janzen, J.E.. *Understanding the Nature of Autism: A Guide to*

the *Autism Spectrum Disorders.*
San Antonio, TX: Harcourt
Assessment, 2003.

Andrea Bress *is a student in the
Communication Sciences and Disorders*
*program at Florida State University.
She is working on Project PALS, an
interdisciplinary project with Dr. Juliann
Woods at the FSU Autism Institute and Dr.
Nancy Everhart at the FSU PALM Center.
Project PALS is promoting professional
development for librarians in regard*
*to dealing with patrons on the autism
spectrum.*

Bress, Andrea, (2013). Making your school
library more functional to individuals with
autism. *LMC, 32*(1), 46–47.

Inquiry Learning: Is Your Selection Policy Ready?

By Elizabeth E. G. Friese

The United States Constitution . . . The First Amendment . . . the American Library Association Library Bill of Rights . . . Your Library Media Center Selection Policy.

It's an inspiring series of documents that outline and protect our freedoms. But your selection policy? What is *that* doing there? Believe it or not, the stalwart selection policy, often overlooked in favor of more exciting topics, belongs on this list of freedom protectors. What does your selection policy do to preserve and enhance the intellectual freedom of your school community?

Last year's announcement of the Standards for the 21st Century Learner by the American Association of School Librarians (AASL, 2007) started me thinking about selection policies and how the new learning standards affect how we select materials. Inquiry is central to the new learning standards. One of the common beliefs underlying the learning standards is that "Inquiry provides a framework for learning." Three of the four learning standards discuss the steps of the inquiry process, starting from seeking information on topics of curricular and personal interest to sharing the new knowledge created. In the inquiry process, students use a wide variety of resources to develop questions, collaborate, and construct new knowledge that is both meaningful and authentic.

Placing inquiry learning at the center of the library media program both celebrates and necessitates intellectual freedom. In an inquiry-centered library media center, we recognize that students are not just locating and receiving information, and that there are different perspectives on and ways to present knowledge about all kinds of topics. Facilitating inquiry requires that we provide access to these different points of view to students as they work to create new knowledge. It also leads to collecting a wide variety

of formats on a range of topics. Not only do a variety of formats allow information to be presented in different ways, it provides access to information for the full range of learners, as well as mirroring the complex information environment students negotiate outside of school.

The requirement of a variety of perspectives and formats is enough to cause concern about challenges to materials. In an age where challenges to materials in the library media center collection are not uncommon, the reconsideration procedure, which outlines the process for dealing with materials challenges, may seem to be the most important part of a selection policy. However, as formats of information and the role of the library media center evolve, we need to think about our selection policies as a whole and the collections they create. I am a firm believer that library media center collections have an enormous impact on the quality and richness of student learning opportunities, and that an effective selection policy is key to an outstanding collection. What does your collection make possible for your school community? What possibilities might a different collection create?

In the face of materials challenges, we also cannot forget that inquiry in the library media center goes hand in hand with the teaching of information literacy skills. Inquiry isn't just about the resources, although the resources are necessary to making inquiry possible. Along with this variety of resources, library media specialists provide instruction in the habits of inquiry, evaluation of information, and knowledge creation (Kuhlthau, Maniotes & Caspari, 2007). It is the teaching of inquiry and information literacy that allows us to expand the collection in ways leading to authentic engagement and the development of skills for lifelong learning.

The selection policy is meant to ensure that the collection meets the

needs of the school community as comprehensively and effectively as possible. Instead of restrictive, the selection policy should be expansive, created, and carried out with the intention of fostering intellectual freedom for each member of the population the library media center serves. Are our selection policies written to facilitate inquiry learning?

The First Step: Who Is Involved in Selection?

Step back for a moment and think about your current selection process. How long has it been since you read your selection policy? When was the last time it was revised or reaffirmed? Pull it out and have a look. As you read through your selection policy, the first question you should ask is: Who is included in the resource selection process?

This question is a critical starting point. A committee of administrators, teachers from all grade levels or subject areas, technology leaders in the school, parents, students, and community members should be involved in the resource selection process. The input of all these groups is invaluable in creating a collection that supports curricular needs, personal learning, and the community at large. This variety of voices can also balance any bias in the process. The role of students in creating the library media center is of particular importance. While we develop collections to support the curriculum as a matter of course, we should also encourage student involvement in creation of the library media center, a central part of their information environment.

This is not to minimize the role of the library media specialist in selection. Of course, library media specialists are professionally trained in selection. It is part of our job to stay at the forefront of the latest in resources, and we have a central position in selecting those resources. But in order to effectively understand

and meet the resource needs of the populations we serve, all the groups in those populations should be represented in the selection process.

What follows are a few points to consider with your committee. Many of these discussions are open-ended, because ultimately selection is a local matter. Every collection is different, and should be tailored to meet the needs of the specific school community. Even if your selection policy is written at the district level, you'll have approaches that are individual to your school. Think about these points with an eye toward how your policy and practice might need to be updated to expand freedoms of students and to provide an atmosphere that facilitates inquiry.

> *To keep selection policies up to date, with an eye toward providing the most expansive collection possible, they should be revisited on a regular basis.*

New Formats: What Are We Collecting?

The library media center is transforming into a flexible space for inquiry learning. Inquiry learning requires many "raw materials" for the creation of knowledge. These include information in a wide variety of formats, including print, audio, visual, artifacts, multimedia, online and digital resources, and many others. Look around your library media center for a moment. How many of these formats do you have in your collection? How many are you planning to purchase or select?

Now look at your selection policy. Consider what formats are included, and how thoroughly they are discussed. What resources do you have in your collection that are not mentioned in your selection policy? Is the policy strictly written for books and other print materials? In my opinion, a comprehensive selection policy should be explicit about what is included in the collection, including new formats as they are integrated.

Now that you know what is actually in your collection, think about the formats and materials are that are missing. What would make your collection better equipped for student inquiry?

Consider a few recent examples.

- There have been several efforts connecting games and gaming with the new AASL standards (School Library System of Genesee Valley BOCES, 2008; Mayer, 2008). Both board games and electronic games can be used in the inquiry learning process, both to teach inquiry skills and curricular content. Growing interest virtually guarantees that there will be more games to choose from in the near future.

- Primary sources are resources being discussed more and more, especially with the explosion of them now available through digital libraries and other online collections. Primary sources are excellent resources to include in the inquiry process when learning about history and other subjects (Pappas, 2006).

- Graphic novels are gaining in popularity among students. While they are often thought of as reading motivators, there is also a growing number of graphic nonfiction and other graphic texts that relate directly to curricular topics and could be used in inquiry projects.

There are benefits to including all of these formats in a library media center. You may already have one, two, or all of these formats in your collection. I can also easily imagine objections to resources in each of these formats. Does your selection policy explicitly include them and how they are selected?

> *If inquiry and intellectual freedom are core considerations for the selection process, seeking diversity of format and content may be the most important criteria to keep in mind when choosing resources.*

Selection Criteria: How Do We Know What to Select?

Library media specialists often use a number of standard criteria in their selection policies. These might include accuracy, authority, and favorable reviews from standard sources, among others. Taking the example of games, what criteria might be used in evaluating games for inclusion in your collection? Many of the traditional criteria for selection such as accuracy and authority don't seem to apply in quite the same way as they do to print materials. The standard reviewing authorities often won't include games. We could simply collect them, applying the standard criteria as best we can. However, as these new formats emerge and become candidates for inclusion in our resource collection, we should carefully consider how the current criteria do or do not apply and how we might adapt or invent new criteria to encourage the inclusion of new formats in the service of inquiry learning and intellectual freedom. Conversations about format-specific criteria should happen with every format in the collection, and perhaps especially with new formats as they are considered for addition. Digital formats of all kinds, such as e-books, Web sites, databases, and primary sources should be included in these discussions as well. Selection of online materials is largely overlooked, and yet these formats are quickly becoming a dominant portion of our collections.

Inquiry learning as a focus in library media centers also brings one of the standard criteria to the forefront of the collection program: presenting many different points of view. While this criterion is traditionally applied to controversial topics, the proliferation of information and content make it possible to include different points of view on all kinds of subjects, not just controversial ones. The provision of different formats is in itself a way of presenting different points of view on a topic. If inquiry and intellectual freedom are core considerations for the selection process, seeking this diversity of format and content may be the most important criteria to keep in mind when choosing resources.

Review and Renew: How Can the Selection Process Be Improved in the Future?

The possibilities for our collections and library media centers are evolving. To keep selection policies up to date, with an eye toward providing the most expansive collection possible, they should be revisited on a regular basis. As we review them, we should keep in mind not only our changing populations and curricula, but also new formats of information that can facilitate inquiry learning, and how current criteria may need to be updated to expand access and intellectual freedom. Even if your district dictates a selection policy, there is room for discussion of how that policy will be applied at the school level. If your selection policy does come from the district, try to find ways to provide input into district policy to encourage inclusion of new formats and the expansion of intellectual freedom.

Instead of restrictive, the selection policy should be expansive, created, and carried out with the intention of fostering intellectual freedom for each member of the population the library media center serves.

Selection is not simple. Keeping in mind the guiding principle that we are not seeking to protect ourselves, but the rights and freedoms of our students, the selection process should be one of expanding diversity of format and content. As library media specialists, we should push to increase student access and freedom as much as possible, but realize that we are not alone in the process of setting standards and establishing criteria. Our school communities, as well as our professional communities, should engage in ongoing debate about these topics, and how student inquiry and intellectual freedom can be most effectively supported.

This discussion has only touched on a few aspects of a resource selection policy, leaving aside the gift policy and weeding among other elements in order to focus on these fundamental concerns. Throughout this discussion I've called it a "resource" selection policy instead of a "materials" selection policy, with good reason. "Materials," in my mind, refers to a time when the majority of the collection was made up of tangible forms of information, most often print. But now and into the future, a large percentage of our collections will be virtual. My suspicion is that our current policies are largely unprepared for the new formats of information we can collect and provide access to, and for the inquiry-centered vision of the library media center that the new AASL Standards point toward. We need to develop and share new templates for this document that open the door to emerging formats and active student inquiry. As the concept of what a collection is continues to evolve, our thinking about how we form our collections should evolve as well. It is through these discussions and debates, as we advocate for student access and intellectual freedom, that the possibility of true inquiry learning emerges.

References

"AASL Standards for the 21st Century Learner." Weblog entry. Gaming. n.d. School Library System of Genesee Valley BOCES. 6 July 2008 <http://sls.gvboces.org/gaming/standards>.

Kuhlthau, Carol C., Leslie K. Maniotes and Ann K. Caspari. *Guided Inquiry: Learning in the 21st Century.* Westport, CT: Libraries Unlimited, 2007.

Mayer, Brian. "AASL Standards Pt. I: Inquire, think critically and gain knowledge." Weblog entry. Library Gamer. 5 May 2008. 6 July 2008 <http://librarygamer.wordpress.com/2008/05/>.

Pappas, Marjorie L. "Primary Sources and Inquiry Learning." *School Library Media Activities Monthly* 23.1 (2006), 23–26.

Standards for the 21st Century Learner. Chicago: American Association of School Librarians, 2007.

Elizabeth E.G. Friese *is a school library media specialist currently working on her doctorate at the University of Georgia in Athens, Georgia. She can be reached at egfriese@uga.edu.*

Friese, Elizabeth E.G. (2008). Inquiry learning: Is your selection policy ready? *LMC*, 27(3), 14–16.

Parental Involvement in Selection: Mandated or Our Choice?

By John B. Harer

The sight of a parent with fire in their eyes, waving a book as they approach you in the school media center, can strike fear in a school library media specialist. In my early days of school librarianship, it did not take long for me to realize that this was not the time to first think of how to involve parents in support of my selections for the library. A lot of good advice exists that suggests ways for parents to be involved that will help support intellectual freedom, as well as lessons learned from the experience of being burnt by a censorship complaint. For example, ALA's advice on conducting a reconsideration hearing on challenged materials suggests that librarians should solicit speakers for the hearing, such as parents, who they have identified from past experience are in support of the freedom to read. I knew one junior high school librarian in the 1970s who created a parent book club to share in reading and discussing young adult novels. The relationships she developed with the parents who participated created a common "freedom to read" bond.

Legislating Parental Involvement in Materials Selection

While our profession knows the benefits of parental involvement, the forces of censorship have harnessed parental involvement as well. In 2005, parental involvement in the selection process was almost mandated by law. Using the innocuous sounding phrase "parent review boards," the idea was introduced into the United States Congress in 2005 by North Carolina Congressman Walter Jones, labeled H. R. 2295 and called the "Parental Empowerment Act." It was intended to mandate parent review boards that would recommend inclusion or exclusion of books and resources for all school districts receiving federal funding prior to any review by school

library media specialists. Reaction in the library community was swift and unequivocal. ALA President Carol Brey-Casiano (2005) issued a statement that said, in part, "The American Library Association is deeply concerned about H.R. 2295, which would deprive schools of much-needed funding unless the community adopts a federally mandated review panel to judge books purchased for classrooms and school libraries." No information existed at the time about how much authority these boards would have, nor what impact these boards would have on selection.

An expressed purpose of the Parental Empowerment Act was to give parents an awareness of controversial books and materials before they were purchased, and a voice in blocking their acquisition before librarians could make appropriate selection decisions using proper selection policy guidelines.

After several of my current students could not discover any information on these boards, my investigation into this topic suggests that the idea may have gone the way of the Neanderthal. Since this legislation was introduced by my own congressman, a call to his Washington legislative aide confirmed that the bill may have had little chance from the outset. Congressman Jones introduced it in the 108th Congress (2005–2007) when the Republicans held a majority in the House and Senate. However, Jones' legislative aide told me that

the Republican leadership always considered it a very low priority. The bill never made it out of committee in the 108th Congress. Jones resubmitted it in the 109th Congress (2007–2009), numbered H. R. 681, but the Republicans had lost their majority in the 2006 elections, and again the bill languished in committee. Congressman Jones' legislative aide indicated that Jones does not intend to reintroduce the bill.

Legislative Failure, Successful Idea?

There may still be reason to be concerned about this concept despite its apparent legislative demise. Jones' motivation was sparked by a book challenge in Wilmington, North Carolina over *King and King* (de Haan, Linda and Stern Nijland. Berkeley: Tricycle Press, 2002), a children's book about a prince who wanted to marry another prince. I was told that Congressman Jones met with constituents during a church meeting who expressed shock that such books existed. An expressed purpose of the Parental Empowerment Act was to give parents an awareness of controversial books and materials before they were purchased, and a voice in blocking their acquisition before librarians could make appropriate selection decisions using proper selection policy guidelines.

Setting aside the argument that a parental review board interferes with the professional responsibilities of the school library media specialist, and quite possibly strips them of their professional judgment in selection, what concerns me is that while the bill hangs out there without a mandate, there are too many ambiguities in it should a school district use it for guidance on creating a parent review board of their own. This lack of clarity empowers school boards to define this concept to their liking and permits a very biased process to be created. For example, the language of H.R. 2295 did not make it clear how a parental review board was to be created; only stating a majority of the board had to be parents of current or recent students in the district. Nor does any language exist on whether school boards are to appoint or elect members. This tells me that representativeness is, apparently, not a desired factor. We might assume that a "parent board" should be made up of all parents, but even that is not clear. Because of the omissions in this legislation, school boards taking their cue from this effort would be able stack it with a very biased viewpoint, and ignore any kind of accountability to citizens, should they form a parent review board on their own.

I can envision a worse-case scenario whereby a school district forms a parent review board of parents from one political or religious point of view, and given no standards or criteria for how to judge a selection, end up banning some of the best young adult literature from that district's schools on little more than a political whim. Consider what happened in Georgia in 2006. Laura Mallory, a parent of children in the Gwinnett County school system,

fought the inclusion of the Harry Potter series using unsubstantiated "evidence" she found on the Internet of a teen's alleged personal account of being turned to witchcraft by these stories. She was unable to substantiate the authenticity of this claim when she appealed to the Georgia State Board of Education. However, Ms. Mallory continues to insist on its accuracy. This lack of guidance on selection criteria would permit a board to accept such inaccurate information because parents would control the review board and school districts would have no obligation to ensure such boards use any acceptable selection criteria.

Though the demise of the Parental Empowerment Act seems certain, the concept of a parent review board may still exist, but with far less national impact. I fear that some states or school systems may feel such an idea is worthwhile. The idea of boards of citizens and parents reviewing materials before inclusion is not new, as can be attested to by the work of the Educational Research Analysts and their influence on the Texas State Education Agency's school textbook adoption process. This can only serve as a reminder that school library media specialists need to build collaboration and working

relationships with parents in support of the freedom to read.

Works Cited

Brey-Casiano, Carol. (2005) American Library Association against proposed bill to federally mandate school library purchases. Retrieved 2/18/2009 from <http://www.ala.org/ala/newspresscenter/news/pressreleases2005/may2005/schllibmandate.cfm>

Complete text of the legislation and its legislative history available from Govtrack.us at <http://www.govtrack.us/congress/bill.xpd?bill=h109-2295>

For more information on Laura Mallory's challenge of the Harry Potter series, go to the Wikipedia article on "Religious debates over the Harry Potter series" at <http://en.wikipedia.org/wiki/Laura_Mallory#Laura_Mallory>

John B. Harer *is an Assistant Professor of Library Science at East Carolina University, an NCATE/AASL accredited program, and former school librarian.*

Harer, John B. (2009). Parental involvement in selection: Mandated or our choice? *LMC, 28*(3), 18–19.

Print to Digital: Opportunities for Choice

By Ellen McNair

At a recent networking event, a discussion started with the question, "Are all of the books really going away?" My colleagues described new print acquisitions, purchased to support various upcoming class projects. In more than one instance, multiple digital resources were identified that students could use, but print sources were ordered for reasons that were not easily articulated. It made me wonder, "What is our map? How will we navigate this transition from print to more and more digital resources? Will this be a marginally random endeavor, our decisions driven by the timeline of resources as they become available, or should we craft a plan?"

The Continuing Value of Print

Many colleagues agreed that print sources will continue to have value as we move forward in the digital age. This is true, not because some of us simply like books, or because we are sentimental about holding a book in a cozy corner by the fireplace, or even because we are worried that if books go, we will go with them. Print sources will continue to have value in different schools for different reasons. Perhaps there will simply be fewer of them, or perhaps hardware purchases might not keep up with public education demands. Or perhaps funds are not available to purchase the same number of books at the same rate we have in the past *and* increase the digital resources students need to transition into a global, digital workforce. Knowing that fewer print books will be purchased increases the significance of our choices. How will we make those choices? How will we establish a bar to measure our progress? Although a pre-determined map (up 40 percent in databases, down 40 percent in books?) may be too formulaic, we need a deliberate focus as we chart new territory.

A Map for the Transition

The decisions about which print sources to order and which ones to weed into extinction are based on several variables: the unique demographic in each school, how student reading levels align to available digital sources, required student projects and essential content, and the subjects and reading levels represented by the digital resources in our libraries. The expectation is that we will make an enormous contribution to student success because the infrastructure of learning is about information access and literacy. Incorporating these factors into a plan is integral to meeting this expectation.

> How will we navigate this transition from print to more and more digital resources? Will this be a marginally random endeavor, our decisions driven by the timeline of resources as they become available, or should we craft a plan?

One School's Plan

Based on the above factors, with an emphasis on the student population and needs in J.E.B. Stuart High School (58 percent free and reduced lunch and 34 percent English as a second language learners) and the existing relevant academic content in our current research databases, we are narrowing the focus of our print source acquisitions. This year the list has six areas of interest for ordering print resources. Next year, we will have three, perhaps four. The list will narrow each year.

Narrative nonfiction: There is increasing emphasis on this genre.

At this time, students will be more likely to discover it in print sources than online or in a digital download format. A marketing or project plan to lead students to "discover" this genre in digital format will be part of the roll-out before we move to more digital narrative nonfiction.

Ancient Civilizations: Level 3 (out of 4) English as a second language students prefer print sources for longer projects, where pages of text are robustly supported by pictures and captions. Digital resources, including databases, are being revised continually, addressing the increased need for pairing graphics and text appropriate for hi/lo readers at the high school level. We have incorporated some new resources in this content area, making it possible for students to alternate between their preferred print sources and the digital ones.

Countries and Immigration: Students who are new to the United States often have projects related to their countries of origin. In reducing barriers to learning and leveling the playing field, these students must have a choice in order to locate text that works for them. They clearly benefit from alternating between computers/digital resources and print resources.

Civil War: We have a robust collection of print sources related to Civil War battles. We also have salient content information in our social studies databases. Considering your print strengths is important in the transition. We will likely not order any more Civil War books, but we will not be weeding the ones we have for some time. They are in excellent condition, and the information is not outdated. While we have digital sources on this topic, the books have a variety of valuable information with better pictures that support the text—something that even our strongest, highest level readers appreciate when studying this topic, rich with facts and nuance.

New Popular Fiction: We need these books in print until we

are prepared to put e-readers and downloadable books into the hands of all students.

Memoirs: Multiple classes have memoir assignments each year. With consideration to the assignments and to the limitations of the digital resources available onsite, memoirs will be on the print acquisition radar for another one to two years. After that time, we anticipate having enough digital resources in downloadable format to limit print orders. Once again, until we are sure that our students have adequate access to enough online resources, we will maintain this part of our print collection.

Collection Development and Professional Responsibility

As a profession, we have always been poignantly sensitive about collection development, making sure that each acquisition aligns with standards for student achievement, content, reading levels, targeted interests, and identified gaps in the collection. It is exciting to move aggressively from this generic model of print source ordering to digital source selection in a systematic elimination of obsolete materials and acquisition of critical new ones. These are going to be library specific decisions.

While we have digital sources on the Civil War, our print books have a variety of valuable information with better pictures that support the text—something that even our strongest, highest level readers appreciate when studying this topic.

The replacement sequence of print resources with digital ones is going to be different in each library, but each librarian can develop a map, moving forward based on these or self-selected variables. A thoughtful analysis is a powerful asset in the task of teaching research skills and multiple literacies.

Publishing delays are not new, but the dilemma was recently highlighted in a conversation with a science teacher. After mentioning that anything published in print about cancer, or any genetic disease, is outdated before it reaches our hands, we enjoyed thinking: Now we can *do* something about it. How true is that of science and technology books in general? On the other hand, science databases are updated *daily*.

Funding Alternatives

At a recent tri-state consortium, the discussion of budget limitations for purchasing digital resources was a lively one. Money is all about choices. Funding for new databases is sparse. Consider alternatives:

- Put 80 percent of your new science, technology, poetry, and biography print source orders (or other subject areas in which you might consider leaning more heavily on digital sources) on hold for one year in order to reallocate the funds for one content-specific database. For funds that disappear if they are not encumbered, try negotiating a shorter contract with the digital vendor.

- Set a goal. Decide which print sources you can afford to reduce or eliminate based on the variables described above. Revisit your goals at the end of the year. Some will change each year based on your analysis of new variables and new resources. It's important to start looking at and discussing digital resources in order to understand the choices.

- Explore the option of re-allocating funds to purchase a database for all schools in a district to share.

- Expand student horizons by providing instruction in appropriate use of the web—good digital citizenship, website assessment with an emphasis on authenticity and bias, and web-based citation tools. When database offerings cannot be increased, introducing these concepts through a generic search engine with web assessment goals can provide essential 21st century skills.

The decisions about which print sources to order and which ones to weed into extinction are based on several variables.

Setting Your Sail

If you think this approach is too slow and you might be left in the dust by libraries that are moving at lightning speed, acquiring several new databases, multiple e-readers each year, you are wrong. We are trusted to make decisions about the best resources to purchase based on our demographics and standards. As you transition into using more digital resources, consider with each decision that you will be giving your 21st century students many advantages: current information, technology skills, more opportunities to learn about ethical use of information on the web, productive searching, web assessment, and appropriate, discriminate use of Google and Wikipedia. Our students are in a digital world and they like it. They are engaged with it and they know how to access it. Let's give it to them with purpose, a plan, and wrapped in the highest ethical use imaginable.

Empty Shelves: NOT!

All of these changes beg the question "What will happen to our shelving?" Here are a few ideas:

- Take out a few shelves and add more tables, perhaps a few more comfortable chairs, an inviting rug, or a life-size art project that inspires witty conversation and stimulates questions for critical thinking.

- Display more student work and projects. The signage inviting students to view the work of their peers should be celebratory ("Look! Mr. Vanderburgh's class brings life to ancient civilizations!")

- Display more fiction and book covers. The cover sells a book. Spreading books out to showcase more book covers will be more enticing.

- Display database logos and their focus of learning. We are advertising learning.

- Use large signage with great literary quotes, quotes from new fiction, and URLs that lead to author blogs and book trailers. Showcase photos of upcoming school field trips and pair them with the research database logos leading to robust topical information.

- Think big: Use a flat panel monitor to display signage and directions to these new resources, alternating this information with student-created book trailers, Web 2.0 projects, database features, and advantages.

Change Is Good

Dream big and plan for success. Instead of wondering whether or not you are going to reduce the number of print sources you will be ordering, start by sharing information with your colleagues about which sections of your print collection will need to stay intact for the next two years, based your demographics, your standards, and the pricing of the digital resources you need. Start planning which shelves to move to make room for more seating. Share thoughts about the emerging formula in your library: 60 percent less on print, 60 percent more on electronic resources and e-readers? Forge a new path.

Ellen McNair *is the school librarian at J.E.B. Stuart High School in Fairfax County Public Schools, Falls Church, Virginia. She regularly presents on Web 2.0 tools and is an adjunct instructor in multimedia at Catholic University. Librarianship is her second career. You may email her at elmcnair@FCPS.edu.*

McNair, Ellen. (2012). Print to digital: Opportunities for choice. *LMC, 30*(6), 28–30.

Evaluating Multicultural Literature Made Easy!

By Kasey Garrison and Roxanne Mills

How do I evaluate multicultural literature when I am unfamiliar with the cultures represented within it? This question presents a huge challenge for librarians and teachers. In her memoir *Journey to the People*, educator and Newbery Award-winning author Ann Nolan Clark outlined five basic qualities of books "true to the pattern of the people in them" that form a useful framework for assessing the quality and integrity of multicultural literature (90). Review the book, ask yourself the listed questions, and include supportive comments.

Roxanne Mills *and* **Kasey Garrison** *work for the Librarianship Upgrades for Children and Youth Services (LUCY) project at Old Dominion University.*

LUCY is a multicultural continuing education program for librarians, made possible by a grant from the U.S. Institute of Museum and Library Services. Check out

Garrison, Kasey, & Mills, Roxanne. (2012). Tools of the trade: Evaluating multicultural literature made easy! *LMC, 30*(5), 24.

Elements of Quality Multicultural Literature for Children and Teens

Quality	Questions	Observed	Comments
Honesty	■ Is the cultural group depicted in a truthful and sincere way? ■ Does the book avoid sensationalizing the group's cultural experiences or historical events?	Y / N	
Accuracy	■ Is there evidence that the information presented is factual in content and nature? (e.g., list of sources used) ■ Does the author include varying points of view?	Y / N	
Reality	■ Does the book portray the realities of the individual ethnic group as well as the universality of the human experience? ■ Does it maintain respect for its young readers by including all facets of life? (e.g., joyous celebrations of life as well as somber inclusions of death)	Y / N	
Imagination	■ Is the book creative, artistic, and imaginative in its text, illustrations, and the combination of both? ■ Will kids enjoy reading it?	Y / N	
Appreciation	■ Does the book convey a feeling of appreciation for the individual cultures represented as well as more universal themes in the story?	Y / N	

Clark, Ann Nolan. *Journey to the People*. Viking Press, 1969.

Educate the Educators about Graphic Novels: Five Tips for Success

By Julie Rick

School libraries can hardly keep graphic novels on their shelves. Enthusiasm for the genre has led many librarians to question how such novels might be infused into normal curricula. However, many librarians who have proposed such an integration have learned that their colleagues do not share their enthusiasm. From their perspective, it may sound like a proposal to replace Twain and London with Spiderman and Archie. They are skeptical, at best, as to whether graphic novels are sufficiently challenging, and worried about how selecting such novels might be perceived by those outside the classroom.

When faced with knee-jerk resistance, don't just retreat back to the library. Consider some of these helpful tips for convincing educators of the value of graphic novels in the classroom.

Tip 1: Educate Teachers about Graphic Novels

Skepticism about the pedagogical value of graphic novels is almost as ubiquitous as the novels themselves. Researchers have found that educators often resist utilizing graphic novels in the classroom because they are perceived as "subliterature" (Viadero 1). Others worry that graphic novels will diminish the importance of text, replace quality texts, or discourage the reading of other genres (Butcher and Manning 68). And with the pressures produced by the No Child Left Behind Act, some teachers feel they cannot justify inclusion of graphic novels in the curriculum given that such novels are not covered on standardized tests (Schwarz, "Expanding Literacies" 63).

Perhaps the most important impediment is confusion over the distinction between comic books and graphic novels. Schwarz defines the graphic novel as "a longer and more artful version of the comic book bound as a 'real book'" ("Expanding Literacies" 58). Thus, while graphic novels resemble comic books in format, there is great divergence when it comes to substance. Graphic novels have covered topics as serious as the Holocaust (Spiegelman's Maus: A Survivor's Tale), Hurricane Katrina (Neufeld's A.D.: New Orleans after the Deluge), and even September 11 (Jacobsen and Colón's The 9/11 Report: A Graphic Adaptation). Making educators aware of this distinction is a crucial first step toward incorporating graphic novels in school curricula.

The academic value of graphic novels is difficult to dispute. Schwarz, for example, argues that "reading graphic novels requires students to use more complex cognitive skills than reading the text alone" ("Graphic Novels" 262–263). The genre is also increasingly embraced within academia. For instance, in January 2009 the first academic conference for "Graphica in Education" was held at Fordham University's Graduate School of Education. Thus, although the novels are embraced by large segments of students, librarians, and academics, there is still a need to educate and persuade school teachers and administrators.

Tip 2: Demonstrate the Literary Merit of Graphic Novels

Graphic novels are gaining recognition in the literary world with books like Art Spiegelman's Maus: A Survivor's Tale winning the Pulitzer Prize in 1992. And while author Brian Selznick doesn't consider The Invention of Hugo Cabret to be a pure graphic novel, as it is told in both pictures and words, this 2008 Caldecott winner represents a definitive shift in what is perceived as high-quality children's literature. Some scholars and teachers are beginning to realize "that in a media-dominated society, one traditional literacy—reading and writing of print—is no longer sufficient" (Schwarz, "Expanding Literacies" 59). Today's students must be able to read, comprehend, and analyze a variety of modes and forms of texts, and that includes graphic novels. By continuing to push traditional methods of text onto our students, we will only continue to "drive a wedge between what is focused on in school and what children are actually reading" (Fitzsimmons 19). As educators, we must attempt to harness the value of these resources and use them in such a way that maximizes the benefits for students.

Tip 3: Show Teachers the Natural Connections between Graphic Novels and the Curricula

In the past, many educators were under the impression that graphic novels were only for reluctant readers, boys, and ELL students. While these students certainly benefit from exposure to graphic novels, students of all levels (even gifted) can be challenged by graphic novels. Graphic novels can "relate big themes and topics by tapping into the way students are already learning naturally" (Cleaver 34).

Perhaps the most promising opportunity for graphic novel usage is as a supplement to existing curriculum elements (Carter 2009). A number of nonfiction titles, historical fiction works, biographies, and even autobiographies have been published recently in the graphic novel world that would be positive additions or supplements to the current curriculum. For example, Icon Books' Introducing . . . series offers an array of graphic guides for secondary students on everything from capitalism and Hinduism to quantum theory and Shakespeare. Rosen Publishing has also released a graphic nonfiction series that contains graphic battles of the Civil War, mythology, and discoveries, as well as "junior" titles for younger students. Given the chance, these titles could appear outside the English and language arts classroom, contributing to interdisciplinary thematic units, or even serving as an introduction to a new concept or content area. But this will only happen if school librarians make teachers aware of these interesting enrichment possibilities.

> *Graphic novels are gaining recognition in the literary world with books like Art Spiegelman's* Maus: A Survivor's Tale *winning the Pulitzer Prize in 1992.*

Tip 4: Illustrate the Potential Avenues of Study Made Possible by Using Graphic Novels in the Classroom

In English and language arts classrooms, many of the literary elements and plot devices studied in traditional texts can also be examined in graphic form. Characterization, plot development, analysis, and concepts like suspense, onomatopoeia, and many more can be explored through graphic novels. Visual literacy can also be promoted in the study of graphic novels. Kids may be at ease combining text information and the visuals, but with graphic novels, the difficult skill of making inferences can be practiced. Students have to make sense of what is happening in the story based on what is and is not present in the frames. This makes for excellent practice for readers of any level and age.

Beyond literary elements and analysis, graphic novels offer unique opportunities for writing and art activities. Looking at a page of frames from a graphic novel that has minimal dialog or narration, students could be given the task to add dialog to the scene. Or, more advanced students could be given the task of taking a page from a picture book for mature audiences, like Shaun Tan's The Arrival, and making it into narrative work. Students would need to fill in the blanks for their potential readers by describing the scene, explaining the action, developing the conflict, and if necessary, creating dialog between the characters.

Allowing students the opportunity to examine the power of color and visuals combined with text is a worthwhile task. While this can be done in isolation by having students reflect on the effect of the author's choice of colors (or lack thereof), students can also compare works that have been done in both color and black and white (like Jeff Smith's Bone series). And, of course, there is always the idea of having students create their own graphic novels. When I taught seventh grade English, I included a graphic novel unit that culminated with students transforming a one-page memoir they had written earlier in the year into a graphic novel. Although the project was time-intensive and required a great deal of scaffolding, the students' final products were powerful, meaningful, and a great source of pride for them.

Tip 5: Offer to Collaborate with Your Colleagues to Create Meaningful and Authentic Learning Experiences Using Graphic Novels

Make use of your expertise and experience with this genre to help educators select appropriate titles to complement their units of study. Teachers will appreciate your review and selection of the titles for overall appropriateness, and willingness to help them create subjects for lessons. Or, if you see a specific title that you feel could greatly benefit the students, do not hesitate to bring it to the attention of the curriculum supervisor of the relevant department. If your educators are concerned about complaints from parents, help them craft a rationale to support the use of the book. If there is controversial material in the graphic novel, address how it will be explained in class.

Concluding Thoughts

The fact that students are already voraciously reading graphic novels cannot be ignored. As librarians we need to capitalize on this opportunity and look for ways to implement this genre across the curriculum—not as a replacement but as a supplement or a study of the genre in isolation. We must also emphasize the legitimacy of graphic novels as literature. Specifically, we must address the confusion regarding the distinction between comic books and graphic novels. Through conversation and the sharing of resources, help your colleagues see how this genre can support and supplement the curricula. Something as simple as dropping a book in a teacher's mailbox can go a long way when a message is attached directing them to the curricular connection. Finally, don't leave your colleagues hanging. Offer yourself as a resource for selecting appropriate texts, and collaborate on lesson plans that will encourage and develop meaningful learning. If we can take advantage of the popularity of this genre, in the process we may be able to build bridges between teachers and students, promote literacy, and provide innovative ways of learning across the curriculum.

Works Cited

Butcher, Katherine, and M. Lee Manning. "Bringing Graphic Novels into a School's Curriculum." *The Clearing House* 78.2 (2004): 67–72. Print.

Carter, James Bucky. "Going Graphic." *Literacy 2.0* 66.6 (2009): 68–73. Print.

Cleaver, Samantha. "Ms. Grundy's Right! You Can Teach Reading with Comics and Graphic Novels." *Instructor* 117.6 (2008): 28–34. Print.

Fitzsimmons, Phil. "What Adolescents Are Reading and What Their Teachers Are Not:

Between the Deformed Discourse and Disdain of the Graphic Novel." *Literacy Learning: The Middle Years* 15.2 (2007): 18–22. Print.

Schwarz, Gretchen. "Expanding Literacies through Graphic Novels." *English Journal* 95.6 (2006): 58–64. Print.

Schwarz, Gretchen. "Graphic Novels for Multiple Literacies." *Journal of Adolescent and Adult Literacy* 46.3 (2002): 262–265. Print.

Viadero, Debra. "Scholars See Comics as No Laughing Matter." *Education Week* 28.21 (2009): 1.

Julie Rick *is a second-year graduate student studying school library media at the University of Michigan's School of Information.*

Rick, Julie. (2011). Educate the educators about graphic novels: Five tips for success. *LMC, 30*(2), 34–35, 38.

Facts: Just the Facts! Evaluating Your Nonfiction Collection

By Deborah B. Ford

Gone are the days of 100 page biographies and nonfiction books for the K-8 crowd. Today's nonfiction is often less than 50 pages with lots of illustrations, photographs, and supportive text features. How can you determine if you have the best nonfiction on your shelves? Where do you find the best new nonfiction to replace the weeds?

- **Begin by doing a collection analysis.** Most circulation systems and book sellers have an analysis component. Evaluate the results by identifying the weakest areas.

- **Target the key Dewey ranges.** Areas such as technology, social problems, and astronomy become outdated very quickly. These books should be the most current. In many cases, no information is better than misinformation.

- **Weed the worst.** Most book vendor analysis programs, Titlewave for example, will give you a list of the books over 15 years old. Start by discarding the oldest in your nonfiction sections.

- **Use your senses.** If you don't have a program that helps you find the oldies, just follow your nose. Books that smell musty or moldy need to be deleted from your collection. Look at the condition of the book. Are the pages falling out? Are there color pictures? Today's students aren't interested in black and white pictures of foreign countries.

- **Get strength in numbers.** Invite some of your colleagues over for a weeding party. Assign partners and sections that need attention. Give them your bottom line criteria—"books 20 years old must go," for example. Partners can discuss the books and give them to you for final approval. Set up a couple of deleting stations to speed up the process. Your district may provide you with a gaylord box on a pallet so you don't have to box up every book.

- **Put your money where your holes are.** If you target key areas for weeding, be sure to create wish lists for those areas. If you delete a book about Pluto for example, add one to your online book vendor list. Be sure to include multiple reading levels.

- **Ask the experts.** In addition to ALA, there are other national organizations that choose the best nonfiction titles in their subject area. The National Council for the Social Studies and the National Science Teachers Association, for example, both annually create a Notable Trade Book list for K-12. You might also ask your subject area specialists to help you weed and shop for replacement titles.

- **Judge for yourself.** Look at the newest award winning nonfiction. There are many text features that work well with today's students. Is there an index? A bibliography? A glossary? What qualifications does the writer hold? What websites support the text? Is there an online site that constantly supports the changing of websites?

Resources

CREW method (http://www.tsl.state.tx.us/ld/pubs/crew/)

Follett Titlewave (http://www.titlewave.com/login/)

National Council for the Social Studies (http://www.socialstudies.org/)

National Science Teachers Association (http://nsta.org/)

Deborah B. Ford blog (http://deborahford.blogspot.com/)

Deborah B. Ford *is an award-winning library media specialist and international speaker with over 25 years of experience as a classroom teacher and librarian in K-12 schools.*

Ford, Deborah B. (2011). Facts: Just the facts! Evaluating your nonfiction collection. *LMC, 29*(5), 5.

Weed 'Em and Reap: The Art of Weeding to Avoid Criticism

By Melissa Allen

Introduction

Today media centers provide students the opportunity to learn and explore subjects of their interest in depth. The media center is the largest classroom in the school providing service to every student and every teacher in all curricular areas. The library should be a place to encourage students' interests and a place to broaden their horizons by introducing them to new perspectives and concepts. To ensure a quality library collection, weeding is as critical as selection of new materials. A quality media collection should result in students actively engaged, working, reading, and learning in libraries.

A well-known Taoist proverb states, "Fertile fields cannot produce good crops as long as the weeds are not cleared away." Students cannot efficiently find quality information if outdated, wrong, or poorly presented information is overcrowding your library shelves. Many media specialists feel the need to weed in the dead of night to avoid criticism from patrons who hate to see "good" books being thrown away. It is hard to explain to everyone that books eventually "expire" by going past their usefulness. Although books that are well taken care of will last many years, they are not meant to last forever. People want to think that every book will always have some value. Destruction of books brings up images of censorship and book burning, but it is better to have worthless books in the trash than have trash on your shelves. While weeding can be controversial, a carefully prepared and fully documented policy on weeding (or deselection) can lessen or alleviate misunderstandings. Media collections should be tailored to meet the needs of the students and the curriculum. Curriculum is constantly being revised and student populations are ever changing; thus school library media collections should also be in a continuous state of change.

> Overflowing shelves give an overall impression of chaos and make it harder for people to find the resources they really need.

New technology developments and advancements occurring on a daily basis have created an atmosphere of unrelenting change. Once stocked mainly with books and other print materials, today's media centers include a wide range of multimedia resources. Technology and nonprint media should be weeded on a regular schedule just like print materials, although it can be harder to judge content and quality without spending a great deal of time watching or listening to each item. Other issues to consider when evaluating nonprint materials include format and condition. Discard obsolete technologies—transferring outdated materials to another format (e.g., VHS to DVD, cassette tape to CD) does not update the information.

Why Weed?

Continual evaluation of media resources will result in a highly effective and quality library collection. Try to avoid a situation where weeding is a massive project that is done once in ten years requiring you to weed hundreds of items. It is much better to make weeding an ongoing process that is tackled with a strategic plan to weed small sections at a time throughout the year. Here are a few reasons to continually weed your collection:

1. Most libraries face space restraints; thus it is important to keep the best resources in the library. Unnecessary or outdated materials weaken a collection.
2. A library needs to be uncluttered to make it easier for patrons to find what they are looking for. Overflowing shelves give an overall impression of chaos and make it harder for people to find the resources they really need.
3. Library patrons want attractive, clean books that are in good condition. Shelves crammed with soiled, worn, torn, moldy, or unattractive books will send patrons running from the library.
4. Collections that are not weeded often contain unacceptable stereotypes and misinformation, not the reliable, accurate, unbiased, up-to-date materials your patrons need.

How to Get Started Weeding

Media specialists need to work with their media committees to develop a weeding policy as part of the overall collection development policy. Weeding should be based on a list of criteria such as copyright date, condition of the material, date last circulated, relevance to the curriculum, inclusion of biases and/or stereotypes, duplicates, and accuracy and appropriateness of material for patrons' reading and interest level. The main question you should ask is, Does this resource serve an appropriate purpose in this learning community? For an overview of the criteria for weeding, the acronym **MUSTY** can be used:

M Misleading and/or factually inaccurate

U Ugly and worn beyond mending or rebinding

S Superseded by a newer edition or by a much better book

T Trivial with no discernible value

Y Your collection has no use for this material, irrelevant to the needs of your clientele

If weeding has not been done on a regular basis, identify areas which need immediate attention. Address these sections first due to currency issues: most career materials are outdated within five years; most computer/technology instruction books are outdated within three years; general encyclopedia and atlases are outdated after five years; and titles that imply currency (e.g., *Today*, *Modern*) that are older than seven years. As a general rule, the following materials should have a copyright date of less than ten years: Social Studies (300s) books, except for fairy tales and holidays; Science (500s) books, except most dinosaurs, animals, and plants; Technology/Health (600s), except for many pet books; Social Studies (900s), except for war history books; and Reference books. If the paper is yellowed or torn or the cover or pages are missing, then weed that book.

Only resources that actually circulate have a value within the collection. Most automated cataloging system can generate a list of all items that have not circulated for at least two or three years. Circulation reports can also be run on all the materials that are being discarded for poor physical condition since the condition may be due to the high usage of the material. Items that are discarded but have a high circulation rate will need to be replaced. Weigh the cost of repairing and rebinding against the cost of replacement. Finally, weed after hours, on planning days, and during the summer to avoid inconveniencing patrons.

Do not make your weeded books a problem for someone else by just passing the buck.

What to Do with the Books

Now that you have resources that fit the criteria to be weeded from your collection, you need to decide what to do with those resources. First, all county and school procedures for discarding school properties should be followed. Media specialists can often avoid criticism about weeding simply by finding another use for books that no longer belong in a media collection. Many books have no proper place but in the trash due to their poor physical condition or outdated information. Often books that are being weeded have information in them that is no longer relevant or contain misinformation that you would not want to pass on to others so those books should be recycled or placed in the trash. Do not make your weeded books a problem for someone else by just passing the buck. Many books may work as donations if they are no longer appropriate for the clientele (e.g., a high school-level topic would not work at an elementary or middle school); the resource is a duplicate copy; or the resource is not circulating even though it is a reliable material. Some charitable organizations collect books to send to needy individuals. Check out their websites for requirements.

- Books for Africa—A nonprofit organization that is the largest shipper of donated books to the African continent: <http://www.booksforafrica.org/>
- Better World Books—A for-profit organization that partners with charitable causes to raise money by selling donated books: <http://www.betterworldbooks.com>
- The Prison Book Club—A nonprofit organization that sends free books to prisoners: <http://www.prisonbookprogram.org/>
- Contact your local public library to see if they have a Friends of the Library organization that works to raise money for the library through the sale of used books.
- Find local shelters, hospitals, prisons, or thrift stores that accept book donations.
- Find local recycling centers that accept books. (Note that paperbacks can be recycled as they are but hardcover books must have the covers and spine removed because only the pages of the book are recyclable).

A well-known Taoist proverb states, "Fertile fields cannot produce good crops as long as the weeds are not cleared away."

Delete all weeded holdings and/or bibliographic records from your cataloging and circulation system. All items not destroyed should have all identifying marks removed and/or be clearly marked as "discarded." If all other options have been reviewed and the weeded materials cannot be placed somewhere else then don your black clothes and come to the school in the dead of night to haul your double bagged discarded books to the dumpster or look for additional ways to use the resources. Involve the staff at your school in the weeding process and removal of the discarded materials. Many staff members may have creative ideas for ways to recycle the weeded resources within the school. Here are some examples of projects that I have seen used in the past:

- Paint the pages of the books in white paint in order to use the book as a diary or journal.
- Pages can be torn out to build a jewelry type box by building up the sides so that the cover of the book is the top of the box.
- Books can become scrapbooks or memory books by allowing students to decorate each page any way they want.
- Books can be used for pictures and text to cut out for use in art assignments and poster projects.
- Books can be glued into a stack to serve as an artistic end table that is perfect for holding a reading lamp at the end of a couch.

Conclusion

Although weeding is one more thing that requires some of your time, the benefits are well worth the effort. Media collection reports, such as a TitleWise collection analysis obtained for free <http://www .titlewave.com>, can be used to justify your media budget allotment. In these hard economic times, media center budgets are getting cut or media specialists are losing control over their designated funds (which allows school administrators to use media funds in other ways besides on vital media resources). Not only is it important to document media purchases, but it is equally important to document resources that you weed from your collection and note why those resources no longer fill a need in your collection. Instead of getting huffy when confronted about weeding items, be prepared to answer criticism about discards and stress the positive aspects of weeding—print a brochure with your media program's mission statement, selection and weeding policy, and statistics about the collection analysis such as average age and number of resources per students.

Melissa Allen *is a library media specialist at Glynn Academy in Brunswick, Georgia, and teaches a class in the instructional technology department at Georgia Southern University.*

Allen, Melissa. (2010). Weed 'em and reap: The art of weeding to avoid criticism. *LMC, 28*(6), 32–33.

Ditching Dewey

By Kristie Miller

From Frustration to Satisfaction

It all started, as most things do in a library, with a frustrated searcher. In graduate school I worked at a branch of the Queens Borough Public Library. We had a large population of teens and an unfortunately small YA collection. Our teens were dedicated readers but liked to read specific styles of books. Their attention lagged when browsing the collection for the types of books they wanted. I got permission from the branch manager to do some rearranging. I couldn't change the records in the library catalog, which were centrally controlled at the main library in our sixty-two branch system, but I could rearrange the books on the shelves as long as I did the re-shelving when the books were returned. I took that deal. I subdivided the YA section into genres that were meaningful to the patrons who frequently browsed the small collection. I didn't have access to the circulation stats to prove with numbers that the shift was a success, but anecdotal information (praise from patrons) proved the changes were appreciated, and the empty shelves proved the changes made it easier for them to find what they wanted.

> *Telling a student to look for the label with the court jester wasn't enough.*

The Goal: Self-Directed Readers

Fast-forward to two years ago. I am a school librarian in a small rural district in upstate New York, with a much different population but the same frustrations. Students would come to me and say, "I like reading this and I would like more books like it" or "I need to get a historical fiction novel for class, and I don't know where to look." I would take them to the shelves and give them some suggestions or point them to the popular authors in the genre they were looking for, or authors that I have read and thought they would like—all common reader's advisory "stuff." It worked okay, but I knew there was a better way, a way that would make the students more independent in their quests for books, would expose them to more authors in a genre than even I knew about, and would be all around more efficient.

In the meantime, The Book Whisperer by Donalyn Miller and The Reading Zone by Nancy Atwell were being passed around the English department. There was a groundswell of support for moving toward a reading workshop style of instruction in reading classes. I started offering the English classes time to come to the library for genre-based booktalks. The teachers started booking library time like crazy. It quickly became apparent to all of us that the current traditional arrangement—alphabetical by the author's last name—was not working, even with the new genre stickers. Telling a student to look for the label with the court jester wasn't enough.

Supporting Student Learning

I started looking at the New York State English Language Arts exams, given annually to students in grades three to eight. Students were expected to be able to identify the genres of reading passages. This was an area I thought I could support and reinforce in the library. Looking at books that are arranged by genre naturally makes people think about the characteristics of that genre and heightens their awareness.

> *Nothing that improves the user experience for the students and teachers in my school is a waste of time.*

A Doable Project with Results!

The teachers and I had a discussion, and I shared my previous experience in Queens rearranging the collection by genre. A plan was made, people stepped up to volunteer, dates were picked, and we all met at the middle school/high school library during the summer to get to work. There were only three or four of us, but it didn't take us long to re-shelve the fiction section by genre. We picked the major genres: realistic, historical, science fiction, fantasy, mystery, and horror. I also pulled all graphic novels from oblivion in the 700s section of nonfiction and created an additional genre section for them. It only took us two days, working for a couple of hours to get everything rearranged. I added signs to the shelves and additional genre-related spine labels. At the start of the school year my assistant changed the catalog records so students could find a book by browsing or searching. It took her a couple of weeks, but changing the records was well worth it.

How was it received? Circulation tripled the first year, and we have been maintaining the new high ever since! Before the first year was over, we tackled the fiction collection in the elementary library as well. Circulation statistics there are always steady because we are on a fixed schedule, but students are much happier with the browsing capability of the fiction collection. The "genre of the month" projects go much more smoothly and we have happy student and teacher customers.

Turning Our Attention to Nonfiction

While the fiction section was taking off, the nonfiction collection wasn't seeing much action. Dewey just hadn't been doing it for me for a long time. Of course, we had hot spots where the students memorized the location of their favorite subjects— animals, motorized vehicles, war books, and drawing books—but large chunks of the collection went unused. I had tried many different ways to draw attention to the hidden gems students might be missing (displays, booktalks, etc.) and taught the Dewey Decimal System many different ways, but students never seemed to be completely comfortable finding what they wanted. Using the catalog was great, but once they had that number written down, students seemed intimidated and then frustrated if they couldn't find the book quickly. I will admit to being frustrated too. Every June, when I did the end of the year inventory, I ended up with large stacks of books I thought belonged somewhere other than where good old Melville thought they belonged.

The Book Store Model

The book store model was the most predominantly used alternative to Dewey. Public libraries have been ahead in making the switch, and the book store model seemed to be the leading choice. Looking at the book store model, I was mostly convinced that it was the way to go, but I wanted to be sure that books were in related neighborhoods.

Positive user experiences translate into repeat customers, and in our business that means lifelong readers and learners, the ultimate goal in what we do.

My colleague Christopher Harris, head of the school library system at the Genesee Valley Educational Partnership (an educational consortia that supports the districts in our region), helped me brainstorm. He sat at the computer and I walked up and down the stacks picking apart the places where I thought Dewey didn't work. We came up with a framework of categories that didn't reflect the book store model but was more like Dewey without the decimals, aligned to how books are actually used in schools—centered around the curriculum, not aligned to a philosophical taxonomy of how things should be.

Now we are looking at this process not just as one library or even both libraries in my district but as something that could be scaled for all the libraries in our region who would like to ditch Dewey. We are currently working on creating a tool that would match the previous Dewey category with the new category from our new classification schema. The tool would automate the reorganization process and make the process more streamlined for future non-Dewey convertors. We are also designing new spine labels that use words and symbols instead of numbers that have no meaning to the end user. The elementary collection will be converted by the end of the school year and the middle/high school collection will follow by the beginning of the next school year.

And the Verdict Is . . .

Since we have gone public with this concept, reactions have ranged from "a huge waste of time" to "that's what book displays are for" to people cheering us on

---

Other Library Practices We Have Dropped or Added

The vertical file. I inherited a well-tended vertical file that no one used. Except for some local history items, it has gone to the great recycling bin in the sky.

Waiting for a teacher to show up to collaborate with me. When I see something interesting or have an idea on how to tweak an existing project, I don't wait to be asked to the dance, I do the asking. And it works. Just today I was given freshly baked cookies for a suggestion I made on a long-existing elementary exit project.

Only maintaining a traditional collection. Yes, we have all the usual suspects in our library—books, magazines, audiobooks, movies, databases, etc. If you look closer, however, you will also find board games, textbooks, embroidery hoops, and, our

newest addition since last spring, the "Prom Dress Lending Library." This winter we will be collaborating with a new apparel sewing class and staging a fashion show to highlight the dresses in the collection, available to students for prom season free of charge.

Leveling the elementary library. We did it and I am glad. I know it is rare to find a librarian who favors marking the books by reading level, and I was one of them, but after looking more closely at the issue, I did it. One of the many functions of a school library is to give students books that they can use to practice their reading skills. In a collection of 10,000 volumes, it is impossible to know the reading level on everything, especially if the publisher doesn't include it on the cover. We used Accelerated Reader to level the collection. We picked the

eight major levels and assigned them a color code. Yes, students need to pick books that interest them to further their desire to read, but they also need experience reading books at their level. In our community we are often the only library our students are exposed to. We are a centralized district that encompasses several towns that do not have public libraries. Picking titles that are of interest and provide the appropriate practice is essential. Putting little colored dots on the spines of the books helped immensely with this task. Students still get their free choice. They get to choose two books every time they come to the library—one on their level and one free choice. The process has been a huge PR gain with the elementary teachers too!

and wanting progress reports. Nothing that improves the user experience for the students and teachers in my school is a waste of time. By the time this project is done, there will be hundreds of hours logged on our end, but those hundreds of hours will translate into positive user experiences. Positive user experiences translate into repeat customers, and in our business that means lifelong readers and learners, the ultimate goal in what we do.

Kristie Miller *is a preK-12 school media specialist at Alexander (New York) Central Schools.*

Miller, Kristie. (2013). Ditching Dewey. *LMC, 31*(6), 24–26.

Internet Safety and Teens Today

By Cheyenne Gray

When a teacher, librarian, or mentor comes to a classroom and says, "We are going to learn about Internet safety today," some students will perk up and listen while others instantly put their heads down or tune out the lesson. Many teens and children think that they already know how to be safe on the Internet; some even believe that they are already safe. In fact, 33 percent of high school teens have been victimized by cyber bullying, 16 percent of teens considered meeting someone they have never met but talked to online, and 8 percent have actually met an online friend in person (Cyber Safety Statistics).

Beyond Learning by Listening

In our school district we have a family life nurse come and speak to the students in the seventh grade about Bullying and Stalking Online, in the ninth grade about Cyber Relationships, and in the tenth grade about Pornography. The librarians come to English classes to discuss Malicious Code and Intellectual Property in the eleventh grade. Social Networks are addressed by government teachers in the twelfth grade. All of these programs are part of the Internet Safety curriculum (ISafe). Now you may say that's enough Internet safety right there, but most students really don't take the time to listen and understand. Often students don't feel a connection with an outside teacher, nurse, or mentor coming into their classroom. If other students came in to talk about Internet safety or prepared a public service announcement (PSA), don't you think it would be more effective?

All teens know how it is when you get on your Facebook or MySpace page. The ability to access information about someone is powerful, sometimes too powerful, and can lead to bullying. Your personal information such as your social security number, your address, or even your name shouldn't be leaked online. It is valuable and can give a stranger access to steal your identity and invade your personal life.

> *Many teens and children think that they already know how to be safe on the Internet; some even believe that they are already safe.*

A Student-Led Internet Safety Project

In my high school, library science students have been organized into four Internet safety groups: Internet Dating, Identity Theft, Computer Viruses, and Cyber Bullying. Each group will develop PSAs to raise awareness and prepare students to safely use the social networks and search engines that most teens access daily.

Each team has a team leader, and each team member will be creating an online Glogster poster which the group team leader will organize as a Glogster PSA project. In addition, students are encouraged to check out the library cameras and create short video scenarios to upload on their Glogs. Teams are made up of members across seven periods and are sharing information through the school's online discussion board and the library's wiki. As project manager, my job will be to guide the teams to completion through the team wikis and put all the projects together into one final project. We will post paper printouts of the posters around the library and school with the web link to view the online versions.

Student Concerns

Below are some comments students made on our discussion board as we opened the discussion to decide which issues to address. They reflect students' awareness of the dangers lurking on the Internet and on social networks.

- "The three concerns I have about the Internet involve social networks. Internet bullying is a threat that has recently become a known issue since many deaths have occurred recently because of this problem. Also, talking to people you don't know can be dangerous. If you don't know the person who you are talking to, they could be a criminal and might hurt you in the future. The last threat with the Internet is identify theft. With so much information available and easy to find about everyone, having your information stolen is extremely easy to do."

- "I spend on average about an hour or so a day on the computer using many different websites. I spend most of my time on Facebook, Hulu, MySpace, and YouTube. All of these sites are pages where you can upload personal information and various videos. Of these websites, Facebook and MySpace are the BIG two social networks because in these websites you create a page about yourself by giving out huge amounts of personal information. Teens need to worry about three different things: identity theft, Internet stalkers, and various things in your pictures. Identity theft is a huge problem in today's society. This can lead to huge losses of money and other dangerous things. Internet stalkers are another problem. By putting personal information out there, you are giving them a path right to your front steps. Third are things in your pictures. As a high school student you are bound to go to parties but you have to watch yourself and be sure you are not in any picture where alcohol or drugs are present because this can jeopardize jobs and can get you in trouble in school."

- "The three main concerns I believe teens should be aware of while on the Internet are cyber bullying, stalkers, and identity theft. There have been many incidents where teens have been harassed and bullied over the Internet. There have also been many cases of teens putting too much information on the Internet, and therefore someone either stalks them or takes their identity."

- "Most of my time on the Internet is spent on Facebook and YouTube. The only social network I use is Facebook, although I had a MySpace. Teens on the Internet should mainly be concerned with illicit websites, i.e. pornography. Studies have shown that nearly 90 percent of the Internet is indeed pornographic material. Also, on social networks, bullying and identity theft are critical issues. Bullying can make someone's morale drop and can even lead some people to suicide. Reports have shown that teenagers are now the leading candidates for identity theft because of all the personal information that they post on the web for others to see."

- "When I am on the Internet I'm usually on Facebook or Pandora. Facebook is a social network, and Pandora is a music site specifically designed for you to hear new music. The biggest concerns one should know about the Internet is that nothing on the net is private. Legally, when something is posted on the web, it becomes public. Another danger is stalking. People can figure out how to get in touch with you on the Internet and constantly contact you. Last are viruses. A virus can mess up your computer and cause you to lose a large sum of money."

- "When using the Internet, you have to be careful of what you choose for everyone to view. What most teens don't understand is that there are sexual predators out there on Facebook and chat rooms. [You must] be careful of what you say because giving out personal information isn't the best choice. In some cases sexting has become a major issue today. With the sending of pictures, you are mostly going to end up on the Internet. With jobs doing checks on your personal information on the web now, you have to be careful of what you say, do, and, most importantly, take a picture of."

As you can see from my classmates' comments, teens taking our class are very aware of the risks and dangers. In this project we hope to gather important information to justify our concerns, give students strategies they can use to keep safe, and spread the word through our PSAs.

Making an Impact

You may wonder how this project will impact the students around the school. Students listen to other students more than anyone else. When the PSAs are online along with little videos and catchy posters, many students will look at it just because it caught their eye. The more students talk about the project, the more aware they will become, and before the students know it, they have learned about Internet safety the fun way! Personally, this project has opened my eyes to how easy it is for danger to come knocking at your computer screen. When you get on the computer, you don't think about identity theft, hackers, and predators. With the right precautions, when you get online you can prevent unwanted solicitations, exposures and harassment. It comes down to what you do online, who you are talking to, and what you say. The computer can be a dangerous place if you let it, so be aware and stay safe.

Works Cited

"Cyber Safety Statistics." NetLingo. Web. 10 Dec. 2010. www.netlingo .com/tips/cyber-safety-statistics .php.

Glogster EDU—21st Century Multimedia Tool for Educators, Teachers and Students. Web. 10 Dec. 2010. http://edu.glogster.com.

I-SAFE Inc. Web. 8 Dec. 2010. www .isafe.org.

"Internet Safety and Your Tween— Online Threats Statistics." Norton. 19 Feb. 2007. Web. 10 Dec. 2010. http://us.norton.com/library/ familyresource/article.jsp?aid=pr_ internetsafety_and_your_tween.

"Internet Safety Statistics." *Parents & Guardians.* Web. 18 Jan. 2011. <http://www.netsmartz.org/Safety/ Statistics>.

SafeWave—Creating ILANDS of Safety for Kids Online. Web. 10 Dec. 2010. www.safewave.org.

Cheyenne Gray *is a senior at Thomas Dale High School in Chester, Virginia.*

Gray, Cheyenne. (2011). Internet safety and teens today. *LMC, 29*(6), 32–33.

Creating a Safe School Environment: How to Prevent Cyberbullying at Your School

By Terry Diamanduros and Elizabeth Downs

Technology has changed the school yard or neighborhood bully. While we were growing up, bullies usually used physical domination to intimidate other children. It no longer requires physical intimidation to be a bully. In fact, bullying can be done anonymously, on or off campus, and physical size does not enter into the scenario. Every year headlines identify children who take their own lives as a result of being victims of various forms of bullying. When technology is used to send the message or intimidate, it becomes cyberbullying. Using computers and cell phones, bullies can send threatening or harassing emails, set up offensive websites about the victim, and send harassing text messages or embarrassing photographs.

Hiding behind Digital Devices

Unfortunately, bullies can hide their cowardice through digital devices. Temporary email addresses and pseudonyms in chat rooms can conceal the bully's identity. Because of such anonymity, today's students may feel uninhibited to do things they would never do in person. Some estimates indicate that eighty-five percent of middle school children have been cyberbullied (Aftab, 2010).

The School's Responsibility

Cyberbullying can occur outside of school hours and off school grounds, which initially lead some schools to debate whether schools were responsible for addressing incidents. Several states have instituted legislation that includes cyberbullying and holds schools responsible for providing safe learning environments for students. For example, Georgia's House Bill 927 (2009) legislation, passed in 2010, expands the definition of bullying to include cyberbullying and applies to students in grades K-12. This bill permits schools to

separate the identified bully from the victim by placing the bully in a school outside his/her attendance area, requires school employees to report suspected cases of cyberbullying, and establishes procedures to investigate incidences of cyberbullying. Georgia's House Bill 310 (2011), The End to Cyberbullying Act, includes acts of bullying that involve computers and electronic communication devices even if such acts do not originate on school property or school computers, as long as the act is directed to a student or to personnel of the school system. Arkansas' ACT115, An Act to Define Bullying and to Include Cyberbullying in Public School District Anti-bullying Policies, allows schools to address cyberbullying that originates off school property (Arkansas House Bill 1072).

> *Several states have instituted legislation that includes cyberbullying and holds schools responsible for providing safe learning environments for students.*

The Media Specialist's Role

As the library media specialist, you are in a unique position to guide students, faculty, staff, and administration through steps to create an awareness of cyberbullying. These steps include development of a cyberbullying policy and promoting awareness and prevention. Fortunately, there are many resources to guide you.

State Mandates

Where to begin? As part of your annual policy "check-up," make sure that your media center has an

up-to-date cyberbullying policy that aligns with the school and district cyberbullying policies. If there are no existing policies, begin your search at the state level. To get information about state legislation on the inclusion of cyberbullying in school policies, contact your state's Department of Education. Hinduja and Patchin (2011) summarized state laws on bullying and cyberbullying, indicating whether a state has legislation that includes cyberbullying and whether a cyberbullying policy is mandated.

Policy Essentials

Several key components should be included in a policy to create an environment in which students feel safe: definitions, delegation of responsibility, complaint procedures, consequences of cyberbullying behavior, description of on-campus vs. off-campus school policies, and district or board policies (Downs, 2010). Of course, the policy should identify what happens after an incident of cyberbullying has occurred. Schools should strive to create an environment that will raise awareness and help to prevent such incidents.

Public Service Announcements and Videos

What can you do to prevent cyberbullying in your school? Promoting awareness is a critical step in helping students understand what cyberbullying entails and the potential effects on other students. One teaching strategy that can be used to start conversations among students involves video-clips and public service announcements (PSA). Some suggested PSAs include the National Crime Prevention Council's (NCPC) *In the Kitchen with Megan* and Concerned Children's Advertisers (CCA-Kids) *Words Hurt*. For elementary school, you may want to consider Disney's *Get Cybersmart with Phineas and Ferb*. Such videos help students understand the power of words and engage students in discussions about cyberbullying. They are easily accessible on YouTube.

Animated videos can also be effective for teaching students about cyberbullying. One such animation series that teens and tweens might find interesting is Angels and Warriors from WiredSafety.org. In this video, three "angels" offer a victim information and advice about cyberbullying. WiredSafety.org also has other videos designed to teach students, parents, and teachers about online harassment. An animated video for younger students, Professor Garfield Cyberbullying, can be found on the website of Common Sense Media.

Promoting Awareness

Have students participate in a cyberbullying campaign in which they develop projects designed to raise awareness. Students can create posters that can be placed in the media center and school hallways. Older students might enjoy developing a wiki or blog about cyberbullying. These Web 2.0 tools can provide students with an outlet to voice the message that posting negative comments, spreading rumors, or posting inappropriate pictures about peers is degrading and that there are consequences for such actions. Working on the projects in groups helps students to get to know others and start conversations about cyberbullying.

Curriculum and Collaboration

To reach students outside the media center, collaborate with teachers to educate students about cyberbullying, how it impacts others, and how to respond if it happens to them. Collaborating with teachers to incorporate a cyberbullying prevention curriculum in the classroom is an effective way of making both students and teachers aware of cyberbullying. One such curriculum (free) is *Cyberbullying: Encouraging Ethical Online Behavior*, developed by the Media Literacy Network of Canada. This curriculum includes a series of lesson plans for grades 5–12 that promote an understanding of cyberbullying and its ethical and legal implications. It can be used to support anti-bullying and empathy building programs already in use. Another free curriculum designed for K-12 is the *Cyberbullying Lessons and Activities* package developed by CyberSmart. This package is available online and consists of nonsequential lesson plans and activity sheets that can be integrated readily into the regular classroom curriculum. Both packages include handouts and materials to educate teachers and parents about cyberbullying.

Breaking the Cycle

Make sure to provide students with information about what to do if they are the victim of a cyberbully. Students need to understand that retaliation is not an option when responding to a cyberbully's cruelty. Such actions would result in their becoming a cyberbully and a cycle of online harassment. StopCyberbullying.org's "Stop, Block, Tell" technique emphasizes the need to stop before responding impulsively in a negative way, suggests blocking the cyberbully to prevent further communication, and telling an adult about the incident. Students need to understand the importance of reporting incidences of cyberbullying so that others do not become victims. Parry Aftab, an Internet privacy and security lawyer, has been instrumental in providing students, parents, teachers, and schools with self-help presentations on how to respond when a cyberbullying incident occurs.

Working with Parents

Teaching parents about Internet safety and helping them establish rules for Internet use is another way to play an active role in the prevention of cyberbullying. On their website, Common Sense Media offers "Parent Tips," helping parents establish a code of conduct for technology use. These tips include such items as appropriate online behavior, limiting online socialization, privacy issues such as password and identification information, and communication about cyberbullying incidents. Additionally, you can help parents develop Internet and smartphone use contracts with their children to ensure that children understand what is considered appropriate and non-appropriate online behavior. Examples of such contracts have been developed by Hinduja and Patchin (2009). Tips for establishing online rules and Internet/cell phone use contracts can be included in a written brochure designed for parents or presented to parents at school functions, such as Family Fun Night or PTA meetings.

Taking a Leadership Role

Cyberbullying is an increasing challenge for 21st century educators. School library media specialists can have an active role in addressing cyberbullying in schools through establishing policies on cyberbullying and promoting awareness and prevention of this form of bullying.

References

Aftab, P. "Statistics and a Snapshot of Cyberbulling Trends." Aftab. com, 2010. Web. 15 April 2011. http://aftab.com/index. php?page=cyberbullying-statistics.

"Arkansas House Bill 1072. ACT115: An Act to Define Bullying and to Include Cyberbullying in Public School District Anti-bullying Policies." Arkansas State Legislature, 2007. Web. 15 April 2011. www.arkleg.state.ar.us/ assembly/2007/R/Bills/HB1072.pdf.

"Classroom Resources to Counter Cyberbullying." Media Literacy Network of Canada. Web. 17 April 2011. www.media-awareness.ca/ english/resources/educational/ lessons/cyberbullying.cfm.

"CyberSmart! Curriculum on Cyberbullying." CyberSmart. Web. 17 April 2011. http:// cybersmartcurriculum.org.

Downs, E. *The School Library Media Specialist's Policy & Procedure Writer*. New York: Neal-Schuman Publishers, 2010. Print.

"Georgia House Bill 927." Georgia General Assembly, 2009. Web. 15 April 2011. www1.legis.ga.gov/ legis/2009_10/fulltext/hb927.htm.

"Georgia House Bill 310. The End to Cyberbullying Act." Georgia

General Assembly, 2011. Web. 16 April 2011. www.legis.ga.gov/ Legislation/20112012/110632.pdf.

Hinduja, S., and J. W. Patchin. "Family Cell Phone Contracts." Cyberbullying, 2009. 16 April 2011. www.cyberbullying.us/cyber bullying_cell_phone_contract.pdf.

Hinduja, S., and J. W. Patchin. Family Internet Contracts. Cyberbullying, 2009. Web. 16 April 2011. www. cyberbullying.us/cyberbullying_ internet_use_contract.pdf.

Hinduja, S., and J. W. Patchin. State Cyberbullying Laws: A Brief Review of State Cyberbullying Laws and Policies. Cyberbullying, 2011. Web. 16 April 2011. www. cyberbullying.us/Bullying_and_ Cyberbullying_Laws.pdf

"Parent Tips: Common Sense on Cyberbullying." Common Sense Media, 2010. Web. 16 April 2011. www.commonsensemedia.org/ sites/default/files/Cyberbullying-Tip.pdf.

"Stop, Block and Tell." Stop Cyberbullying.org. Web. 17 April 2011. www.stopcyberbullying. org/take_action/stop_block_and_ tell.html.

"Cyber Stalking and Harassment Self-help." WiredSafety.org. Web. 15 April 2011. http://wiredsafety.com/ cyberstalking_harassment/index. html.

Dr. Terry Diamanduros *is an associate professor in the Leadership, Technology, and Human Development Department in the College of Education, Georgia Southern University in Athens, Georgia. Terry may be reached at tdiamanduros@ georgiasouthern.edu.*

Dr. Elizabeth Downs *is a professor in the Leadership, Technology, and Human Development Department in the College of Education, Georgia Southern University in Athens, Georgia. She may be reached at edowns@georgiasouthern .edu.*

Diamandurous, Terry, & Downs, Elizabeth. (2011). Creating a safe school environment: How to prevent cyberbullying at your school. *LMC, 30*(2). 36–39, and Tools of the Trade: Cyberbullying resources.

From Communication to Cooperation to Collaboration: School and Public Librarians as Partners for Student Success

By Mary Wepking

When they hear the word "collaboration," today's teacher-librarians immediately think of their teaching faculty and the need to incorporate 21st century information skills into the school's curriculum. But there may be another professional or two in your community who would also be very valuable collaborators, helping you to reach and teach children beyond the school day and school year. Have you extended a collaborative hand to your local public library?

In a 1986 survey of medium-sized Indiana public libraries (serving populations between 10,000 and 35,000), Daniel Callison discovered that the majority of public librarians (57%) could not name a librarian in their community's secondary schools. Only slightly better than that, just 46% of the library media specialists surveyed could name a librarian from their community's public library staff. Many years have passed since this survey, but one wonders exactly how much has changed over the years. Limits on time and resources make communication, much less cooperation and collaboration, with our public library counterparts increasingly challenging.

Another reason that teacher-librarians may not reach out to their public library colleagues is that many of us have worked exclusively in schools as teachers and as teacher-librarians. Perhaps we don't understand the work and the mission of public library staff and therefore can't envision the benefits of working together to serve the same children and teens. A review of recent literature and the ALA Web site on best practices in school and public library efforts (Fig. 1) reveals many great ideas for true collaboration with your public library counterparts. The following examples are just a few simple ways to make this kind of collaboration happen.

Limits on time and resources make communication, much less cooperation and collaboration, with our public library counterparts increasingly challenging.

Assignment Alerts

Ask any public children's librarian about their pet peeves with respect to school assignments and most will quickly share this one: having the first student who comes to the library for books on birds check out *all* the best books on birds before the librarian learns that she'll have 25 more students coming in this week with the same request. Some public libraries have constructed online forms for teachers or teacher-librarians to complete to inform them of upcoming research assignments (Fig. 2), but these impersonal forms, hidden away on library Web sites, may sit unused. Collaborate instead by dropping a quick email to the children's librarian, perhaps even attaching a copy of the research assignment. This will aid the public library not only in reference but also in collection development. If they know that the local third graders study birds each spring, they'll be likely to improve their collection and resources in that area.

Traveling Collections

The library media center budget may be unable to meet the demands of classroom teachers for topical books for use in the classroom. Have you checked with your local public library for support? Larger library systems such as Multnomah County

Library in Oregon offer a wide range of circulating collections on topics suitable for use in local schools. Their Bucket of Books (Fig. 3) sets include not only collections of books by topic but even teacher guides with Web resources and other support materials. Your local public library will not likely have this depth of resources, but they may have materials that would supplement those available in your own school library collection. Are educator cards readily available to help you or your teachers borrow these materials, with extended loan periods? This is another excellent service your public library may be willing to extend to assist teachers and students in your school.

Creating Lifelong Readers

So much of the teacher-librarian's time is necessarily consumed with instruction, often allowing much less time than we'd like to promote reading. Are you aware that the local public library shares this important goal? Think about meeting with the children's or YA (Young Adult) librarian in your community for joint planning of a lunchtime or after-school book club, regularly scheduled booktalks for students in their language arts classrooms, and for collaboration on Battle of the Books or other reading incentive programs. Public librarians who serve children envy the teacher-librarian's easy access to nearly all of the children in the community. Share that access to your students by inviting the public librarian into the school. Many youth services librarians would be glad to reach so many students with booktalks and other promotions. Make the most of your collaboration by getting a list of the titles that will be booktalked by the public librarian and create a display of your copies in your own library.

Summer Library Reading Programs

Many of us welcome the public librarian into our schools each spring to promote their summer library reading program. It seems like a nice thing to do. But did you know that it's an absolutely critical thing to do if we're concerned about student achievement? Many recent empirical studies have confirmed that children who do not engage in recreational reading over the summer months suffer from summer reading loss. This research summary says it best:

> A review of 13 empirical studies representing approximately 40,000 students found that, on average, the reading proficiency levels of students from lower income families declined over the summer months, while the reading proficiency levels of students from middle-income families improved modestly. In a single academic year, this decline resulted in an estimated three-month achievement gap between more advantaged and less advantaged students. Between grades 1 and 6, the potential cumulative impact of this achievement gap could compound to 1.5 years' worth of reading development lost in the summer months alone. (Mraz & Rasinski)

Beyond welcoming public librarians into your schools for promotion of their program, get behind the effort by offering incentives for children who participate. How about a pizza party or other special event in September for all of the children who participated in the public library's summer reading program? Inform your administration of the importance of recreational reading over the summer to keep your students, especially economically disadvantaged students, moving ahead in reading achievement, and it's likely that administration will support this critical partnership.

Library Cards for Students

This is another area that seems, on the surface, like a nice thing to do.

But the value of every student in your school having a public library card goes beyond reading. Many public libraries also offer remote authentication to databases that will extend the school library's resources tremendously. In the late 1990s, Houston, Texas, launched their acclaimed Power Card Challenge, offering prizes and banners for schools that have the largest percentage of their students with public library cards. With a goal of getting a library card into the hands of every child in the city's schools, the result was not merely an increase in library cards but also increased participation in summer reading, after-school reading clubs, and more.

> *Think about meeting with the children's or YA (Young Adult) librarian in your community for joint planning of a lunchtime or after-school book club, regularly scheduled booktalks for students in their language arts classrooms, and for collaboration on Battle of the Books or other reading incentive programs.*

Conclusion

Most of us recognize that the teacher-librarian is a unique "hybrid librarian," straddling two professions. It's important that we do not let this dual role set us apart from librarians who work in other settings. We tend, as a group, to attend our regional and state school library conferences, but eschew our state's overall library association membership. With limited professional development funding and time, focusing our continuing education and professional involvement in school library associations seems wise. However, with today's expansive opportunities

for online communication and collaboration, coupled with decreasing budgets and cuts to school library staff, there has never been a better time to help your students succeed through collaboration with those who serve young people evenings, weekends, and in the summer—the youth services librarian at your local public library.

Sources

"Bucket of Books—School Corps-." *Multnomah County Library.* 21 Jan. 2009 <http://www.multcolib.org/schoolcorps/bucket.html>.

Callison, Daniel. "Expanding Collaboration for Literacy Promotion in Public and School Libraries." *Youth Services in Libraries* 11 (1997): 37–48.

"Class Assignment Alert Form." *Milwaukee Public Library.* 21 Jan. 2009 <http://www.mpl.org/coldfusion/email_clcr.cfm>.

Mraz, Maryann, and Timothy V. Rasinski. "Summer Reading Loss." *Reading Rockets.* 2007. 21 Jan. 2009 <http://www.readingrockets.org/article/15218>.

"'Power Card Challenge' Draws Houston's Students to Libraries." *The United States Conference of Mayors* 21 Jan. 2009 <http://www.usmayors.org/USCM/us_mayor_newspaper/documents/02_21_00/power_article.htm>.

"School/public library cooperative programs." *American Library Association.* 21 Jan. 2009 <http://www.ala.org/ala/mgrps/divs/alsc/initiatives/partnerships/coopacts/schoolplcoopprogs.cfm>.

Mary Wepking *is a Senior Lecturer in the School of Information Studies at the University of Wisconsin-Milwaukee.*

Wepking, Mary. (2009). From communication to cooperation to collaboration: School and public librarians as partners for student success. *LMC, 28*(3), 24–26.

Marketing Your School Library Media Center: What Can We Learn from National Bookstores

By Terrence E. Young, Jr.

"You never get a second chance to make a first impression."

During these tough economic times it's important to promote your school library media center's program and collection as integral parts of the learning process. The changing landscape of librarianship demands a wide selection of approaches to promote library resources. Ideas, strategies, and lessons can be learned from the marketing techniques of the national bookstore chains.

Look around your school library media center. Where do you focus your eyes? What really catches your attention? Pretend you are coming into the center as a student or teacher for the first time. Now what do you like or dislike about what you see and feel? Were you greeted by the school library media specialist?

Ask yourself similar questions on your next visit to a national chain bookstore. What are the similarities and differences? What ideas can you take away from your visit and use to improve your library media center image and increase student and teacher use?

We can communicate better with our students and faculty if we study and apply techniques that bookstores use to communicate with customers. Here is one tip to get you started: Experts in customer behavior claim that people entering a store drift toward the right so a store's prime display area is five to twenty steps inside the store to the right of the front door. What can *you* display in this prime location?

Let's begin with the basics:

Effective Library Signage

Welcoming students as they arrive in the library is the most important and basic premise of marketing and public relations. Students, like the rest of us, are used to being bombarded constantly by messages at all times from television, the Internet, and instant messaging as well as billboards and other advertisements. Signage plays a critical role in creating an appealing and user-friendly environment. This is so important when you consider the fact that you are usually the only "real person" to assist users.

Organize the media center and its collection with students in mind. Can they readily find your Online Public Access Catalog (OPAC)? Can they look up from that OPAC and see a library sign (range finders) that shows them where to go to locate the item? Can they read your library signs from a distance? Does your library signage give them answers at every point where they need to make a decision?

> *Effective displays recommend books by being located where the display will be easily noticed, attract the eye with color and signage, and reflect the books' importance.*

In the many school library media centers that I have visited I have seen every kind of DDC poster. When I return years later, I see the same set of DDC posters in the same media center. This must change. The stagnant nature of signage is no longer acceptable. You can keep the same content but vary the color, style, and format of the information. Swap DDC signs with another library. Bilingual/multilingual signage may be necessary for your student population.

Sign readability is a combination of the color contrast between the letters and their background, the shape of the letters, and the size of the letters. The format, color, and type style should be geared toward the grade levels of the students. All signage should have a distinct purpose and message that would benefit all users. Signs that benefit only a few contribute to visual clutter—something that must be avoided.

Signs that fit the needs of the patrons might announce upcoming events, new books, movie tie-ins, and award-winning titles, or represent a particular genre. Use hook and loop fastener tabs when you put up new signs. By using a tab at the corner of each sign, alternating between the fuzzy and smooth sides, you can easily change or move signs and save wear and tear on your walls.

Free Is Good

Major database vendors supply publicity materials for school library media centers. From posters and tent cards to marketing and public relations tools, these free materials increase awareness of your library's offerings. You may also find downloadable graphics for your webpage, PowerPoint presentations, research tools, and lesson plans for staff development. The major publisher websites often have pages devoted to teachers and librarians. Check out some of these exceptional resources.

ABC-CLIO's Social Studies Database Resource Center: http://www.abc-clio.com/schoolresources
Greenwood Skills Center: http://skillscenter.greenwood.com
EBSCO: http://www.ebscohost.com/customerSuccess/default.php?id=13
Gale/Cengage: http://www.gale.cengage.com/power/request_materials.htm, http://www.gale.cengage.com/power/k12.htm
Hyperion: http://www.hyperionbooks forchildren.com/teachers/index.asp

Simon & Schuster: http://www
.simonandschuster.net/
Penguin Putnam: http://
us.penguingroup.com/#
ProQuest: http://www.proquestk12
.com/productinfo/marketingkits/
ELKIT.shtml
Random House: http://www
.randomhouse.com/teachers/
Scholastic: http://www2.scholastic
.com/browse/home.jsp

The two major bookstore chains aggressively target educators. Barnes & Noble has the B&N Educator Program <http://www. barnesandnoble.com/bn-at-school/ educator.asp>, which provides 20 percent off the publisher's list price on all purchases for classroom use and up to 25 percent off the publisher's list price during Educator Appreciation Days. Borders has a similar program at <http://www.borders.com/online/ store/MediaView_teachingzone> and offers a 25 percent discount for classroom purchases, 30 percent during Educator Appreciation Week.

Indoor/Outdoor Banners

Well-designed banners that include graphics can be a great marketing tool. High traffic areas are the best locations to hang a banner: snack bar area, stadium fencing, cafeteria ceiling, bus loading/unloading areas, and the main entrance to the campus. Let everyone who enters your campus know that the school library media center is important. Design your banner online and e-mail the proof back and forth until you are satisfied. The fixed prices vary according to banner size.

BiblioBanners: <http://www
.bibliobanners.com/index.htm>
BuyaBanner: <http://buyabanner
.com/>

Merchandising

When students and teachers come to the school library media specialist, what are they looking for? How will they find it? In the chain bookstores you will probably find new titles prominently placed at the front and center of the store. Books of local interest, books with movie tie-ins, and books featured in the media

(e.g., Oprah, newspapers) make great displays in high traffic areas. You may also see culturally driven displays. Display newly released titles and award-winning titles. Face-out/displayed titles can highlight a popular author, series, or theme.

Book displays are the most effective way to recommend books. Standing books up on a low table is boring and suggests that the books are insignificant. Effective displays recommend books by being located where the display will be easily noticed, attract the eye with color and signage, and reflect the books' importance. DEMCO, Gaylord, and Highsmith all have book display merchandise, which ranges from easels to mobile display carts, acrylic sign holders, and display cases.

> Experts in customer behavior claim that people entering a store drift toward the right so a store's prime display area is five to twenty steps inside the store to the right of the front door. What can you display in this prime location?

One of the best places to display titles is on your shelving end panels. Retailers claim end panel displays sell more items that half of one-side of a range of shelves. If you are fortunate to have slatwall end panels, then purchase a variety of acrylic display items to use on the slatwall. If your end panels are flat, try end panel bins available from North American Enterprise. Most of their products are available in national library supply catalogs. You will save 30 percent or more by ordering directly from the North American Enterprise website <http://northamericanenterprise .com/>.

Trends

National bookstores buyers and local staff have expertise in their areas of book selection. Often you will see

"Staff Recommendation" next to titles. Would this work in your school? Ask faculty and students to write a recommendation for a book they have read and post it with the book. Identify the highest circulating titles and ask readers what they liked about the titles. Don't forget movie promotions, a new title in a popular series, required or summer reading, or just simply a display of titles with a similar theme. Newsletters (print or electronic) are terrific vehicles for delivering your messages. Just make sure the newsletter targets your primary prospects and you have a strong message. Use your library automation system to its fullest. Follett's Destiny home page allows graphics, messages, and category viewing. Create a category "New Books 09/10" so students can read about the new titles purchased during the school year. Change the graphic, message, and background color on your library home page often to attract attention.

Atmosphere

Without fail the chain bookstores are cozy and welcoming with warm colors, comfortable furniture, a strategic floor plan, and of course the café. Has the furniture placement and atmosphere in your school library media center changed recently? Consider some of the following ideas:

1. Change the paint color to an accent color on a single wall.
2. Add some comfortable and colorful furniture such as bean bag chairs, sofas (with laptop arms), and arm chairs.
3. Create a reading nook.
4. Provide an area for social opportunities.
5. Add area theme rug(s).

> Think of every interaction, big or small, online or off, in terms of your approachability.

Customer Service

The bottom line for any bookstore is to put the book in the customer's hand. If the book is unavailable, then employees offer to find or order a copy. It's the same way with student and faculty requests—put the information in their hands (print or electronic). In the school library media center, customer service starts with greeting everyone. Next, the signage should direct students to the appropriate resources and/or encourage them to ask questions. All of the above works best when the school library media specialist is approachable, that is, easy to meet or deal with. Think of every interaction, big or small, online or off, in terms of your approachability.

Students and faculty will chose to communicate with you in different ways. Some will choose face to face, some will e-mail, others will call, while others will do a little of everything. Make all of these ways available and let students know that they can get in touch with you in whatever manner they choose. Sure, you might prefer e-mail. But what matters most is the comfort level of the other person and his or her ability to communicate effectively.

Marketing Your Library Using Web 2.0 Tools

Web 2.0 marketing is the future, but how do you decide what Web 2.0 tools to use? Web 2.0 technologies provide new and exciting ways of extending marketing reach with little effort and cost. Blogs, wikis, and podcasts can help spread your message 24/7. They can help you better understand your patrons (their problems, needs, likes, dislikes, fears, and opinions). Peer-to-peer network sites that support rich media and user-generated content, such as LimeWire, YouTube, SlideShare, and micro-blogging sites such as Twitter can be used to market library programs and services. The use of Web 2.0

should be planned carefully and used strategically. Web 2.0 techniques will continue to reshape how we market our products to our students and teachers.

Community of Stakeholders

The daily activities of our jobs are demanding. Sometimes we believe that once beginning-of-the-year library orientation sessions have been completed everyone knows everything about the school library media center. This is a fallacy! New students are constantly entering our schools. How does a new student receive information about the center? Design and publish a student brochure that every student can understand and that includes hours, staff names, printing/photocopy costs, book checkout/return policy, databases, and access information from campus and home. (If you post the brochure on a public network, omit the login and password information.)

Focusing on your mission to ensure that all students and faculty are effective users of ideas and information requires many approaches. Get the message out to your community through your webpage, monthly calendar of events, e-mails, mailing lists, and news media (print and television). Your professional association, the American Association of School Librarians, has numerous resources on their public relations webpage at <http://www.ala.org/ala/mgrps/divs/aasl/aaslarchive/resourceguides/publicrelations.cfm>.

Students love to be involved in library activities, so consider some of the following: display of student projects in the school library media center, book fairs, costume character visits, book discussion groups, Skype with an author, and poetry slams. The book Bite-Sized Marketing: Realistic Solutions for the Overworked Librarian

by Nancy Dowd, Mary Evangeliste, and Jonathan Silberman provides a plethora of strategies. LaPerriere and Christiansen take a retail vision and apply it to libraries while understanding the differences between libraries and retail stores. Their book shows you how to create branding—and foster customer loyalty—through signage, arrangement, and displays.

As the school library media specialist, it is your professional responsibility to actively market your library media programs and services both inside and outside the school library media center. A productive partnership with your local public library can be effective in promoting lifelong learning. The possibilities are endless. Make communication your priority. What will be your marketing slogan?

Works Mentioned

Dowd, Nancy, Mary Evangeliste, and Jonathan Silberman. *Bite-Sized Marketing: Realistic Solutions for the Overworked Librarian*. Chicago, IL: American Library Association, 2009. 978-0-8389-1000-9.

LaPerriere, Jenny, and Trish Christiansen. *Merchandising Made Simple: Using Standards and Dynamic Displays to Boost Circulation*. Santa Barbara, CA: Libraries Unlimited, 2008. 978-1-59158-561-9.

Terrence E. Young, Jr., *MEd, MLS, is a library media specialist at West Jefferson High School in Harvey, Louisiana and Adjunct Instructor at the University of New Orleans and LSU School of Library and Information Science.*

Young. Terrence E., Jr. (2010). Marketing your school library media center: What we can learn from national bookstores. *LMC,* 28(6), 18–20.

Librarians as Leaders in Professional Learning Communities through Technology, Literacy, and Collaboration

By Dianne Dees, Alisande Mayer, Heather Morin, and Elaine Willis

Do you see yourself as a leader within the professional learning community? Black (2007) discussed professional learning communities from the aspect of school leadership, but her statements are equally applicable to school librarians. Black (41) referred to research done at the University of Lethbridge, identifying several key elements that contribute to the success of learning communities:

- effective communication and a clear set of goals along with administrative support
- focus on improving teaching and learning
- use of data to plan for instructional needs
- sharing of collective knowledge and expertise

According to the Professional Development Web site from the North Carolina Department of Instruction, professional learning communities are composed of a "collegial group who are united in their commitment to an outcome . . . student learning." Many school librarians exemplify the leadership role and contribute to the overall learning community.

Librarians promote student learning through technology, literacy, and collaboration with teachers. Each element provides ample opportunities to offer leadership and to learn as a member of the learning community. The librarian demonstrates leadership within the professional learning community (PLC) by providing professional development for classroom technology integration, sharing information about new resources, and demonstrating innovative instructional tools. The standards of the American Association of School Librarians (AASL) support the librarian's role in promoting literacy and a love of reading. Providing resources and

novel approaches to appreciating and understanding literature connects the library to the classroom. As instructional partners, the school librarian and the classroom teacher learn from each other and improve instructional strategies. When a project is particularly successful, other teachers want to have the same learning experience for their students. Networking within the school builds a strong sense of community and shared goals. From instructional partner to program administrator, the librarian can have a great impact on student learning through modeling good instructional practices and providing relevant curriculum materials.

> *Utilizing the "whole school" view, the librarian is in a key position to contribute to the development of strong professional learning communities through professional development and technology integration.*

Since student learning is the underlying motivation for developing professional learning communities and the theme of the AASL Standards for the 21st Century Learner, it seems only natural for librarians to be at the forefront of developing strong professional learning communities. The ultimate goal of improving student learning and utilizing the best practices school-wide requires all stakeholders in the learning community to work together. Utilizing the "whole school" view, the librarian is in a key position to contribute to the development of strong professional learning communities through professional development and

technology integration. As a supervisor of school library media interns, I see first-hand how mentors in the field demonstrate their leadership within the learning community. The librarians included below are examples of how many others are leading from the "center" of their professional learning communities. Each contributes to the success of the academic program of their schools and places the library program right in the center of the learning community.

Building the Professional Learning Community through Technology Integration and Training

Debra Martin and Heather Morin, media specialists at Hahira Middle School, Georgia's 2008 Library Media Program of the Year, fully understand the need for collaboration with their teachers. In fact, these media specialists offer a full-day staff development where academic area teachers come together to learn the latest and greatest educational technology and see how it can be implemented in their classrooms. The training day has evolved, growing from basic uses of email, word processing, and Internet searches to modeling use of interactive whiteboards, incorporating wikis, and podcasting. The development of the training is a process steeped in collaboration. First, Debra and Heather closely monitor their online resource scheduler to determine which resources are used most and which are not and by whom. Once this information is determined, they begin providing lesson ideas, resource suggestions, and collaboration opportunities to various teachers, and they begin constructing the format for that school year's teacher technology training.

Recently, Debra and Heather created an entirely different sort of technology training opportunity. They set up a classroom with an interactive whiteboard, student response system, laptop carts, and then modeled effective teaching practices that incorporated the everyday use of not only these components but also wikis, blogs, podcasts, and video editing software. Throughout the day, teachers participated in the lesson as students, creating podcasts, wikis, blogs, and videos. From this training, Debra and Heather created wiki spaces for 23 of their 40 academic teachers, assisted five teachers in creating classroom blogs, and collaborated with nine teachers on video editing projects. Hahira Middle School teachers have begun expressing an interest in moving toward a paperless classroom, and more teachers than ever have stopped using their overhead projectors in favor of LCD projectors and document cameras.

> *As a school librarian, the goal should be to look at what students are learning and what teachers are teaching in the classroom and see where your knowledge and skills can fit into that plan.*

Immediately following the technology training, Debra and Heather begin scheduling collaboration opportunities with teachers. Many of the teachers want to create wiki spaces for their students to store, share, and collaborate on writing projects. Whatever the need expressed by the teacher, Debra and Heather make certain each teacher is comfortable with that level of technology integration. Collaborative sessions result in lessons that include integration of student response systems, interactive whiteboards, or wikis. The learning community here expands to include students who also contribute ideas or requests for lessons utilizing the new technology. In fact, Debra

and Heather have taught many lessons for classroom teachers at the request of students who heard about a great project that another teacher assigned.

Another example of the PLC in action is the development of the teacher wiki. This space is a collaborative work area where the middle school teachers share quizzes, study guides, vocabulary lists, Web sites, interactive whiteboard lessons, and videos they have created and a space for documentation of departmental, grade-level, and interdepartmental meetings. Because of this workspace, teachers can stay abreast of issues regardless of grade or academic area. Off campus teachers are also included so they continue to be active participants in the learning community. Several teachers are developing wikis that will serve as their online classrooms. Through these wikis, students will view the daily agenda, look for lost handouts, view assessment rubrics, turn in assignments, edit documents, and work in a digital environment much like they will in their future workplace.

Collaboration of this nature does not happen by chance. Hahira Middle School teachers have grown to value the technical knowledge and instructional expertise of these two school librarians. Over time their collective efforts to provide both necessary equipment and instructional support to the teachers has impacted classroom instructional practices. Ten years ago, nearly every teacher posted an agenda on the marker board. Now, teachers have multimedia displays welcoming their students to class with problems of the day, introductory videos, or curriculum reviews. Instead of traditional paper and pencil projects, teachers allow students to choose from an assortment of technology based projects to culminate their units of study. Through listening to and surveying teacher needs, providing equipment to meet their goals, and patiently guiding teachers through the process, the Hahira Middle School learning community is enriched by technology with the media specialists squarely at the center.

Literacy is this Librarian's Focus within the Learning Community

Elaine Willis is the school librarian at Irwin County Middle/High School. Even though she considers information access skills an important aspect of student learning, her focus is on developing a lifelong love of reading. She often quotes Mark Twain, "A person who won't read has no advantage over one who can't read." She is consistently on the lookout for new ways to promote particular titles, as well as new ways to hook the reluctant reader.

Earlier this year, Elaine promoted AASL's Teens' Top Ten (TTT) program in her high school. An avid reader herself and wanting to be prepared for the upcoming TTT event, she purchased the approximately 25 titles to read over the summer. Many of the books were a part of a series, and knowing how much her students enjoyed series, she ended up reading far more than the titles on the list. Her preparation enabled her to match the books to the right students.

Elaine collaborated with her English teachers, including the Gifted teacher, to promote these books on the TTT list. Two of the English teachers used the books with Literature Circles while the Gifted teacher included the list of TTTs as alternates to her original reading list. Without her leadership, the teachers would not have known about the books or thought to consider them as alternatives for traditional reading lists. In October, the students participated in the online voting for the Teens' Top Ten books. Elaine plans to have a "voting booth" for the TTT next year.

Incorporating technology with the Literature Circles, Elaine and one of the English teachers developed a wiki for the students to use with their Literature Circles. Each group had their own page on which they discussed the books. The teacher included a rubric for the students to follow which was also posted on each page. Now there were no more worries about lost rubrics. The wiki was so successful that the teacher increased the number of groups from four the first semester it was implemented to 10 in the next semester.

Ever mindful of how technology can motivate all students, even reluctant readers, Elaine observed how the incorporation of wikis encouraged some of the more reluctant readers to participate in the Literature Circles. To help keep interest high, she has recently added 90 Sony Touch Readers (purchased with grant funds) to the library collection. The readers are currently being used in Literature Circles, during extended learning, and as a reward for students who have completed their work. Following the wiki experiment with the Literature Circles, more teachers incorporated wikis as part of their instruction, including the Spanish teacher who uses wikis to plan daily activities for his classes.

> *Be an active participant in your professional learning community, contributing both as a leader and learner.*

As a technology leader in her school, Elaine knows most of her teachers are receptive to incorporating new technology into their lessons, but the teachers do not really have the time to explore the variety of tools available to them. In response, Elaine organized and delivered after-school sessions called "Tech Tuesday" for the teachers. Each series consists of 12 sessions, and teachers can earn one PLU credit (10 Tech Tuesday sessions). Elaine focuses on free Web 2.0 tools and different ways they can be used in the classroom. The classes have become so popular that some of the teachers do not even apply for the PLUs; they are just interested in the information. Including students as a part of the learning community, Elaine plans to incorporate Web 2.0 tools such as Diigo (http://www.diigo.com/) and Evernote (http://www.evernote.com/) with her student research classes in the fall. Utilizing Diigo and Google Reader, Elaine keeps up with new resources for her own professional development and to provide quick access to resources

for the teachers. She spends a lot of time searching out curriculum-related resources to share. Elaine certainly illustrates how a school librarian can take a strong leadership role within the PLC to make a difference in the instructional program of the school and integrate technology and literacy with young adults. In her words, "I consider myself a catalyst. The teachers carry the torch to the students."

Innovative and Tasty Approach to Writing Instruction at Moulton-Branch Elementary School

Alisande Mayer considers collaboration to be one of the most rewarding aspects of being a school librarian. Writing was an area of need within her school community, therefore a 30-minute period was set aside each day during which all classes would concentrate on writing and the writing process. Alisande saw this as an opportunity to work with teachers on a specific need and one in which she could be an instructional partner.

Alisande approached the kindergarten teachers with an idea to increase student vocabulary and spelling skills. She approached the kindergarten teachers first because she thought kindergartners might have the most difficult time with writing. She decided to make writing a class project in which she taught them how to use "sparkle" words to "decorate" their writing. With input from the kindergarten teachers on which skills needed to be addressed, she created a lesson geared toward expanding their use of descriptive words in writing.

She started by baking a large sugar cookie for each class. When they came to visit the media center, they all gathered around a large table with the sugar cookie on it. As the students and she decorated the sugar cookie, the teacher wrote their description of it on the SMARTboard so they could see what they had accomplished. By doing this, the librarian, teacher, and students could pre-write and revise and edit as they progressed through the lesson by changing words such as "big" to more descriptive words like "enormous,

humongous, and gigantic" and so forth. With the addition of green icing, white and multicolored sprinkles, pink and yellow decorator icing and neon sour gummy worms, students were asked to provide descriptive words for each of these additions. The completed project was a yummy treat with a descriptive paragraph that was far from the typical kindergarten writing.

Word got around about the tasty new way to improve writing skills so it was not long before Alisande was approached by the first and second grade teachers for a repeat performance. While discussing plans for the first and second graders, the collaborative group recognized that this activity could be extended to include thesaurus skills. Since Alisande had originally anticipated only completing this project with the kindergartners, she needed assistance with the ingredients required for the baking and decorating of multiple pizza-sized cookies. So in true PLC fashion, she approached her principal and explained the activity and its cost. The principal (a very good PLC leader herself) agreed to cover the cost for these two grade levels. So, as first and second graders decorated their cookies, they were asked not only to provide more descriptive words but to actually use the thesaurus to find more appropriate words.

The administrators wanted to see what the buzz was all about so they attended one of the "cookie writing" sessions. They were so impressed with how well this lesson demonstrated the writing process that they ultimately agreed to fund cookies for third, fourth, and fifth grades as well. What had begun as a project to overcome the obstacle of teaching kindergartners to write had been revised for each grade level to address the writing process and reference skills appropriate to each grade.

Alisande illustrates what it means to "provide leadership . . . and establish connections with . . . the education community . . . that focus on students learning . . . " (ALA/AASL, Standard 3). Many times it may be difficult for a school librarian to see herself as a part of the classroom learning experience.

However, as a school librarian, the goal should not be to create a standalone lesson on a skill you feel needs to be addressed, but to look at what students are learning and what teachers are teaching in the classroom and see where your knowledge and skills can fit into that plan. Approach teachers with ideas that you may have and ask for their input. Provide openings for teachers to approach you and ask for your knowledge in lesson planning. They may love your idea and feel it fits with what they are teaching or the conversation may spark another idea that would be better suited. The ultimate goal is to provide opportunities for your teachers to see you as an instructional partner and a valuable resource in increasing student achievement.

AASL guidelines dictate that our focus will be on student learning. As part of the learning community, we are challenged to serve as leaders who can identify needs based on data and observation and then provide positive feedback to the community for addressing those needs. Teaching and learning through collaboration is another significant element of a learning community (Pennell 26). Who best to demonstrate and encourage that process than the school librarian? Being an active participant in a professional learning community is not for the faint of heart as explained by Black (41). It involves dedication and determination as illustrated by Heather and Debra, Elaine, and Alisande. Be an active participant in your professional learning community, contributing both as a leader and learner.

References

"ALA/AASL Standards for Initial Programs for School Library Media Specialist Preparation." American Library Association/ American Association of School Librarians. 2010. Web. 12 Feb. 2010.

Black, Susan. "A Community of Learners." *American School Board Journal* Nov. 2007: 40–41, 47. *Academic Search Premier*. Web. 15 Apr. 2010.

North Carolina Department of Instruction. "Professional Development." n.d. Web. 13 Apr. 2010.

Pennell, Susan. "Teacher Librarians in Professional Learning Communities." *CSLA Journal* 32.1 (Fall 2008): 25–26. *Academic Search Premier*. Web. 15 Apr. 2010.

Dr. Dianne Dees *is the facilitator for the School Library Media Program at Valdosta (Georgia) State University and can be reached at ecdees@valdosta.edu.*

Mrs. Alisande Mayer *is a school librarian at Moulton-Branch Elementary School in Valdosta, Georgia and can be reached at amayer@lowndes.k12.ga.us.*

Mrs. Heather Morin *is a school librarian at the Hahira (Georgia) Middle School and can be reached at hmorin@lowndes.k12.ga.us.*

Dr. Elaine Willis is *a school librarian at the Irwin County Middle/High School in Ocilla, Georgia and can be reached at drewillis@gmail.com.*

Dees, Dianne, Mayer, Alisande, Morin, Heather, & Willis, Elaine. (2010). Librarians as leaders in professional learning communities through technology, literacy, and collaboration. *LMC, 29*(2), 10–13.

Library Advisory Councils

By Natalie Teske

Library Advisory Councils (LACs) go by many names—Media Technology Committees, Reader Advisory Boards, and Faculty Feedback Forums, among others. They may target different segments of the patron base, or be established for a specified amount of time. Most of us are aware of Teen Advisory Councils, but there are Senior Advisory Councils as well as committees that serve the needs of homeschoolers. This article draws on my own experiences with starting a Library Advisory Council at my K-12 private school library media center.

Why Have an LAC?

An LAC is beneficial to every library, of every size. It increases buy-in from stakeholders, distributes responsibility for decisions, increases library usage, and assists the library governing body (even if it's only one person, like me) in crafting a strategic plan understood by stakeholders and the community the library serves. Without an LAC, the librarian/media specialist does the best she can by using informal survey techniques to determine the needs of her educational community. In this case, the most vocal of users will get more materials and more support for their curriculum, while the low-users or non-users will continue to believe the library has "nothing they want." In my school, these users are typically the faculty of math/higher science-oriented subjects: just the areas where America's students lag behind. When we follow this course to its logical conclusion, our school libraries will have a variety of history, humanities, and language arts materials, but less than robust collections in math and higher sciences. I frequently hear from these same teachers that "they don't have time" to bring their classes to the library. Presented with the argument that research skills cross all boundaries and disciplines, they agree, but the school year passes without a class visit to the library, or a research project.

If each high school department was required to nominate an LAC member, their department would become more informed about tools the library offers. When their department realizes that the library is asking for input on how its budget is spent to better to support them in the classroom, more requests would flood in. As these non-users realize that the library now has the materials they requested, they would increase their usage. At first, LAC members may resist or resent being required to take on another duty, but as they begin to realize that it will eventually make their load easier, as they get technology, web 2.0, and research skills support from the media specialist, they will become enthusiastic LAC members.

> A Library Advisory Council increases buy-in from stakeholders, distributes responsibility for decisions, increases library usage, and assists the library governing body.

An LAC also builds relationships and assists in beneficial conflict resolution between faculty/library, parents/library, and student/library users. In cases where a teacher may not feel comfortable speaking directly with the librarian, they can go to their faculty representative, who will present their request at the next LAC meeting.

Steps to Starting an LAC

The supervisory librarian first needs to establish several policies and procedures that answer some critical questions.

- Establishing procedures: How often/how long will the LAC meet? Does everyone get an equal voice?

How will you handle challenges to budgetary decisions? How will you handle disputes between members? You must emphasize that this is an *advisory* council: you will note, and consider everyone's comments and opinions, but you will, in the end, make the best decision for the library. Members may feel that their time was "wasted" if their advice was not followed—continuously reiterate how much you value their time and contribution to the library. They are helping make your job easier, even if it doesn't feel like it at the time!

- Designating an LAC leader: This should *not* be the librarian. You need an independent person to call "time." You don't want a teacher to think you're biased just because time for their topic was up. You also want someone to consult with when making the agenda for the meetings. This should be someone who the other faculty members feel free to come and talk to if there is an issue they want addressed. Teachers don't always feel comfortable coming to the librarian and telling them that they feel the computer lab schedule is unfairly biased towards a certain teacher. The LAC leader is your liaison to the faculty body.

- Creating an LAC mission statement: The librarian should work with the LAC leader to create a rough draft, and ask for input from the committee for the final draft.

- Nominating members: In middle and high schools, members should be nominated by department. What a 6th grade science teacher needs is much different from what a 6th grade English teacher needs. In elementary school, divisions by grade level make more sense. A parent and student representative will give your committee more depth, and help all involved remember the end-user they all serve. The parent/student need not be invited to every meeting, or stay the whole time. An Administrative representative is also necessary. When you create your LAC, you must decide if this representative gets a "voice" or if they are only there to support.

> *In cases where a teacher may not feel comfortable speaking directly with the librarian, they can go to their faculty representative, who will present their request at the next LAC meeting.*

Obstacles You May Encounter

If you create an LAC, leadership will no longer be solely in your hands, or the hands of the administration. If your administration believes that they "know best" what teachers, parents or students want, you will face opposition. Your principal/supervisor may fear loss of control, fear of transparency, and fear of new ideas. All of these fears have a common root—a lack of trust in other educational professionals in our schools. This subject has been extensively explored in the business world by Margaret Wheatly in her 1997 article "Goodbye Command and Control" in *Leader to Leader.* That institutions still struggle with this concept 12 years later illustrates how deeply ingrained the top-down management model is in our culture. A carefully reasoned proposal may be sufficient to calm your principal's fears and convince him to trust you and your fellow teachers. It also may not. If you manage to implement a Library Advisory Council at your school, you will have done your part in furthering collaboration and improving the state of education and school libraries in America. I wish you luck!

Natalie Teske *is the sole library media specialist in a private school in Orlando, Florida. Her Web site and blog can be found at www.wilylibrarian.com and she can be reached at teskenatalie@gmail .com.*

Teske, Natalie. (2010). Library advisory councils. *LMC, 28*(4), 40–41.

Parents, Reading Partners, Library Advocates

By Liz Deskins

One of my most important goals as a school librarian is to inspire my students to become lifelong lovers of reading. I recognize that I cannot do this alone, and one of my most powerful partners is a parent (feel free to insert grandparent, guardian, or other caring adult). I can encourage a child to check out a book that may open their eyes to the wonders of literature, but if there is no one at home to encourage the child to read it, that potentially life-altering book may never get finished. An advocate at home is essential to reading. But how does one begin to build this partnership? I can suggest several strategies that have worked for me.

Family Literacy Nights

Family literacy nights are one great way to bring families into the school library, couched within a fun event that asks nothing of parents. Many of the parents in my building have less than fond memories of being in school; they are reluctant to attend parent-teacher conferences and do not join the parent teacher organization (PTO). But attending an evening of family fun can be enticing. Once you have families in the media center a time or two without any negative repercussions, they will begin to pop in for other reasons—and become your library advocates.

How to host this fun event? First, elicit support from other adults: folks from the local public library, teachers, and the PTO. The public library is a great support for many reasons, particularly because you are building extended community support for your program and they have the same goals you do. Teachers are usually willing to pitch in because they also strive to build a positive rapport with parents, and they love reading as well. PTOs are a potential source of monetary funds, and their mission is to support families and teachers as they work together to support student learning.

Once you have a group to work with, start brainstorming ideas for your theme, the organizational plan for the evening, and what materials you will need to make the evening a success. One tip: Keep things as easy as possible. Don't get so wrapped up in decorations and excess incidentals that you miss the point of the evening. My goal is always to find a way to help families connect with reading, be it through books in print form, online, or extending the literary experience.

Pick a Creative Theme

Here's an example of an evening we offered. We picked a "Winter Wonderland" theme with these components: a storyteller (from the public library), a cozy read by the fireplace (made out of cardboard and construction paper) with various winter-themed books set out for groups of readers, and a techno space which shared a variety of online reading resources via laptops with bookmarks and a SMART Board (bookmarks with directions to get to the library homepage were provided). There was also a game room with board and card games with a literary theme, and a cookies and hot chocolate station. As you can imagine, none of these stations were difficult to create or maintain. Costs were minimal and it was low stress.

Other successful themes and stations included themed rooms where each open classroom would host a different topic or genre with a guest reader and booklists. There were rooms for dragons, Mother Goose, community helpers (our DARE officer hosted this room and read Officer Buckle and Gloria), Dr. Seuss, not so scary books, poetry, and facts and fun reading, to name a few. Extended activities have included making reading journals and bookmarks, games, songs with books, and even a writing space for young authors.

> Building a foundation of trust and collaboration with parents has positive long-term consequences.

Be a Reading Advocate!

While everyone was enjoying the evening, I made a point of engaging with as many families as possible, talking about books their children enjoyed and what they might want to share as a family. This easy activity let parents know that I knew their children as individuals with their own reading interests and that I cared enough to continue to support each child as they developed lifelong reading habits. Once parents see me as a caring adult in the school building, it makes it easier for them to stop by if they have a minute, if they are early picking up their child, or even if they want to call and ask for birthday or Christmas book suggestions. Over the course of the six years a child typically spends at the elementary school, these points of contact translate into parents who become advocates for you and your library program.

Family Book Clubs

A successful offshoot of the reading nights has been my family book club. Families who enjoy reading books together were ready for the next step. So I sent out an invitation to all families in the school, inviting them to read a selected book together as a family and then join me in the media center one evening to talk about the book in a relaxed setting. It was fun to watch family friendships build and parent confidence in book choices grow. I chose the first three books and everyone just abided by that choice, but by the fourth book they were making suggestions and deciding for themselves. Listening to the students take leadership roles in the discussion is very enjoyable. Sometimes the discussions would get loud with several children wanting to share their point of view at the same time, but they would just as quickly settle down and respond more appropriately to one another. As our get-togethers continued, parents became comfortable enough to add to the conversation. It was even suggested that everyone send in some money and we order pizzas, so no one had to worry about cooking dinner on book club nights. This ownership of the book club was another opportunity to build parent interest and advocacy for the library and the media program. This interest also resulted in several nights of talking about technology tools and tips, sharing with parents the Internet tools and software products students use daily and giving students the opportunity to share projects they had created.

> *Once you have families in the media center a time or two without any negative repercussions, they will begin to pop in for other reasons—and become your library advocates.*

Building Blocks for a Community of Lifelong Readers and Advocates

All of these events have been effective for many reasons. I know I am working toward my goal of building lifelong readers as well as encouraging the important 21st century tools of communication, collaboration, creativity, and critical thinking. Because learning is enhanced by opportunities to share and learn with others, I am also building a community of learners that reaches beyond the walls of the school, and finally, I am creating advocates who understand the value of a well-supported media center staffed by a certified media specialist.

This careful building of a foundation of trust and collaboration with my parents has positive longterm consequences. Parents and other community members are interested in the services the media center provides, they support it at formal meetings and informal gatherings. I have parents advocating for a new, larger space for the media center, parents who want to see

more technology available to students, and parents who want to talk books. This kind of support is priceless and gives me opportunities to educate further with parent technology events, summer activities, and family book checkouts.

The more parents and community members realize the myriad of resources available, especially the services of a school librarian who is educated and certified, the more strongly they feel about continued support for this program. As Henry Ward Beecher said, "A library is not a luxury but one of the necessities of life." It has even garnered me several new parent volunteers who love to read the books as much as shelve them!

Liz Deskins *is a library media specialist at J. W. Reason (Ohio) Elementary School and can be reached at Liz.library@gmail .com.*

Deskins, Liz. (2011). Parents, reading partners, library advocates. *LMC, 30*(3), 34–35.

Survival Tactics for the Warrior Librarian

By Cathy Collins

Truth be told, I wanted to be a music teacher. My high school English teacher father steered me instead toward work as a school librarian. He confessed to secretly admiring their world, which seemed so far apart from that of the rest of the school. He saw the world of the school library as a safe haven, a student refuge for independent learning, an open space, free of educational politics. He could not have foreseen that as public education's funding started to whittle away, that sacred learning space and the professionals that staff it might be jeopardized.

Advocacy

Politics have not been so important since the birth of this nation's first lending libraries, back in Ben Franklin's day. The school librarian who ignores political forces does so at his or her own peril. Gone are the days of my father's era, when school librarians could focus solely on guiding young readers toward those books that would light the fires of lifelong learning. This is not all bad news.

We tend to glorify the past rather than to accept our current position in the universe. The vision of the school library as the heart and hub of knowledge and its exchange has not changed, except to encompass more: more software, hardware, electronic resources; more of a role of librarian as teacher-leader, more staff development, more teaching of important information literacy skills, more collaboration, more district and site-level initiatives that call upon the credentialed library media specialist's full participation. On the down side, we are expected to do more with less: less support staffing, less time as some of us are now covering multiple sites, shrinking budgets, and fewer available resources.

Yet in spite of nationwide budget cuts, the potential of school libraries to positively impact student achievement has never been higher. When one considers the school librarian's role in providing technology training and information literacy skills to both students and staff and the collaborative efforts and school-wide leadership that a skilled school librarian accomplishes, it becomes a "no brainer." Schools cannot afford to do without strong school library programs. It is our professional responsibility to fight for our programs, using warrior tactics to survive and thrive through tough economic times.

> It is our professional responsibility to fight for our programs, using warrior tactics to survive and thrive through tough economic times.

School librarians who have not made politics their business must now put advocacy at the top of their "to do" list, by showcasing their "value add" on a daily basis. It is our responsibility to "toot our own horn." By focusing efforts closest to classroom learning and increased student achievement, the task of advocacy winds up being shared by allies at the site and district level.

How can we best prioritize time so that work with students and staff remains strong? The answer lies in focusing on three areas: leadership, technology, and collaboration.

Leadership

When I moved to California from Massachusetts, I was appalled to discover the librarian-to-student ratio in the public schools. According to the National Center for Education statistics, the national average ratio of librarians to students is 1 to 916. In California, the ratio is one librarian per 5,124 students. Only one in every eight California schools employs a credentialed teacher librarian. Due to the chronic state budget crisis, and the lack of a mandate for teacher librarians, the cuts become more severe each year.

Having to share time at multiple sites was a new challenge for me. I knew that my best plan for success would involve aligning my vision for the library media center with administrators' visions for their schools. I scheduled several individual meetings with the principals, sharing goals, and coming up with a joint plan of attack at each site. Seasoned administrators who had worked in schools with strong library programs jumped on board immediately. Newer administrators who had not been exposed to the potential of strong school library programs required great public relations efforts from me, with little result.

I began to consciously focus the bulk of my work on schools with the strongest level of administrative support. By doing so, I was able to maximize my impact at those sites, and to create a ripple public relations effect as the more library-friendly administrators spread the word about the work I was doing.

For example, at one of my elementary sites, the Accelerated Reader (AR) program was given a priority. Since interest was already high around AR, it was a simple task to develop a year-long Read-a-Thon charting student progress around books read and AR test results. I am not a big fan of AR, but I am an enormous fan of motivating students to read more and to read better. By combining a school-wide goal with a library program goal, collaboration and student success were natural results. I had automatic buy-in from my principal, which was passed along to the teaching staff. Increased book circulation, improved reading comprehension scores, and community spirit were the results, which we celebrated at an all-school assembly at the end of the year. From initial planning through the final assembly, co-leadership between the principal and me was necessary. From staff development in the use of AR software, to presentations at staff meetings to instruct teachers in use of the software, to presentations at site council meetings to involve parents, and through ongoing meetings with the principal, the school library truly became the hub of the school in spite of the fact that I wasn't present all days of the week. The program also allowed me the opportunity to establish myself as a teacher leader in technology as well as in motivational reading techniques.

> *By combining a school-wide goal with a library program goal, collaboration and student success were natural results.*

Delegation is critical when juggling multiple sites. Librarians, fearing further job cutbacks, often limit the range of tasks they direct their clerks and technicians to perform. The reality is that our time is limited, and we need to take full advantage of whatever clerical support is available to us. For the Read-a-Thon, the clerk who was on site four days a week charted student progress and awarded prizes based on improved reading scores. I handled the organizational, staff development, and teaching components of the program.

Keep in mind the link to student achievement when facing one's "to do" list. For instance, cataloging, while important, should not keep us hiding in the back room all day. It is low priority in that it does not directly impact student achievement, and thus, needs to fall to the bottom of the "to do" list. Book shelving, gathering of materials related to specific subject areas, compiling overdue lists and hotlists, processing book check-in and check-out, are all tasks that can and should be delegated to free us up to focus on collaborative teaching and learning activities. Remember that we are in charge of our time, and it

is up to us to manage it in a way that allows us to have maximum impact.

To prove our value, we must lead by sharing our knowledge and keeping current in instructional methods, technology, educational trends, and resource materials that impact student learning. Librarianship is, at heart, the job of sharing resources, so this should be a natural area in which we excel.

Technology

Another tool at our disposal is technology. By posting reading lists on specific topics, creating Web-based resources using sites such as Page-Flakes and WallWisher, we avoid duplicating requests for information, and allow ourselves opportunities to share and teach. The need for folks on site who are skilled in technology integration has never been higher. As the range of technology tools has expanded, the number of technology teachers and troubleshooters on campus is generally shrinking as a result of budget cuts. The librarian who embraces technology, keeps current, and becomes skillful at teaching and modeling technology integration will always be highly marketable.

I jumped at the chance this year to serve as the school's newspaper advisor. It allowed me to strengthen relationships with students and staff and showcase our school's activities. By taking the initiative to transition from print to multimedia (including clips produced by the school's video production class), readership grew and I became firmly established as someone knowledgeable about technology.

Likewise, when my principal expressed interest in Web 2.0, I shared my own knowledge and interest. We met, and sought out another teacher with similar interests to plan Web 2.0 staff development. I met with that teacher several times over the next few weeks to formulate a plan of attack, to outline areas of emphasis, and brainstorm about ways to engage our teacher audience. From feedback received, the effort was a success.

I doubt that this effort would have succeeded had firm relationships not been in place prior to the start

of the planning process. The most valuable time spent as a leader is that of building strong, trusting relationships. Whether our task is to manage a library, a school, or a country, it is the quality of the relationships developed that will determine our success or failure.

Collaboration

One of the simplest strategies for relationship building is to serve on school and district-wide leadership committees. When I first began my current position, I joined the Principal's Advisory Committee, the Technology Committee, the Professional Learning Community Committee, and an International Baccalaureate/ Middle Years Program Steering Committee. Had I not become part of those groups, I would not have understood the challenges facing the staff, nor been in a position to assist them in brainstorming efforts.

> *By seeking out needs and finding ways to serve, we create a circle of activity that places the school library at the hub of student learning.*

Our Professional Learning Community chose to focus on community service efforts as a school-wide goal. Knowing that one of my elementary sites was in need of children's books, a student-led book drive allowed me to serve needs at two sites through one project. By sharing the need for books at a meeting of the high school's community service club, instant buy-in resulted, since many of the students had attended the elementary school, and looked forward to working with teachers and students from their former school through the book drive.

One of my most rewarding alliances was created by working with the counseling team. The school had lost a career resource counselor. By working with our school site council and the local Rotary club, I was able to find funding for career explorations software that had expired, and to develop a collection of career-related materials. I then collaborated with classroom teachers and counselors involved in a student group, "Will Work for Success," to develop units related to career exploration. By seeking out needs and finding ways to serve, we create a circle of activity that places the school library at the hub of student learning.

As teacher librarians, we are in a truly unique position to have maximum impact on students across all grade levels and subject areas. It is a privileged position that endows us with great freedom and equally great responsibility. It is up to us to be proactive leaders at our sites and to manage our time effectively, by focusing on those goals and collaborative activities that will best move our students forward toward success.

Cathy Collins *is a teacher librarian for Montgomery High School, Santa Rosa, California and can be reached at cathy-swish2004@yahoo.com.*

Collins, Cathy. (2010). Survival tactics for the warrior librarian. *LMC, 29*(3), 18–19.

ONE QUESTION SURVEY RESULTS
Do You Leave the Library to Provide Service?

By Gail K. Dickinson

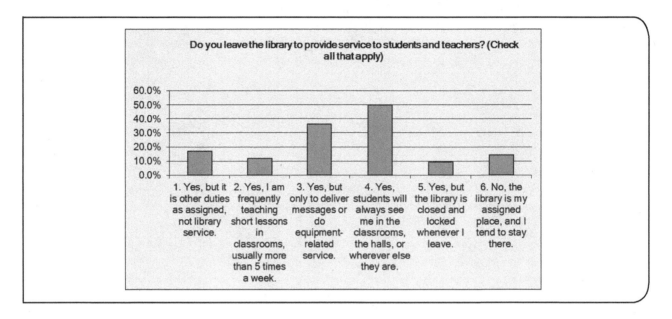

It's a dilemma. Good librarians build programs, curate collections, and lobby intensely to create busy active libraries. Nothing worries a good librarian more than an empty room. What makes that end result difficult to achieve is that students are assigned to classrooms, classrooms are supervised by teachers, and all of that happens outside of the library. So, should the librarian stay in the library and hope to catch teachers on quick breaks in the hall or by emails and texts? Or is it more effective to be out where the teachers are, pushing transliteracy knowledge and skills into the classroom? One of the foundational precepts of the profession is for the library to be open and accessible throughout the school day, so how can we justify closing and locking the library door? And if the library is open, is the librarian responsible for what could happen with no adult supervision? It's a dilemma. Should librarians stay in their assigned place and supervise a busy library or should

a librarian be out drumming up more business?

Librarians call the library home, but our survey shows that for outgoing strong and skilled librarians, it's not a cage with iron bars. Even with the anecdotal reports of cuts in support staff, only 14% of our 708 respondents said that the library was their assigned place and they tended to stay there. Another nearly 17% do venture out of the library, not necessarily because they want to, but because they have to as a result of being assigned tasks and duties that have nothing to do with the library.

With the pressure on classroom teachers to use every instructional minute preparing for testing, it is harder and harder to get classes scheduled for library time. Savvy librarians are using different ways to embed library learning in subject content. Face-to-face instruction, whether it is in the library or the classroom, is only one of those ways.

Perhaps the best way to use this survey is to advocate for the strategies that would work best in your library. Discuss with your administrator how you can be one of the 50% of respondents who are highly visible to students and staff. Decide as a district-level department whether you want to be one of the 10% who are always locked in the library or one of the 10% who are always teaching in other teachers' classrooms. This survey is a snapshot. Where are you in the picture?

Find data for past One-Question Surveys at www.librarymediaconnection.com. Have a good question? Be sure to let us know at lmc@librarymediaconnection.com.

Dickinson, Gail K. (2012). Do you leave the library to provide service? *LMC, 31*(1), 55.

ONE QUESTION SURVEY RESULTS
Library Advisory Committees

By Gail K. Dickinson

If the best questions are the simplest, then we have failed miserably. Try as we might, we could not come up with one question that adequately covered what our readers would want to know about Library Advisory Committees, so we asked two. First, we asked if you had a library advisory committee at your school, then second, we asked who served on that committee.

We had 358 respondents to the survey, and I suspect we may have had more, since there may have been respondents who did not want to answer no to this question. The need for library advisory committees has been taught in library school for centuries, was required by Library Power grants, and is a major component of the Empowering Learners Planning

Guide and Rubric. Yet nearly 90 percent of our respondents said that no, they do not have a Library Advisory Committee.

The 41 respondents who said yes, only slightly more than 11% of the total, went on to answer the second question, which focused on who served on those committees. By far, the strongest representation came from teachers, with nearly 80% of committees reporting teacher membership. It is interesting that the number of parents nearly equaled the number of students who serve. For the Other category, with only three respondents, no true conclusions can be drawn, but one respondent did note that they had a student advisory committee separate from the library advisory committee.

What does this mean? How can something that is held as a tenet of a strong library program exist in only one out of ten. True, there is little help in the literature or on conference schedules touting how to build strength in a library advisory committee. And, even though the need is taught in library school, I confess that there are few examples to point to.

Clearly there is a need for more research here. In the places where the advisory committees are working, we need to find out how they started, where they found their strength, and how they have aided the library program. A good place to start is writing an article in Library Media Connection on your Library Advisory Committee, or doing a panel presentation at your state conference. This is how the world gets changed.

Library Media Connection encourages the use of evidence-based practices to help you ensure that your students have the libraries they deserve. Use these graphs to illustrate the importance of your job in the school and your work to create strong library programs.

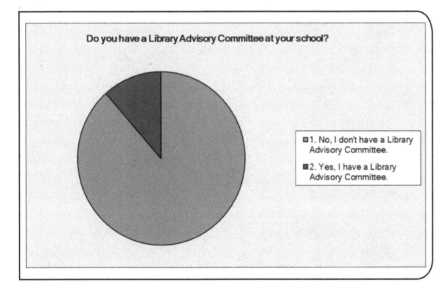

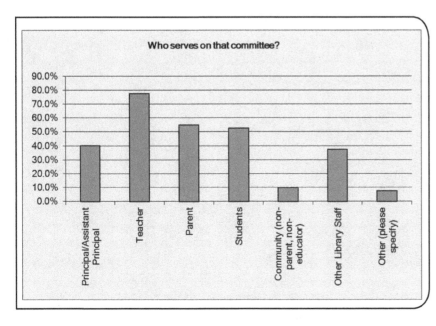

Find data for past One-Question Surveys at www.librarymediaconnection.com. Have a good question? Be sure to let us know at lmc@librarymediaconnection.com.

Dickinson, Gail K. (2012). Library advisory committees. *LMC, 31*(2), 35.

ONE QUESTION SURVEY RESULTS

How Many Books Are Students Allowed to Have Checked Out at One Time, According to Your Library Policy?

By Gail K. Dickinson

Whenever I think about limiting students in the number of books allowed to be checked out, a scene from a Western novel comes to mind. Although I have long forgotten author, title, or plot, I do remember vividly that the hard-bitten rancher, each time he came home to an unappreciated dinner, first roamed the small yard of hard-packed earth looking for blades of grass. When he found any of the tender shoots daring to break through the surface, he ground his booted heel into it, killing any chance for survival. "Varmints hide in grass." was his excuse. Meanwhile his wife slowly wasted away from the lack of any beauty in her life.

In the same way, sometimes I think overzealous librarians, cautious of the varmints who may not return books, stamp out any hope of the joy of reading. The only things in life that are limited are those bad for us. We limit caffeine, sugar, and dessert. Why on earth do we limit reading? It makes no sense to do our best to encourage reading on one hand, and then limit those that have the greatest joy of reading to one or two books at a time.

There is hope. The survey below shows encouraging news. Nearly 16% of the 853 respondents have established unlimited checkout.

Approximately 1/3 of the respondents allow students to check out five or more books. Unfortunately, 33% of the respondents also only allow students to only check out one or two books. In order to create libraries that students and teachers cannot live without, we have to ensure that we don't care more about keeping the books safe than we care about whether or not people are reading them. Books only work if they are in the hands of readers.

Linworth encourages the use of evidence-based practices to assure your students have the libraries they deserve. Use this chart to lobby for open access to books, reading, and resources for your students.

Next month we will report on if you have considered getting administrative certification. Curious about our previous surveys? All are available online at www.linworth.com.

Dickinson, Gail K. (2009). How many books are students allowed to have checked out at one time, according to your library policy? *LMC, 28*(2), 47.

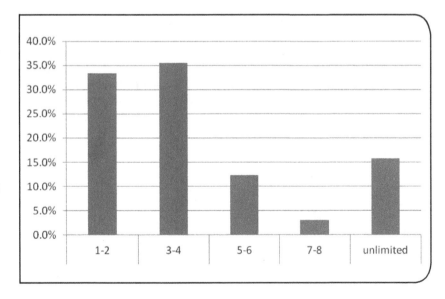

ONE QUESTION SURVEY RESULTS
How Many Books Are Lost in Your Library Each Year?

By Gail K. Dickinson

For most school library media specialists, the bliss of summer vacation cannot be reached until they struggle through the agony of getting all of the books and other materials returned. "How many books do you lose?" is a perennial question to be asked at conferences and over late night e-mails. "A lot" or "too many" is too often the vague answer. Even the most experienced school library professionals cannot put a magic number on what the field considers an acceptable number of losses. This One Question Survey tells us that almost all libraries lose books on a regular basis. Only one respondent reported no books lost. The largest category of responses, 28.8%, reported losses of 11–25 books. More than half of the respondents (65%) reported losing 40 or fewer books per year. What this survey does not report, of course, is the loss rate. To find your loss rate, divide the total number of books circulated by the number of books lost. That calculation will give you the percentage of the circulated books total that you have lost. If research holds, it will be a very small percentage, sometimes as tiny as .1%, meaning only one book lost out of every thousand books circulated. Of course, some would argue that every book lost from the library is a book

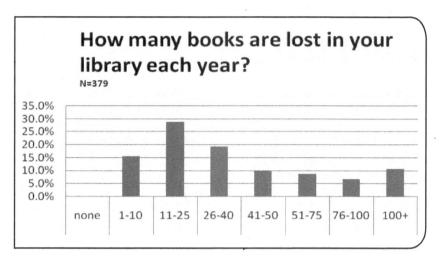

removed from the hands of a child. Others would argue that lost books are somewhere, in some household, and maybe they are in a household in which that is the only book. Some libraries report the dollar value of lost books by multiplying the number of books lost by the reported average price of a new book. Others write off losses as a natural form of weeding. Regardless, these survey results will help place your library's losses (averaged over the last three years) in context and tell you how your losses compare with those of other libraries.

Linworth encourages the use of evidence-based practices to assure your students have the libraries they deserve. Use these results to continue to advocate for the improvement of school libraries.

Next month we will report on how many students your library can seat (and how many students you have in your building). Curious about our previous surveys? All are available online at www.linworth.com.

Dickinson, Gail K. (2009). How many books are lost in your library each year? *LMC, 27*(6), 51.

Tips

BYOD (Bring Your Own Device) Overdues

Encouraging students to use the book renewal feature in your circulation system is easy. Create a bookmark with the QR code for your system and stamp the bookmark with the due date. Whenever students see the bookmark, they will be reminded that they can manage their library accounts with a smartphone. Overdues will be reduced and students will learn to use their phones as a management tool.

Daniel Russo
Batavia (Illinois) High School

Russo, Daniel. (2012). BYOD (Bring Your Own Device) overdues. *LMC, 31*(1), 9.

One Night Only!

Book fairs don't have to last for days. Try one after school on PTA Open House night, or at PTA special events like our December PTA choral concert. It's only one night after school (4–8 p.m.), so there are no interruptions to instruction. There are a lot of parents at school on those nights and it's like a one stop shop deal! This year we sold 260 books in four hours at the September Open House. That is approximately 46,800 reading minutes. (We also offer the books online for two weeks; however, we don't get many sales.) My crew consists of book club members and my goal is to sell enough books for each member to have a copy of the books we read each semester.

Mitzy O. Cromwell
Plaza Middle School
Virginia Beach, Virginia

Cromwell, Mitzi O. (2013). One night only! *LMC, 31*(5), 8.

From Trash to Treasures

Our copies of past book club books were sitting in a storage room. We recently cataloged them and made a "Book Club Reads" display in the library. Kids were drawn to the books and assumed they were good books since we had multiple copies and they had been used in our book club. We now circulate all of our past book club selections, and we encourage teachers to use them as classroom sets for teaching.

Christy Banton
Wynne (Arkansas) High School
Library

Banton, Christy. (2013). From trash to treasures. *LMC, 31*(5), 8.

Read This!

I purchased a big screen TV with a wall mount and a splitter for my computer with the intention of using the TV screen as a second screen and advertisement billboard for the library. Each month I've made a simple slide presentation that features the cover art and a descriptive blurb about each new book purchased, as well as the collection titles based on a particular theme (Thanksgiving, Christmas, spring, classics, etc.) This presentation runs on an endless loop on the TV, and the splitter allows me to still work on my computer monitor with privacy.

Lu Ann Brobst Staheli
Payson (Utah) Jr. High

Staheli, Lu Ann Brobst. (2013). Read this! *LMC, 32*(1), 8.

CHAPTER 5

What Does the Future Hold?

Editor's Note

Librarians as Deep-Water Sailors

"He's a deep-water sailor, he'll be fine," my husband said to me. Since we weren't talking about a work-related issue at the shipyard, I looked confused. "It means he's been around; he knows the ropes; it isn't the first time he's had to face and solve a problem," my husband further explained. Ah, I see. The phrase appealed to me as a good descriptor of people who tackle problems instead of avoiding them and who navigate seas instead of criticizing the navigation skills of others. As always, I immediately applied the analogy to librarianship. It fit exactly.

Great librarians don't hang around port, safely tying up each night. They are up for the challenge of an open-water crossing, knowing there are few safe havens along the way. They don't need the sky to always be sunny and cloud-free, and they know before they set out on their journeys that rain will inevitably fall. They plan the trip down to the tiniest detail to ensure that their supplies will last, but they are wise enough to know that plans have to be flexible. You have to plan for both the storms and the calm. Each can delay a trip and can spell disaster for the unprepared.

It takes good planning to be a deep-water sailor. You must have enough provisions to last the trip, an accurate chart map, and a sound boat. You must also have confidence in your skills and judgment: confidence born of past experiences. And you can't be arrogant. Deep-water sailors respect the wind and the tides. They know that the sea has dark tales to tell, and they read the waters thoughtfully and reflect on their role as part of the grand tradition of sailors. They make bold moves when the time is right, and at other times they are submissive to the greater power of

The handwritten margin note reads: "Hope for the best but prepare for the worst" the sea. There are faster ways to get to a destination, but for deep-water sailors it's the journey that is the real goal.

I opened my newspaper this morning to see yet another headline about deep cuts in the state budget for education and wondered what else can possibly be cut. How can the educational system carefully built over centuries survive the beyond-minimalist approach to school funding? Where will any library, whether it is academic, public, or school, stand at the end of the long, dark tunnel created by an either willful or spiteful ignorance of the importance of education by politicians and public alike? It's a scary time to be battling the elements, but safe ports are not where our passion drives us. Our students need us, and some of our administrators and teachers will pledge to follow where we lead.

We the school librarians are deep-water sailors, and we have to be. Otherwise, fear will keep us too tightly tied to tradition, hoping just not to be noticed, afraid to move from the dock lest our slip be taken by some lesser vessel. Like deep-water sailors, off sailing into the horizons, sometimes we have only the stars to guide us, along with modern technologies, best practices, and healthy doses of luck. Some storms we can avoid, others we can't, and some we simply choose not to, reveling instead in the power of wind and rain to take us where we need to go.

Lead on.

Gail K. Dickinson
Editorial Director

Dickinson, Gail K. (2012). Librarians as deep-water sailors. *LMC, 30*(6), 6.

The Class of 2022: How Will We Meet Their Needs and Expectations?

By Elizabeth Haynes

This fall's kindergarten class will graduate in 2022 and recent history indicates that those 13 years will likely bring an ever-increasing pace of technological change. Those wiser and more knowledgeable have said that predicting technology that far out is an exercise in crystal ball gazing with about as much validity. However, if we look at the background that many of these children bring with them as they enter school, and at how technology is likely to change in the next few years, we can make some assumptions about where we are headed and how school libraries will need to reach out to meet their needs.

It's a High-Tech World for a Kindergartner

What are some of the experiences these children have had by the time they entered kindergarten this fall? How have those experiences shaped their view of the world?

- Some have never seen a videocassette.
- Many live in homes that do not have landline telephones.
- More than a third of them have a television in their bedroom (Vandewater, p. e1010).
- At least a quarter of them have used a computer on a typical day (Vandewater, p. e1011).
- Four-fifths of them live in households with at least one computer (Vandewater, p. e1010).
- They can (and do) learn to use a mouse and navigate easily on a computer to find what they need or want.
- They can use a remote control to operate a television or media player and can load CDs and DVDs.
- A few already have their own cell phones.
- Reading aloud/being read to is still valued by parents and children.

- Many have their own books.
- They enjoy listening to music.
- Almost a fifth of them have played console or hand-held video games (Vandewater, p. e1011). Even more of them play games on a computer.
- They expect their toys to "do something."

(The figures given above are from 2007—the percentages likely would be higher today.)

We can debate whether or not the environment in which these children are growing up is a good one, but the fact remains that it is reality.

These children are immersed in a world of technology—even those on the wrong side of the digital divide almost always have access to television and are likely to live in a home with cell phones. This has shaped the way they view the world and expect to interact with it. But when they come to school do they find the technology they are used to? Should they? How do we, as librarians, provide instruction, materials, and access that capitalize on the knowledge that these students bring? How can we guide and instruct them in efficient, ethical, and fulfilling use of these technologies? How can we make our libraries educational yet relevant and fun places for the post-millenial generation? The answers to those questions are determined by many factors, not the least of which are budgetary constraints, personal teaching styles, training (or lack thereof), and personal philosophies.

What Does it REALLY Mean to Be a Digital Native?

Much has been written about digital natives vs. digital immigrants. But being a digital native is more than being able to learn and use technology intuitively. It also implies a mind-set, a "language" or "culture," if you will, that those who are digital

immigrants have a hard time learning and understanding. A story related by Zevenbergen illustrates this. A six-year-old boy (in Australia) told his mother he was going to play cricket with the boy next door. This happened several afternoons in a row before the mother, who thought her son was outside playing, discovered that the boys were playing cricket on an Xbox. The boys' conception of playing cricket was quite different from that of adults and involved digital interaction rather than physical activity (Zevenbergen, p. 25–26).

> Being a digital native is more than being able to learn and use technology intuitively. It implies a "language" or "culture" that those who are digital immigrants have a hard time learning and understanding.

What does the future look like for these children in terms of digital technology developments? It seems relatively safe to say that mobile and hand-held technologies will become even more dominant. The development of cloud computing means that small devices will have access to applications and files that could previously only be stored on hard drives with hundreds of gigabytes of storage. Hand-held devices will be capable of meeting most communication, information, and entertainment needs and laptops or desktop computers may only be used for larger projects that require greater visualization than a small screen can provide. The day when textbooks will reside on electronic readers along with recreational reading titles might not be too far in the future. Wireless Internet access will become even more ubiquitous than it is now. These and other trends are discussed each year in the annual *Horizon Report*, which has a K–12 edition (Johnson, et al.).

Impact on the Elementary Media Program

What does all this mean for elementary school libraries? As noted earlier, many librarians are constrained in their use of digital technologies by lack of money, school policy, Internet filters, aging equipment, uncertain connectivity, and other factors. However, these can be looked at as opportunities rather than challenges. Today's students are used to interactivity—with their toys, on the computer, and in their games. Even low-tech activities can be planned to provide a maximum amount of interactivity and collaboration. Where possible, the use of high-tech tools such as smart boards, clicker technology, and online collaborative activities can be used. If Internet filters preclude using online blog and wiki sites, see if similar software can be loaded on a school or district server so that students can use them collaboratively. Activities that incorporate problem-solving and require hands-on application extend the skills that these students have exhibited in learning computer navigation, playing digital games, and figuring out remote control technology.

Kindergarten and primary children can do more with digital technologies than you may expect. Kindergartners can learn presentation software such as PowerPoint. Using word processing software can enable younger children to write more easily and fluently. Educational digital games can hone problem-solving skills. Even younger children may be adept at interacting with simulated and virtual environments. Many are at home manipulating avatars, thanks to the popular Wii game system and other games. But the librarian also needs to design activities that are related to real life. The *Horizon Report* points out that real-life

learning experiences don't occur enough in schools. Such experiences need not always be high-tech. "Use of technology tools that are already familiar to students, project-based learning practices that incorporate real-life experiences, and mentoring from community members are a few practices that support increased engagement" (Johnson, et al., p. 7). And, of course, engagement leads to increased learning.

What will school library collections look like in the near future? One school in the news reacted to the challenge of ever-increasing digital technologies by totally doing away with books. Even the most die-hard "techies" in our ranks would find that solution extreme. But increasingly school librarians are changing from "keepers of the books" to information managers who assist students and teachers in finding and using information in the most appropriate sources and formats, whether print or digital. Hand in hand with that is our mission to promote "reading as a foundational skill for learning, personal growth, and enjoyment" (American Association of School Librarians, p. 21). It's my belief that the hard-copy book will still lend itself to that goal for some time to come. Still, online information sources and the Google scanned books project may make many of our print information sources obsolete.

Challenging Our Assumptions

As educators we cannot assume that these children think and learn in the ways that we thought and learned. In many ways their "culture" is alien to us. It requires a shift in our own mind-sets to adapt our practices to meet them where they are and engage them in educational activities that will be meaningful. We must always be challenging our own assumptions about what is right or best for our students. The world in which they will grow up to live and work will be vastly different from anything we have experienced or, possibly, can even imagine. Yet we are the ones who are charged with preparing them for that world. It will take all of our

imagination, creativity, and ingenuity to do so.

Sources and Resources

American Association of School Librarians. *Empowering Learners: Guidelines for School Library Media Programs.* Chicago: American Association of School Librarians, 2009.

American Association of School Librarians. *Standards for the 21st-Century Learner in Action.* Chicago: American Association of School Librarians, 2009

Ferriter, Bill. "The Kindle in My Classroom." *The Horn Book* (2008): 641–643.

Johnson, L., et al. "Horizon Report: 2009 K–12 Edition." 2009. 13 September 2009. <http://www.nmc.org/publications>.

Rideout, Victoria J., Vandewater, Elizabeth A., and Ellen A. Wartella. "Zero to Six: Electronic Media in the Lives of Infants, Toddlers, and Preschoolers." 2003. 13 September 2009. <http://www.kff.org/entmedia/upload/Zero-to-Six-Electronic-Media-in-the-Lives-of-Infants-Toddlers-and-Preschoolers-PDF.pdf>.

Vandewater, Elizabeth A., et al. "Digital Childhood: Electronic Media and Technology Use Among Infants, Toddlers, and Preschoolers." *Pediatrics* 119 (2007): e1006–1015.

Walton-Hadlock, Madleine. "Tots to Tweens: Age-Appropriate Technology Programming for Kids." *Children and Libraries* (2008): 52–55.

Zevenbergen, Robyn. "Digital Natives Come to Preschool." *Contemporary Issues in Early Childhood* 3.1 (2007): 19–29.

Elizabeth Haynes *is a faculty member in the School of Library and Information Science at the University of Southern Mississippi and a former school librarian. She can be reached at ehaynes@netdoor.com*

Haynes, Elizabeth. (2010). The class of 2022: How will we meet their needs and expectations? *LMC, 28*(4), 10–11.

Digital Resourcing and Access in the School Library: A Pandora's Box of Problems, Ponderings, and Potential

By Dianne McKenzie

The landscape of school libraries has been changing with the overwhelming and rapid introduction of different of e-readers, e-books, audiobooks, podcasts, and databases. This is all great for the consumer, but what about the management of these resources in a school library?

The many advantages to supplying fiction and nonfiction in a digital format include:

- There is no need for expensive and time-consuming shipping or processing for shelving.
- Resources are in your collection immediately, without taking up physical space.
- Items are available 24/7.
- E-versions are easier to surf, scan, and skim using keyword searches.
- The font can be changed according to needs.
- The text can be read aloud for the person who needs or wants it delivered in this format.
- Hyperlinks can be embedded and followed.
- Editions can be quickly updated.
- E-versions can be downloaded on portable devices and read anywhere.

With so many positives, why doesn't every school embrace the digital format?

Libraries have been about organizing physical 'things' so they can be located when required. Books, magazines, CDs, DVDs, VHS tapes, microfiche, and audio cassettes are all easy to store, organize, and retrieve, but now we have a resource that is intangible and proves a little difficult to organize and manage, especially when we need to consider copyright implications.

> *Instilling a culture of academic honesty and respect for intellectual property is an important strategy.*

A Growing Student Population and a Growing Number of E-Resources

I manage a school library that is relatively small but will eventually serve 1,400 students from grades 1 to 13, all undertaking the International Baccalaureate programs, which are based on inquiry and resource-based learning. We do not have the space to accommodate the printed word for every direction of independent inquiry or interest that a student has in thirteen years of schooling. As we grow larger in population and take on the higher grades, our collection will be taking on more of a digital focus with the adoption of databases and digital libraries. We are a 1:1 laptop school from grade 6 with a high computer to student ratio in the lower grade levels and one hundred percent home access to computers. Many of the secondary students have portable devices that are able to host e-books. I would like to be able to offer a format of reading that takes advantage of all these digital tools.

Currently, our focus is to provide access to nonfiction in the digital form for the upper grades. Print fiction books are still popular for the reasons of convenience, portability, and browsing. We have access through the National Library to Naxos AudioBooks and a limited version of NetLibrary. We subscribe to some databases with e-book content, such as Gale InfoTrac, Global Issues in Context, Encyclopædia Britannica, and BookFlix. We also make use of Google Books and have lists of free digital libraries available for student access. Links to online manga, comics, and graphic novels are also provided, with iTunes and podcasts offering further free resources to access. In many cases these sites do not allow downloading of their resources, so access requires an active Internet connection.

The major problem is ease of access and the number of access points. The student needs to go to each individual site to search, read or listen. They need to be motivated, have a good understanding of what they want, and know how to navigate the different sites. The integration of the digital resources into our OPAC to allow for one point searching of all our resources is appealing.

Using the Capabilities of the OPAC

Our library OPAC (Oliver by Softlink) allows for cataloging Web sites and electronic files. Utilizing its capability to do integrated federated searches with all the databases we have, students can do one-keyword searches in the OPAC to access database articles, e-books, video, Web sites, and images alongside the printed books we have in the library. While the OPAC helps with databases and Web sites, how can a student access free downloadable e-books without going to each site and having to figure out how to navigate, identify the format they need, choose the method required to download the item to the desired location, and open it?

Some of the strategies that will be implemented include using e-books and magazines that are free, open source, and have an independent Web site that can be given a catalog record that has a direct and active link to the page the student can select and be directed to. This would work well with Google Books, Google Scholar, and similar services. An example can be found at this link to our OPAC: **http://tinyurl.com/dcopac1** (click twice to access, then select the link itself).

This again only allows you to look at the e-book on the computer rather than download and read offline. It would also be accessible on an iPad with Wi-Fi or 3G capabilities, though the interface is not distraction free and space is lost to peripheral information.

Similarly, a free site that allows downloads could be cataloged with a direct link to the page with the specific title and download options so the title is still searchable in the OPAC. Free-ebooks (http://www.free-ebooks.net) allows downloads in various formats and has a number of titles. Although you do need to be a member to download, you could create a school account and give all students the access code for this one account.

Copyright Questions and Concerns

Loading the e-books on our server would be ideal. Students could search the OPAC, find the entry, and download the title from the server. Does this breach copyright? Probably, as there are now multiple copies of the book where there used to be one. If the resources were legally free and public domain downloads, is there a copyright issue if multiple copies are made from the one download? What formats would be required? All this discussion and research seems to create more questions than answers!

What about digital resources that have been purchased? It would be a blatant breach of copyright to allow students and staff to make a copy of the book and retain the original on the server. Can I trust students and staff to remove the copy from their electronic device when they are finished? We are working on instilling a culture of academic honesty and respect

for intellectual property, so these considerations are important.

Potential Solutions Using an Audiobook Model

A monthly subscription to Audible allows for one original download of the audiobook and a transfer to four computers and three mobile devices. After that, the system indicates you have reached the limit and need to de-activate one or more copies of the borrowed resource. One strategy is to have a dedicated audiobook storage machine, using iTunes, where students can access the catalog to find the titles, which can then be downloaded. This brings up another question: Will their personal devices allow them to do this when synching is so specific to their own computers?

> There is a digital management minefield out there, which requires creative thinking, understanding of copyright laws and many hours of research to find the best fit for your library.

Other schools purchase mp3 players. They have all downloads on a central machine and load one book onto a single device, which can be lent to a student. This brings the intangible digital back to being physical. It also prevents accidental breach of copyright. A similar system could be used with e-books—purchasing a number of readers and lending them with the e-books on them. However, this is a very expensive option in terms of setup costs, and if a reader is lost or damaged, most parents would not be happy replacing one.

Personally, I do not believe it is the library's responsibility to supply the readers to students when we still have options for print. However, having said that, we are looking at purchasing cheap mp3 players for students who do not have their own

device for downloading and listening to audio resources. We are also investigating purchasing iPads for in-library use to take advantage of the more interactive e-books that are becoming available.

Subscription Solutions

Subscription services such as NetLibrary, Follett, OverDrive, MyiLibrary, eLibrary, ebrary, Teachingbooks.net, and Gale Virtual Reference Library seem to have answered and solved most of the copyright and management issues. However, the services can be expensive. They also tend to lock you in to their individual platforms so you cannot change providers without losing your digital collection. Some have their own interface and download software/managers while others do not. They all offer MARC records for catalog integration and formats compatible for different e-readers.

The resources are 'loaned' to the student when they are downloaded, and after a specified time, they disappear or are disabled from the e-reader, computer, or mobile device. In most cases, only one resource can be borrowed at a time, which sorts out the copyright issues, and most allow for reserves. They mostly deliver nonfiction, with a few exceptions, and they all enable you to customize the resources according to your collection and school curriculum. They also supply usage statistics, which could be useful and supplement the library's circulation records. Adoption of one of these services will need research and reflection on what your library needs and can afford before the choice is made as it will be a longterm decision.

The most efficient and cost effective method of storing and accessing digital resources is through your own library management system, with functionality as mentioned above, but this does not seem to be in development.

There is a digital management minefield out there, which requires creative thinking, understanding of copyright laws, and many hours of research to find the best fit for your library. Until issues of formatting, copyright, accessibility, and costs are standardized, it will continue to be an area where we need to share our strategies and best practice for management. Digital resourcing is an issue with rapid growth and huge potential. We need to keep abreast of developments and offer our customers the best service and access to retain credibility and currency.

Dianne McKenzie *is head of library and MYP teacher librarian at Discovery College, Hong Kong. Read her blog at http://librarygrits.blogspot.com.*

McKenzie, Dianne. (2011). Digital resourcing and access in the school library: A Pandora's box of problems, ponderings and potential. *LMC, 29*(4), 56–57.

BYO What?

By Mark Ray

BYOD or BYOT stands for Bring Your Own Device (or Technology.) For many educators it is an acronym that may sound vaguely familiar. As an educational idea, it may lead to more questions than answers. Like some other districts and schools, Vancouver Public Schools has been exploring the use of BYOD as one of many strategies to promote 21st century skills, foster entrepreneurial teaching and learning, and increase engagement in the classroom. Vancouver Public Schools is by no means the first district to dabble in BYOD, but as a public school district with nearly 21,000 students, our exploration of wireless access for students represents a significant shift in philosophy and policy, not to mention strategic investments and changes to our network infrastructure. Here are some questions and answers based on what we've learned so far.

What does BYOD stand for? "Bring Your Own Device" is a program where staff and students can bring their personal computing devices (PCDs) on campus and connect them to a district wireless network that provides filtered Internet access. During the 2011–12 school year, this program was piloted at two high schools and one middle school with the goal of informing district decision-making for educational technology integration. As a result of its success, wireless expanded to all K–12 sites, with BYOD implementations at all secondary schools in fall 2012.

What is a PCD? A PCD is a personally owned laptop, netbook, tablet computer, mobile device or smartphone, e-reader, or any other personal computing device.

How is this different from 1:1? 1:1 models presume that all students have devices at most times in the instructional day, often with a prescribed device or product and specific expectations of use and integration into the curriculum. In many 1:1 implementations, devices are purchased by the district and checked out to students. In some 1:1 models, parents are expected to purchase devices for their children. In BYOD, there may be instances in which all or most students have devices in a given classroom, but that is not an assumption. Parent, teacher, and student choice define when and, more importantly, *if* PCDs are used at school. In addition, not one but a variety of personal computing devices may be used as part of individual, small group, or large group instruction.

Are teachers or students required to bring devices to school? No.

Can a teacher require students to have a personal computing device in their class? Teachers cannot require students to have devices, nor expect their use for any given class.

> *In BYOD a variety of personal computing devices may be used as part of individual, small group, or large group instruction.*

Are teachers required to implement the use of personal computing devices in their instruction? No. Some teachers opted to be part of a district pilot to serve as test beds for learning about BYOD. In these classrooms there was an expectation of increased instructional use of personal computing devices. This pilot provided proof of concept and led to a broader implementation of BYOD in the district. It has also helped inform decision-making regarding the use of PCDs as educational tools. The pilot model is being replicated as the project expands to other schools. Small teams of teachers will serve as first adopters at each site and be provided additional support. Nevertheless, all teachers are encouraged to do their own explorations and use BYOD as they see fit.

What about board and district approval for such use? In anticipation of the BYOD and wireless pilots, existing policy and guidelines were reviewed and modified to allow personal computing devices to be used in an approved instructional setting. A policy review of other districts with similar programs was done to inform and modify guidelines and policies.

What is the level of technical support provided? Aside from providing filtered Internet access, BYOD was not actively supported by district personnel or the IT help desk. In general, teachers and district staff are not expected to provide troubleshooting or technical assistance to users. Given the number and variety of possible devices that might be used in schools, expert support for users would be difficult, if not impossible. To date, most users have been able to access and use the wireless networks without difficulty. Additionally, because the devices are personal, students and teachers already have expertise in their operation and use.

Was anything done with respect to digital citizenship with students? A digital social contract was developed by students to focus on the responsibilities that come with BYOD. Several schools have used the digital social contract as a means for framing the project and instructing students on acceptable and appropriate use of technology in schools. Individual schools and teachers developed additional lessons and guidelines to help students connect BYOD to digital citizenship learning.

Are students at a disadvantage if they don't have a personal computing device for use at school? No. The district instructional program and curriculum remains the same. The district continues to purchase basic and supplementary textbooks, support materials, computers, and software to support student learning.

Who decides when students can use their devices? When students are under a teacher's supervision, that teacher has complete and final say on the use of PCDs for either the entire class or individuals in that classroom. The school may have developed specific guidelines for common spaces outside of classrooms.

A digital social contract is one means for framing the project and instructing students on acceptable and appropriate use of technology in schools.

Are any spaces designated Wi-Fi lounges for access to the network? School libraries may be designated as locations where users who are not part of scheduled classes can use personal computing devices—subject to district approved policy and guidelines. Buildings can opt to designate other areas as "anytime" spaces as well. Different buildings have adopted different approaches and policies regarding access beyond the classroom.

What network or software access do users have with their own devices? Students and teachers are only provided district-filtered Internet access. Users do not have access to district-purchased software or network storage. Students and teachers are free to purchase and use apps, resources, or cloud storage of their own choosing so long as they adhere to technology ethics and acceptable use policies. In this respect, access will be similar to the wireless access in hotels and cafés.

Are there recommended devices for students or teachers? No. Because BYOD is not intended as a 1:1 initiative and the district offers no formal support for personally owned devices, it is up to students and teachers to choose the

devices they wish to use at school. Interestingly, our surveys have shown that smartphones and non-phone handhelds like iPod Touch or Android devices were far more likely to be used in BYOD classrooms than laptops or tablets.

Are students and teachers still bound to district technology ethics policies and guidelines if they bring 3G/4G devices to use at school? Yes. District policies clearly specify that users must follow acceptable use guidelines regardless of ownership of the device or the network that they use. Students and teachers are encouraged, but not required, to use the district wireless network.

Can a teacher opt to restrict the use of personal computing devices in their classroom or specify which type of devices can be used? Yes. At this point in the implementation, teachers define when and where personal computing devices are used in their respective classrooms. Many teachers develop classroom protocols that specify when devices can be out and used and when they need to be stowed. Teachers could conceivably allow the use of laptops and tablet computers rather than cell phones.

Are cell phones and smartphones considered personal computing devices? Yes. Some teachers have made it a point to encourage students to use their phones for just-in-time research and informal polling using Poll Everywhere.

What if a personal computing device is stolen or lost at school? Users bring devices at their own risk and choice. Loss or damage of personal computing devices by students and/or teachers is not covered by the district or school. Our surveys have shown that concerns about theft or loss of devices by students was cited as one of the main reasons they did not bring the devices to school or use them in the classroom. Interestingly, due to the absence of lockers in most schools, this issue appears to be a greater barrier to widespread technology use than filtering or district policy.

Was there staff development in the use of personal computing devices? Compared to other technology pilots, BYOD adopted a hands-off approach to support and staff development. Even among the specified pilot participants, teachers were encouraged to explore the use of devices in the classroom on their own. As the pilot expands to all secondary schools, instructional technology facilitators will work with core teacher teams at each site to plan and support instruction with personal computing devices. There will remain an attempt to encourage students and teachers to be entrepreneurial in their use of personal technologies in the classroom and to promote exploration and experimentation. Teacher participating in the initial pilot has already provided examples of best practices, recommended classroom management, instructional integration, and other useful information. That guidance will help inform how we support teachers and students in the coming year.

What was the biggest surprise? The sky didn't fall. Despite a fear of the unknown by many, there were no significant disciplinary, media, or educational cataclysms. Because choice was central to the project—and since teachers controlled if, when, and where BYOD fit into their instruction—it was something that educators could explore in a safe way on their own timeline.

Despite a fear of the unknown by many, there were no significant disciplinary, media, or educational cataclysms when BYOD was implemented.

What did you learn from teachers? Teachers indicated that the most significant impact to the classroom environment was less connected with wireless access or the ability to use personal devices, and more about the change in culture that occurred for students and teachers.

The physical and philosophical shift toward owning and personalizing the use of technology in the classroom conveyed a sense of opportunity, exploration, and innovation.

What did you learn from students? Students surprised us in two ways. Despite assumptions that digitally native students are naturally innovative in their thinking about how to use technology, an initial focus group with juniors and seniors revealed some traditional ideas about how they would work differently in BYOD classrooms. Note-taking, research, and word processing were identified by many as likely uses. Few students considered using their devices as creative tools for video or audio production, leveraging personal apps, or using the network to connect, collaborate, and communicate with

one another. Another surprise was that students were very aware of the social and practical implications of the program. In the same focus group, issues of equity and safety/security were raised even before the project began.

What will you do differently based on what you've learned so far? As we go to scale with BYOD, we will expand our professional development and integration support based both on what we've learned and the rapidly emerging body of best practices. We plan to implement a digital professional learning community to connect teachers who are exploring BYOD to allow sharing of insights, lessons, and best practices. This will add an additional layer of support and reinforce the entrepreneurial goals of the project.

As we move BYOD to schools with higher levels of poverty, we will be looking at a variety of ways to ensure students have access to technology. One idea under consideration is the purchase of classroom sets of devices to allow teachers to easily deploy devices for specific projects. Additionally, schools may allow devices to be checked out from the library. In the end, we are learning that while BYOD removes some barriers, it reveals others. And the lessons have only begun.

Mark Ray *is a media specialist at Skyview High School in Vancouver, Washington. He can be reached at mark.ray@vansd.org.*

Ray, Mark. (2013). BYO what? *LMC, 31*(4), 8–10.

Bring Your Own Excitement

By Wendy Stephens and Sarah Fanning

support & expectations

It's Time for New Ways of Thinking

At the National Association of Secondary School Principals National Conference in 2009, Dr. Kipp Rogers, then principal of Passage Middle School in Newport News, Virginia, and now director of secondary instruction for York County (Virginia) Schools, presented a session on the whole-school integration of cell phone technology in his building.

That was a turning point in our local thinking. Previously, we had focused on purchasing classroom response systems to share among our departments. Dr. Rogers showcased several smartphone-based applications to replicate polling interactivity without the initial capital outlay or recurring expense of batteries. He also discussed the offline applications of cell phones, including using the calculator, camera, and calendar functionality, and showcased the text-based Google search and dictionary definition features. All of this led us to revisit the handy devices so many of our high school students already possessed.

In our cash-strapped district we are never going to be able to provide a device for every student in the building. It is already a challenge to keep teacher computers operational. Our district policy allows students to bring devices into schools. However, students are officially not allowed to use them during the school day. We sought an exception from our district administration to begin experimenting with these devices for instructional purposes. Several teachers were enthusiastic about incorporating them into their teaching. The first experiment involved a social studies elective using a backchannel to post observations about World War I as students watched the film *The Lost Battalion*.

> In our cash-strapped district, we are never going to be able to provide a device for every student in the building.

A Very Enthusiastic Response

The next year, we decided to participate in the first national Digital Learning Day project. Our school has a relationship with the Alliance for Excellent Education, which helped sponsor the event, and it gave some credibility to our desire to incorporate a range of technologies, particularly student-owned devices.

We laid the groundwork for BYOD ("Bring Your Own Device") with a mandatory professional development session embedded in the school day. The librarian had done a workshop for a district technology conference two years prior on using smartphones in the classroom, and she updated that for the faculty. Teachers were given hands-on experience with live polling, finding definitions, and retrieving search results. Because of the enthusiasm and the many creative ideas teachers had when presented with the capabilities of the mobile devices, the four sessions ended up being longer and more interactive than we had anticipated. Teachers shared previous experiences, including allowing students to use cell phones as calculators in algebra, which one teacher said required some additional vigilance but had been an overall positive experience. We discussed the fact that, if students could cheat on a test via text messaging, that assessment was probably not the most authentic sort. Only a couple of members of our large faculty were hesitant about the idea of turning students loose online outside of the school network. The administration spoke to each group, punctuating the

expectation that teachers would seize this opportunity to think outside the normal strictures of the classroom and do something truly innovative.

On Digital Learning Day the excitement was palpable. Students emerged from their first block classes buzzing about their learning. The faculty was invited to spend their planning period watching a nationally televised webcast that showcased the same types of activities they were already implementing. Our state superintendent of education, Dr. Tommy Bice, was featured in the webcast. He announced that in Alabama the entire month would be devoted to digital learning. We welcomed the opportunity to extend the rich, instructional experiences for our students for another twenty-eight days.

Limited Bandwith? Go Mobile! *us too*

Only district-owned devices are allowed on the wireless network in our school, so even teachers are unable to use personal hardware. Don Knezek, former CEO of ISTE, proposed that schools invest in multiple wireless networks to separate those handling district business from those oriented around student-owned devices (Schachter 32). We knew that many students have access to cellular data. One of our math teachers had a student bring in a mobile hotspot. Through this hardware, all students in the class were able to get online, even with laptops. The teacher contrasted the quality of engagement and interaction in that class section with that of another section where students pooled cellular-capable hardware. He said having one-to-one online access made an appreciable difference in the quality of learning in his classroom that day.

From Twitter hashtags and Poll Everywhere to Wiffiti, Facebook, and digital camera images to capture everything from angles for math class to landscapes for art composition, we have never seen more enthusiasm among our students than during our digital learning push. These technologies allowed our classroom conversations to be more inclusive. As Principal Eric Sheninger reported about BYOD initiatives at New Milford (New Jersey) High School, "In a typical classroom, a teacher will ask a question and maybe a few students will raise their hands to answer, but with Poll Everywhere, every student has to answer the question" (Puente 64). The feedback from our faculty and students was entirely positive. One parent said it was the first time her tenth grader had ever enjoyed school.

this!

From Twitter hashtags and Poll Everywhere to Wiffiti, Facebook, and digital camera images to capture everything from angles for math class to landscapes for art composition, we have never seen more enthusiasm among our students than during our digital learning push.

Setting Boundaries

As long as there have been schools, some students have chosen to misuse the available tools. Teens will push the boundaries with language, images, and innuendo through whatever medium. But educators haven't banned crayons, pencils, or pens just because a student might inscribe a textbook with profanity or a lewd image. Recognizing the distinction between the behavior and the materials with which students choose to express themselves was a fundamental element of our implementation of BYOD in our building. The administration stressed that it was the inappropriate conduct which should be addressed, as with any other infraction, rather than the means students used to violate school policy.

Addressing Equity

Our faculty worried about students who might not have hardware of their own, but they were surprised about the technology their students did possess, regardless of their economic backgrounds. In fact, as has been demonstrated by national research, many teens, especially from minority groups, are more likely to have web-enabled cell phones than Internet access at home. Some teachers expressed concern that they did not know how to use the range of devices their students possessed, something that has been called "the heterogeneity challenge" of BYOD programs (Norris 94). But we were actually eliminating the initial learning curve by promoting technology with which students themselves were already quite comfortable.

In his presentation on cell phone technology integration, Rogers proposed an excellent solution for students who might not have cell phones of their own. Once his initiative was underway, he found many people willing to donate their older devices to the school. These phones could be employed offline at no expense, and with minimal pay-as-you-go expenditures they were useful for polling and searching. Lake Travis (Texas) Independent School District found another solution. Equity was ensured with a bond issue to fund devices for low-income families, and middle-income families were able to purchase or lease devices from a variety of vendors at a negotiated discount ("BYOD Strategies" 34). Some cellular service providers have started gearing products for education settings by offering data-only plans (Williams 29).

Building Trust

We combined much of the evidence of the excitement and the innovative student work from Digital Learning Day in a short film to share with our district. It won the Digital Learning Day follow-up video contest in the Teacher Implementation category, demonstrating that, with appropriate professional development led by a tech-savvy librarian and significant administrative support, students could use their own technology tools to enhance their work in myriad ways and provide teachers with formative assessment data. Students also learned transferable skills, including text-based searching and dictionary features to support their own independent and everyday

life learning. And, by modeling appropriate and productive uses of technology, teachers actually gained credibility for their own skills among these digital natives.

While the use of student-owned hardware is still not officially sanctioned by our district, teachers are working with the tools and concepts they picked up through our Digital Learning Day experience. For example, one biology class recently took advantage of app-based instrumentation to monitor the local environment. These were the same tools, the teacher asserted, that working scientists use.

Now, instead of operating under a mandate that links communication to criminality, we choose to trust our students to remain engaged and on task, and they have not disappointed us.

Works Cited

"BYOD Strategies." *Technology & Learning* Feb. 2012: 34. Print.

Norris, Cathleen, and Elliot Soloway. "From Banning to BYOD: This Inevitable Shift Is at the Heart of School Change." *District Administration* May 2011: 94. Print.

Puente, Kelly. "High School Pupils Bring Their Own Devices." *District Administration* Feb. 2012: 34–37. Print.

Schachter, Ron. "Creating a Robust and Safe BYOD Program: Plan to Upgrade Your District's Infrastructure for Increased Capacity and Security." *District Administration* Apr. 2012: 28–32. Print.

Williams, Courtney. "Student Engagement Soars with Smartphones." *District Administration* Feb. 2012: 29. Print.

Wendy Stephens *is the school librarian at Buckhorn High School in New Market, Alabama, and may be reached at wstephens@madison.k12.al.us.*

Sarah Fanning *is the assistant principal for curriculum and instruction at Buckhorn High School.*

Stephens, Wendy, & Fanning, Sarah. (2013). Bring your own excitement. *LMC, 31*(4), 12–13.

E-books Draw a Crowd!

By Kristin Steingraeber

Yesterday I met with a newly hired teacher librarian at a small school in southeast Iowa. By the end of our conversation, we had been joined by the superintendent, both high school and elementary principals, and two tech coordinators. The focus was on e-books, and they were enthusiastic about this conversation.

The e-reader Conversation

My conversation that day started with questions about e-readers. People have seen the ads. Many received a Kindle for Christmas, or are using a Nook Simple Touch and learning to download books from an online store or library. As you will see, e-readers are not the complete solution yet, but using them is helping all of us understand e-books—both options and limitations.

Make that step and get an e-reader and account. Purchase a title and transfer it to the device. Each step helps you understand how this works, and also how it doesn't work for the large number of students we have! For example:

- When we were talking on Friday, one of the teachers shared that there is a waiting list for *The Hunger Games* at her public library—123 people.
- When the ALA Awards were announced and I did not have a copy of *Dead End in Norvelt*, Jack Gantos' Newbery winner, I probably did what anyone with an account would do. I used my credit card, downloaded the title to my computer and also to my WhisperSync iPad app, and started to read. Today, when I am at my computer, it automatically asks me if I want to "sync to furthest page read" from another device. That is pretty powerful. I wish I could provide an e-reader to every student.

The challenge? I serve 36,800 students in forty school districts. Our school populations have forced us to look at multi-use, simultaneous access. The information I have learned about accessibility issues has helped me see how important audio and text features are with e-books.

Simultaneous, Multi-use Access: The Series Nonfiction Solution

While I encourage experimentation with a few devices for checkout—because only then can we have conversations with people about single use, file types, and limitations (namely, fiction)—we have a great opportunity here to enable students to discover series nonfiction through multi-use, simultaneous access.

Our GPAEA pilot began with initial purchases from Rosen's ePoint books and Capstone's Acorn Read-Aloud series. All 600 of the titles are multi-use, simultaneous access and do not require an e-reader. (We also found support for this based on a December 2011 survey of our teachers: 62 percent of respondents were using laptops, and only 1 percent were using an e-reader to read e-books.)

1. Access. Key is the ability to provide e-books to student devices (including smartphones) with no waiting lists.

Background information

In Iowa, nine Area Education Agencies (AEAs) use their media centers to provide resources to schools via an intermediate library and van system. In the past year at Great Prairie AEA, where I am the media specialist, we are seeing our e-book collection increase in usage, challenging some of our print delivery numbers (which are remaining relatively stable). The data shows we are checking out three times as many e-books as we did in the first six months of 2011. When we opened up access to e-books to student readers, they became our top users immediately.

In 2011, the AEAs worked together to find out more about e-books and the market. Conference phone calls were set up with individuals around the country, including

- Ric Hasenyager, director for library services, North East ISD, San Antonio
- Christopher Harris, school library system coordinator, Genesee Valley Educational Partnership, New York
- Ken Petri, the director of the Web Accessibility Center at Ohio State University
- Ira Socol, a graduate student and Universal Design for Learning Technology researcher at Michigan State University;

assistive technology specialist at Michigan Rehab Services; and author.

Presentations from several vendors were available, including Mackin, Rosen, Capstone, Overdrive, and Follett. We visited Barnes and Noble for a demonstration of the Nook and how it could be used in the classroom. We also surveyed teachers who were just starting to think about using e-books and e-readers, as well as some who had. We started pilots in our own AEAs and as a state purchased BookFlix for all K-3 students in Iowa this past summer.

> *Our school populations have forced us to look at multi-use, simultaneous access to e-books.*

I use a graphic organizer for my conversations, which includes a column for the media they work with as well as some of the titles we are talking about.

Having this organizer with me helps move our conversations along, and I can share demonstrations of what we find in our e-book collection. I use the actual e-books when we have an Internet connection, but also a series of page images I captured with an iPad, to demonstrate e-books when there is no Internet connection.

2. Our e-books are web-based and not dependent on a certain device. Some of them include options to download, so they can be read with software like Adobe Digital Editions or as a PDF without Internet access.
3. Online text features are part of what makes nonfiction e-books a positive experience for young readers.

   - Ability to search within the title, with results highlighted in the text
   - Table of contents
   - Links to websites
   - Ability to create individual accounts and take notes

Johnson describes the text design of online e-books in "Every Student's Reading Teacher: The School Librarian" (*SLM*, February 2012). It is helpful to explain to teachers how text design helps manage the reading experience.

4. While not all of our e-books have audio options, we feature that in our CyberSmarts e-books. Accessibility is something we, as a school library community, should continue to request. With CyberSmarts, students can listen to text and the quoted material in the sidebars has audio as well.

5. There are so many options with series nonfiction in relation to content. We have only scratched the surface in our small pilot, and I look forward to working with other publishers. The quality of the text has been excellent and is very important now as we move to Common Core and recommendations for 50 percent informational text.

Getting the Word Out

To make all of this happen we have to tell the teachers. I agree with Julie Rick when she writes about Rosen's nonfiction series:

"Rosen Publishing has also released a nonfiction series that contains graphic battles of the Civil War, mythology and discoveries, as well as "junior" titles for younger students. Given the chance, these titles could appear outside the English and language arts classroom, contributing to interdisciplinary thematic units, or even serving as an introduction to a new concept or content area. But this will only happen if school librarians make teachers aware of these interesting enrichment possibilities." (*LMC*, October 2011)

What is possible with e-books? It does not take long before we make connections between the recent science news on solar storms and the e-book in the collection that focuses on solar flares. I can even show how the title includes a video of a solar flare. Here are some other connections to share:

- Bring a print text and have the computer ready for a corresponding e-book example. Take the U.S. history textbook *Exploring America's Past* (Holt, Rinehart and Winston, 1998), bookmarked with three short references to the 13th Amendment and Jim Crow laws. Then look at the e-book *Rosa Parks: The Life of a Civil Rights Heroine* (Rosen, 2007). Four pages talk about those same subjects but go beyond the textbook in terms of length. Those pages are followed by a graphic nonfiction story with engaging graphics and detailed text.

> *What is possible with e-books? It does not take long before we make connections between the recent science news on solar storms and the e-book in the collection that focuses on solar flares.*

- Connect with teachers by simply sending a screenshot as part of your "advertisement" of what is new. I can take a great screenshot with my iPad, and by sending that partial image to a teacher, it brings them to the catalog to explore the e-book. For example, three sections of a graphic nonfiction title work well to "advertise" *Rosa Parks: The Life of a Civil Rights Heroine*:
  1. The images from the explosion of Martin Luther King's house, January 30, 1956
  2. The color choices in the graphics on the page describing her life as she was growing up
  3. The artistic design of one of the bus scenes on page 29

Share this not only with social studies content area teachers because of the topic, but also with art teachers and gifted/talented teachers as well. Who might benefit from a quick visual of what is available in your catalog of e-books? That is the guiding question.

- Use Jing to create short video clips that demonstrate something as simple as moving around the media catalog to select e-books, as well as the process of getting to the reading part.
- Model how to move across the e-book pages in a web browser.
- Model how to use the personal workspaces, including taking notes and jumping from place to place with the table of contents, or finding the citation information.
- Demonstrate downloading to a PDF and opening in Adobe Digital Editions.
- Connect your Nook and then transfer from Adobe Digital Editions to the Nook.

- Use new technologies like QR codes to move from older print titles to newer material. An earlier title, *Everything You Need to Know: Bird Flu* (Icon, 2005), can be updated by simply adding a QR code to the book jacket. The code links to the newer title *Frequently Asked Questions about Avian Flu* (Rosen, 2009). By sharing examples like this, the group you are visiting will brainstorm other ideas of how they could move students from older materials to newer e-book titles.

- Reference your work that supports the content. I share my review blog for a simple reason. In the blog, I try to suggest ways to use media resources, especially nonfiction books, and I'm starting to make connections with nonfiction e-books. One example: http://amrc-reviews.blogspot.com/2011/11/many.html. This post suggests pairing *The Many Faces of George Washington: Remaking a Presidential Icon* (Carolrhoda, 2011) not only with NCSS titles but also with a great e-book in our collection.

Finally, it's important to get feedback from teachers and librarians. We want to know subject areas, questions they are raising, and their plans for instruction. This helps us build our e-book collection and provide examples to share with other teachers/librarians.

References

Foote, Carolyn. "E-books: Just Jump In!" *Library Media Connection* 29.4 (2011): 58–59. Print.

Johnson, Mary J. "Every Student's Reading Teacher: The School Librarian." *School Library Monthly* 28.5 (2012): 27–28. Print.

Rick, Julie. "Educate the Educators about Graphic Novels: Five Tips for Success." *Library Media Connection* 30.2 (2011): 34+. Print.

Shone, Rob. *Rosa Parks: The Life of a Civil Rights Heroine.* Rosen, 2007. ePoint Books. Web. 1 Dec. 2011. www.epointbooks.com.

Kristin Steingreaber *is a library media specialist at Great Prairie (Iowa) Area Education Agency and can be reached at @ksteingr.*

Steingraeber, Kristin. (2012). E-books draw a crowd! *LMC, 31*(1), 30–33.

E-book implementation ideas

- A.W. (2011) shares that she uses e-books for whole group instruction to model reading for facts with the Mysteries series (UFO, Bermuda Triangle, and Bigfoot). She also models reading for facts in science (earthquakes). Students are not yet using e-books on their smartphones, but that will be a possible conversation in the future. They can read these nonfiction titles on a web browser on their phones.

- S.K. (2011) has used an interactive whiteboard with the e-book *Learning about the Effects of Natural Events with Graphic Organizer* (Rosen, 2005). From that e-book, she posted a graphic, editing it with a cover screen. Students were able to complete this as a pre-reading activity before reading.

- I surveyed teachers to find out if e-books were helpful in their instruction. Based on the Gradual Release of Responsibility framework (Fisher and Frey), 30 percent of the teachers were using e-books with whole group instruction, 19 percent for independent, and 7 percent each for productive or guided.

- One teacher used e-books for independent "listen to reading" work. She is pushing me to find more audio options. I discovered a free option for older students from a conversation with Mary Nemeth, coordinator for INFOhio Services: ThoughtAudio, www.thoughtaudio.com. That is how we move forward. Continually be aware of possibilities and participate in conversations about e-reading and e-books as often as you can.

Above all, we want to make student reading possible—print and online. Based on the enthusiasm at a small table on a Friday morning in Iowa, I am very confident that we will succeed!

Selecting a Web 2.0 Presentation Tool

By Charles B. Hodges and Kenneth Clark

Presentations in the Cloud

Online presentation tools, an emerging type of Web 2.0 tool, can be used in many different ways in education. This article covers online presentation tools suitable for K–12 settings and offers an evaluation instrument for selecting the tool that best matches your skills and needs.

The 2010 K–12 edition of the *Horizon Report* (Johnson, et al., 2010) includes key trends in the educational implementation of technologies forecasted for adoption in one year or less, two to three years, and four to five years. Cloud computing and collaborative environments were on this year's list in the "one year or less" time frame. Both of these concepts also were mentioned in the 2009 edition (Johnson, et al., 2009). Since these technologies have made the list two years in a row, it is clear that they are on their way to prominence.

Cloud computing refers to data storage and software tools that do not reside on a single user's computer but instead exist on servers and data centers across the world, accessible via the Internet. A common example of cloud computing is Google's Gmail service, which stores all of your e-mail on Google's servers.

Collaborative environments are defined as "online spaces where the focus is on making it easy to collaborate and work in groups" (Johnson, et al., 2010) regardless of the physical location of the group members. Wikis and shared document services like Google Apps are common examples of the types of collaborative environments the *Horizon Report* highlights.

PowerPoint for the 21st Century

Web-based presentation tools are sometimes referred to as "next generation presentation tools" (EDUCAUSE, 2010). At the most basic level, these tools are simply online versions of traditional presentation software, such as Microsoft's PowerPoint or Apple's Keynote, but some services offer features like web-based collaboration, online presentation sharing, and non-traditional authoring schemes that offer interesting alternatives to the old standards. Most are free to use, and since they are based on the cloud computing concept, all that is typically needed is a computer with an Internet connection and a web browser. Table 1 lists popular online presentation tools.

Table 1 **Popular Online Presentation Tools**

Presentation Tools	
These programs allow you to create linear presentations that are similar to PowerPoint.	
Tool	**URL**
Ahead	http://ahead.com
280 Slides	http://280slides.com
Emprssr	http://www.emressr.com
Google Docs	http://www.google.com/google-d-s/presentations
MyBrainShark	http://my.brainshark.com
PreZentit	http://prezentit.com
Prezi	http://prezi.com
SlideRocket	http://www.sliderocket.com
Vuvox	http://www.vuvox.com
Zoho Show	http://show.zoho.com
Free-Form Presentation Tools	
These programs were not created to be presentations tools, but can be used by a creative	
individual for non-linear, free-form presentations.	
Tool	**URL**
Glogster	www.glogster.com

Magnoto	www.magnoto.com
Wall Wisher	www.wallwisher.com
Slideshow Storage Sites	
These sites allow you to store and share your presentations via the cloud. Some sites will allow you to store not only PowerPoint presentations but also Keynote presentations, Word documents, and PDFs.	
Tool	**URL**
AuthorStream	www.authorstream.com
MyPlick	www.myplick.com
SlideBoom	www.slideboom.com
SlideServe	www.slideserve.com
SlideShare	www.slideshare.net
SlideSix	http://slidesix.com

Meeting the Standards

Marshall Jones (2008) provides tips and resources for using PowerPoint that could easily be adapted for use with these next generation presentation tools. Some of Jones' ideas include using presentation tools as multimedia authoring tools, for digital storytelling, and for electronic portfolios. Roblyer and Doering (2010) comment that "the most powerful strategy for integrating presentation multimedia is for students to create individual or small-group presentations to document and display the results of research they have done and/or to practice making persuasive presentations" (188). Roblyer and Doering go on to say that this is a strategy for using presentation software in any content area, "from art history to math to science to social studies and beyond" (188).

It does not take a lot of imagination to see how projects using these new presentation tools would satisfy technology standards. For example, "use technology and other information tools to analyze and organize information" and "use the writing process, media and visual literacy, and technology skills to create products that express new understandings" are part of the *Standards for the 21st-Century Learner* (AASL, 2007). Likewise, NETS-S, the International Society for Technology in Education's National Educational Technology Standards for Students (ISTE, 2007)

include standards for (1) creativity and innovation; (2) communication and collaboration; (3) research and information fluency; (4) digital citizenship; and (5) technology operations and concepts. The use of an online presentation tool in a group project can allow indicators of the NETS-S to be met, such as "interact, collaborate, and publish with peers, experts, or others employing a variety of digital environments and media" (2a), and "understand and use technology systems" (6a).

Matching Users, Purpose, and Tools

Once you decide to use an online presentation tool, your next step is to select one. The tools listed in Table 1 are just a small sampling of the number of tools available. Even a quick search for presentation tools will yield several possible choices along with online tools that were not originally designed for presentations but can be utilized for such with a little creativity. Presentation tools are constantly changing. Use your favorite search engine to discover tools not listed in Table 1.

A two part Online Presentation Tool Evaluation Instrument (Figure 1) is provided to help. Part A includes criteria that are considered to have "make or break" status. Ease of Use and Technical Compatibility can be determined rather quickly by exploring the tool yourself and checking that it works in your classroom or school. Accessibility

and Security will take some more effort. You may need to consult school or district policies regarding technology use, and you may need to ask for guidance from knowledgeable persons in your professional context, such as a school instructional technology specialist. Take the time to consider Part A carefully.

Part B can be completed without consulting others, but you will want to dig into the tool's website in detail to make sure it offers what you and your students need. The first category, Development Status/Longevity, should be tempered with your own comfort-level regarding new software. The instrument is designed to rate mature and established tools higher than others. Mature and established tools will usually be more reliable in terms of functioning features and availability. If you are comfortable working with a system that might have a few bugs or that might not exist tomorrow, then experiment with a newer tool. You will sometimes find unique and interesting features in the newer tools. To help you create a list of features that you want to consider, several current features of online presentation tools are listed in Tables 2 and 3 along with an explanation of those features. Due to the ever evolving list of tools available on the Internet, this list will get you started thinking about the features offered. As you explore other tools, make note of features that you want or need, and add them to your own list.

EXAMPLES OF ADAPTATIONS AND USE OF ASSISTIVE TECHNOLOGY

For a student who experiences difficulty with writing:

Instructional Strategies	Task Modifications	Adaptive or No/Low AT	Alternative or Mid/High AT
• tracing exercises • "talk through" letter formation • dot-to-dot • multisensory instruction • chalkboard practice • avoid using short pencils • utilize cross-age tutoring • cooperative learning • keyboarding instruction	• adapt tests to fill-in-the-blank, multiple choice or true/false • allow more time • shorten assignments • photocopy notes • change paper position • change student position	• tape paper to desk • clipboard to hold paper • different writing tools • pencil holders/grips • different texture/color paper • different line spacing • acetate sheets w/ markers • talking pen • stencils/templates • rubber stamps • magnetic letters • slant board/easel • wrist support • arm stabilizer	• typewriter • word processor • keyguard • alternative input devices for computer • software providing macros • spell checker • talking word processor • word prediction • abbreviation expansion • onscreen keyboard • voice recognition

For a student who experiences difficulty with reading

Instructional Strategies	Task Modifications	Adaptive or No/Low AT	Alternative or Mid/High AT
• story mapping • read aloud guests • multisensory instruction • structured study guides • utilize cross-age tutoring • cooperative learning	• highlight key concepts • allow more time • shorten assignments • simplify text • use chapter outlines	• study carrel • tactile letters/words • magnifying bars • colored acetate • word window • flash cards • highlighter • post-it flags • color coded paper clips	• tape recorder • books on tape • Language Master • electronic dictionary • scanner with OCR • talking word processor • Reading Pen

From the Web site of the Hawaii State Department of Education, "Welcome to A.T. the Forefront Online." http://doc.k12.hi.us/specialeducation/chapter56/appendix.htm

Making an Informed Choice

After completing the instrument, make a judgment regarding the suitability of the tool or tools you are considering. If you are comparing two or more tools, then the total score for Part B should give you some insight into which tool is more appropriate for your needs.

If you are considering only one tool, the instrument provides a structure that will allow you to consider important criteria before deciding whether a tool is an appropriate choice.

This instrument is fairly generic and could be used to select other Web 2.0 tools or more traditional educational software offerings. If you are working with advanced students, you may actually be able to include them in the selection process, enabling them to achieve additional standards aimed at higher level learning outcomes, such as analyzing, evaluating, or drawing conclusions.

Table 2 Features Available in Online Presentation Tools

Feature	Explanation
Import PowerPoint	Will the program allow you to import an existing PowerPoint presentation?
Export PowerPoint	Will the program allow you to download your presentation to your computer as a PowerPoint presentation?
Import Other	Will the program allow you to import a presentation created by a presentation program other than PowerPoint? What formats?
Export Other	Will the program allow you to export your presentation in a format other than PowerPoint? What formats?
Create from Scratch	Will the program allow you to create a presentation from scratch?
Host Presentation	Can you store your presentation on the program's server?
Collaboration	Does the program allow collaboration in the creation of the presentation? Can multiple people work on the presentation at the same time?

Table 3 Presentation-Level Features Available in Online Presentation Tools

Feature	Explanation
Text	Does the program allow you to use different font faces, styles, and effects?
Images	Does the program allow you to upload images from your computer? Can you import from online photo sites like Flickr?
Import Other	Will the program allow you to import a presentation created by a presentation program other than PowerPoint? What formats?
Audio	Does the program allow you to upload audio from your computer? Can you add narration to your slides from within the program?
Transitions	What types of transitions does the program have available?
Builds	Does the program support builds?
Hyperlinks	Does the program allow you to link to an external website? Can you hyperlink to another slide in the same presentation?
Drawing Tools	Does the program provide drawing tools?
Templates	Does the program provide background templates?

References

AASL. *Standards for the 21st-Century Learner*. AASL, 2007. Web. 4 Feb 2011. www.ala.org/ala/mgrps/divs/aasl/guidelinesandstandards/learningstandards/AASL_LearningStandards.pdf.

ISTE. "NETS for Students 2007." ISTE, 2007. Web. 8 Dec 2010. www.iste.org/standards/nets-for-students/nets-student-standards-2007.aspx.

Johnson, L., A. Levine, R. Smith, and T. Smythe. *The Horizon Report: 2009 Edition*. Austin: The New Media Consortium, 2009. Print.

Johnson, L., R. Smith, A. Levine, and K. Haywood. *The Horizon Report: 2010 Edition*. Austin: The New Media Consortium, 2010. Print.

Jones, M. "Using the Power of PowerPoint for Good, and Not for Evil." 2008. Web. 8 Dec 2010. http://coe.winthrop.edu/jonesmg/lti/pal/PAL_PowerPoint.htm.

Roblyer, M. D. and A. H. Doering. *Integrating Educational Technology into Teaching*. 5th ed. Boston: Pearson Education Inc., 2010. Print.

"Seven Things You Should Know bout . . . Next-Generation Presentation Tools." EDUCAUSE, 2010. Web. 8 Dec 2010. http://net.educause.edu/ir/library/pdf/ELI7056.pdf.

Charles B. Hodges, Ph.D., *is an assistant professor, Leadership, Technology & Human Development at Georgia Southern University in Statesboro, Georgia. He can be reached at chodges@georgiasouthern.edu.*

Kenneth Clark, Ph.D., *is a professor, Leadership, Technology & Human Development at Georgia Southern University in Statesboro, Georgia. He can be reached at kclark@georgiasouthern.edu.*

Hodges, Charles B., & Clark, Kenneth. (2011). Selecting a Web 2.0 presentation tool. *LMC, 30*(3), 42–45.

Reader's Advisory for Net-Gen Students

By Judi Repman and Stephanie Jones

Admit it, when you look up a book title on Amazon, you enjoy reading the reviews. Maybe you have even purchased another title based on the suggestions provided in "frequently bought together" or "customers who bought this item also bought" links. If you think about it, the purpose of reader's advisory is to *sell* the next book to the eager (or reluctant) reader. Amazon and other online booksellers have done a terrific job of developing ways to let customers share their opinions about books with the goal of getting you to buy more books. They have also made effective use of the bottom line, which is what a customer spends those hard-earned dollars on, to further entice us to add one more item to our cart.

In this article, we are going to share non-commercial ways to do some of the same things in your school library. The reader's advisory (RA) concept, to link books with readers, hasn't changed much from the days of the card catalog. All of us probably have some of the classic print resources about RA on our bookshelves, but these days it's easy, fun, and often free to use tools that can get students, teachers, librarians, parents, and others involved in a dynamic conversation about reading.

The Net-Gen Approach

Today's students can make many choices when it comes to the format of the materials they choose to read. Print, e-books, fanfiction, graphic novels, manga and/or anime, and cell phone novels are some of the most popular. No matter what format they choose, our highly connected net-gen students want to share their opinions about what they've read, see what their friends have enjoyed reading, and perhaps even engage in discussions about their reading. And where do they look to find this information? The web, of course! While many excellent print resources are available to help school librarians provide reader's advisory services, our students expect more. Most importantly, they expect to be involved in building the network of resources about what *they* want to read.

One-Stop Shopping

You shouldn't overlook resources you may already have on hand or can easily build to involve students in RA. Many current versions of library automation software incorporate Amazon-like features. For instance, Follett's Destiny Quest (www.follettsoftware.com/pg110/destiny-quest) allows students to rate titles they've read in addition to adding their own reviews. One interesting feature, which is part of the opening page, is Top 10 Books Checked Out. As students mouse over the titles on the list, the availability of the title is indicated along with brief plot summaries. Check with your library automation vendor to see if features like this are available for your system.

If you'd like to do a little web construction, there are many good examples to check out. Clovis East High School in California uses LibGuides (www.springshare.com/libguides/index.html) to build content for their Good Reads section (http://cehs.clovisusd.libguides.com/content.php?pid=72201&sid=662295). LibGuides is a fee-based service, but a similar product could be created with free tools such as Netvibes (www.netvibes.com), Pageflakes (www.pageflakes.com), or Jog the Web (www.jogtheweb.com). Jog the Web makes it easy to add comments, instructions, and explanations with each of the websites included on the list.

Sqworl (http://sqworl.com) is a bookmarking tool, but instead of seeing a list of site titles or URLs, the results show the front page of each website. Using the sites listed in the Other Approaches section of our Reader's Advisory wiki (http://itec7134resources.pbworks.com/Reader%27s-Advisory-Resources), here is an example of Sqworl: http://sqworl.com/c99tmu.

> *Our highly connected net-gen students want to share their opinions about what they've read, see what their friends have enjoyed reading, and perhaps even engage in discussions about their reading.*

Joyce Valenza has used a combination of a wiki and Glogster to create the appealing Book Leads site for high school students (http://bookleads.wikispaces.com). While this approach might take a little more time and skill, the visual appeal may be well worth the effort.

Many public libraries have developed websites with ideas worth considering. The Eugene (Oregon) Public Library has a comprehensive You Might Like website (www.eugene-or.gov/portal/server.pt?open=512&objID=489&PageID=0&cached=true&mode=2). This site links to reader reviews, lists of new arrivals, the library catalog, and NoveList.

NoveList

NoveList is a powerful reader's advisory tool from Ebsco Publishing (www.ebscohost.com/novelist). Users can search NoveList's extensive database by title, author, series, and keyword, or they can browse lists by genre and reading level. Perhaps the most useful feature for teens is the ability to locate read-alikes for their favorite books. Teens can enter a description of the type of book they like and NoveList will provide a list of recommended titles. The results can be filtered by age, genre, storyline, tone, writing style, subject, and location. Each book entry includes a color image of the book cover, a description, reviews of the book, and recommended readings. With more than 125,000 titles in the database, users are sure to find titles they want to read. NoveList can tie into your school library catalog, allowing students to know whether the books they want are available in the media center. NoveList also has a version for mobile devices.

RA in the Palm of Your Hand

The ubiquitous use of cell phones has prompted libraries to take advantage of mobile technology for reader's advisory. One way is through the use of QR (Quick Response) codes, two-dimensional barcodes that, when scanned by a phone, can link the user to a website or give them the ability to send a text message or email. Librarians can use QR codes to make traditional book displays interactive and thus more appealing to teens. At California's Contra Costa

County Libraries (https://snapngo .ccclib.org) all copies of the YALSA Teens' Top Ten nominees were tagged with QR codes. Users with the QR app could access a webpage where they could leave comments, find other book nominees, and vote for their favorite title. At Abilene Christian University QR codes are being used in the library exhibits to link users to songs, videos, websites, and real-time searches of the library catalog. We all know that book covers and informative blurbs can entice readers. Imagine then the uses of QR codes that have the ability to instantly link teens to further information, including book reviews, author information, movie tie-ins, and suggested readings.

Engaged, Involved Readers

The idea of creating a one-stop shopping resource list is important. We know that net-gen students want all of their information in one place. Our own experience tells us that having to click more than two or three times to get to a desired destination may mean that we will

either get distracted or give up in frustration. As you think about the best way to share RA resources with your learners, keep the one-stop principle in mind. We want to promote our own resources, from our catalog to subscription databases, but we also want to guide our students to resources they can use to develop their own love of reading.

All of the resources listed here, along with many others, can be found at our Reader's Advisory Resources wiki, http:// itec7134resources.pbworks.com/ Reader%27s-Advisory-Resources.

Judi Repman *(jrepman@ georgiasouthern.edu) and* **Stephanie Jones** *(sjones@georgiasouthern.edu) are faculty members in the Instructional Technology Program at Georgia Southern University in Statesboro. They both teach online classes for prospective school library media specialists. Judi is also the consulting editor of Library Media Connection.*

Repman, Judi, & Jones, Stephanie. (2012). Reader's advisory for net-gen students. *LMC, 30*(4), 34–35.

Augmenting Reality in Your School's Library

By Heather Moorefield-Lang

A New and Exciting Idea for Educators

Augmented reality is a direct or indirect view of what is real in the actual, physical world with a layer of augmentation. This layer can include computer-generated sound, data, and visuals. It is meant to enhance a person's perception of reality (Mashable, 2013). For example, a mapping site lets a user view a street but enhances the sight with information about restaurants, shops, and other establishments. An educational site that focuses on anatomy can enable users to look at the human body and layer each level from skeleton to complete human frame. A library site could show students the books on the shelves and enhance the image with information about books, videos about titles, and even recommendations from peers. Augmented reality is only limited by the imagination; it is a relatively new and very exciting idea for our school libraries.

Many wonderful free sites and apps help librarians, educators, and students get started with augmented reality. They can range from image and video embedding to knowledge absorption. Take a look, try them out, and see which can be the most useful for creating learning experiences in your school library.

Images

Thinglink (www.thinglink.com): With this user-friendly site, students, librarians, and teachers can upload images and embed information into each image. Any item that can be linked can be embedded into the image. Describe a person in the photo with text; explain important information in a photo with a linked article; record a video and link it to describe what is occurring in the picture; embed polls—anything is possible. With every link an icon shows up on the image for viewers to float their mouse over. Thinglink is an interesting site to view and interact with images.

> *Augmented reality is only limited by the imagination; it is a relatively new and very exciting idea for our school libraries.*

Marqueed (www.marqueed .com): Marqueed allows users to embed information, links, video, and text into images in the same way as Thinglink, and it also gives patrons the opportunity to mark up images and collaborate with others. This site takes the experience of working on an image from an individual experience to a group endeavor. As each person works on the image they can also write messages and chat. It's a wonderful tool for group projects.

Taggstar (www.taggstar.com): Similar to Thinglink and Marqueed, Taggstar offers users opportunities to make their images interactive by embedding links, video, text, and other types of information. One interesting twist to this site is that users can also shop their images and earn from them.

Video

Mad Video (www.themadvideo .com): Several months ago I was unable to recommend sites where information could be embedded into video. The problem being, video moves. Then I was introduced to Mad Video, a site where information and links could be inserted into video. The idea is simple: Record your video and add needed information, links, and more. When users are finished, they publish the video online. This is a great way to create video information with augmented information contained within.

Wirewax (www.wirewax.com): Similar to Mad Video, Wirewax allows users to embed information into video. Simply upload video, click on the item or person that needs embedded information, and proceed to add. Users are also able to pull available videos, post the links, and add information to already produced videos (giving proper citation and credit, of course). This is very useful for instructional videos and further explanation for questions that might arise in video content.

Apps

Anatomy 4D: Teaching anatomy has never been more fun. This free app, available in iOS and Droid formats, allows users to view the human skeleton and body in a new way. Students can print out a hospital gurney/focus target and point the camera of their tablet devices at the target. Over top of the gurney will be a human body. From there users can build the skeleton up, including muscles, various bodily systems, and skin. Some users have printed the gurney/target using a plotter or poster printer. Having the hospital gurney printed on a poster sheet makes the experience even more realistic since the body is larger. Students can choose a male or female. Warning: This app does have an age rating because it shows the parts of the body.

> *Adding a layer of augmentation can certainly be an intriguing way to deliver education to students and information to educators, parents, and administrators.*

Spacecraft 3D: Similar to Anatomy 4D in operation, educators print a sheet of spacecraft target codes. Once those have been printed, students can point their tablets as well as iPhones at the code sheets and robotic explorers will appear with which they can interact. The explorers look a great deal like the Mars Rover. For space exploration this is an incredibly engaging tool for students.

Zooburst (www.zooburst.com): Zooburst is a website and an app; it is also an AASL Best Websites for Teaching and Learning winner. This wonderful storytelling resource offers students the opportunity to create their own 3D pop books that can include sound, narration, and images. Not only is Zooburst a great resource for increasing creative writing experiences but it is also wonderful for reading and story sharing.

Augmented reality is a way to enhance instruction. As with many technology tools, you will have to see for yourself if the recommended sites and apps in this article would be a good fit for your lessons and teaching. Each of these tools has the ability to add to instruction. They are fun to work with and students will enjoy them. Adding a layer of augmentation can certainly be an intriguing way to deliver education to students and information to educators, parents, and administrators. Give them a try and see how you can augment reality in your library!

Work Cited

Mashable. "Augmented Reality." Web. 20 Mar. 2013. http://mashable .com/category/augmented-reality.

Heather Moorefield-Lang *is the Education and Applied Social Sciences librarian at Virginia Tech and can be reached at hmlang@vt.edu. To see more of Heather's work, visit her website at www .actinginthelibrary.com or follow her on Twitter @actinginthelib.*

Moorefield-Lang, Heather. (2013). Augmenting reality in your school's library. *LMC, 31*(1), 26–27.

AT, UD, and Thee: Using Assistive Technology and Universal Design for Learning in 21st Century Media Centers

By Karen Gavigan and Stephanie Kurtts

Gretchen Linville, library media specialist at Hawkins Middle School, watched closely as Ramone, Lisa, and Sam, three sixth grade students in Lou Madden's science class, grappled with the online research assignment on global warming they had been assigned. Lou had shared with Gretchen that he had been working closely with Carl Edwards, the special education teacher, to meet the needs of the all of the students in Lou's class. Carl and Lou were co-teaching in this science class and several of the students were receiving individualized instructional accommodations that provided them greater access to the curriculum. As Gretchen watched the students' intense expressions and furrowed brows, she thought to herself, "Should I be doing more to make sure all the students have access to the information available in the media center? Is it really my job to do this? If it is, where do I begin?" As the bell rang for the class period to end, she watched the children end their work and continued to ponder these questions.

As stated in the American Association of School Librarians' new document, *Standards for the 21st-Century Learner*, "All children deserve equitable access to books and reading, to information, and to information technology in an environment that is safe and conducive to learning" (AASL, 2007, p. 1). It is the social and legal responsibility of all educators to serve the learning needs of every student in their schools, regardless of that student's age, ability, ethnicity, race, gender, sexual orientation, socioeconomic status, or exceptionalities. In fact, the Individuals with Disabilities in Education Act, or IDEA, mandates that all students with disabilities receive a free and appropriate public education meeting their individual needs in the least restrictive environment (U.S. Dept. of Education, 2005).

As such, educational professionals, including media specialists, continually seek innovative and effective instructional approaches that provide access to curricula for increasingly diverse student populations. For many media specialists and teachers, using assistive technology (AT) combined with the components of universal design for learning (UDL) can facilitate meaningful learning experiences for all students by providing equitable access and delivery of information (Hopkins, 2004; Orkwis, 2003; Rose & Meyer, 2002).

> It is the social and legal responsibility of all educators to serve the learning needs of every student in their schools, regardless of that student's age, ability, ethnicity, race, gender, sexual orientation, socioeconomic status, or exceptionalities.

Assistive Technology and Universal Design for Learning

Assistive technology is defined by the Individuals with Disabilities Education Act (IDEA) as, "any item, piece of equipment, or product system, whether acquired commercially off the shelf, modified, or customized, that is used to increase, maintain, or improve functional capabilities of individuals with disabilities (U.S. Dept. of Education, 2005). Assistive technology services are further defined as "any service that directly assists an individual with a disability in the selection, acquisition, or use of an assistive technology device." (Smith, 1999). Assistive technology has historically been considered part of service delivery for children with special needs. However, the emphasis of universal design for learning in the

creation of accessible and effective curriculum-based instruction can support the educational needs of all learners (Center for Applied Special Technology, 2008; Orkwis, 2002).

The concept of universal design, on which UDL is based, originated in the field of architecture and puts forth that all physical spaces and structures are accessible to a wide range of individuals with disabilities and will offer substantial benefit for the population at large (Pisha & Coyne, 2001). When educators plan and support instruction using universal design for learning, there is the expectation that a wide range of learning styles and abilities will be served in the classroom. As such, UDL provides flexible, multifaceted instruction supported by multiple opportunities for representation, expression, and engagement (Orkwis & McLane, 1998). Each of these components

- representation, providing content through varied modes such as visual, auditory, and graphic so that all students have access to information,

- expression, offering students many opportunities to demonstrate what they know, and

- engagement, including multiple means of involving students in learning

is essential in ensuring that the curriculum is accessible to all students (Curry, Cohen & Lightbody, 2006).

The Media Specialist's Role in AT and UDL

There is often apprehension and confusion on the part of media specialists as to the role they should play in implementing assistive technology services. Many media specialists may assume that they do not have any specific responsibilities for assistive technology resources and programming in their schools. When it comes to meeting the assistive technology needs of students with disabilities, these media specialists may feel that the issues are best handled through special education teachers and instructional technology departments.

Furthermore, while Hopkins (2004) references UDL as part of school reform initiatives, the approach is rarely referenced in the literature regarding the role of media specialists in providing resources and services to diverse learners. Finally, some media specialists may believe that they do not have the funding, resources, time, or skill set to implement the instructional supports integral to serving students with special needs (Wojahn, 2006).

However, as Dr. Gail Dickinson, Co-Chairman of the AASL Learning Standards Rewrite Task Force states, "The process of how we are teaching our 21st-century learners has to be reconsidered" (Dickinson, Library Media Connection, March 2008, p. 12). Media specialists must collaborate with classroom teachers to continually assess the needs of their students and reinvent their instructional materials, learning environment, and teaching strategies to engage all learners (Hopkins, 2004).

Making the Connection: Strategies for Implementation

Once the special needs of students have been identified, media specialists can help them, and their teachers and parents, become aware of existing resources available in their media centers. For example, big books, audiobooks, Playaways®, and interactive books are excellent tools to use with students with visual difficulties. DVDs and videotapes are other popular materials used to facilitate learning for disabled and non-disabled students.

While there are numerous high-tech AT resources available on the market such as voice recognition software and talking word processors, there are also many other no / low tech tools that support instruction using universal design for learning at minimal cost. These tools can address the needs of students with disabilities at the same time that they enhance learning for all students.

Figure 1 lists several examples of no / low tech and mid / high tech tools along with the skill areas and instructional strategies they support:

Figure 1 Examples of Adaptations and Use of Assistive Technology

For a student who experiences difficulty with writing:

Instructional Strategies	Task Modifications	Adaptive or No/Low AT	Alternative or Mid/High AT
■ tracing exercises ■ "talk through" letter formation ■ dot-to-dot ■ multisensory instruction ■ chalkboard practice ■ avoid using short pencils ■ utilize cross-age tutoring ■ cooperative learning ■ keyboarding instruction	■ adapt tests to fill-in-the-blank, multiple choice or true/false ■ allow more time ■ shorten assignments ■ photocopy notes ■ change paper position ■ change student position	■ tape paper to desk ■ clipboard to hold paper ■ different writing tools ■ pencil holders/grips ■ different texture/color paper ■ different line spacing ■ acetate sheets w/markers ■ talking pen ■ stencils/templates ■ rubber stamps ■ magnetic letters ■ slant board/easel ■ wrist support ■ arm stabilizer	■ typewriter ■ word processor ■ keyguard ■ alternative input devices for computer ■ software providing macros ■ spell checker ■ talking word processor ■ word prediction ■ abbreviation expansion ■ onscreen keyboard ■ voice recognition

For a student who experiences difficulty with reading

■ story mapping ■ read aloud guests ■ multisensory instruction ■ structured study guides ■ utilize cross-age tutoring ■ cooperative learning	■ highlight key concepts ■ allow more time ■ shorten assignments ■ simplify text ■ use chapter outlines	■ study carrel ■ tactile letters/words ■ magnifying bars ■ colored acetate ■ word window ■ flash cards ■ highlighter ■ post-it flags ■ color coded paper clips	■ tape recorder ■ books on tape ■ Language Master ■ electronic dictionary ■ scanner with OCR ■ talking word processor ■ Reading Pen

From the Web site of the Hawaii State Department of Education, "Welcome to A.T. the Forefront Online." http://doc.k12.hi.us/specialeducation/chapter56/appendix.htm

As in the case of Gretchen, Lou, and Carl, media specialists can collaborate with administrators, special education teachers, and instructional technology specialists to ensure that the appropriate resources, equipment, and infrastructure are available to facilitate learning for all students. Media specialists can also serve on school improvement or leadership teams to develop effective policies and procedures regarding AT services. They can provide their peers with information about the laws, policies, and use of assistive technology resources and universal design for learning. Media specialists can also collaborate with instructional technology specialists to ensure that their media centers' Web sites utilize adaptive technology tools.

In order to support the use of AT and UDL in schools, in-service media specialists need to be provided with quality initial and ongoing professional development opportunities. These opportunities can be provided through local and state education agencies online, or face to face through certification programs such as the California State University Northridge Assistive Technology Applications Certificate Program (CSUN, 2008).

Furthermore, schools of Library and Information Science (LIS) need to align professional standards with best practices by requiring pre-service media specialists to take courses that integrate information regarding assistive technology and universal design for learning in the curriculum. For example, some library schools currently offer assistive technology certificate courses. Additionally, LIS and Schools of Education, as well as K–12 school districts, should provide opportunities for inservice and preservice media specialists to visit model programs that offer opportunities for hands-on experiences with AT and UDL.

Finally, there are a variety of publications and Web sites available about AT and UDL issues, such as those listed in the references at the end of this article. For example, Hopkin's (2004) *Assistive Technology: An Introductory Guide for K–12 Library Media Specialists,*

is an excellent resource for media specialists who want to learn more about the field of assistive technology and universal design for learning. The Center for Applied Specialist Technology provides a "Teaching Every Student" Web page that can help media specialists make their library curriculums more user-friendly to students with disabilities (Wojahn, 2006). Moreover, the Hawaii State Department of Education's TeleSchool Division offers an online resource, "Welcome to A.T. the Forefront Online!" which provides videos, PowerPoint® presentations, PDF files, lesson plans, and instructions on how to create your own AT tools. This invaluable site is available at <www.teleschool.k12 .hi.us/attf>.

> When educators plan and support instruction using universal design for learning, there is the expectation that a wide range of learning styles and abilities will be served in the classroom.

As library media specialists consider how to use assistive technology and implement universal design for learning, it may change the way they view their role in meeting diverse learner needs. Media specialists who embrace the concept of an accessible and equitable curricula will find themselves at the center of effective collaborative partnerships that open up unlimited learning opportunities for all students in the media center and beyond.

References

American Association of School Librarians. *The information powered school.* Chicago, IL: American Library Association and the Public Education Network, 2001.

American Association of School Librarians. *Position statement on flexible scheduling.* Chicago, IL.

22 June 2008. <http://www .ala.org/ala/aasl/aaslproftools/ positionstatements/ aaslpositionstatement.cfm>.

American Association of School Librarians. *School libraries count! A National survey of school library media programs. 2007.* Chicago, IL. 22 June 2008. <http://www .ala.org/ala/aasl/school_libraries_ count07_report.pdf>.

American Association of School Librarians and Association for Educational Communications and Technology. (1988). *Information Power: Guidelines for school library media programs.* Chicago, IL: American Library Association and Washington, D.C.: Association for Educational Communications and Technology.

Bishop, K. *The Collection program in schools: Concepts, practices and information sources.* 4th edition. Westport, CT: Libraries Unlimited, 2007.

Haycock, K. "The impact of scheduling on cooperative program planning and teaching (CPPT) and information skills instruction." *School Libraries in Canada.* 18 no. 3 (1998): 20–23.

Hurley, C. A. "Fixed vs. flexible scheduling in school library media centers: A Continuing Debate." *Library Media Connection.* 23 (November/December 2004): 3, 36–41.

Krashen, S. *Power of reading: Insights from the research.* Englewood, CO: Libraries Unlimited, 1993.

Krashen, S. *Power of reading: Insights from the research.* 2nd edition. Portsmouth, NH: Heinemann, 2004.

Lance, K.C. "The impact of school library media centers on academic Achievement" {in Colorado}. *School Library Media Quarterly.* 22 (1994): 167–170.

Lance, K.C. "The impact of school library media centers on academic achievement." *Teacher Librarian.* 29 (3) (2002): 29–34.

Lance, K.C. "What research tells us about the importance of school libraries." *Teacher Librarian:*

The Journal for School Library Professionals. 30 (2002): 1, 76–78

Lance, K.C., Wellburn, L. and C. Hamilton-Pennell. *The impact of school library media centers on academic achievement.* Castle Rock, CO: Hi Willow Research & Publishing, 1993.

Lance, K.C., Rodney, M. and C. Hamilton-Pennell. *How school libraries improve outcomes for children: The New Mexico study.* San Jose, CA: Hi Willow Press, 2003.

Lance, K.C., Rodney, M. and C. Hamilton-Pennell. *The impact of Michigan school librarians on academic achievement: Kids who have libraries succeed.* Lansing, MI: Library of Michigan, 2003.

McCracken, A. "School library media specialists' perceptions of practice and importance of roles described in Information Power." *School Library Media Research.* 4, 2001. 24 Aug. 2008. <http://libproxy.uncg.edu:2072/hww/results/results_single_fulltext.jhtml;hwwilsonid=04ZOFLZVZS2YPQA3DILCFGOADUNGIIV0>

McGregor, J. "Flexible scheduling: Implementing an innovation." *School Library Media Research.* 9 (2006): 1–27.

Michie, J. and B. Chaney. *Assessment of the role of school and public libraries in support of educational reform.* (2000). General Audience Report. 24 Aug. 2008. <http://www.eric.ed.gov/ERICWebPortal/custom/portlets/recordDetails/detailmini.jsp?_nfpb=true&_&ERICExtSearch_SearchValue_0=ED440627&ERICExtSearch_SearchType_0=no&accno=ED440627>

Miller, M. and M. Shontz. "The SLJ Spending survey: While funding takes a hit, libraries expand their services." *School Library Journal.* 49 (October, 2003): 10, 52–59.

Shannon, D. "Tracking the transition to a flexible access library program in two Library Power elementary schools." *School Library Media Quarterly.* 24, no. 3 (1996): 155–63.

Van Deusen, J.D. "An analysis of the time use of elementary school library media specialists and factors that influence it." *School Library Media Quarterly.* 24, no. 2 (1996): 85–92.

Van Deusen, J.D. and J. Tallman. "The impact of scheduling on curriculum consultation and information skills instruction." Part one: The 1993–1994 AASL/Highsmith Research Award Study. *School Library Media Quarterly* 23, no. 1 (1994): 7–25.

Zweizig, D.L. "Access and use of library resources in Library Power." *School Libraries Worldwide* 5, no. 2 (1999): 16–28.

Karen Gavigan *is the Director of the Teaching Resources Center at the University of North Carolina at Greensboro. She can be reached at karen_gavigan@uncg.edu.*

Dr. Stephanie Kurtts *is an assistant professor in the School of Specialized Education Services at the University of North Carolina at Greensboro. She can be reached at sakurtts@uncg.edu.*

Gavigan, Karen, & Kurtts, Stephanie. (2009). AT, UD, and thee: Using assistive technology and universal design for learning in 21st century media centers. *LMC, 27*(4), 54–56.

Why Go International? Professional Benefits

By Lesley Farmer

As the world grows closer, as access to resources worldwide increases, as more students move from country to country, the need to connect with other librarians around the globe increases. Over the past few years, my participation in international associations and other professional activities has grown, which has expanded my own expertise and networking opportunities. How, and why, can you get involved in international professional associations? Examples that can impact school library programs follow.

Benefits

Besides getting flowers and gifts, there are many benefits for being a part of an association, the most important probably being opportunities to network with other librarians.

As a member of an association you can join a committee, which is an excellent venue for actually making a difference: creating policies, developing projects and writing publications that can help people in school library services. You also have access to directories of other members. Because many school librarians work "solo," it's good to know that there are other people out there who can help you, so you can be mutually supportive.

Professional education is a core value within associations, so whether you're going to live conferences and seminars or looking at Web tutorials or other resources available just for members, professional organizations can enrich your own career life.

Professional organizations also have free and discounted resources that are available just to members. And you can contribute your own experiences and knowledge in these associations through publications and seminars.

Associations can wield considerable power so that they can make policy statements, have international projects, and make a difference. Quite frankly, in today's global society, we school librarians really need to step up to the plate and show what we can do.

> *Professional education is a core value within associations, so whether you're going to live conferences and seminars or looking at Web tutorials or other resources available for members, professional organizations can enrich your own career life.*

American Library Association

ALA has several different ways to parse out international activities. The International Relations Round Table (IRRT) offers conferences, exchanges, sister library activity, and publications. They also note Web sites that help you travel internationally or pursue international exchanges. The International Relations Council focuses on current international policies and projects such as book donations and disaster relief. The AASL International Relations Community's charge is to provide a clearing house of information about international opportunities and ways to promote global understanding. This is a fairly new group, so I really encourage you to participate and make it viable.

International Association of School Librarianship

The International Association of School Librarianship (IASL) is the premier association that links school librarians throughout the world. International School Library Month, started by IASL as a day celebration, is now a month-long celebration with events and activities such as an international bookmark exchange. It's just one of the projects within IASL to foster international relationships and mutual support across the globe. Several SIGs offer different approaches to international connections: Children's and Young Adult Literature, Information Literacy, Technology, School Library Research. The International Focus SIG is now developing library and librarian standards for International Baccalaureate schools, which might interest those kinds of libraries in the U.S. GiggleIT is a project of Children's and Young Adult Literature SIG that promotes the idea of students contributing jokes, riddles, and other fun stories that are reflective of their culture. These stories are being put into an anthology, which is a way for your students to connect with children around the world.

IASL also publishes the *School Libraries Worldwide* journal, which features current research, as well as a newsletter. IASL's Web site (http://www.iasl-online.org) also has a "ping" and links to a ning so you can get more connected with these different SIGs. Another fun feature on the IASL Web site are pictures of school libraries throughout the world. As a member, you can submit your picture as well, which is a simple way to share "your" library with others.

IASL offers grants, and meets at conferences once a year throughout the world in sites such as Lisbon, Brisbane, Padua, and Durban, South Africa. In 2011 they will meet in Jamaica, and in 2012 the conference will be held in Texas. IASL provides videocasts and podcasts of some of the sessions that are accessible even if you're not a member. IASL is also starting regional conferences; I presented at the Latin American regional conference in Sao Paulo, and keynoted at a School Librarians conference in Nepal (pictured here).

Special Libraries Association

The Special Libraries Association (SLA) has the Education Division (http://sladedu.typepad.com) which publishes *Education Libraries*, a peer reviewed journal. The journal also has a section on Web sites done topically and a feature about new reference materials. SLA conferences are very active, very techy, and draw people from around the world.

International Federation of Library Associations

International Federation of Library Associations (IFLA) is a high powered group; they have different regions with their own caucuses as well as thematic sections. The most relevant to school librarians is the School Libraries and Resource Centers Division. Their newsletter is available online at <http://www .ifla.org/en/publications/52>. IFLA meets yearly; Gothenburg in 2010 and Puerto Rico in 2011. The 2010 conference also features a pre-conference on the future of school libraries, and a post-conference event in Copenhagen about school-public library collaboration.

Other sections that could be of interest to school librarians include Education Research, Libraries for Higher Education, Reference, and Information Services. Information Literacy is very interesting, and I was recently selected as the YALSA representative for the Literacy and Reading Section. They are developing a brochure on research about literacy and reading, which is targeted to librarians and other stakeholders.

IFLA produces many publications and works with other organizations such as UNESCO. They develop policy statements such as the School Library Manifesto, and are talking about new ways to configure libraries (for example, their Digital Library Future Conference).

The Information Literacy Section developed *Guidelines for Info Literacy Assessment*, which would be of particular interest to school librarians. That section is also a leader in looking at and maintaining the Web site (http:// www.infolitglobal.info/en/),

which links to information literacy resources and learning objects from around the world. So if you serve students who are non-English speakers, this resource helps explain library-related concepts in their primary language.

International Society for Technology in Education

The International Society for Technology in Education (ISTE) leverages the strength of several affiliate groups to foster the meaningful and responsible integration of technology in lifelong education, with a focus on K12 settings. Based in the United States, ISTE does have an international flavor.

Within ISTE is the Media Specialists SIG, which promotes school libraries and provides a means for school librarians to share their knowledge and concerns about educational technology. The International Committee within the SIG strives to identify and address international school librarianship issues of interest to Media Specialist SIG members. The committee maintains a wiki (http://sigms.iste.wikispaces.net/ International+Librarianship) and holds a monthly online chat about topics that draw upon international issues, such as ebooks and sister libraries.

Goethe Institute

The Goethe Institute is a private organization that has global reach. They do professional training and provide teaching materials, with special emphasis on learning about education in Germany. They also underwrite educational opportunities; in May 2009, six librarians were selected (including me) to participate a study tour in Germany in order to find out about library education in Germany. They are setting up a student study group this year.

> No matter where you are, there are ways for you to connect with others.

Fulbright

The Fulbright program is probably of most interest to library educators because it requires that participants be affiliated with the university. Some of its projects last half a year or a full academic year in terms of studying and teaching, but two- and six-week projects are available for senior specialists who are over 55. Fulbright projects are developed by non-U.S. countries, who request the Fulbright program to find someone who is a good match for them.

You can be a part of that pool, and apply for those opportunities. I participated in a project in Brazil, giving talks to pre-service librarians and library educators and visiting outstanding school libraries, such as the International School Library in Sao Paulo.

U.S. Department of State

The U.S. Department of State also offers several kinds of opportunities. For example, the Sustainable Library Development group connected with IRRT includes members of the Department of State so that you can find out about local projects to connect with.

The U.S. Department of State maintains International Resource Centers throughout the world; Library of Congress Centers also exist in some of those areas. One State Department project is "American Corners." The department donates a small collection, usually maintained in a public library or an academic library, which gives a picture of the United States and helps people to understand American perspectives. The State Department also offers cultural programs highlighting both U.S. and that nation's ways of expressing ideas.

This is a picture from a National Center for Book Reviews for K12 schools, which these women started from scratch. I was supported by the U.S. Department of State in Brazil where I talked with public and school librarians about library services for youth.

Getting Involved

No matter where you are, there are ways for you to connect with others.

International associations are a great way for doing that. It can be as simple as joining an association, and participating in SIG activities such as conference sessions and contributing content for wiki pages.

Representing a professional organization is a special honor and responsibility. As a representative, you are the "face" of the organization. When I work with other professional associations, I am the communication lynchpin. I have to listen well to make sure I understand what concerns and trends are emerging, using my experience as a YALSA or IASL member as my hearing timbre. How do these ideas potentially impact YALSA or IASL? Likewise, I listen for opportunities to insert the concerns, values, and possible contributions of the association I represent. I also have to listen to the silence, the unspoken, to make sure that the voice of YALSA and IASL ideas are heard.

So what does it take to become a representative? First, you need to be a knowledgeable member of the association you are representing.

Participating in the association's events and serving on committees gives you the grounding to build credibility within the organization—and with other organizations. Usually, you should already be involved in the target organization. In other words, you like and know both organizations.

To be a representative for IFLA, you need to be nominated by a sponsoring organization. Even if you are nominated, there's no guarantee that you will be voted in by the existing committee members, but you can't win if you don't play. In any case, you can usually still attend the meetings for which you have been designated as a representative. Usually the role of representative brings access to people and ideas and worthwhile activities, but not material advantage. You have to pay for all expenses, and are expected to fulfill your duties for the extent of your term of duty.

What do I do? I am an IASL corresponding member of the School Libraries and Resource Centers section; I attend the meetings, help plan programs, present, and edit the

newsletter. As the YALSA (Young Adult Library Services Association of ALA) representative to the Literacy and Reading section of IFLA, I participate actively in the section business meetings. I make sure that teen reading and literacy is addressed. I volunteered to be a table facilitator for the section's program. I also volunteered to serve on the research brochure sub-committee to help others access and use research about literacy and reading. Obviously, planning and attending the conference takes weeks, and writing up the report takes a few hours. But I keep my representative "jobs" as part of my everyday mindset. And I feel that I'm making a contribution to these organizations, to myself, and to students around the world.

Lesley Farmer *is a professor of Library Media in the Advanced Studies in Education & Counseling Department at California (Long Beach) State University.*

Farmer, Lesley. (2010). Why go international? Professional benefits. *LMC, 29*(2), 34–36.

The Embedded Librarian for K–12 Schools

By Robin Henry

The embedded librarian model has been around for a while. According to *Embedded Librarians: Moving beyond One-Shot Instruction*, the term was first applied in 2004 in an article by Barbara Dewey (Kvenild and Calkins vii). However, the model has been in use since the late 1960s in medical libraries. From there the practice spread to academic libraries, where it continues to be a viable service model. Embedded librarianship involves "focusing on the needs of one or more specific groups, building relationships with these groups, developing a deep understanding of their work, and providing information services that are highly customized and targeted to their greatest needs" (Brower 3). This may involve leaving the confines of the library to offer these services.

Liaison Model vs. Embedded Model

Most school libraries currently use a service model that is more closely related to the liaison model in academic libraries, where librarians offer a variety of services to departments to which they are assigned based on expertise. These services may include bibliographies, ordering materials, information literacy instruction, etc. The difference is in the depth of service. Like the one-shot lesson, liaison services tend to only scratch the surface of what a librarian can really do to help faculty and students. It is like trying to hit a target with a shot gun when what you really need is a guided missile.

> Embedded librarianship is one way to be remarkable. K–12 libraries will have to scale down the embedded model to fit them, but it can be done.

Two of the most striking examples of the embedded librarian model in higher education are California State University at Stanislaus and the Arizona State University Herberger Institute School of Dance. Warren Jacobs' 2010 article is one of the few to record quantitative data about the difference it made to be embedded. During the course of 2009, Jacobs' office was relocated to the Department of Education because of a library renovation project. He used the opportunity to become embedded in the department. He emailed, he visited with faculty, he visited classes; he marketed his services like crazy. Even he admits that the embedded model, if done correctly, will increase the workload (Jacobs 6). In the end, two numbers stood out. Jacobs provided over 150 research consultations with faculty and 45 with students within the Department of Education during 2009. Normally, the *entire* library staff provided about 100 research appointments each year beyond the reference desk. He increased his instructional sessions (entire class sessions) by 20 percent. Embedding himself in the department worked.

The Arizona State University Herberger Institute School of Dance provides more qualitative data. After a large donation to the school made a special collection for dance possible, Christopher Miller, the librarian for the collection, was invited into the dance department as an equal member with faculty. Miller doesn't offer hard numbers, but he lists the observed advantages he found, such as being completely integrated into the department, being a departmental colleague, having greater input into the curriculum and the ability to teach information literacy, and finding that the librarian was perceived by students as having a more "pronounced role" in their educational experience (Miller 98). These are outcomes that many school librarians would give their book carts to have.

How Can We Translate the Embedded Librarian Model to K–12?

How do we get there from here? Academic libraries have larger staffs, bigger budgets, and the freedom to leave the library. How can K–12 librarians manage to offer embedded services in a school setting? Here is the more important question: How can we afford not to? The value of school libraries is being questioned from all sides. Sometimes it seems that school librarians are the only ones who care about what school libraries can offer. But what if that were not the case? In *Purple Cow* (2009), Seth Godin writes about being remarkable. He says that being remarkable is what will keep you viable. Embedded librarianship is one way to be remarkable. K–12 libraries will have to scale down the embedded model to fit them, but it can be done.

Jake Carlson and Ruth Kneale offer advice for making the embedded model work. First, be a team player. Embedded means working with others, so play nice, which includes taking the time to build relationships. Next, be willing to accept some risk—and this might mean moving outside your comfort zone. Remember the old saying "If you haven't failed, you haven't tried." Not every attempt you make will be successful, but make the attempts anyway. In K–12 schools it is important to work out a plan. Target the departments or teachers you will work with first, remembering the definition of embedded librarianship. It is okay to target some teachers or departments and not others. As a K–12 librarian, your staff is small, so you have to make your efforts count. Don't waste time on a teacher or department where you do not have a reasonable expectation of success. Save them for when everyone is talking about how remarkable the library is, then they will make their way to you. Remember your goal, which is to provide information literacy instruction to your students.

Know What You Have to Offer

Practical strategies for embedding yourself into a department are based on the definition of the embedded librarian. Make sure you know what is being taught and when. Always be ready with a suggestion for how the library could help with the unit. Go to departmental or team meetings to make yourself available. If you haven't already done so, move your pathfinders into the digital age and put them online. See if you can embed yourself into online class activities by offering to create a links page, a citation tip sheet, or other valuable services to teachers and students. If you can arrange coverage by an aide or a volunteer, offer to go to computer labs and instruct students in databases, searching, or research-specific topics for a class. Talk to your administrator about what it means to be embedded. Advertise, advertise, advertise through whatever means you have at your disposal. Make sure that the staff knows what services they can get from you and the library.

Embedded Librarianship as a Process

A word about assessment: Keep records of all the lessons you collaborate on and the teachers you work with to share with administration and to promote the value of embedded librarianship. Get students to share stories about their success. Remember that the transformation won't happen overnight. There are stages of embedded librarianship, and like any process, you may move between the stages and be at different levels with different staff members.

> *Remember the old saying "If you haven't failed, you haven't tried." Not every attempt you make will be successful, but make the attempts anyway.*

The first stage is the introductory phase in which you begin the process of marketing by introducing yourself, going to meetings, and targeting key people with whom to build relationships. Next comes awareness, when you brand the library, create subject and course guides, and engage in other outreach activities. Third is the timely instruction services phase. Here you get the chance to give instruction to students. Make it count. Partnerships make up the fourth stage when you begin to work on specific courses with instructors and become more directly involved in classes. The final phase is information competency, which means that you work to get information literacy fully integrated into the course work, measure your progress, and provide feedback to faculty team members (Krkoska 122–124). This fifth stage is where all school librarians would like to be, and it is a laudable goal that will help students be better prepared for life after their K–12 experience.

The embedded librarian model can be a successful service model for K–12 libraries. By concentrating on the targeting and customizing aspects of embedded librarianship, K–12 librarians can make it work and make a difference.

References

Brower, M. "A Recent History of Embedded Librarianship: Collaboration and Partnership Building with Academics in Learning and Research Environments." In C. Kvenild and K. Calkins (eds.). *Embedded Librarians: Moving beyond One-Shot Instruction*. Chicago: Association of College and Research Libraries, 2011: 3–16.

Carlson, J., and R. Kneale. "Embedded Librarianship in the Research Context: Navigating New Waters." *College and Research Libraries News* 72.3 (2011): 167–70.

Godin, S. *Purple Cow: Transform Your Business by Being Remarkable*. New York: Portfolio, 2009.

Jacobs, W. N. "Embedded Librarianship Is a Winning Proposition." *Education Libraries* 33.2 (2010): 3–10.

Krkoska, B. B., C. Andrews, and J. Morris-Knower. "A Tale of Three Disciplines: Embedding Librarians and Outcomes-based Information Literacy Competency in Business, Biology, and Communication." In C. Kvenild and K. Calkins (eds.). *Embedded Librarians: Moving beyond One-Shot Instruction*. Chicago: Association of College and Research Libraries, 2011: 121–137.

Kvenild, C., and K. Calkins. (eds.). *Embedded Librarians: Moving beyond One-shot Instruction*. Chicago: Association of College and Research Libraries, 2011.

Miller, C. "Embedded and Embodied: Dance Librarianship within the Academic Department." In C. Kvenild and K. Calkins (eds.). *Embedded Librarians: Moving beyond One-Shot Instruction*. Chicago: Association of College and Research Libraries, 2011: 95–105.

Robin Henry *is the library systems administrator at Richardson (Texas) ISD. She may be reached at robin.henry@risd.org.*

Henry, Robin. (2013). The embedded librarian for K–12 schools. *LMC, 31*(4), 22–23.

Confessions of a Commoner

By Robin Cicchetti

"A rose by any other name. . . ." Really? What if a rose were called a thorny phlegm-arachnid? Would we really enjoy the fragrance as much? What if *Romeo and Juliet* were titled *Ernie and Agnes* and were written by Freddie Buckets?

Words and names matter. They are containers for ideas, associations, memories, and emotions. So what does the term 'library' mean? Wordnet, a lexical database from Princeton, provides the following entry: "a room where books are kept; *they had brandy in the library*." Putting aside the apparent news that libraries at Princeton serve brandy, the definition fits with the common usage of 'library.' It's a place for books.

While many school libraries are quickly evolving, the term 'library' is not. Traditional libraries still exist. Rare books libraries, academic archives, libraries of record, and personal libraries often are libraries in the customary sense of the definition. That doesn't mean, however, that these types of libraries are stuck in the past—far from it. Many are among the most modern and technologically advanced libraries, whether they offer books, artifacts, or information in a digital format.

The activities in our school library have expanded the definition of 'library' to the extent that the word itself was holding us back. I was hearing over and over again, 'how can you do THAT in the library?' We can do *that* because it's not a library, it's a learning commons.

The cultural idea of a library bears little resemblance to the skills, services, and activities we provide to students and staff on a daily basis. So deeply ingrained are the associations and emotions tied to the traditional view of the role of libraries that it was time give our vocabulary a shake. We officially completed the transition and renamed our school library a learning commons last April, in honor of National Library Week.

> *Few people really know what it means to walk into a learning commons. This uncertainty is our greatest opportunity.*

A reasonable analogy is the term "telephone." We all know what a telephone is, but would we use that term to describe an iPhone or a Blackberry? At first we used terms like "cell phone" to describe the mobility of these new communications tools. Now we use evolving terms like "smartphone" to describe that they are capable not only of mobile audio calls, but of video calls, text-messaging, email, and taking and editing photos and videos. In fact, students today text, email, and use Facebook on their mobile devices far more than they make voice calls. Telephone is now only a partial and somewhat anachronistic description for these devices.

So What Happens in Our Learning Commons?

Our learning commons does, of course, hold books, periodicals, reference materials, and information in video and audio formats. We are still a place that has areas reserved for quiet individual study. But there is more going on here:

- The learning commons is a teaching space with up to three classes going on simultaneously during our busiest blocks.
- The learning commons is a 'doing' space with a new, advanced media center for the creation of video projects and ample space for noisy collaborative projects.
- The learning commons is a performance space. We have hosted everything from Wii gaming on the last day of school to Taiko drumming at closing time. We also have student art generously displayed throughout the room.
- The learning commons is a communications space. Our projects and research often include Skype conversations, such as with our town's sister city in Nanae, Japan, and the creation of student wikis to provide a communication platform with classrooms in China. Connecting students with other students and experts around the world is one of our new missions.

Changing the name was the signal that the worlds of books, learning, communication, and work have changed dramatically. Everybody knows what it is like to walk into a library. Few people really know what it means to walk into a learning commons. This uncertainty is our greatest opportunity. When students and classes are in the learning commons, they are there to learn about tools to help them research, assemble, and create. We spend our time teaching skills to find, evaluate, and organize information, and then produce a result that can be shared. Nobody shows up to "get" information, because it isn't that easy anymore. Information has to go through an evaluation process where it has to prove itself worthy of consideration. And there are now so many places to look for information! We are the guides in a global search for quality information.

Teachers and students are beginning to push the boundaries of what it means to be in the learning commons. We encourage collaborative study within an atmosphere of academic purpose. Of course, the distinctions are not clear as to what is appropriate for the learning commons, and our own standards are evolving, but that's what makes it so interesting.

Here are some ways in which we draw our admittedly fuzzy lines.

- We invited the jazz band to perform with amplifiers. Unfortunately, it seemed the amps were turned up to eleven. I was told the music could be heard out in the football field. We will not do that again. Next time, we'll go for an unplugged, coffee house vibe.
- When a lively Scrabble game gets a little loud and requires adjudication and multiple dictionaries, it is still a learning commons activity. But, if it devolves into sketchy word creation, then it is not.
- When a statistics class shows up asking to head to the stacks to do an exercise in figuring out how many books we have with red spines and scatters through the stacks, calling each other for feedback, it is a learning commons activity. When couples head to the stacks and it gets quiet, we have a problem.
- When eighty extra students appear during a lunch block during March Madness to check their team rankings, it does not mean they have a right to take over all twenty-five desktop stations. That is what web-enabled phones are for. Go to the cafeteria. The day a statistics teacher assigns a basketball-based regression analysis is the day it becomes a learning commons activity.

What about Facebook?

Facebook is the elephant in the room when we talk about technology in schools. Ask any college professor and they will tell you that when their students have their laptops open in a lecture, and they always do, Facebook occupies at least part of the screen. Facebook is the current indispensable communications medium for students. We should not only learn to live with that fact but embrace it.

> Facebook is the current indispensable communications medium for students. We should not only learn to live with that fact but embrace it.

One teacher approached me asking about students he saw using Facebook during school hours and how I rationalized this use. I asked him if he was on Facebook and he admitted that he had never visited the site. I helped him set up an account, recommended privacy settings, gave him a quick overview of the platform, and had him friend me. Over the next couple of weeks he was friending people, poking, throwing sheep, and connecting with family and friends with whom he had lost touch. Today he is a regular—not only on Facebook but in the learning commons, frequently asking for new tech tools and advice on assignments. His technology skills have grown exponentially. He gets it.

We are late in rolling out a Facebook page for our learning commons, but this is the year. As I feel increasingly frustrated by the limits of my monthly newsletter, Facebook and Twitter feel like appropriate evolutions in upping our level of communicating with students, faculty, and our parent community.

Our students are online all the time. We teach, guide, and encourage them to be aware of their digital footprint. Studies indicate that most of them are careful about their privacy settings on social media sites. This year we are going to go a step further and introduce the idea of drafting a personal "brand." What comes up when you Google yourself? What do you *want* to come up when you Google yourself and why is this important? Creating a Google profile, for instance, can give students the power to form their digital footprint.

(This program will be offered as an evening session with parents invited as well.)

Another goal this year will be to get up to speed with widgets and mobile apps that are available for some of our databases. This was on my to-do list last year and never got crossed off. Anything that improves our students' ability to access information from whatever device they are using is a good thing.

We are also rolling out a new media server that will allow us to archive diverse material, which will be accessible through our online catalog. Teachers and students will be learning how to access the catalog in new ways, for new needs.

Included in those needs will be continued advocacy for our SpEd population. Students on individual education plans need ease of access. We have to continue to make sure that specialized e-books and audio materials are available and easily accessible—both in the learning commons and online.

Just as the debate over print versus digital has evolved toward recognizing that it is about the reading and not the medium, school libraries have evolved, too. The learning commons is about teaching, learning, creating, and community. A name change is the device that helps our community understand that their old assumptions and expectations are no longer relevant. It signifies that it is time to develop a new understanding.

Considering our space is no longer called a library, am I still a librarian? If not, what am I? Am I a commoner? I think I will need new business cards.

Robin Cicchetti *is head of the learning commons at Concord-Carlisle Regional High School, Concord, Massachusetts. She can be reached at rcicchetti@colonial.net.*

Cicchetti, Robin. (2011). Confessions of a commoner. *LMC, 29*(5), 52–53.

Pivots for Change: Libraries and Librarians

By Buffy J. Hamilton

The Power of a Personal Learning Network

Heeding the wisdom of Anne Ruggles Gere who once said, "I propose that we listen to the signals that come through the walls of our classrooms from the outside," I have been adding many people who are innovative thinkers regarding business, social media, and cultural trends to my personal learning network. What is a personal learning network? David Warlick defines a personal learning network (PLN) as "the people and information sources that help you accomplish your goals, either on the job or in your personal pursuits" (Warlick). In the past, one's personal learning network might consist of people, professional journals, the occasional conference experience, and list-serv subscriptions. In today's connected world, though, one can use social media tools such as Twitter, social networking services like Facebook, blog subscriptions, RSS feeds, webinars, Flickr, YouTube and other video services, wikis, social bookmarking services, podcasts, and chat through services like Google to connect with library professionals, educators, and other experts around the world. The PLN is a means to build professional knowledge and a medium for connecting, creating, and collaborating with others who share similar interests and passions.

How do you manage your personal learning network? Tools like Google Reader and group features available in Facebook and Tweetdeck for Twitter allow me to organize my contacts and RSS feeds. For example, RSS feeds from blog posts, favorite Web resources, and Twitter friends in my Google Reader account are organized into folders like "librarian blogs," "social media," "edtech," and other categories to help me effectively manage my PLN. You can also use tools like iGoogle <http://www .google.com/ig> and Netvibes <http:// www.netvibes.com> to organize the RSS feeds from your favorite resources in your network to create a customized learning portal for yourself.

Re-Thinking the Concept of Change

While working on a project this summer, I revisited one of these innovative-thinker voices, Seth Godin, and his post, "Pivots for Change." Godin, a marketing and business expert, prefaces his points by beginning with this sage observation:

When industry norms start to die, people panic. It's difficult to change when you think that you must change everything in order to succeed. Changing everything is too difficult.

I immediately began thinking about how these statements apply to libraries, particularly school libraries. We are in the midst of a sea-change in which we as school librarians and our "brand" are ". . . in serious need of redefinition" (Valenza). How do we go about reinventing our brand and our role in today's schools? How do we help school librarians who may feel overwhelmed see that change can be effected? Godin suggests that we pick some selected "pivot points for change" rather than trying to redo all aspects of our practice and programs at once.

Here is Godin's original list of "pivot points for change":

- Keep the machines in your factory, but change what they make.
- Keep your customers, but change what you sell to them.
- Keep your providers, but change the profit structure.
- Keep your industry but change where the money comes from.
- Keep your staff, but change what you do.
- Keep your mission, but change your scale.
- Keep your products, but change the way you market them.
- Keep your customers, but change how much you sell each one.
- Keep your technology, but use it to do something else.
- Keep your reputation, but apply it to a different industry or problem.

So what might these "pivot points of change" look like in a school library? Here are some examples that may help your library program take another step forward.

Changes in Thinking, Changes in Practice

Keep books and print materials in your library, but add and promote the formats in which their content appears (i.e. audio books, databases, e-books, downloadable books such as NetLibrary, Google Books, free online versions of periodicals).

As school libraries face funding cuts, it is more important than ever that we make thoughtful collection development decisions to get the most for our money and to best meet the needs of today's learners. While print books may be the most popular format for some genres, other genres, such as reference, lend themselves to digital format so that the greatest number of students may access them with the least risk of material loss. In addition, digital formats of books provide more options for manipulation by students, including language translation, PDF formats, vocabulary aid tools, hot links, and read aloud options (usually in MP3 format) to aid struggling readers and to support audio learners.

Keep teaching evaluation of online resources, but teach students (and teachers) to apply those same principles of information to traditional sources of information— they are not immune from bias or inaccurate information.

For too long, we have not questioned the integrity of traditional information sources. However, we should be teaching students to apply principles of information evaluation to all sources as the format doesn't make information immune from bias or inaccuracy. Teach students to be critical evaluators of all information sources regardless of the "container" in which they are housed.

Keep your traditional sources of authoritative information, but let the research topic and mode of research guide the integration of social media information sources and tools for delivering that content.

YouTube, RSS feeds, Google News, podcasts, Twitter feeds, mashups, and blogs are emerging as authoritative sources of information. If a student is researching the Iran elections of 2009, it makes more sense to use YouTube as a primary source than a print book as the information is more timely and immediate. If students are researching current events, RSS feeds from saved searches in Google News or news service podcasts will provide rich content that is constantly updated to give students the latest information.

Keep teaching information literacy skills, but focus on the bigger picture of helping students devise personal learning networks that they can apply to any learning situation instead of a topic specific research task.

Standards for the 21st Century Learner emphasizes the ideals of connected learning and inquiry. By teaching students how to find resources for their personal learning network and the tools to help organize that PLN, we are taking a significant step in nurturing learners who are information fluent and who have a deeper understanding of when and how to use specific information sources.

Use pivots for change as a lens for evaluating what is working in your program and to re-imagine the possibilities to embed your program as an integral part of your school.

Keep teaching students Internet safety principles, but also shift your focus on the concept of digital footprints and teaching students how to create and maintain a positive online identity.

While many school librarians feel comfortable teaching principles of online safety, how many provide guidance on how to be a responsible digital citizen? Students need to know how to be an ethical user and producer of information; they need to know how to establish a professional and positive online identity. Who better to teach students these principles than school librarians?

Continue creating a warm and welcoming physical library environment, but give equal attention to developing a virtual library presence that is accessible to students 24/7 with elements such as a virtual learning commons, screencasts, video tutorials, or online classrooms through a platform like Elluminate v-classroom.

Today's 21st century learners expect a strong Web presence from their libraries. Creating an attractive Web site featuring widgets streaming helpful content allow you to create a dynamic Web presence. Free and easy-to-learn tools are plentiful to help you create and host your tutorial screencasts. In addition, tools such as YouTube and Flickr allow you to share videos and photos that spotlight special activities or demonstrations in your library.

Keep teaching quality subscription based resources like NoodleTools for managing and citing information, but teach additional free tools for managing, citing, and organizing information sources.

Tools like CiteULike and Zotero enable learners to easily document information sources and publicly share resources with others. These tools allow learners to organize resources by topic and to engage in more transparent scholarship. Social bookmarking tools like delicious and Diigo empower students to access their traditional and emerging authoritative sources of information from any computer. In addition, Diigo provides students tools for annotating their bookmarked sources using sticky notes and for easily capturing snapshots of a digital resource. These tools also allow learners to network with others who have similar research interests to engage in collaborative knowledge sharing and resource list building.

Keep school rules in mind, but explore ways to tap into the power of devices like cell phones and iPods for student learning and present a plan for using these tools to your administrator so that you can provide service where your students are.

Engage students by allowing them to use their smartphones and mobile devices for virtual polls. Also show students free apps they can use to access reading materials, such as the complete works of a classic author, learning tools, and study aids for specific content areas.

Establishing a presence in social networks is a free yet powerful way to reach out to the parents in your learning community and to advocate for your program by highlighting library activities and services through these social networks.

Keep writing a vision statement and annual PDEP (Program Design and Evaluation Plan) and monthly reports, but compose them in a different format, such as a mindmap, video, or other multimedia/visualization medium.

Tools like Animoto can help you combine the power of words and images to communicate information about what is happening in your library. You can also make your library reports come alive using tools like Google Sites to document unit/lesson plans, the accompanying research pathfinders, and student learning artifacts. Mindmapping tools like Mindomo <http://www.mindomo.com/> are wonderful for creating visual concept maps to help your stakeholders envision your program goals and initiatives for the upcoming year.

Keep positing literacy as a primary focal point of your library program, but expand that definition of literacy to include new media literacy and information literacy as mainstream literacies equal in importance to traditional literacy.

Reports from research groups like the Pew Foundation and the Knight Commission on the Information Needs of Communities in a Democracy underscore the fact that digital and media literacy are no longer optional literacies; they are now essential literacies for participating in a democratic society. Cultivate a library environment that privileges **transliteracy**, "the ability to read, write and interact across a range of platforms, tools and media from signing and orality through handwriting, print, TV, radio and film, to digital social networks (*Transliteracy Research Group*).

Market your library in places such as Twitter or Facebook where your parents may "be" to share news about your library program and to network with your parent community.

Think about where your students dwell: YouTube, MySpace, Facebook, mobile phones? Consider creating a presence in these social networks to create conversations about your library and to stream information to your students. If your students are too young to participate in these networks, consider that their parents are not! Establishing a presence in social networks is a free yet powerful way to reach out to the parents in your learning community and to advocate for your program by highlighting library activities and services through these social networks.

Keep reading your print journals, but use a feed aggregator to access and organize your favorite blogs, journals, podcasts, YouTube

videos, and Twitter RSS feeds to stay on the cutting edge.

Today's read/write world provides librarians the opportunity to connect with colleagues and other content area specialists on a global scale. Tap into the wisdom of the crowd and join the conversations to better inform your practice and philosophy.

Keep your traditional sources of authoritative information, but let the research topic and mode of research guide the integration of social media information sources and tools for delivering that content.

RSS feeds, videos, podcasts, Flickr streams, blog posts, Twitter feeds, and mashups provide relevant and timely delivery of information and conversations about topics for today's learners. Incorporate social media streams of quality information so that your students can explore concepts of social scholarship and emerging sources of authoritative information.

Leadership in a Time of Change

AASL's *Empowering Learners: Guidelines for School Library Media Programs* identifies **leader** as a primary role for school library media specialists. Establishing a presence in social networks is a free yet powerful way to reach out to the parents in your learning community and to advocate for your program by highlighting library activities and services through these social networks. Use pivots for change as a lens for evaluating what is working in your program and to re-imagine the possibilities to embed your program as an integral part of your school. Think about how pivots for change can help your students enjoy the library as an experience. By using pivots for change as a framework

for ongoing program evaluation, you can provide leadership in your school through bold innovation and purposeful change.

Works Cited

The Art Amp Technique of Cultivating Your Personal Learning Network. Weblog post. *Transliteracy Research Group*. N.p., n.d. Web. 14 Oct. 2009. <http://nlabnetworks.typepad.com/transliteracy/>.

Godin, Seth. "Pivots for change." *Seth Godin's Blog*. N.p., 12 Mar. 2009. Web. 13 Sept. 2009. <http://sethgodin.typepad.com/seths_blog/2009/03/pivots-for-change-swords-and-plowshares.html>.

Hamilton, Buffy. "Pivots for Change and Libraries." *The Unquiet Librarian*. N.p., 25 July 2009. Web. 13 Sept. 2009. <http://theunquietlibrarian.wordpress.com/2009/07/25/pivots-for-change-and-libraries/>.

Valenza, Joyce. "Free The Standards." *Neverending Search*. School Library Journal, 13 July 2009. Web. 11 Oct. 2009. <http://www.schoollibraryjournal.com/blog/1340000334/post/.html>.

Warlick, David. "The Art & Technique of Personal Learning Networks." *David Warlick's CoLearners Wiki*. N.p., n.d. Web. 11 Oct. 2009. <http://davidwarlick.com/wiki/pmwiki.php/Main/

Buffy J. Hamilton *is the school library media specialist at Creekview High School in Canton, Georgia. She can be reached at buffy.hamilton@gmail.com.*

Hamilton, Buffy J. (2010). Pivots for change: Libraries and librarians. *LMC*, 28(6), 54–56.

ONE QUESTION SURVEY RESULTS
Will You Be Retiring within the Next 2 Years?

By Gail K. Dickinson

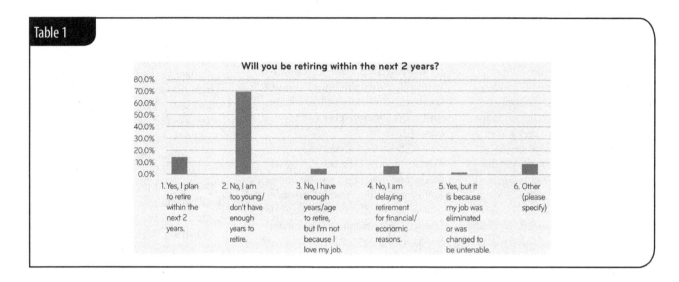

Table 1

The problem with dire warnings is that after a point, they get too unbelievable and will just get ignored. We've all heard about the graying of the library profession and the astonishing number of school librarians who will reach retirement age in the next several years. We at LMC believe that the best questions are the simplest, so we asked our respondents if they planned to retire in the next two years. We chose two years, because we thought that it would capture people who had definite plans. Any more than that and the decision becomes less of a plan and more of an opinion.

The very good news is that out of our 514 total respondents, only 2, less than half of one percent, are retiring because the job was eliminated, or because they were placed in a job that they found untenable. More good news is that a whopping 70% are either too young or do not have enough retirement system years to retire. We received several comments on this question, mostly from librarians who told us

how much they appreciated being able to answer to anything that they were too young. The fact is, though, that librarianship is usually based on the platform of another career, whether that is classroom teaching or something outside of education. It is a rare librarian who starts in a library at a fresh 22 and continues for the next 30 years.

It does our heart good to see that for nearly 6 %; the job is keeping them in the job. These respondents are old enough to retire, but just don't want to yet. Even the figure of 13% of those planning to retire in the next two years is not nearly as threatening as it could be, even when those delaying for economic reasons or just simply loving the job are added to the totals.

For the other category, the top three categories are a definite plan to retire in more years than two (usually three), already retired, or surprisingly, retired but returned to the field as a half-time or even full-time librarians.

The library field has always had a faster turnover rate than other fields.

Many, but certainly not all, school librarians arrive at the profession from the platform of another career. Classroom teachers may be able to look back at their first classroom at age 21, put in their 30 years, and retire. For the librarian, though, the library beginning may have been in their 30's, or even older. That's one reason why simply looking at age as an indicator of retirement does not work for the library field.

LMC One Question Surveys provide data-based snapshots of issues in school librarianship. You can find past surveys at our website at www.librarymediaconnection.com. Have an issue? We are always looking for great questions.

Dickinson, Gail K. (2012). Will you be retiring within the next 2 years? *LMC*, *30*(4), 54.

ONE QUESTION SURVEY RESULTS
Does Your School Allow Student-Owned Devices (Smartphones, iPods, e-readers) to Be Used during the School Day?

By Gail K. Dickinson

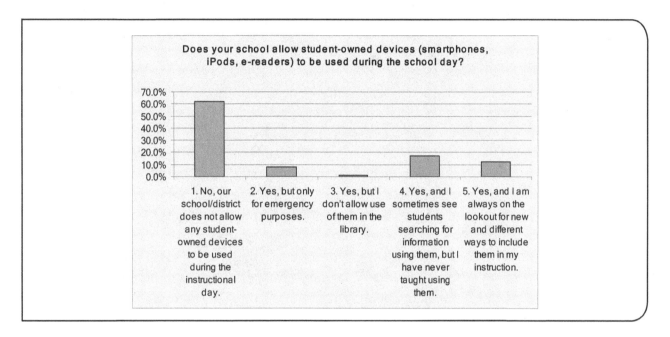

Anecdotal evidence has policies banning student-owned devices falling like dominos as school districts bow to the inevitable. School districts who restrict the use to emergency purposes only will find that rule impossible to police. We will repeat this survey next year for comparison purposes, and it will be interesting to see the number of school districts still outlawing any device. For sure, it will be lower than the nearly 62% reported in this survey.

Interestingly, comments by participants indicated that some districts are qualifying the use of these devices. Some librarians reported that e-readers are allowed, but cell phones strictly forbidden. Others only allowed the use of tablets and laptops. Some only allowed iPods or MP3 players. Over time, though, this will change as well as single-

purpose devices merge into more universal devices. Some librarians who responded that such devices are currently not allowed also noted that changes are underway, and they expect that barrier to fall shortly.

Some respondents noted that lack of a robust Internet infrastructure is preventing open access. Updating the wifi access was in the works in several cases. Another barrier seemed to be the lack of a specific policy. "Awaiting a policy to be formed" was a typical quote focusing on policies.

Subversion or disregard of an outright ban was also reported, thus bolstering the argument that such bans are difficult to enforce. "I do know that some teachers use them instructionally even though it is against our policy," "We only allow the use of e-readers though I often allow students to use iPods in the

library," and "No, but the students can use them in the library" are typical responses. Comments such as "Our official policies haven't really kept up with our day-to-day operations" and "but they use them anyway" illustrate the enforcement problem.

Of interest, and with some dismay, the survey also found that only 12% of librarians are pursuing instructional applications for these devices. This is a wave that is on its way to shore, and savvy school librarians will need to quickly learn how to surf. The profession is missing the opportunity to lead the use of these devices and to lobby for ways to use them for direct instructional purposes. Whether or not schools currently allow such devices, change is on the horizon, and school librarians need to be in front of the parade, not passively watching from the sidelines.

Use LMC One-Question Surveys to support evidence-based practices in your library. You can find past surveys at our website at www. librarymediaconnection.com. Have an issue? We are always looking for great questions.

Dickinson, Gail K. (2012). Does your school allow student-owned devices (smartphones, iPods, e-readers) to be used during the school day? *LMC, 30*(6), 55.

ONE QUESTION SURVEY RESULTS
What Reference Tools Are the Most Used in Your Library Program?

By Gail K. Dickinson

Some one-question surveys appeal to a wide variety of readers, with a tremendous outpouring of responses. This one had a response rate that is one of our lowest, at only 30 respondents. That is enough of a variety of respondents, though, to draw meaning for the future of reference resources in schools.

Deciding the future of reference is an important topic. Terri Kirk, in the October issue of LMC (see page 28) is one of those making the move to a greatly reduced reference area. Only a few (3.3 %) of the respondents in our latest survey agree with her. On the other hand, the peaks below tell the story of the two-headed monster that is today's reference services. Slightly over 1/3 of the respondents reported using web browsers as their most popular avenue for reference sources. Slightly less than 1/3 of the respondents report that subject series or individual specific books are their most popular sources.

The reference standards of encyclopedias and dictionaries, now in a subscription online format, are holding their own in about 25% of respondent's libraries as the most popular resource. And, thankfully, only about 6% of our respondents report using a free source such as Wikipedia most of the time.

Decades ago, reference sections in school libraries were nearly identical. No matter what library you entered, you could expect to see the brown shades of encyclopedias shelved beside the green books of magazine indexes. The only real difference in the libraries may be the size of the collection. Things are changing, and with the wealth of authoritative sources available in a variety of formats, school librarians are making decisions on how to best use reference sources and reference funding.

Library Media Connection encourages the use of evidence-based practices to assure your students have the libraries they deserve. Use this chart to help you make the best decisions regarding reference services for your students.

Curious about our previous surveys? All are available online at www.librarymediaconnection.com.

Dickinson, Gail K. (2010). What reference tools are most used in your library program? *LMC, 29*(3), 53.

May/June 2010 Library Media Connection		
What Reference Tools are the most used in your library program?		
Answer Options	**Response Percent**	**Response Count**
We have no reference resources.	3.3%	1
Subject specific reference sets, series, or individual books.	30.0%	9
Subscription online encyclopedias or dictionaries.	23.3%	7
World Wide Web (i.e. Google, Ask.com).	36.7%	11
Free online resources (such as Wikipedia).	6.7%	2
answered question		**30**
skipped question		**0**

ONE QUESTION SURVEY RESULTS
What Devices Are You Using for eBooks

By Gail K. Dickinson

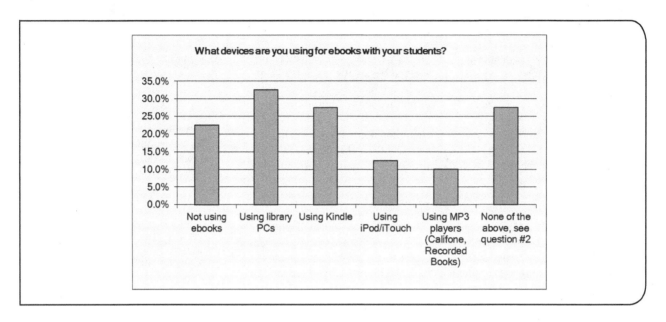

What devices are you using for ebooks with your students?

This is the third year that we have asked this question, and with only 40 respondents, it's time to move on to other questions. Still, a review of the data from the past two years reveals some interesting trends. In 2010, nearly 50% of our respondents said that they were not using ebooks. In 2011, the percentage dropped to just under 40%, and now in 2012, it is just over 20%. In three years, that is a steady decrease in the number of school libraries without ebooks.

There was little change over three years in the percentage of respondents using library PC's for ebooks. That has remained right about 30%. The percentage using Kindle's, though, has grown from about 5 % in 2010 to 10% in 2011 to over 25% in 2012, a figured that was almost the same as the percentage of participants who reported using other devices than the choices that we offered. The open question regarding other devices was interesting, as some participants reported using multiple devices, most often Nook Simple Touch. Several

respondents reported that their school had a 1–1 initiative, and two reported that the students used their own devices.

So what does this tell us about ebooks in libraries? First of all, it tells us that they are becoming commonplace. This change is not restricted by grade level. Only 12% of our respondents were elementary, so ebooks are becoming a K–12 fixture. Second, it tells us that the field, over three years, has not found one common device to use as an e-book reader. If anything, judging by the increased percentage in the "None of the Above" category, school librarians are branching out in their selection of e-readers. This category rose from just under 10% in 2010 to 20% in 2011, and in 2012 was well on its way to 30%.

There are, of course, a lot of questions that we did not ask. Certainly we did not ask what percentage e-reading was of the total circulation, and I am not sure that counting e-circulation

is even possible in today's cloud environment. We did not ask how e-books are used instructionally, and we did not ask school librarians to predict which e-reader would be the device of the future. We also did not ask them to predict the percentage of their collection that would remain print five years from now. Either question would be fascinating and informative.

But for now, though, all we can say is that more school librarians are including e-books in their collections. We can say additionally that the numbers do not point to any one clear winner in the e-reader competition. School librarians continue to make the best decisions for their schools and students based on their unique needs. All is as it should be.

LMC encourages the use of evidence-based planning to improve school libraries. To review previous LMC One-Question Surveys, visit

www.librarymediaconnection.
com. Have a good question? Submit
it to lmc@librarymediaconnection.
com. We will be waiting to hear
from you.

This survey question was
identical to the October 2010 and
October 2011 LMC One-Question
Survey.

Dickinson, Gail K. (2013). What devices
are you using for ebooks? *LMC, 31*(5), 29.

Tips

Bookmark It!

Want to share database password information on bookmarks with your students but don't want to create and print all new bookmarks? Using Word, create labels with login information and affix the labels to the back of bookmarks purchased from a library supply vendor. This allows you to get important information to students, but on attractive, full color bookmarks.

Stacy Cameron
Pioneer Heritage Middle School
McKinney, Texas

Cameron, Stacy. (2013). Bookmark it! *LMC, 31*(5), 8.

Common Core Implementation

We asked the LMC EdWeb community (www.edweb.net/lmcforefront) for their best tips on Common Core implementation. Here is a sampling:

- Use the AASL Crosswalk as you take part in content meetings
- Attend content leader meetings
- Post an AASL Crosswalk link on your library's page
- Get out of the library—go into the classrooms

Peg Becksvoort
Librarian
Falmouth (Maine) Middle School

Take the TRAILS assessments and crosswalk the info lit standards into Common Core with each question. Upload the scores into Data Director to see the growth of the students throughout the year and easily map out which Common Core standards are being reached or not. If you're not familiar with TRAILS, you may want to check it out at www.trails-9.org.

Walter Butler
Marshall Fundamental
Pasadena, California

Remember C. V. S.

- C—Understand what *complex text* is all about and how this is critical to raising rigor and writing from sources.
- V—Embrace *vocabulary* as this will be a big spotlight to build the brain.
- S—Become an information *superhero*.

Take a look at writing standards 6–9: "Research to build and present knowledge." If they are not coming to you for research and information, they are probably not handling WI 6–9 correctly. The information superhero in you should come to their rescue. Use your imagination on that one!

Paige Jaeger
WSWHE BOCES
Saratoga Springs, New York

Thoroughly understand text complexity, provide great nonfiction selections for teachers and students, attend all the webinars and workshops you can on CCSS, and make yourself an expert. Another suggestion would be to become a part of the planning/curriculum teams for CCSS lessons (if that's possible).

Kerrlita Westrick
Litchfield Elem. School District
Litchfield Park, Arizona

EdWeb Community (various authors). (2013). Common core implementation. *LMC, 32*(1), 8.

Virtually Yours

With the purchase of more e-books and databases, the physical bookshelf can be stuck in time. In order to move users from physical to virtual, add signage on the physical bookshelf with the addition of "googly eyes." The sign points shelf browsers to the online access where the latest information can be found. Imagine if a person browsing the shelves is looking in the right place, but the book is no longer current or not in its place! The sign will direct them to a current virtual version. Consider placing a netbook where there is room on the shelf, so it becomes the access point for the user. A great place to start this project is on the periodicals and newspapers rack where a magazine or newspaper is available online, either through the state digital library or open access.

Sue Lantelme
Ledyard (Connecticut) High School

Lantelme, Sue. (2013). Virtually yours. *LMC, 32*(1), 8.

PDF Magic

Embedding a video in a .pdf (using Adobe Acrobat software) makes it easy for a student to access and view a short video. For example, try teaching a lesson about using an online encyclopedia. Use the screencast-o-matic (www.screencastomatic.com) tool to record various aspects of the online encyclopedia. Then embed and use the video to introduce the online encyclopedia information. Questions or activities can be inserted in the same document. There are instructional YouTube videos on how to embed a video in a .pdf and other written tutorials online. It's a great way to create student-centered activities!

Tom Johnson
The Hockaday School
Dallas, Texas

Johnson, Tom. (2012). PDF magic. *LMC, 31*(2), 8.

Index